T0384861

Graphics & Visualization

A K Peters/CRC Press
Taylor & Francis Group
6000 Broken Sound Parkway NW, Suite 300
Boca Raton, FL 33487-2742

© 2008 by Taylor and Francis Group, LLC
A K Peters/CRC Press is an imprint of Taylor & Francis Group, an Informa business

No claim to original U.S. Government works

International Standard Book Number: 978-1-56881-274-8 (Hardback)

Visit the Taylor & Francis Web site at
http://www.taylorandfrancis.com

and the A K Peters Web site at
http://www.akpeters.com

Graphics & Visualization
Principles & Algorithms

T. Theoharis
G. Papaioannou
N. Platis
N. Patrikalakis

With contributions by
P. Dutré
A. Nasri, F. A. Salem, and G. Turkiyyah

A K Peters, Ltd.
Wellesley, Massachusetts

Contents

Contents

Preface

Graphics & Visualization: Principles and Algorithms is aimed at undergraduate and graduate students taking computer graphics and visualization courses. Students in computer-aided design courses with emphasis on visualization will also benefit from this text, since mathematical modeling techniques with parametric curves and surfaces as well as with subdivision surfaces are covered in depth. It is finally also aimed at practitioners who seek to acquire knowledge of the fundamental techniques behind the tools they use or develop. The book concentrates on established principles and algorithms as well as novel methods that are likely to leave a lasting mark on the subject.

The rapid expansion of the computer graphics and visualization fields has led to increased specialization among researchers. The vast nature of the relevant literature demands the cooperation of multiple authors. This book originated with a team of four authors. Two chapters were also contributed by well-known specialists: Chapter 16 (Global Illumination Algorithms) was written by P. Dutré. Chapter 8 (Subdivision for Graphics and Visualization) was coordinated by A. Nasri (who wrote most sections), with contributions by F. A. Salem (section on Analysis of Subdivision Surfaces) and G. Turkiyyah (section on Subdivision Finite Elements).

A novelty of this book is the integrated coverage of computer graphics and visualization, encompassing important current topics such as scene graphs, subdivision surfaces, multi-resolution models, shadow generation, ambient occlusion, particle tracing, spatial subdivision, scalar and vector data visualization, skeletal animation, and high dynamic range images. The material has been developed, refined, and used extensively in computer graphics and visualization courses over a number of years.

Some prerequisite knowledge is necessary for a reader to take full advantage of the presented material. Background on algorithms and basic linear algebra

Some prerequisite knowledge is necessary for a reader to take full advantage of the presented material. Background on algorithms and basic linear algebra principles are assumed throughout. Some, mainly advanced, sections also require understanding of calculus and signal processing concepts. The appendices summarize some of this prerequisite material.

Each chapter is followed by a list of exercises. These can be used as course assignments by instructors or as comprehension tests by students. A steady stream of small, low- and medium-level of difficulty exercises significantly helps understanding. Chapter 3 (2D and 3D Coordinate Systems and Transformations) also includes a long list of worked examples on both 2D and 3D coordinate transformations. As the material of this chapter must be thoroughly understood, these examples can form the basis for tutorial lessons or can be used by students as self-study topics.

The material can be split between a basic and an advanced graphics course, so that a student who does not attend the advanced course has an integrated view of most concepts. Advanced sections are indicated by an asterisk ⊛. The visualization course can either follow on from the basic graphics course, as suggested below, or it can be a standalone course, in which case the advanced computer-graphics content should be replaced by a more basic syllabus.

Course 1: Computer Graphics–Basic. This is a first undergraduate course in computer graphics.

- Chapter 1 (Introduction).

- Chapter 2 (Rasterization Algorithms).

- Chapter 3 (2D and 3D Coordinate Systems and Transformations). Section 3.9 (Quaternions) should be excluded.

- Chapter 4 (Projections and Viewing Transformations). Skip Section 4.5 (Extended Viewing Transformation).

- Chapter 5 (Culling and Hidden Surface Elimination Algorithms). Skip Section 5.4 (Occlusion Culling). Restrict Section 5.5 (Hidden Surface Elimination) to the Z-buffer algorithm.

- Chapter 6 (Model Representation and Simplification).

- Chapter 7 (Parametric Curves and Surfaces). Bézier curves and tensor product Bézier surfaces.

- Chapter 9 (Scene Management).

- Chapter 11 (Color in Graphics and Visualization).

- Chapter 12 (Illumination Models and Algorithms). Skip the advanced topics: Section 12.3 (The Lambert Illumination Model), Section 12.7 (The Cook–Torrance Illumination Model), Section 12.8 (The Oren–Nayar Illumination Model), and Section 12.9 (The Strauss Illumination Model), as well as Section 12.10 (Anisotropic Reflectance) and Section 12.11 (Ambient Occlusion).

- Chapter 13 (Shadows). Skip Section 13.4 (Shadow Maps).

- Chapter 14 (Texturing). Skip Section 14.4 (Texture Magnification and Minification), Section 14.5 (Procedural Textures), Section 14.6 (Texture Transformations), Section 14.7 (Relief Representation), Section 14.8 (Texture Atlases), and Section 14.9 (Texture Hierarchies).

- Chapter 17 (Basic Animation Techniques). Introduce the main animation concepts only and skip the section on interpolation of rotation (page 622), as well as Section 17.3 (Rigid-Body Animation), Section 17.4 (Skeletal Animation), Section 17.5 (Physically-Based Deformable Models), and Section 17.6 (Particle Systems).

Course 2: Computer Graphics–Advanced. This choice of topics is aimed at either a second undergraduate course in computer graphics or a graduate course; a basic computer-graphics course is a prerequisite.

- Chapter 3 (2D and 3D Coordinate Systems and Transformations). Review this chapter and introduce the advanced topic, Section 3.9 (Quaternions).

- Chapter 4 (Projections and Viewing Transformations). Review this chapter and introduce Section 4.5 (Extended Viewing Transformation).

- Chapter 5 (Culling and Hidden Surface Elimination Algorithms). Review this chapter and introduce Section 5.4 (Occlusion Culling). Also, present the following material from Section 5.5 (Hidden Surface Elimination): BSP algorithm, depth sort algorithm, ray-casting algorithm, and efficiency issues.

- Chapter 7 (Parametric Curves and Surfaces). Review Bézier curves and tensor product Bézier surfaces and introduce B-spline curves, rational B-spline curves, interpolation curves, and tensor product B-spline surfaces.

- Chapter 8 (Subdivision for Graphics and Visualization).

- Chapter 12 (Illumination Models and Algorithms). Review this chapter and introduce the advanced topics, Section 12.3 (The Lambert Illumination Model), Section 12.7 (The Cook–Torrance Illumination Model), Section 12.8 (The Oren–Nayar Illumination Model), and Section 12.9 (The Strauss Illumination Model), as well as Section 12.10 (Anisotropic Reflectance) and Section 12.11 (Ambient Occlusion).

- Chapter 13 (Shadows). Review this chapter and introduce Section 13.4 (Shadow Maps).

- Chapter 14 (Texturing). Review this chapter and introduce Section 14.4 (Texture Magnification and Minification), Section 14.5 (Procedural Textures), Section 14.6 (Texture Transformations), Section 14.7 (Relief Representation), Section 14.8 (Texture Atlases), and Section 14.9 (Texture Hierarchies).

- Chapter 15 (Ray Tracing).

- Chapter 16 (Global Illumination Algorithms).

- Chapter 17 (Basic Animation Techniques). Review this chapter and introduce the section on interpolation of rotation (page 620), as well as Section 17.3 (Rigid-Body Animation), Section 17.4 (Skeletal Animation), Section 17.5 (Physically-Based Deformable Models), and Section 17.6 (Particle Systems).

Course 3: Visualization. The topics below are intended for a visualization course that has the basic graphics course as a prerequisite. Otherwise, some of the sections suggested below should be replaced by sections from the basic graphics course.

- Chapter 6 (Model Representation and Simplification). Review this chapter.

- Chapter 3 (2D and 3D Coordinate Systems and Transformations). Review this chapter.

- Chapter 11 (Color in Graphics and Visualization). Review this chapter.

- Chapter 8 (Subdivision for Graphics and Visualization).

- Chapter 15 (Ray Tracing).

- Chapter 17 (Basic Animation Techniques). Review this chapter and introduce Section 17.3 (Rigid-Body Animation) and Section 17.6 (Particle Systems).

- Chapter 10 (Visualization Principles).

- Chapter 18 (Scientific Visualization Algorithms).

About the Cover

The cover is based on M. Denko's rendering *Waiting for Spring*, which we have renamed *The Impossible*. Front cover: final rendering. Back cover: three aspects of the rendering process (wireframe rendering superimposed on lit 3D surface, lit 3D surface, final rendering).

Acknowledgments

The years that we devoted to the composition of this book created a large number of due acknowledgments. We would like to thank G. Passalis, P. Katsaloulis, and V. Soultani for creating a large number of figures and M. Sagriotis for reviewing the physics part of light-object interaction. A. Nasri wishes to acknowledge support from URB grant #111135-788129 from the American University of Beirut, and LNCSR grant #111135-022139 from the Lebanese National Council for Scientific Research. Special thanks go to our colleagues throughout the world who provided images that would have been virtually impossible to recreate in a reasonable amount of time: P. Hall, A. Helgeland, L. Kobbelt, L. Perivoliotis, G. Ward, D. Zorin, G. Drettakis, and M. Stamminger.

Introduction

There are no painting police—just have fun.
—Valerie Kent

1.1 Brief History

Out of our five senses, we spend most resources to please our vision. The house we live in, the car we drive, even the clothes we wear, are often chosen for their visual qualities. This is no coincidence since vision, being the sense with the highest information bandwidth, has given us more advance warning of approaching dangers, or exploitable opportunities, than any other.

This section gives an overview of milestones in the history of computer graphics and visualization that are also presented in Figures 1.1 and 1.2 as a time-line. Many of the concepts that first appear here will be introduced in later sections of this chapter.

1.1.1 Infancy

Visual presentation has been used to convey information for centuries, as images are effectively comprehensible by human beings; a picture is worth a thousand words. Our story begins when the digital computer was first used to convey visual information. The term *computer graphics* was born around 1960 to describe the work of people who were attempting the creation of vector images using a digital computer. Ivan Sutherland's landmark work [Suth63], the Sketchpad system developed at MIT in 1963, was an attempt to create an effective bidirectional man-machine interface. It set the basis for a number of important concepts that defined the field, such as:

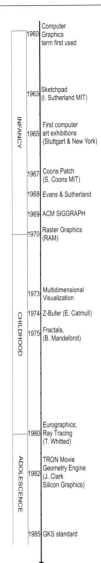

- hierarchical display lists;

- the distinction between object space and image space;

- interactive graphics using a light pen.

At the time, *vector displays* were used, which displayed arbitrary vectors from a *display list*, a sequence of elementary drawing commands. The length of the display list was limited by the refresh rate requirements of the display technology (see Section 1.6.1).

As curiosity in synthetic images gathered pace, the first two *computer art* exhibitions were held in 1965 in Stuttgart and New York.

The year 1967 saw the birth of an important modeling concept that was to revolutionize computer-aided geometric design (CAGD). The *Coons patch* [Coon67], developed by Steven Coons of MIT, allowed the construction of complex surfaces out of elementary patches that could be connected together by providing continuity constraints at their borders. The Coons Patch was the precursor to the Bézier and B-spline patches that are in wide CAGD use today.

The first computer graphics related companies were also formed around that time. Notably, Evans & Sutherland was started in 1968 and has since pioneered numerous contributions to graphics and visualization.

As interest in the new field was growing in the research community, a key conference ACM SIGGRAPH was established in 1969.

1.1.2   Childhood

The introduction of transistor-based random access memory (RAM) around 1970 allowed the construction of the first *frame buffers* (see Section 1.5.2). *Raster displays* and, hence, *raster graphics* were born. The frame buffer decoupled the creation of an image from the refresh of the display device and thus enabled the production of arbitrarily complicated synthetic scenes, including filled surfaces, which were not previously possible on vector displays. This sparked the interest in the development of *photo-realistic algorithms* that could simulate the real visual appearance of objects, a research area that has been active ever since.

The year 1973 saw an initial contribution to the visualization of multidimensional data sets, which are hard to perceive as our brain is not used to dealing with more than three dimensions. Chernoff [Cher73] mapped data dimensions onto characteristics of human faces, such as the length of the nose or the curvature of the mouth, based on the innate ability of human beings to efficiently "read" human faces.

Figure 1.1.
Historical milestones
in computer graphics
and visualization
(Part 1).

Edward Catmull introduced the *depth buffer* (or *Z-buffer*) (see Section 1.5.3) in 1974, which was to revolutionize the elimination of hidden surfaces in synthetic image generation and to become a standard part of the graphics accelerators that are currently used in virtually all personal computers.

In 1975, Benoit Mandelbrot [Mand75] introduced *fractals*, which are objects of non-integer dimension that possess self-similarity at various scales. Fractals were later used to model natural objects and patterns such as trees, leaves, and coastlines and as standard visualization showcases.

1.1.3 Adolescence

The increased interest for computer graphics in Europe led to the establishment of the Eurographics society in 1980. Turner Whitted's seminal paper [Whit80] set the basis for ray tracing in the same year. Ray tracing is an elegant image-synthesis technique that integrates, in the same algorithm, the visualization of correctly depth-sorted surfaces with elaborate illumination effects such as reflections, refractions, and shadows (see Chapter 15).

The year 1982 saw the release of *TRON*, the first film that incorporated extensive synthetic imagery. The same year, James Clark introduced the Geometry Engine [Clar82], a sequence of hardware modules that undertook the geometric stages of the graphics pipeline (see Section 1.4), thus accelerating their execution and freeing the CPU from the respective load. This led to the establishment of a pioneering company, Silicon Graphics (SGI), which became known for its revolutionary real-time image generation hardware and the IrisGL library, the predecessor of the industry standard OpenGL application programming interface. Such hardware modules are now standard in common graphics accelerators.

The spread in the use of computer graphics technology, called for the establishment of standards. The first notable such standard, the Graphical Kernel System (GKS), emerged in 1975. This was a two-dimensional standard that was inevitably followed by the three-dimensional standards ANSI PHIGS and ISO GKS-3D, both in 1988.

The year 1987 was a landmark year for visualization. A report by the US National Science Foundation set the basis for the recognition and funding of the field. Also a classic visualization algorithm, *marching cubes* [Lore87], appeared that year and solved the problem of visualizing raw three-dimensional data by converting them to surface models. The year 1987 was also important for the computer graphics industry, as it saw the collapse of established companies and the birth of new ones.

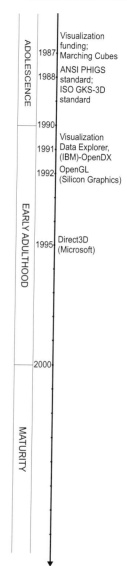

Figure 1.2.
Historical milestones in computer graphics and visualization (Part 2).

Two-dimensional graphics accelerators (see Section 1.6.1) became widely available during this period.

1.1.4   Early Adulthood

The 1990s saw the release of products that were to boost the practice of computer graphics and visualization. IBM introduced the Visualization Data Explorer in 1991 that was similar in concept to the Application Visualization System (AVS) [Upso89] developed by a group of vendors in the late 1980s. The Visualization Data Explorer later became a widely used open visualization package known as OpenDX [Open07a]. OpenDX and AVS enabled non-programmers to combine pre-defined modules for importing, transforming, rendering, and animating data into a re-usable data-flow network. Programmers could also write their own re-usable modules.

De-facto graphics standards also emerged in the form of application programming interfaces (APIs). SGI introduced the OpenGL [Open07b] API in 1992 and Microsoft developed the Direct3D API in 1995. Both became very popular in graphics programming.

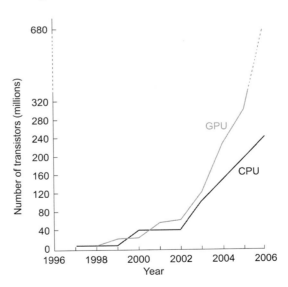

Figure 1.3. The rise of graphics accelerators: the black line shows the number of transistors incorporated in processors (CPU) while the gray line shows the number of transistors incorporated in graphics accelerators (GPU).

Three-dimensional graphics accelerators entered the mass market in the mid-1990s.

1.1.5 Maturity

The rate of development of graphics accelerators far outstripped that of processors in the new millenium (see Figure 1.3). Sparked by increased demands in the computer games market, graphics accelerators became more versatile and more affordable each year.

In this period, 3D graphics accelerators are established as an integral part of virtually every personal computer. Many popular software packages require them. The capabilities of graphics accelerators were boosted and the notion of the specialized graphics workstation died out. State-of-the-art, efficient synthetic image generation for graphics and visualization is now generally available.

1.2 Applications

The distinction between applications of computer graphics and applications of visualization tends to be blurred. Also application domains overlap, and they are so numerous that giving an exhaustive list would be tedious. A glimpse of important applications follows:

Special effects for films and advertisements. Although there does not appear to be a link between the use of special effects and box-office success, special effects are an integral part of current film and spot production. The ability to present the impossible or the non-existent is so stimulating that, if used carefully, it can produce very attractive results. Films created entirely out of synthetic imagery have also appeared and most of them have met success.

Scientific exploration through visualization. The investigation of relationships between variables of multidimensional data sets is greatly aided by visualization. Such data sets arise either out of experiments or measurements (acquired data), or from simulations (simulation data). They can be from fields that span medicine, earth and ocean sciences, physical sciences, finance, and even computer science itself. A more detailed account is given in Chapter 10.

Interactive simulation. Direct human interaction poses severe demands on the performance of the combined simulation-visualization system. Applications such as flight simulation and virtual reality require efficient algorithms and high-performance hardware to achieve the necessary interaction rates and, at the same time, offer appropriate realism.

Computer games. Originally an underestimated area, computer games are now the largest industry related to the field. To a great extent, they have influenced the development of graphics accelerators and efficient algorithms that have delivered low-cost realistic synthetic image generation to consumers.

Computer-aided geometric design and solid modeling. Physical product design has been revolutionized by computer-aided geometric design (CAGD) and solid modeling, which allows design cycles to commence long before the first prototype is built. The resulting computer-aided design, manufacturing, and engineering systems (CAD/CAM/CAE) are now in wide-spread use in engineering practice, design, and fabrication. Major software companies have developed and support these complex computer systems. Designs (e.g., of airplanes, automobiles, ships, or buildings) can be developed and tested in simulation, realistically rendered, and shown to potential customers. The design process thus became more robust, efficient, and cost-effective.

Graphical user interfaces. Graphical user interfaces (GUIs) associate abstract concepts, non-physical entities, and tasks with visual objects. Thus, new users naturally tend to get acquainted more quickly with GUIs than with textual interfaces, which explains the success of GUIs.

Computer art. Although the first computer art exhibitions were organized by scientists and the contributions were also from scientists, computer art has now gained recognition in the art community. Three-dimensional graphics is now considered by artists to be both a tool and a medium on its own for artistic expression.

1.3 Concepts

Computer graphics harnesses the high information bandwidth of the human visual channel by digitally synthesizing and manipulating visual content; in this manner, information can be communicated to humans at a high rate.

An aggregation of primitives or elementary drawing shapes, combined with specific rules and manipulation operations to construct meaningful entities, constitutes a three-dimensional *scene* or a two-dimensional drawing. The scene usually consists of multiple elementary *models* of individual objects that are typically collected from multiple sources. The basic building blocks of models are *primitives*, which are essentially mathematical representations of simple shapes such as points in space, lines, curves, polygons, mathematical solids, or functions.

Typically, a scene or drawing needs to be converted to a form suitable for digital output on a medium such as a computer display or printer. The majority of visual output devices are able to read, interpret, and produce output using a raster image as input. A *raster image* is a two-dimensional array of discrete picture elements (*pixels*) that represent intensity samples.

Computer graphics encompasses *algorithms* that generate (*render*), from a scene or drawing, a raster image that can be depicted on a display device. These algorithms are based on *principles* from diverse fields, including geometry, mathematics, physics, and physiology. Computer graphics is a very broad field, and no single volume could do justice to its entirety.

The aim of *visualization* is to exploit visual presentation in order to increase the human understanding of large data sets and the underlying physical phenomena or computational processes. Visualization algorithms are applied to large data sets and produce a *visualization object* that is typically a surface or a volume model (see below). Graphics algorithms are then used to manipulate and display this model, enhancing our understanding of the original data set. Relationships between variables can thus be *discovered* and then checked experimentally or proven theoretically. At a high level of abstraction, we could say that visualization is a function that converts a data set to a displayable model:

$$\text{model} = \text{visualization (data set)}.$$

Central to both graphics and visualization is the concept of *modeling*, which encompasses techniques for the representation of graphical objects (see Chapters 6, 7 and 8). These include surface models, such as the common polygonal mesh surfaces, smoothly-curved polynomial surfaces, and the elegant subdivision surfaces, as well as volume models. Since, for non-transparent objects, we can only see their exterior, surface models are more common because they dispense with the storage and manipulation of the interior.

Graphics encompasses the notion of the *graphics pipeline*, which is a sequence of stages that create a digital image out of a model or scene:

$$\text{image} = \text{graphics pipeline (model)}.$$

The term *graphics pipeline* refers to the classic sequence of steps used to produce a digital image from geometric data that does not consider the interplay of light between objects of the scene and is differentiated in this respect from approaches such as ray-tracing and global illumination (see Chapters 15 and 16). This approach to image generation is often referred to as *direct rendering*.

1.4   Graphics Pipeline

A line drawing, a mathematical expression in space, or a three-dimensional scene needs to be *rasterized* (see Chapters 2 and 5), i.e., converted to intensity values in an image buffer and then propagated for output on a suitable device, a file, or used to generate other content. To better understand the necessity of the series of operations that are performed on graphical data, we need to examine how they are specified and what they represent.

From a designer's point of view, these shapes are expressed in terms of a coordinate system that defines a modeling space (or "drawing" canvas in the case of 2D graphics) using a user-specified unit system. Think of this space as the desktop of a workbench in a carpenter's workshop. The modeler creates one or more objects by combining various pieces together and transforming their shapes with tools. The various elements are set in the proper pose and location, trimmed, bent, or clustered together to form sub-objects of the final work (for object aggregations refer to Chapter 9). The pieces have different materials, which help give the result the desired look when properly lit. To take a snapshot of the finished work, the artist may clear the desktop of unwanted things, place a hand-drawn cardboard or canvas backdrop behind the finished arrangement of objects, turn on and adjust any number of lights that illuminate the desktop in a dramatic way, and finally find a good spot from which to shoot a digital picture of the scene. Note that the final output is a digital image, which defines an *image space* measured in and consisting of pixels. On the other hand, the objects depicted are first modeled in a three-dimensional *object space* and have objective measurements. The camera can be moved around the room to select a suitable viewing angle and zoom in or out of the subject to capture it in more or less detail.

For two-dimensional drawings, the notion of rasterization is similar. Think of a canvas where text, line drawings, and other shapes are arranged in specific locations by manipulating them on a plane or directly drawing curves on the canvas. Everything is expressed in the reference frame of the canvas, possibly in real-world units. We then need to display this mathematically defined document in a window, e.g., on our favorite word-processing or document-publishing application. What we define is a virtual window in the possibly infinite space of the

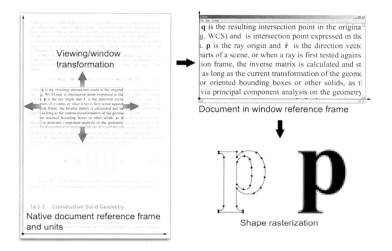

Figure 1.4. Rasterization steps for a two-dimensional document.

document canvas. We then "capture" (render) the contents of the window into an image buffer by converting the transformed mathematical representations visible within the window to pixel intensities (Figure 1.4).

Thinking in terms of a computer image-generation procedure, the objects are initially expressed in a local reference frame. We manipulate objects to model a scene by applying various operations that deform or geometrically transform them in 2D or 3D space. *Geometric object transformations* are also used to express all object models of a scene in a common coordinate system (see Figure 1.5(a) and Chapter 3).

We now need to define the viewing parameters of a virtual camera or window through which we capture the three-dimensional scene or rasterize the two-dimensional geometry. What we set up is a viewing transformation and a projection that map what is visible through our virtual camera onto a planar region that corresponds to the rendered image (see Chapter 4). The *viewing transformation* expresses the objects relative to the viewer, as this greatly simplifies what is to follow. The *projection* converts the objects to the projection space of the camera. Loosely speaking, after this step the scene is transformed to reflect how we would perceive it through the virtual camera. For instance, if a perspective projection is used (pinhole-camera model), then distant objects appear smaller (perspective shortening; see Figure 1.5(b)).

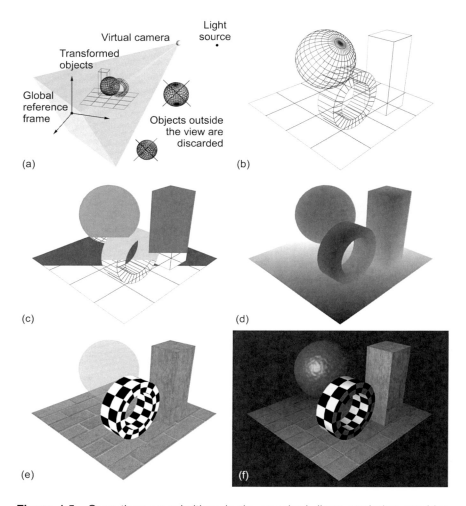

Figure 1.5. Operations on primitives in the standard direct rendering graphics pipeline. (a) Geometry transformation to a common reference frame and view frustum culling. (b) Primitives after viewing transformation, projection, and back-face culling. (c) Rasterization and (d) fragment depth sorting: the darker a shade, the nearer the corresponding point is to the virtual camera. (e) Material color estimation. (f) Shading and other fragment operations (such as fog).

Efficiency is central to computer graphics, especially so when direct user interaction is involved. As a large number of primitives are, in general, invisible from a specific viewpoint, it is pointless to try to render them, as they are not going to appear in the final image. The process of removing such parts of the scene is referred to as *culling*. A number of culling techniques have been developed to remove as many such primitives as possible as early as possible in the graphics pipeline. These include back-face, frustum, and occlusion culling (see Chapter 5). Most culling operations generally take place after the viewing transformation and before projection.

The projected primitives are clipped to the boundaries of the virtual camera field of view and all visible parts are finally rasterized. In the rasterization stage, each primitive is sampled in image space to produce a number of *fragments*, i.e., elementary pieces of data that represent the surface properties at each pixel sample. When a surface sample is calculated, the fragment data are interpolated from the supplied primitive data. For example, if a primitive is a triangle in space, it is fully described by its three vertices. Surface parameters at these vertices may include a surface normal direction vector, color and transparency, a number of other surface parameters such as texture coordinates (see Chapter 14), and, of course, the vertex coordinates that uniquely position this primitive in space. When the triangle is rasterized, the supplied parameters are interpolated for the sample points inside the triangle and forwarded as fragment tokens to the next processing stage. Rasterization algorithms produce coherent, dense and regular samples of the primitives to completely cover all the projection area of the primitive on the rendered image (Figure 1.5(c)).

Although the fragments correspond to the sample locations on the final image, they are not directly rendered because it is essential to discover which of them are actually directly visible from the specified viewpoint, i.e., are not occluded by other fragments closer to the viewpoint. This is necessary because the primitives sent to the rasterization stage (and hence the resulting fragments) are not ordered in depth. The process of discarding the hidden parts (fragments) is called *hidden surface elimination* (HSE; see Figure 1.5(d) and Chapter 5).

The fragments that successfully pass the HSE operation are then used for the determination of the color (Chapter 11) and shading of the corresponding pixels (Figure 1.5(e,f)). To this effect, an illumination model simulates the interplay of light and surface, using the material and the pose of a primitive fragment (Chapters 12 and 13). The colorization of the fragment and the final appearance of the surface can be locally changed by varying a surface property using one or more *textures* (Chapter 14). The final color of a fragment that corresponds to a ren-

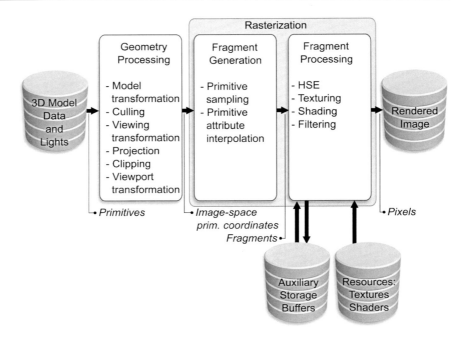

Figure 1.6. Three-dimensional graphics pipeline stages and data flow for direct rendering.

dered pixel is filtered, clamped, and normalized to a value that conforms to the final output specifications and is finally stored in the appropriate pixel location in the raster image.

An abstract layout of the graphics pipeline stages for direct rendering is shown in Figure 1.6. Note that other rendering algorithms do not adhere to this sequence of processing stages. For example, ray tracing does not include explicit fragment generation, HSE, or projection stages.

1.5   Image Buffers

1.5.1   Storage and Encoding of a Digital Image

The classic data structure for storing a digital image is a two-dimensional array (either row-major or column-major layout) in memory, the *image buffer*. Each

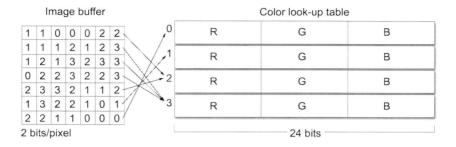

Figure 1.7. Paletted image representation. Indexing of pixel colors in a look-up table.

cell of the buffer encodes the color of the respective pixel in the image. The color representation of each pixel (see Chapter 11) can be monochromatic (e.g., grayscale), multi-channel color (e.g., red/green/blue), or paletted. For an image of $w \times h$ pixels, the size of the image buffer is at least[1] $w \times h \times \text{bpp}/8$ bytes, where bpp is the number of bits used to encode and store the color of each pixel. This number (bpp) is often called the *color depth* of the image buffer.

For monochromatic images, usually one or two bytes are stored for each pixel that map quantized intensity to unsigned integer values. For example, an 8 bpp grayscale image quantizes intensity in 256 discrete levels, 0 being the lowest intensity and 255 the highest.

In multi-channel color images, a similar encoding to the monochromatic case is used for each of the components that comprise the color information. Typically, color values in image buffers are represented by three channels, e.g., red, green, and blue. For color images, typical color depths for integer representation are 16, 24 and 32 bpp.

The above image representations are often referred to as *true-color*, a name that reflects the fact that full color intensity information is actually stored for each pixel. In *paletted* or *indexed* mode, the value at each cell of the image buffer does not directly represent the intensity of the image or the color components at that location. Instead, an index is stored to an external *color look-up table* (CLUT), also called a *palette*. An important benefit of using a paletted image is

---

[1]In some cases, word-aligned addressing modes pose a restriction on the allocated bytes per pixel, leading to some overhead. For instance, for 8-bit red/green/blue color samples, the color depth may be 32 instead of 24 (3×8) because it is faster to address multiples of 4 than multiples of 3 bytes in certain computer architectures.

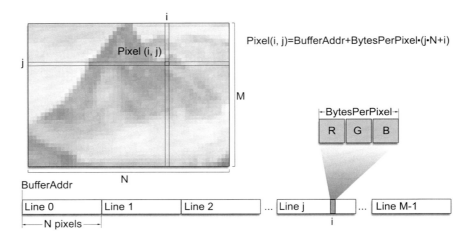

Figure 1.8. Typical memory representation of an image buffer.

that the bits per pixel do not affect the accuracy of the displayed color, but only the number of different color values that can be simultaneously assigned to pixels. The palette entries may be true-color values (Figure 1.7). A typical example is the image buffer of the Graphics Interchange Format (GIF), which uses 8 bpp for color indexing and 24-bit palette entries. Another useful property of a palette representation is that pixel colors can be quickly changed for an arbitrarily large image. Nevertheless, true-color images are usually preferred as they can encode 2^{bpp} simultaneous colors (large look-up tables are impractical) and they are easier to address and manipulate.

An image buffer occupies a contiguous space of memory (Figure 1.8). Assuming a typical row-major layout with interleaved storage of color components, an image pixel of BytesPerPixel bytes can be read by the following simple code:

```
unsigned char * GetPixel( int i, int j, int N, int M,
      int BytesPerPixel, unsigned char * BufferAddr )
{
   // Index-out-of-bounds checks can be inserted here.
   return BufferAddr + BytesPerPixel*(j*N+i);
}
```

Historically, apart from the above scheme, color components were stored contiguously in separate "memory planes."

1.5.2 The Frame Buffer

During the generation of a synthetic image, the calculated pixel colors are stored in an image buffer, the *frame buffer*, which has been pre-allocated in the main memory or the graphics hardware, depending on the application and rendering algorithm. The frame buffer's name reflects the fact that it holds the current *frame* of an animation sequence in direct analogy to a film frame. In the case of real-time graphics systems, the frame buffer is the area of graphics memory where all pixel color information from rasterization is accumulated before being driven to the graphics output, which needs constant update.

The need for the frame buffer arises from the fact that rasterization is primitive-driven rather than image-driven (as in the case of ray tracing, see Chapter 15) and therefore there is no guarantee that pixels will be sequentially produced. The frame buffer is randomly accessed for writing by the rasterization algorithm and sequentially read for output to a stream or the display device. So pixel data are pooled in the frame buffer, which acts as an interface between the random write and sequential read operations.

In the graphics subsystem, frame buffers are usually allocated in pairs to facilitate a technique called *double buffering*,[2] which will be explained below.

1.5.3 Other Buffers

We will come across various types of image buffers that are mostly allocated in the video memory of the graphics subsystem and are used for storage of intermediate results of various algorithms. Typically, all buffers have the same dimensions as the frame buffer, and there is a one-to-one correspondence between their cells and pixels of the frame buffer.

The most frequently used type of buffer for 3D image generation (other than the frame buffer) is the *depth buffer* or *Z-buffer*. The depth buffer stores distance values for the fragment-sorting algorithm during the hidden surface elimination phase (see Chapter 5). For real-time graphics generation, it is resident in the memory of the graphics subsystem.

Other specialized auxiliary buffers can be allocated in the graphics subsystem depending on the requirements of the rendering algorithm and the availability of

---

[2] *Quad buffering* is also utilized for the display of stereoscopic graphics where a pair of double-buffered frame buffers is allocated, corresponding to one full frame for each eye. The images from such buffers are usually sent to a single graphics output in an interleaved fashion ("active" stereoscopic display).

video RAM. The *stencil buffer* (refer to Chapter 13 for a detailed description) and the *accumulation buffer* are two examples. Storage of transparency values of generated fragments is frequently needed for blending operations with the existing colors in the frame buffer. This is why an extra channel for each pixel, the *alpha channel*, is supported in most current graphics subsystems. A transparency value is stored along with the red (R), green (G) and blue (B) color information (see Chapter 11) in the frame buffer. For 32-bit frame buffers, this fourth channel, alpha (A), occupies the remaining 8 bits of the pixel word (the other 24 bits are used for the three color channels).

1.6   Graphics Hardware

To display raster images on a matrix display, such as a *cathode ray tube* (CRT) or a digital flat panel display, color values that correspond to the visible dots on the display surface are sequentially read. The input signal (pixel intensities) is read in *scanlines* and the resulting image is generated in row order, from top to bottom. The source of the output image is the frame buffer, which is sequentially read by a video output circuit in synchrony with the refresh of the display device. This minimum functionality is provided by the graphics subsystem of the computer (which is a separate board or circuitry integrated on the main board). In certain cases, multiple graphics subsystems may be hosted on the same computing system to drive multiple display devices or to distribute the graphics processing load for the generation of a single image. The number of rows and the number of pixels per row of the output device matrix display determines the resolution at which the frame buffer is typically initialized.

1.6.1   Image-Generation Hardware

Display adapters. The early (raster) graphics subsystems consisted of two main components, the frame buffer memory and addressing circuitry and the output circuit. They were not unreasonably called *display adapters*; their sole purpose was to pool the randomly and asynchronously written pixels in the frame buffer and adapt the resulting digital image signal to a synchronous serial analog signal that was used to drive the display devices. The first frame buffers used paletted mode (see Section 1.5.1). The CPU performed the rasterization and randomly accessed the frame buffer to write the calculated pixel values. On the other side of the frame buffer a special circuit, the RAMDAC (random access memory digital-to-analog converter), was responsible for reading the frame buffer line by line and for the color look-up operation using the color palette (which constituted the RAM part of the circuit). It was also responsible for the conversion of the color values to the appropriate voltage on the output interface. The color look-up table progressively became obsolete with the advent of true color but is still integrated or emulated for compatibility purposes. For digital displays, such as the ones supporting the DVI-Digital and HDMI standard, the digital-to-analog conversion step is not required and is therefore bypassed. The output circuit operates in a synchronous manner to provide timed signaling for the constant update of the output devices. An internal clock determines its conversion speed and therefore its maximum *refresh rate*. The refresh rate is the frequency at which the display device performs a complete redisplay of the whole image. Display devices can be updated at various refresh rates, e.g., 60, 72, 80, 100, or 120 Hz. For the display adapter to be able to feed the output signal to the monitor, its internal clock needs to be adjusted to match the desired refresh rate. Obviously, as the output circuit operates on pixels, the clock speed also depends on the resolution of the displayed image. The maximum clock speed determines the maximum refresh rate at the desired resolution. For CRT-type displays the clocking frequency of the output circuit (RAMDAC clock) is roughly $f_{\mathrm{RAMDAC}} = 1.32 \cdot w \cdot h \cdot f_{\mathrm{refresh}}$, where w and h are the width and height of the image (in number of pixels) and f_{refresh} is the desired refresh rate. The factor 1.32 reflects a typical timing overhead to retrace the beam of the CRT to the next scanline and to the next frame (see Section 1.6.2 below).

Double buffering. Due to the incompatibility between the reading and writing of the frame buffer memory (random/sequential), it is very likely to start reading a scanline for output that is not yet fully generated. Ideally, the output circuit should wait for the rendering of a frame to finish before starting to read the frame buffer. This cannot be done as the output image has to be constantly updated at a very specific rate that is independent of the rasterization time. The solution to this problem is *double buffering*. A second frame buffer is allocated and the write and read operations are always performed on different frame buffers, thus completely decoupling the two processes. When buffer 1 is active for writing (this frame buffer is called the *back* buffer, because it is the one that is hidden, i.e., not currently displayed), the output is sequentially read from buffer 2 (the *front* buffer). When the write operation has completed the current frame, the roles of the two buffers are interchanged, i.e., data in buffer 2 are overwritten by the rasterization and pixels in buffer 1 are sequentially read for output to the display device. This exchange of roles is called *buffer swapping*.

Buffer swaps can take place immediately after the data in the back buffer become ready. In this case, if the sequential reading of the front buffer has not completed a whole frame, a "tearing" of the output image may be noticeable if the contents of the two buffers have significant differences. To avoid this, buffer swapping can be synchronously performed in the interval between the refresh of the previous and the next frame (this interval is known as vertical blank interval, or VBLANK, of the output circuit). During this short period, signals transmitted to the display device are not displayed. Locking the swaps to the VBLANK period eliminates this source of the tearing problem but introduces a lag before a back buffer is available for writing.[3]

Two-dimensional graphics accelerators. The first display adapters relied on the CPU to do all the rendering and buffer manipulation and so possessed no dedicated graphics processors. Advances in VLSI manufacturing and the standardization of display algorithms led to the progressive migration of rasterization algorithms from the CPU to specialized hardware. As graphical user interfaces became commonplace in personal computers, the drawing instructions for windows and graphical primitives and the respective APIs converged to standard sets of operations. Display drivers and the operating systems formed a *hardware abstraction layer* (HAL) between API-supported operations and what the underlying graphics subsystem actually implemented. Gradually, more and more of the operations supported by the standard APIs were implemented in hardware. One of the first operations that was included in specialized graphics hardware was "blitting," i.e., the efficient relocation and combination of "sprites" (rectangular image blocks). Two-dimensional primitive rasterization algorithms for lines, rectangles, circles, etc., followed. The first graphical applications to benefit from the advent of the (2D) graphics accelerators were computer games and the windowing systems themselves, the latter being an obvious candidate for acceleration due to their standardized and intensive processing demands.

Three-dimensional graphics accelerators. A further acceleration step was achieved by the standardization of the 3D graphics rendering pipeline and the wide adoption of the Z-buffer algorithm for hidden surface elimination (see Chapter 5). 3D graphics accelerators became a reality by introducing special processors and rasterization units that could operate on streams of three-dimensional primitives and corresponding instructions that defined their properties, lighting, and global operations. The available memory on the graphics accelerators was in-

---

[3]This is a selectable feature on many graphics subsystems.

creased to support a Z-buffer and other auxiliary buffers. Standard 3D APIs such as OpenGL [Open07b] and Direct3D focused on displaying surfaces as polygons, and the hardware graphics pipeline was optimized for this task. The core elements of a 3D graphics accelerator expanded to include more complex mathematical operations on matrices and vectors of floating-point data, as well as bitmap addressing, management, and paging functionality. Thus, special geometry processors could perform polygon set-up, geometric transformations, projections, interpolation, and lighting, thus completely freeing the CPU from computations relating to the display of 3D primitives. Once an application requests a rasterization or 3D set-up operation on a set of data, everything is propagated through the driver to the graphics accelerator. A key element to the success of the hardware acceleration of the graphics pipeline is the fact that operations on primitives and fragments can be executed in a highly parallel manner. Modern geometry processing, rasterization, and texturing units have multiple parallel stages. Ideas pioneered in the 1980s for introducing parallelism to graphics algorithms have found their way to 3D graphics accelerators.

Programmable graphics hardware. Three-dimensional acceleration transferred the graphics pipeline to hardware. To this end, the individual stages and algorithms for the various operations on the primitives were fixed both in the order of execution and in their implementation. As the need for greater realism in real-time graphics surpassed the capabilities of the standard hardware implementations, more flexibility was pursued in order to execute custom operations on the primitives but also to take advantage of the high-speed parallel processing of the graphics accelerators. In modern *graphics processing units* (GPUs), see Figure 1.9, both the fixed geometry processing and the rasterization stages of their predecessors were replaced by small, specialized programs that are executed on the graphics processors and are called *shader programs* or simply *shaders*.

Two types of shaders are usually defined. The *vertex shader* replaces the fixed functionality of the geometry processing stage and the *fragment shader* processes the generated fragments and usually performs shading and texturing (see Chapter 12 for some shader implementations of complex illumination models). Vendors are free to provide their specific internal implementation of the GPU so long as they remain compliant with a set of supported shader program instructions. Vertex and fragment shader programs are written in various shading languages, compiled, and then loaded at runtime to the GPU for execution. Vertex shaders are executed once per primitive vertex and fragment shaders are invoked for each generated fragment. The fixed pipeline of the non-programmable 3D

Figure 1.9. Typical consumer 3D graphics accelerator. The board provides multiple output connectors (analog and digital). Heat sinks and a cooling fan cover the on-board memory banks and GPU, which operate at high speeds.

graphics accelerators is emulated via shader programs as the default behavior of a GPU.

1.6.2   Image-Output Hardware

Display monitors are the most common type of display device. However, a variety of real-time as well as non-real-time and hard-copy display devices operate on similar principles to produce visual output. More specifically, they all use a raster image. Display monitors, regardless of their technology, read the contents of the frame buffer (a raster image). Commodity printers, such as laser and inkjet printers, can prepare a raster image that is then directly converted to dots on the printing surface. The rasterization of primitives, such as font shapes, vectors, and bitmaps, relies on the same steps and algorithms as 2D real-time graphics (see Section 1.4).

Display monitors. During the early 2000s, the market of standard raster image-display monitors made a transition from cathode ray tube technology to liquid crystal flat panels. There are other types of displays, suitable for more specialized types of data and applications, such as vector displays, lenticular autostereoscopic displays, and volume displays, but we focus on the most widely available types.

  Cathode ray tube (CRT) displays (Figure 1.10 (top right)) operate in the following manner: An electron beam is generated from the heating of a cathode of a

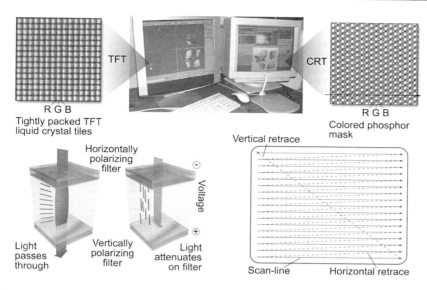

Figure 1.10. Color display monitors. (Top left) TFT liquid crystal tile arrangement. (Bottom left) Standard twisted nematic liquid crystal display operation. (Top right) Cathode ray tube dot arrangement. (Bottom right) CRT beam trajectory.

special tube called an electron gun that is positioned at the back of the CRT. The electrons are accelerated due to voltage difference towards the anodized glass of the tube. A set of coils focuses the beam and deflects it so that it periodically traces the front wall of the display left to right and top to bottom many times per second (observe the trajectory in Figure 1.10 (bottom right)). When the beam electrons collide with the phosphor-coated front part of the display, the latter is excited, resulting in the emission of visible light. The electron gun fires electrons only when tracing the scanlines and remains inactive while the deflection coils move the beam to the next scanline or back to the top of the screen (vertical blank interval). The intensity of the displayed image depends on the rate of electrons that hit a particular phosphor dot, which in turn is controlled by the voltage applied to the electron gun as it is modulated by the input signal. A color CRT display combines three closely packed electron guns, one for each of the RGB color components. The three beams, emanating from different locations at the back of the tube, hit the phosphor coating at slightly different positions when focused properly. These different spots are coated with red, green, and blue phosphor, and as they are tightly clustered together, they give the impression of a combined additive color (see Chapter 11). Due to the beam-deflection principle, CRT displays suffer from distortions and focusing problems, but provide high brightness and contrast as well as uniform color intensity, independent of viewing angle.

The first *liquid crystal displays* (LCDs) suffered from slow pixel intensity change response times, poor color reproduction, and low contrast. The invention and mass production of color LCDs that overcame the above problems made LCD flat panel displays more attractive in many ways to the bulky CRT monitors. Today, their excellent geometric characteristics (no distortion), lightweight design, and improved color and brightness performance have made LCD monitors the dominant type of computer display.

The basic twisted nematic (TN) LCD device consists of two parallel transparent electrodes that have been treated so that tiny parallel grooves form on their surface in perpendicular directions. The two electrode plates are also coated with linear polarizing filters with the same alignment as the grooves. Between the two transparent surfaces, the space is filled with liquid crystal, whose molecules naturally align themselves with the engraved (brushed) grooves of the plates. As the grooves on the two electrodes are perpendicular, the liquid crystal molecules form a helix between the two plates. In the absence of an external factor such as voltage, light entering from the one transparent plate is polarized and its polarization gradually changes as it follows the spiral alignment of the liquid crystal (Figure 1.10 (bottom left)). Because the grooves on the second plate are aligned with its polarization direction, light passes through the plate and exits the liquid crystal. When voltage is applied to the electrodes, the liquid crystal molecules align themselves with the electric field and their spiraling arrangement is lost. Polarized light entering the first electrode hits the second filter with (almost) perpendicular polarization and is thus blocked, resulting in black color. The higher the voltage applied, the more intense the blackening of the element. LCD monitors consist of tightly packed arrays of liquid crystal tiles that comprise the "pixels" of the display (Figure 1.10 (top left)). Color is achieved by packing three color-coated elements close together. The matrix is back-lit and takes its maximum brightness when no voltage is applied to the tiles (a reverse voltage/transparency effect can also be achieved by rotating the second polarization filter). TFT (thin-film transistor) LCDs constitute an improvement of the TN elements, offering higher contrast and significantly better response times and are today used in the majority of LCD flat panel displays.

In various application areas, where high brightness is not a key issue, such as e-ink solutions and portable devices, other technologies have found ground to flourish. For instance, organic light-emitting diode (OLED) technology offers an attractive alternative to TFT displays for certain market niches, mostly due to the fact that it requires no backlight illumination, has much lower power consumption, and can be literally "printed" on thin and flexible surfaces.

Projection systems. Digital video projectors are visual output devices capable of displaying real-time content on large surfaces. Two alternative methods exist for the projection of an image, *rear projection* and *front projection*. In rear-projection set-ups, the projector is positioned at the back of the display surface relative to the observer and emits light, which passes through the translucent material of the projection medium and illuminates its surface. In front-projection set-ups, the projector resides at the same side as the observer and illuminates a surface, which reflects light to the observer.

There are three major projector technologies: CRT, LCD, and DLP (digital light processing). The first two operate on the same principles as the corresponding display monitors. DLP projectors, characterized by high contrast and brightness, are based on an array of micro-mirrors embedded on a silicon substrate (digital micromirror devices (DMD)). The mirrors are electrostatically flipped and act as shutters which either allow light to pass through the corresponding pixel or not. Due to the high speed of these devices, different intensities are achieved by rapidly flipping the mirrors and modulating the time interval that they remain shut. High quality DLP systems use three separate arrays to achieve color display, while single-array solutions require a transparent color wheel to alternate between color channels. In the latter case, the time available for each mirror to perform the series of flips required to produce a shade of a color is divided by three, resulting in lower color resolutions.

Printer graphics. The technology of electronic printing has undergone a series of major changes and many types of printers (such as dot-matrix and daisywheel printers and plotters) are almost obsolete today. The dominant mode of operation for printers is graphical, although all printers can also work as "line printers," accepting a string of characters and printing raw text line by line. In graphics mode, a raster image is prepared that represents a printed page or a smaller portion of it, which is then buffered in the printer's memory and is finally converted to dots on the printing medium.

The generation of the raster image can take place either in the computing system or inside the printer itself, depending on its capabilities. The raster image corresponds to the dot pattern that will be printed. Inexpensive printers have very limited processing capabilities and therefore the rasterization is done by the CPU via the printer driver. Higher-end printers (usually laser printers) are equipped with raster image processing units (common microprocessors are often used for this task) and enough memory to prepare the raster image of a whole page locally. The vector graphics and bitmaps are directly sent to the printer after conversion to an appropriate *page description language* that the raster image processor can understand, such as Adobe *PostScript* [Adob07]. PostScript describes two-dimensional graphics and text using *Bézier* curves (see Chapter 7), vectors, fill patterns, and transformations. A document can be fully described by this printing language, and PostScript was adopted early on as a portable document specification across different platforms as well. Once created, a PostScript document can be directly sent for printing to a PostScript printer or converted to the printer's native vector format if the printer supports a different language (e.g., Hewlett-Packard's PCL). This process is done by a printer driver. The PostScript document can also be rasterized by the computer in memory for viewing or printing, using a PostScript interpreter application.

Apart from the dynamic update of the content, an important difference between the image generated by a display monitor and the one that is printed is that color intensity on monitors is modulated in an analog fashion by changing an electric signal. A single displayed pixel can be "lit" at a wide range of intensities. On the other hand, ink is either deposited on the paper or other medium or not (although some technologies do offer a limited control of the ink quantity that represents a single dot). In Chapter 11, we will see how the impression of different shades of a color can be achieved by *halftoning*, an important printing technique where pixels of different intensity can be printed as patterns of colored dots from a small selection of color inks.

Printer technology. The two dominant printing technologies today are inkjet and laser. *Inkjet printers* form small droplets of ink on the printing medium by releasing ink through a set of nozzles. The flow of droplets is controlled either by heating or by the piezoelectric phenomenon. The low cost of inkjet printers, their ability to use multiple color inks (four to six) to form the printed pixel color variations (resulting in high quality photographic printing), and the acceptable quality in line drawings and text made them ideal for home and small-office use. On the other hand, the high cost per page (due to the short life of the ink cartridges), low printing speed, and low accuracy make them inappropriate for demanding printing tasks, where laser printers are preferable.

Laser printers operate on the following principle: a photosensitive drum is first electrostatically charged. Then, with the help of a mechanism of moving mirrors and lenses, a low-power laser diode reverses the charge on the parts of each line that correspond to the dots to be printed. The process is repeated while the drum rotates. The "written" surface of the drum is then exposed to the toner, which is a very fine powder of colored or black particles. The toner is charged with the same electric polarity as the drum, so the charged dust is attracted and deposited only on the drum areas with reversed charge and repelled by the rest. The paper or other medium is charged opposite to the toner and rolled over the drum, causing the particles to be transferred to its surface. In order for the fine particles of the toner to remain on the printed medium, the printed area is subjected to intense heating, which fuses the particles with the printing medium. Color printing is achieved by using three (color) toners and repeating the process three times. The high accuracy of the laser beam ensures high accuracy line drawings and halftone renderings. Printing speed is also superior to that of the inkjet printers and toners last far longer than the ink cartridges of the inkjet devices. A variation of the laser printer is the light-emitting diode (LED) printer: a dense row of fixed LEDs shines on the drum instead of a moving laser head, while the rest of the mechanism remains identical. The fewer moving parts make these printers cheaper, but they cannot achieve the high resolution of their laser cousins.

1.7 Conventions

The following mathematical notation conventions are generally used throughout the book.

- *Scalars* are typeset in italics.

- *Vector quantities* are typeset in bold. We distinguish between points in $\mathbb{E}^k$, which represent locations, and vectors in $\mathbb{R}^k$, which represent directions; see also Appendix A. Specifically,

  - *points* in $\mathbb{E}^k$ are typeset in upright bold letters, usually lowercase, e.g., **a**, **b**;

  - *vectors* in $\mathbb{R}^k$ are typeset in upright bold letters, usually lowercase, with an arrow on top, e.g., $\overrightarrow{\mathbf{a}}$, $\overrightarrow{\mathbf{b}}$, $\overrightarrow{\mathbf{Oa}}$;

  - *unit vectors* are typeset in upright bold letters, usually lowercase, with a "hat" on top, e.g., $\hat{\mathbf{e}}_1$, $\hat{\mathbf{n}}$.

- *Matrices* are typeset in uppercase upright bold letters, e.g., $\mathbf{M}$, $\mathbf{R}_x$.

Column vectors are generally used; row vectors are marked by the "transpose" symbol, e.g., $\vec{\mathbf{v}}^{\mathrm{T}} = [0,1,2]$. However, for ease of presentation, the alternative notation (x,y,z) will also be used for points.

- *Functions* are typeset as follows:

    - *Standard mathematical functions* and *custom functions* defined by the authors are in upright letters, e.g., $\sin(\theta)$.

    - Functions follow the above conventions for scalar and vector quantities, e.g., $\vec{\mathbf{F}}(\vec{\mathbf{x}})$ is a vector function of a vector variable, $\vec{\mathbf{g}}(x)$ is a vector function of a scalar variable, etc.

- *Norms* are typeset with single bars, e.g., $|\vec{\mathbf{v}}|$.

- *Standard sets* are typeset using "black board" letters, e.g., $\mathbb{R}$, $\mathbb{C}$.

Algorithm descriptions are given in pseudocode based on standard C and C++. However, depending on the specific detail requirements of each algorithm, the level of description will vary.

Advanced sections are marked with an asterisk ⊛ and are aimed at advanced courses.

2

Rasterization Algorithms

A line is a dot that went for a walk.
—Paul Klee

2.1 Introduction

Two-dimensional display devices consist of a discrete grid of pixels, each of which can be independently assigned a color value. *Rasterization*[1] is the process of converting two-dimensional primitives[2] into a discrete pixel representation. In other words, the pixels that best describe the primitives must be determined.

Given that we want to rasterize P primitives for a particular frame, and assuming that each primitive consists of an average of p pixels, the complexity of rasterization is in general $O(Pp)$. Previous stages in the graphics pipeline (e.g., transformations and culling) work with the vertices of primitives only. In general, the complexity of these previous stages is $O(Pv)$, where v is the average number of vertices of a primitive. Usually $p \gg v$, so we must ensure that rasterization algorithms are extremely efficient in order to avoid making the rasterization stage a bottleneck in the graphics pipeline.

The pixels of a raster device form a two-dimensional regular grid. There are two main ways of viewing this grid (Figure 2.1).

---

[1]*Scan-conversion* is a synonym.
[2]E.g., lines and polygons.

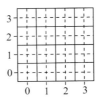

Figure 2.1. Two ways to view a pixel.

- *Half-integer centers.* Pixels are separated by imaginary horizontal and vertical border lines, just like graph paper. The border lines are at integer coordinates; hence, pixel centers are at half-integer coordinates.

- *Integer centers.* When the pixel grid is considered as a set of samples, it is natural to place sampling points (pixel centers) at integer coordinates.

We shall use the integer centers metaphor here. When considering a pixel as a point (e.g., a point in primitive inclusion tests) we shall be referring to the center of a pixel.

An important concept in rasterization is that of *connectedness*. What does it mean for a set of pixels to form a connected curve or area? For example, if a curve-drawing algorithm steps from a pixel to its diagonal neighbor, is there a gap in the curve? The key question to answer is, which are the neighbors of a pixel? There are two common approaches to this: 4-connectedness and 8-connectedness (Figure 2.2). In 4-connectedness the neighbors are the 4 nearest pixels (up, down, left, right) while in 8-connectedness the neighbors are the 8 nearest pixels (they include the diagonal pixels). Whichever type of connectedness we use, we must make sure that our rasterization algorithms consistently output curves that obey it. We shall use 8-connectedness.

There are two main challenges in designing a rasterization algorithm for a primitive:

1. to determine the pixels that *accurately* describe the primitive;

2. to be *efficient*.

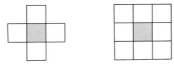

Figure 2.2. 4-connectedness and 8-connectedness.

The first challenge is essential for correctness, and it implies that a rasterization algorithm modifies the pixels that best describe a primitive, that it modifies only these pixels, and that it modifies the values of these pixels correctly. The second challenge is also extremely important, as our scenes may be composed of very large numbers of primitives and a real-time requirement may exist.

This chapter provides the mathematical principles and the algorithms necessary for the rasterization of common scene primitives: line segments, circles, general polygons, triangles, and closed areas. It also explains perspective correction and antialiasing which improve the result of the rasterization process. Finally, it deals with clipping algorithms that determine the intersection of a primitive and a clipping object and that are useful, among other things, in culling primitives that lie outside the field of view.

2.2 Mathematical Curves and Finite Differences

Among the mathematical forms that can be used to define two-dimensional primitive curves, the *implicit* and the *parametric* forms are most useful in rasterization. In the implicit form, a curve is defined as a function $f(x,y)$ that produces three possible types of result:

$$f(x,y) \begin{cases} < 0, & \text{implies point } (x,y) \text{ is inside the curve;} \\ = 0, & \text{implies point } (x,y) \text{ is on the curve;} \\ > 0, & \text{implies point } (x,y) \text{ is outside the curve.} \end{cases}$$

The terms inside and outside have no special significance, and in some cases (e.g., a line) they are entirely symmetrical. A curve thus separates the plane into two distinct regions: the inside region and the outside region.

For example, the implicit form of a line is

$$l(x,y) \equiv ax + by + c = 0, \tag{2.1}$$

where a, b, and c are the line coefficients. Points (x,y) on the line have $l(x,y) = 0$. For a line from $\mathbf{p_1} = (x_1, y_1)$ to $\mathbf{p_2} = (x_2, y_2)$, we have $a = y_2 - y_1$, $b = x_1 - x_2$ and $c = x_2 y_1 - x_1 y_2$. The line divides the plane into two half-planes; points with $l(x,y) < 0$ are on one half-plane, while points with $l(x,y) > 0$ are on the other.

The implicit form of a circle with center $\mathbf{c} = (x_c, y_c)$ and radius r is

$$c(x,y) \equiv (x - x_c)^2 + (y - y_c)^2 - r^2 = 0. \tag{2.2}$$

A point (x,y) for which $c(x,y) = 0$ is on the circle; if $c(x,y) < 0$ the point is inside the circle, while if $c(x,y) > 0$ the point is outside the circle.

The parametric form defines the curve as a function of a parameter t, which roughly corresponds to arc length along the curve. For example, the parametric form of a line defined by $\mathbf{p_1} = (x_1, y_1)$ and $\mathbf{p_2} = (x_2, y_2)$ is

$$\mathbf{l}(t) = (x(t), y(t)), \qquad (2.3)$$

where

$$x(t) = x_1 + t(x_2 - x_1), \qquad y(t) = y_1 + t(y_2 - y_1).$$

As t goes from 0 to 1, the line segment from $\mathbf{p_1}$ to $\mathbf{p_2}$ is traced; extending t beyond this range traces the line defined by $\mathbf{p_1}$ and $\mathbf{p_2}$.

Similarly, a parametric equation for a circle with center (x_c, y_c) and radius r is

$$\mathbf{c}(t) = (x(t), y(t)),$$

where

$$x(t) = x_c + r\cos(2\pi t), \qquad y(t) = y_c + r\sin(2\pi t).$$

As t goes from 0 to 1 the circle is traced; if the values of t are extended beyond this range, the circle is retraced.

The functions that define primitives often need to be evaluated on the pixel grid, for example, as part of the rasterization process or in eliminating hidden surfaces. Simply evaluating a function for each pixel independently is wasteful. For example, the evaluation of the implicit line function costs two multiplications and two additions, while the circle function costs three multiplications and four additions per point (pixel). Fortunately, since the pixel grid is regular, it is possible to cut this cost by taking advantage of the *finite differences* of the functions [Krey06]. The first *forward difference* of a function f at x_i is defined as

$$\delta f_i = f_{i+1} - f_i,$$

where $f_i = f(x_i)$. Similarly, its second forward difference at x_i is

$$\delta^2 f_i = \delta f_{i+1} - \delta f_i,$$

and, generalizing, its kth forward difference is defined recursively

$$\delta^k f_i = \delta^{k-1} f_{i+1} - \delta^{k-1} f_i.$$

For a polynomial function of degree n, all differences from the nth and above will be constant (and those from $(n+1)$th and above will be 0). Take the implicit line equation (2.1). Let us calculate its forward differences for a step in the x direction, i.e., from pixel x to pixel $x+1$. Since the line equation is of degree 1 in x, we only need to compute the (constant) first forward difference along x:

$$\delta_x l(x, y) = l(x+1, y) - l(x, y) = a, \qquad (2.4)$$

where δ_x stands for the forward difference on the x parameter. Similarly $\delta_y l(x,y)$ $= b$. We can thus evaluate the line function incrementally, from pixel to pixel. To go from its value $l(x,y)$ at pixel (x,y) to its value at pixel $(x+1,y)$, we simply compute $l(x,y) + \delta_x l(x,y) = l(x,y) + a$, while to go from (x,y) to $(x,y+1)$, we compute $l(x,y) + \delta_y l(x,y) = l(x,y) + b$. Each incremental evaluation of the line function thus costs only one addition.

Let us compute the forward differences on the x parameter for the circle equation (2.2). Since it has degree 2, there will be a first and a second forward difference. Evaluating them for a point (x,y) gives

$$\delta_x c(x,y) = c(x+1,y) - c(x,y) = 2(x-x_c) + 1,$$
$$\delta_x^2 c(x,y) = \delta_x c(x+1,y) - \delta_x c(x,y) = 2. \tag{2.5}$$

To incrementally compute the circle function from $c(x,y)$ to $c(x+1,y)$ we need two additions:

$$\delta_x c(x,y) = \delta_x c(x-1,y) + \delta_x^2 c(x,y);$$
$$c(x+1,y) = c(x,y) + \delta_x c(x,y).$$

Similarly, we can incrementally compute its value from $c(x,y)$ to $c(x,y+1)$ by adding $\delta_y c(x,y)$ and $\delta_y^2 c(x,y)$.

To rasterize a primitive, we must determine the pixels that accurately describe it. One way of doing this is to define a Boolean-valued mathematical function that, given a pixel (x,y), decides if it belongs to the primitive or not. Implicit functions can be used for this purpose. For example, the distance of a pixel (x,y) from a line described by the implicit function (2.1) is

$$\frac{|l(x,y)|}{\sqrt{a^2+b^2}}.$$

A test for the inclusion of pixel (x,y) in the rasterized line could thus be

$$|l(x,y)| < e,$$

where e is related to the required line width. Unfortunately, it is rather costly to evaluate such functions blindly over the pixel grid, even if done incrementally using their finite differences. Instead methods that track a primitive are usually more efficient.

2.3 Line Rasterization

To design a good line-rasterization[3] algorithm, we must first decide what it means
for such an algorithm to be correct (i.e., satisfy the accuracy requirement). Since
the pixel grid has finite resolution, it is not possible to select pixels that are exactly
on the mathematical path of the line; it is necessary to approximate it. The desired
qualities of a line-rasterization algorithm are:

1. selection of the nearest pixels to the mathematical path of the line;

2. constant line width, independent of the slope of the line;

3. no gaps;

4. high efficiency.

The derivation of line-rasterization algorithms will follow the exposition of
Sproull [Spro82], Harris [Harr04], and Rauber [Raub93].

Suppose that we want to draw a line starting at pixel $\mathbf{p_s} = (x_s, y_s)$ and ending at
pixel $\mathbf{p_e} = (x_e, y_e)$ in the first octant[4] (Figure 2.3). If we let $s = (y_e - y_s)/(x_e - x_s)$
be the slope of the line, then the pixel sequence we select can be derived from the
explicit line equation

$$y = y_s + round(s \cdot (x - x_s));$$
$$x = x_s, ..., x_e.$$

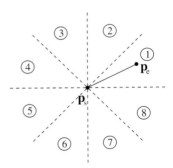

Figure 2.3. The eight octants with an example line in the first octant.

---

[3]In this section we liberally use the term "line" to refer to "line segment." "Line drawing" is often
used as a synonym for "line rasterization."

[4]The other seven octants can be treated in a similar manner, as discussed at the end of this section.

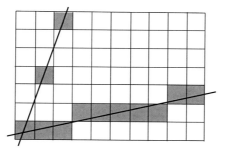

Figure 2.4. Using the `line1` algorithm in the first and second octants.

The `line1` algorithm selects the above pixel sequence:

```
line1 ( int xs, int ys, int xe, int ye, color c )  {
    float s; int x,y;

    s=(ye-ys) / (xe-xs);
    (x,y)=(xs,ys);
    while (x <= xe) {
        setpixel(x,y,c);
        x=x+1;
        y=ys + round(s * (x-xs));
    }
}
```

The `while` loop is based on the variable of the *major axis* of the line (x). The major axis is x if $|x_e - x_s| > |y_e - y_s|$; otherwise it is y. The non-major axis is called the *minor axis*. If the `line1` algorithm is used to draw a line whose major axis is y, then gaps appear (Figure 2.4). Instead, a variant which runs the `while` loop on the y variable should be used in that case. Also note that we should check for the condition $x_e - x_s = 0$ to avoid a division by 0; line rasterization becomes trivial in this case.

The value being rounded is increased by s at every iteration of the loop. The expensive `round` operation can be avoided if we split the y value into an integer and a float part e and compute its value incrementally. The `line2` algorithm does this:

```
line2 ( int xs, int ys, int xe, int ye, color c )  {
    float s,e; int x,y;
```

```
e=0;
s=(ye-ys) / (xe-xs);
(x,y)=(xs,ys);
while (x <= xe) {
    /* assert -1/2 <= e < 1/2 */
    setpixel(x,y,c);
    x=x+1;
    e=e+s;
    if (e >= 1/2) {
        y=y+1;
        e=e-1;
    }
}
}
```

Notice how the `line2` algorithm resembles the leap-year calculation. The slope is added to the *e* variable at each iteration until it makes up more than half a unit, and then the line leaps up by 1; the integer *y* variable is incremented and *e* is correspondingly reduced, so that the sum of the two variables is unchanged. In a similar manner, there are approximately 365.25 days per year, but calendars are designed with an integer number of days. Hence we add a day every fourth year to make up for the error being accumulated [Harr04].

With suitable scaling, the floating point variables in `line2` can be replaced by integer variables. Multiplying the leap-decision variables by $dx = x_e - x_s$ makes *s* and *e* integers. The leap decision becomes $e \geq dx/2$, but since *e* is now integer, we can replace $dx/2$ by the integer value $\lfloor dx/2 \rfloor$, which can be computed by a numerical shift without changing the algorithm semantics. We can also replace the test $e \geq \lfloor dx/2 \rfloor$ by $e \geq 0$ (which is more efficient) using an initial subtraction of $\lfloor dx/2 \rfloor$ from *e*. We thus arrive at the Bresenham algorithm [Bres65]:

```
line3 ( int xs, int ys, int xe, int ye, color c )  {
    int x,y,e,dx,dy;

    e=-(dx >> 1);
    dx=(xe-xs);
    dy=(ye-ys);
    (x,y)=(xs,ys);
    while (x <= xe) {
        /* assert -dx <= e < 0 */
        setpixel(x,y,c);
        x=x+1;
        e=e+dy;
        if (e >= 0) {
```

```
                y=y+1;
                e=e-dx;
            }
        }
    }
```

where >> stands for the right shift integer operator (right shifting by 1 bit is equivalent to dividing by 2 and taking the floor). The algorithm line3 is suitable for lines in the first octant. The major axis for each of the eight octants and the action on the variable of the minor axis are given in Table 2.1.

Octant	Major axis	Minor axis variable
1	x	increasing
2	y	increasing
3	y	decreasing
4	x	increasing
5	x	decreasing
6	y	decreasing
7	y	increasing
8	x	decreasing

Table 2.1. Line-rasterization requirements per octant.

Lines in the eighth octant can be handled by decrementing the y value in the loop and negating dy so that it is positive. Lines in the fourth and fifth octants are dealt with by swapping their endpoints, thus converting them to the eighth and first octants, respectively. Lines in the second, third, sixth, and seventh octants have y as the major axis and use a symmetrical version of the algorithm which runs the while loop on the y variable. An optimized Bresenham line-rasterization code usually contains two versions, one for when x is the major axis and one for when y is the major axis.

Notice how the Bresenham algorithm meets the requirements of a good line-rasterization algorithm. First, it selects the closest pixels to the mathematical path of the line since it is equivalent to line1 which rounded to the nearest pixel to the value of the mathematical line. Second, the major axis concept ensures (roughly) constant width and no gaps in an 8-connected sense. Third, it is highly efficient since it uses only integer variables and simple operations on them (additions, subtractions, and shifts).

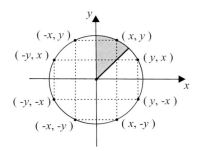

Figure 2.5. 8-way symmetry of a circle.

2.4   Circle Rasterization

The circle is mainly used as a primitive in design and information presentation
applications, and we shall now explore how to efficiently rasterize the perimeter
of a circle. Circles possess 8-way symmetry (Figure 2.5), and we take advantage of this in the rasterization process. Essentially, we only compute the pixels
of one octant, and the rest are derived using the 8-way symmetry (by taking all
combinations of swapping and negating the x and y values).

We shall give a variation of Bresenhem's circle algorithm [Bres77] due to
Hanrahan [Hanr98]. Suppose that we draw a circular arc that belongs to the second octant (shown shaded in Figure 2.5) of a circle of radius r centered at the
origin, starting with pixel $(0, r)$. In the second octant, x is the major axis and
$-y$ the minor axis, so we increment x at every step and sometimes we decrement y. The algorithm traces pixels *just below* the circle, incrementing x at every
step; if the value of the circle function becomes non-negative (pixel not inside the

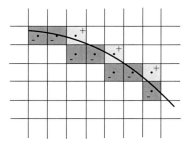

Figure 2.6. Tracing the circle in the second octant.

circle)[5] y is decremented (Figure 2.6). The value of the circle function is always
kept updated for the current pixel in variable e.

As described, the algorithm treats inside and outside pixels asymmetrically.
To center the selected pixels on the circle, we use a circle function which is displaced by half a pixel upwards; the circle center becomes $(0, \frac{1}{2})$:

$$c(x,y) = x^2 + (y - \frac{1}{2})^2 - r^2 = 0.$$

The following algorithm results:

```
circle ( int r, color c )  {
    int x,y,e;

    x=0
    y=r
    e=-r
    while (x <= y) {
        /* assert e == x^2 + (y - 1/2)^2 - r^2 */
        set8pixels(x,y,c);
        e=e+2*x+1;
        x=x+1;
        if (e >= 0) {
            e=e-2*y+2;
            y=y-1;
        }
    }
}
```

The error variable must be initialized to

$$c(0,r) = (r - \frac{1}{2})^2 - r^2 = \frac{1}{4} - r,$$

but since it is an integer variable, the $\frac{1}{4}$ can be dropped without changing the
algorithm semantics. For the incremental evaluation of e (which keeps the value
of the implicit circle function), we use the finite differences of that function for
the two possible steps that the algorithm takes:

$$c(x+1,y) - c(x,y) = (x+1)^2 - x^2 = 2x+1;$$
$$c(x,y-1) - c(x,y) = (y - \frac{3}{2})^2 - (y - \frac{1}{2})^2 = -2y+2.$$

---

[5]The implicit circle function $c(x,y)$ (Equation (2.2)) evaluates to 0 for points on the circle, takes
positive values for points outside the circle, and negative values for points inside the circle.

The above algorithm is very efficient, as it uses only integer variables and simple operations (additions / subtractions and multiplications by powers of 2) and only traces $\frac{1}{8}$ of the circle's circumference. The other $\frac{7}{8}$ are computed by symmetry :

```
set8pixels ( int x,y, color c )  {

    setpixel(x,y,c);
    setpixel(y,x,c);
    setpixel(y,-x,c);
    setpixel(x,-y,c);
    setpixel(-x,-y,c);
    setpixel(-y,-x,c);
    setpixel(-y,x,c);
    setpixel(-x,y,c);
}
```

2.5   Point-in-Polygon Tests

Perhaps the most common building block for surface models is the polygon and, in particular, the triangle. Polygon rasterization algorithms that rasterize the perimeter as well as the interior of a polygon, are based on the condition necessary for a point (pixel) to be inside a polygon. We shall define a *polygon* as a closed piecewise linear curve in $\mathbb{R}^2$. More specifically, a polygon consists of a sequence of n vertices $\mathbf{v_0}, \mathbf{v_1}, ..., \mathbf{v_{n-1}}$ that define n edges that form a closed curve $\mathbf{v_0 v_1}, \mathbf{v_1 v_2}, ..., \mathbf{v_{n-2} v_{n-1}}, \mathbf{v_{n-1} v_0}$. The *Jordan Curve Theorem* [Jord87] states that a continuous simple closed curve in the plane separates the plane into two distinct regions, the inside and the outside. (If the curve is not simple, i.e., it intersects itself, then the inside and outside regions are not necessarily connected). In order to efficiently rasterize polygons we need a test which, for a point (pixel) $\mathbf{p}(x,y)$ and a polygon P, decides if $\mathbf{p}$ is inside P (discussed here) and efficient algorithms for computing the inside pixels (see Section 2.6).

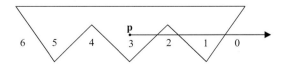

Figure 2.7. The parity test for a point in a polygon.

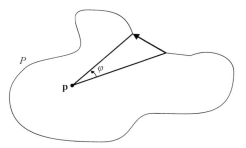

Figure 2.8. The winding number.

There are two well-known inclusion tests, which decide if a point **p** is inside a polygon *P*. The first is the *parity* test and states that if we draw a half-line from **p** in any direction such that the number of intersections with *P* is finite, then if that number is odd, **p** is inside *P*; otherwise, it is outside. This is demonstrated in Figure 2.7 for a horizontal half-line.

The second test is the *winding number*. For a closed curve *P* and a point **p**, the winding number $\omega(P, \mathbf{p})$ counts the number of revolutions completed by a ray from **p** that traces *P* once (Figure 2.8). For every counterclockwise revolution $\omega(P, \mathbf{p})$ is incremented and for every clockwise revolution $\omega(P, \mathbf{p})$ is decremented:

$$\omega(P, \mathbf{p}) = \frac{1}{2\pi} \int d\varphi.$$

If $\omega(P, \mathbf{p})$ is odd then **p** is inside *P*, otherwise it is outside (Figure 2.9). A simple way to compute the winding number counts the number of right-handed minus the number of left-handed crossings of a half-line from **p**, performed by tracing *P* once (Figure 2.10).

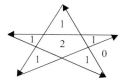

Figure 2.9. The winding-number test for a point in a polygon.

Figure 2.10. Simple computation of the winding number.

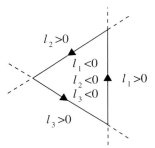

Figure 2.11. The sign test for a point in a convex polygon.

In the special case of a convex polygon whose n edges are defined by lines $l_0...l_{n-1}$, a simpler test can be used. If all edges are given in a consistent walk around the convex polygon (i.e., clockwise or counterclockwise), we can define the associated line functions so that points on the inside half-plane of every edge give evaluations of the same sign. If all edge functions have the same sign for a pixel $\mathbf{p}$, then $\mathbf{p}$ is inside the convex polygon:

$$\text{sign}(l_0(\mathbf{p})) = \text{sign}(l_1(\mathbf{p})) = \ldots = \text{sign}(l_{n-1}(\mathbf{p})). \qquad (2.6)$$

For example, if the line coefficients a, b, and c are derived as for Equation (2.1), and assuming a counterclockwise polygon traversal, inside points will give negative values to the line functions (Figure 2.11). If the line functions of all edges are negative for a point $\mathbf{p}$, then $\mathbf{p}$ is inside the convex polygon.

2.6   Polygon Rasterization

We shall first consider algorithms suitable for rasterizing arbitrary polygons (as defined in the previous section) and then specialized algorithms for triangles. Triangles are, in practice, the most widespread primitive. The triangle algorithms are simpler, and variants of them can be found implemented on graphics accelerators. For general polygons, the rasterization algorithms of Sections 2.6.1, 2.6.3, and 2.6.4 can be used, or alternatively, such polygons can be split into triangles using triangulation algorithms. Area-filling algorithms work directly on the contents of the frame buffer and are suitable for some 2D drawing applications.

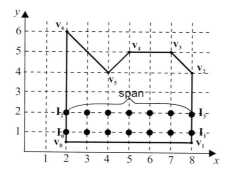

Figure 2.12. Spans and singularities.

2.6.1   Basic Polygon-Rasterization Algorithm

This is a simple algorithm based on the parity test. The steps are:

1. Compute the intersections $\mathbf{I}(x,y)$ of every polygon edge with all the scan-lines it intersects and store them in a list.

2. Sort the intersections by (y,x).

3. Extract spans (pairs of successive intersection points) from the list and set the pixels between them.

The basic algorithm computes the intersections of the polygon edges with the scanlines, sorts them with y (scanline) as the primary key and x as the secondary key, and then extracts them in pairs from the sorted list and sets the pixels between each such pair. A pair of successive intersection points in the sorted list is called a *span* and represents a sequence of pixels that are inside the polygon, according to the parity test (Figure 2.12). The simple setting of the pixels of a span may be replaced by the interpolation of a property, such as color.

2.6.2   Singularities

Figure 2.12 shows some problematic cases in polygon rasterization. If a polygon vertex falls exactly on a scanline, does it count as 2, 1, or 0 intersections? Unfortunately, none of these choices will work universally. For example, vertices $\mathbf{v_2} - \mathbf{v_6}$ should be treated differently. For correct rasterization results, vertex $\mathbf{v_2}$ should count as 1 intersection, vertices $\mathbf{v_5}$ and $\mathbf{v_6}$ should count as 0 or 2 intersections, and vertices $\mathbf{v_3}$ and $\mathbf{v_4}$ as 1 or 0 intersections. What is the general rule?

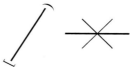

Figure 2.13. Rule for treating intersection singularities.

A simple solution is to regard a polygon edge as closed on the vertex with the minimum y- and open on the vertex with the maximum y-coordinate; horizontal edges are ignored (Figure 2.13). Thus, in the example of Figure 2.12, v_2 would count as 1 intersection (with edge v_2v_3), v_5 as 2, v_6 as 0, and v_3 and v_4 also as 0 intersections since v_3v_4 is a horizontal edge. The singularities problem is solved, but the polygon is then rasterized asymmetrically in the y direction: horizontal edges on the upper part of the polygon and vertices that represent local maxima are rasterized while horizontal edges on the lower part of the polygon and verticies that represent local minima are not rasterized. However this will hardly be noticeable in practice. The effect of this rule on the singularities is shown in Figure 2.14.

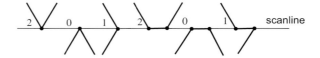

Figure 2.14. Effect of singularities rule on singularities.

2.6.3   Scanline Polygon-Rasterization Algorithm

The basic polygon rasterization algorithm is inefficient. Intersection computations are costly. Fortunately it is possible to take advantage of *scanline coherence* and *edge coherence* in order to improve efficiency. Scanline coherence exploits the fact that there is usually little change between the polygon edges that intersect successive scanlines. It therefore makes sense to *cache* these intersection points and update them incrementally for each scanline. This cache is called the *active edge table* (AET) .

Edge coherence refers to the fact that an edge changes in a predictable manner over its length; specifically, the edge-scanline intersection point can be incrementally computed from scanline to scanline by adding the inverse slope of the line defined by the edge ($\frac{1}{s} = \frac{\Delta x}{\Delta y}$).

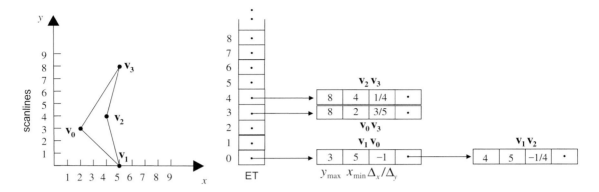

Figure 2.15. A polygon and its edge table.

An *edge table* (ET) is used to bucket-sort the polygon edges in order to aid the incremental update of the AET. Each bucket in the ET corresponds to a scanline (Figure 2.15). A record containing the necessary information for an edge is inserted in the bucket of its minimum y-coordinate.

The steps of the scanline algorithm are as follows:

1. Construct the ET for the polygon containing the maximum y, the minimum x and the inverse slope of each edge $(y_{max}, x_{min}, \frac{1}{s})$. The record of an edge is inserted in the bucket of its minimum y-coordinate.

2. For every scanline y that intersects the polygon in an upward sweep:

   (a) Update the AET edge intersections for the current scanline: $x = x + \frac{1}{s}$.

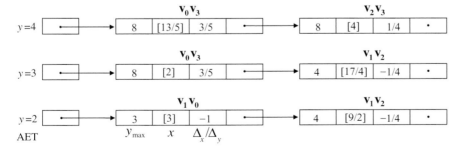

Figure 2.16. Example states of the AET.

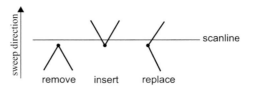

Figure 2.17. Updating the AET.

(b) Insert edges from the y bucket of ET into AET.

(c) Remove edges from AET whose $y_{\max} \leq y$.

(d) Re-sort AET on x.

(e) Extract spans from the AET and set their pixels.

Three examples of the state of the AET for scanlines 2, 3, and 4 are shown in Figure 2.16.

In the scanline algorithm, the edges that populate the AET change at polygon vertices according to Figure 2.17. A local maximum will remove two edges, a local minimum will insert two edges, and other vertices will result in the replacement of an edge.

2.6.4   Critical Points Polygon-Rasterization Algorithm

In the previous algorithm we noted that new edges are only inserted at polygon vertices that are local minima. The sole purpose of the ET is to maintain edge information for insertion in the AET during the processing of the proper scanline. The critical points algorithm [Gord94] makes the ET redundant and avoids its expensive creation by using the local minima explicitly. The local minima (polygon vertices that are local minima with respect to their y-coordinate) are called *critical points*.

The main steps of the critical points polygon-rasterization algorithm are:

1. Find and store the critical points of the polygon.

2. For every scanline y that intersects the polygon in an upward sweep:

    (a) For every critical point $\mathbf{c}(c_x, c_y) \mid (y - 1 < c_y \leq y)$ track the perimeter of the polygon in both directions starting at $\mathbf{c}$. Tracking stops if scanline y is intersected or a local maximum is found. For every intersection with scanline y, create an AET record $(v, \pm 1, x)$ containing the start vertex number v of the intersecting edge, the tracking direction

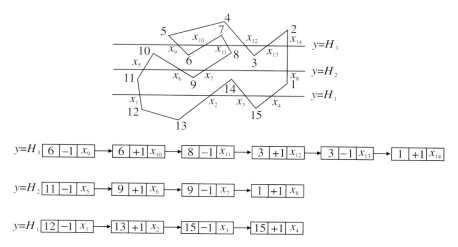

Figure 2.18. The critical points polygon-rasterization algorithm. An example polygon (above) and the contents of the AET for 3 scanlines (below) are shown.

along the perimeter of the polygon (-1 or $+1$ depending on whether it is clockwise or counterclockwise), and the x-coordinate of the point of intersection.

(b) For every AET record that pre-existed step (a), track the polygon perimeter in the direction stored within it. If an intersection with scanline y is found, the record's start vertex number and intersection x-coordinate are updated. If a local maximum is found, the record is deleted from the AET.

(c) Sort the AET on x if necessary.

(d) Extract spans from the AET and set their pixels.

Figure 2.18 shows a polygon being rasterized and the contents of the AET for three successive scanlines.

2.6.5 Triangle-Rasterization Algorithms

The triangle is the simplest polygon and is guaranteed, by definition, to be both planar and convex. Triangles are the most common building block of our models, and algorithms exist for the conversion of most surface representations (e.g., bicubic surfaces, volumetric isosurfaces) into triangle meshes. Hence, triangles deserve special attention.

One way of determining the pixels covered by a triangle is to perform an *inside test* on all the pixels in the triangle's bounding box. Since the triangle is a convex polygon, the inside test can be the evaluation of the three line functions defined by the triangle edges. For each pixel **p** of the bounding box, if the three line functions give results of the same sign, then **p** is inside the triangle. This test can be specialized to an all-positive or all-negative check if the order of the vertices is fixed to clockwise or counterclockwise. For efficiency, the line functions are incrementally evaluated using their forward differences.

```
triangle1 ( vertex v0, v1, v2, color c );  {
    line l0, l1, l2;
    float e0, e1, e2,   e0t, e1t, e2t;

    /* Compute the line coefficients (a,b,c) from the vertices */
    mkline(v0, v1, &l0);
    mkline(v1, v2, &l1);
    mkline(v2, v0, &l2);

    /* Compute bounding box of triangle */
    bb_xmin = min(v0.x, v1.x, v2.x);
    bb_xmax = max(v0.x, v1.x, v2.x);
    bb_ymin = min(v0.y, v1.y, v2.y);
    bb_ymax = max(v0.y, v1.y, v2.y);

    /* Evaluate linear functions at (bb_xmin, bb_ymin) */
    e0 = l0.a * bb_xmin + l0.b * bb_ymin + l0.c;
    e1 = l1.a * bb_xmin + l1.b * bb_ymin + l1.c;
    e2 = l2.a * bb_xmin + l2.b * bb_ymin + l2.c;

    for (y=bb_ymin; y<=bb_ymax; y++)  {
        e0t = e0; e1t = e1; e2t = e2;
        for (x=bb_xmin; x<=bb_xmax; x++)  {
            if (sign(e0)==sign(e1)==sign(e2))  setpixel(x,y,c);

            e0 = e0 + l0.a;
            e1 = e1 + l1.a;
            e2 = e2 + l2.a;
        }
        e0 = e0t + l0.b;
        e1 = e1t + l1.b;
        e2 = e2t + l2.b;
    }
}
```

If the bounding box is large compared to the area of a triangle (e.g., thin diagonal triangle) then the `triangle1` algorithm will be wasteful as it will evaluate the line functions for a large number of outside pixels. Another approach to triangle rasterization is *edge walking*. Three Bresenham line-rasterization algorithms are used to walk the edges of the triangle. The tracing is done per scanline by synchronizing the line rasterizers. Thus, the endpoints of a span of inside pixels are computed for every scanline that intersects the triangle, and the pixels of the span are set. Special attention must be paid to special cases, e.g., if the triangle has one horizontal edge, then only two line rasterizers must be used.

The simplicity of the above algorithms makes them ideal for hardware implementation, and variants of them can be found implemented on graphics accelerators.

2.6.6 Area-Filling Algorithm

A simple way to set the pixels covered by a closed polygon (or indeed any closed curve) is to first draw its perimater and then *flood-fill* it starting from a seed point inside it. Area-filling algorithms work directly on the contents of the frame buffer and are suitable for some 2D drawing applications:

1. Draw the perimeter of the polygon/curve.

2. Identify or specify a seed pixel inside it.

3. Recursively set the inside pixels by expanding from the seed pixel in all directions until the perimeter is met.

In pseudocode the algorithm is as follows:

```
flood_fill ( polygon P, color c );  {
    point s;
    draw_perimeter ( P, c );
    s = get_seed_point ( P );
    flood_fill_recur ( s, c );
}

flood_fill_recur ( point (x,y), color fill_color );  {
    color c;
    c = getpixel(x,y);    /* read current pixel color */
    if (c != fill_color)   {
        setpixel(x,y,fill_color);
        flood_fill_recur ( (x+1,y), fill_color );
        flood_fill_recur ( (x-1,y), fill_color );
        flood_fill_recur ( (x,y+1), fill_color );
```

```
              flood_fill_recur ( (x,y-1), fill_color );
    }
}
```

Simple variants of the flood-fill algorithm use a different color for the perimeter and the interior or fill while a specific color or other criteria are met. The type of connectedness assumed is critical to this algorithm. For 4-connected areas the above four recursive calls are sufficient. For 8-connected areas, four more recursive calls in the diagonal directions must be added: $(x+1,y+1)$, $(x+1,y-1)$, $(x-1,y+1)$, and $(x-1,y-1)$. The perimeter must also be carefully drawn ensuring that no 4-connected/8-connected holes exist; otherwise, the flood-fill algorithm will escape the intended area.

A basic problem with the flood-fill algorithm is its inefficiency. A pixel may be visited up to 4 times (4-connected) or 8 times (8-connected); the large number of recursive calls introduces delays and may result in stack overflow. A non-recursive version involves marking visited pixels and is more efficient.

2.7 Perspective Correction

The rasterization process for lines, polygons, and other objects is performed in 2D screen space while the properties of objects are associated with 3D object vertices. Such properties include texture values (u,v), color values (r,g,b), normals, and depth values. Unfortunately, the general projection transformation does not preserve ratios of distances (see figure in margin and also Figure 4.2). It is therefore incorrect to linearly interpolate the values of properties in screen space. For example, looking again at the figure, **b** is the midpoint of the line segment **ad** in 3D space, but **b**$'$ will not necessarily be the midpoint of **a**$'$**d**$'$ in screen space. Thus, the value of a property at **b**$'$ should not be halfway between its value at **a**$'$ and **d**$'$.

Perspective correction can be used to obtain the correct value at a projected point [Heck91]. This is based on the fact that projective transformations preserve cross-ratios (see Chapter 4). For the same example line,

$$\frac{\frac{ac}{cd}}{\frac{ab}{bd}} = \frac{\frac{a'c'}{c'd'}}{\frac{a'b'}{b'd'}}, \qquad (2.7)$$

which means that we can obtain the complete image of the line by projecting three points. Suppose that, apart from its endpoints, we also project its midpoint

b onto **b′**. Then for a point **c′** on the image of the line, we want to find the corresponding point **c** on the 3D line, or equivalently the ratio $\frac{ac}{cd}$ for the interpolation. Since **b** is the midpoint of **ad** and **b′** is its known projection, $\frac{ab}{bd} = 1$; let $\frac{a′b′}{b′d′} = q$. We can also compute $\frac{a′c′}{c′d′}$ from the screen coordinates of **c′**. Thus, we can solve (2.7) for $\frac{ac}{cd}$ obtaining the perspective correction formula

$$\frac{\mathbf{ac}}{\mathbf{cd}} = \frac{\mathbf{a′c′}}{q\ \mathbf{c′d′}}. \tag{2.8}$$

Heckbert [Heck91] provides an efficient solution to perspective correction by showing that a property must go through perspective division (see Chapter 4) just like the position coordinates. Let the pre perspective division coordinates of a vertex be $[x, y, z, c, w]^T$, where c is the value of a property. After the perspective division by w, we store $[\frac{x}{w}, \frac{y}{w}, \frac{z}{w}, \frac{c}{w}, \frac{1}{w}]^T$ for the projected vertex. Interpolation in screen coordinates then takes place, on both the property values $\frac{c}{w}$ and the $\frac{1}{w}$ value of each vertex. After interpolation, the property values are adjusted for each pixel by dividing them by the interpolated value of $\frac{1}{w}$.

2.8 Spatial Antialiasing

The primitive rasterization algorithms presented in the previous sections make a binary decision as to whether a pixel belongs to a primitive or not. However, pixels are not mathematical points; they have a small area. The binary decision was based on the positioning of the pixel center with regard to the primitive being rasterized; in other words, the pixel was represented as a point. A number of adverse visible *aliasing* effects can result out of this simplification [SIGG01]:

1. Lines and polygon edges (and, in general, the silhouettes of objects) can appear *jagged* (Figure 2.19).

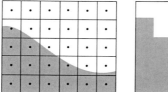 

Figure 2.19. The jagged appearance of object silhouettes.

2. *Small objects* can be improperly rasterized, appearing too small, too large, or of the wrong shape (Figure 2.20). Even worse, animated small objects may appear and disappear from frame to frame, depending on whether they fall on pixel centers.

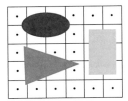 

Figure 2.20. Improperly rasterized small objects.

3. *Fine detail*, such as texture, can be incorrectly rasterized (Figure 2.21).

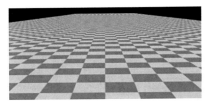

Figure 2.21. Incorrectly rasterized detail.

In sampling theory, the aliasing problem is well known and occurs when the signal being sampled contains frequencies higher than half the sampling frequency (Nyquist theorem), see Appendix E. In computer graphics, the signal being sampled is the mathematical model of the image[6] (consisting, for example, of lines and polygons) and the sampling frequency is the resolution of the pixel grid. The pixel centers are the sampling points. While it is not easy to measure the exact maximum frequency of the mathematical model of an image, *antialiasing* techniques founded on sampling theory can be applied; their result can be judged from their visual effect.

Essentially antialiasing trades intensity resolution to gain spatial resolution, which is the opposite of the halftoning technique discussed in Chapter 11.

---

[6]A still image is assumed here with spatial dimensions x and y, hence the name *spatial antialiasing*. Aliasing also occurs across frames in animation (i.e., in the time dimension); temporal antialiasing techniques are used there (see Chapter 17).

Depending on the approach for handling high frequencies, antialiasing techniques are divided into two categories:

- *Pre-filtering* which extract high frequencies before sampling; essentially the pixel is treated as a finite area and the percentage contribution of each primitive that overlaps the pixel area is computed.

- *Post-filtering* which extract the high frequencies after sampling; essentially the sampling frequency is increased and the results are averaged down.

2.8.1 Pre-Filtering Antialiasing Methods

Catmull's algorithm for antialiased polygon rasterization. Catmull [Catm78] suggested that each pixel be considered as a square window against which all overlapping polygons are clipped (see Section 2.9.3). After removing the hidden surfaces, the visible area of each polygon is estimated, as a percentage of pixel coverage, and this is the contribution of the respective polygon's color to the color value of the pixel (Figure 2.22). Specifically, the following steps are needed:

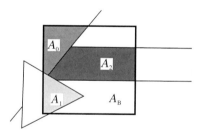

Figure 2.22. Example pixel coverage by polygons.

1. Clip all polygons against the pixel window; let the surviving polygon pieces be $P_0...P_{n-1}$.

2. Eliminate hidden surfaces; this can be achieved by depth-ordering the polygons $P_0...P_{n-1}$ and clipping against the area formed by subtracting the polygons from the (remaining) pixel window in depth order. Let the visible parts of polygons be $P_0...P_{m-1}$, and their respective areas be $A_0...A_{m-1}$.

3. Compute the final pixel color as $A_0C_0 + A_1C_1 + ... + A_{m-1}C_{m-1} + A_BC_B$ where C_i is the color of polygon i and A_B and C_B represent the area of the background (not covered by any polygon) and its color, respectively.

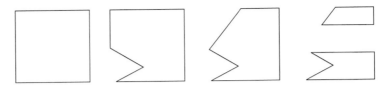

Figure 2.23. Successive clipping windows.

A general polygon-clipping algorithm, such as the Greiner-Hormann, is needed for the second step (see Section 2.9.3). The successive clipping windows for the second step using the above example are shown in Figure 2.23.

Catmull's algorithm can be considered as the ideal against which to evaluate antialiasing algorithms but, in most cases, is not practically viable due to its extraordinary computational requirements. It also assumes that each polygon has a constant color within the area of a pixel, an assumption which is no longer valid given the use of texture-mapping techniques.

A discrete version of Catmull's algorithm is the A-buffer [Carp84]. It uses masks and logical operators to discretely approximate the pixel coverage computations, avoiding the expensive general clipping algorithms.

Antialiased line rasterization. Lines drawn using the Bresenham algorithm have a jagged appearance (Figure 2.24 (left)); the same is true for polygon edges. This jaggedness results from the binary decision made when selecting the closest pixel to the mathematical path of the line. However, for drawn lines to be visible, they must have a certain width and could be modelled as long thin parallelograms. In this case, it is wrong to select pixels in a binary manner; pixels should rather acquire a color value that is proportional to the part of them that is covered by the line (Figure 2.24 (right)).

Let us again consider a line in the first octant and the two pixels that it partially covers at a certain (horizontal) step in its path. Figure 2.25 shows the relationship between the top boundary of the parallelogram, which represents the line and the

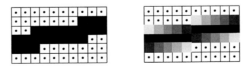

Figure 2.24. Jagged (left) versus antialiased (right) line.

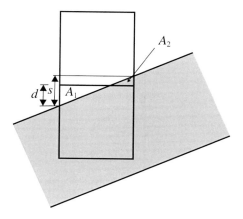

Figure 2.25. Relationship between first octant line and two pixels in its path.

two pixels. Assume that the thickness of the parallelogram is enough to fully cover the part of the lower pixel below the top boundary of the parallelogram. Considering the pixels as unit-area squares, we must determine the portions of unit area A_1 and A_2 covered by the triangles shown. The top pixel will then acquire the color of the line at a portion A_2 while the bottom pixel at a portion $1 - A_1$. Let the slope of the line be $s = -\frac{a}{b}$ (see Equation (2.1)). The areas of the two triangles are then

$$A_1 = \frac{d^2}{2s},$$
$$A_2 = \frac{(s-d)^2}{2s}.$$

As the evaluation of the above expressions is expensive, incremental approximations have been developed. Pitteway and Watkinson [Pitt80] is one such approximation suitable for lines that represent polygon edges. Unfortunately this incremental algorithm only adjusts the value of one pixel (not two as shown above); it uses the Bresenham error term to adjust the pixel that would be selected by the Bresenham line-rasterization algorithm at each step.

2.8.2 Post-Filtering Antialiasing Methods

In post-filtering,[7] we take more than one sample per pixel. This corresponds to creating the image at a higher resolution. The extra samples are taken at regularly

---

[7] *Super-sampling* is a synonym.

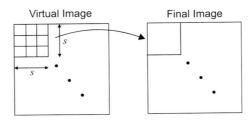

Figure 2.26. Post-filtering example.

spaced intervals, which form a denser grid than the pixel grid. The results are
then averaged down to the resolution of the pixel grid. For example, to create an
image of resolution 1024×1024 we may take 3072×3072 samples, corresponding to nine samples per pixel (three horizontally times three vertically); the nine
samples are then averaged to compute the final color for a pixel (Figure 2.26).
Post-filtering is the most common antialiasing technique, due to its simplicity.

More formally, post-filtering can be described as a three-step algorithm:

1. The continuous image is sampled at s times the final pixel resolution
   (s horizontally $\times$ s vertically) creating a virtual image I_v.

2. The virtual image is low-pass filtered to eliminate the high frequencies that
   cause aliasing.

3. The filtered virtual image is re-sampled at the pixel resolution to produce
   the final image I_f.

Usually, rather than simply averaging the $s \times s$ virtual image pixels that correspond to a final image pixel, an $s \times s$ convolution filter h (see Appendix E) is used
for the low-pass filtering. A typical convolution operation takes place: the filter
is placed over the virtual image pixels that correspond to a final image pixel, its
weights are multiplied by the virtual image pixel values, and summed to produce
the final image pixel value. The filter is then moved by s virtual image pixels in
scanline order. Thus,

$$I_f(i,j) = \sum_{p=0}^{s-1} \sum_{q=0}^{s-1} I_v(i*s+p, j*s+q) \cdot h(p,q).$$

Examples of practical convolution filters for post-filtering are shown in Figure 2.27 [Crow81]. These filters give more weight to the central virtual image
pixel, and the weights fade out as one moves away from the center. Odd dimensions are used ($s = 2k + 1$) in order to allow for a central sample. To avoid color

```
                                              1   2   3   4   3   2   1
                                              2   4   6   8   6   4   2
                               1  2  3  2  1   3   6   9  12   9   6   3
                               2  4  6  4  2   4   8  12  16  12   8   4
             1   2   1         3  6  9  6  3   3   6   9  12   9   6   3
             2   4   2         2  4  6  4  2   2   4   6   8   6   4   2
             1   2   1         1  2  3  2  1   1   2   3   4   3   2   1
           ─────────        ─────────────   ───────────────────────
              3 x 3               5 x 5                 7 x 7
```

Figure 2.27. Examples of convolution filters useful in antialiasing.

shifts, the weights of the convolution filter should be normalized:[8]

$$\sum_{p=0}^{s-1} \sum_{q=0}^{s-1} h(p,q) = 1.$$

There are thus two parameters that drive the basic post-filtering algorithm: the size s of the convolution filter and the choice of weights. The larger s is, the better the results.

The main drawbacks of the post-filtering algorithm are

1. Increasing s raises proportionately the image-generation time and the amount of memory required to store the virtual image. Thus, in practice, s is a small number.

2. Theoretically, since the frequencies in an image are unlimited, no matter how big s becomes, the aliasing problem will remain; the Nyquist limit is only pushed to a higher frequency. Practically, if the human eye is content then the method is successful.

3. Post-filtering is not sensitive to image complexity; the resolution is blindly increased by s regardless of whether it is necessary. Thus, a lot of wasted computations may be performed.

Adaptive post-filtering only increases the sampling rate in parts of the image where high frequencies exist. However, this algorithm is more complex.

Stochastic post-filtering [Cook89] samples the continuous image at non-uniformly spaced positions (Figure 2.28). Aliasing effects (spurious low frequencies that result from sampling high-frequencies above the Nyquist limit) are then converted to noise which is naturally ignored by the human eye.

---

[8]This can be easily seen by considering an area of constant color in the virtual image; only a normalized filter will preserve this color in the final image.

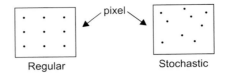

Figure 2.28. Regular versus stochastic sampling.

2.9 Two-Dimensional Clipping Algorithms

Clipping algorithms arose out of the need to avoid giving out-of-range values to a display device. For example, requesting the rasterization of a line from $(-10, 3)$ to $(8, 4)$ can create problems if the range of addresses of the display pixels start at 0. The display device is usually, but not necessarily, modelled as a rectangular parallelogram which defines the within-range values and is called the *clipping object*.[9] In what follows, let *subject* refer to a line, polygon, or other primitive of a model scene.

An important application of clipping algorithms is the frustum-culling stage of the graphics pipeline. 3D clipping algorithms are used there (clipping after projection is theoretically incorrect (see Section 4.6)). We shall start by presenting 2D clipping algorithms, which are easier to describe and have useful applications in 2D graphics. Their generalization to 3D is relatively straightforward.

When rasterizing a subject there are three possible ways that it may relate to the clipping object:

1. The subject is *entirely inside* the clipping object. In this case, the subject is rasterized in its entirety and nothing needs to be done.

2. The subject is *entirely outside* the clipping object. In this case, the subject is not rasterized and nothing needs to be done.

3. The subject *intersects* the clipping object. The intersection of the two must be computed and rasterized.

Clipping algorithms deal with the third case, as the other two cases are trivial. Thus they may be regarded as geometrical intersection algorithms, and theoretically it makes no difference which is the clipping object and which is the subject, since intersection is a commutative operation. In practice, however, they pose restrictions on both objects in order to gain efficiency (e.g., the clipping object must

---

[9]In two-dimensional clipping, if the clipping object is an axis-aligned rectangular parallelogram, it is often called the *clipping window*.

be a parallelogram, and the subject must be a convex polygon). Practical clipping algorithms are designed for a single type of subject, and we shall explore three such categories here: point, line, and polygon.

2.9.1 Point Clipping

Point clipping is trivial. We merely need to establish if the subject point $\mathbf{p}(x, y)$ is inside the clipping object. If the clipping object is a rectangular parallelogram defined by its two opposite vertices $(x_{\min}, y_{\min}), (x_{\max}, y_{\max})$, then the inclusion test is simply

$$x_{\min} \leq x \leq x_{\max} \quad \text{and} \quad y_{\min} \leq y \leq y_{\max}.$$

2.9.2 Line Clipping

The line-clipping algorithms that follow are suitable for clipping a line segment (subject) against an axis-aligned rectangular parallelogram (clipping window). Some of them generalize easily to any convex clipping window.

Cohen-Sutherland algorithm. The philosophy of the Cohen-Sutherland (CS) line-clipping algorithm is to first perform a low-cost test that, in most cases, decides if a line segment is entirely inside or entirely outside the clipping window. This test uses the overlap of the x-extents and the y-extents of the line segment and the window. For example, in Figure 2.29, line segment **ab** is easily established to be entirely outside, **cd** to be entirely inside, but the decision for **ef** and **gh** is not trivial.

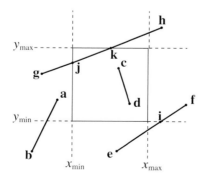

Figure 2.29. Examples of line segments to be clipped.

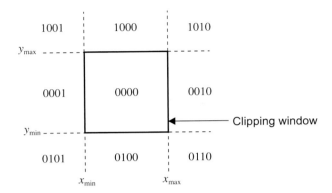

Figure 2.30. Region codes in the CS algorithm.

If the extents test is not conclusive, we compute the intersection of the line segment with one of the lines defined by the window boundary. The line segment is thus split into two, and the CS algorithm is recursively applied to both parts. For example, the **ef** line segment of Figure 2.29 can be split by the line $y = y_{min}$ into the parts **ei** and **if**.

To perform the extent tests efficiently, the plane of the clipping window is divided into nine regions and each region is assigned a 4-bit binary code, as shown in Figure 2.30. The code of a region is determined by the relationship of the region to the clipping window. Each of the four lines that define the clipping window divides the plane into two half-planes: the inside half-plane, which includes the clipping window, and the outside half-plane. The four code bits are set according to the following rules:

- *First bit.* Set to 1 for $y > y_{max}$, else set to 0;

- *Second bit.* Set to 1 for $y < y_{min}$, else set to 0;

- *Third bit.* Set to 1 for $x > x_{max}$, else set to 0;

- *Fourth bit.* Set to 1 for $x < x_{min}$, else set to 0.

Each endpoint (x, y) of the line segment to be clipped is assigned a 4-bit region code according to the above rules. The four bits, respectively, correspond to the sign of the expressions $(y_{max} - y)$, $(y - y_{min})$, $(x_{max} - x)$, and $(x - x_{min})$. Let the 4-bit codes of the endpoints of a line segment be $c1$ and $c2$. Then the extent tests are:

- If $c1 \vee c2 = 0000$, then the line segment is entirely inside.

- If $c1 \wedge c2 \neq 0000$, then the line segment is entirely outside.

If the extent tests are not conclusive, we estimate an intersection point between the line segment and one of the lines that define the clipping window. We select a clipping window line that corresponds to a bit with different values in $c1$ and $c2$ and compute the intersection of the line segment with that line. Then, we recurse with the inside part of the line segment (i.e., the part that had the 0-valued bit). For example, referring to Figure 2.29, the 4-bit code assignments are:

Endpoint	Code	Endpoint	Code
a	0001	e	0100
b	0101	f	0010
c	0000	g	0001
d	0000	h	1010

Segment **ab** is entirely outside since $0001 \wedge 0101 \neq 0000$; **cd** is entirely inside since $0000 \vee 0000 = 0000$. For **ef** and **gh**, the extent tests are not conclusive, so we have to compute intersection points. We intersect **ef** with the line $y = y_{min}$ since the second bit of the code is different at **e** and **f**. Next, we recurse with the **if** line segment since the second bit of of the code of the **f** vertex has value 0 (inside). Similarly, for **gh** we compute one of the intersection points (say **k**) and recurse with **gk** which then computes the intersection **j** and recurses with a trivial inside decision for **jk**. The CS pseudocode follows:

```
CS_Clip ( vertex p1, p2, float xmin, xmax, ymin, ymax );  {
    int c1, c2;
    vertex i;
    edge e;

    c1=mkcode (p1);
    c2=mkcode (p2);
    if ((c1 | c2) == 0)         /* p1p2 is inside */
    else if ((c1 & c2) != 0)    /* p1p2 is outside */
    else  {
        e= /* window line with (c1 bit != c2 bit) */
        i = intersect_lines (e, (p1,p2));
        if outside (e, p1)  CS_Clip(i, p2, xmin, xmax, ymin, ymax);
        else                CS_Clip(p1, i, xmin, xmax, ymin, ymax);
    }
}
```

Two auxiliary routines are used. The `intersect_lines` routine computes the intersection of the line segment from **p1** to **p2** with the window line e. The planar line-line intersection problem is discussed in Appendix C. The `outside` routine decides if a point lies on the inside or the outside half-plane of window edge e and, for an axis-aligned edge, it involves a simple comparison.

The CS algorithm is efficient when most line segments can be handled by the low-cost extent tests. Its recursive case is rather costly.

Skala algorithm. Skala [Skal05] showed that it is possible to achieve a gain in efficiency over the CS algorithm by additionally classifying the vertices of the clipping window relative to the line segment being clipped. To this end, a binary code c_i is assigned to each clipping window vertex $\mathbf{v_i} = (x_i, y_i)$ according to the rule

$$c_i = \begin{cases} 1, & l(x_i, y_i) \geq 0; \\ 0, & \text{otherwise,} \end{cases}$$

where $l(x,y)$ is the function defined by the line segment to be clipped from $\mathbf{p_1}$ to $\mathbf{p_2}$, as per Equation (2.1). The code c_i essentially indicates which side of the line segment the vertex $\mathbf{v_i}$ lies on. If the codes are computed by taking the vertices in a consistent order around the clipping window (e.g., counterclockwise), then a clipping-window edge is intersected by the line segment for every change in the coding of the vertices (from 0 to 1 or from 1 to 0). For example, if the code vector for clipping window vertices $(\mathbf{v_0}, \mathbf{v_1}, \mathbf{v_2}, \mathbf{v_3})$ is $(0,0,1,0)$, then the line segment intersects clipping window edges $\mathbf{v_1 v_2}$ and $\mathbf{v_2 v_3}$.[10] A pre-computed table directly gives the clipping window edges intersected by the line segment from the code vector (c_0, c_1, c_2, c_3), and this replaces the recursive case of the CS algorithm. In the example of Figure 2.29, the Skala algorithm can immediately decide the fate of line segments **ef** and **gh**.

Liang-Barsky algorithm. The Liang-Barsky (LB) algorithm [Lian84] solves the line-clipping problem in a direct way, avoiding the possible recursive calls of the CS algorithm. Tests have shown that LB provides more than 30% performance increase over CS for typical scenes. In its basic form, it is suitable for clipping a line segment against an axis-aligned rectangular parallelogram, but it can be extended to any convex 2D or 3D clipping object.

The LB algorithm is based on the parametric equation of the line segment to be clipped from $\mathbf{p_1}(x_1, y_1)$ to $\mathbf{p_2}(x_2, y_2)$ (see Equation (2.3)). For $t \in [0,1]$, the

---

[10] Actually, the line defined by the line segment has these intersections; the line segment may end sooner and this case requires special handling.

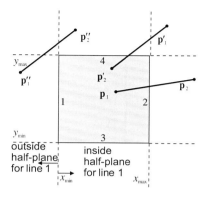

Figure 2.31. Extended clipping window and line segments to be clipped.

line segment from $\mathbf{p_1}$ to $\mathbf{p_2}$ is traced. For $t \in [-\infty, +\infty]$ the entire line through $\mathbf{p_1}$ and $\mathbf{p_2}$ is defined. Now consider the extended clipping window which consists of the lines defined by the clipping window edges (Figure 2.31). The directed line segment from $\mathbf{p_1}$ to $\mathbf{p_2}$ is *incoming* or *outgoing* with respect to each clipping-window line, depending on whether its direction is from the outside to the inside half-plane or vice versa. If the two are parallel, the clipping problem becomes trivial. For example, in Figure 2.31, line segments $\mathbf{p_1 p_2}$ and $\mathbf{p_1'' p_2''}$ are incoming with respect to line 1 while line segment $\mathbf{p_1' p_2'}$ is outgoing.

An important observation that leads to the LB algorithm is that, for a point on the line segment to be inside the clipping window, it has to be on the inside half-plane of every clipping-window line. Thus, if we imagine travelling on the line from $\mathbf{p_1}$ to $\mathbf{p_2}$, we should not "exit" with respect to any window line before "entering" with respect to another. For example, the sequence of intersections [enter, enter, exit, exit] signifies intersection with the clipping window (Figure 2.32 (left)) while the sequence [enter, exit, enter, exit] does not (Figure 2.32 (right)).

If a line segment intersects the clipping window, it will enter it at its intersection point with a window line for which it is incoming and leave it at its intersection point with a window line for which it is outgoing, with the exception of endpoints within the clipping window. The LB algorithm computes the maximum parametric value of the incoming intersections t_{in} and the minimum parametric value of the outgoing intersections t_{out}. It then checks if these parametric values correspond to points on the line segment (i.e., fall in the range $[0, 1]$) and, if not, they are replaced by 0 and 1, respectively. If $t_{\text{in}} \leq t_{\text{out}}$, then an intersection of the line segment and the window exists (the intersection order is of type

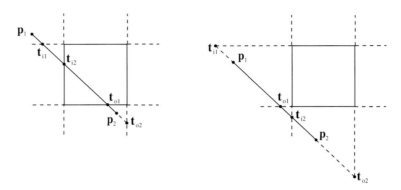

Figure 2.32. Ordering the intersections.

[enter, enter, exit, exit]); otherwise, it does not (the intersection order is of type
[enter, exit, enter, exit]). In the examples of Figure 2.32, t_{i1} and t_{i2} represent
the incoming intersections, while t_{o1} and t_{o2} represent the outgoing intersections;
$t_{in} = \max(t_{i1}, t_{i2}) = t_{i2}$ and $t_{out} = \min(t_{o1}, t_{o2}) = t_{o1}$. In the left part of the figure,
$t_{in} < t_{out}$, so the line segment intersects the clipping window, while in the right
part $t_{in} > t_{out}$, so there is no intersection.

More formally, the theory behind the LB algorithm is the following. Define
$\Delta x = x_2 - x_1$, $\Delta y = y_2 - y_1$ for the line segment from $\mathbf{p_1}(x_1, y_1)$ to $\mathbf{p_2}(x_2, y_2)$. The
part of the line segment that is inside the clipping window satisfies (see Equa-
tion (2.3) and Figure 2.31)

$$x_{min} \leq x_1 + t\Delta x \leq x_{max},$$
$$y_{min} \leq y_1 + t\Delta y \leq y_{max},$$

or

$$-t\Delta x \leq x_1 - x_{min},$$
$$t\Delta x \leq x_{max} - x_1,$$
$$-t\Delta y \leq y_1 - y_{min},$$
$$t\Delta y \leq y_{max} - y_1.$$

These inequalities have the common form

$$t\, p_i \leq q_i, \qquad i : 1..4,$$

where

$$p_1 = -\Delta x, \qquad q_1 = x_1 - x_{\min};$$
$$p_2 = \Delta x, \qquad q_2 = x_{\max} - x_1;$$
$$p_3 = -\Delta y, \qquad q_3 = y_1 - y_{\min};$$
$$p_4 = \Delta y, \qquad q_4 = y_{\max} - y_1.$$

Each inequality corresponds to the relationship between the line segment and the respective clipping-window edge, where the edges are numbered according to Figure 2.31. Note the following:

- If $p_i = 0$ the line segment is parallel to window edge i and the clipping problem is trivial.

- If $p_i \neq 0$ the parametric value of the point of intersection of the line segment with the line defined by window edge i is $\frac{q_i}{p_i}$.

- If $p_i < 0$ the (directed) line segment is incoming with respect to window edge i.

- If $p_i > 0$ the (directed) line segment is outgoing with respect to window edge i.

Therefore, t_{in} and t_{out} can be computed as

$$t_{\text{in}} = \max(\{\frac{q_i}{p_i} \mid p_i < 0, \ i : 1..4\} \cup \{0\}),$$
$$t_{\text{out}} = \min(\{\frac{q_i}{p_i} \mid p_i > 0, \ i : 1..4\} \cup \{1\}).$$

The sets $\{0\}$ and $\{1\}$ are added to the above expressions in order to clamp the starting and ending parametric values at the endpoints of the line segment. If $t_{\text{in}} \leq t_{\text{out}}$ the parametric values t_{in} and t_{out} are plugged into the parametric line equation to get the endpoints of the clipped line segment; otherwise, there is no intersection with the clipping window.

Example 2.1 (Liang-Barsky.) Use the LB algorithm to clip the line segment defined by $\mathbf{p_1}(x_1, y_1) = (0.5, 0.5)$ and $\mathbf{p_2}(x_2, y_2) = (3, 3)$ by the window with $x_{\min} = y_{\min} = 1$ and $x_{\max} = y_{\max} = 4$ (see Figure 2.33).

- Compute $\Delta x = 2.5$ and $\Delta y = 2.5$.

- Compute the p_i's and q_i's:
$$\begin{cases} p_1 = -2.5, & q_1 = -0.5; \\ p_2 = 2.5, & q_2 = 3.5; \\ p_3 = -2.5, & q_3 = -0.5; \\ p_4 = 2.5, & q_4 = 3.5. \end{cases}$$

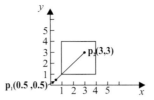

Figure 2.33. Liang-Barsky example.

- Compute

$$t_{\text{in}} = \max(\{\frac{q_1}{p_1}, \frac{q_3}{p_3}\} \cup \{0\}) = 0.2,$$

$$t_{\text{out}} = \min(\{\frac{q_2}{p_2}, \frac{q_4}{p_4}\} \cup \{1\}) = 1.$$

- Since $t_{\text{in}} < t_{\text{out}}$ compute the endpoints $\mathbf{p_1}'(x_1', y_1')$ and $\mathbf{p_2}'(x_2', y_2')$ of the clipped line segment using the parametric line equation

$$x_1' = x_1 + t_{\text{in}}\Delta x \ = 0.5 + 0.2 \cdot 2.5 = 1,$$
$$y_1' = y_1 + t_{\text{in}}\Delta y \ = 0.5 + 0.2 \cdot 2.5 = 1,$$
$$x_2' = x_1 + t_{\text{out}}\Delta x = 0.5 + 1 \quad \cdot 2.5 = 3,$$
$$y_2' = y_1 + t_{\text{out}}\Delta y = 0.5 + 1 \quad \cdot 2.5 = 3.$$

2.9.3 Polygon Clipping

In two-dimensional polygon clipping, the subject and the clipping object are both polygons. The clipping object is sometimes restricted to a convex polygon or a clipping window. We shall refer to the two polygons as *subject polygon* and *clipping polygon*.

A natural first question to ask is why are special polygon-clipping algorithms required at all? Why do we not simply consider the subject polygon as a set of line segments and use line-clipping algorithms to clip these line segments independently? The example of Figure 2.34 should answer this. If we simply clip a polygon as a set of line segments, we can get the wrong result. In the example, the results of clipping the edges of the triangle $\mathbf{v_0 v_1 v_2}$ against the clipping polygon are the line segments $\mathbf{v_0 v_{i0}}$ and $\mathbf{v_0 v_{i1}}$. First, these do not represent a closed polygon. And second, assuming that we draw the closing line segment $\mathbf{v_{i0} v_{i1}}$, they represent the wrong polygon; the result should be the polygon $\mathbf{v_0 v_{i0} v_w v_{i1}}$ and not $\mathbf{v_0 v_{i0} v_{i1}}$. The problem with line-clipping algorithms is that they regard a subject

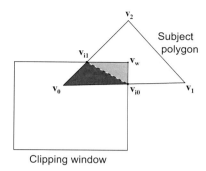

Figure 2.34. Polygon clipping cannot be regarded as multiple line clipping.

polygon as a set of line segments. Instead, a subject polygon should be regarded as the area that it covers, and a polygon-clipping algorithm must compute the *intersection* of the subject polygon area with the area of the clipping polygon.

Specialized polygon-clipping algorithms are thus required, and we shall see two such algorithms here. The Sutherland-Hodgman algorithm is an efficient and widespread polygon-clipping algorithm which poses the restriction that the clipping polygon must be convex. The Greiner-Hormann algorithm is a general polygon-clipping algorithm.

A polygon is given as a sequence of n vertices $\mathbf{v}_0, \mathbf{v}_1, ..., \mathbf{v}_{n-1}$ that define n edges that form a closed curve $\mathbf{v}_0\mathbf{v}_1, \mathbf{v}_1\mathbf{v}_2, ..., \mathbf{v}_{n-2}\mathbf{v}_{n-1}, \mathbf{v}_{n-1}\mathbf{v}_0$. The vertices are given in a consistent direction around the polygon; we shall assume a counter-clockwise traversal here.

Sutherland-Hodgman algorithm. The Sutherland-Hodgman (SH) algorithm [Suth74a] clips an arbitrary subject polygon against a convex clipping polygon. It has m pipelined stages which correspond to the m edges of the clipping polygon. Stage $i \mid i : 0...m-1$ clips the subject polygon against the line defined by edge i of the clipping polygon[11] (it essentially computes the intersection of the area of the subject polygon with the inside half-plane of clipping line i). This is why the clipping polygon must be convex: it is regarded as the intersection of the m inside half-planes defined by its m edges. The input to stage $i \mid i : 1...m-1$ is the output of stage $i - 1$. The subject polygon is input to stage 0 and the clipped polygon is the output of stage $m - 1$. An example is shown in Figure 2.35.

---

[11]We shall refer to this line as *clipping line i*.

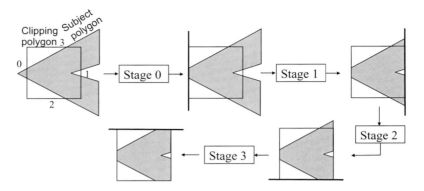

Figure 2.35. Sutherland-Hodgman example.

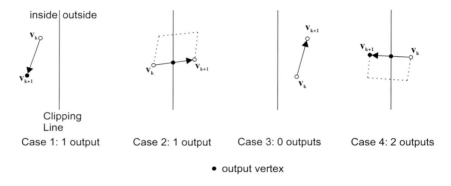

Figure 2.36. The four possible relationships between a clipping line and an input (subject) polygon edge $v_k v_{+1}$.

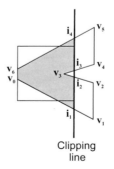

Figure 2.37. One stage of the SH algorithm in detail.

v_k	v_{k+1}	Case	Output
v_0	v_1	2	i_1
v_1	v_2	3	-
v_2	v_3	4	i_2, v_3
v_3	v_4	2	i_3
v_4	v_5	3	-
v_5	v_6	4	i_4, v_6
v_6	v_0	1	v_0

Table 2.2. Stage 1 of the algorithm for the example of Figure 2.35.

We shall next describe the operation of a single stage of the SH pipeline. Each edge $v_k v_{k+1}$ of the input polygon is considered in relation to the clipping line of the stage. There are four possibilities which result in four different appendages to the output polygon list of vertices. From zero to two vertices are added as shown in Figure 2.36.

Table 2.2 traces stage 1 of the SH algorithm for the example of Figure 2.35. The situation at this stage is shown in more detail in Figure 2.37.

The pseudocode for the SH algorithm follows:

```
polygon SH_Clip ( polygon C, S ); {  /*C must be convex*/
    int i,m;
    edge e;
    polygon InPoly, OutPoly;

    m=getedgenumber(C);
    InPoly=S;
    for (i=0; i<m; i++) {
        e = getedge(C,i);
        SH_Clip_Edge(e,InPoly,OutPoly);
        InPoly = OutPoly
    }
    return OutPoly
}

SH_Clip_Edge ( edge e, polygon InPoly, OutPoly ); {
    int k,n;
    vertex vk, vkplus1, i;

    n=getedgenumber(InPoly);
    for (k=0; k<n; k++) {
        vk=getvertex(InPoly,k);
        vkplus1=getvertex(InPoly,(k+1) mod n);
```

```
        if (inside(e, vk) and inside(e, vkplus1))
            /* Case 1 */
            putvertex(OutPoly,vkplus1)
        else if (inside(e, vk) and !inside(e, vkplus1)) {
            /* Case 2 */
            i=intersect_lines(e, (vk,vkplus1));
            putvertex(OutPoly,i)
        }
        else if (!inside(e, vk) and !inside(e, vkplus1))
            /* Case 3 */
        else {
            /* Case 4 */
            i=intersect_lines(e, (vk,vkplus1));
            putvertex(OutPoly,i);
            putvertex(OutPoly,vkplus1)
        }
    }
}
```

Two auxiliary routines are used. The intersect_lines routine was described in the Cohen-Sutherland algorithm and the mathematical details of the planar line-line intersection problem are discussed in Appendix C.

The inside routine decides if a point lies on the inside or the outside half-plane of clipping line e and, if e is axis-aligned, it involves a simple comparison. In the general case, the sign of the evaluation of the line equation (2.1) for the coordinates of the point can be checked.

The complexity of the SH algorithm is $O(mn)$ where m and n are the numbers of vertices of the clipping and subject polygons, respectively. However, the m stages can be pipelined in hardware, since the clipping polygon is, in general, constant. No complex data structures or operations are required so the SH algorithm is quite efficient.

Greiner-Hormann algorithm. The Greiner-Hormann (GH) algorithm [Grei98] is suitable for general polygons.[12] Both the clipping polygon (C) and the subject polygon (S) can be arbitrary closed polygons, even self-intersecting. In fact the GH algorithm views the S and C polygons symmetrically; since their area of intersection is computed it does not matter which is which.

The GH algorithm is based on the winding-number test for a point in a polygon (see Section 2.5). The winding number $\omega(P, \mathbf{p})$ of a point $\mathbf{p}$ with respect to a polygon P does not change as long as the topological relation of the two remains

---

[12]An earlier solution to general polygon clipping was given by Vatti [Vatt92].

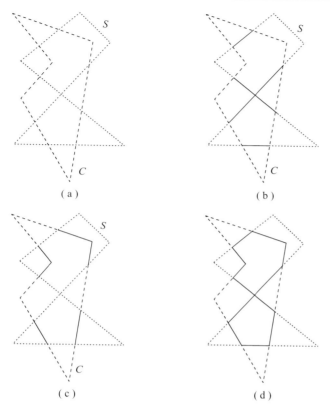

Figure 2.38. Greiner-Hormann example: (a) the initial S and C polygons; (b) after Step 1 of GH; (c) after Step 2 of GH; (d) the final result.

constant. If $\mathbf{p}$ crosses P then $\omega(P, \mathbf{p})$ is incremented or decremented. If $\omega(P, \mathbf{p})$ is odd then $\mathbf{p}$ is inside P; otherwise, it is outside. Thus, every time a moving point crosses P it switches from the inside to the outside of P or vice versa.

Consider the S and C polygons of Figure 2.38 (a). The GH algorithm has three steps:

1. Trace the perimeter of S starting from a vertex $\mathbf{v}_{s0}$. An imaginary stencil toggles between an *on* and an *off* state every time the perimeter of C is crossed. Its initial state is *on* if $\mathbf{v}_{s0}$ is inside C and *off* otherwise. It thus computes the part of the perimeter of S that is inside C (Figure 2.38 (b)).

2. Similar to Step 1 but reverse the roles of S and C. The part of the perimeter of C that is inside S is thus computed (Figure 2.38 (c)).

3. The union of the results of Steps 1 and 2 is the result of clipping S against C (or equivalently C against S) (Figure 2.38 (d)).

The output of the GH algorithm may be composed of disconnected components. The implementation suggested in the original paper proposes the use of doubly linked lists for the vertices of C and S with extra pointers for the linkage of the disconnected components.

The toggling of the stencil state described in the algorithm essentially involves the computation of all intersections between the edges of S and C. These intersections can be computed by the intersect_lines routine mentioned in previous clipping algorithms and Appendix C. The complexity of step 1 (and 2) is $O(mn)$, where m and n are the numbers of vertices of the C and S polygons, respectively, and this is the overall complexity of the GH algorithm. In practice, the complex data structures used make it less efficient than the SH algorithm.

As described, the GH algorithm computes the intersection of the areas of the two polygons, $C \cap S$. It easily generalizes to compute $C \cup S$, $C - S$ and $S - C$ by changing the initial states of the stencils for S and C (there are four possible combinations of initial state). These generalizations are not useful for the clipping problem.

2.10   Exercises

1. Generalize the line3 algorithm so that it works in all octants.

2. Implement the line1, line2, and line3 algorithms and compare their performance by timing them on a large set of line segments.

3. Modify the line3 algorithm so that it includes an extra parameter thickness which defines the thickness of the line, in pixels. Thickness is measured on the minor axis.

4. Change the circle algorithm so that it draws circles with arbitrary integer center (x_c, y_c).

5. The triangle1 algorithm can be generalized to convex1 which rasterizes arbitrary convex polygons, by incrementally evaluating their edge (line) functions at all pixels within their bounding box. Implement this algorithm.

6. Design a non-recursive flood-filling algorithm. *Hints:* think of ways to fill multiple pixels simultaneously; 'branching' points (where filling on a neighboring scanline can commence) may have to be stored in a list.

7. Implement an antialiased line-rasterization algorithm, ignoring performance. The line width should be given as a real-valued parameter in pixel units.

8. Define a simple two-dimensional scene using a small set of triangles, and associated colors. Use the `triangle1` algorithm to rasterize the scene. Rasterize it again at three times the resolution ($s = 3$) and then post-filter it using

   (a) the 3×3 convolution filter given in Section 2.8.2;

   (b) a 3×3 filter with all weights equal.

   Compare the results. *Note*: the weights of both filters should be normalized.

9. Implement the CS and LB line-clipping algorithms and compare their performance. To this end you will have to construct an experiment which includes a generator that produces arbitrary line segments.

10. Implement the SH and GH polygon-clipping algorithms and compare their performance. To this end you will have to construct an experiment which includes a generator that produces arbitrary polygons.

11. Generalize the GH algorithm to compute

   • $C \cup S$;

   • $C - S$;

   • $S - C$.

12. Implement the SH clipping algorithm for a rectangular clipping polygon using a pipeline of four stages, running on a pipeline of four processors. Compute the speed-up over the sequential implementation. You must run the algorithms on a large number of input polygons to allow the pipeline-filling cost to become negligible.

3

2D and 3D Coordinate Systems and Transformations

There is nothing wrong with change, if it is in the right direction.
—Winston Churchill

3.1   Introduction

In computer graphics, it is often necessary to *change* the form of objects or, equivalently, change the coordinate system. For example the digitized form of a car may be used in several instances in the model of a scene, positioned at various points and directions, and in different sizes. In animation, an object may be transformed from frame to frame; this transformation may involve its position, orientation, size, or even shape. Also, as objects traverse the graphics pipeline, their coordinate system is changed several times, e.g., from object coordinates to world coordinates, from world coordinates to eye coordinates, etc.

All the above changes use a common element for their implementation: *coordinate transformations*. Coordinate transformations are the most important and classic topic in computer graphics; they are *the tools of change*.

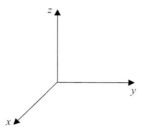

Figure 3.1. Right-handed coordinate system.

In this book we shall represent points[1] in three-dimensional Euclidean space $\mathbb{E}^3$ as 3×1 column vectors

$$\mathbf{p} = \left[\begin{array}{c} p_x \\ p_y \\ p_z \end{array} \right].$$

Linear transformations are represented by 3×3 matrices which are post-multiplied by a point to produce another point

$$\left[\begin{array}{c} p'_x \\ p'_y \\ p'_z \end{array} \right] = \left[\begin{array}{ccc} m_1 & m_2 & m_3 \\ m_4 & m_5 & m_6 \\ m_7 & m_8 & m_9 \end{array} \right] \cdot \left[\begin{array}{c} p_x \\ p_y \\ p_z \end{array} \right].$$

Note that if points were represented by 1×3 row vectors, then the transpose of the above matrices should be pre-multiplied by the point:

$$\left[\begin{array}{ccc} p'_x & p'_y & p'_z \end{array} \right] = \left[\begin{array}{ccc} p_x & p_y & p_z \end{array} \right] \cdot \left[\begin{array}{ccc} m_1 & m_4 & m_7 \\ m_2 & m_5 & m_8 \\ m_3 & m_6 & m_9 \end{array} \right].$$

Throughout this book we make use of right-handed three-dimensional coordinate systems (Figure 3.1).

3.2 Affine Transformations

In mathematics, a *transformation* is defined as a mapping whose domain and range are the same set; for example, from $\mathbb{E}^3$ to $\mathbb{E}^3$. In computer graphics and

---

[1]For a formal definition of points and vectors, see Section A.2.

visualization we are mainly interested in *affine transformations*, those which preserve important geometric properties of the objects being transformed (see Section 3.10). In particular they preserve *affine combinations* (which include line
segments and convex polygons: the building blocks of our models).

An *affine combination* of points $\mathbf{p_0}, \mathbf{p_1}, ..., \mathbf{p_n} \in \mathbb{E}^3$ is a point $\mathbf{p} \in \mathbb{E}^3$ defined
as

$$\mathbf{p} = \sum_{i=0}^{n} a_i \mathbf{p_i}, \qquad (3.1)$$

with $a_0, a_1, ..., a_n \in \mathbb{R}$ and $\sum_{i=0}^{n} a_i = 1$. The $a_0, a_1, ..., a_n$ are the *affine coordinates*
of $\mathbf{p}$ with respect to $\mathbf{p_0}, \mathbf{p_1}, ..., \mathbf{p_n}$. An affine combination is *convex* if all the affine
coordinates a_i are non-negative; in this case the affine combination $\mathbf{p}$ is within the
convex hull of the original points $\mathbf{p_0}, \mathbf{p_1}, ..., \mathbf{p_n}$.[2]

Instances of affine combinations are line segments, triangles, and tetrahedra
(the usual buildings blocks of our models). A line segment between points $\mathbf{p_1}$
and $\mathbf{p_2}$ can be defined as the set of points $\mathbf{p}$ which satisfy $\mathbf{p} = a_1 \cdot \mathbf{p_1} + a_2 \cdot \mathbf{p_2}$
with $0 \leq a_1 \leq 1$ and $a_2 = 1 - a_1$. Thus, $a_1 + a_2 = 1$ and $a_1, a_2 \geq 0$, so we have a
convex affine combination. Similarly, a triangle with vertices $\mathbf{p_1}$, $\mathbf{p_2}$, and $\mathbf{p_3}$ can
be defined as the set of points $\mathbf{p}$ which satisfy $\mathbf{p} = a_1 \cdot \mathbf{p_1} + a_2 \cdot \mathbf{p_2} + a_3 \cdot \mathbf{p_3}$ with $0 \leq$
$a_1, a_2, a_3 \leq 1$ and $a_1 + a_2 + a_3 = 1$, which is another convex affine combination.

An *affine transformation* is defined as a transformation which preserves affine
combinations; that is, a transformation which retains the inter-relationship of the
points of the affine combination. In mathematical terms, a transformation $\Phi :$
$\mathbb{E}^3 \to \mathbb{E}^3$ is affine if

$$\Phi(\mathbf{p}) = \sum_{i=0}^{n} a_i \Phi(\mathbf{p_i}), \qquad (3.2)$$

where $\mathbf{p} = \sum_{i=0}^{n} a_i \mathbf{p_i}$ is an affine combination. In other words, the result of the
application of an affine transformation onto the result $\mathbf{p}$ of an affine combination
should equal the affine combination of the result of performing the affine transformation on the defining points, with the same weights a_i. For example, an affine
transformation will convert the midpoint of a line segment to the midpoint of the
transformed line segment.

The above definition has an extremely important practical consequence; to
perform an affine transformation on an affine combination, internal points of the
affine combination need not be transformed; it suffices to transform the defining
points. Thus, to perform an affine transformation on a triangle, it is theoretically

---

[2]Informally, the convex hull is defined as the minimum convex shape that encloses the given points.

correct to transform its three vertices, and it is not necessary to transform its (infinite) interior points.

Mappings of the form

$$\Phi(\mathbf{p}) = \mathbf{A} \cdot \mathbf{p} + \overrightarrow{\mathbf{t}}, \tag{3.3}$$

where $\mathbf{A}$ is a 3×3 matrix and $\overrightarrow{\mathbf{t}}$ is a 3×1 vector, are affine transformations in $\mathbb{E}^3$.

Proof: We shall show that transformation (3.3) preserves affine combinations:

$$\begin{aligned}
\Phi(\sum_{i=0}^{n} a_i \mathbf{p_i}) &= \mathbf{A}(\sum_{i=0}^{n} a_i \mathbf{p_i}) + \overrightarrow{\mathbf{t}} \\
&= \sum_{i=0}^{n} a_i \mathbf{A} \mathbf{p_i} + \sum_{i=0}^{n} a_i \overrightarrow{\mathbf{t}} \\
&= \sum_{i=0}^{n} a_i (\mathbf{A} \mathbf{p_i} + \overrightarrow{\mathbf{t}}) \\
&= \sum_{i=0}^{n} a_i \Phi(\mathbf{p_i}).
\end{aligned}$$

$\square$

The four basic affine transformations of translation, scaling, rotation, and shear are special cases of Equation (3.3), as we shall see in Section 3.3.

3.3   2D Affine Transformations

We shall start by describing the basic two-dimensional (2D) affine transformations for reasons of simplicity; it is much easier to show the effect of 2D transformations on the 2D pages of a book. The previous discussion on three-dimensional (3D) affine transformations holds true for the 2D case and the 2D results readily generalize to three dimensions.

The affine transformations that we shall describe transform a point into another point. To transform an object, we simply transform all the points that define it (e.g., the vertices of its polygons). The defining property of affine transformations (preservation of affine combinations) ensures that the result is valid, and it is not necessary to transform all the internal points of the objects.

3.3.1   2D Translation

Translation defines movement by a certain distance in a certain direction, both specified by the translation vector. The translation of a 2D point $\mathbf{p} = [x, y]^{\mathrm{T}}$ by a

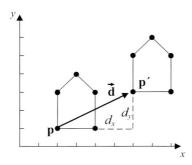

Figure 3.2. 2D translation.

vector $\overrightarrow{\mathbf{d}} = [d_x, d_y]^{\mathrm{T}}$ gives another point $\mathbf{p}' = [x', y']^{\mathrm{T}}$ which is the result of adding $\overrightarrow{\mathbf{d}}$ to $\mathbf{p}$:

$$\mathbf{p}' = \mathbf{p} + \overrightarrow{\mathbf{d}}. \tag{3.4}$$

This is an instantiation of the general affine transformation of Equation (3.3), where $\mathbf{A} = \mathbf{I}$ and $\overrightarrow{\mathbf{t}} = \overrightarrow{\mathbf{d}}$ ($\mathbf{I}$ is the 2×2 identity matrix). Figure 3.2 shows the effect of a translation on a simple object.

3.3.2 2D Scaling

The *scaling* transformation changes the size of objects. The change of size in each dimension is specified by the respective scaling factor; for two dimensions we have two scaling factors, s_x and s_y, which are multiplied by the respective coordinates of a 2D point $\mathbf{p} = [x, y]^{\mathrm{T}}$ to give $\mathbf{p}' = [x', y']^{\mathrm{T}}$

$$\mathbf{p}' = \mathbf{S}(s_x, s_y) \cdot \mathbf{p} \tag{3.5}$$

where

$$\mathbf{S}(s_x, s_y) = \begin{bmatrix} s_x & 0 \\ 0 & s_y \end{bmatrix}.$$

It is not possible to observe the effect of scaling on a single point; Figure 3.3 shows its effect on a simple object. Notice that scaling is an instantiation of the general affine transformation of Equation (3.3), where $\mathbf{A} = \mathbf{S}(s_x, s_y)$ and $\overrightarrow{\mathbf{t}} = \overrightarrow{\mathbf{0}}$.

If a scaling factor is less than 1, the object's size is reduced in the respective dimension, while if it is greater than 1 it is increased.

Scaling has a translation side-effect that is proportional to the scaling factor; notice how the object of Figure 3.3 has moved toward the origin on the x-axis (scaling factor < 1) and away from the origin on the y-axis (scaling factor > 1).

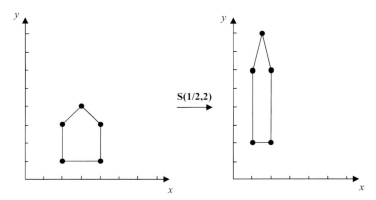

Figure 3.3. 2D scaling.

A scaling transformation is called *isotropic*, if all the scaling factors are equal.[3] In the two-dimensional case this implies $s_x = s_y$. Isotropic scaling preserves the similarity of objects (angles) whereas non-isotropic scaling does not (see also Section 3.10).

Mirroring about an axis can be described as a special case of the scaling transformation, using a -1 scaling factor. Mirroring about the x-axis is $\mathbf{S}(1, -1)$, and mirroring about the y-axis is $\mathbf{S}(-1, 1)$.

3.3.3   2D Rotation

The *rotation* transformation has the effect of turning objects about the origin. The distance from the origin does not change, only the orientation changes. We follow the convention that a counterclockwise rotation is positive; thus in Figure 3.4 (a), the object is rotated by $+90°$.

Looking at Figure 3.4 (b), we can estimate $\mathbf{p}' = [x', y']^{\mathrm{T}}$ from $\mathbf{p} = [x, y]^{\mathrm{T}}$:

$$x' = l\cos(\phi + \theta) = l(\cos\phi \ \cos\theta - \sin\phi \ \sin\theta) = x \ \cos\theta - y \ \sin\theta;$$

$$y' = l\sin(\phi + \theta) = l(\cos\phi \ \sin\theta + \sin\phi \ \cos\theta) = x \ \sin\theta + y \ \cos\theta.$$

Thus,

$$\mathbf{p}' = \mathbf{R}(\theta) \cdot \mathbf{p}, \tag{3.6}$$

---

[3]This is also referred to as *uniform* scaling. By contrast, when $s_x \neq s_y$, we have *non-uniform* scaling.

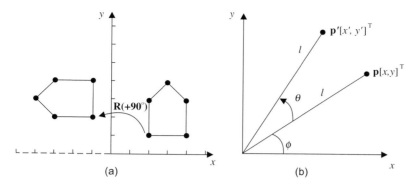

Figure 3.4. 2D rotation.

where

$$\mathbf{R}(\theta) = \begin{bmatrix} \cos\theta & -\sin\theta \\ \sin\theta & \cos\theta \end{bmatrix}.$$

Rotation is an instantiation of the general affine transformation of Equation (3.3), where $\mathbf{A} = \mathbf{R}(\theta)$ and $\overrightarrow{\mathbf{t}} = \overrightarrow{\mathbf{0}}$.

3.3.4 2D Shear

The shear is the final basic affine transformation and has the effect of increasing one of the object's coordinates by an amount equal to the other coordinate times a shearing factor.[4] A physical example can be observed by placing a stack of cards flat on a table and then taking a hard book, placing it vertically adjacent to the stack of cards and tilting it against them. The higher up a card's original position is, the more it will be 'sheared'; note that a card's vertical position will not change but its horizontal position will change by an amount proportional to its vertical position (unless the stack topples over!). Figure 3.5 shows the effect of a shear along the x-axis by a shear factor of 2.

The shear of a point $\mathbf{p} = [x, y]^\mathrm{T}$ along the x-axis results in $\mathbf{p}' = [x', y']^\mathrm{T}$, defined by

$$x' = x + ay, \quad y' = y,$$

while the shear along the y-axis is

$$x' = x, \quad y' = bx + y,$$

---

[4]In higher (say d) dimensions, as we shall see in Section 3.7 for the 3D case, shear increases $d - 1$ coordinates by an amount equal to one coordinate times the respective shearing factors.

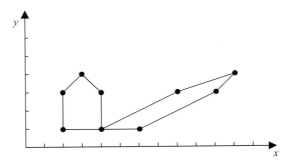

Figure 3.5. 2D shear.

where a and b are the respective shear factors. In matrix form, the x-axis shear is

$$\mathbf{p}' = \mathbf{SH_x}(a) \cdot \mathbf{p}, \qquad (3.7)$$

where

$$\mathbf{SH_x}(a) = \left[\begin{array}{cc} 1 & a \\ 0 & 1 \end{array} \right],$$

while the y-axis shear is

$$\mathbf{p}' = \mathbf{SH_y}(b) \cdot \mathbf{p}, \qquad (3.8)$$

where

$$\mathbf{SH_y}(b) = \left[\begin{array}{cc} 1 & 0 \\ b & 1 \end{array} \right].$$

The shear is an instantiation of the general affine transformation of Equation (3.3), where $\mathbf{A} = \mathbf{SH_x}(a)$ or $\mathbf{A} = \mathbf{SH_y}(b)$ and $\overrightarrow{\mathbf{t}} = \overrightarrow{\mathbf{0}}$.

3.4   Composite Transformations

Useful transformations in computer graphics and visualization rarely consist of a single basic affine transformation; they typically consist of two or more steps (see the 2D and 3D examples of Sections 3.6 and 3.8). Such transformations must typically be applied to objects of a scene that are defined by thousands or even millions of vertices.

For example, suppose that we wish to rotate a 2D object by $45°$ and then isotropically scale it by a factor of 2. We must first apply the rotation matrix

$$\mathbf{R}(45°) = \left[\begin{array}{cc} \frac{\sqrt{2}}{2} & -\frac{\sqrt{2}}{2} \\ \frac{\sqrt{2}}{2} & \frac{\sqrt{2}}{2} \end{array} \right]$$

and then the scaling matrix

$$\mathbf{S}(2,2) = \begin{bmatrix} 2 & 0 \\ 0 & 2 \end{bmatrix}$$

to every vertex of the object.

While it is possible to apply the matrices sequentially to every vertex $\mathbf{p}$: $\mathbf{S}(2,2) \cdot (\mathbf{R}(45°) \cdot \mathbf{p})$, it is more efficient to exploit the *associative* property[5] of matrix multiplication and apply the pre-computed composite matrix that describes the composite transformation to the vertices: $(\mathbf{S}(2,2) \cdot \mathbf{R}(45°)) \cdot \mathbf{p}$. The composite transformation is only computed once and the composite matrix is applied to the vertices, which generally saves a large amount of computation (see Exercises, Section 3.11).

Matrix multiplication is *not* in general *commutative*,[6] so the order of multiplying the transformation matrices is important. Having chosen the column representation of points (which implies that transformation matrices are right-multiplied by the points), we must write the matrix composition in the reverse of the order of application. In the above example, we compute the composite matrix $\mathbf{S}(2,2) \cdot \mathbf{R}(45°)$ to apply the rotation first and the scaling second. In general, to apply the sequence of transformations $T_1, T_2, ..., T_m$, we compute the composite matrix $\mathbf{T_m} \cdot ... \cdot \mathbf{T_2} \cdot \mathbf{T_1}$.

Unfortunately, there is a problem with the translation transformation. Translation can not be described by a linear transformation matrix, i.e., it can not be described as $x' = ax + by$ and $y' = cx + dy$. Thus, translation can not be included in a composite transformation. Fortunately there is a simple solution to this problem: homogeneous coordinates.

3.4.1 Homogeneous Coordinates

Homogeneous coordinates use one additional dimension than the space that we want to represent. In the two-dimensional case, homogeneous points have the form

$$\begin{bmatrix} x \\ y \\ w \end{bmatrix},$$

where w is the new coordinate that corresponds to the extra dimension, with $w \neq 0$.

Fixing $w = 1$ maintains our original dimensionality by taking the slice $w = 1$. In the 2D case, we use the plane $w = 1$ instead of the xy-plane (Figure 3.6). Points

---

[5] $(\mathbf{A} \cdot \mathbf{B}) \cdot \mathbf{C} = \mathbf{A} \cdot (\mathbf{B} \cdot \mathbf{C})$.
[6] $\mathbf{A} \cdot \mathbf{B} \neq \mathbf{B} \cdot \mathbf{A}$.

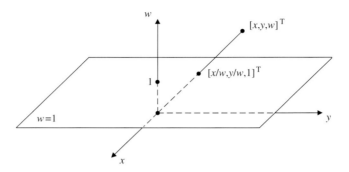

Figure 3.6. 2D homogeneous coordinates.

whose homogeneous coordinates are multiples of each other are equivalent. Thus $[1,2,3]^T$ and $[2,4,6]^T$ represent the same point; the actual point that they represent is given by their unique *basic representation*, which has $w = 1$ and is obtained by dividing all coordinates by w: $[x/w, y/w, w/w]^T = [x/w, y/w, 1]^T$. For example, the above pair of equivalent points has the basic representation $[\frac{1}{3}, \frac{2}{3}, 1]^T$. Equivalent points (i.e., points with the same basic representation) lie on the same line through the origin, (Figure 3.6). In general, we use the basic representation for points, and we ensure that our transformations preserve this property.

Let us see how homogeneous coordinates help homogenize the treatment of the translation transformation. We take advantage of the fact that points have $w = 1$, in order to represent the translation of a point $\mathbf{p} = [x, y, w]^T$ by a vector $\overrightarrow{\mathbf{d}} = [d_x, d_y]^T$, as a linear transformation

$$
\begin{aligned}
x' &= 1x + 0y + d_x w &&= x + d_x, \\
y' &= 0x + 1y + d_y w &&= y + d_y, \\
w' &= 0x + 0y + 1w &&= 1.
\end{aligned}
\tag{3.9}
$$

The transformation on the w-coordinate ensures that the resulting point $\mathbf{p}' = [x', y', w']^T$ has $w' = 1$. The above linear expressions can be encapsulated in matrix form as we shall see in the next section, thus treating translation in the same way as the other basic affine transformations.

For the simple affine transformation matrices of Section 3.3, the origin $[0,0]^T$ is a *fixed point*, i.e., a point that does not change under transformation:

$$
\begin{bmatrix} a & b \\ c & d \end{bmatrix} \cdot \begin{bmatrix} 0 \\ 0 \end{bmatrix} = \begin{bmatrix} 0 \\ 0 \end{bmatrix}.
$$

A secondary positive effect of homogeneous coordinates is that there is no fixed point under homogeneous affine transformations, because the 2D origin is now $[0,0,1]^T$ which is not a fixed point for the homogeneous affine-transformation matrices. The $[0,0,0]^T$ point is outside the $w = 1$ plane and, furthermore, is disallowed since it has $w = 0$.

In Section 3.5, points will be represented by homogeneous coordinates. The homogeneous representation of a 2D point will thus be $[x,y,1]^T$ and that of a 3D point will be $[x,y,z,1]^T$. For brevity of presentation we shall often omit the homogeneous coordinate. Coercion[7] between homogeneous and non-homogenous matrices, points, and vectors will be assumed.

3.5   2D Homogeneous Affine Transformations

The linear expressions (3.9) that define 2D translation can be represented as a homogeneous matrix:

$$\mathbf{T}(\vec{\mathbf{d}}) = \begin{bmatrix} 1 & 0 & d_x \\ 0 & 1 & d_y \\ 0 & 0 & 1 \end{bmatrix}. \tag{3.10}$$

Thus, $\mathbf{p}' = \mathbf{T}(\vec{\mathbf{d}}) \cdot \mathbf{p}$ and translation is treated by matrix composition, like the other basic affine transformations. The last row of a homogeneous transformation matrix is always $[0,0,1]$ in order to preserve the unit value of the w-coordinate. Homogeneous matrices can be obtained for the other basic affine transformations. *2D homogeneous scaling* matrix:

$$\mathbf{S}(s_x, s_y) = \begin{bmatrix} s_x & 0 & 0 \\ 0 & s_y & 0 \\ 0 & 0 & 1 \end{bmatrix}. \tag{3.11}$$

2D homogeneous rotation matrix:

$$\mathbf{R}(\theta) = \begin{bmatrix} \cos\theta & -\sin\theta & 0 \\ \sin\theta & \cos\theta & 0 \\ 0 & 0 & 1 \end{bmatrix}. \tag{3.12}$$

2D homogeneous shear matrices:

$$\mathbf{SH_x}(a) = \begin{bmatrix} 1 & a & 0 \\ 0 & 1 & 0 \\ 0 & 0 & 1 \end{bmatrix}; \tag{3.13}$$

---

[7]Coercion is implicit type conversion.

$$\mathbf{SH_y}(b) = \begin{bmatrix} 1 & 0 & 0 \\ b & 1 & 0 \\ 0 & 0 & 1 \end{bmatrix}. \tag{3.14}$$

It is often necessary to reverse a transformation, as will become evident in the examples that follow. To this end, it is useful to have the inverse of the basic affine transformations. A translation is reversed by negating the translation vector:

$$\mathbf{T}^{-1}(\overrightarrow{\mathbf{d}}) = \mathbf{T}(-\overrightarrow{\mathbf{d}}) = \begin{bmatrix} 1 & 0 & -d_x \\ 0 & 1 & -d_y \\ 0 & 0 & 1 \end{bmatrix}. \tag{3.15}$$

A scaling is reversed by inverting the scaling factors:

$$\mathbf{S}^{-1}(s_x, s_y) = \mathbf{S}(\frac{1}{s_x}, \frac{1}{s_y}) = \begin{bmatrix} \frac{1}{s_x} & 0 & 0 \\ 0 & \frac{1}{s_y} & 0 \\ 0 & 0 & 1 \end{bmatrix}. \tag{3.16}$$

A rotation is reversed by negating the rotation angle:

$$\mathbf{R}^{-1}(\theta) = \mathbf{R}(-\theta) = \begin{bmatrix} \cos\theta & \sin\theta & 0 \\ -\sin\theta & \cos\theta & 0 \\ 0 & 0 & 1 \end{bmatrix}. \tag{3.17}$$

A shear is reversed by negating the shear factor:

$$\mathbf{SH_x}^{-1}(a) = \mathbf{SH_x}(-a) = \begin{bmatrix} 1 & -a & 0 \\ 0 & 1 & 0 \\ 0 & 0 & 1 \end{bmatrix}; \tag{3.18}$$

$$\mathbf{SH_y}^{-1}(b) = \mathbf{SH_y}(-b) = \begin{bmatrix} 1 & 0 & 0 \\ -b & 1 & 0 \\ 0 & 0 & 1 \end{bmatrix}. \tag{3.19}$$

Applying a transformation on an object (*object transformation*) is equivalent to the application of the inverse transformation on the coordinate system (*axis transformation*). For example, isotropically scaling an object by 2 is equivalent to isotropically scaling the coordinate system axes by $\frac{1}{2}$ (shrinking).

Some simple but useful properties of homogeneous affine transformation matrices under composition are:

- $\mathbf{T}(\overrightarrow{\mathbf{d1}}) \cdot \mathbf{T}(\overrightarrow{\mathbf{d2}}) = \mathbf{T}(\overrightarrow{\mathbf{d2}}) \cdot \mathbf{T}(\overrightarrow{\mathbf{d1}}) = \mathbf{T}(\overrightarrow{\mathbf{d1}} + \overrightarrow{\mathbf{d2}})$;

- $\mathbf{S}(s_{x1}, s_{y1}) \cdot \mathbf{S}(s_{x2}, s_{y2}) = \mathbf{S}(s_{x2}, s_{y2}) \cdot \mathbf{S}(s_{x1}, s_{y1}) = \mathbf{S}(s_{x1} \cdot s_{x2}, s_{y1} \cdot s_{y2})$;

- $\mathbf{R}(\theta 1) \cdot \mathbf{R}(\theta 2) = \mathbf{R}(\theta 2) \cdot \mathbf{R}(\theta 1) = \mathbf{R}(\theta 1 + \theta 2)$;

- $\mathbf{S}(s_x, s_y) \cdot \mathbf{R}(\theta) = \mathbf{R}(\theta) \cdot \mathbf{S}(s_x, s_y)$ for isotropic scaling only, i.e., for $s_x = s_y$.

Similar homogeneous matrices can be obtained for 3D affine transformations as we shall see in Section 3.7.

3.6 2D Transformation Examples

Example 3.1 (Rotation about an Arbitrary Point.) Determine the transformation matrix $\mathbf{R}(\theta, \mathbf{p})$ required to perform rotation about an arbitrary point $\mathbf{p}$ by an angle θ (Figure 3.7).

The 2D rotation matrix $\mathbf{R}(\theta)$ (Equation (3.12)) rotates graphical objects about the origin. To rotate about an arbitrary point $\mathbf{p} = [p_x, p_y]^{\mathrm{T}}$, we first have to translate $\mathbf{p}$ to the origin, rotate about the origin, and finally undo the translation.

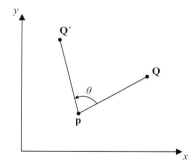

Figure 3.7. Rotation about an arbitrary point.

Step 1. Translate by $-\vec{\mathbf{p}}$, $\mathbf{T}(-\vec{\mathbf{p}})$.

Step 2. Rotate by θ, $\mathbf{R}(\theta)$.

Step 3. Translate by $\vec{\mathbf{p}}$, $\mathbf{T}(\vec{\mathbf{p}})$.

$$\mathbf{R}(\theta,\mathbf{p}) = \begin{bmatrix} 1 & 0 & p_x \\ 0 & 1 & p_y \\ 0 & 0 & 1 \end{bmatrix} \cdot \begin{bmatrix} \cos\theta & -\sin\theta & 0 \\ \sin\theta & \cos\theta & 0 \\ 0 & 0 & 1 \end{bmatrix} \cdot \begin{bmatrix} 1 & 0 & -p_x \\ 0 & 1 & -p_y \\ 0 & 0 & 1 \end{bmatrix}$$

$$= \begin{bmatrix} \cos\theta & -\sin\theta & p_x - p_x\cos\theta + p_y\sin\theta \\ \sin\theta & \cos\theta & p_y - p_x\sin\theta - p_y\cos\theta \\ 0 & 0 & 1 \end{bmatrix}.$$

Example 3.2 (Rotation of a Triangle about a Point.) Rotate the triangle $\triangle\mathbf{abc}$ by $45°$ about the point $\mathbf{p} = [-1,-1]^{\mathrm{T}}$, where $\mathbf{a} = [0,0]^{\mathrm{T}}$, $\mathbf{b} = [1,1]^{\mathrm{T}}$ and $\mathbf{c} = [5,2]^{\mathrm{T}}$.

The triangle can be represented by a matrix $\mathbf{T}$, the columns of which contain the homogeneous coordinates of its vertices:

$$\mathbf{T} = \begin{bmatrix} 0 & 1 & 5 \\ 0 & 1 & 2 \\ 1 & 1 & 1 \end{bmatrix}.$$

We shall apply the $\mathbf{R}(\theta,\mathbf{p})$ matrix of Example 3.1 to the triangle

$$\mathbf{R}(45°, [-1,-1]^{\mathrm{T}}) \cdot \mathbf{T} = \begin{bmatrix} \frac{\sqrt{2}}{2} & -\frac{\sqrt{2}}{2} & -1 \\ \frac{\sqrt{2}}{2} & \frac{\sqrt{2}}{2} & \sqrt{2}-1 \\ 0 & 0 & 1 \end{bmatrix} \cdot \begin{bmatrix} 0 & 1 & 5 \\ 0 & 1 & 2 \\ 1 & 1 & 1 \end{bmatrix}$$

$$= \begin{bmatrix} -1 & -1 & \frac{3}{2}\sqrt{2}-1 \\ \sqrt{2}-1 & 2\sqrt{2}-1 & \frac{9}{2}\sqrt{2}-1 \\ 1 & 1 & 1 \end{bmatrix}.$$

The rotated triangle is thus $\triangle\mathbf{a'b'c'}$ with

$$\mathbf{a'} = [-1, \sqrt{2}-1]^{\mathrm{T}},$$
$$\mathbf{b'} = [-1, 2\sqrt{2}-1]^{\mathrm{T}}, \text{ and}$$
$$\mathbf{c'} = [\frac{3}{2}\sqrt{2}-1, \frac{9}{2}\sqrt{2}-1]^{\mathrm{T}}.$$

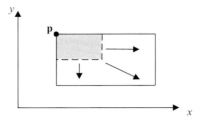

Figure 3.8. Scaling about an arbitrary point.

Example 3.3 (Scaling about an Arbitrary Point.) Determine the transformation matrix $\mathbf{S}(s_x, s_y, \mathbf{p})$ required to perform scaling by s_x and s_y about an arbitrary point $\mathbf{p}$ (Figure 3.8).

The 2D scaling matrix $\mathbf{S}(s_x, s_y)$ (Equation (3.11)) scales about the origin; in particular, its translation side-effect is relative to the origin. To scale about an arbitrary point $\mathbf{p} = [p_x, p_y]^\mathrm{T}$, we first have to translate $\mathbf{p}$ to the origin, scale about the origin, and finally undo the translation.

Step 1. Translate by $-\overrightarrow{\mathbf{p}}$, $\mathbf{T}(-\overrightarrow{\mathbf{p}})$.

Step 2. Scale by s_x, s_y, $\mathbf{S}(s_x, s_y)$.

Step 3. Translate by $\overrightarrow{\mathbf{p}}$, $\mathbf{T}(\overrightarrow{\mathbf{p}})$.

$$\mathbf{S}(s_x, s_y, \mathbf{p}) = \begin{bmatrix} 1 & 0 & p_x \\ 0 & 1 & p_y \\ 0 & 0 & 1 \end{bmatrix} \cdot \begin{bmatrix} s_x & 0 & 0 \\ 0 & s_y & 0 \\ 0 & 0 & 1 \end{bmatrix} \cdot \begin{bmatrix} 1 & 0 & -p_x \\ 0 & 1 & -p_y \\ 0 & 0 & 1 \end{bmatrix}$$

$$= \begin{bmatrix} s_x & 0 & p_x - p_x s_x \\ 0 & s_y & p_y - p_y s_y \\ 0 & 0 & 1 \end{bmatrix}.$$

Example 3.4 (Scaling of a Triangle about a Point.) Double the lengths of the sides of triangle $\triangle \mathbf{abc}$ keeping its vertex $\mathbf{c}$ fixed. The coordinates of its vertices are $\mathbf{a} = [0,0]^\mathrm{T}, \mathbf{b} = [1,1]^\mathrm{T}$ and $\mathbf{c} = [5,2]^\mathrm{T}$.

Since this is the same triangle as in Example 3.2, it can be represented by the matrix $\mathbf{T}$. We shall apply the matrix $\mathbf{S}(s_x, s_y, \mathbf{p})$ of Example 3.3 to the triangle $\triangle \mathbf{abc}$, setting the scaling factors equal to 2 and $\mathbf{p} = \mathbf{c}$:

$$\mathbf{S}(2,2,[5,2,1]^{\mathrm{T}}) \cdot \mathbf{T} = \begin{bmatrix} 2 & 0 & -5 \\ 0 & 2 & -2 \\ 0 & 0 & 1 \end{bmatrix} \cdot \begin{bmatrix} 0 & 1 & 5 \\ 0 & 1 & 2 \\ 1 & 1 & 1 \end{bmatrix}$$

$$= \begin{bmatrix} -5 & -3 & 5 \\ -2 & 0 & 2 \\ 1 & 1 & 1 \end{bmatrix}.$$

The scaled triangle is thus $\triangle \mathbf{a'b'c'}$ with $\mathbf{a'} = [-5, -2]^{\mathrm{T}}, \mathbf{b'} = [-3, 0]^{\mathrm{T}}$, and $\mathbf{c'} = [5, 2]^{\mathrm{T}}$. A simple calculation reveals that the lengths of its sides have indeed doubled.

Example 3.5 (Axis Transformation.) Suppose that the coordinate system is translated by the vector $\overrightarrow{\mathbf{v}} = [v_x, v_y]^{\mathrm{T}}$. Determine the matrix that describes this effect.

This is an example of an axis transformation, i.e., a transformation of the coordinate system. The coordinate system is translated by $\overrightarrow{\mathbf{v}} = [v_x, v_y]^{\mathrm{T}}$ relative to the objects (Figure 3.9).

The required transformation matrix must produce the coordinates of the objects with respect to the new coordinate system. This is achieved by applying the inverse translation to the objects; that is,

$$\mathbf{T}(-\overrightarrow{\mathbf{v}}) = \begin{bmatrix} 1 & 0 & -v_x \\ 0 & 1 & -v_y \\ 0 & 0 & 1 \end{bmatrix}.$$

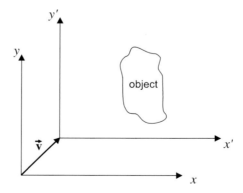

Figure 3.9. Axis translation.

A similar argument holds for any other axis transformation; its effect is encapsulated by applying the inverse transformation to the objects.

Example 3.6 (Mirroring about an Arbitrary Axis.) Determine the transformation matrix required to perform mirroring about an axis specified by a point $\mathbf{p} = [p_x, p_y]^T$ and a direction vector $\overrightarrow{\mathbf{v}} = [v_x, v_y]^T$ (Figure 3.10).

We shall proceed as follows. First, the general axis will be made to coincide with the x-axis, then we shall perform x-axis mirroring, and finally the axis will recover its original position. Making the general axis coincide with the x-axis requires two simple steps: a translation by $-\overrightarrow{\mathbf{p}}$ and a rotation by the angle θ formed between $\overrightarrow{\mathbf{v}}$ and the x-axis. It can easily be seen that

$$\sin\theta = \frac{v_y}{\sqrt{v_x^2 + v_y^2}} \text{ and } \cos\theta = \frac{v_x}{\sqrt{v_x^2 + v_y^2}}.$$

The required steps are the following:

Step 1. Translate by $-\overrightarrow{\mathbf{p}}$, $\mathbf{T}(-\overrightarrow{\mathbf{p}})$.

Step 2. Rotate by $-\theta$ (negative as it is clockwise), $\mathbf{R}(-\theta)$.

Step 3. Perform mirroring about the x-axis, $\mathbf{S}(1, -1)$.

Step 4. Rotate by θ, $\mathbf{R}(\theta)$.

Step 5. Translate by $\overrightarrow{\mathbf{p}}$, $\mathbf{T}(\overrightarrow{\mathbf{p}})$.

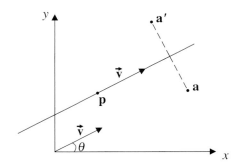

Figure 3.10. Mirroring about a general axis.

$$\mathbf{M}_{\text{SYM}} = \begin{bmatrix} 1 & 0 & p_x \\ 0 & 1 & p_y \\ 0 & 0 & 1 \end{bmatrix} \cdot \begin{bmatrix} \cos\theta & -\sin\theta & 0 \\ \sin\theta & \cos\theta & 0 \\ 0 & 0 & 1 \end{bmatrix}$$

$$\cdot \begin{bmatrix} 1 & 0 & 0 \\ 0 & -1 & 0 \\ 0 & 0 & 1 \end{bmatrix} \cdot \begin{bmatrix} \cos\theta & \sin\theta & 0 \\ -\sin\theta & \cos\theta & 0 \\ 0 & 0 & 1 \end{bmatrix} \cdot \begin{bmatrix} 1 & 0 & -p_x \\ 0 & 1 & -p_y \\ 0 & 0 & 1 \end{bmatrix}$$

$$= \begin{bmatrix} \cos^2\theta - \sin^2\theta & 2\sin\theta\cos\theta & p_x - p_x(\cos^2\theta - \sin^2\theta) - 2p_y\sin\theta\cos\theta \\ 2\sin\theta\cos\theta & \sin^2\theta - \cos^2\theta & p_y - p_y(\sin^2\theta - \cos^2\theta) - 2p_x\sin\theta\cos\theta \\ 0 & 0 & 1 \end{bmatrix}.$$

Example 3.7 (Mirror Polygon.) Given a polygon, determine its mirror polygon with respect to (a) the line $y = 2$ and (b) the axis specified by the point $\mathbf{p} = [0,2]^T$ and the vector $\overrightarrow{\mathbf{v}} = [1,1]^T$. The polygon is given by its vertices $\mathbf{a} = [-1,0]^T$, $\mathbf{b} = [0,-2]^T$, $\mathbf{c} = [1,0]^T$ and $\mathbf{d} = [0,2]^T$.

The polygon can be represented by a 3×4 matrix Π, the columns of which are the homogeneous coordinates of its vertices:

$$\Pi = \begin{bmatrix} -1 & 0 & 1 & 0 \\ 0 & -2 & 0 & 2 \\ 1 & 1 & 1 & 1 \end{bmatrix}.$$

We shall pre-multiply the $\mathbf{M}_{\text{SYM}}$ matrix of Example 3.6 by the matrix of the vertices Π.

In case (a), $\mathbf{p} = [0,2]^T$ and $\overrightarrow{\mathbf{v}} = [1,0]^T$; thus $\theta = 0°$, $\sin\theta = 0$, $\cos\theta = 1$, and we have

$$\Pi' = \mathbf{M}_{\text{SYM}} \cdot \Pi$$

$$= \begin{bmatrix} 1 & 0 & 0 \\ 0 & -1 & 4 \\ 0 & 0 & 1 \end{bmatrix} \cdot \begin{bmatrix} -1 & 0 & 1 & 0 \\ 0 & -2 & 0 & 2 \\ 1 & 1 & 1 & 1 \end{bmatrix}$$

$$= \begin{bmatrix} -1 & 0 & 1 & 0 \\ 4 & 6 & 4 & 2 \\ 1 & 1 & 1 & 1 \end{bmatrix}.$$

In case (b), $\mathbf{p} = [0,2]^T$ and $\vec{\mathbf{v}} = [1,1]^T$, so $\sin\theta = \cos\theta = \frac{1}{\sqrt{2}}$, and we have

$$\Pi' = \mathbf{M}_{\mathrm{SYM}} \cdot \Pi$$

$$= \begin{bmatrix} 0 & 1 & -2 \\ 1 & 0 & 2 \\ 0 & 0 & 1 \end{bmatrix} \cdot \begin{bmatrix} -1 & 0 & 1 & 0 \\ 0 & -2 & 0 & 2 \\ 1 & 1 & 1 & 1 \end{bmatrix}$$

$$= \begin{bmatrix} -2 & -4 & -2 & 0 \\ 1 & 2 & 3 & 2 \\ 1 & 1 & 1 & 1 \end{bmatrix}.$$

Example 3.8 (Window-to-Viewport Transformation.) A common transformation in computer graphics and visualization but also in entertainment is the window-to-viewport transformation, where the contents of a 2D "window" must be transferred to a 2D "viewport" (Figure 3.11). The window and the viewport are both rectangular parallelograms with sides parallel to the x- and y-axes. For example, the window/viewport pair may be a theater-sized screen $(16:9)$ and a television-sized screen $(4:3)$, respectively. Determine the window to viewport transformation matrix. Also determine how objects are deformed by this transformation.

Suppose that the window and the viewport are defined by two opposite vertices $[w_{\mathrm{xmin}}, w_{\mathrm{ymin}}]^T$, $[w_{\mathrm{xmax}}, w_{\mathrm{ymax}}]^T$ and $[v_{\mathrm{xmin}}, v_{\mathrm{ymin}}]^T$, $[v_{\mathrm{xmax}}, v_{\mathrm{ymax}}]^T$ of the window and viewport, respectively (Figure 3.11).

The window-to-viewport transformation $\mathbf{M}_{\mathrm{WV}}$ can be implemented in three basic steps:

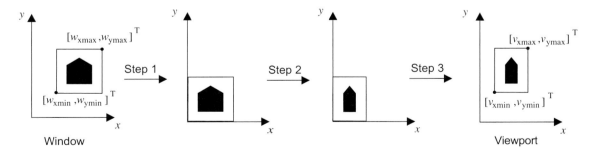

Figure 3.11. Window-to-viewport transformation.

Step 1. Translate $[w_{\text{xmin}}, w_{\text{ymin}}]^{\text{T}}$ to the origin, using $\mathbf{T}(-\overrightarrow{\mathbf{w}}_{\text{min}})$ where $\overrightarrow{\mathbf{w}}_{\text{min}} = [w_{\text{xmin}}, w_{\text{ymin}}]^{\text{T}}$.

Step 2. Scale the window to the size of the viewport, using $\mathbf{S}(s_x, s_y)$ where $s_x = \frac{v_{\text{xmax}} - v_{\text{xmin}}}{w_{\text{xmax}} - w_{\text{xmin}}}$ and $s_y = \frac{v_{\text{ymax}} - v_{\text{ymin}}}{w_{\text{ymax}} - w_{\text{ymin}}}$.

Step 3. Translate to the minimum viewport vertex $[v_{\text{xmin}}, v_{\text{ymin}}]^{\text{T}}$, using $\mathbf{T}(\overrightarrow{\mathbf{v}}_{\text{min}})$ where $\overrightarrow{\mathbf{v}}_{\text{min}} = [v_{\text{xmin}}, v_{\text{ymin}}]^{\text{T}}$.

$$\mathbf{M}_{\text{WV}} = \mathbf{T}(\overrightarrow{\mathbf{v}}_{\text{min}}) \cdot \mathbf{S}(s_x, s_y) \cdot \mathbf{T}(-\overrightarrow{\mathbf{w}}_{\text{min}})$$

$$= \begin{bmatrix} 1 & 0 & v_{\text{xmin}} \\ 0 & 1 & v_{\text{ymin}} \\ 0 & 0 & 1 \end{bmatrix} \cdot \begin{bmatrix} \frac{v_{\text{xmax}} - v_{\text{xmin}}}{w_{\text{xmax}} - w_{\text{xmin}}} & 0 & 0 \\ 0 & \frac{v_{\text{ymax}} - v_{\text{ymin}}}{w_{\text{ymax}} - w_{\text{ymin}}} & 0 \\ 0 & 0 & 1 \end{bmatrix} \cdot \begin{bmatrix} 1 & 0 & -w_{\text{xmin}} \\ 0 & 1 & -w_{\text{ymin}} \\ 0 & 0 & 1 \end{bmatrix}$$

$$= \begin{bmatrix} \frac{v_{\text{xmax}} - v_{\text{xmin}}}{w_{\text{xmax}} - w_{\text{xmin}}} & 0 & v_{\text{xmin}} - w_{\text{xmin}} \frac{v_{\text{xmax}} - v_{\text{xmin}}}{w_{\text{xmax}} - w_{\text{xmin}}} \\ 0 & \frac{v_{\text{ymax}} - v_{\text{ymin}}}{w_{\text{ymax}} - w_{\text{ymin}}} & v_{\text{ymin}} - w_{\text{ymin}} \frac{v_{\text{ymax}} - v_{\text{ymin}}}{w_{\text{ymax}} - w_{\text{ymin}}} \\ 0 & 0 & 1 \end{bmatrix}.$$

$$(3.20)$$

Since the $\mathbf{M}_{\text{WV}}$ transformation contains non-isotropic scaling ($s_x \neq s_y$) objects will be deformed during the transition from the window to the viewport (angles will change). Thus, a circle will become an ellipse, and a square will become a rectangular parallelogram. The *aspect ratios* of the window and the viewport are defined as the ratios of their x- to their y-sizes:

$$a_w = \frac{w_{\text{xmax}} - w_{\text{xmin}}}{w_{\text{ymax}} - w_{\text{ymin}}}, \quad a_v = \frac{v_{\text{xmax}} - v_{\text{xmin}}}{v_{\text{ymax}} - v_{\text{ymin}}}.$$

If $a_w \neq a_v$ then objects will be deformed. A simple way to avoid this deformation is to use the largest part of the viewport which has the same aspect ratio as the window. For example, we can change the v_{xmax} or the v_{ymax} boundary of the viewport in the following manner: if $(a_v > a_w)$ then $v_{\text{xmax}} = v_{\text{xmin}} + a_w * (v_{\text{ymax}} - v_{\text{ymin}})$ else if $(a_v < a_w)$ then $v_{\text{ymax}} = v_{\text{ymin}} + \frac{(v_{\text{xmax}} - v_{\text{xmin}})}{a_w}$.

Example 3.9 (Window-to-Viewport Transformation Instances.) Determine the window to viewport transformation from the window $[w_{\text{xmin}}, w_{\text{ymin}}]^{\text{T}} = [1, 1]^{\text{T}}$, $[w_{\text{xmax}}, w_{\text{ymax}}]^{\text{T}} = [3, 5]^{\text{T}}$ to the viewport $[v_{\text{xmin}}, v_{\text{ymin}}]^{\text{T}} = [0, 0]^{\text{T}}$, $[v_{\text{xmax}}, v_{\text{ymax}}]^{\text{T}} = [1, 1]^{\text{T}}$. If there is deformation, how can it be corrected?

Direct application of the $\mathbf{M}_{WV}$ matrix of Example 3.8 for the window and viewport pair gives

$$\mathbf{M}_{WV} = \begin{bmatrix} \frac{1}{2} & 0 & -\frac{1}{2} \\ 0 & \frac{1}{4} & -\frac{1}{4} \\ 0 & 0 & 1 \end{bmatrix}.$$

Now $a_w = \frac{1}{2}$ and $a_v = \frac{1}{1}$, so there is distortion since $(a_v > a_w)$. It can be corrected by reducing the size of the viewport by setting $v_{xmax} = v_{xmin} + a_w * (v_{ymax} - v_{ymin}) = \frac{1}{2}$.

Example 3.10 (Tilted Window–to-Viewport Transformation.) Suppose that the window is tilted as in Figure 3.12 and given by its four vertices $\mathbf{a} = [1,1]^T$, $\mathbf{b} = [5,3]^T$, $\mathbf{c} = [4,5]^T$, and $\mathbf{d} = [0,3]^T$. Determine the transformation $\mathbf{M}_{WV}^{TILT}$ that maps it to the viewport $[v_{xmin}, v_{ymin}]^T = [0,0]^T$, $[v_{xmax}, v_{ymax}]^T = [1,1]^T$.

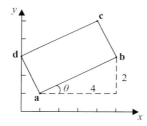

Figure 3.12. Tilted window to viewport.

The angle θ formed by side $\mathbf{ab}$ of the window and the horizontal line through $\mathbf{a}$ has $\sin \theta = \frac{1}{\sqrt{5}}$ and $\cos \theta = \frac{2}{\sqrt{5}}$. The required transformation $\mathbf{M}_{WV}^{TILT}$ will be the composition of the following steps:

Step 1. Rotate the window by angle $-\theta$ about point $\mathbf{a}$. For this we shall use the matrix $\mathbf{R}(\theta, \mathbf{p})$ of Example 3.1, instantiating it as $\mathbf{R}(-\theta, \mathbf{a})$.

Step 2. Apply the window to viewport transformation $\mathbf{M}_{WV}$ to the rotated window.

Before we can apply Step 2 we must determine the maximum x- and y-coordinates of the rotated window by computing

$$\mathbf{c}' = \mathbf{R}(-\theta, \mathbf{a}) \cdot \mathbf{c} = \begin{bmatrix} 1 + 2\sqrt{5} \\ 1 + \sqrt{5} \\ 1 \end{bmatrix}.$$

Thus, $[w_{\text{xmin}}, w_{\text{ymin}}]^{\text{T}} = \mathbf{a}$, $[w_{\text{xmax}}, w_{\text{ymax}}]^{\text{T}} = \mathbf{c}'$, and we have

$$
\mathbf{M}_{\text{WV}}^{\text{TILT}} = \mathbf{M}_{\text{WV}} \cdot \mathbf{R}(-\theta, \mathbf{a}) =
\begin{bmatrix}
\frac{1}{2\sqrt{5}} & 0 & -\frac{1}{2\sqrt{5}} \\
0 & \frac{1}{\sqrt{5}} & -\frac{1}{\sqrt{5}} \\
0 & 0 & 1
\end{bmatrix}
\cdot
\begin{bmatrix}
\frac{2}{\sqrt{5}} & \frac{1}{\sqrt{5}} & 1-\frac{3}{\sqrt{5}} \\
-\frac{1}{\sqrt{5}} & \frac{2}{\sqrt{5}} & 1-\frac{1}{\sqrt{5}} \\
0 & 0 & 1
\end{bmatrix}
$$

$$
=
\begin{bmatrix}
\frac{1}{5} & \frac{1}{10} & -\frac{3}{10} \\
-\frac{1}{5} & \frac{2}{5} & -\frac{1}{5} \\
0 & 0 & 1
\end{bmatrix}.
$$

3.7   3D Homogeneous Affine Transformations

In three dimensions homogeneous coordinates work in a similar way to two dimensions (see Section 3.4.1). An extra coordinate is added to create the quadruplet $[x, y, z, w]^{\text{T}}$, where w is the coordinate that corresponds to the additional dimension. Again, points whose homogeneous coordinates are multiples of each other are equivalent, e.g., $[1, 2, 3, 2]^{\text{T}}$ and $[2, 4, 6, 4]^{\text{T}}$ are equivalent. The (unique) *basic representation* of a point has $w = 1$ and is obtained by dividing by w:

$$
[x/w, y/w, z/w, w/w]^{\text{T}} = [x/w, y/w, z/w, 1]^{\text{T}}
$$

where $w \neq 0$. For example for the above pair of equivalent points,

$$
[\frac{1}{2}, \frac{2}{2}, \frac{3}{2}, \frac{2}{2}]^{\text{T}} = [\frac{2}{4}, \frac{4}{4}, \frac{6}{4}, \frac{4}{4}]^{\text{T}} = [\frac{1}{2}, 1, \frac{3}{2}, 1]^{\text{T}}.
$$

By setting $w = 1$ (basic representation) we obtain a 3D projection of 4D space.

Since points are represented by 4×1 vectors, transformation matrices are 4×4. As in the 2D case, for brevity of presentation we shall often omit the homogeneous coordinate, but it will be assumed. All the transformations that follow are affine transformations.

3.7.1   3D Homogeneous Translation

Three-dimensional translation is specified by a three-dimensional vector $\vec{\mathbf{d}} = [d_x, d_y, d_z]^{\text{T}}$ and is encapsulated in matrix form as

$$
\mathbf{T}(\vec{\mathbf{d}}) =
\begin{bmatrix}
1 & 0 & 0 & d_x \\
0 & 1 & 0 & d_y \\
0 & 0 & 1 & d_z \\
0 & 0 & 0 & 1
\end{bmatrix}.
\tag{3.21}
$$

As in two dimensions, the main advantage of homogeneous coordinates is that the translation matrix can be combined with other affine transformation matrices by matrix multiplication.

For the inverse translation we use the inverse of the translation matrix $\mathbf{T}^{-1}(\overrightarrow{\mathbf{d}}) = \mathbf{T}(-\overrightarrow{\mathbf{d}})$.

3.7.2   3D Homogeneous Scaling

Three-dimensional scaling is entirely analogous to two-dimensional scaling. We now have three scaling factors, s_x, s_y, and s_z. If a scaling factor is less than 1, then the object's size is reduced in the respective dimension, while if it is greater than 1 it is increased. Again, scaling has a translation side-effect which is proportional to the scaling factor. The matrix form is

$$\mathbf{S}(s_x, s_y, s_z) = \begin{bmatrix} s_x & 0 & 0 & 0 \\ 0 & s_y & 0 & 0 \\ 0 & 0 & s_z & 0 \\ 0 & 0 & 0 & 1 \end{bmatrix}. \tag{3.22}$$

A scaling transformation is called *isotropic*, if $s_x = s_y = s_z$. Isotropic scaling preserves the similarity of objects (angles).

Mirroring about one of the major planes (xy, xz, or yz) can be described as a special case of the scaling transformation, by using a -1 scaling factor. For example, mirroring about the xy-plane is $\mathbf{S}(1, 1, -1)$.

For the inverse scaling we use the inverse of the scaling matrix $\mathbf{S}^{-1}(s_x, s_y, s_z) = \mathbf{S}(\frac{1}{s_x}, \frac{1}{s_y}, \frac{1}{s_z})$.

3.7.3   3D Homogeneous Rotation

Three-dimensional rotation is quite different from the two-dimensional case as the object about which we rotate is an *axis* and not a point. The axis of rotation can be arbitrary, but the basic rotation transformations rotate about the three main axes x, y, and z. It is possible to combine them in order to describe a rotation about an arbitrary axis, as will be shown in the examples that follow. In our right-handed coordinate system, we specify a *positive rotation* about an axis a as one which is in the *counterclockwise* direction when looking from the positive part of a toward the origin. Figure 3.13 shows the direction of positive rotation about the y-axis.

In three-dimensional rotation, the distance from the axis of rotation of the object being rotated does not change; thus, rotation does not affect the coordinate that corresponds to the axis of rotation. Simple trigonometric arguments, similar

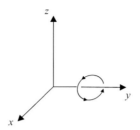

Figure 3.13. Positive rotation about the *y*-axis.

to the two-dimensional case, result in the following rotation matrices about the main axes x, y, and z:

$$\mathbf{R_x}(\theta) = \begin{bmatrix} 1 & 0 & 0 & 0 \\ 0 & \cos\theta & -\sin\theta & 0 \\ 0 & \sin\theta & \cos\theta & 0 \\ 0 & 0 & 0 & 1 \end{bmatrix}; \qquad (3.23)$$

$$\mathbf{R_y}(\theta) = \begin{bmatrix} \cos\theta & 0 & \sin\theta & 0 \\ 0 & 1 & 0 & 0 \\ -\sin\theta & 0 & \cos\theta & 0 \\ 0 & 0 & 0 & 1 \end{bmatrix}; \qquad (3.24)$$

$$\mathbf{R_z}(\theta) = \begin{bmatrix} \cos\theta & -\sin\theta & 0 & 0 \\ \sin\theta & \cos\theta & 0 & 0 \\ 0 & 0 & 1 & 0 \\ 0 & 0 & 0 & 1 \end{bmatrix}. \qquad (3.25)$$

For the inverse rotation transformations, we use the inverse of the rotation matrices $\mathbf{R_x}^{-1}(\theta) = \mathbf{R_x}(-\theta)$, $\mathbf{R_y}^{-1}(\theta) = \mathbf{R_y}(-\theta)$ and $\mathbf{R_z}^{-1}(\theta) = \mathbf{R_z}(-\theta)$.

Rotations can also be expressed using quaternions as will be described in Section 3.9.

3.7.4   3D Homogeneous Shear

The three-dimensional shear transformation "shears" objects along one of the major planes. In other words it increases two coordinates by an amount equal to the third coordinate times the respective shearing factors. We therefore have three cases of shear in three dimensions, which correspond to the three major planes xy, xz, and yz.

The *xy* shear increases the *x*-coordinate by an amount equal to the *z*-coordinate times the shear factor *a* and the *y*-coordinate by an amount equal to the *z*-coordinate times the shear factor *b*:

$$\mathbf{SH_{xy}}(a,b) = \begin{bmatrix} 1 & 0 & a & 0 \\ 0 & 1 & b & 0 \\ 0 & 0 & 1 & 0 \\ 0 & 0 & 0 & 1 \end{bmatrix}. \tag{3.26}$$

The *xz* and *yz* shears are similar:

$$\mathbf{SH_{xz}}(a,b) = \begin{bmatrix} 1 & a & 0 & 0 \\ 0 & 1 & 0 & 0 \\ 0 & b & 1 & 0 \\ 0 & 0 & 0 & 1 \end{bmatrix}; \tag{3.27}$$

$$\mathbf{SH_{yz}}(a,b) = \begin{bmatrix} 1 & 0 & 0 & 0 \\ a & 1 & 0 & 0 \\ b & 0 & 1 & 0 \\ 0 & 0 & 0 & 1 \end{bmatrix}. \tag{3.28}$$

The inverse of a shear is obtained by negating the shear factors: $\mathbf{SH_{xy}^{-1}}(a,b) = \mathbf{SH_{xy}}(-a,-b)$, $\mathbf{SH_{xz}^{-1}}(a,b) = \mathbf{SH_{xz}}(-a,-b)$, $\mathbf{SH_{yz}^{-1}}(a,b) = \mathbf{SH_{yz}}(-a,-b)$.

3.8   3D Transformation Examples

Example 3.11 (Composite Rotation.) We use the term "bending" to define a rotation about the *x*-axis by θ_x followed by a rotation about the *y*-axis by θ_y. Compute the bending matrix and determine whether the order of the rotations matters.

From its definition, the bending matrix is computed as

$$\mathbf{M}_{\text{BEND}} = \mathbf{R_y}(\theta_y) \cdot \mathbf{R_x}(\theta_x)$$

$$= \begin{bmatrix} \cos\theta_y & 0 & \sin\theta_y & 0 \\ 0 & 1 & 0 & 0 \\ -\sin\theta_y & 0 & \cos\theta_y & 0 \\ 0 & 0 & 0 & 1 \end{bmatrix} \cdot \begin{bmatrix} 1 & 0 & 0 & 0 \\ 0 & \cos\theta_x & -\sin\theta_x & 0 \\ 0 & \sin\theta_x & \cos\theta_x & 0 \\ 0 & 0 & 0 & 1 \end{bmatrix}$$

$$= \begin{bmatrix} \cos\theta_y & \sin\theta_x\sin\theta_y & \cos\theta_x\sin\theta_y & 0 \\ 0 & \cos\theta_x & -\sin\theta_x & 0 \\ -\sin\theta_y & \sin\theta_x\cos\theta_y & \cos\theta_x\cos\theta_y & 0 \\ 0 & 0 & 0 & 1 \end{bmatrix}.$$

To determine whether the order of the rotations matters, we shall compute the composition in reverse order:

$$\mathbf{M}'_{\mathrm{BEND}} = \mathbf{R_x}(\theta_x) \cdot \mathbf{R_y}(\theta_y)$$

$$= \begin{bmatrix} 1 & 0 & 0 & 0 \\ 0 & \cos\theta_x & -\sin\theta_x & 0 \\ 0 & \sin\theta_x & \cos\theta_x & 0 \\ 0 & 0 & 0 & 1 \end{bmatrix} \cdot \begin{bmatrix} \cos\theta_y & 0 & \sin\theta_y & 0 \\ 0 & 1 & 0 & 0 \\ -\sin\theta_y & 0 & \cos\theta_y & 0 \\ 0 & 0 & 0 & 1 \end{bmatrix}$$

$$= \begin{bmatrix} \cos\theta_y & 0 & \sin\theta_y & 0 \\ \sin\theta_x \sin\theta_y & \cos\theta_x & -\sin\theta_x \cos\theta_y & 0 \\ -\cos\theta_x \sin\theta_y & \sin\theta_x & \cos\theta_x \cos\theta_y & 0 \\ 0 & 0 & 0 & 1 \end{bmatrix}.$$

Since $\mathbf{M}_{\mathrm{BEND}} \neq \mathbf{M}'_{\mathrm{BEND}}$, we deduce that the order of the rotations matters.

Note that in a composite rotation about the $x-, y-$ and $z-$ axes, a problem known as *gimbal lock* may be encountered; see Section 17.2.1.

Example 3.12 (Alignment of Vector with Axis.) Determine the transformation $\mathbf{A}(\overrightarrow{\mathbf{v}})$ required to align a given vector $\overrightarrow{\mathbf{v}} = [a, b, c]^{\mathrm{T}}$ with the unit vector $\hat{\mathbf{k}}$ along the positive z-axis.

The initial situation is shown is Figure 3.14 (a). One way of accomplishing our aim uses two rotations:

Step 1. Rotate about x by θ_1 so that $\overrightarrow{\mathbf{v}}$ is mapped onto $\overrightarrow{\mathbf{v_1}}$ which lies on the xz-plane (Figure 3.14 (b)), $\mathbf{R_x}(\theta_1)$.

Step 2. Rotate $\overrightarrow{\mathbf{v_1}}$ about y by θ_2 so that it coincides with $\hat{\mathbf{k}}$ (Figure 3.14 (c)), $\mathbf{R_y}(\theta_2)$.

The alignment matrix $\mathbf{A}(\overrightarrow{\mathbf{v}})$ is then

$$\mathbf{A}(\overrightarrow{\mathbf{v}}) = \mathbf{R_y}(\theta_2) \cdot \mathbf{R_x}(\theta_1).$$

We need to compute the angles θ_1 and θ_2. Looking at Figure 3.14 (b), angle θ_1 is equal to the angle formed between the projection of $\overrightarrow{\mathbf{v}}$ onto the yz-plane and the z-axis. For the tip $\mathbf{p}$ of $\overrightarrow{\mathbf{v}}$, we have $\mathbf{p} = [a, b, c]^{\mathrm{T}}$, therefore the tip of its projection on yz is $\mathbf{p}' = [0, b, c]^{\mathrm{T}}$. Assuming that b and c are not both equal to 0, we get

$$\sin\theta_1 = \frac{b}{\sqrt{b^2 + c^2}}, \qquad \cos\theta_1 = \frac{c}{\sqrt{b^2 + c^2}}.$$

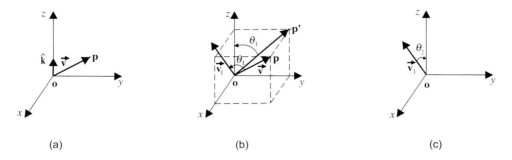

Figure 3.14. Alignment of an arbitrary vector with $\hat{\mathbf{k}}$.

Thus,

$$\mathbf{R_x}(\theta_1) = \begin{bmatrix} 1 & 0 & 0 & 0 \\ 0 & \frac{c}{\sqrt{b^2+c^2}} & -\frac{b}{\sqrt{b^2+c^2}} & 0 \\ 0 & \frac{b}{\sqrt{b^2+c^2}} & \frac{c}{\sqrt{b^2+c^2}} & 0 \\ 0 & 0 & 0 & 1 \end{bmatrix}.$$

We next apply $\mathbf{R_x}(\theta_1)$ to $\overrightarrow{\mathbf{v}}$ [8] in order to get its xz projection $\overrightarrow{\mathbf{v_1}}$:

$$\overrightarrow{\mathbf{v_1}} = \mathbf{R_x}(\theta_1) \cdot \overrightarrow{\mathbf{v}} = \mathbf{R_x}(\theta_1) \cdot \begin{bmatrix} a \\ b \\ c \\ 1 \end{bmatrix} = \begin{bmatrix} a \\ 0 \\ \sqrt{b^2+c^2} \\ 1 \end{bmatrix}.$$

Note that $|\overrightarrow{\mathbf{v_1}}| = |\overrightarrow{\mathbf{v}}| = \sqrt{a^2+b^2+c^2}$. From Figure 3.14 (c), we can now compute

$$\sin\theta_2 = \frac{a}{\sqrt{a^2+b^2+c^2}} \qquad \cos\theta_2 = \frac{\sqrt{b^2+c^2}}{\sqrt{a^2+b^2+c^2}}.$$

Thus,

$$\mathbf{R_y}(\theta_2) = \begin{bmatrix} \frac{\sqrt{b^2+c^2}}{\sqrt{a^2+b^2+c^2}} & 0 & \frac{a}{\sqrt{a^2+b^2+c^2}} & 0 \\ 0 & 1 & 0 & 0 \\ -\frac{a}{\sqrt{a^2+b^2+c^2}} & 0 & \frac{\sqrt{b^2+c^2}}{\sqrt{a^2+b^2+c^2}} & 0 \\ 0 & 0 & 0 & 1 \end{bmatrix}.$$

---

[8]This is equivalent to rotating the tip of the vector **p**.

The required matrix $\mathbf{A}(\overrightarrow{\mathbf{v}})$ can now be computed:

$$\mathbf{A}(\overrightarrow{\mathbf{v}}) = \mathbf{R_y}(\theta_2) \cdot \mathbf{R_x}(\theta_1) = \begin{bmatrix} \frac{\lambda}{|\overrightarrow{\mathbf{v}}|} & -\frac{ab}{\lambda|\overrightarrow{\mathbf{v}}|} & -\frac{ac}{\lambda|\overrightarrow{\mathbf{v}}|} & 0 \\ 0 & \frac{c}{\lambda} & -\frac{b}{\lambda} & 0 \\ \frac{a}{|\overrightarrow{\mathbf{v}}|} & \frac{b}{|\overrightarrow{\mathbf{v}}|} & \frac{c}{|\overrightarrow{\mathbf{v}}|} & 0 \\ 0 & 0 & 0 & 1 \end{bmatrix}, \qquad (3.29)$$

where $|\overrightarrow{\mathbf{v}}| = \sqrt{a^2 + b^2 + c^2}$ and $\lambda = \sqrt{b^2 + c^2}$.

We shall also compute the inverse matrix $\mathbf{A}(\overrightarrow{\mathbf{v}})^{-1}$ as it will prove useful in Example 3.13:

$$\mathbf{A}^{-1}(\overrightarrow{\mathbf{v}}) = (\mathbf{R_y}(\theta_2) \cdot \mathbf{R_x}(\theta_1))^{-1} = \mathbf{R_x}(\theta_1)^{-1} \cdot \mathbf{R_y}(\theta_2)^{-1}$$

$$= \mathbf{R_x}(-\theta_1) \cdot \mathbf{R_y}(-\theta_2) = \begin{bmatrix} \frac{\lambda}{|\overrightarrow{\mathbf{v}}|} & 0 & \frac{a}{|\overrightarrow{\mathbf{v}}|} & 0 \\ -\frac{ab}{\lambda|\overrightarrow{\mathbf{v}}|} & \frac{c}{\lambda} & \frac{b}{|\overrightarrow{\mathbf{v}}|} & 0 \\ -\frac{ac}{\lambda|\overrightarrow{\mathbf{v}}|} & -\frac{b}{\lambda} & \frac{c}{|\overrightarrow{\mathbf{v}}|} & 0 \\ 0 & 0 & 0 & 1 \end{bmatrix}.$$

If b and c are both equal to 0, then $\overrightarrow{\mathbf{v}}$ coincides with the x-axis, and we only need to rotate about y by $90°$ or $-90°$, depending on the sign of a. In this case, we have

$$\mathbf{A}(\overrightarrow{\mathbf{v}}) = \mathbf{R_y}(-\theta_2) = \begin{bmatrix} 0 & 0 & -\frac{a}{|a|} & 0 \\ 0 & 1 & 0 & 0 \\ \frac{a}{|a|} & 0 & 0 & 0 \\ 0 & 0 & 0 & 1 \end{bmatrix}.$$

Example 3.13 (Rotation about an Arbitrary Axis using Two Translations and Five Rotations.) Find the transformation which performs a rotation by an angle θ about an arbitrary axis specified by a vector $\overrightarrow{\mathbf{v}}$ and a point $\mathbf{p}$ (Figure 3.15).

Using the $\mathbf{A}(\overrightarrow{\mathbf{v}})$ transformation, we can align an arbitrary vector with the z-axis. We thus reduce the problem of rotation about an arbitrary axis to a rotation around z. Specifically, we perform the following composite transformation:

Step 1. Translate $\mathbf{p}$ to the origin, $\mathbf{T}(-\overrightarrow{\mathbf{p}})$.

Step 2. Align $\overrightarrow{\mathbf{v}}$ with the z-axis using the $\mathbf{A}(\overrightarrow{\mathbf{v}})$ matrix of Example 3.12.

Step 3. Rotate about the z-axis by the desired angle θ, $\mathbf{R_z}(\theta)$.

Step 4. Undo the alignment, $\mathbf{A}^{-1}(\overrightarrow{\mathbf{v}})$.

Step 5. Undo the translation, $\mathbf{T}(\overrightarrow{\mathbf{p}})$.

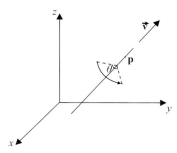

Figure 3.15. Rotation about an arbitrary axis.

Thus the required transformation is

$$\mathbf{M}_{\mathrm{ROT-AXIS}} = \mathbf{T}(\overrightarrow{\mathbf{p}}) \cdot \mathbf{A}^{-1}(\overrightarrow{\mathbf{v}}) \cdot \mathbf{R_z}(\theta) \cdot \mathbf{A}(\overrightarrow{\mathbf{v}}) \cdot \mathbf{T}(-\overrightarrow{\mathbf{p}}). \qquad (3.30)$$

Example 3.14 (Coordinate System Transformation using One Translation and Three Rotations.) Determine the transformation $\mathbf{M}_{\mathrm{ALIGN}}$ required to align a given 3D coordinate system with basis vectors $(\hat{\mathbf{l}}, \hat{\mathbf{m}}, \hat{\mathbf{n}})$ with the xyz coordinate system with basis vectors $(\hat{\mathbf{i}}, \hat{\mathbf{j}}, \hat{\mathbf{k}})$; the origin of the first coordinate system relative to xyz is $\mathbf{O}_{\mathrm{lmn}}$.

Note that this is an axis transformation; aligning the $(\hat{\mathbf{l}}, \hat{\mathbf{m}}, \hat{\mathbf{n}})$ basis to the $(\hat{\mathbf{i}}, \hat{\mathbf{j}}, \hat{\mathbf{k}})$ basis corresponds to changing an object's coordinate system from $(\hat{\mathbf{i}}, \hat{\mathbf{j}}, \hat{\mathbf{k}})$ to $(\hat{\mathbf{l}}, \hat{\mathbf{m}}, \hat{\mathbf{n}})$. The solution is a simple extension of the $\mathbf{A}(\overrightarrow{\mathbf{v}})$ transformation described in Example 3.12. Three steps are required:

Step 1. Translate by $-\mathbf{O}_{\mathrm{lmn}}$ to make the two origins coincide, $\mathbf{T}(-\overrightarrow{\mathbf{O}}_{\mathrm{lmn}})$.

Step 2. Use $\mathbf{A}(\overrightarrow{\mathbf{v}})$ of Example 3.12 to align the $\hat{\mathbf{n}}$ basis vector with the $\hat{\mathbf{k}}$ basis vector. The new situation is depicted in Figure 3.16. Transformation matrix $\mathbf{A}(\hat{\mathbf{n}})$.

Step 3. Rotate by φ around the z-axis to align the other two axes, $\mathbf{R_z}(\varphi)$.

$$\mathbf{M}_{\mathrm{ALIGN}} = \mathbf{R_z}(\varphi) \cdot \mathbf{A}(\hat{\mathbf{n}}) \cdot \mathbf{T}(-\overrightarrow{\mathbf{O}}_{\mathrm{lmn}}) \qquad (3.31)$$

It is necessary to transform the $\hat{\mathbf{l}}$ or the $\hat{\mathbf{m}}$ vector by $\mathbf{A}(\hat{\mathbf{n}})$ in order to be able to subsequently estimate φ: e.g., $\hat{\mathbf{m}}' = \mathbf{A}(\hat{\mathbf{n}}) \cdot \hat{\mathbf{m}}$. The $\sin\varphi$ and $\cos\varphi$ values required for the rotation are then just the x and y components of $\hat{\mathbf{m}}'$, respectively.

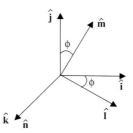

Figure 3.16. Aligning two coordinate systems.

Let us take a concrete example. Suppose that the orthonormal basis vectors of the two coordinate systems are

$$\hat{\mathbf{i}} = \begin{bmatrix} 1 \\ 0 \\ 0 \end{bmatrix}, \quad \hat{\mathbf{j}} = \begin{bmatrix} 0 \\ 1 \\ 0 \end{bmatrix}, \quad \hat{\mathbf{k}} = \begin{bmatrix} 0 \\ 0 \\ 1 \end{bmatrix};$$

$$\hat{\mathbf{l}} = \begin{bmatrix} \frac{3}{\sqrt{29}} \\ \frac{4}{\sqrt{29}} \\ \frac{2}{\sqrt{29}} \end{bmatrix}, \quad \hat{\mathbf{m}} = \begin{bmatrix} -\frac{32}{\sqrt{1653}} \\ \frac{25}{\sqrt{1653}} \\ -\frac{2}{\sqrt{1653}} \end{bmatrix}, \quad \hat{\mathbf{n}} = \begin{bmatrix} -\frac{2}{\sqrt{57}} \\ -\frac{2}{\sqrt{57}} \\ \frac{7}{\sqrt{57}} \end{bmatrix},$$

and that the origins of the two coordinate systems coincide ($\mathbf{O_{lmn}} = [0,0,0]^{\mathrm{T}}$). The basis vectors of the second system are expressed in terms of the first. Then, from the coordinates of $\hat{\mathbf{n}}$, $a = -\frac{2}{\sqrt{57}}$, $b = -\frac{2}{\sqrt{57}}$, $c = \frac{7}{\sqrt{57}}$ and $\lambda = \sqrt{b^2 + c^2} = \sqrt{(-\frac{2}{\sqrt{57}})^2 + (\frac{7}{\sqrt{57}})^2}$ (see Example 3.12).

Thus,

$$\mathbf{A}(\hat{\mathbf{n}}) = \begin{bmatrix} \sqrt{\frac{53}{57}} & -\frac{4}{\sqrt{3021}} & \frac{14}{\sqrt{3021}} & 0 \\ 0 & \frac{7}{\sqrt{53}} & \frac{2}{\sqrt{53}} & 0 \\ -\frac{2}{\sqrt{57}} & -\frac{2}{\sqrt{57}} & \frac{7}{\sqrt{57}} & 0 \\ 0 & 0 & 0 & 1 \end{bmatrix},$$

and

$$\hat{\mathbf{m}}' = \mathbf{A}(\hat{\mathbf{n}}) \cdot \hat{\mathbf{m}} = \mathbf{A}(\hat{\mathbf{n}}) \cdot \begin{bmatrix} -\frac{32}{\sqrt{1653}} \\ \frac{25}{\sqrt{1653}} \\ -\frac{2}{\sqrt{1653}} \\ 1 \end{bmatrix} = \begin{bmatrix} -\frac{32}{\sqrt{1537}} \\ 3\sqrt{\frac{57}{1537}} \\ 0 \\ 1 \end{bmatrix},$$

so

$$\sin\varphi = -\frac{32}{\sqrt{1537}} \text{ and } \cos\varphi = 3\sqrt{\frac{57}{1537}}.$$

Hence,

$$\mathbf{R_z}(\varphi) = \begin{bmatrix} 3\sqrt{\frac{57}{1537}} & \frac{32}{\sqrt{1537}} & 0 & 0 \\ -\frac{32}{\sqrt{1537}} & 3\sqrt{\frac{57}{1537}} & 0 & 0 \\ 0 & 0 & 1 & 0 \\ 0 & 0 & 0 & 1 \end{bmatrix}.$$

Finally, since the origins of the two coordinate systems coincide, Equation (3.31) becomes

$$\mathbf{M}_{\text{ALIGN}} = \mathbf{R_z}(\varphi) \cdot \mathbf{A}(\hat{\mathbf{n}}) \cdot \mathbf{ID}$$

$$= \begin{bmatrix} 3\sqrt{\frac{57}{1537}} & \frac{32}{\sqrt{1537}} & 0 & 0 \\ -\frac{32}{\sqrt{1537}} & 3\sqrt{\frac{57}{1537}} & 0 & 0 \\ 0 & 0 & 1 & 0 \\ 0 & 0 & 0 & 1 \end{bmatrix} \cdot \begin{bmatrix} \sqrt{\frac{53}{57}} & -\frac{4}{\sqrt{3021}} & \frac{14}{\sqrt{3021}} & 0 \\ 0 & \frac{7}{\sqrt{53}} & \frac{2}{\sqrt{53}} & 0 \\ -\frac{2}{\sqrt{57}} & -\frac{2}{\sqrt{57}} & \frac{7}{\sqrt{57}} & 0 \\ 0 & 0 & 0 & 1 \end{bmatrix}$$

$$= \begin{bmatrix} \frac{3}{\sqrt{29}} & \frac{4}{\sqrt{29}} & \frac{2}{\sqrt{29}} & 0 \\ -\frac{32}{\sqrt{1653}} & \frac{25}{\sqrt{1653}} & -\frac{2}{\sqrt{1653}} & 0 \\ -\frac{2}{\sqrt{57}} & -\frac{2}{\sqrt{57}} & \frac{7}{\sqrt{57}} & 0 \\ 0 & 0 & 0 & 1 \end{bmatrix}.$$

Example 3.15 (Change of Basis.) Determine the transformation $\mathbf{M}_{\text{BASIS}}$ required to change the orthonormal basis of a coordinate system from $B1 = (\hat{\mathbf{i}}_1, \hat{\mathbf{j}}_1, \hat{\mathbf{k}}_1)$ to $B2 = (\hat{\mathbf{i}}_2, \hat{\mathbf{j}}_2, \hat{\mathbf{k}}_2)$ and vice versa.

Let the coordinates of the same vector in the two bases be $\overrightarrow{\mathbf{v}}_{B1}$ and $\overrightarrow{\mathbf{v}}_{B2}$, respectively. If the coordinates of the $\hat{\mathbf{i}}_2$, $\hat{\mathbf{j}}_2$, and $\hat{\mathbf{k}}_2$ basis vectors in $B1$ are

$$\hat{\mathbf{i}}_{2,B1} = \begin{bmatrix} a \\ b \\ c \end{bmatrix}, \quad \hat{\mathbf{j}}_{2,B1} = \begin{bmatrix} d \\ e \\ f \end{bmatrix}, \text{ and } \hat{\mathbf{k}}_{2,B1} = \begin{bmatrix} p \\ q \\ r \end{bmatrix},$$

then it is simple to show that (see Exercises, Section 3.11)

$$\overrightarrow{\mathbf{v}}_{B1} = \begin{bmatrix} a & d & p \\ b & e & q \\ c & f & r \end{bmatrix} \cdot \overrightarrow{\mathbf{v}}_{B2}. \tag{3.32}$$

Thus,

$$\mathbf{M}_{BASIS}^{-1} = \begin{bmatrix} a & d & p \\ b & e & q \\ c & f & r \end{bmatrix}.$$

Since $B2$ is an orthonormal basis, $\mathbf{M}_{BASIS}^{-1}$ is an orthogonal matrix, and, therefore its inverse equals its transpose. Thus,

$$\mathbf{M}_{BASIS} = (\mathbf{M}_{BASIS}^{-1})^T = \begin{bmatrix} a & b & c \\ d & e & f \\ p & q & r \end{bmatrix},$$

whose homogeneous form is

$$\mathbf{M}_{BASIS} = \begin{bmatrix} a & b & c & 0 \\ d & e & f & 0 \\ p & q & r & 0 \\ 0 & 0 & 0 & 1 \end{bmatrix}. \tag{3.33}$$

Example 3.16 (Coordinate System Transformation using Change of Basis.)
Use the change-of-basis result of Example 3.15 to align a given 3D coordinate system with basis vectors $(\hat{\mathbf{l}}, \hat{\mathbf{m}}, \hat{\mathbf{n}})$ with the xyz-coordinate system with basis vectors $(\hat{\mathbf{i}}, \hat{\mathbf{j}}, \hat{\mathbf{k}})$; the origin of the first coordinate system relative to xyz is $\mathbf{O}_{lmn}$ [Cunn90].

As in Example 3.14, the required transformation is an axis transformation; it corresponds to changing an object's coordinate system from $(\hat{\mathbf{i}}, \hat{\mathbf{j}}, \hat{\mathbf{k}})$ to $(\hat{\mathbf{l}}, \hat{\mathbf{m}}, \hat{\mathbf{n}})$. The change of basis can replace the three rotational transformations of Example 3.14. Thus, the steps required in order to align the former coordinate system with the latter are:

Step 1. Translate by $-\mathbf{O}_{lmn}$ to make the two origins coincide, $\mathbf{T}(-\overrightarrow{\mathbf{O}}_{lmn})$.

Step 2. Use $\mathbf{M}_{BASIS}$ to change the basis from $(\hat{\mathbf{i}}, \hat{\mathbf{j}}, \hat{\mathbf{k}})$ to $(\hat{\mathbf{l}}, \hat{\mathbf{m}}, \hat{\mathbf{n}})$.

$$\begin{aligned} \mathbf{M}_{ALIGN2} &= \mathbf{M}_{BASIS} \cdot \mathbf{T}(-\overrightarrow{\mathbf{O}}_{lmn}) \\ &= \begin{bmatrix} a & b & c & -(a\,o_x + b\,o_y + c\,o_z) \\ d & e & f & -(d\,o_x + e\,o_y + f\,o_z) \\ p & q & r & -(p\,o_x + q\,o_y + r\,o_z) \\ 0 & 0 & 0 & 1 \end{bmatrix}, \end{aligned} \tag{3.34}$$

where the basis vectors $(\hat{\mathbf{l}}, \hat{\mathbf{m}}, \hat{\mathbf{n}})$ expressed in the basis $(\hat{\mathbf{i}}, \hat{\mathbf{j}}, \hat{\mathbf{k}})$ are $\hat{\mathbf{l}} = [a, b, c]^T$, $\hat{\mathbf{m}} = [d, e, f]^T$, $\hat{\mathbf{n}} = [p, q, r]^T$, and $\mathbf{O}_{lmn} = [o_x, o_y, o_z]^T$.

For a concrete example, let us take the numerical values of Example 3.14 for the $(\hat{\mathbf{i}}, \hat{\mathbf{j}}, \hat{\mathbf{k}})$ and $(\hat{\mathbf{l}}, \hat{\mathbf{m}}, \hat{\mathbf{n}})$ bases. No translation is required since the two origins coincide. The latter basis is expressed in terms of the former, so we can immediately write down the change of basis matrix as

$$\mathbf{M}_{\text{BASIS}} = \begin{bmatrix} \frac{3}{\sqrt{29}} & \frac{4}{\sqrt{29}} & \frac{2}{\sqrt{29}} \\ -\frac{32}{\sqrt{1653}} & \frac{25}{\sqrt{1653}} & -\frac{2}{\sqrt{1653}} \\ -\frac{2}{\sqrt{57}} & -\frac{2}{\sqrt{57}} & \frac{7}{\sqrt{57}} \end{bmatrix},$$

whose homogeneous form is

$$\mathbf{M}_{\text{BASIS}} = \begin{bmatrix} \frac{3}{\sqrt{29}} & \frac{4}{\sqrt{29}} & \frac{2}{\sqrt{29}} & 0 \\ -\frac{32}{\sqrt{1653}} & \frac{25}{\sqrt{1653}} & -\frac{2}{\sqrt{1653}} & 0 \\ -\frac{2}{\sqrt{57}} & -\frac{2}{\sqrt{57}} & \frac{7}{\sqrt{57}} & 0 \\ 0 & 0 & 0 & 1 \end{bmatrix},$$

which is equivalent to the $\mathbf{M}_{\text{ALIGN}}$ matrix of Example 3.14 for the same basis vectors.

Example 3.17 (Rotation about an Arbitrary Axis using Change of Basis.) Use the change-of-basis result of Example 3.15 to find an alternative transformation which performs a rotation by an angle θ about an arbitrary axis specified by a vector $\overrightarrow{\mathbf{v}}$ and a point $\mathbf{p}$ (Figure 3.15) [Cunn90].

Let

$$\overrightarrow{\mathbf{v}} = \begin{bmatrix} a \\ b \\ c \end{bmatrix} \quad \text{and} \quad \mathbf{p} = \begin{bmatrix} x_p \\ y_p \\ z_p \end{bmatrix}.$$

Then the equation of the plane perpendicular to $\overrightarrow{\mathbf{v}}$ through $\mathbf{p}$ is

$$a(x - x_p) + b(y - y_p) + c(z - z_p) = 0.$$

Let $\mathbf{q}$ be a point on that plane, such that $\mathbf{q} \neq \mathbf{p}$ (this can be trivially obtained from the plane equation by selecting an x and a y value and solving for z). Also let $\overrightarrow{\mathbf{m}} = \mathbf{q} - \mathbf{p}$ and $\overrightarrow{\mathbf{l}} = \overrightarrow{\mathbf{m}} \times \overrightarrow{\mathbf{v}}$. We normalize the vectors $\overrightarrow{\mathbf{l}}$, $\overrightarrow{\mathbf{m}}$ and $\overrightarrow{\mathbf{v}}$ to define a coordinate system basis $(\hat{\mathbf{l}}, \hat{\mathbf{m}}, \hat{\mathbf{v}})$ with one axis being $\overrightarrow{\mathbf{v}}$ and the other two axes on the given plane. It is thus possible to use the $\mathbf{M}_{\text{BASIS}}$ transformation in order to align it with the xyz-coordinate system and then perform the desired rotation by θ around the z-axis. The required steps therefore are:

Step 1. Translate $\mathbf{p}$ to the origin, $\mathbf{T}(-\vec{\mathbf{p}})$.

Step 2. Align the $(\hat{\mathbf{l}}, \hat{\mathbf{m}}, \hat{\mathbf{v}})$ basis with the $(\hat{\mathbf{i}}, \hat{\mathbf{j}}, \hat{\mathbf{k}})$ basis, $\mathbf{M}_{\text{BASIS}}$.

Step 3. Rotate about the z-axis by the desired angle θ, $\mathbf{R_z}(\theta)$.

Step 4. Undo the alignment, $\mathbf{M}_{\text{BASIS}}^{-1}$.

Step 5. Undo the translation, $\mathbf{T}(\vec{\mathbf{p}})$.

$$\mathbf{M}_{\text{ROT-AXIS2}} = \mathbf{T}(\vec{\mathbf{p}}) \cdot \mathbf{M}_{\text{BASIS}}^{-1} \cdot \mathbf{R_z}(\theta) \cdot \mathbf{M}_{\text{BASIS}} \cdot \mathbf{T}(-\vec{\mathbf{p}}). \qquad (3.35)$$

Compared to the geometrically derived $\mathbf{M}_{\text{ROT-AXIS}}$ matrix, the algebraic derivation of the $\mathbf{M}_{\text{ROT-AXIS2}}$ matrix is conceptually simpler.

Example 3.18 (Rotation of a Pyramid.) Rotate the pyramid defined by the vertices $\mathbf{a} = [0,0,0]^T$, $\mathbf{b} = [1,0,0]^T$, $\mathbf{c} = [0,1,0]^T$ and $\mathbf{d} = [0,0,1]^T$ by $45°$ about the axis defined by $\mathbf{c}$ and the vector $\vec{\mathbf{v}} = [0,1,1]^T$ (Figure 3.17).

The pyramid can be represented by a matrix $\mathbf{P}$ whose columns are the homogeneous coordinates of its vertices:

$$\mathbf{P} = \begin{bmatrix} \mathbf{a} & \mathbf{b} & \mathbf{c} & \mathbf{d} \end{bmatrix} = \begin{bmatrix} 0 & 1 & 0 & 0 \\ 0 & 0 & 1 & 0 \\ 0 & 0 & 0 & 1 \\ 1 & 1 & 1 & 1 \end{bmatrix}.$$

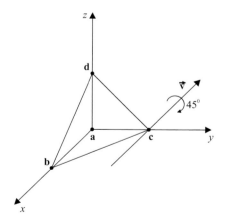

Figure 3.17. Rotation of a pyramid about an axis.

We shall use the $\mathbf{M}_{\text{ROT}-\text{AXIS}}$ matrix (Equation (3.30)) to rotate the pyramid. The required submatrices are

$$\mathbf{T}(-\overrightarrow{\mathbf{c}}) = \begin{bmatrix} 1 & 0 & 0 & 0 \\ 0 & 1 & 0 & -1 \\ 0 & 0 & 1 & 0 \\ 0 & 0 & 0 & 1 \end{bmatrix}, \qquad \mathbf{A}(\overrightarrow{\mathbf{v}}) = \begin{bmatrix} 1 & 0 & 0 & 0 \\ 0 & \frac{1}{\sqrt{2}} & -\frac{1}{\sqrt{2}} & 0 \\ 0 & \frac{1}{\sqrt{2}} & \frac{1}{\sqrt{2}} & 0 \\ 0 & 0 & 0 & 1 \end{bmatrix},$$

$$\mathbf{R}_{\mathbf{z}}(45^\circ) = \begin{bmatrix} \frac{1}{\sqrt{2}} & -\frac{1}{\sqrt{2}} & 0 & 0 \\ \frac{1}{\sqrt{2}} & \frac{1}{\sqrt{2}} & 0 & 0 \\ 0 & 0 & 1 & 0 \\ 0 & 0 & 0 & 1 \end{bmatrix}, \quad \mathbf{A}^{-1}(\overrightarrow{\mathbf{v}}) = \begin{bmatrix} 1 & 0 & 0 & 0 \\ 0 & \frac{1}{\sqrt{2}} & \frac{1}{\sqrt{2}} & 0 \\ 0 & -\frac{1}{\sqrt{2}} & \frac{1}{\sqrt{2}} & 0 \\ 0 & 0 & 0 & 1 \end{bmatrix},$$

$$\mathbf{T}(\overrightarrow{\mathbf{c}}) = \begin{bmatrix} 1 & 0 & 0 & 0 \\ 0 & 1 & 0 & 1 \\ 0 & 0 & 1 & 0 \\ 0 & 0 & 0 & 1 \end{bmatrix}.$$

The above are combined according to Equation (3.30) giving

$$\mathbf{M}_{\text{ROT}-\text{AXIS}} = \begin{bmatrix} \frac{\sqrt{2}}{2} & -\frac{1}{2} & \frac{1}{2} & \frac{1}{2} \\ \frac{1}{2} & \frac{2+\sqrt{2}}{4} & \frac{2-\sqrt{2}}{4} & \frac{2-\sqrt{2}}{4} \\ -\frac{1}{2} & \frac{2-\sqrt{2}}{4} & \frac{2+\sqrt{2}}{4} & \frac{\sqrt{2}-2}{4} \\ 0 & 0 & 0 & 1 \end{bmatrix},$$

and the rotated pyramid is computed as

$$\mathbf{P}' = \mathbf{M}_{\text{ROT}-\text{AXIS}} \cdot \mathbf{P} = \begin{bmatrix} \frac{1}{2} & \frac{1+\sqrt{2}}{2} & 0 & 1 \\ \frac{2-\sqrt{2}}{4} & \frac{4-\sqrt{2}}{4} & 1 & \frac{2-\sqrt{2}}{2} \\ \frac{\sqrt{2}-2}{4} & \frac{\sqrt{2}-4}{4} & 0 & \frac{\sqrt{2}}{2} \\ 1 & 1 & 1 & 1 \end{bmatrix}.$$

Thus the vertices of the rotated pyramid are $\mathbf{a}' = [\frac{1}{2}, \frac{2-\sqrt{2}}{4}, \frac{\sqrt{2}-2}{4}]^{\text{T}}$, $\mathbf{b}' = [\frac{1+\sqrt{2}}{2}, \frac{4-\sqrt{2}}{4}, \frac{\sqrt{2}-4}{4}]^{\text{T}}$, $\mathbf{c}' = [0, 1, 0]^{\text{T}}$ and $\mathbf{d}' = [1, \frac{2-\sqrt{2}}{2}, \frac{\sqrt{2}}{2}]^{\text{T}}$.

3.9   Quaternions[⊛]

Rotations around an arbitrary axis have been already described in Examples 3.13 and 3.17. In this section, we will present yet another alternative way to express such rotations, using *quaternions*. As we shall see, this expression of rotations has interesting properties, and, most importantly, it is very useful when *animating* rotations, as will be described in Section 17.2.1. Quaternions were conceived by Sir William Hamilton in 1843 as an extension of complex numbers.

3.9.1   Mathematical Properties of Quaternions

A quaternion q consists of four real numbers,

$$q = (s, x, y, z),$$

of which s is called the *scalar* part of q and $\overrightarrow{\mathbf{v}} = (x, y, z)$ is called the *vector* part of q; thus, we also write q as

$$q = (s, \overrightarrow{\mathbf{v}}). \tag{3.36}$$

Quaternions can be viewed as an extension of complex numbers in four dimensions: using "imaginary units" i, j, and k such that $i^2 = j^2 = k^2 = -1$ and $ij = k$, $ji = -k$, and so on by cyclic permutation, the quaternion q may be written as

$$q = s + xi + yj + zk. \tag{3.37}$$

A real number u corresponds to the quaternion $(u, \overrightarrow{\mathbf{0}})$; an ordinary vector $\overrightarrow{\mathbf{v}}$ corresponds to the quaternion $(0, \overrightarrow{\mathbf{v}})$ and, similarly, a point $\mathbf{p}$ to the quaternion $(0, \mathbf{p})$.

Let $q_i = (s_i, \overrightarrow{\mathbf{v}}_i)$.

Addition between quaternions is defined naturally as

$$q_1 + q_2 = (s_1, \overrightarrow{\mathbf{v}}_1) + (s_2, \overrightarrow{\mathbf{v}}_2) = (s_1 + s_2, \ \overrightarrow{\mathbf{v}}_1 + \overrightarrow{\mathbf{v}}_2). \tag{3.38}$$

Multiplication between quaternions is more complex, and its result can be obtained by using the form (3.37) of the quaternions and the properties of the imaginary units. Below are some useful formulas for the quaternion product:

$$\begin{aligned}
q_1 \cdot q_2 = (s_1 s_2 - \overrightarrow{\mathbf{v}}_1 \cdot \overrightarrow{\mathbf{v}}_2, \qquad & s_1 \overrightarrow{\mathbf{v}}_2 + s_2 \overrightarrow{\mathbf{v}}_1 + \overrightarrow{\mathbf{v}}_1 \times \overrightarrow{\mathbf{v}}_2) \\
= (s_1 s_2 - x_1 x_2 - y_1 y_2 - z_1 z_2, & \ s_1 x_2 + x_1 s_2 + y_1 z_2 - z_1 y_2, \\
& \ s_1 y_2 + y_1 s_2 + z_1 x_2 - x_1 z_2, \\
& \ s_1 z_2 + z_1 s_2 + x_1 y_2 - y_1 x_2).
\end{aligned} \tag{3.39}$$

Multiplication between quaternions is associative; however, it is *not* commutative, as manifested by the first of the above formulas, since the cross product $\overrightarrow{\mathbf{v}}_1 \times \overrightarrow{\mathbf{v}}_2$ is involved.

The *conjugate* quaternion of q is defined as

$$\bar{q} = (s, -\overrightarrow{\mathbf{v}}), \tag{3.40}$$

and it can easily be verified that

$$\overline{q_1 \cdot q_2} = \overline{q_2} \cdot \overline{q_1}. \tag{3.41}$$

The *norm* of q is defined as

$$|q|^2 = q \cdot \bar{q} = \bar{q} \cdot q = s^2 + |\overrightarrow{\mathbf{v}}|^2 = s^2 + x^2 + y^2 + z^2, \tag{3.42}$$

and it can be shown that $|q_1 \cdot q_2| = |q_1| \, |q_2|$. A *unit* quaternion is one whose norm is equal to 1.

The *inverse* quaternion of q is defined as

$$q^{-1} = \frac{1}{|q|^2} \, \bar{q}, \tag{3.43}$$

and therefore $q \cdot q^{-1} = q^{-1} \cdot q = 1$. If q is a unit quaternion, then $q^{-1} = \bar{q}$.

3.9.2 Expressing Rotations using Quaternions

As already mentioned, quaternions can be used to express arbitrary rotations. Specifically, a rotation by an angle θ about an axis *through the origin* whose direction is specified by a unit vector $\hat{\mathbf{n}}$, is represented by the *unit* quaternion

$$q = (\cos\frac{\theta}{2}, \ \sin\frac{\theta}{2}\,\hat{\mathbf{n}}), \tag{3.44}$$

and it is applied to a point $\mathbf{p}$, represented by the quaternion $p = (0, \mathbf{p})$, using the formula

$$p' = q \cdot p \cdot q^{-1} = q \cdot p \cdot \bar{q} \tag{3.45}$$

(the second equality holds since q is a unit quaternion). This yields

$$p' = \left(0, \ (s^2 - \overrightarrow{\mathbf{v}} \cdot \overrightarrow{\mathbf{v}})\mathbf{p} + 2\overrightarrow{\mathbf{v}}(\overrightarrow{\mathbf{v}} \cdot \mathbf{p}) + 2s(\overrightarrow{\mathbf{v}} \times \mathbf{p})\right), \tag{3.46}$$

where $s = \cos\frac{\theta}{2}$ and $\overrightarrow{\mathbf{v}} = \sin\frac{\theta}{2}\,\hat{\mathbf{n}}$. Notice that the resulting quaternion p' represents an ordinary point $\mathbf{p}'$ since it has zero scalar part; below we show that $\mathbf{p}'$ is

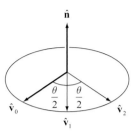

Figure 3.18. Rotation of unit vector.

exactly the image of the original point $\mathbf{p}$ after rotation by angle θ about the given axis.

Using this formulation, it is algebraically very easy to express the outcome of two consecutive rotations. Supposing that they are represented by unit quaternions q_1 and q_2, the outcome of the composite rotation is

$$q_2 \cdot (q_1 \cdot p \cdot \overline{q_1}) \cdot \overline{q_2} = (q_2 \cdot q_1) \cdot p \cdot (\overline{q_1} \cdot \overline{q_2}) = (q_2 \cdot q_1) \cdot p \cdot \overline{(q_2 \cdot q_1)};$$

therefore, the composite rotation is represented by the quaternion $q = q_2 \cdot q_1$ (which is also a unit quaternion). Compared to the equivalent multiplication of rotation matrices, quaternion multiplication is simpler, requires fewer operations, and is therefore numerically more stable.

Let us now verify relations (3.44) and (3.45). Consider a unit vector $\hat{\mathbf{v}}_0$, a rotation axis $\hat{\mathbf{n}}$, and the images $\hat{\mathbf{v}}_1$ and $\hat{\mathbf{v}}_2$ of $\hat{\mathbf{v}}_0$ after two consecutive rotations by $\frac{\theta}{2}$ around $\hat{\mathbf{n}}$ (Figure 3.18); the respective quaternions are $p_0 = (0, \hat{\mathbf{v}}_0)$, $p_1 = (0, \hat{\mathbf{v}}_1)$, $p_2 = (0, \hat{\mathbf{v}}_2)$.

Our initial aim is to show that $p_2 = q \cdot p_0 \cdot \overline{q}$ for $q = (\cos\frac{\theta}{2}, \sin\frac{\theta}{2}\,\hat{\mathbf{n}})$. We observe that $\cos\frac{\theta}{2} = \hat{\mathbf{v}}_0 \cdot \hat{\mathbf{v}}_1$ and $\sin\frac{\theta}{2}\,\hat{\mathbf{n}} = \hat{\mathbf{v}}_0 \times \hat{\mathbf{v}}_1$, therefore we may write q as $q = (\hat{\mathbf{v}}_0 \cdot \hat{\mathbf{v}}_1,\ \hat{\mathbf{v}}_0 \times \hat{\mathbf{v}}_1) = p_1 \cdot \overline{p_0}$. Similarly, we may also conclude that $q = p_2 \cdot \overline{p_1}$. Then,

$$\begin{aligned}
q \cdot p_0 \cdot \overline{q} &= (p_1 \cdot \overline{p_0}) \cdot p_0 \cdot \overline{(p_2 \cdot \overline{p_1})} \\
&= (p_1 \cdot \overline{p_0}) \cdot p_0 \cdot p_1 \cdot \overline{p_2} \\
&= p_1 \cdot p_1 \cdot \overline{p_2} \\
&= p_2,
\end{aligned}$$

since $p_1 \cdot p_1 = (-1, \vec{\mathbf{0}}) = -1$ because $|\hat{\mathbf{v}}_1| = 1$, and also $(-1) \cdot \overline{p_2} = -(0, -\hat{\mathbf{v}}_2) = (0, \hat{\mathbf{v}}_2) = p_2$. This proves that $q \cdot p_0 \cdot \overline{q}$ results in the rotation of $\hat{\mathbf{v}}_0$ by angle θ about $\hat{\mathbf{n}}$.

Using similar arguments, it can be proven that $q \cdot p_1 \cdot \overline{q}$ results in the same rotation for $\hat{\mathbf{v}}_1$, whereas $q \cdot (0, \hat{\mathbf{n}}) \cdot \overline{q}$ yields $\hat{\mathbf{n}}$, which agrees with the fact that $\hat{\mathbf{n}}$ is the axis of rotation.

We are now able to generalize the above for an arbitrary vector: the three vectors $\hat{\mathbf{v}}_0$, $\hat{\mathbf{v}}_1$, and $\hat{\mathbf{n}}$ are linearly independent; therefore, a vector $\vec{\mathbf{p}}$ may be written as a linear combination of three components, $\vec{\mathbf{p}} = \lambda_0 \hat{\mathbf{v}}_0 + \lambda_1 \hat{\mathbf{v}}_1 + \lambda \hat{\mathbf{n}}$. Then,

$$
\begin{aligned}
q \cdot (0, \vec{\mathbf{p}}) \cdot \overline{q} &= q \cdot (0, \lambda_0 \hat{\mathbf{v}}_0 + \lambda_1 \hat{\mathbf{v}}_1 + \lambda \hat{\mathbf{n}}) \cdot \overline{q} \\
&= q \cdot (0, \lambda_0 \hat{\mathbf{v}}_0) \cdot \overline{q} + q \cdot (0, \lambda_1 \hat{\mathbf{v}}_1) \cdot \overline{q} + q \cdot (0, \lambda \hat{\mathbf{n}}) \cdot \overline{q} \\
&= \lambda_0 (q \cdot (0, \hat{\mathbf{v}}_0) \cdot \overline{q}) + \lambda_1 (q \cdot (0, \hat{\mathbf{v}}_1) \cdot \overline{q}) + \lambda (q \cdot (0, \hat{\mathbf{n}}) \cdot \overline{q}),
\end{aligned}
$$

which is exactly a quaternion with zero scalar part and vector part made up of the rotated components of $\vec{\mathbf{p}}$.

3.9.3 Conversion between Quaternions and Rotation Matrices

If rotations using quaternions are to be incorporated in a sequence of transformations represented by matrices, it will be necessary to construct a rotation matrix starting from a given unit quaternion, and vice versa. Recall that, contrary to the rotations described in Examples 3.13 and 3.17, quaternions represent rotations around an axis through the origin; if this is not the case, then the usual sequence of transformations (translation to the origin, rotation, translation back) is necessary.

It can be proven [Shoe87] that the rotation matrix corresponding to a rotation represented by the unit quaternion $q = (s, x, y, z)$ is

$$
\mathbf{R}_q = \begin{bmatrix} 1 - 2y^2 - 2z^2 & 2xy - 2sz & 2xz + 2sy & 0 \\ 2xy + 2sz & 1 - 2x^2 - 2z^2 & 2yz - 2sx & 0 \\ 2xz - 2sy & 2yz + 2sx & 1 - 2x^2 - 2y^2 & 0 \\ 0 & 0 & 0 & 1 \end{bmatrix}. \tag{3.47}
$$

For the inverse procedure, if a matrix

$$
\mathbf{R} = \begin{bmatrix} m_{00} & m_{01} & m_{02} & 0 \\ m_{10} & m_{11} & m_{12} & 0 \\ m_{20} & m_{21} & m_{22} & 0 \\ 0 & 0 & 0 & 1 \end{bmatrix}
$$

represents a rotation, the corresponding quaternion $q = (s,x,y,z)$ may be computed as follows. In $\mathbf{R}_q$ we sum the elements in the diagonal, and, therefore,

$$m_{00} + m_{11} + m_{22} + 1 = 1 - 2y^2 - 2z^2 + 1 - 2x^2 - 2z^2 + 1 - 2x^2 - 2y^2 + 1$$
$$= 4 - 4(x^2 + y^2 + z^2) = 4 - 4(1 - s^2) = 4s^2$$

(3.48)

(remembering that q is a unit quaternion and thus $s^2 + x^2 + y^2 + z^2 = 1$), so

$$s = \frac{1}{2}\sqrt{m_{00} + m_{11} + m_{22} + 1}.$$

(3.49)

The other coordinates x, y, and z of q may be computed by subtracting elements of $\mathbf{R}_q$ that are symmetric with respect to the diagonal. Thus, if $s \neq 0$,

$$x = \frac{m_{21} - m_{12}}{4s}, \quad y = \frac{m_{02} - m_{20}}{4s}, \quad z = \frac{m_{10} - m_{01}}{4s}.$$

(3.50)

If $s = 0$ (or if s is near zero and in order to improve numerical accuracy) a different set of relations may be used, for instance,

$$x = \frac{1}{2}\sqrt{m_{00} - m_{11} - m_{22} + 1},$$

$$y = \frac{m_{01} + m_{10}}{4x}, \quad z = \frac{m_{02} + m_{20}}{4x}, \quad s = \frac{m_{21} - m_{12}}{4x}.$$

The reader can refer to [Shoe87] for a complete presentation.

Example 3.19 (Rotation of a Pyramid.) We will re-work Example 3.18 using quaternions.

The prescribed rotation is by $45°$ about an axis defined by point $\mathbf{c} = [0,1,0]^T$ and direction $\overrightarrow{\mathbf{v}} = [0,1,1]^T$. Since the axis does not pass through the origin, we must translate it by $-\overrightarrow{\mathbf{c}}$, perform the rotation using matrix $\mathbf{R}_q$ from (3.47), and translate it back. We must also normalize the direction vector to get $\hat{\mathbf{v}} = \overrightarrow{\mathbf{v}}/|\overrightarrow{\mathbf{v}}| = [0,1/\sqrt{2},1/\sqrt{2}]^T$.

The quaternion that expresses the rotation by $45°$ about an axis with direction $\overrightarrow{\mathbf{v}}$ is

$$q = \left(\cos\frac{45°}{2}, \sin\frac{45°}{2}\hat{\mathbf{v}}\right) = (\cos 22.5°, 0, \frac{\sin 22.5°}{\sqrt{2}}, \frac{\sin 22.5°}{\sqrt{2}}).$$

From the double-angle trigonometric identities, we get

$$\cos^2 22.5° = \frac{1 + \cos 45°}{2} = \frac{2 + \sqrt{2}}{4},$$

$$\sin^2 22.5° = \frac{1 - \cos 45°}{2} = \frac{2 - \sqrt{2}}{4}.$$

Therefore,

$$\mathbf{R}_q = \begin{bmatrix} \frac{\sqrt{2}}{2} & -\frac{1}{2} & \frac{1}{2} & 0 \\ \frac{1}{2} & \frac{2+\sqrt{2}}{4} & \frac{2-\sqrt{2}}{4} & 0 \\ -\frac{1}{2} & \frac{2-\sqrt{2}}{4} & \frac{2+\sqrt{2}}{4} & 0 \\ 0 & 0 & 0 & 1 \end{bmatrix},$$

and the final transformation matrix is

$$\mathbf{M}_{\mathrm{ROT-AXIS3}} = \mathbf{T}(\overrightarrow{\mathbf{c}}) \cdot \mathbf{R}_q \cdot \mathbf{T}(-\overrightarrow{\mathbf{c}}),$$

which is equal to $\mathbf{M}_{\mathrm{ROT-AXIS}}$ of Example 3.18.

3.10 Geometric Properties

The wide adoption of affine transformations in computer graphics and visualization is owed to the fact that they preserve important geometric features of objects. For example, if Φ is an affine transformation and $\mathbf{p}$ and $\mathbf{q}$ are points, then

$$\Phi(\lambda \mathbf{p} + (1-\lambda)\mathbf{q}) = \lambda\Phi(\mathbf{p}) + (1-\lambda)\Phi(\mathbf{q}), \tag{3.51}$$

for $0 \leq \lambda \leq 1$. Since the set $\{\lambda \mathbf{p} + (1-\lambda)\mathbf{q}, \ \lambda \in [0,1]\}$ is the line segment between $\mathbf{p}$ and $\mathbf{q}$, Equation (3.51) states that the affine transformation of a line segment under Φ is another line segment; furthermore, ratios of distances on the line segment $\lambda/(1-\lambda)$ are preserved.

Table 3.1 summarizes the properties of affine transformations and three subclasses of them.

The basic affine transformations that belong to the subclasses *linear*, *similitudes*, and *rigid* are shown in Figure 3.19.

Linear transformations can be represented by a matrix $\mathbf{A}$ which is post-multiplied by the point to be transformed. All homogeneous affine transformations are

Property preserved	Affine	Linear	Similitude	Rigid
Angles	No	No	Yes	Yes
Distances	No	No	No	Yes
Ratios of distances	Yes	Yes	Yes	Yes
Parallel lines	Yes	Yes	Yes	Yes
Affine combinations	Yes	Yes	Yes	Yes
Straight lines	Yes	Yes	Yes	Yes
Cross ratios	Yes	Yes	Yes	Yes

Table 3.1. Geometric properties preserved by transformation classes.

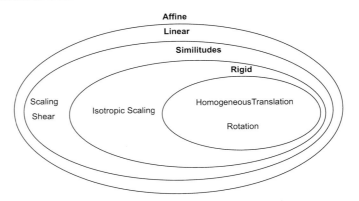

Figure 3.19. Classification of affine homogeneous transformations.

linear. Of the non-homogeneous basic transformations, translation is not linear. Affine and linear transformations preserve most important geometric properties except angles and distances (for a discussion of cross ratios see Chapter 4).

Similitudes preserve the similarity of objects; the result of the application of such a transformation on an object will be identical to the initial object, except for its size which may have been uniformly altered. Thus, similitudes preserve angles but not distances. Similitudes are: rotation, homogeneous translation, isotropic scaling, and their compositions.

The most restrictive class is that of rigid transformations which preserve all of the geometric features of objects. Any sequence of rotations and homogeneous translations is a rigid transformation.

3.11   Exercises

1. If three-dimensional points are represented as row vectors $[x, y, z, 1]$ instead of column vectors, determine what impact this has on the composition of transformations.

2. If a left-handed three-dimensional coordinate system is used instead of a right-handed system, determine how the basic three-dimensional affine transformations change.

3. Suppose that a composite transformation which consists of m basic 3D affine transformations must be applied to n object vertices. Compare the

cost of applying the basic matrices to the vertices sequentially against the cost of composing them and then applying the composite matrix to the vertices. The comparison should take into account the total numbers of scalar multiplications and scalar additions. Instantiate your result for $m = 2, 4, 8$ and $n = 10, 10^3, 10^6$.

4. Prove that Equation (3.32) (in Example 3.15) holds.

5. Determine *two* transformations (matrices) that align the vector $\overrightarrow{\mathbf{op}}$ with the unit vector $\hat{\mathbf{j}}$ along the positive y-axis, where $\mathbf{o}$ is the coordinate origin and $\mathbf{p}$ is a given 3D point.

6. Show which of the following pairs of 3D transformations are commutative:

    (a) Translation and rotation;

    (b) Scaling and rotation;

    (c) Translation and scaling;

    (d) Two rotations;

    (e) Isotropic scaling and rotation.

7. Determine a 3D transformation that maps an axis-aligned orthogonal parallelepiped defined by two opposite vertices $[x_{min}, y_{min}, z_{min}]^T$ and $[x_{max}, y_{max}, z_{max}]^T$ into the space of the unit cube without deformation (maintain aspect ratio) and then rotates it by an angle θ about the axis specified by a point $\mathbf{p}$ and a vector $\overrightarrow{\mathbf{v}}$.

8. Determine the affine matrices required to transform the unit cube, defined by the matrix of its vertices

$$\mathbf{C} = \begin{bmatrix} \mathbf{A} & \mathbf{B} & \mathbf{C} & \mathbf{D} & \mathbf{E} & \mathbf{F} & \mathbf{G} & \mathbf{H} \end{bmatrix} = \begin{bmatrix} 0 & 0 & 0 & 0 & 1 & 1 & 1 & 1 \\ 0 & 0 & 1 & 1 & 0 & 0 & 1 & 1 \\ 0 & 1 & 0 & 1 & 0 & 1 & 0 & 1 \\ 1 & 1 & 1 & 1 & 1 & 1 & 1 & 1 \end{bmatrix}$$

into each of the following shapes:

$$\mathbf{S1} = \begin{bmatrix} 0 & 0 & 0 & 0 & 1 & 1 & 1 & 1 \\ y & y & y+1 & y+1 & y & y & y+1 & y+1 \\ 0 & 1 & 0 & 1 & 0 & 1 & 0 & 1 \\ 1 & 1 & 1 & 1 & 1 & 1 & 1 & 1 \end{bmatrix};$$

$$
\mathbf{S2} = \begin{bmatrix} 0 & 0 & 0 & 0 & 1 & 1 & 1 & 1 \\ y^2 & y^2 & y(y+1) & y(y+1) & y^2 & y^2 & y(y+1) & y(y+1) \\ 0 & 1 & 0 & 1 & 0 & 1 & 0 & 1 \\ 1 & 1 & 1 & 1 & 1 & 1 & 1 & 1 \end{bmatrix};
$$

$$
\mathbf{S3} = \begin{bmatrix} 0 & 0 & 0 & 0 & 1 & 1 & 1 & 1 \\ 0 & -1 & 0 & -1 & 0 & -1 & 0 & -1 \\ 0 & 0 & 1 & 1 & 0 & 0 & 1 & 1 \\ 1 & 1 & 1 & 1 & 1 & 1 & 1 & 1 \end{bmatrix},
$$

where y is the last digit of your year of birth.

9. Determine the three-dimensional window to viewport transformation matrix. The window and the viewport are both axis-aligned rectangular parallelepipeds specified by two opposite vertices $[w_{xmin}, w_{ymin}, w_{zmin}]^T$, $[w_{xmax}, w_{ymax}, w_{zmax}]^T$ and $[v_{xmin}, v_{ymin}, v_{zmin}]^T$, $[v_{xmax}, v_{ymax}, v_{zmax}]^T$, respectively.

10. Determine the three-dimensional transformation that performs mirroring with respect to a plane defined by a point $\mathbf{p}$ and a normal vector $\overrightarrow{\mathbf{v}}$.

11. Use the $\mathbf{M}_{ROT-AXIS2}$ matrix (Equation (3.35)) to rotate the pyramid of Example 3.18. Check that you get the same result.

12. Suppose that n consecutive rotations about different axes through the origin are to be applied to a point. Compare the cost of computing the composite rotation by using rotation matrices and by using quaternions to express the rotations. Include in your computation the cost of constructing the required rotation matrices (using, for example, the result of Equation (3.30) without the translations) and quaternions (using Equation (3.44)), and in the case of quaternions the cost of conversion to the final rotation matrix (Equation (3.47)).

4

Projections and Viewing Transformations

Perspective is to painting what the bridle is to the horse, the rudder to a ship.
—Leonardo da Vinci

4.1   Introduction

In computer graphics, models are generally three-dimensional, but the output devices (displays and printers) are two-dimensional.[1] A *projective mapping*, or simply *projection*, must thus take place at some point in the graphics pipeline and is usually placed after the culling stages and before the rendering stage. The projection parameters are specified as part of the *viewing transformation*[2] that defines the transition from the world coordinate system (WCS) to canonical screen space

---

[1] Three-dimensional display devices do exist and are an active topic of research; however, current systems are expensive and offer a limited advantage to the human visual system.

[2] The term "viewing transformation" is widely used in computer graphics, although it is not a transformation in the strict mathematical sense (i.e., a mapping with the same domain and range sets).

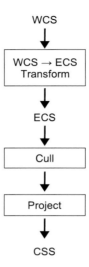

Figure 4.1. Overview of coordinate systems involved in the viewing transformation.

coordinates (CSS) via the eye coordinate system (ECS) (Figure 4.1). The viewing transformation also specifies the clipping bounds (for frustum culling) in ECS.

The rationale behind these coordinate systems is the following: All objects are initially defined in their own local coordinate system which may, for example, be the result of a digitization or design process. These objects are unified in WCS where they are placed suitably modified; the WCS is essentially used to define the model of a three-dimensional synthetic world. The transition from WCS to ECS, which involves a change of coordinates, is carried out in order to simplify a number of operations including culling (e.g., the specification of the clipping bounds by the user) and projection. Finally, the transition from ECS to CSS ensures that all objects that survived culling will be defined in a canonical space (usually ranging from -1 to 1) that can easily be scaled to the actual coordinates of any display device or viewport and that also maintains high floating-point accuracy.

4.2   Projections

In mathematics, *projection* is a term used to describe techniques for the creation of the *image* of an object onto another simpler object such as a line, plane, or

Property preserved	Affine	Projective
Angles	No	No
Distances	No	No
Ratios of distances	Yes	No
Parallel lines	Yes	No
Affine combinations	Yes	No
Straight lines	Yes	Yes
Cross ratios	Yes	Yes

Table 4.1. Properties of affine transformations and projective mappings.

surface. A *center of projection*, along with points on the object being projected, is used to define the *projector* lines; see Figure 4.3. The intersection of a projector with the simpler object (e.g., the plane of projection) forms the image of a point of the original object. Projections can be defined in spaces of arbitrary dimension.

In computer graphics and visualization we are generally concerned with projections from 3D space onto 2D space (the 2D space is referred to as the *plane of projection* and models our 2D output device). Two such projections are of interest:

- *Perspective projection*, where the distance of the center of projection from the plane of projection is finite;

- *Parallel projection*, where the distance of the center of projection from the plane of projection is infinite.

Projective mappings are *not* affine transformations and, therefore, cannot be described by affine transformation matrices. Table 4.1 summarizes the differences between affine transformations and projective mappings in terms of which object properties they preserve.

Parallel lines are not projected onto parallel lines unless their plane is parallel to the plane of projection; their projections seem to meet at a *vanishing point*. A straight line will map to a straight line, but ratios of distances on the straight line will not be preserved. Therefore, affine combinations are not preserved by projections (in contrast, ratios on the straight line are preserved by affine transformations by their definition). For example, looking at Figure 4.2,

$$\frac{\mathbf{ab}}{\mathbf{bd}} \neq \frac{\mathbf{a'b'}}{\mathbf{b'd'}}.$$

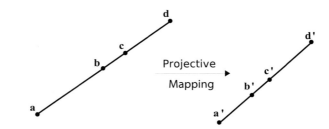

Figure 4.2. Straight-line ratios under projective mapping.

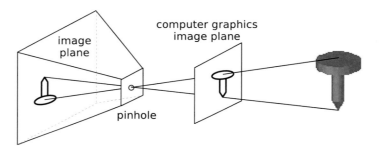

Figure 4.3. Pinhole-camera model for perspective projection.

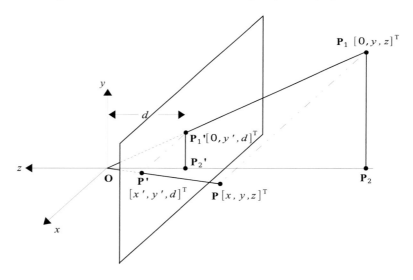

Figure 4.4. Perspective projection.

Projections do, however, preserve cross ratios; looking again at Figure 4.2,

$$\frac{\frac{\mathbf{ac}}{\mathbf{cd}}}{\frac{\mathbf{ab}}{\mathbf{bd}}} = \frac{\frac{\mathbf{a'c'}}{\mathbf{c'd'}}}{\frac{\mathbf{a'b'}}{\mathbf{b'd'}}}.$$

The implication is that in order to fully describe the projective image of a line we need the image of three points on the line, in contrast to affine transforms where we needed just two. (This generalizes to planes and other objects defined by sets of points; for the projective image of an object we need the image of a set of points with one element more than for its affine image). This result has important implications when mapping *properties* of an object under projective mappings; for example, although the "straightness" of a line is preserved and can be described by mapping two points, properties such as the depth or color of the line must be mapped using three points (see Section 2.7).

4.2.1 Perspective Projection

Perspective projection models the viewing system of our eyes and can be abstracted by a pinhole camera (Figure 4.3). The pinhole is the center of projection, and the plane of projection, where the image is formed, is the image plane. The pinhole-camera model creates an inverted image but in computer graphics an upright image is derived by placing the image plane "in front" of the pinhole.

Suppose that the center of projection coincides with the origin and that the plane of projection is perpendicular to the negative z-axis at a distance d from the center (Figure 4.4). A three-dimensional point $\mathbf{P} = [x, y, z]^T$ is projected onto the point $\mathbf{P'} = [x', y', d]^T$ on the plane of projection. Consider the projections $\mathbf{P_1}$ and $\mathbf{P'_1}$ of $\mathbf{P}$ and $\mathbf{P'}$, respectively, onto the yz-plane. From the similar triangles $\triangle \mathbf{OP_1P_2}$ and $\triangle \mathbf{OP'_1P'_2}$, we have

$$\frac{\mathbf{P'_1P'_2}}{\mathbf{OP'_2}} = \frac{\mathbf{P_1P_2}}{\mathbf{OP_2}}.$$

Since $y' = \mathbf{P'_1P'_2}$, $d = \mathbf{OP'_2}$, $y = \mathbf{P_1P_2}$, and $z = \mathbf{OP_2}$,

$$y' = \frac{d \cdot y}{z}. \tag{4.1}$$

The expression for x' can similarly be derived:

$$x' = \frac{d \cdot x}{z}. \tag{4.2}$$

The perspective-projection equations are not linear, since they include division by z, and therefore a small trick is needed to express them in matrix form. The matrix

$$\mathbf{P_{PER}} = \begin{bmatrix} d & 0 & 0 & 0 \\ 0 & d & 0 & 0 \\ 0 & 0 & d & 0 \\ 0 & 0 & 1 & 0 \end{bmatrix} \tag{4.3}$$

alters the homogeneous coordinate and maps the coordinates of a point $[x, y, z, 1]^{\mathrm{T}}$ as follows:

$$\mathbf{P_{PER}} \cdot \begin{bmatrix} x \\ y \\ z \\ 1 \end{bmatrix} = \begin{bmatrix} x \cdot d \\ y \cdot d \\ z \cdot d \\ z \end{bmatrix}.$$

To achieve the desired result, a division with the homogeneous coordinate must be performed, since its value is no longer 1:

$$\begin{bmatrix} x \cdot d \\ y \cdot d \\ z \cdot d \\ z \end{bmatrix} /z = \begin{bmatrix} \frac{x \cdot d}{z} \\ \frac{y \cdot d}{z} \\ d \\ 1 \end{bmatrix}.$$

An important characteristic of the perspective projection is *perspective shortening*, the fact that the size of the projection of an object is inversely proportional to its distance from the center of projection (Figure 4.5).

Perspective shortening was known to the ancient Greeks, but the laws of perspective were not thoroughly studied until Leonardo da Vinci. This explains why

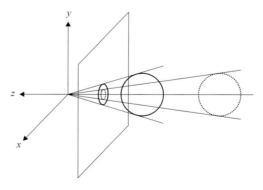

Figure 4.5. Perspective shortening.

some older paintings present distant figures unrealistically large. In fact, it was only in the last few centuries that paintings attempt to model human vision. Before that, other symbolic criteria often prevailed; for example, the size of characters was proportional to their importance.

4.2.2 Parallel Projection

In parallel projection, the center of projection is at an infinite distance from the plane of projection and the projector lines are therefore parallel to each other. To describe such a projection one must specify the *direction of projection* (a vector) and the plane of projection. We shall distinguish between two types of parallel projections: *orthographic*, where the direction of projection is normal to the plane of projection, and *oblique*, where the direction of projection is not necessarily normal to the plane of projection.

Orthographic projection. Orthographic projections usually employ one of the main planes as the plane of projection. Suppose that the xy-plane is used (Figure 4.6). A point $\mathbf{P} = [x, y, z]^{\mathrm{T}}$ will then be projected onto $[x', y', z']^{\mathrm{T}} = [x, y, 0]^{\mathrm{T}}$. The following matrix accomplishes this:

$$\mathbf{P_{ORTHO}} = \begin{bmatrix} 1 & 0 & 0 & 0 \\ 0 & 1 & 0 & 0 \\ 0 & 0 & 0 & 0 \\ 0 & 0 & 0 & 1 \end{bmatrix}, \tag{4.4}$$

so that $\mathbf{P'} = \mathbf{P_{ORTHO}} \cdot \mathbf{P}$.

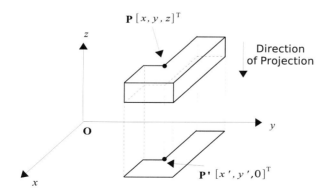

Figure 4.6. Orthographic projection onto the *xy*-plane.

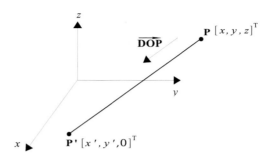

Figure 4.7. Oblique projection.

Oblique projection. Here the direction of projection is not necessarily normal to the plane of projection. Let the direction of projection be

$$\overrightarrow{\mathbf{DOP}} = [DOP_x, DOP_y, DOP_z]^{\mathrm{T}}$$

and the plane of projection be the xy-plane (Figure 4.7).

Then, the projection $\mathbf{P'} = [x', y', 0]^{\mathrm{T}}$ of a point $\mathbf{P} = [x, y, z]^{\mathrm{T}}$ will be

$$\mathbf{P'} = \mathbf{P} + \lambda \cdot \overrightarrow{\mathbf{DOP}} \qquad (4.5)$$

for some scalar λ. But the z-coordinate of $\mathbf{P'}$ is 0, so Equation (4.5) becomes

$$0 = z + \lambda \cdot DOP_z \quad \text{or} \quad \lambda = -\frac{z}{DOP_z}$$

The other two coordinates of $\mathbf{P'}$ can now be determined from Equation (4.5):

$$x' = x + \lambda \cdot DOP_x = x - \frac{DOP_x}{DOP_z} \cdot z$$

and, similarly,

$$y' = y - \frac{DOP_y}{DOP_z} \cdot z.$$

These equations can be expressed in matrix form as

$$\mathbf{P_{OBLIQUE}}(\overrightarrow{\mathbf{DOP}}) = \begin{bmatrix} 1 & 0 & -\frac{DOP_x}{DOP_z} & 0 \\ 0 & 1 & -\frac{DOP_y}{DOP_z} & 0 \\ 0 & 0 & 0 & 0 \\ 0 & 0 & 0 & 1 \end{bmatrix}, \qquad (4.6)$$

so that $\mathbf{P'} = \mathbf{P_{OBLIQUE}}(\overrightarrow{\mathbf{DOP}}) \cdot \mathbf{P}$.

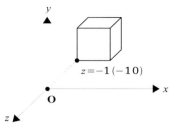

$z = -1 (-10)$

Figure 4.8. Perspective projection example: cube.

4.3 Projection Examples

Example 4.1 (Perspective Projection of a Cube.) Determine the perspective projections of a cube of side 1 when (a) the plane of projection is $z = -1$ and (b) the plane of projection is $z = -10$. The cube is placed on the plane of projection as shown in Figure 4.8.

The vertices of the cube can be represented as the columns of a 4×8 matrix. In case (a), the cube is

$$
\mathbf{C} = \begin{bmatrix}
0 & 1 & 1 & 0 & 0 & 1 & 1 & 0 \\
0 & 0 & 1 & 1 & 0 & 0 & 1 & 1 \\
-1 & -1 & -1 & -1 & -2 & -2 & -2 & -2 \\
1 & 1 & 1 & 1 & 1 & 1 & 1 & 1
\end{bmatrix}.
$$

The result of the projection of the cube is obtained by multiplying the perspective projection matrix of Equation (4.3) $(d = -1)$ by $\mathbf{C}$:

$$
\mathbf{P_{PER}} \cdot \mathbf{C} = \begin{bmatrix}
-1 & 0 & 0 & 0 \\
0 & -1 & 0 & 0 \\
0 & 0 & -1 & 0 \\
0 & 0 & 1 & 0
\end{bmatrix} \cdot \mathbf{C} = \begin{bmatrix}
0 & -1 & -1 & 0 & 0 & -1 & -1 & 0 \\
0 & 0 & -1 & -1 & 0 & 0 & -1 & -1 \\
1 & 1 & 1 & 1 & 2 & 2 & 2 & 2 \\
-1 & -1 & -1 & -1 & -2 & -2 & -2 & -2
\end{bmatrix},
$$

which must be normalized by the homogeneous coordinate to give

$$
\begin{bmatrix}
0 & 1 & 1 & 0 & 0 & \frac{1}{2} & \frac{1}{2} & 0 \\
0 & 0 & 1 & 1 & 0 & 0 & \frac{1}{2} & \frac{1}{2} \\
-1 & -1 & -1 & -1 & -1 & -1 & -1 & -1 \\
1 & 1 & 1 & 1 & 1 & 1 & 1 & 1
\end{bmatrix}.
$$

The result can be seen in Figure 4.9(a).

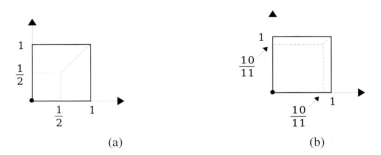

(a) (b)

Figure 4.9. Perspective projection of a cube onto (a) the plane $z = -1$ and (b) the plane $z = -10$.

In case (b), the original cube is

$$\mathbf{C}' = \begin{bmatrix} 0 & 1 & 1 & 0 & 0 & 1 & 1 & 0 \\ 0 & 0 & 1 & 1 & 0 & 0 & 1 & 1 \\ -10 & -10 & -10 & -10 & -11 & -11 & -11 & -11 \\ 1 & 1 & 1 & 1 & 1 & 1 & 1 & 1 \end{bmatrix}.$$

Multiplying the perspective projection matrix ($d = -10$) by $\mathbf{C}'$ gives

$$\begin{bmatrix} -10 & 0 & 0 & 0 \\ 0 & -10 & 0 & 0 \\ 0 & 0 & -10 & 0 \\ 0 & 0 & 1 & 0 \end{bmatrix} \cdot \mathbf{C}' = \begin{bmatrix} 0 & -10 & -10 & 0 & 0 & -10 & -10 & 0 \\ 0 & 0 & -10 & -10 & 0 & 0 & -10 & -10 \\ 100 & 100 & 100 & 100 & 110 & 110 & 110 & 110 \\ -10 & -10 & -10 & -10 & -11 & -11 & -11 & -11 \end{bmatrix},$$

and normalizing by the homogeneous coordinate gives

$$\begin{bmatrix} 0 & 1 & 1 & 0 & 0 & \frac{10}{11} & \frac{10}{11} & 0 \\ 0 & 0 & 1 & 1 & 0 & 0 & \frac{10}{11} & \frac{10}{11} \\ -10 & -10 & -10 & -10 & -10 & -10 & -10 & -10 \\ 1 & 1 & 1 & 1 & 1 & 1 & 1 & 1 \end{bmatrix}.$$

The result can be seen in Figure 4.9(b). Note how the "far" face of the cube has been projected differently in the two cases.

Example 4.2 (Perspective Projection onto an Arbitrary Plane.) Compute the perspective projection of a point $\mathbf{P} = [x, y, z]^T$ onto an arbitrary plane Π which is specified by a point $\mathbf{R_0} = [x_0, y_0, z_0]^T$ and a normal vector $\overrightarrow{\mathbf{N}} = [n_x, n_y, n_z]^T$. The center of projection is the origin $\mathbf{O}$.

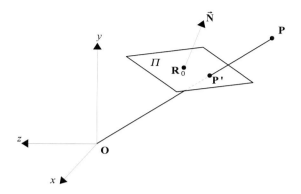

Figure 4.10. Perspective projection onto an arbitrary plane.

Consider the projection $\mathbf{P'} = [x',y',z']^T$ of $\mathbf{P} = [x,y,z]^T$ (Figure 4.10). Since the vectors $\overrightarrow{\mathbf{OP'}}$ and $\overrightarrow{\mathbf{OP}}$ are collinear, $\overrightarrow{\mathbf{OP'}} = a \cdot \overrightarrow{\mathbf{OP}}$ for some scalar a and the projection equations for each coordinate are

$$x' = ax, \quad y' = ay, \quad z' = az. \tag{4.7}$$

We need to determine the scalar a. The vector $\overrightarrow{\mathbf{R_0P'}}$ is on the plane of projection, therefore its inner product with the plane normal $\vec{\mathbf{N}}$ is 0:

$$\vec{\mathbf{N}} \cdot \overrightarrow{\mathbf{R_0P'}} = 0,$$

or

$$n_x(x' - x_0) + n_y(y' - y_0) + n_z(z' - z_0) = 0,$$

or

$$n_x x' + n_y y' + n_z z' = n_x x_0 + n_y y_0 + n_z z_0.$$

Substituting the values of x', y', and z' from Equation (4.7), setting $c = n_x x_0 + n_y y_0 + n_z z_0$, and solving for a gives

$$a = \frac{c}{n_x x + n_y y + n_z z}.$$

Note that the projection equations include a division by a combination of x, y, and z (in simple perspective we had only z in the denominator). We can express the projection equations in matrix form by changing the homogeneous coordinate, just as for simple perspective:

$$\mathbf{P}_{\text{PER},\Pi} = \begin{bmatrix} c & 0 & 0 & 0 \\ 0 & c & 0 & 0 \\ 0 & 0 & c & 0 \\ n_x & n_y & n_z & 0 \end{bmatrix}. \tag{4.8}$$

To project the point $\mathbf{P}$ onto the plane Π, we thus apply $\mathbf{P}_{\text{PER},\Pi}$ and then divide by the homogeneous coordinate $n_x x + n_y y + n_z z$.

Example 4.3 (Oblique Projection with Azimuth and Elevation Angles.) Sometimes, particularly in the field of architectural design, oblique projections are specified in terms of the azimuth and elevation angles ϕ and θ that define the relation of the direction of projection to the plane of projection. Determine the projection matrix in this case.

Define xy as the plane of projection and let ϕ and θ, respectively, be the azimuth and elevation angles of the direction of projection (Figure 4.11). One can show, by simple trigonometry (see Exercises, Section 4.8), that the direction of the projection vector is $\overrightarrow{\mathbf{DOP}} = [\cos\theta\cos\phi, \cos\theta\sin\phi, \sin\theta]^{\text{T}}$. Thus, the $\mathbf{P}_{\text{OBLIQUE}}$ matrix of Equation (4.6) becomes

$$\mathbf{P}_{\text{OBLIQUE}}(\phi, \theta) = \begin{bmatrix} 1 & 0 & -\frac{\cos\phi}{\tan\theta} & 0 \\ 0 & 1 & -\frac{\sin\phi}{\tan\theta} & 0 \\ 0 & 0 & 0 & 0 \\ 0 & 0 & 0 & 1 \end{bmatrix}. \tag{4.9}$$

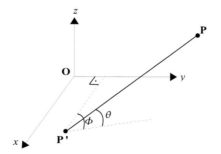

Figure 4.11. Azimuth and elevation angles for oblique projection.

Example 4.4 (Oblique Projection onto an Arbitrary Plane.) Determine the oblique projection mapping onto an arbitrary plane Π that is specified by a point $\mathbf{R_0} = [x_0, y_0, z_0]^T$ and a normal vector $\overrightarrow{\mathbf{N}} = [n_x, n_y, n_z]^T$. The direction of projection is given by the vector $\overrightarrow{\mathbf{DOP}} = [\mathrm{DOP}_x, \mathrm{DOP}_y, \mathrm{DOP}_z]^T$.

We shall first transform the plane Π so that it coincides with the xy-plane; we shall next use the oblique projection matrix of Equation (4.6), and finally we shall undo the first transformation. This requires five steps:

Step 1. Translate $\mathbf{R_0}$ to the origin, $\mathbf{T}(-\overrightarrow{\mathbf{R_0}})$.

Step 2. Align $\overrightarrow{\mathbf{N}}$ with the positive z-axis; this is accomplished by matrix $\mathbf{A}(\overrightarrow{\mathbf{N}})$ of Example 3.12.

Step 3. Use the oblique projection matrix of Equation (4.6) with the direction of projection transformed according to Steps 1 and 2:

$$\overrightarrow{\mathbf{DOP}'} = \mathbf{A}(\overrightarrow{\mathbf{N}}) \cdot \mathbf{T}(-\overrightarrow{\mathbf{R_0}}) \cdot \overrightarrow{\mathbf{DOP}}.$$

Step 4. Undo the alignment, $\mathbf{A}(\overrightarrow{\mathbf{N}})^{-1}$.

Step 5. Undo the translation, $\mathbf{T}(\overrightarrow{\mathbf{R_0}})$.

Thus,

$$\mathbf{P_{OBLIQUE,\Pi}}(\overrightarrow{\mathbf{DOP}}) = \mathbf{T}(\overrightarrow{\mathbf{R_0}}) \cdot \mathbf{A}(\overrightarrow{\mathbf{N}})^{-1} \cdot \mathbf{P_{OBLIQUE}}(\overrightarrow{\mathbf{DOP}'}) \cdot \mathbf{A}(\overrightarrow{\mathbf{N}}) \cdot \mathbf{T}(-\overrightarrow{\mathbf{R_0}}). \tag{4.10}$$

4.4 Viewing Transformation

A *viewing transformation* (VT) defines the process of coordinate conversion all the way from the world coordinate system (WCS) to canonical screen space (CSS) via the intermediate eye coordinate system (ECS). At the same time, it defines the clipping boundaries (for frustum culling) in ECS. All coordinate systems used are right-handed. We shall split its description into two parts; the first part will describe the WCS-to-ECS conversion while the second part will describe the ECS-to-CSS conversion. The second part will be further split to consider orthographic and perspective projections separately. Extensions deal with oblique projection and non-symmetrical viewing volume for perspective projection. Note that the z-coordinate is maintained by the ECS-to-CSS conversion, as stages following the viewing transformation (such as hidden surface elimination) require three-dimensional information.

4.4.1   WCS to ECS

The first step is the transition from WCS to ECS. ECS can be defined within the WCS by the following intuitive parameters:

- the ECS origin $\mathbf{E}$;

- the direction of view $\overrightarrow{\mathbf{g}}$;

- the up direction $\overrightarrow{\mathbf{up}}$.

The origin $\mathbf{E}$ represents the point of view, where an imaginary observer is located. The vector $\overrightarrow{\mathbf{up}}$ defines the up direction and need not be perpendicular to $\overrightarrow{\mathbf{g}}$. Having chosen to use a right-handed coordinate system, we have sufficient information to define the ECS axes x_e, y_e, and z_e.

The x_e- and y_e-axes must be aligned with the corresponding CSS axes with the usual convention that x_e is the horizontal axis and increases to the right and y_e is the vertical axis and increases upwards. At the same time, a right-handed ECS must be constructed. Thus, we have to select a z_e-axis that points toward the observer; in other words, the direction of view $\overrightarrow{\mathbf{g}}$ is aligned with the negative z_e-axis. The vectors that define the other two axes are computed by cross products as follows (Figure 4.12):

$$\overrightarrow{\mathbf{z_e}} = -\overrightarrow{\mathbf{g}},$$
$$\overrightarrow{\mathbf{x_e}} = \overrightarrow{\mathbf{up}} \times \overrightarrow{\mathbf{z_e}},$$
$$\overrightarrow{\mathbf{y_e}} = \overrightarrow{\mathbf{z_e}} \times \overrightarrow{\mathbf{x_e}}.$$

Having defined the ECS, we next need to perform the WCS-to-ECS conversion. In practice, once the conversion matrix $\mathbf{M_{WCS \to ECS}}$ is established, the

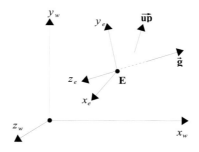

Figure 4.12. WCS to ECS.

vertices of all objects are pre-multiplied by it. As was shown in Example 3.16, this conversion can be accomplished by two transformations: a translation by $-\overrightarrow{\mathbf{E}} = [E_x, E_y, E_z]^T$ followed by a rotational transformation which can be expressed as a change of basis. Let the WCS coordinates of the ECS unit axis vectors be $\hat{\mathbf{x}}_e = [a_x, a_y, a_z]^T$, $\hat{\mathbf{y}}_e = [b_x, b_y, b_z]^T$, and $\hat{\mathbf{z}}_e = [c_x, c_y, c_z]^T$. Then:

$$\mathbf{M}_{\mathbf{WCS} \rightarrow \mathbf{ECS}} = \begin{bmatrix} a_x & a_y & a_z & 0 \\ b_x & b_y & b_z & 0 \\ c_x & c_y & c_z & 0 \\ 0 & 0 & 0 & 1 \end{bmatrix} \cdot \begin{bmatrix} 1 & 0 & 0 & -E_x \\ 0 & 1 & 0 & -E_y \\ 0 & 0 & 1 & -E_z \\ 0 & 0 & 0 & 1 \end{bmatrix}. \qquad (4.11)$$

4.4.2 ECS to CSS

We now convert our scene from ECS to CSS. Here, we must distinguish two cases: orthographic projection on one of the three basic coordinate planes (we shall use the xy-plane) and perspective projection.

Orthographic projection. Suppose that we perform an orthographic projection onto the xy-plane. We need to select a region of space that will be mapped to CSS. This region is called the *view volume* and takes the form of a rectangular parallelepiped. It can be defined by two opposite vertices, which also define the clip planes used for frustum culling (Figure 4.13):

- $x_e = l$, the *left* clip plane;

- $x_e = r$, the *right* clip plane, $(r > l)$;

- $y_e = b$, the *bottom* clip plane;

- $y_e = t$, the *top* clip plane, $(t > b)$;

- $z_e = n$, the *near* clip plane;

- $z_e = f$, the *far* clip plane, $(f < n$, since the z_e axis points toward the observer.)

Given that we want to maintain the z-coordinate, the orthographic projection matrix (see Equation (4.4)) onto the xy-plane is simply the identity matrix. The view volume can be converted into CSS by a translation and a scaling transformation. We want to map the (l, b, n) values to -1 and the (r, t, f) values to 1; the required mapping is

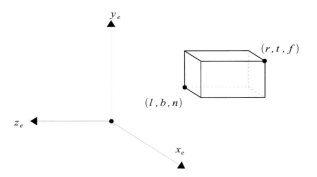

Figure 4.13. View volume for orthographic projection.

$$
\mathbf{M}^{\text{ORTHO}}_{\text{ECS}\rightarrow\text{CSS}} = \mathbf{S}(\frac{2}{r-l}, \frac{2}{t-b}, \frac{2}{f-n}) \cdot \mathbf{T}(-\frac{r+l}{2}, -\frac{t+b}{2}, -\frac{n+f}{2}) \cdot \mathbf{ID}
$$

$$
= \begin{bmatrix} \frac{2}{r-l} & 0 & 0 & 0 \\ 0 & \frac{2}{t-b} & 0 & 0 \\ 0 & 0 & \frac{2}{f-n} & 0 \\ 0 & 0 & 0 & 1 \end{bmatrix} \cdot \begin{bmatrix} 1 & 0 & 0 & -\frac{r+l}{2} \\ 0 & 1 & 0 & -\frac{t+b}{2} \\ 0 & 0 & 1 & -\frac{n+f}{2} \\ 0 & 0 & 0 & 1 \end{bmatrix}
$$

$$
= \begin{bmatrix} \frac{2}{r-l} & 0 & 0 & -\frac{r+l}{r-l} \\ 0 & \frac{2}{t-b} & 0 & -\frac{t+b}{t-b} \\ 0 & 0 & \frac{2}{f-n} & -\frac{n+f}{f-n} \\ 0 & 0 & 0 & 1 \end{bmatrix}.
$$

$$(4.12)$$

Thus, using orthographic projection, a WCS point $\mathbf{X_w} = [x_w, y_w, z_w, 1]^{\text{T}}$ can be converted into CSS by

$$
\mathbf{X_s} = \mathbf{M}^{\text{ORTHO}}_{\text{ECS}\rightarrow\text{CSS}} \cdot \mathbf{M}_{\text{WCS}\rightarrow\text{ECS}} \cdot \mathbf{X_w}.
$$

Perspective projection. In the case of perspective projection, the view volume is a truncated pyramid that is symmetrical about the $-z_e$-axis; Figure 4.14 shows its yz-view shaded. This view volume can be specified by four quantities:

- θ, the angle of the field of view in the y-direction;

- *aspect*, the ratio of the width to the height of a cross section of the pyramid;[3]

---

[3]For example, for the cross section defined by the plane $z = n$, height is the distance between t and b (Figure 4.14), and width is the distance between l and r.

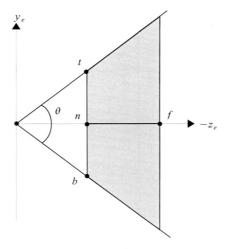

Figure 4.14. View volume for perspective projection (*yz*-view).

- $z_e = n$, the near clipping plane;

- $z_e = f$, the far clipping plane ($f < n$).

Projection is assumed to take place onto the near clipping plane $z_e = n$. The top, bottom, right, and left clipping boundaries at the near clipping plane can be derived from the above parameters as

$$t = |n| \cdot \tan(\frac{\theta}{2}),$$
$$b = -t,$$
$$r = t \cdot \text{aspect},$$
$$l = -r.$$

A modified version of the perspective projection matrix can be used (P_{PER} from Equation (4.3)). Special consideration must be given to the z-coordinate, which must be preserved for hidden surface and other computations in screen space. However, simply keeping the z_e-coordinate will deform objects. We want a mapping that preserves lines and planes, i.e., ECS lines and planes must map to lines and planes in CSS. As shown in [Newm81], a mapping that achieves this is $z_s = A + B/z_e$, where A and B are constants; by inverting the z-coordinate this mapping resembles the mappings for the x- and y-coordinates. We require that

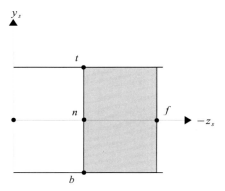

Figure 4.15. The perspective view volume transformed into a rectangular parallelepiped (*yz*-view).

$(z_e = n) \Rightarrow (z_s = n)$ and $(z_e = f) \Rightarrow (z_s = f)$, and so we get two equations with two unknowns, which results in $A = (n+f)$ and $B = -nf$.[4] The selected mapping will not alter the boundary values $z_e = n$ and $z_e = f$, but this will not be true for z_e values between the two boundaries. Thus, the perspective projection matrix is

$$\mathbf{P_{VT}} = \begin{bmatrix} n & 0 & 0 & 0 \\ 0 & n & 0 & 0 \\ 0 & 0 & n+f & -nf \\ 0 & 0 & 1 & 0 \end{bmatrix},$$

which makes the w-coordinate equal to z_e and must therefore be followed by a division by z_e (this is called the *perspective division*). The transformation $\mathbf{P_{VT}}$ has the effect of transforming the truncated pyramid of Figure 4.14 into the rectangular parallelepiped of Figure 4.15. The clipping boundaries are not affected by $\mathbf{P_{VT}}$.

We now have a situation that is similar to the setting before the orthographic projection, except that the view volume is already symmetrical about the $-z_e$-axis. In order to complete the ECS-to-CSS conversion, we therefore need to follow $\mathbf{P_{VT}}$ by a translation along z_e only and a scaling transformation

---

[4]Note that we could have alternatively required that $(z_e = n) \Rightarrow (z_s = -n)$ and $(z_e = f) \Rightarrow (z_s = -f)$ so that larger z_s values correspond to greater distance from the viewpoint; this results in $A = -(n+f)$ and $B = nf$.

$$\mathbf{M}^{\mathbf{PERSP}}_{\mathbf{ECS}\rightarrow\mathbf{CSS}} = \mathbf{S}(\frac{2}{r-l}, \frac{2}{t-b}, \frac{2}{f-n}) \cdot \mathbf{T}(0,0,-\frac{n+f}{2}) \cdot \mathbf{P}_{\mathbf{VT}}$$

$$= \begin{bmatrix} \frac{2}{r-l} & 0 & 0 & 0 \\ 0 & \frac{2}{t-b} & 0 & 0 \\ 0 & 0 & \frac{2}{f-n} & 0 \\ 0 & 0 & 0 & 1 \end{bmatrix} \cdot \begin{bmatrix} 1 & 0 & 0 & 0 \\ 0 & 1 & 0 & 0 \\ 0 & 0 & 1 & -\frac{n+f}{2} \\ 0 & 0 & 0 & 1 \end{bmatrix} \cdot \begin{bmatrix} n & 0 & 0 & 0 \\ 0 & n & 0 & 0 \\ 0 & 0 & n+f & -nf \\ 0 & 0 & 1 & 0 \end{bmatrix}$$

$$= \begin{bmatrix} \frac{2n}{r-l} & 0 & 0 & 0 \\ 0 & \frac{2n}{t-b} & 0 & 0 \\ 0 & 0 & \frac{n+f}{f-n} & -\frac{2nf}{f-n} \\ 0 & 0 & 1 & 0 \end{bmatrix}.$$

(4.13)

A WCS point $\mathbf{X_w} = [x_w, y_w, z_w, 1]^T$ can thus be converted into CSS using perspective projection as follows:

$$\begin{bmatrix} x \\ y \\ z \\ w \end{bmatrix} = \mathbf{M}^{\mathbf{PERSP}}_{\mathbf{ECS}\rightarrow\mathbf{CSS}} \cdot \mathbf{M}_{\mathbf{WCS}\rightarrow\mathbf{ECS}} \cdot \mathbf{X_w},$$

followed by the perspective division by the w-coordinate (which equals z_e). Frustum culling is usually performed just before the perspective division (see Section 4.6) ensuring that the x-, y-, and z-coordinates of every point on every object are within the clipping bounds:

$$-w \leq x, y, z \leq w.$$

The perspective division then completes the transition into CSS; every point of every object is now in the range $[-1, 1]$:

$$\mathbf{X_s} = \begin{bmatrix} x \\ y \\ z \\ w \end{bmatrix} / w.$$

Let us follow a couple of specific points through the above mapping to make the process clear. Take the boundary points with ECS coordinates $[l, b, n, 1]^T$ and $[0, 0, f, 1]^T$ (Figure 4.14). Applying the perspective projection matrix $\mathbf{P}_{\mathbf{VT}}$ gives

$$\mathbf{P}_{\mathbf{VT}} \cdot \begin{bmatrix} l \\ b \\ n \\ 1 \end{bmatrix} = \begin{bmatrix} ln \\ bn \\ n^2 \\ n \end{bmatrix} \qquad \mathbf{P}_{\mathbf{VT}} \cdot \begin{bmatrix} 0 \\ 0 \\ f \\ 1 \end{bmatrix} = \begin{bmatrix} 0 \\ 0 \\ f^2 \\ f \end{bmatrix}.$$

We can see that the homogeneous coordinate is no longer 1. Next, we apply the combination of the scaling and translation matrices:

$$\mathbf{S} \cdot \mathbf{T} \cdot \begin{bmatrix} ln \\ bn \\ n^2 \\ n \end{bmatrix} = \begin{bmatrix} -n \\ -n \\ -n \\ n \end{bmatrix} \qquad \mathbf{S} \cdot \mathbf{T} \cdot \begin{bmatrix} 0 \\ 0 \\ f^2 \\ f \end{bmatrix} = \begin{bmatrix} 0 \\ 0 \\ f \\ f \end{bmatrix}.$$

Note that $r - l = -2l$ and $t - b = -2b$, since $r = -l$ and $t = -b$ due to the symmetry of the truncated pyramid about $-z_e$. Finally, the perspective division gives the CSS values of the points:

$$\begin{bmatrix} -n \\ -n \\ -n \\ n \end{bmatrix} / n = \begin{bmatrix} -1 \\ -1 \\ -1 \\ 1 \end{bmatrix} \qquad \begin{bmatrix} 0 \\ 0 \\ f \\ f \end{bmatrix} / f = \begin{bmatrix} 0 \\ 0 \\ 1 \\ 1 \end{bmatrix}.$$

4.5 Extended Viewing Transformation

While the above viewing transformation is sufficient for most settings, there are a number of extensions to the viewing transformation that are of interest.

4.5.1 Truncated Pyramid Not Symmetrical about z_e-Axis

A generalization of the perspective projection is depicted in Figure 4.16. The truncated pyramid view volume is not symmetrical about the z_e-axis; this situation arises for example in stereo viewing where two viewpoints are slightly offset on the x_e-axis.

The above viewing volume can be specified by giving the parameters of the clipping planes directly:

- $z_e = n_0$, the near clipping plane (as before);

- $z_e = f_0$, the far clipping plane, $f_0 < n_0$ (as before);

- $y_e = b_0$, the y_e-coordinate of the bottom clipping plane at its intersection with the near clipping plane;

- $y_e = t_0$, the y_e-coordinate of the top clipping plane at its intersection with the near clipping plane;

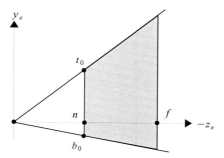

Figure 4.16. Truncated pyramid view volume not symmetrical about z_e (yz-view).

- $x_e = l_0$, the x_e-coordinate of the left clipping plane at its intersection with the near clipping plane;

- $x_e = r_0$, the x_e-coordinate of the right clipping plane at its intersection with the near clipping plane.

A shear transformation on the xy-plane can convert the above pyramid so that it is symmetrical about z_e. We must determine the A and B parameters of the general xy shear matrix,

$$\mathbf{SH_{xy}} = \begin{bmatrix} 1 & 0 & A & 0 \\ 0 & 1 & B & 0 \\ 0 & 0 & 1 & 0 \\ 0 & 0 & 0 & 1 \end{bmatrix}. \tag{4.14}$$

Taking the shear on the y_e-coordinate, we want to map the midpoint of the line segment $t_0 b_0$ to 0. In terms of the shear,

$$\frac{b_0 + t_0}{2} + B \cdot n_0 = 0,$$

and solving for the shear factor B gives $B = -\frac{b_0 + t_0}{2n_0}$. Similarly the x_e shear factor is $A = -\frac{l_0 + r_0}{2n_0}$. The required shear transformation is

$$\mathbf{SH_{NON-SYM}} = \begin{bmatrix} 1 & 0 & -\frac{l_0 + r_0}{2n_0} & 0 \\ 0 & 1 & -\frac{b_0 + t_0}{2n_0} & 0 \\ 0 & 0 & 1 & 0 \\ 0 & 0 & 0 & 1 \end{bmatrix}.$$

The clipping boundaries must also be altered to reflect the symmetrical shape of the new pyramid:

$$n = n_0, \qquad\qquad f = f_0,$$
$$l = l_0 - \frac{l_0 + r_0}{2}, \qquad r = r_0 - \frac{l_0 + r_0}{2},$$
$$b = b_0 - \frac{b_0 + t_0}{2}, \qquad t = t_0 - \frac{b_0 + t_0}{2}.$$

If we substitute the above equivalences into the $\mathbf{M}^{\mathbf{PERSP}}_{\mathbf{ECS} \rightarrow \mathbf{CSS}}$ matrix and do the simplifications we get

$$\mathbf{M}^{\mathbf{PERSP}}_{\mathbf{ECS} \rightarrow \mathbf{CSS}} = \begin{bmatrix} \frac{2n_0}{r_0 - l_0} & 0 & 0 & 0 \\ 0 & \frac{2n_0}{t_0 - b_0} & 0 & 0 \\ 0 & 0 & \frac{n_0 + f_0}{f_0 - n_0} & -\frac{2n_0 f_0}{f_0 - n_0} \\ 0 & 0 & 1 & 0 \end{bmatrix},$$

which is equivalent to the original $\mathbf{M}^{\mathbf{PERSP}}_{\mathbf{ECS} \rightarrow \mathbf{CSS}}$ matrix with the clipping bounds replaced by the initial clipping bounds. Thus, it is not necessary to have initial clipping bounds and convert them after the shear; we can name them n, f, l, r, b, t from the start.

The symmetry transformation $\mathbf{SH}_{\mathbf{NON-SYM}}$ should precede $\mathbf{M}^{\mathbf{PERSP}}_{\mathbf{ECS} \rightarrow \mathbf{CSS}}$, and the ECS $\rightarrow$ CSS mapping in the case of non-symmetrical perspective projection becomes

$$\mathbf{M}^{\mathbf{PERSP-NON-SYM}}_{\mathbf{ECS} \rightarrow \mathbf{CSS}} = \mathbf{M}^{\mathbf{PERSP}}_{\mathbf{ECS} \rightarrow \mathbf{CSS}} \cdot \mathbf{SH}_{\mathbf{NON-SYM}}$$

$$= \begin{bmatrix} \frac{2n}{r-l} & 0 & 0 & 0 \\ 0 & \frac{2n}{t-b} & 0 & 0 \\ 0 & 0 & \frac{n+f}{f-n} & -\frac{2nf}{f-n} \\ 0 & 0 & 1 & 0 \end{bmatrix} \cdot \begin{bmatrix} 1 & 0 & -\frac{l+r}{2n} & 0 \\ 0 & 1 & -\frac{b+t}{2n} & 0 \\ 0 & 0 & 1 & 0 \\ 0 & 0 & 0 & 1 \end{bmatrix}$$

$$= \begin{bmatrix} \frac{2n}{r-l} & 0 & -\frac{l+r}{r-l} & 0 \\ 0 & \frac{2n}{t-b} & -\frac{b+t}{t-b} & 0 \\ 0 & 0 & \frac{n+f}{f-n} & -\frac{2nf}{f-n} \\ 0 & 0 & 1 & 0 \end{bmatrix}.$$

$$(4.15)$$

4.5.2 Oblique Projection

Although orthographic projections are the most frequently used form of parallel projection, there are applications where the more general case of oblique parallel projection is required. An example is the computation of oblique views for three-dimensional displays [Theo90]. In such cases the $\mathbf{M}_{\text{ECS}\to\text{CSS}}^{\text{ORTHO}}$ mapping is not sufficient, and the direction of projection must be taken into account. The view volume is now a six-sided parallelepiped (Figure 4.17) and can be specified by the six parameters used for the non-symmetrical pyramid $(n_0, f_0, b_0, t_0, l_0, r_0)$ plus the direction of projection vector $\overrightarrow{\textbf{DOP}}$.

We first translate the view volume so that the (l_0, b_0, n_0)-point moves to the ECS origin and then perform a shear in the xy-plane (see Equation (4.14)) to transform the parallelepiped into a rectangular parallelepiped. Take the point defined by the origin and the vector $\overrightarrow{\textbf{DOP}} = [\text{DOP}_x, \text{DOP}_y, \text{DOP}_z]^{\text{T}}$. The (DOP_y) coordinate must be sheared to 0:

$$\text{DOP}_y + B \cdot \text{DOP}_z = 0,$$

and solving for the y shear factor gives $B = -\frac{\text{DOP}_y}{\text{DOP}_z}$. Similarly the x shear factor is $A = -\frac{\text{DOP}_x}{\text{DOP}_z}$. The required transformation is therefore

$$\textbf{SH}_{\text{PARALLEL}} \cdot \textbf{T}_{\text{PARALLEL}} = \begin{bmatrix} 1 & 0 & -\frac{\text{DOP}_x}{\text{DOP}_z} & 0 \\ 0 & 1 & -\frac{\text{DOP}_y}{\text{DOP}_z} & 0 \\ 0 & 0 & 1 & 0 \\ 0 & 0 & 0 & 1 \end{bmatrix} \cdot \begin{bmatrix} 1 & 0 & 0 & -l_0 \\ 0 & 1 & 0 & -b_0 \\ 0 & 0 & 1 & -n_0 \\ 0 & 0 & 0 & 1 \end{bmatrix}.$$

Note that the $\textbf{SH}_{\text{PARALLEL}}$ matrix is almost identical to the oblique projection matrix $\textbf{P}_{\text{OBLIQUE}}$ (Equation (4.6)) with the exception that it preserves the

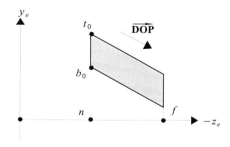

Figure 4.17. Parallel projection view volume (*yz*-view).

z-coordinate. The clipping boundaries must also be altered to reflect the new rectangular parallelepiped:

$$n = 0,$$
$$f = f_0 - n_0,$$
$$l = 0,$$
$$r = r_0 - l_0,$$
$$b = 0,$$
$$t = t_0 - b_0.$$

The symmetry transformation $\mathbf{SH_{PARALLEL}} \cdot \mathbf{T_{PARALLEL}}$ should precede $\mathbf{M^{ORTHO}_{ECS \to CSS}}$ and the ECS $\to$ CSS mapping in the case of a general parallel projection is

$$\mathbf{M^{PARALLEL}_{ECS \to CSS}} = \mathbf{M^{ORTHO}_{ECS \to CSS}} \cdot \mathbf{SH_{PARALLEL}} \cdot \mathbf{T_{PARALLEL}}.$$

4.6 Frustum Culling and the Viewing Transformation

As discussed in Section 5.3, frustum culling is implemented by 3D clipping algorithms. The viewing transformation defines the 3D clipping boundaries. Clipping takes place in CSS, after the application of $\mathbf{M^{PERSP}_{ECS \to CSS}}$ or $\mathbf{M^{ORTHO}_{ECS \to CSS}}$, respectively, but before the division by w in the former. Thus the clipping boundaries for perspective projection are

$$-w \le x, y, z \le w$$

and for orthographic or parallel projection

$$-1 \le x, y, z \le 1.$$

A question that is often asked is, "Why perform frustum culling by clipping in 3D and not in 2D, after throwing away the *z*-coordinate?" There are good reasons for clipping 3D objects in 3D rather than 2D. First, in the case of perspective projection, after throwing away the *z*-coordinate, there is not sufficient information to clip out objects behind the center of projection $\mathbf{E}$; such objects would appear upside-down. Second, again in the case of perspective projection, we avoid the perspective division by 0 (for points with $z_e = 0$), provided the near clipping plane is suitably set, and the cost of the perspective division is saved for points that are clipped out. Third, the near and far clipping planes limit the depth range and enable the optimal allocation of the bits of the depth buffer; for this reason one should choose as narrow a depth range as possible for the view volume.

The 2D clipping algorithms of Chapter 2 easily generalize to 3D as shown in Chapter 5.

4.7 The Viewport Transformation

The *viewport* is the rectangular part of the screen where the contents of the view volume are displayed; this could be the entire screen area. A viewport is usually defined by its bottom-left and top-right corners $[x_{min}, y_{min}]^T$ and $[x_{max}, y_{max}]^T$ in pixel coordinates or, to maintain the z-coordinate, $[x_{min}, y_{min}, z_{min}]^T$ and $[x_{max}, y_{max}, z_{max}]^T$. The *viewport transformation* converts objects from CSS into the viewport coordinate system (VCS). It involves a scaling and a translation:

$$
\mathbf{M}_{\text{CSS}\rightarrow\text{VCS}}^{\text{VIEWPORT}} =
\begin{bmatrix}
1 & 0 & 0 & \frac{x_{min}+x_{max}}{2} \\
0 & 1 & 0 & \frac{y_{min}+y_{max}}{2} \\
0 & 0 & 1 & \frac{z_{min}+z_{max}}{2} \\
0 & 0 & 0 & 1
\end{bmatrix}
\cdot
\begin{bmatrix}
\frac{x_{max}-x_{min}}{2} & 0 & 0 & 0 \\
0 & \frac{y_{max}-y_{min}}{2} & 0 & 0 \\
0 & 0 & \frac{z_{max}-z_{min}}{2} & 0 \\
0 & 0 & 0 & 1
\end{bmatrix}
$$

$$
=
\begin{bmatrix}
\frac{x_{max}-x_{min}}{2} & 0 & 0 & \frac{x_{min}+x_{max}}{2} \\
0 & \frac{y_{max}-y_{min}}{2} & 0 & \frac{y_{min}+y_{max}}{2} \\
0 & 0 & \frac{z_{max}-z_{min}}{2} & \frac{z_{min}+z_{max}}{2} \\
0 & 0 & 0 & 1
\end{bmatrix} . \qquad (4.16)
$$

This is a generalization of the 2D window-to-viewport transformation (see Example 3.8). Note that the z-coordinate is maintained by the viewport transformation for use by screen-space algorithms, such as Z-buffer hidden surface elimination (see Section 5.5.1).

Since the entire contents of the view volume are displayed in the viewport, the size of the viewport defines the final size of the objects on the screen. Choosing a large viewport (e.g., the entire screen area) will enlarge objects while a small viewport will show them smaller.

4.8 Exercises

1. Determine the perspective projection matrix when the plane of projection is the xy-plane and the center of projection is on the positive z-axis at a distance d from the origin.

2. Determine the perspective projection matrix when the plane of projection is $z = -5$ and the center of projection is $[0,0,7]^T$.

3. Use any perspective projection matrix to compute the projection of a simple object (e.g., triangle) that lies "behind" the observer, having named its vertices. Can you thus see one important reason for performing frustum culling (clipping) *before* projection?

4. Prove that $\overrightarrow{\mathbf{DOP}} = [\cos\theta\cos\phi, \cos\theta\sin\phi, \sin\theta]^T$ in Example 4.3.

5. Two important cases of oblique projection in design applications are the *Cavalier* and the *Cabinet* projections. These correspond to elevation angles of $\theta = 45°$ and $\theta = 63°$, respectively (see Example 4.3). Using an azimuth angle of your choice, determine the projection of the unit cube onto the xy-plane. Hence, measure the length of the projections of cube sides that were originally normal to the xy-plane. What useful observation can you make?

6. Write a simple program which allows the user to interactively rotate the unit cube around the x-, y-, or z-axes. Use three windows to display a perspective projection and the Cavalier and Cabinet oblique projections, respectively (see previous exercise).

7. Write a simple program which allows the user to experiment with the viewing transformation using perspective projection. Specifically, the user must be able to interactively change θ, aspect, n and f on a scene of your choice. *Note*: You will have to include a 3D clipping algorithm.

5

Culling and Hidden Surface Elimination Algorithms

...the 'total overpaintings' developed... through incessant reworking. The original motif peeped through the edges. Gradually it vanished completely.
—Arnulf Rainer

5.1 Introduction

The world we live in consists of a huge number of objects. We can only see a tiny portion of these objects at any one time, due to restrictions pertaining to our field of view as well as occlusions among the objects. For example, if we are in a room we can not see objects behind the walls as they are occluded by the walls themselves; we can also not see objects behind our back as they are outside our field of view. Analogously, a typical synthetic world is composed of a very large number of primitives, but the portion of these primitives that are relevant to the rendering of any single frame is very small.

Culling algorithms remove primitives that are not relevant to the rendering of a specific frame because

- they are outside the field of view (*frustum culling*);

- they are occluded by other objects (*occlusion culling*);

- they are occluded by front-facing primitives of the same object (*back-face culling*).[1]

---

[1]This is only considered as a special case because a very efficient method exists for its solution.

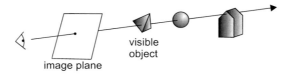

Figure 5.1. The occlusion problem.

Frustum culling removes primitives that are outside the field of view, and it is implemented by 3D clipping algorithms.

Back-face culling filters out primitives that face away from the point of view and are thus invisible as they are hidden by front-facing primitives of the same object. This can be achieved by a simple test on their normal vector.

The *occlusion* (or *visibility*) problem refers to the determination of the visible object in every part of the image. It can be solved by computing the first object intersected by each relevant ray[2] emanating from the viewpoint[3] (Figure 5.1).

It is not possible to produce correct renderings without solving the occlusion problem. Not surprisingly, therefore, it was one of the first problems to be addressed by the computer graphics community [Appe68, Suth74b]. Theoretically, the occlusion problem is now considered solved and a number of *hidden surface elimination* (HSE) algorithms have been proposed. HSE algorithms directly or indirectly involve sorting of the primitives. Primitives must be sorted in the z (depth) dimension as visibility is dependent on depth order. Sorting in the x and y dimensions can reduce the size of the task of sorting in z, as primitives which do not overlap in x or y can not possibly occlude each other.

According to the space in which they work, HSE algorithms are classified as belonging to the *object space* class or *image space* class. Object space algorithms operate in eye coordinate space (before the perspective projection) while image space algorithms operate in screen coordinates (after the perspective projection);[4] see Chapter 4.

The general form of object space HSE algorithms is

```
for each primitive
    find visible part (compare against all other primitives)
    render visible part
```

which has complexity $O(P^2)$ where P is the number of primitives. The general

---

[2]Ray refers to a semi-infinite line, i.e., a line from a point to infinity. A ray can be defined by a point and a vector.

[3]This assumes opaque objects.

[4]Note that the reason for maintaining the z-coordinate after projection is HSE (see Section 5.5).

form of image space HSE algorithms is

```
for each pixel
    find closest primitive
    render pixel with color of closest primitive
```

which has complexity $O(pP)$ where p is the number of screen pixels.[5] From the early days of computer graphics, HSE algorithms were identified as a computational bottleneck in the graphics pipeline. For this reason, special-purpose architectures were developed, based mainly on parallel processing [Deer88,Fuch85, Theo89a]. The experience gained was inherited by the modern graphics accelerators.

Applications requiring interactive walk-throughs of complex scenes, such as games and site reconstructions, made the computational cost of HSE algorithms overwhelming even with hardware support. It was noticed that large numbers of primitives could easily be discarded without the expensive computations of an HSE algorithm, simply because they are occluded by a large object. *Occlusion culling* algorithms thus arose.

Back-face culling eliminates approximately half of the primitives (the back-faces) by a simple test, at a total cost of $O(P)$, where P is the number of primitives. Frustum culling removes those remaining primitives that fall outside the field of view (i.e., most of them in the usual case) at a cost of $O(Pv)$ where v is the average number of vertices per primitive.[6] Occlusion culling also costs $O(P)$ in the usual case. The performance bottleneck are the HSE algorithms which cost $O(P^2)$ or $O(pP)$ depending on the type of algorithm, as mentioned above, where p is the number of screen pixels; for this reason it is worth expending effort on the culling stages that precede HSE.

5.2   Back-Face Culling

Suppose that an opaque sphere, whose surface is represented by a number of small polygons, is placed directly in front of the viewer. Only about half of the polygons will be visible—those that lie on the hemisphere facing the viewer. If models are constructed in such a way that the back sides of polygons are never visible, then we can cull polygons showing their *back-faces* to the viewer.

---

[5] As will be seen later in this chapter, the above complexity figures are amenable to optimizations.

[6] As v is often fixed and equal to three (triangles), frustum culling can be regarded as having cost $O(P)$.

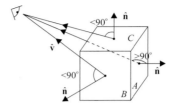

Figure 5.2. Detecting the back-faces of a cube.

The required constraints on the solid models for back-faces to be invisible are that their surfaces have no boundary, are two-dimensional manifolds, and are opaque. Note that convexity is not a constraint. Usual solid models (e.g., most of those used in 3D games and computer-aided design applications) fulfill these constraints.

Back-faces can be detected by computing the angle formed by a polygon's normal vector $\hat{\mathbf{n}}$ (pointing outwards from the opaque solid) and the view vector $\hat{\mathbf{v}}$. If the angle is greater than $90°$, the polygon is a back-face polygon. In Figure 5.2, A is a back-face polygon while B and C are not. Taking the inner product of the vectors, the back-face test becomes

$$\hat{\mathbf{v}} \cdot \hat{\mathbf{n}} < 0. \tag{5.1}$$

The vectors $\hat{\mathbf{n}}$ and $\hat{\mathbf{v}}$ can be computed as shown in Section 12.5. The back-face cull is extremely effective as it eliminates about 50% of the polygons.

Since the back-face test and the computation of the normal and view vectors for each polygon take constant time, the cost of back-face culling is proportional to the number of polygons $O(P)$.

5.3 Frustum Culling

The viewing transformation of Chapter 4 defines the field of view of the observer.[7] Usually this is restricted by a minimum and maximum depth value,[8] thus defining a three-dimensional solid, the *view volume*. Depending on the type of projection used, the view volume takes the form of a truncated pyramid or a rectangular parallelepiped and is also known as the *(view) frustum*.

---

[7]A monocular observer is usually assumed. For stereoscopic viewing, two separate fields of view can be used.

[8]The depth restrictions are placed for reasons of computational efficiency and numerical accuracy.

The objective of frustum culling is to eliminate those primitives, or parts of primitives, that lie outside the view frustum and are thus irrelevant to the specific view. As discussed in Section 4.6, frustum culling must take place after the transformation from ECS to CSS (i.e., after the application of the $\mathbf{M}^{\text{PERSP}}_{\text{ECS}\rightarrow\text{CSS}}$ or $\mathbf{M}^{\text{ORTHO}}_{\text{ECS}\rightarrow\text{CSS}}$ matrix) but before the division by w in the case of perspective projection. That is, frustum culling must be performed in three dimensions rather than two, for the reasons discussed in Section 4.6.

Frustum culling is implemented by extending the two-dimensional clipping algorithms of Section 2.9 to three dimensions. The objects to be clipped are primitives such as points, line segments, and polygons, as in the case of two-dimensional clipping. Point clipping is trivial. Both line segment and polygon clipping reduce to the computation of the intersection of a line segment with the planes of the clipping object.

In three dimensions the interior of the clipping object can be defined as

$$
\begin{aligned}
x_{\min} \leq x \leq x_{\max}, \\
y_{\min} \leq y \leq y_{\max}, \\
z_{\min} \leq z \leq z_{\max}.
\end{aligned}
\tag{5.2}
$$

In the case of orthographic or parallel projection we use the $\mathbf{M}^{\text{ORTHO}}_{\text{ECS}\rightarrow\text{CSS}}$ matrix of Section 4.4.2 which maps the clipping planes to -1 and 1 so that

$$x_{\min} = y_{\min} = z_{\min} = -1$$

and

$$x_{\max} = y_{\max} = z_{\max} = 1.$$

In the case of perspective projection, the $\mathbf{M}^{\text{PERSP}}_{\text{ECS}\rightarrow\text{CSS}}$ matrix of Section 4.4.2 (before the division by w) maps the clipping planes to $-w$ and w so that

$$x_{\min} = y_{\min} = z_{\min} = -w$$

and

$$x_{\max} = y_{\max} = z_{\max} = w.$$

The value of w is not constant (it is equal to a point's eye coordinate z_e). Clipping against the homogeneous coordinate w is called *homogeneous clipping*.

For a parametric line segment $\mathbf{l}(t) = (1-t)\mathbf{p_1} + t\mathbf{p_2}$ from $\mathbf{p_1} = [x_1, y_1, z_1, w_1]^{\text{T}}$ to $\mathbf{p_2} = [x_2, y_2, z_2, w_2]^{\text{T}}$, the value of w can be interpolated as $(1-t)w_1 + tw_2$. Then the inequalities (5.2) can be used to define the part of the line segment within the clipping object:

$$-((1-t)w_1+tw_2) \le (1-t)x_1+tx_2 \le (1-t)w_1+tw_2,$$
$$-((1-t)w_1+tw_2) \le (1-t)y_1+ty_2 \le (1-t)w_1+tw_2, \qquad (5.3)$$
$$-((1-t)w_1+tw_2) \le (1-t)z_1+tz_2 \le (1-t)w_1+tw_2,$$

and the six intersections of the line defined by the line segment with the clipping object planes are obtained by solving relations (5.3), used as equalities, for t:

$$\text{left: } t = \frac{x_1+w_1}{(x_1-x_2)+(w_1-w_2)},$$

$$\text{right: } t = \frac{x_1-w_1}{(x_1-x_2)+(w_2-w_1)},$$

$$\text{bottom: } t = \frac{y_1+w_1}{(y_1-y_2)+(w_1-w_2)},$$

$$\text{top: } t = \frac{y_1-w_1}{(y_1-y_2)+(w_2-w_1)}, \qquad (5.4)$$

$$\text{near: } t = \frac{z_1+w_1}{(z_1-z_2)+(w_1-w_2)},$$

$$\text{far: } t = \frac{z_1-w_1}{(z_1-z_2)+(w_2-w_1)}.$$

5.3.1   Three-Dimensional Clipping Algorithms

Most clipping algorithms extend easily to three dimensions by addressing

- the intersection computation;

- the inside/outside test.

Clipping algorithms essentially compute the intersection of the clipping object and the subject, so to go from two to three dimensions we replace the two-dimensional clipping object by the three-dimensional one (the view frustum). We shall consider the Cohen–Sutherland and Liang–Barsky [Lian84] line clipping algorithms and the Sutherland–Hodgman [Suth74a] polygon clipping algorithm.

3D Cohen–Sutherland line clipping.   First study the two-dimensional Cohen–Sutherland (CS) algorithm of Section 2.9.2. In 3D, six bits are used to code the 27 partitions of three-dimensional space defined by the view frustum planes. The significance of these bits is (see inequalities (5.2)):

First bit. Set to 1 for $z > z_{max}$, else set to 0

Second bit. Set to 1 for $z < z_{min}$, else set to 0

Third bit. Set to 1 for $y > y_{max}$, else set to 0

Fourth bit. Set to 1 for $y < y_{min}$, else set to 0

Fifth bit. Set to 1 for $x > x_{max}$, else set to 0

Sixth bit. Set to 1 for $x < x_{min}$, else set to 0.

A six-bit code can thus be assigned to a three-dimensional point according to which one of the 27 partitions of three-dimensional space it lies in. If $c1$ and $c2$ are the six-bit codes of the endpoints $\mathbf{p_1}$ and $\mathbf{p_2}$ of a line segment, the trivial accept test is $c1 \vee c2 = 000000$ and the trivial reject test is $c1 \wedge c2 \neq 000000$, where $\vee$ and $\wedge$ denote bitwise disjunction and conjunction, respectively. The pseudocode for the three-dimensional CS algorithm follows:

```
CS_Clip_3D ( vertex p1, p2 );  {
    int c1, c2;
    vertex i;
    plane R;

    c1=mkcode (p1);
    c2=mkcode (p2);
    if ((c1 | c2) == 0)          /* p1p2 is inside */
    else if ((c1 & c2) != 0)     /* p1p2 is outside */
    else    {
        R = /* frustum plane with (c1 bit != c2 bit) */
        i = intersect_plane_line (R, (p1,p2));
        if outside (R, p1)  CS_Clip_3D(i, p2);
        else                CS_Clip_3D(p1, i);
    }
}
```

This differs from the two-dimensional algorithm in the intersection computation and the outside test. A 3D plane-line intersection computation is used (instead of the 2D line-line intersection). Notice that we have not given the clipping limits in the pseudocode; in the case of orthographic or parallel projection, these are constant planes (e.g., $x = -1$) and the plane-line intersections of Appendix C are used; in the case of perspective projection and homogeneous coordinates, the plane-line intersections of Equations (5.4) are used. The outside test can be implemented by a sign check on the evaluation of the plane equation R with the coordinates of $\mathbf{p_1}$.

Three-dimensional Liang–Barsky line clipping. First study the two-dimensional Liang–Barsky (LB) algorithm [Lian84] of Section 2.9.2. A parametric 3D line segment to be clipped is represented by its starting and ending points $\mathbf{p_1}$ and $\mathbf{p_2}$ as above.

In the case of orthographic or parallel projection, the clipping object is a cube and the LB computations extend directly to 3D simply by adding a third inequality to address the z-coordinate:

$$z_{min} \le z_1 + t\Delta z \le z_{max}.$$

The rest of the LB algorithm remains basically the same as in the 2D case.

In the case of perspective projection and homogeneous coordinates, we can rewrite inequalities (5.3), which define the part of a parametric line segment within the clipping object, as

$$-(w_1 + t\Delta w) \le x_1 + t\Delta x \le w_1 + t\Delta w,$$
$$-(w_1 + t\Delta w) \le y_1 + t\Delta y \le w_1 + t\Delta w,$$
$$-(w_1 + t\Delta w) \le z_1 + t\Delta z \le w_1 + t\Delta w,$$

where $\Delta x = x_2 - x_1$, $\Delta y = y_2 - y_1$, $\Delta z = z_2 - z_1$, and $\Delta w = w_2 - w_1$. These inequalities have the common form $tp_i \le q_i$ for $i = 1, 2, ..6$, where

$$
\begin{aligned}
p_1 &= -\Delta x - \Delta w, & q_1 &= x_1 + w_1, \\
p_2 &= \Delta x - \Delta w, & q_2 &= w_1 - x_1, \\
p_3 &= -\Delta y - \Delta w, & q_3 &= y_1 + w_1, \\
p_4 &= \Delta y - \Delta w, & q_4 &= w_1 - y_1, \\
p_5 &= -\Delta z - \Delta w, & q_5 &= z_1 + w_1, \\
p_6 &= \Delta z - \Delta w, & q_6 &= w_1 - z_1.
\end{aligned}
$$

Notice that the ratios $\frac{q_i}{p_i}$ correspond to the parametric intersection values of the line segment with clipping plane i and are equivalent to Equations (5.4). The rest of the LB algorithm remains basically the same as in the 2D case.

Three-dimensional Sutherland–Hodgman polygon clipping. First study the two-dimensional Sutherland–Hodgman (SH) algorithm [Suth74a] of Section 2.9.3. In 3D the clipping object is a convex volume, the view frustum, instead of a convex polygon. The algorithm now consists of six pipelined stages, one for each face of the view frustum, as shown in Figure 5.3.[9]

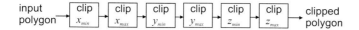

Figure 5.3. Sutherland–Hodgman 3D polygon clipping algorithm.

The logic of the algorithm remains similar to the 2D case; the main differences are:

Inside test. The `inside` test must be altered so that it tests whether a point is on the inside half-space of a plane. In the general case, this is equivalent to testing the sign of the plane equation for the coordinates of the point.

Intersection computation. The `intersect_lines` subroutine must be replaced by `intersect_plane_line` to compute the intersection of a polygon edge against a plane of the clipping volume. Such an intersection test is given in Appendix C; a solution for homogeneous coordinates and perspective projection is given by Equations (5.4).

5.4 Occlusion Culling

In large scenes, it is usually the case that only a very small portion of the primitives are visible for a given set of viewing parameters. The rest are hidden by other primitives nearer to the observer (Figure 5.4(b)). Occlusion culling aims at *efficiently* discarding a large number of primitives before computationally expensive hidden surface elimination (HSE) algorithms are applied. Let us define the *visible set* as the subset of primitives that are rendered on at least one pixel of the final image (Figure 5.4(a)). The objective of occlusion culling algorithms is to compute a tight superset of the visible set so that the rest of the primitives can be discarded; this superset is called the *potentially visible set* (PVS) [Aire91, CO03][10] (Figure 5.4(c)).

Occlusion culling algorithms do not expend time in determining exactly which parts of primitives are visible, as HSE algorithms do. Instead they determine which primitives are entirely *not* visible and quickly discard those, computing the PVS. The PVS is then passed to the classical HSE algorithms to determine the exact solution to the visibility problem.

---

[9]The SH algorithm can be applied to any other convex clipping volume; the number of stages in the pipeline is then equal to the number of bounding planes of the convex volume.

[10]Occlusion culling algorithms that compute the *exact* visible set have also been developed, but their computational cost is high.

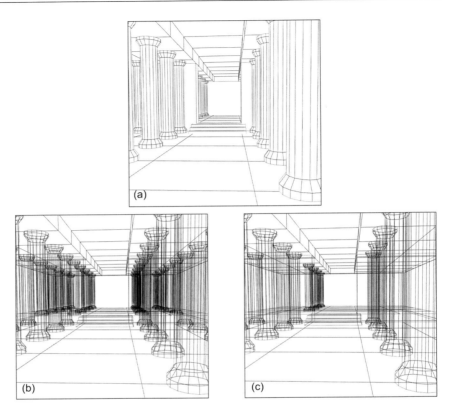

Figure 5.4. Line renderings of the primitives of a scene: (a) the visible set; (b) all primitives; (c) the potentially visible set.

The performance goal of occlusion culling algorithms is to have a cost proportional to the size of the visible set or the PVS. In practice their cost is often proportional to the input size, $O(P)$.

There are a number of categorizations of occlusion culling algorithms; see, for example, [CO03, Nire02]. We shall distinguish between two major classes here that essentially define the applicability of the algorithms: *from-point* and *from-region*. The former solve the occlusion problem for a single viewpoint and are more suitable for general outdoor scenes while the latter solve it for an entire region of space and are more suitable for densely populated indoor scenes. From-region approaches also require considerable pre-computation and are therefore applicable to static scenes.

5.4.1 From-Region Occlusion Culling

A number of applications, such as architectural walk-throughs and many games, consist of a set of convex regions, or *cells*, that are connected by transparent *portals*. In its simplest form the scene can be represented by a 2D floor plan, and the cells and portals are parallel to either the *x*- or the *y*-axis [Tell91] (Figure 5.5(a)). Assuming the walls of cells to be opaque, primitives are only visible between cells via the portals. Cell visibility is a recursive relationship: cell c_a may be visible from cell c_b via cell c_m, if appropriate *sightlines* exist that connect their portals.

The algorithm requires a preprocessing step, but this cost is only paid once assuming the cells and portals to be static, which is a reasonable assumption since they usually represent fixed environments. At preprocessing, a PVS matrix and a BSP tree [Fuch80] are constructed. The PVS matrix gives the PVS for every cell that the viewer may be in (Figure 5.5(c)). Since visibility is symmetric, the PVS matrix is also symmetric. To construct the PVS matrix, we start from each cell c and recursively visit all cells reachable from the cell adjacency graph, while

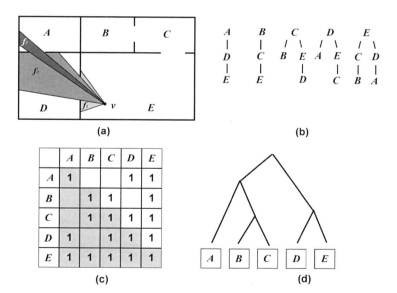

Figure 5.5. (a) A scene modeled as cells and portals; (b) the stab trees of the cells; (c) the PVS matrix; (d) the BSP tree.

sightlines exist that allow visibility from c. Thus the *stub tree* of c is constructed which defines the PVS of c (Figure 5.5(b)). All nodes in the stub tree become 1s in the appropriate PVS matrix row (or column).

A BSP tree (see Section 5.5.2) is also constructed during preprocessing (Figure 5.5(d)). The BSP tree uses separating planes, which may be cell boundaries, to recursively partition the scene. The leafs of the BSP tree represent the cells. A balanced BSP tree can be used to quickly locate the cell that a point (such as the viewpoint) lies in, in $O(\log_2 n_c)$ time, where n_c is the number of cells.

At runtime, the steps that lead to the rendering of the PVS for a viewpoint $\mathbf{v}$ are

- determine cell c of $\mathbf{v}$ using the BSP tree;

- determine PVS of cell c using the PVS matrix;

- render PVS.

Notice that the PVS does not change as long as $\mathbf{v}$ remains in the same cell (this is the essence of a from-region algorithm). The first two steps are therefore only executed when $\mathbf{v}$ crosses a cell boundary. At runtime only the BSP tree and the PVS matrix data structures are used.

During a dynamic walk-through, the culling algorithm can be further optimized by combining it with frustum and back-face culling. The rendering can be further restricted to primitives that are both within the view frustum and the PVS. The view frustum must be recursively constricted from cell to cell on the stab tree. The following pseudocode incorporates these ideas (but it does not necessarily reflect an implementation on modern graphics hardware)

```
portal_render(cell c, frustum f, list PVS); {
    for each polygon R in c {
        if ((R is portal) & (c' in PVS)) {
            /* portal R leads to cell c' */
            /* compute new frustum f' */
            f'=clip_frustum(f, R);
            if (f' <> empty) portal_render(c', f', PVS);
        }
        else if (R is portal) {}
        else { /* R is not portal */
            /* apply back-face cull */
            if !back_face(R) {
                /* apply frustum cull */
                R'=clip_poly(f, R);
```

```
                    if (R' <> empty) render(R);
                }
            }
        }
    }

main() {
    determine cell c of viewpoint using BSP tree;
    determine PVS of cell c using PVS matrix;
    f=original view frustum;
    portal_render(c, f, PVS);
}
```

Looking at the 2D example superimposed on Figure 5.5(a), the cell E that the viewer **v** lies in is first determined. Objects in that cell are culled against the original frustum f_1. The first portal leading to PVS cell D constricts the frustum to f_2, and objects within cell D are culled against this new frustum. The second portal leading to cell A reduces the frustum to f_3, and objects within cell A are culled against the f_3 frustum. The recursive process stops here as there are no new portal polygons within the f_3 frustum.

The f'=clip_frustum(f, R) command computes the intersection of the current frustum f and the volume formed by the viewpoint and the portal polygon R. This can give rise to odd convex shapes, losing the ability to use hardware support. A solution is to replace f' by its bounding box. Figure 5.6 shows a 2D example.

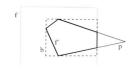

Figure 5.6. The original frustum (f), the portal polygon (p), the new frustum (f'), and its bounding box (b).

5.4.2 From-Point Occlusion Culling

For indoor scenes consisting of cells and portals, Luebke and Georges [Lueb95] propose a from-point image space approach that renders the scene starting from the current cell. Any other primitives must be visible through the image space projection of the portals, if these fall within the clipping limits. Recursive calls are made for the cells that the portals lead to, and at each step the new portals are intersected with the old portals until nothing remains. An overestimate (axis-aligned bounding window) of the intersection of the portals is computed to reduce complexity (Figure 5.7).

In the general case (e.g., outdoor scenes), it can not be assumed that a scene consists of cells and portals. Partitioning such scenes into regions does not then make much sense, since the regions would not be coherent with regard to their occlusion properties. From-point occlusion culling methods solve the problem

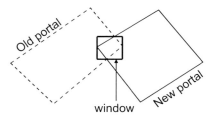

Figure 5.7. Intersection of old and new projected portals producing axis-aligned window through which other cells may be visible.

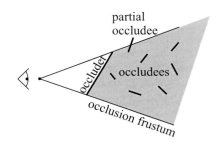

Figure 5.8. Occluder and occludees.

for a single viewpoint and consequently do not require as much pre-processing as from-region methods, since they do not pre-compute the PVS.

The main idea behind from-point techniques is the *occluder*. An occluder is a primitive, or a combination of primitives, that occludes a large number of other primitives, the *occludees*, with respect to a certain viewpoint (Figure 5.8). The region of space defined by the viewpoint and the occluder is the *occlusion frustum*. Primitives that lie entirely within the occlusion frustum can be culled. Partial occludees must be referred to the HSE algorithm. In practice, the occlusion test checks the bounding volume of objects (see Section 5.6.1) for inclusion in the occlusion frustum.

Two main steps are required to perform occlusion culling for a specific viewpoint **v**:

- create a small set of good occluders for **v**;

- perform occlusion culling using the occluders.

Coorg and Teller [Coor97] use *planar occluders* (i.e., planar primitives such as triangles) and rank them according to the area of their screen space projections. The larger that area is, the more important the occluder. Their ranking function f_{planar} is

$$f_{\text{planar}} = \frac{-A(\hat{\mathbf{n}} \cdot \hat{\mathbf{v}})}{|\vec{\mathbf{v}}|^2},$$

(5.5)

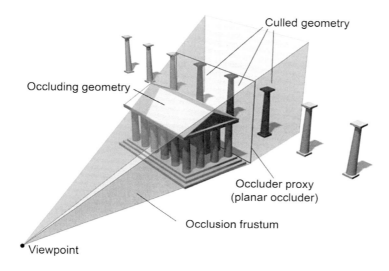

Figure 5.9. Using a planar occluder.

where A is the area of a planar occluder, $\hat{\mathbf{n}}$ is its unit normal vector and $\overrightarrow{\mathbf{v}}$ is the vector from the viewpoint to the center of the planar occluder.[11]

A usual way of computing a planar occluder is as the *proxy* for a primitive or object (Figure 5.9). The proxy is a convex polygon perpendicular to the view direction *inscribed* within the occlusion frustum of the occluder object or primitive.

The occlusion culling step can be made more efficient by keeping a hierarchical bounding volume description of the scene [Huds97]. Starting at the top level, a bounding volume that is entirely inside or entirely outside an occlusion frustum is rejected or rendered, respectively. A bounding volume that is partially inside and partially outside is split into the next level of bounding volumes, which are then individually tested against the occlusion frustum (see also Chapter 9).

Simple occlusion culling as described above suffers from the problem of partial occlusion (Figure 5.10(a)). An object may not lie in the occlusion frustum of any individual primitive and, therefore, cannot be culled, although it may lie in the occlusion frustum of a combination of adjacent primitives. For this reason algorithms that merge primitives or their occlusion frusta have been developed (Figure 5.10(b)). Papaioannou et al. [Papa06] proposed an extension to the basic

---

[11]The square in the denominator is due to the fact that projected area is inversely proportional to the square of the distance.

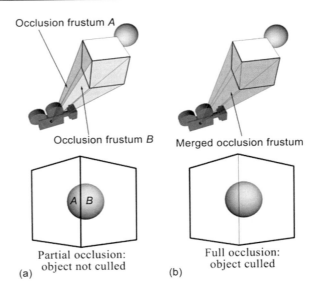

Figure 5.10. (a) The partial occlusion problem; (b) a solution by merging occluders.

planar occluder method, *solid occluders*, to address the partial occlusion problem. It dynamically produces a planar occluder for the entire volume of an object.

5.5   Hidden Surface Elimination

Hidden surface elimination (HSE) algorithms must provide a complete solution to the occlusion problem. The primitives or parts of primitives that are visible must be determined or rendered directly. To this end HSE algorithms (directly or indirectly) sort the primitives intersected by the projection rays. This reduces to the comparison of two points $\mathbf{p_1}=[x_1,y_1,z_1,w_1]^T$ and $\mathbf{p_2}=[x_2,y_2,z_2,w_2]^T$ for occlusion. If two such points are on the same ray then they form an *occluding pair* (the nearer one will occlude the other). We have to distinguish two cases here (see Section 4.4.2).

Orthographic projection. Assuming the projection rays to be parallel to the z_e-axis (Figure 5.11(a)), the two points will form an occluding pair if

$$(x_1 = x_2) \text{ and } (y_1 = y_2).$$

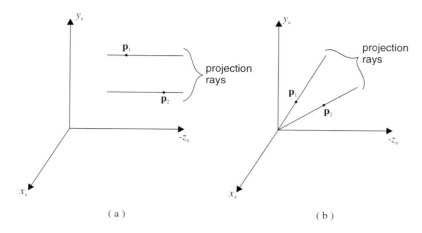

Figure 5.11. Projection rays in (a) orthographic and (b) perspective projection.

Perspective projection. In this case (Figure 5.11 (b)) the perspective division must be performed to determine if the two points form an occluding pair

$$(x_1/z_1 = x_2/z_2) \text{ and } (y_1/z_1 = y_2/z_2).$$

In the case of perspective projection, the (costly) perspective division is performed anyway within the ECS to CSS part of the viewing transformation (see Section 4.4.2). It essentially transforms the perspective view volume into a rectangular parallelepiped (see Figure 4.15) making direct comparisons of x- and y-coordinates possible for the determination of occluding pairs. For this reason HSE takes place *after* the viewing transformation into CSS; note that it is for the purpose of HSE that the viewing transformation maintains the z-coordinates.

Most HSE algorithms take advantage of *coherence*, the property of geometric primitives (such as polygons or lines) to maintain certain characteristics locally constant or predictably changing. For example, to determine the depth z of a planar polygon at each of the pixels it covers, it is not necessary to compute the intersection of its plane with the ray defined by each pixel, a rather costly computation. Instead, noting that depth changes linearly over the surface of the polygon, we can start from the depth at a certain pixel and add the appropriate depth increment for each neighboring pixel visited. Thus, by taking advantage of *surface coherence*, the costly ray-polygon intersection calculation can be replaced by an incremental computation; this is actually used in the Z-buffer algorithm described below. Other types of coherence used in HSE as well as other computer graphics algorithms are: *edge coherence*, *object coherence*, *scan-line coherence* and *frame coherence* [Suth74b].

5.5.1   Z-Buffer Algorithm

The Z-buffer is a classic image space HSE algorithm [Catm74] that was originally dismissed because of its high memory requirements; today a hardware implementation of the Z-buffer can be found on every graphics accelerator.

The idea behind the Z-buffer is to maintain a two-dimensional memory of depth values, with the same spatial resolution as the frame buffer (Figure 5.12). This is called the *depth* (or *Z*) *buffer*. There is a one-to-one correspondence between the frame- and Z-buffer elements.

Every element of the Z-buffer maintains the minimum depth for the corresponding pixel of the frame buffer. Before rendering a frame, the Z-buffer is initialized to a maximum value (usually the depth f of the far clipping plane). Sup-

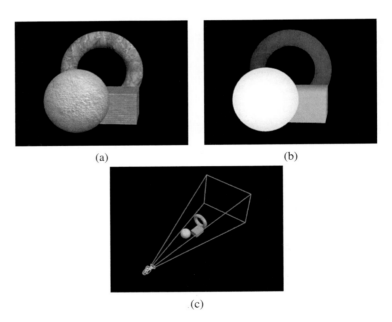

(a)   (b)

(c)

Figure 5.12. (a) The frame buffer; (b) the depth buffer; (c) the 3D scene. In the depth buffer image, lighter colors correspond to object points closer to the observer.

pose that during the rendering of a primitive[12] we compute its attributes (z_p, c_p) at pixel $\mathbf{p} = (x_p, y_p)$, where z_p is the depth of the primitive at $\mathbf{p}$ (distance from the viewpoint) and c_p its color at $\mathbf{p}$. Assuming that depth values decrease as we move away from the viewpoint (the $+z$ axis points toward the viewpoint), the main Z-buffer test is

```
if (z-buffer[xp, yp] < zp)  {
    f-buffer[xp, yp] = cp;   /* update frame buffer */
    z-buffer[xp, yp] = zp;   /* update depth buffer */
}
```

Note that the primitives can be processed in any order; this is due to the indirect depth sorting that is performed by the Z-buffer memory.

An issue that has direct consequence on the efficiency of the Z-buffer algorithm is the computation of the depth value z_p at each of the pixels that a primitive covers. Computing the intersection of the ray defined by the viewpoint and the pixel with the primitive is rather expensive. Instead we take advantage of the surface coherence of the primitive to compute the depth values incrementally. For planar primitives (e.g., triangles) this amounts to 1 addition per pixel. Let the plane equation of the primitive be

$$F(x, y, z) = ax + by + cz + d = 0$$

or, since we are interested in the depth,

$$F'(x, y) = z = -\frac{d}{c} - \frac{a}{c}x - \frac{b}{c}y.$$

The value of F' is incrementally computed from pixel (x, y) to pixel $(x+1, y)$ as

$$F'(x+1, y) - F'(x, y) = -\frac{a}{c}.$$

Thus, by adding the constant first forward difference of F' in x or y (see Chapter 2), we can compute the depth value from pixel to pixel at a cost of 1 addition. In practice, the depth values at the vertices of the planar primitive are interpolated across its edges and then between the edges (across the scanlines).

The same argument applies to the color value. Simple color interpolation can be performed in a manner similar to depth interpolation. Alternatively, texture mapping algorithms can provide color values per pixel.

---

[12]We use the word "primitive" here, instead of "polygon," as the Z-buffer is suitable for any geometric object whose depth we can determine. In practice we usually have polygons and most often these are triangles.

The complexity of the Z-buffer algorithm is $O(Ps)$, where P is the number of primitives and s is the average number of pixels covered by a primitive. However, practice dictates that as the number of primitives P increases, their size s decreases proportionately, maintaining a roughly constant depth complexity.[13] Thus, the cost of the Z-buffer can be regarded as proportional to the image resolution, $O(p)$, where p is the number of pixels.

The main advantages of the Z-buffer are its simplicity, its constant performance, roughly independent of scene complexity, and the fact that it can process primitives in any order. Its constant performance makes it attractive in today's highly complex scenes, while its simplicity led to its implementation on every modern graphics accelerator. Its weaknesses include the difficulty to handle some special effects (such as transparency) and the fixed resolution of its result which is inherited from its image space nature. The latter leads to arithmetic depth sorting inaccuracies for wide clipping ranges, a problem known as *Z-fighting*.

The Z-buffer computed during the rendering of a frame can be kept and used in various ways. A simple algorithm allows the depth-merging of two or more images created using the Z-buffer [Duff85, Port84]. This can be useful, for example, when constituent parts of a scene are generated by different software packages. Suppose that (F_a, Z_a) and (F_b, Z_b) represent the frame and Z-buffers for two parts of a scene. These can be merged in correct depth order by selecting the part with the nearest depth value at each pixel[14]

```
for (x=0; x<XRES; x++)
    for (y=0; y<YRES; y++)  {
        Fc[x,y] = (Za[x,y]>Zb[x,y])?Fa[x,y]:Fb[x,y];
        Zc[x,y] = (Za[x,y]>Zb[x,y])?Za[x,y]:Zb[x,y];
    }
```

Many more computations can be performed using Z-buffers, including shadow determination [Will78, Will98], voxelization [Kara99, Pass04], Voronoi computations [Hoff99], object reconstruction [Papa02], symmetry detection, and object retrieval [Pass06]. A survey of Z-buffer applications can be found in [Theo01].

5.5.2 Binary Space Partitioning Algorithm

The binary space partitioning (BSP) algorithm [Fuch80, Fuch83] is an object space algorithm that uses a binary tree that recursively subdivides space. In its

---

[13]Depth complexity is the average number of primitives intersected by a ray through the viewpoint and a pixel.

[14]Again, this corresponds to maximum z value as we have assumed the $+z$-axis to point toward the viewpoint.

pure form, each node of the binary tree data structure represents a polygon of the scene. Internal nodes, additionally, split space by the plane of their polygon, so that children on their left subtree are on one side of the plane and children on their right subtree are on the other (Figure 5.13).

To construct the BSP tree, the following algorithm is used:

```
BuildBSP(BSPnode, polygonDB);  {
    Select a polygon (plane) Pi from polygonDB;
    Assign Pi to BSPnode;
    /* Partition scene polygons into those that lie on either side
    of plane Pi, splitting polygons that intersect Pi */
    Partition(Pi, polygonDB, polygonDBL, polygonDBR);
    if (polygonDBL != empty) BuildBSP(BSPnode->Left,polygonDBL);
    if (polygonDBR != empty) BuildBSP(BSPnode->Right,polygonDBR);
}
```

The selection of the partitioning plane P_i is critical since we would like to end up with a balanced BSP tree; a plane is therefore selected that divides the scene into two parts of roughly equal cardinality. During the partitioning, polygons that intersect the partitioning plane must be split into two to enforce the partitioning.

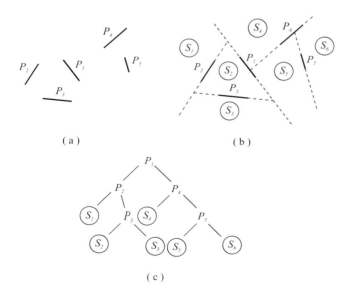

Figure 5.13. (a) A scene; (b) a space partitioning based on the scene polygons; (c) the corresponding BSP tree. The example is two-dimensional for simplicity.

This can be achieved by extending a clipping algorithm to deliver both the "inside" and the "outside" parts of a clipped polygon.

The BSP tree can then be used to display the scene with the hidden surfaces removed. For a specific viewpoint **v** and BSP node (representing a partitioning plane), all polygons that lie in the same partition as **v** cannot possibly be hidden by polygons that lie in the other partition. Thus the polygons of the other partition should be displayed first (further from **v**). This argument holds recursively and leads to the BSP display algorithm that performs HSE by an in-order traversal of the BSP tree:

```
DisplayBSP(BSPnode, v); {
    if IsLeaf(BSPnode) Render(BSPnode->Polygon)
    else if (v in ''left'' subspace of BSPnode->Polygon) {
        DisplayBSP(BSPnode->Right, v);
        Render(BSPnode->Polygon);
        DisplayBSP(BSPnode->Left, v);
    }
    else  /* v in ''right'' subspace of BSPnode->Polygon */  {
        DisplayBSP(BSPnode->Left, v);
        Render(BSPnode->Polygon);
        DisplayBSP(BSPnode->Right, v);
    }
}
```

The `DisplayBSP` algorithm visits every polygon once and thus costs $O(P)$. The `BuildBSP` algorithm costs $O(P^2)$ since, in the partitioning step, the selected polygon must be compared to all other polygons in the current partition, and this is repeated for every polygon. The overall complexity of the BSP tree algorithm is therefore $O(P^2)$.

For static scenes the `BuildBSP` algorithm need only be used once, as a preprocessing step, and then for every new position of the viewpoint only the `DisplayBSP` algorithm must be run. The BSP tree algorithm is therefore extremely suitable for static scenes but not suitable for dynamic scenes where the relative position of primitives changes often.

5.5.3 Depth Sort Algorithm

This algorithm sorts polygons according to their distance from the observer and displays them in reverse order (back to front) [Newe72]. This resembles the way a painter works, drawing the background in full first and then objects in the foreground, so the algorithm is often referred to as the *painter's* algorithm.

The minimum depth value[15] of polygons is often used for the sorting. The basic structure of the depth sort algorithm is the following:

```
DepthSort(polygonDB);    {
    /* Sort polygonDB according to minimum z */
    for each polygon in polygonDB find MINZ and MAXZ;
    sort polygonDB according to MINZ;
    resolve overlaps in z;
    display polygons in order of sorted list;
}
```

Overlaps in z arise when the z extents[16] of polygons overlap. When this happens the sorting becomes ambiguous as it is not clear which polygon obscures the other. In fact there are cases when they cannot be sorted (Figure 5.14).

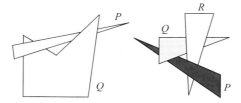

Figure 5.14. Examples of polygons that cannot be sorted in z in an order that will permit correct display.

When the z extents of two polygons R and Q overlap, a sequence of tests of increasing complexity are employed to resolve the ambiguity of their order in the display list. A positive conclusion of one of the following tests establishes that Q can not be occluded by R:

1. The x extents of R and Q do not overlap.

2. The y extents of R and Q do not overlap.

3. R lies entirely in the half-space of Q which does not include the viewpoint $\mathbf{v}$. This can be established by checking that the sign of the plane

---

[15]When the $+z$-axis points toward the observer, the minimum z corresponds to the maximum distance from the observer.

[16]By z *extent* we mean the region of space bounded by the planes $z = \text{MINZ}$ and $z = \text{MAXZ}$, where MINZ and MAXZ represent the minimum and maximum z-coordinates of a polygon. Similar extents can be defined for x and y.

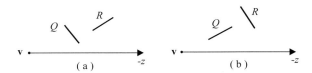

Figure 5.15. (a) R behind Q and (b) Q in front of R.

equation of Q is the same for all vertices of R and different to its sign for $\mathbf{v}$ (Figure 5.15(a)):

$$\text{sign}(f_Q(\mathbf{r_i})) \neq \text{sign}(f_Q(\mathbf{v})) \qquad \forall \mathbf{r_i} \in R,$$

where $f_Q(x,y,z) = a_Q x + b_Q y + c_Q z + d_Q = 0$ is the plane equation of polygon Q.

4. Q lies entirely in the half-space of R which includes the viewpoint $\mathbf{v}$. This can be established by checking that the sign of the plane equation of R is the same for all vertices of Q and for $\mathbf{v}$ (Figure 5.15(b)):

$$\text{sign}(f_R(\mathbf{q_i})) = \text{sign}(f_R(\mathbf{v})) \qquad \forall \mathbf{q_i} \in Q,$$

where $f_R(x,y,z) = a_R x + b_R y + c_R z + d_R = 0$ is the plane equation of polygon R.

5. The projections of R and Q do not overlap.

If none of the above tests is positive, the roles of R and Q are swapped and Tests 3 and 4 are repeated, in an attempt to establish that Q does not occlude R. Tests 1, 2, and 5 need not be repeated as they are symmetric. If the order is still not resolved, then R is divided into two polygons using the plane of Q (or equivalently Q is divided using the plane of R), the new polygons replace R in the list, and the process is repeated.

The depth sort is clearly an object space algorithm, except for the last step (display) which takes place in image space. An optimization is to draw the polygons in reverse order (front to back) in the display step, using the rule that succeeding polygons are only drawn on pixels that have not been written to before by nearer polygons. Then the display step can stop as soon as all image pixels have been written to at least once.

The cost of the sorting step is $O(P \log_2 P)$. The resolution of z overlaps could cost $O(P^2)$ in the worst case where the z extents of all polygons overlap. Practice dictates that the depth sort is a rather slow algorithm in typical scenes of great complexity. On the positive side, the depth sort algorithm can straightforwardly handle transparency.

5.5.4 Ray-Casting Algorithm

As its name implies, a *ray* is followed for every pixel $\mathbf{p}$; the ray is defined by the viewpoint $\mathbf{v}$ and the vector $\overrightarrow{\mathbf{p} - \mathbf{v}}$. Intersections with all scene primitives are computed and the nearest intersection to $\mathbf{v}$ defines the visible primitive. An efficient ray-triangle intersection algorithm is given in Appendix C; the ray-casting algorithm is, however, applicable to any primitive for which we can define a ray-intersection algorithm. The basic form of the algorithm is:

```
RayCasting(primitiveDB, v);    {
    for each pixel p    {
        minp = MAXINT;
        for each primitive R in primitiveDB  {
            /* compute intersection of ray (v,p) with R */
            i=intersect_primitive_ray(R,v,p); /* MAXINT if none */
            if (|i-v| < minp)   {
                p->nearest_primitive = R;
                minp = |i-v|
            }
        }
    }
}
```

Even with efficient intersection computations and the use of bounding volumes (see Section 5.6.1), the ray-casting algorithm is slow, $O(pP)$, as it takes no advantage of coherence. On the other hand, it is very general since it can be easily applied to most primitive types. It can be speeded up in a straight-forward manner, by distributing the rays among parallel processors and duplicating the primitives database (see Chapters 15 and 9 for more details).

The ray-casting algorithm can be applied either before or after the perspective projection; in the former case the rays are the projection rays themselves, in the latter case the rays are all parallel to each other and orthogonal to the projection plane. Hence, the ray-casting algorithm can be classified as either object or image space.

HSE algorithm	Complexity	Space
Z-Buffer	$O(Ps) \simeq O(p)$	Image
BSP	$O(P^2)$	Object
Depth Sort	$O(P^2)$	Object
Ray Casting	$O(pP)$	Image/Object

Table 5.1. Complexities and application spaces of HSE algorithms.

In summary, the complexities and application spaces of the presented HSE algorithms are given in Table 5.1.

5.6   Efficiency Issues

This section includes techniques that can increase the performance of intersection computations, often required in culling, HSE, ray tracing (Chapter 15), and other algorithms.

5.6.1   Bounding Volumes

Whenever intersection tests between complex objects are involved, *bounding volumes* can be used to improve efficiency.

Most models created for synthetic worlds tend to be quite complex, as they usually attempt to represent real-life objects using simple geometric primitives. A natural way of reducing the cost of computing intersections with a complex model, is to cluster its primitives in a bounding volume, such as a rectangular parallelepiped or a sphere (Figure 5.16). A bounding volume need not be closed; for example the extent of a model in a single coordinate axis has often been used (Figure 5.16(b)).

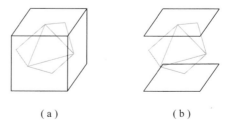

(a)   (b)

Figure 5.16. (a) Bounding volume example; (b) open bounding volume.

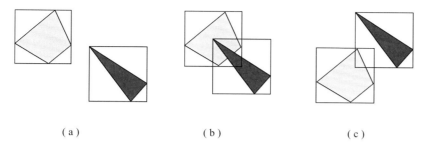

(a)   (b)   (c)

Figure 5.17. 2D examples of bounding volume intersections: (a) non-intersecting; (b), (c) intersecting; (c) false alarm.

Intersection with the bounding volume does not necessarily imply an intersection with the model since the bounding volume usually includes some *void space* between itself and the model. "False alarms" can be generated if only the void space is intersected; these false alarms are costly as they require detailed intersection tests against all of the primitives that define the model. On the other hand, non-intersection with the bounding volume does imply no intersection with the enclosed model. Figure 5.17 gives 2D examples.

Whenever the bounding volume is not intersected, no detailed intersection tests against the model need take place, potentially saving large amounts of computational effort. For a bounding volume to be successful it must possess two qualities: be simple and minimize void space.

The first quality is necessary in order to make the intersection tests against the bounding volume efficient. The second quality ensures that as few false alarms as possible are generated. However, the achievement of both of these qualities is contradictory, and a compromise usually has to be reached.

Rectangular parallelepiped bounding volumes with faces parallel to the xy, yz and xz planes can be created simply by taking the minima and maxima of the models' vertex coordinates; they are the intersection of half-spaces defined by six planes perpendicular to the coordinate axes and are thus called *axis-aligned bounding boxes* (AABBs) (Figure 5.18). AABBs generally suffer from large amounts of void space. *Oriented bounding boxes* (OBBs) [Gott96] are arbitrarily oriented rectangular parallelepipeds; with a careful selection of orientation, OBBs result in less void space than AABBs. Hierarchical bounding volumes provide a better compromise between simplicity and void space. These include hierarchies of *k-DOPs* [Klos98] (polyhedra whose faces may only have predefined orientations) and hierarchies of OBBs. Both of the above construct trees of nested vol-

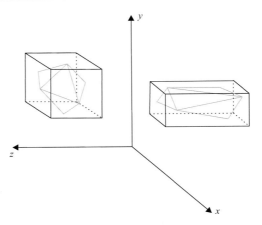

Figure 5.18. Axis-aligned bounding boxes.

umes. The root of the tree represents a bounding volume that encloses the entire model; this contains smaller volumes enclosing parts of the model more tightly, up to individual primitives. During intersection queries, the tree structure helps to quickly restrict the area of potential intersection. Another hierarchical method with good results for complex models is *progressive hulls*, i.e., a succession of hulls that enclose the model more tightly [Plat03] (Figure 5.19). Each hull in this hierarchy encloses all successive hulls (and of course all hulls enclose the model). The outer hulls are simpler but leave more void space, while inner hulls are more complex and leave less void space. The hulls are used starting from the outermost (simplest), while intersections are found.

The pseudocode for the hierarchical intersection test of a model M follows:

```
IntersectionTest(M);  {
    if BottomLevel(M)  return(LLIntersectionTest(M))
    else
        if LLIntersectionTest(BoundingVolume(M))  {
            v = false;
            for each component M->C
                v = (v || IntersectionTest(M->C));
            return(v);
        }
        else return(false);
}
```

Figure 5.19. Progressive hulls as bounding volumes; a horse model with 96,966 polygons followed by its 2,000 and 200 polygon hulls.

where `LLIntersectionTest` performs an exhaustive intersection test with the primitives of its parameter and `M->C` represents a component one level below in the object hierarchy.

5.6.2   Space Subdivision

Space subdivision techniques, as their name implies, divide space into an ordered set of *cells*. The cells occupied by a model indirectly determine its spatial relationship with respect to other models and objects such as the view frustum. We can thus infer if two objects potentially intersect by checking if they occupy common cells. Furthermore, we can use the ordering of the cells to infer if an object A potentially occludes another object B. Space subdivision techniques require specialized cell data structures and a preprocessing step to assign objects to these data structures.

A common hierarchical 3D space subdivision technique is the *octree* (Figure 5.20). An octree recursively subdivides an initial cell (finite region of 3D space, e.g., cube) into eight sub-cells that partition the space of the original cell. Depending on the implementation, this subdivision stops

- when an elementary cell size (called *voxel*) is reached, or

- when the object complexity within a cell is below a certain limit (e.g., the cell contains a single primitive).

In a culling application, models that do not occupy the cells of interest can be discarded. For example, in frustum culling only models that occupy cells common to the view frustum need be considered. In occlusion culling, only objects that occupy cells with the same x- and y-coordinates need be tested for occlusion. Furthermore, this cell-sharing property can be decided at the highest level possible to save computational time; the octree will have more levels where higher scene complexity exists.

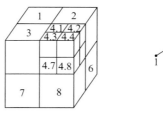

Figure 5.20. Finite 3D space and octree.

5.7 Exercises

1. Reformulate the 3D Liang–Barksy algorithm so that it can be used for an arbitrary convex clipping polyhedron. The polyhedron is given as a set of n planes P_i, $i = 1, 2, ..n$ with their normal vectors $\overrightarrow{\mathbf{N}}_i$, $i = 1, 2, ..n$ that define the "outside" half-space of each plane. The volume of the polyhedron is the intersection of the "inside" half-spaces of the n planes. Assume that the given set of planes form a properly closed convex polyhedron.

2. As above, for the 3D Sutherland–Hodgman algorithm. What problem does the use of an arbitrary convex clipping polyhedron pose to a hardware implementation of this algorithm?

⊛3. (Parallel processing.) Implement the six stages of the 3D Sutherland–Hodgman algorithm as a pipeline of six processors on a parallel processing platform of your choice/access. Measure the speed-up for different numbers of polygons and explain the result. For more details see [Theo89b].

⊛4. (Field programmable gate arrays (FPGA).) As above, but implement the pipeline on an FPGA of your choice/access. If you possess a silicon compiler (e.g., Handel-C), you might want to abstract the code of a clipping stage and instantiate it six times.

5. (Culling efficiency.) Estimate the approximate number of primitives culled by each of the three culling stages. State any assumptions that you need to make about your scene. If you have access to a system that performs the three types of culling, run experiments to actually measure the portion of primitives culled for a number of different viewing parameters.

6. (Depth image combination.) In your rendering system, find a way of exporting the final frame and depth buffers after rendering a scene. Then implement an algorithm to combine *multiple* sets of frame and depth buffer pairs in correct depth order, generalizing the algorithm given at the end of Section 5.5.1.

7. (3D cursor.) In your rendering system, find a way of exporting the final frame and depth buffers after rendering a scene. Then implement an algorithm which will track and display a 3D cursor in the rendered scene, with hidden surfaces eliminated (the cursor may *hide* behind objects). The cursor can be moved in three dimensions, e.g., by using six keys (two for each

dimension). (*Hint:* You will need to implement a small modification to the Z-buffer algorithm).

8. An important advantage of the Z-buffer algorithm is its ability to process primitives in any order. Does this imply that the final contents of the frame and depth buffers will be exactly the same regardless of the order of processing the primitives? Verify your answer experimentally. (*Hint:* Think of "borderline" cases).

9. Implement the depth sort HSE algorithm for a scene consisting of a single convex polyhedron that is arbitrarily translated and rotated within a set of limits, in a screen-saver fashion. (*Note:* The 5 basic steps should suffice; you will not need to divide any of the polyhedron's polygons.)

10. (Bounding volumes.) Implement the ray-triangle intersection algorithm of Appendix C. Then select a complex model consisting of at least 1,000 triangles. Scale the model so that it occupies about 10% of the volume of the unit cube. Determine the bounding box of the scaled model by taking the minima and maxima of its x-, y-, and z-coordinates. Next, write a simple algorithm to generate random rays within the unit cube (essentially, for each ray, you need to generate two random points on different faces of the cube). Fire 1,000-10,000 random rays (in increments of 1,000) across the unit cube and measure the amount of time required to

   - compute the intersection of each ray (if any) with the model *using* the bounding box;
   - compute the intersection of each ray (if any) with the model *without using* the bounding box.

   Plot a graph of the number of rays fired against the total time taken, with and without the use of the bounding box.

6

Model Representation and Simplification

> Art takes nature as its model.
> —Aristotle

6.1 Introduction

The 3D scenes composed in graphics and visualization depict objects of various shapes and structures: geometric primitives such as spheres; free-form surfaces with a known mathematical description, such as NURBS patches (see Chapter 7); arbitrary surfaces with no concrete mathematical description, such as the surface of a scanned object; volume objects where the internal structure of the object is equally important to its boundary surface, such as a human organ; even fuzzy objects such as smoke.

Models are approximate representations of the actual objects, constructed so as to retain as many of the properties of the represented objects as feasible, while at the same time being amenable to the manipulations required by graphics algorithms. *Polygonal models* are the most common representation for surfaces.

As a result of the advances in computer processing power and data-acquisition techniques, the amount of information contained in the models produced is growing constantly; even though the available detail is useful for archival purposes or other specialized uses, mainstream graphics applications often require or benefit from less detailed models. *Model simplification* aims to reduce the amount of information present in a model without significantly sacrificing the quality of representation.

175

6.2   Overview of Model Forms

The two main categories of models are *surface representations* (also called *boundary representations* or *b-reps*) that represent only the surface of an object and *volume representations* (or *space-subdivision representations*) that represent the whole volume that a (closed) 3D object occupies.

Surface representations are used more frequently. Many objects are not closed; therefore, a volume representation is not applicable. Also the majority of objects are not transparent, their interior is not visible, and thus space and processing power may be saved by only representing their surface, which, in all respects, determines their appearance. On the other hand, volume representations are used when displaying semi-transparent objects or, more generally, objects whose internal structure is of interest; a concrete example is the visualization of three-dimensional fields (see Section 18.2.2). Furthermore, space subdivision representations are used as auxiliary structures in several graphics algorithms (see, for example, Section 15.5.1).

Some model forms cannot be classified easily into the above two categories. *Constructive Solid Geometry (CSG) models* represent an object by combining geometric primitives; see Section 15.5.3 for a brief presentation. Also amorphous objects and phenomena may be modelled as point clouds or by aggregating simple surface or volume primitives.

Regarding surface models, we may differentiate between those that have some mathematical description, such as geometric primitives, NURBS surfaces (see Chapter 7), subdivision surfaces (see Chapter 8), or general parametric surfaces (see Appendix B), and those that do not have such a mathematical description. The latter consist of a set of points and of a set of (usually planar) polygons constructed with these points as vertices; hence they are called *polygonal models*. Comparing these two surface model forms, we note that mathematical models are usually exact representations of the respective objects and also allow computations on the objects, such as normal vectors, to be performed exactly; on the other hand, they are limited to specific kinds of objects and cannot describe arbitrary shapes. On the contrary, polygonal models are certainly approximations of the original objects, albeit very precise ones if enough vertices are used; they are the most general ones, since there is virtually no limit to the kind of object they can represent—even mathematical representations are usually rendered in a "discrete" form as polygonal models.

Polygonal models may consist of polygons of any number of vertices; in practice, the most common ones are those comprised of quadrilaterals or triangles. Quadrilateral models are naturally generated when rasterizing parametric surfaces (for example, tensor product surfaces, see Section 7.6). Unfortunately, a quadrilateral in 3D is not necessarily planar, and this limitation either restricts the shape and flexibility of the model, if the planarity of its quadrilaterals is enforced, or makes all computations more difficult, since the constituent polygons are no longer planar. This shortcoming does not exist in triangle models, since a triangle is always planar; additionally any polygon may be triangulated efficiently [Prep85, O'Ro98] and, therefore, a triangle model can be generated from any polygonal model. It is evident that triangle models (also called *triangle meshes*) are almost always preferred for any application that involves polygonal models.

Polygonal models are generalized for volume representations to *polyhedral models*. The most basic polyhedral primitive is the tetrahedron, and *tetrahedral meshes* are the most general and flexible representation for volume models. However, models consisting of parallelepipeds are abundant, mainly as the outcome of space subdivision processes that use rectangular grids; the constituent parallelepipeds are called *voxels* (volume elements). Hierarchical volume representations such as octrees (see Section 15.5.1) and BSP trees (see Section 5.5.2) are also used.

In the remainder of this chapter, we will focus on polygonal models.

6.3 Properties of Polygonal Models

A surface model is a 2-*manifold* (or simply a manifold) if every point on the surface has a neighborhood homeomorphic to an open disk (the open disk is the interior of a circle).[1] In other words, even though the surface exists in three-dimensional space, it is topologically flat when the surface is examined closely in a small enough area around any given point. On a manifold surface, every edge is shared by exactly two faces, and around each vertex there exists a closed loop of faces. Similarly, a surface model is a *manifold with boundary* if every point on the surface has a neighborhood homeomorphic to a half-disk. On a manifold with boundary, some edges (those on the boundary of the model) belong to exactly one face, and around some vertices (those on the boundary) the loop of faces is

---

[1]Two objects are *homeomorphic* if the one can be continuously and invertibly deformed (stretched and bent) onto the other; for instance, a circle and a square are homeomorphic, as are a cube, a sphere and a tetrahedron. Homeomorphic objects have common topological properties, such as number of holes, being a manifold or not, etc.

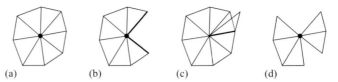

Figure 6.1. (a) Part of a manifold surface; (b) Boundary vertex of a manifold surface with boundary; (c) Non-manifold edge; (d) Non-manifold boundary vertex.

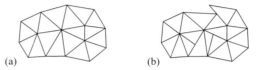

Figure 6.2. The triangle mesh (a) is a simplicial complex, whereas (b) is not.

open. Figure 6.1 presents some manifold and non-manifold triangular models. For the usual, three-dimensional surfaces, a manifold surface without boundary is a *closed* surface.

It is almost always assumed that the polygons constituting a polygonal model meet only along their edges, and the edges of the model intersect only at their endpoints. Triangular models that satisfy this property are termed *simplicial complexes*; Figure 6.2 shows an example of a triangular mesh that is a simplicial complex and one that is not.

Surfaces can also be characterized as *orientable* or not. Intuitively, an orientable surface is one that has two "sides," like a sheet of paper; most of the surfaces encountered in practice are orientable. On closed, orientable surfaces the "external" and the "internal" portions of the surface are distinguishable. Figure 6.3 shows an example of a non-orientable surface, the Möbius strip; this strip has actually just one side, since if we start off at a point and move along the strip, we will arrive at the origin after having travelled on all of its surface. By convention, the *normal vector* of a closed orientable surface points towards the outside of the surface.

Closed manifold models homeomorphic to a sphere satisfy *Euler's formula*,

$$V - E + F = 2, \tag{6.1}$$

where V is the number of vertices, E is the number of edges, and F is the number of faces of the model. Specialized for a closed triangular model (see Exercise 1),

Figure 6.3. The Möbius strip, a non-orientable surface.

this formula reveals that the number of triangles of the model is almost twice the number of its vertices, and also that the average number of triangles around each vertex is six. Euler's formula has been generalized for arbitrary manifold models to

$$V - E + F = 2 - 2G, \qquad (6.2)$$

where G is the *genus* of the model; the genus of a model can be considered as the number of penetrating holes or "handles" of the model; for instance, a torus has genus 1, a double torus has genus 2, and so on.

6.4   Data Structures for Polygonal Models

Several different data structures have been proposed for the representation of polygonal models. They differ in the type of polygonal models that they are able to represent, in the amount and type of information that they capture directly about the model, and in other information that can or cannot be derived indirectly from them about the model. Information that is useful in several graphics operations is the following:

- *Topological information.* Whether the model is manifold; whether it is closed; whether it has a boundary or holes.

- *Adjacency information.* Neighboring faces of a given edge and face; edges and faces around a given vertex; the boundary of an open model.

- *Attributes attached to the model.* Normal vector, colors, material properties (see Chapter 12), texture coordinates (see Chapter 14).

The most primitive data structures that were used are the *explicit list of edges* (the *wireframe representation*) and the *explicit list of faces*, containing, for each

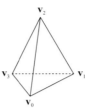

Figure 6.4. The polygonal model of a tetrahedron.

edge or face of the model, the coordinates of its vertices. For example, the list of edges for the tetrahedron in Figure 6.4 is

$$e_0 = \big((x_0,y_0,z_0),(x_1,y_1,z_1)\big), \qquad e_3 = \big((x_1,y_1,z_1),(x_2,y_2,z_2)\big),$$
$$e_1 = \big((x_0,y_0,z_0),(x_2,y_2,z_2)\big), \qquad e_4 = \big((x_1,y_1,z_1),(x_3,y_3,z_3)\big),$$
$$e_2 = \big((x_0,y_0,z_0),(x_3,y_3,z_3)\big), \qquad e_5 = \big((x_2,y_2,z_2),(x_3,y_3,z_3)\big),$$

and the list of faces is

$$f_0 = \big((x_3,y_3,z_3),(x_2,y_2,z_2),(x_1,y_1,z_1)\big),$$
$$f_1 = \big((x_2,y_2,z_2),(x_3,y_3,z_3),(x_0,y_0,z_0)\big),$$
$$f_2 = \big((x_1,y_1,z_1),(x_0,y_0,z_0),(x_3,y_3,z_3)\big),$$
$$f_3 = \big((x_0,y_0,z_0),(x_1,y_1,z_1),(x_2,y_2,z_2)\big).$$

The wireframe representation is actually not a b-rep, since it does not specify the faces of the model; these must be inferred from the edge data, but the procedure is not straightforward and may lead to ambiguities. For example, given the above edges of the tetrahedron, we cannot know whether this tetrahedron is closed or whether one of its faces is missing.

The explicit list of faces also has severe drawbacks and is not currently used. It wastes space, since the coordinates of each vertex are repeated for each edge or face that contains it; it provides no information on the adjacency of edges and faces; computing adjacency information may even be problematic, since common vertices can only be detected by comparing coordinates, and numerical accuracy problems may interfere. Similarly, editing the model incurs significant overhead and risks destroying it, if adjacent faces are not detected correctly.

Several of these shortcomings are addressed by the *indexed list of faces*. This composite data structure contains a list of the vertices of the model and a list of its faces; the vertices of each face are given as references to the list of vertices.

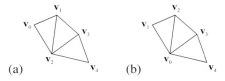

Figure 6.5. (a) A triangle strip $\{v_0,v_1,v_2,v_3,v_4\}$; (b) A triangle fan $\{v_0,v_1,v_2,v_3,v_4\}$.

For instance, the tetrahedron of Figure 6.4 is represented as

$$\begin{aligned}
\mathbf{v}_0 &= (x_0, y_0, z_0), & f_0 &= (\mathbf{v}_3, \mathbf{v}_2, \mathbf{v}_1), \\
\mathbf{v}_1 &= (x_1, y_1, z_1), & f_1 &= (\mathbf{v}_2, \mathbf{v}_3, \mathbf{v}_0), \\
\mathbf{v}_2 &= (x_2, y_2, z_2), & f_2 &= (\mathbf{v}_1, \mathbf{v}_0, \mathbf{v}_3), \\
\mathbf{v}_3 &= (x_3, y_3, z_3), & f_3 &= (\mathbf{v}_0, \mathbf{v}_1, \mathbf{v}_2).
\end{aligned}$$

This data structure can represent any kind of polygonal model, is far more compact than the explicit list of faces, and permits direct modifications to the positions of the vertices of the model. The edges of the model are straightforward to discover, but they are repeated for each polygon that uses them, so some processing is required in order to generate a valid list of unique edges. Furthermore, the indexed list of faces does not provide adjacency information about the model, although the data it contains is sufficient to compute it. When this data structure is used to represent orientable models, it is customary to list the vertices of all faces in a consistent ordering, either clockwise or counterclockwise, when seen from the outside of the model. Using this convention, it is easier to make computations on the model, especially calculations of normal vectors (see Section 12.5.1). Specifically for triangle models, in order to minimize the duplication of data, most graphics packages are able to handle neighboring triangles more efficiently as *triangle strips* or *triangle fans* (see Figure 6.5).

Owing to its generality, simplicity, and compactness, the indexed list of faces is the basis of several common file formats for 3D models, such as the .OBJ (Wavefront Object, [Murr96]) and .PLY [PLY07] formats. In these formats, the structure is augmented with other indexed data for the attributes of the model (see above) that may be bound either to the vertices or the faces of the model; for instance, the representation of a colored cube will include a list of colors and a list of entries indicating the color of each face.

Several more advanced data structures for polygonal model representation exist that capture some adjacency information directly and allow for easy derivation

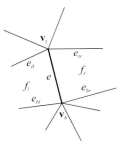

Figure 6.6.   The winged-edge data structure.   The thick edge is
$e(\mathbf{v}_t, \mathbf{v}_b, f_l, f_r, e_{tl}, e_{tr}, e_{bl}, e_{br})$.

of more adjacency relations. All of these data structures are indexed and contain
at least a list of vertices to which the other elements of the model (edges and
faces) refer. Most of the data structures deal with manifold models composed of
arbitrary polygons.

One such data structure is the *winged-edge* representation [Baum72]. In this
data structure, the central node of information is the edge. Each edge stores references to its two vertices, to its two adjacent faces, and to its four neighboring
edges along the adjacent faces (Figure 6.6). The winged-edge data structure also
stores, for each vertex, a reference to one of its incident edges and, for each face,
a reference to one of its edges. This additional information makes it possible to
"navigate" in the topology of the model and compute adjacency queries, several
of them in constant time. The winged-edge data structure can be modified in order
to represent some types of non-manifold models.

The *half-edge* data structure [Weil85] is similar to the winged-edge representation, but uses *oriented* edges: each edge of the model is "decomposed" into two
half-edges, each storing references to its start and end vertex, to its adjacent face,
to its two neighboring half-edges along the adjacent face, and to its opposite half-
edge (Figure 6.7). Since this orientation of edges is natural in manifold models,
the half-edge data structure is more efficient than the winged-edge data structure
for several adjacency queries.

Finally, the *quad-edge* data structure [Guib85] is conceptually similar to the
above representations, but its implementation is more sophisticated [Lisc94], allowing it to compute adjacency queries efficiently and, most notably, enabling it
to represent simultaneously a manifold model and its *dual*. The dual of a model
is constructed by rotating edges by 90 degrees, replacing vertices with faces and
vice versa: the dual of a tetrahedron is also a tetrahedron, the dual of a cube is an

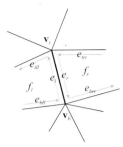

Figure 6.7. The half-edge representation. The thick edge is decomposed into two half edges, $e_l(\mathbf{v}_b, \mathbf{v}_t, f_l, e_{bll}, e_{tll}, e_r)$ and $e_r(\mathbf{v}_t, \mathbf{v}_b, f_r, e_{trr}, e_{brr}, e_l)$.

octahedron and vice versa. This property of the quad-edge data structure is useful in the context of *computational geometry*, the algorithmic study of geometric problems.

6.5 Polygonal Model Simplification

The polygonal models used in practice are most often produced automatically, by rasterization of mathematically defined surfaces, by 3D scanning of real objects, or by other similar procedures. The quest for better accuracy of representation, aided by the steady increase in computing power and the advances in 3D scanning and other data acquisition techniques, leads to the generation of models that capture the finest details of the represented surfaces at the cost of a very large number of vertices and faces. In addition, the size of constituent polygons is usually uniform on the surface of the model due to the techniques used to generate them.

As an example, the *Digital Michelangelo* project [Levo00] was concerned with scanning and reconstructing some of the sculptures made by Michelangelo. Using the most advanced scanning technology available at the time, the sculptures were scanned at a resolution up to 1/4 of a mm, and the triangle meshes produced contain several hundred million triangles (depending on the physical size of the sculptures) and occupy several gigabytes of data storage. Such detail is certainly required for archival purposes, but is probably useless for any other practical application, since it is only visible at very high magnification levels. Furthermore, the amount of data in these models will be difficult or impossible to process by even the most advanced computers for some time to come.

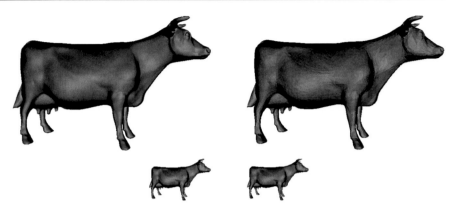

Figure 6.8. Top: The cow model at 5000 triangles (left) and simplified at 1000 triangles (right); Bottom: The same models in smaller size; their differences are not easily discernible. (Simplification performed with QSlim [Garl97].)

On a much smaller scale, models are usually created at the finest level of detail that is expected to be useful in a given application. Even in this case, the application can benefit from multiple *resolutions (levels of detail (LODs))* of the model that can be used in different viewing conditions. For instance, when the screen projection of a model is sufficiently small, only a small amount of detail is discernible and rendering any more would only waste resources (Figure 6.8). In addition, in many situations it would be beneficial to vary the detail in different parts of the model; for instance, coplanar triangles could be merged into fewer larger ones, and areas of the surface that are closer to the viewer would require more detail than those further away. All of this holds particularly for interactive applications that display large graphics scenes, where the total number of polygons that must be processed at any time is considerable.

For these reasons, several model-simplification techniques have been developed. Their common aim is to reduce the number of faces of a polygonal model while retaining, as much as possible for a given number of faces, the appearance and structure of the original model. Then, any application that makes use of simplified models usually employs several levels of detail of the original model and selects dynamically the one that fits the current scene configuration better.

The idea of model simplification is not new [Clar76], but the more interesting simplification techniques have been developed recently. These vary greatly in many respects: they can be applied to different kinds of models, take different paths for the simplification of the models, have different priorities and applications.

With regard to their domain of application, simplification algorithms deal most easily with closed manifold meshes. The boundary of non-closed models is handled in most cases, however, only few algorithms are able to simplify non-manifold models.

A classification of simplification methods may be based on whether the method produces *discrete* or *continuous* levels of detail of the original model. In the former case, a target number of faces is prescribed, and the algorithm generates a new model with the required number of faces; if another level of detail is requested, the algorithm has to be executed again. In the latter case, using local simplifications of the model (removal of single vertices, edges, or faces), the algorithm produces a continuous sequence of increasingly simplified models, from the original detailed model down to a coarse *base* mesh. By recording the simplification steps, any intermediate level of detail may be produced. We present one such algorithm in Section 6.5.1.

Continuous simplification algorithms are far more interesting than discrete ones. In addition to their flexibility in the resolution of the simplified models, several of them are easily *reversible*, allowing the application to move back and forth between intermediate levels of detail. More importantly, some algorithms support the *selective* refinement and coarsening of the mesh, enabling the dynamic adjustment of detail on different parts of the model according to the needs of the application. Finally, it is usually possible to refine or coarsen the mesh *smoothly*, which minimizes visual artifacts due to switching resolutions of the model in interactive applications.

An important issue for all simplification algorithms is how to assess the quality of a simplified model with respect to the original one. Most simplification algorithms are guided by such measures in order to determine where the "best" position to put the new vertex is or which edge should be removed first in order to minimize the discrepancy of the simplified model from the original. These measures also provide a global estimate of the quality of the final model so that different algorithms can be compared [Cign98].

The most widely used method for this assessment is to measure some form of distance between the simplified and the original model. For instance, the *Hausdorff distance* [Prep85] measures the maximum distance between any two points of two surfaces M and M' as

$$d_\infty(M, M') = \max\left(\max_{\mathbf{v} \in M}\{d(\mathbf{v}, M')\}, \max_{\mathbf{v}' \in M'}\{d(\mathbf{v}', M)\}\right),$$

where

$$d(\mathbf{v}, M) = \min_{\mathbf{w} \in M} \{ |\mathbf{v} - \mathbf{w}| \}$$

is the distance of a point $\mathbf{v}$ from a surface M, defined as the distance of $\mathbf{v}$ from the closest point $\mathbf{w}$ of the surface. Alternatively, the *mean square distance* of two surfaces is

$$d_2(M, M') = \frac{1}{s} \int_{\mathbf{v} \in M} d(\mathbf{v}, M') + \frac{1}{s'} \int_{\mathbf{v}' \in M'} d(\mathbf{v}', M),$$

where s and s' are the areas of M and M', respectively. In practice, these formulae must be discretized in order to be computed on polygonal models; this is accomplished by sampling a number of points on both surfaces and using them for the computations. Other approximations of the distance are often used by specific algorithms as they fit better with the calculations performed.

6.5.1 Simplification using Iterative Edge Collapses

As an example of a polygonal model simplification method, we present the simplification of triangle meshes using iterative edge collapses. The reader is referred to [Pupp97, Garl99] for reviews of many more simplification methods.

The edge-collapse operation [Hopp96] is a local operation on a triangle mesh that removes an edge of the model and the two adjacent triangles by collapsing an edge to a single vertex (Figure 6.9). Using edge collapses, it is rather easy to compute a measure of the distance of the simplified mesh from the one before the collapse, since they only differ on the faces around the collapsed edge. Here, we assume that the model is manifold, but variations of this method support non-manifold models as well. The edges to be collapsed are placed in a priority queue, using a measure of the impact of their collapse to the approximation error as their priority, so that those that will have less impact are performed first. The algorithm is summarized as follows:

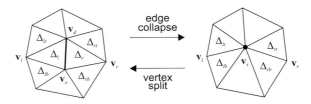

Figure 6.9. Edge collapse and vertex split operations.

1. For each edge of the model that can be collapsed,[2] compute a collapse priority; sort the edges in a priority queue.

2. While more candidate edges exist in the queue and the simplification target (for example, a maximum error or a number of faces for the base mesh) has not been reached

   (a) remove from the queue the edge collapse with highest priority;

   (b) collapse this edge (the mesh only changes locally around the edge);

   (c) re-compute the priorities of all edges affected by the collapse.

The two factors that affect the result of this method are

- the measure used to assess each edge collapse and assign its priority;

- the position of the new vertex for each edge collapse.

Significantly different techniques have been proposed for these two elements of the method, usually trading computational speed for quality of simplification. In some implementations, the position of the new vertex is fixed, for example, at one of the edge endpoints or at its middle. In many other implementations, the above two factors are interrelated: the position of the new vertex is computed as a result of an optimization procedure that seeks to minimize the approximation error (assessed using some suitable measure); the minimum error attained is used as the priority of the edge collapse.

As an example, we present the *quadric error-metric* method [Garl97, Garl98, Heck99] that minimizes the squared distance of the new vertex from the faces around the collapsed edge. If Δ is a triangular face of the model with plane equation

$$ax + by + cz + d = 0,$$

the squared distance of a point $\mathbf{x} = [x, y, z]^T$ from the plane of Δ is

$$Q_\Delta(\mathbf{x}) = \frac{(ax + by + cz + d)^2}{a^2 + b^2 + c^2} = \frac{(\overrightarrow{\mathbf{n}}^T \mathbf{x} + d)^2}{|\overrightarrow{\mathbf{n}}|^2} = (\hat{\mathbf{n}}^T \mathbf{x} + \hat{d})^2$$

$$= \mathbf{x}^T(\hat{\mathbf{n}}\hat{\mathbf{n}}^T)\mathbf{x} + 2\hat{d}\hat{\mathbf{n}}^T \mathbf{x} + \hat{d}^2,$$

---

[2]For instance, if the simplification algorithm must preserve the topology of the model, it will not collapse edges that would create or destroy holes on it.

where $\hat{\mathbf{n}} = \frac{\vec{\mathbf{n}}}{|\mathbf{n}|}$ is the unit normal vector of Δ and $\hat{d} = \frac{d}{|\vec{\mathbf{n}}|}$. Therefore, it can be represented by the quadratic form

$$Q_\Delta = (\mathbf{A}, \mathbf{b}, p) = (\hat{\mathbf{n}}\hat{\mathbf{n}}^\mathsf{T}, \hat{d}\hat{\mathbf{n}}, \hat{d}^2)$$

so that

$$Q_\Delta(\mathbf{x}) = \mathbf{x}^\mathsf{T}\mathbf{A}\mathbf{x} + 2\mathbf{b}^\mathsf{T}\mathbf{x} + p.$$

With this notation, the sum of the squared distances of $\mathbf{x}$ from two triangles Δ_1 and Δ_2 can be computed by summing coordinate-wise the corresponding quadratic forms $Q_{\Delta_1} = (\mathbf{A}_1, \mathbf{b}_1, p_1)$ and $Q_{\Delta_2} = (\mathbf{A}_2, \mathbf{b}_2, p_2)$:

$$\begin{aligned} Q_{\Delta_1}(\mathbf{x}) + Q_{\Delta_2}(\mathbf{x}) &= (Q_{\Delta_1} + Q_{\Delta_2})(\mathbf{x}) \\ &= \mathbf{x}^\mathsf{T}(\mathbf{A}_1 + \mathbf{A}_2)\mathbf{x} + 2(\mathbf{b}_1 + \mathbf{b}_2)^\mathsf{T}\mathbf{x} + (p_1 + p_2). \end{aligned}$$

We observe that this is a quadratic form similar to the ones of the Q_{Δ_i}; also this result generalizes naturally to any number of triangles. The simplification algorithm assigns initially, to each vertex $\mathbf{v}$ of the mesh, the quadratic form that expresses the sum of squared distances of a point from the faces around that vertex (each component of the sum may be weighted by the surface of the respective face, for better scaling):

$$Q_\mathbf{v} = \sum_{\Delta \text{ around } \mathbf{x}} w_\Delta Q_\Delta.$$

Then, when an edge $e(\mathbf{v}_o, \mathbf{v}_d)$ is collapsed, the total squared distance of the resulting vertex $\mathbf{v}_s$ from all the faces around $\mathbf{v}_o$ and $\mathbf{v}_d$ is:

$$Q(\mathbf{v}_s) = Q_{\mathbf{v}_o}(\mathbf{v}_s) + Q_{\mathbf{v}_d}(\mathbf{v}_s),$$

therefore represented by the quadratic form

$$Q = Q_{\mathbf{v}_o} + Q_{\mathbf{v}_d},$$

which is of the familiar form $Q = (\mathbf{A}, \mathbf{b}, p)$. The optimal position for $\mathbf{v}_s$ may be considered the one that minimizes Q. By differentiating Q, it can easily be shown that its minimum is attained at

$$\mathbf{v}_s = \mathbf{A}^{-1}\mathbf{b},$$

and the minimum is

$$Q(\mathbf{v}_s) = -\mathbf{b}^\mathsf{T}\mathbf{A}^{-1}\mathbf{b} + p = \mathbf{b}^\mathsf{T}\mathbf{v}_s + p.$$

If the matrix $\mathbf{A}$ is singular, then the minimization is restricted along the edge $e(\mathbf{v}_o, \mathbf{v}_d)$; if this fails as well, $\mathbf{v}_s$ is selected between $\mathbf{v}_o$ and $\mathbf{v}_d$ depending on which vertex gives the smaller value for Q.

Simplification based on iterative edge collapses has all the desirable properties of continuous level of detail methods. First, it is easily reversible to the coarse base model by performing *vertex splits* (Figure 6.9) in reverse order to the corresponding edge collapses, provided that the position of the original endpoints is kept with each edge collapse. The base mesh, together with the sequence of vertex splits that lead to the original model, is termed a *progressive mesh*. Second, by retaining some more information on the neighboring vertices and faces of each collapsed edge, it is possible to perform selective refinement and coarsening of the mesh on regions of interest [Xia96, Hopp97, DF97a, DF97b, DF98, Pupp98]. In addition, as already mentioned, various error metrics and vertex-positioning strategies may be employed, so the method can be adapted to various intents and available resources.

The simplification of large models is a rather lengthy operation, especially if an optimization procedure is used, and, therefore, it is typically performed offline; nonetheless, the generated levels of detail can be exploited interactively in real time for selectively refining the model. The infrastructure for supporting simplification based on edge collapse is becoming a standard feature in several graphics packages.

6.6 Exercises

1. Show that in the case of *triangular* models, the basic Euler formula (6.1) reduces to $F + 4 = 2V$ or $3V = 6 + E$.

2. Construct an algorithm to generate the list of edges of a model in an indexed list of faces representation. The algorithm must also report the following:

   - if the model is manifold or not;
   - its boundary edges, if it has any.

3. Construct an algorithm to compute the following adjacency information of a model in an indexed list of faces representation:

   - all edges around a given vertex;
   - all faces around a given vertex;
   - the neighboring faces across the edges of a given face.

4. Construct an algorithm to compute the winged-edge representation of a manifold model, given its indexed list of faces representation.

5. Given the winged-edge representation of a polygonal model, construct algorithms to enumerate

   - all vertices of a given face;
   - all edges of a given face;
   - all edges around a given vertex;
   - all faces around a given vertex.

6. Repeat Exercise 5 using the half-edge representation.

7. A simple simplification algorithm for triangular models is based on merging nearly coplanar neighboring faces and re-triangulating the resulting polygon using fewer triangles [Hink93, Kalv96]. Construct a program to implement this simplification method. Does this algorithm produce a continuous sequence of simplified meshes easily?

8. An edge collapse may alter the topology of a triangle mesh. Find a situation in which this occurs; see [Hopp93, Dey99, Cign00] for details.

9. Implement an algorithm to simplify a triangle mesh by iterative edge collapses. You may use the quadric error metric described or a simpler vertex-placement strategy and error approximation computation.

7

Parametric Curves and Surfaces

Equations are just the boring part of mathematics.
I attempt to see things in terms of geometry.
—Stephen Hawking

7.1 Introduction

In Chapter 2 we presented algorithms for the rasterization of basic geometric primitives, lines and circles. However, the composition of realistic graphics scenes calls for more flexible, free-form curves and surfaces. The area of computer graphics that deals with these shapes is *computer-aided geometric design* (CAGD). In this chapter we shall examine representations and properties of the most basic forms of such curves and surfaces; the reader should refer to [Fari01, Hosc96, Bart87] for more advanced topics.

The need for mathematical representations of free-form shapes, suitable for computer processing, became apparent during the 1960s in the automotive and aeronautic industries. Until that time, the specifications by the designers for the shape of cars and planes were implemented only approximately, as no exact descriptions of such shapes were in practical use. When computer-driven machinery that could produce complex-shaped objects was made available to these industries, it became essential to devise suitable mathematical descriptions. Paul de Casteljau and Pierre Bézier, then working at Citroën and Renault, respectively, developed independently the theory of polynomial curves and surfaces that now bears Bézier's name—de Casteljau's work was not published early on—and constitutes the basic tool for describing and rendering free-form shapes.

191

All of the curve and surface descriptions examined in the rest of this Chapter are in parametric form, and the reader is referred to Appendix B (especially Sections B.1.1 and B.2.1) for an overview of the relevant background theory. We remind here that a curve in parametric representation is given as two or three (if it is a plane or space curve, respectively) independent coordinate functions in terms of a parameter t:

$$\mathbf{X}(t) = \begin{bmatrix} x(t) \\ y(t) \end{bmatrix} \quad \text{or} \quad \mathbf{X}(t) = \begin{bmatrix} x(t) \\ y(t) \\ z(t) \end{bmatrix}.$$

Owing to the independence of the coordinate functions, the description of plane and space curves is essentially the same: $z(t)$ may be considered zero everywhere for a plane curve. Similarly, surfaces are given as three independent coordinate functions in terms of two parameters u and v:

$$\mathbf{X}(u,v) = \begin{bmatrix} x(u,v) \\ y(u,v) \\ z(u,v) \end{bmatrix}.$$

The basic geometric primitive utilized in the following is the line segment between two points $\mathbf{p}_0$ and $\mathbf{p}_1$, which in parametric form is

$$\mathbf{P}(t) = (1-t)\,\mathbf{p}_0 + t\,\mathbf{p}_1, \quad t \in [0,1], \tag{7.1}$$

and expresses the *linear interpolation* between these two points.

7.2 Bézier Curves

7.2.1 Quadratic Bézier Curves

Let us consider three points, $\mathbf{p}_0$, $\mathbf{p}_1$, and $\mathbf{p}_2$, and interpolate them in pairs, $(\mathbf{p}_0,\mathbf{p}_1)$ and $(\mathbf{p}_1,\mathbf{p}_2)$, as follows:

$$\begin{aligned} \mathbf{p}_0^1(t) &= (1-t)\,\mathbf{p}_0 + t\,\mathbf{p}_1, \\ \mathbf{p}_1^1(t) &= (1-t)\,\mathbf{p}_1 + t\,\mathbf{p}_2, \end{aligned} \quad t \in [0,1].$$

For each value of t between 0 and 1, $\mathbf{p}_0^1(t)$ and $\mathbf{p}_1^1(t)$ represent points on the respective line segments. In a second step, we interpolate these points for the same value of t as follows:

$$\begin{aligned} \mathbf{p}_0^2(t) &= (1-t)\,\mathbf{p}_0^1(t) + t\,\mathbf{p}_1^1(t) \\ &= (1-t)^2\,\mathbf{p}_0 + 2t(1-t)\,\mathbf{p}_1 + t^2\,\mathbf{p}_2. \end{aligned} \tag{7.2}$$

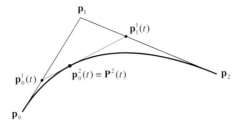

Figure 7.1. Generation of a quadratic Bézier curve.

In $\mathbf{p}_i^r(t)$, the superscript r refers to the interpolation step and the subscript i refers to the index of the first point being interpolated. Notice that as t increases from 0 to 1, the three points $\mathbf{p}_0^1(t)$, $\mathbf{p}_1^1(t)$, and $\mathbf{p}_0^2(t)$ move concurrently on the respective line segments (see Figure 7.1). Equation (7.2) shows that the point $\mathbf{p}_0^2(t)$ traces a quadratic (second-degree) curve with respect to the parameter t; this curve is a *quadratic Bézier curve* (or a *second-degree Bézier curve*), and it will be denoted by $\mathbf{P}^2(t)$. The initial points $\mathbf{p}_0$, $\mathbf{p}_1$, and $\mathbf{p}_2$ are called *control points* of the Bézier curve.

7.2.2 *n*th-Degree Bézier Curves

The process outlined above for the generation of a quadratic Bézier curve from its three control points can be generalized for more control points in a straightforward manner. Figure 7.2 presents the curve generated by four control points: in this case we perform three linear-interpolation steps, and the outcome is a *cubic Bézier curve* (or a *third-degree Bézier curve*) $\mathbf{P}^3(t)$.

In the general case, an *n*th-*degree Bézier curve* $\mathbf{P}^n(t)$ may be constructed given $(n+1)$ *control points* $\mathbf{p}_0, \mathbf{p}_1, \ldots, \mathbf{p}_n$ after n linear interpolation steps. The curve is given by the formula[1]

$$\mathbf{P}^n(t) = \sum_{i=0}^{n} \binom{n}{i} t^i (1-t)^{n-i} \mathbf{p}_i, \quad t \in [0,1]. \tag{7.3}$$

---

[1] The *binomial coefficients* $\binom{n}{i}$ are defined as

$$\binom{n}{i} = \frac{n!}{i!\,(n-i)!}$$

if $0 \le i \le n$ and 0 otherwise.

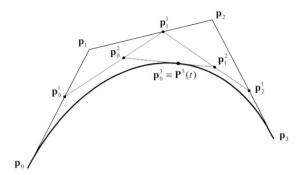

Figure 7.2. Generation of a cubic Bézier curve. For a specific value of t, all intermediate points used for the interpolation steps are denoted.

It is easy to see that this formula gives exactly Equation (7.2) for $n = 2$. The polygon formed by $\mathbf{p}_0, \mathbf{p}_1, \ldots, \mathbf{p}_n$ is called the *control polygon* of the curve.

7.2.3   The de Casteljau Algorithm

Equation (7.3) provides a direct way to compute points on a Bézier curve. Unfortunately, this formula is numerically rather complex and inefficient, requiring computations of binomial coefficients and of powers of t and $(1-t)$. On the contrary, the interpolation steps performed for the generation of the Bézier curve are simple linear relations of t.

The *de Casteljau algorithm* summarizes these linear interpolation steps in a convenient iterative scheme for the computation of Bézier curve points:

1. For the required value of t, set

$$\mathbf{p}_i^0(t) = \mathbf{p}_i, \quad i = 0, 1, \ldots, n. \tag{7.4a}$$

2. Perform the linear interpolation steps

$$\mathbf{p}_i^r(t) = (1-t)\,\mathbf{p}_i^{r-1}(t) + t\,\mathbf{p}_{i+1}^{r-1}(t), \quad \begin{matrix} r = 1, 2, \ldots, n, \\ i = 0, 1, \ldots, n-r. \end{matrix} \tag{7.4b}$$

3. Then the point on the curve corresponding to parametric value t is

$$\mathbf{P}^n(t) = \mathbf{p}_0^n(t).$$

All the intermediate points involved in the de Casteljau algorithm can be written in a triangular arrangement called the *de Casteljau triangle*. For the case of a cubic Bézier curve, the triangle is (omitting the parameter t from $\mathbf{p}_i^r(t)$ for simplicity)

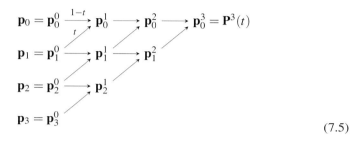

$$(7.5)$$

When implementing this algorithm in a computer program, the above arrangement indicates that we need not store all intermediate points. We may use a one-dimensional array, initialized with the control points of the curve, and overwrite its elements from top to bottom as the algorithm progresses; at the end, the first element of the array will be the point on the curve. The pseudocode in Listing 7.1 provides an implementation of the de Casteljau algorithm.

```
point bezierPoint ( int n, point[] controlPt, float t )
{
    point deCasPt[n+1];

    for (i=0; i <= n; i++)
        deCasPt[i] = controlPt[i];

    for (r=1; r <= n; r++)  {
        for (i=0; i <= n-r; i++)  {
            deCasPt[i] = (1-t)*deCasPt[i] + t*deCasPt[i+1];
        }
    }

    return deCasPt[0];
}
```

Listing 7.1: The de Casteljau algorithm.

Example 7.1 (Bézier Curve Point Evaluation.) Given a Bézier curve with control points

$$\mathbf{p}_0 = \begin{bmatrix} 0 & 0 \end{bmatrix}^{\mathrm{T}}, \quad \mathbf{p}_1 = \begin{bmatrix} 2 & 2 \end{bmatrix}^{\mathrm{T}}, \quad \mathbf{p}_2 = \begin{bmatrix} 6 & 4 \end{bmatrix}^{\mathrm{T}}, \text{ and } \quad \mathbf{p}_3 = \begin{bmatrix} 8 & 2 \end{bmatrix}^{\mathrm{T}},$$

compute the point corresponding to the parametric value $t = 1/4$.

The required point is computed by the following de Casteljau triangle:

$$\begin{bmatrix} 0 \\ 0 \end{bmatrix} \quad \begin{bmatrix} \frac{1}{2} \\ \frac{1}{2} \end{bmatrix} \quad \begin{bmatrix} \frac{9}{8} \\ 1 \end{bmatrix} \quad \begin{bmatrix} \frac{29}{16} \\ \frac{23}{16} \end{bmatrix}$$

$$\begin{bmatrix} 2 \\ 2 \end{bmatrix} \quad \begin{bmatrix} 3 \\ \frac{5}{2} \end{bmatrix} \quad \begin{bmatrix} \frac{31}{8} \\ \frac{11}{4} \end{bmatrix}$$

$$\begin{bmatrix} 6 \\ 4 \end{bmatrix} \quad \begin{bmatrix} \frac{13}{2} \\ \frac{7}{2} \end{bmatrix}$$

$$\begin{bmatrix} 8 \\ 2 \end{bmatrix}$$

Each point is an affine combination of the two points from the column at its left, on the same and on the next line of the triangle, with coefficients $\frac{3}{4}$ and $\frac{1}{4}$, respectively. The required point is

$$\mathbf{P}^3\left(\tfrac{1}{4}\right) = \begin{bmatrix} \frac{29}{16} \\ \frac{23}{16} \end{bmatrix}.$$

7.2.4   Bernstein Polynomials

The coefficients of $\mathbf{p}_i$ in the Bézier curve definition (7.3) are special polynomials called *nth-degree Bernstein polynomials*. They are

$$B_i^n(t) = \binom{n}{i} t^i (1-t)^{n-i}, \quad i = 0, 1, 2, \ldots, n. \tag{7.6}$$

Using the Bernstein polynomials, the Bézier curve can be rewritten as

$$\mathbf{P}^n(t) = \sum_{i=0}^{n} B_i^n(t) \mathbf{p}_i, \quad t \in [0, 1]. \tag{7.7}$$

For the most common cases of $n = 2$ and $n = 3$, the Bernstein polynomials are, respectively,

$$
\begin{aligned}
B_0^2(t) &= (1-t)^2, \\
B_1^2(t) &= 2t(1-t), \\
B_2^2(t) &= t^2,
\end{aligned}
\tag{7.8}
$$

(remember relation (7.2)), and

$$
\begin{aligned}
B_0^3(t) &= (1-t)^3, \\
B_1^3(t) &= 3t(1-t)^2, \\
B_2^3(t) &= 3t^2(1-t), \\
B_3^3(t) &= t^3.
\end{aligned}
\tag{7.9}
$$

Bernstein polynomials possess interesting properties that will help us in the analysis of Bézier curves. The most important of these properties are the following:

- The nth-degree Bernstein polynomials constitute a basis of the vector space of nth-degree polynomials. In other words, any nth-degree polynomial $f(t)$ may be written in the form

$$
f(t) = \sum_{i=0}^{n} B_i^n(t) c_i,
\tag{7.10}
$$

where $c_i, i = 0, 1, 2, \ldots, n$ are suitable (scalar) coefficients.

- Bernstein polynomials satisfy

$$
\sum_{i=0}^{n} B_i^n(t) = 1, \quad \text{for every } t
\tag{7.11}
$$

and

$$
0 \leq B_i^n(t) \leq 1, \quad \text{for } t \in [0,1].
\tag{7.12}
$$

- Bernstein polynomials are symmetric with respect to t and $1 - t$:

$$
B_j^n(t) = B_{n-j}^n(1-t).
\tag{7.13}
$$

7.2.5 Properties of Bézier Curves

The definition given in Equation (7.3) of the Bézier curve and the properties of Bernstein polynomials reveal important properties of Bézier curves.

- *Every nth-degree polynomial curve may be written in the form of a Bézier curve.* This follows from the fact that each of the x, y (and possibly z) components of a polynomial curve is itself an nth-degree polynomial, and therefore it may be written in terms of the Bernstein basis as mentioned above; the Bézier control points of the curve are formed by assembling the coefficients of each Bernstein polynomial.

- *Convex-hull property.* The Bézier curve always lies inside the convex hull of its control points. This is due to properties (7.11) and (7.12) of the Bernstein polynomials, which imply that the Bézier curve is a convex combination of its control points.

- *Invariance under affine transformations.* This stems from property (7.11) of the Bernstein polynomials, which signifies that the Bézier curve is an affine combination of its control points. As a practical consequence, in order to apply an affine transformation to a Bézier curve, it is sufficient to transform its control points.

- *Invariance under affine transformations of its parameter.* The curve remains unaltered if the parametric interval is changed from $t \in [0,1]$ to $u \in [a,b]$; in other words, if an affine transformation of the parameter t to $u = a + (b-a)t$ is performed. In this case the interpolation steps (7.4b) become

$$\mathbf{p}_i^r(t) = \frac{b-u}{b-a}\mathbf{p}_i^{r-1}(t) + \frac{u-a}{b-a}\mathbf{p}_{i+1}^{r-1}(t). \qquad (7.14)$$

- *Symmetry with respect to its control points.* If the control points of the curve are used in reverse order, $\mathbf{p}_n$, $\mathbf{p}_{n-1}, \ldots, \mathbf{p}_0$, the shape of the curve does not change, but the curve is traversed in the opposite direction. This results from the symmetry of Bernstein polynomials, relation (7.13).

- *Linear precision.* If all control points lie on a straight line, then the curve also has the shape of a straight line, since its convex hull becomes a line.

- *Variation-diminishing property.* A planar Bézier curve is intersected by an arbitrary straight line no more than the number of times that the line intersects the control polygon of the curve. Similarly, a non-planar Bézier curve is intersected by an arbitrary line or plane no more than the number of times that the line or plane intersects its control polygon. As a consequence of the variation-diminishing property, a curve with a convex control polygon is convex as well—but note that the inverse is not true: a convex Bézier curve may have a non-convex control polygon.

- *Endpoint interpolation.* It is easy to verify that

$$
\begin{aligned}
\mathbf{P}^n(0) &= \mathbf{p}_0, \\
\mathbf{P}^n(1) &= \mathbf{p}_n;
\end{aligned}
\tag{7.15}
$$

therefore, the curve starts at its first control point and ends at its last one.

- *Derivative.* Using properties of the binomial coefficients, it can be shown that the tangent (first derivative) of a Bézier curve is

$$
\frac{d}{dt}\mathbf{P}^n(t) = n\sum_{i=0}^{n-1} B_i^{n-1}(t)\,(\mathbf{p}_{i+1} - \mathbf{p}_i).
\tag{7.16}
$$

- *Tangents at the endpoints.* The above relation is considerably simplified at the end points. It can be shown that

$$
\begin{aligned}
\frac{d}{dt}\mathbf{P}^n(0) &= n(\mathbf{p}_1 - \mathbf{p}_0), \\
\frac{d}{dt}\mathbf{P}^n(1) &= n(\mathbf{p}_n - \mathbf{p}_{n-1});
\end{aligned}
\tag{7.17}
$$

therefore, the tangent vectors at the endpoints of the curve are parallel to the first and last edge of its control polygon.

If the curve is defined over an arbitrary parametric interval $u \in [a,b]$, the chain rule yields, for the above relations,

$$
\begin{aligned}
\frac{d}{du}\mathbf{P}^n(a) &= \frac{d}{dt}\frac{dt}{du}\mathbf{P}^n(0) = \frac{1}{b-a}n(\mathbf{p}_1 - \mathbf{p}_0), \\
\frac{d}{du}\mathbf{P}^n(b) &= \frac{d}{dt}\frac{dt}{du}\mathbf{P}^n(1) = \frac{1}{b-a}n(\mathbf{p}_n - \mathbf{p}_{n-1}).
\end{aligned}
\tag{7.18}
$$

- *Second derivatives at the endpoints.* It can be shown that the following relations hold for the second derivatives at the endpoints of an nth-degree Bézier curve:

$$
\begin{aligned}
\frac{d^2}{dt^2}\mathbf{P}^n(0) &= n(n-1)(\mathbf{p}_2 - 2\mathbf{p}_1 + \mathbf{p}_0), \\
\frac{d^2}{dt^2}\mathbf{P}^n(1) &= n(n-1)(\mathbf{p}_n - 2\mathbf{p}_{n-1} + \mathbf{p}_{n-2}).
\end{aligned}
\tag{7.19}
$$

If the curve is defined over an arbitrary parametric interval $u \in [a, b]$, the chain rule yields, for the above relations,

$$
\begin{aligned}
\frac{d^2}{du^2} \mathbf{P}^n(a) &= \frac{1}{(b-a)^2} n(n-1)(\mathbf{p}_2 - 2\mathbf{p}_1 + \mathbf{p}_0), \\
\frac{d^2}{du^2} \mathbf{P}^n(b) &= \frac{1}{(b-a)^2} n(n-1)(\mathbf{p}_n - 2\mathbf{p}_{n-1} + \mathbf{p}_{n-2}).
\end{aligned}
\tag{7.20}
$$

- *Pseudo-local control.* Local control implies that moving a control point of a curve has a localized effect on the curve. Bézier curves *do not* possess local control since the Bernstein polynomials $B_i^n(t)$, which are essentially the weights by which the control points contribute to the shape of the curve, are non-zero over the whole parametric interval $[0, 1]$ of the curve; therefore, moving any control point affects the shape of the whole curve. However, we may say that Bézier curves possess pseudo-local control, since the effect of moving $\mathbf{p}_i$ is more pronounced around the parametric value i/n, where the respective Bernstein polynomial $B_i^n(t)$ has its only maximum. Pseudo-local control makes it easier to predict the change of shape of a Bézier curve when moving its control points.

As a result of the above properties, Bézier curves are an important tool for representing curves in computer graphics and geometric design. Cubic Bézier curves are mostly used in practice, since they provide enough shape flexibility, intuitive dependence on their control points, and efficiency for their calculation. Higher-degree curves can produce more complex shapes involving more control points, but the higher cost for their computation and the global effect of changing any control point make them less attractive in practice. In the following sections, we will discuss practical solutions to the problem of defining a curve using more control points.

7.2.6 Bézier Curve Subdivision

Consider the cubic Bézier curve $\mathbf{P}^3(t)$ shown in Figure 7.2. Any specific parametric value $t_0 \in [0, 1]$ divides the curve into two segments, the "left" one with endpoints $\mathbf{P}^3(0) = \mathbf{p}_0$ and $\mathbf{P}^3(t_0)$, and the "right" one with endpoints $\mathbf{P}^3(t_0)$ and $\mathbf{P}^3(1) = \mathbf{p}_3$. Being parts of the initial cubic Bézier curve, these segments are both also cubic curves and, therefore, they may be written in Bézier curve form. Our aim is to determine the Bézier control points of these two segments; as we show below they can be computed using only the control points of the initial curve.

We will work first on the left segment. We denote it by $\mathbf{L}$ and call its control points $\mathbf{l}_i$, $i = 0, 1, 2, 3$, so that

$$\mathbf{L}(t') = \sum_{i=0}^{3} B_i^3(t') \mathbf{l}_i, \quad t' \in [0, 1].$$

(We use a *local* parameter t' for $\mathbf{L}$, different from the parameter t of the original curve, so that $\mathbf{L}(t')$ traces the whole left segment when $t' \in [0, 1]$.)

The first and the last control point can be determined immediately, since the curve interpolates its endpoints, so

$$\mathbf{l}_0 = \mathbf{p}_0 = \mathbf{P}^3(0) = \mathbf{p}_0^0(t_0), \tag{7.21a}$$

$$\mathbf{l}_3 = \mathbf{P}^3(t_0) = \mathbf{p}_0^3(t_0). \tag{7.21b}$$

For $\mathbf{l}_1$, we observe that it is involved in the tangent of $\mathbf{L}(t')$ for $t' = 0$. $\mathbf{P}$ and $\mathbf{L}$ have the same tangent at this point, since they coincide when $t \in [0, t_0]$, therefore

$$\frac{d}{dt} \mathbf{P}^3(0) = \frac{d}{dt} \mathbf{L}(0) = \frac{d}{dt'} \frac{dt'}{dt} \mathbf{L}(0)$$

$$\Leftrightarrow \quad 3(\mathbf{p}_1 - \mathbf{p}_0) = \frac{1}{t_0} 3(\mathbf{l}_1 - \mathbf{l}_0)$$

$$\Leftrightarrow \quad \mathbf{l}_1 = (1 - t_0)\mathbf{p}_0 + t_0 \mathbf{p}_1,$$

and using the notation of the de Casteljau algorithm,

$$\mathbf{l}_1 = \mathbf{p}_0^1(t_0). \tag{7.21c}$$

Similarly, we observe that $\mathbf{l}_2$ is involved in the second derivative of $\mathbf{L}(t')$ for $t' = 0$, and therefore

$$6(\mathbf{p}_2 - 2\mathbf{p}_1 + \mathbf{p}_0) = \frac{1}{t_0^2} 6(\mathbf{l}_2 - 2\mathbf{l}_1 + \mathbf{l}_0)$$

$$\Leftrightarrow \quad \mathbf{l}_2 = (1 - t_0)^2 \mathbf{p}_0 + 2t_0(1 - t_0)\mathbf{p}_1 + t_0^2 \mathbf{p}_2,$$

and using the notation of the de Casteljau algorithm,

$$\mathbf{l}_2 = \mathbf{p}_0^2(t_0). \tag{7.21d}$$

Relations (7.21) can be written concisely as

$$\mathbf{l}_i = \mathbf{p}_0^i(t_0); \tag{7.22}$$

therefore, the control points $\mathbf{l}_i$ of the left segment are exactly the points of the first line of the de Casteljau triangle (7.5). It is important that this property holds for Bézier curves of any degree n, as can be proved by computing higher-degree derivatives of the curve.

The right segment of the curve is the part that corresponds to the parametric interval $[t_0, 1]$ of the initial curve. Its control points $\mathbf{r}_i$ can be computed by working in a similar manner with the tangents at the other end of the curve. They are given by

$$\mathbf{r}_i = \mathbf{p}_i^{n-i}(t_0), \tag{7.23}$$

which are the points of the "hypotenuse" of the de Casteljau triangle (see (7.5) for the cubic case); this result holds as well for Bézier curves of any degree.

It is interesting, thus, that the de Casteljau algorithm not only computes the point on the curve that corresponds to a parametric value t_0, but also provides the control points of the two segments into which the curve is subdivided by this point. The implementation given in Section 7.2.3 readily provides the points $\mathbf{r}_i$ (they are the deCasPt available at the end of the algorithm), and it must be modified slightly in order to provide points $\mathbf{l}_i$ as well: after each column of the triangle is completed, its 0-index element is a control point of the left segment.

Applications of Bézier curve subdivision. The subdivision of a Bézier curve that we just described can be repeated recursively for each of the two segments of the curve. It can be shown that the control points generated during this recursion converge to the initial curve, and that this convergence is rather fast. This result has interesting practical applications.

The most important application is a way to draw Bézier curves. By recursively subdividing the curve into two segments, after a number of steps the control points of the segments will be nearly collinear, up to a tolerance level set in advance; then, the subdivision may be stopped and each segment may be drawn as a line segment between its two endpoints, owing to the linear precision of Bézier curves. This manner of drawing Bézier curves is clearly *adaptive*, since it will draw its flat regions quickly but perform more recursion steps in sections of the curve with high curvature.

During the recursion, subdivision of the curve may be performed at any parametric value t_0. However, the value $t_0 = \frac{1}{2}$ is preferred, since in this case the interpolation steps involve only divisions by 2, which can be implemented efficiently as bit shifts.

Collinearity of the control points can be tested by constructing the line through the two extreme control points $\mathbf{p}_0$ and $\mathbf{p}_n$, computing the distance of every other control point $\mathbf{p}_i$, $i = 1, 2, \ldots, n - 1$, from this line, and ensuring that every such distance is less than the required tolerance. The distance of a control point $\mathbf{p}_i$ from the line through $\mathbf{p}_0$ and $\mathbf{p}_n$ is given by the formula

$$d = \frac{|(\mathbf{p}_n - \mathbf{p}_0) \times (\mathbf{p}_n - \mathbf{p}_i)|}{|\mathbf{p}_n - \mathbf{p}_0|}.$$

If the control points are two-dimensional, the cross product in the numerator of this formula can be computed by constructing three-dimensional points with zero z-coordinate. If the denominator is equal to zero, $\mathbf{p}_0$ and $\mathbf{p}_n$ coincide, and one of them should be changed in the above formula.

A second application of Bézier curve subdivision concerns finding the intersection of the curve with a line. The algorithm is also recursive. First the axis-aligned bounding box (AABB) of the initial curve is constructed and checked for intersection with the line; if an intersection does exist, the curve is subdivided into its left and right segment, and this process continues recursively with the AABB of each segment. The subdivision stops when the AABB of a segment is so small as to be considered a single point, up to a given tolerance level.

The algorithm works correctly since the AABB contains the curve; therefore, if the line does not intersect the AABB, it will not intersect the curve either. When the AABB becomes a point, the curve segment contained therein will also be a single point. Thus, if the line intersects the box it will intersect the curve as well. The AABB is very efficient both to compute (in fact, it is the AABB box of the control points of the curve, since the curve is contained in the convex hull of its control points) and to check for intersection with the line (using one of the algorithms of Section 2.9).

7.2.7 Smoothly Joining Bézier Curves

The complexity of the shape of a single Bézier curve is restricted by its degree, or equivalently by the number of its control points. In many practical applications, there is a need to draw complex shapes and in these cases Bézier curves of high degree are needed. Unfortunately, the use of high-degree Bézier curves is not advisable for two reasons: first, the higher the degree of the curve, the less efficient it is to compute it as more linear interpolation steps are involved and numerical accuracy problems may appear; and second, the lack of local control makes it difficult to create a desirable shape with a single Bézier curve. For these reasons, Bézier curves of degree higher than 5 are not used in practice very often.

The problem of representing complex shapes is solved by using low-degree curves joined in such a way that the resulting shape is smooth at the joins. The most common form of such curves is the B-spline curve, which we will present in the next section. Here we will discuss the core procedure for joining two Bézier curves smoothly, in order to gain insight about its properties and limitations.

Before we continue, we need to formalize the meaning of "smooth joins." Consider two polynomial curves $\mathbf{F}(t)$, $t \in [t_0, t_1]$ and $\mathbf{G}(t)$, $t \in [t_1, t_2]$. We say that these curves join with *parametric continuity* C^r at t_1 if their rth-order derivatives are equal at t_1:

$$\mathbf{F}^{(r)}(t_1) = \mathbf{G}^{(r)}(t_1).$$

It can be proven that C^r continuity at a point implies also C^m continuity for all $0 \le m < r$. For instance, if $\mathbf{F}(t)$ and $\mathbf{G}(t)$ join at t_1 with C^2 continuity, then their values (C^0), their tangents (C^1), and their second derivatives (C^2) are equal at this point; this join is naturally "smooth," since the slope of the curve at the join does not change abruptly. For polynomial curves of degree k, it is meaningful to look for continuity up to C^{k-1}, since their kth-order derivatives are constant and higher-order ones are zero.

Consider now two Bézier curves, $\mathbf{P}^n(t)$, $t \in [0, 1]$ of degree n with control points $\mathbf{p}_0$, $\mathbf{p}_1, \ldots \mathbf{p}_n$ and $\mathbf{Q}^m(t)$, $t \in [1, 2]$ of degree m with control points $\mathbf{q}_0$, $\mathbf{q}_1, \ldots \mathbf{q}_m$. We seek conditions for the two curves to join at $t = 1$ with C^2 continuity.

C^0 continuity implies that the last point of the first curve coincides with the initial point of the second one. Since the curves interpolate their endpoints, it is sufficient to have

$$\mathbf{p}_n = \mathbf{q}_0. \tag{7.24}$$

Similarly, C^1 continuity requires, because of (7.17) and (7.18), that

$$n(\mathbf{p}_n - \mathbf{p}_{n-1}) = m(\mathbf{q}_1 - \mathbf{q}_0) \quad \Leftrightarrow \quad \mathbf{q}_1 - \mathbf{p}_n = \frac{n}{m}(\mathbf{p}_n - \mathbf{p}_{n-1}); \tag{7.25}$$

therefore, $\mathbf{q}_1$ must be placed on the line defined by $\mathbf{p}_{n-1}$ and $\mathbf{p}_n = \mathbf{q}_0$, and its distance from $\mathbf{p}_n$ must be the one given by (7.25).

Because of (7.19) and (7.20), C^2 continuity requires that

$$n(n-1)(\mathbf{p}_n - 2\mathbf{p}_{n-1} + \mathbf{p}_{n-2}) = m(m-1)(\mathbf{q}_2 - 2\mathbf{q}_1 + \mathbf{q}_0) \tag{7.26}$$

from which the position of $\mathbf{q}_2$ can be determined.

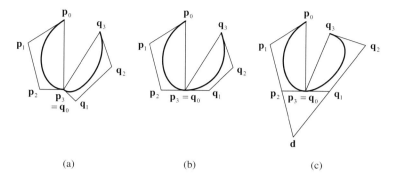

Figure 7.3. Smooth join of cubic Bézier curves. (a) C^0 continuity; (b) C^1 continuity; (c) C^2 continuity.

In the special case where $n = m$, relation (7.25) becomes $\mathbf{q}_1 - \mathbf{p}_n = \mathbf{p}_n - \mathbf{p}_{n-1}$, so the distance $|\mathbf{q}_1\mathbf{p}_n|$ must be equal to the distance $|\mathbf{p}_n\mathbf{p}_{n-1}|$. Additionally, if $n = m = 3$, relation (7.26) becomes $\mathbf{q}_2 - 2\mathbf{q}_1 = \mathbf{p}_1 - 2\mathbf{p}_2$; if we set this point $\mathbf{d} = \mathbf{q}_2 - 2\mathbf{q}_1 = \mathbf{p}_1 - 2\mathbf{p}_2$, then $\mathbf{d}$ must be placed so that $|\mathbf{dp}_2| = |\mathbf{p}_2\mathbf{p}_1|$, and finally $\mathbf{q}_2$ must be placed so that $|\mathbf{dq}_1| = |\mathbf{q}_1\mathbf{q}_2|$ (see Figure 7.3).

From the above, we observe that each additional degree of continuity restricts the position of one more control point of each curve; for $n = m = 3$ with C^2 continuity, which is a fairly usual and practical requirement, only the position of the two extreme endpoints $\mathbf{p}_0$ and $\mathbf{q}_3$ is free.

For greater flexibility, higher-degree curves can be used, which as already mentioned is not very efficient, or alternatively lower continuity could be required, which would probably not produce a satisfactorily smooth curve. There is another alternative, which is to modify the *kind* of continuity required: instead of parametric continuity (C^r), we could require the weaker *geometric continuity* (G^r), which, as its name implies, is based on geometric elements of the curves instead of algebraic ones. We just mention here that G^0 is the same as C^0; G^1 requires that the tangent vector at the join be continuous (only the direction of the tangents should be equal and not their norm as in C^1), and G^2 requires additionally that the curvature be continuous at the join. For details and applications of geometric continuity, the reader should refer to the specialized books mentioned in the beginning of this chapter.

7.3   B-Spline Curves

In the last section, we saw how Bézier curves can be joined together so that the resulting curve is smooth (continuous) at the join. Such curves that are generated by joining parametric curves with continuity constraints are called, in general, *spline curves*. Their name comes from the mechanical spline, a flexible wooden, metal or plastic strip used to draw smooth curves for engineering applications, such as shipbuilding or carmaking; the desired bendings of the strip are created by appropriate pegs (or ducks or weights) that hold it in place.

B-spline curves are specifically spline curves comprised of polynomial segments of degree k joined with C^{k-1} continuity, the highest continuity that we may seek. The degree k of the segments is also the *degree* of the B-spline curve.

Similar to Bézier curves, B-spline curves are defined with the help of *control points*, which we will denote by $\mathbf{p}_0, \mathbf{p}_1, \ldots, \mathbf{p}_n$. Unlike Bézier curves, though, the number $(n+1)$ of control points is independent of the curve degree and only related to the number of polynomial segments that constitute it.

The polynomial segments that form a B-spline curve are defined over consecutive parametric intervals $[t_i, t_{i+1}]$, whose union is an interval $[t_{min}, t_{max}]$ called the *domain* of the curve. The values t_i at the boundaries of the intervals are called *knots* of the B-spline curve. As we shall see, the definition of the B-spline curve requires some additional knots outside its domain; in total, a B-spline curve has a knot sequence

$$t_{first} \leq \ldots \leq t_{min} \leq \ldots \leq t_{max} \leq \ldots \leq t_{last}.$$

The number of knots depends on the degree of the curve and on the number of its control points; we will determine it precisely in the following.

7.3.1   Quadratic B-Spline Curves

We will start by examining quadratic (or second-degree) B-spline curves, in order to facilitate the presentation of general kth-degree B-spline curves.

A quadratic B-spline curve $\mathbf{Q}(t)$ will be comprised of quadratic segments $\mathbf{Q}_i(t)$, defined in parametric intervals $[t_i, t_{i+1}]$. Similar to quadratic Bézier curves, we will use three control points for each segment—but the two linear interpolation steps required will be different, in order to ensure continuity at the joins. For segment $\mathbf{Q}_i(t)$, we will use control points $\mathbf{p}_{i-2}, \mathbf{p}_{i-1}$, and $\mathbf{p}_i$.

In the first step, we interpolate separately $(\mathbf{p}_{i-2}, \mathbf{p}_{i-1})$ and $(\mathbf{p}_{i-1}, \mathbf{p}_i)$ in the parametric intervals $[t_{i-1}, t_{i+1}]$ and $[t_i, t_{i+2}]$, respectively; notice that we do not use $[t_i, t_{i+1}]$ for both as in Bézier curves, but different overlapping intervals for each pair of control points. Thus we get the intermediate points

$$\mathbf{q}_{i-1}^1(t) = \frac{t_{i+1}-t}{t_{i+1}-t_{i-1}}\mathbf{p}_{i-2} + \frac{t-t_{i-1}}{t_{i+1}-t_{i-1}}\mathbf{p}_{i-1}, \qquad t \in [t_{i-1}, t_{i+1}]$$

$$\mathbf{q}_i^1(t) = \frac{t_{i+2}-t}{t_{i+2}-t_i}\mathbf{p}_{i-1} + \frac{t-t_i}{t_{i+2}-t_i}\mathbf{p}_i, \qquad t \in [t_i, t_{i+2}].$$

In the parametric interval of interest $[t_i, t_{i+1}]$, both $\mathbf{q}_{i-1}^1(t)$ and $\mathbf{q}_i^1(t)$ are defined, and for the second step we interpolate them in this interval. Thus, we get

$$\mathbf{Q}_i(t) = \mathbf{q}_i^2(t) = \frac{t_{i+1}-t}{t_{i+1}-t_i}\mathbf{q}_{i-1}^1(t) + \frac{t-t_i}{t_{i+1}-t_i}\mathbf{q}_i^1(t), \quad t \in [t_i, t_{i+1}],$$

and substituting $\mathbf{q}_{i-1}^1(t)$ and $\mathbf{q}_i^1(t)$ from the previous relations, we get an expression for $\mathbf{Q}_i(t)$ in terms of the control points of the curve:

$$\begin{aligned}\mathbf{Q}_i(t) = &\frac{t_{i+1}-t}{t_{i+1}-t_i}\frac{t_{i+1}-t}{t_{i+1}-t_{i-1}}\mathbf{p}_{i-2} \\ &+ \left(\frac{t_{i+1}-t}{t_{i+1}-t_i}\frac{t-t_{i-1}}{t_{i+1}-t_{i-1}} + \frac{t-t_i}{t_{i+1}-t_i}\frac{t_{i+2}-t}{t_{i+2}-t_i}\right)\mathbf{p}_{i-1} \\ &+ \frac{t-t_i}{t_{i+1}-t_i}\frac{t-t_i}{t_{i+2}-t_i}\mathbf{p}_i.\end{aligned} \qquad (7.27)$$

Therefore, the segment $\mathbf{Q}_i(t)$ defined in this way is quadratic with respect to t over the parametric interval $[t_i, t_{i+1}]$. Using (7.27) it can also be shown that consecutive segments $\mathbf{Q}_i(t)$, $t \in [t_i, t_{i+1}]$ and $\mathbf{Q}_{i+1}(t)$, $t \in [t_{i+1}, t_{i+2}]$ join with the desired C^1 continuity: at the common parametric value t_{i+1} they satisfy

$$\mathbf{Q}_i(t_{i+1}) = \mathbf{Q}_{i+1}(t_{i+1}),$$
$$\mathbf{Q}_i'(t_{i+1}) = \mathbf{Q}_{i+1}'(t_{i+1}).$$

In other words, they join at t_{i+1} (C^0) and their tangents coincide (C^1). Overall, the set of quadratic segments generated as described above forms a quadratic B-spline curve.

Formula (7.27) provides a piecewise expression for the B-spline curve that is not very useful for studying the curve; what we need is a uniform expression for the whole curve in terms of its control points and its knots. To derive it, we consider a single control point $\mathbf{p}_i$; from the preceding analysis, we conclude that

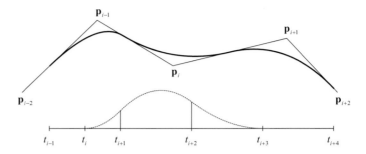

Figure 7.4. A quadratic B-spline curve and the effect of control point $\mathbf{p}_i$ on the curve.

it affects three consecutive segments of the curve, $\mathbf{Q}_i(t)$, $\mathbf{Q}_{i+1}(t)$, and $\mathbf{Q}_{i+2}(t)$ (see Figure 7.4). We rewrite (7.27) for these segments, giving in full only the coefficients of $\mathbf{p}_i$ and abbreviating the others for the sake of simplicity:

$$\mathbf{Q}_i(t) = a_i\,\mathbf{p}_{i-2} + b_i\,\mathbf{p}_{i-1} + \frac{t-t_i}{t_{i+1}-t_i}\,\frac{t-t_i}{t_{i+2}-t_i}\,\mathbf{p}_i,$$

$$t \in [t_i, t_{i+1}],$$

$$\mathbf{Q}_{i+1}(t) = a_{i+1}\,\mathbf{p}_{i-1}$$
$$+ \left(\frac{t_{i+2}-t}{t_{i+2}-t_{i+1}}\,\frac{t-t_i}{t_{i+2}-t_i} + \frac{t-t_{i+1}}{t_{i+2}-t_{i+1}}\,\frac{t_{i+3}-t}{t_{i+3}-t_{i+1}}\right)\mathbf{p}_i + c_{i+1}\,\mathbf{p}_{i+1},$$

$$t \in [t_{i+1}, t_{i+2}],$$

$$\mathbf{Q}_{i+2}(t) = \frac{t_{i+3}-t}{t_{i+3}-t_{i+2}}\,\frac{t_{i+3}-t}{t_{i+3}-t_{i+1}}\,\mathbf{p}_i + b_{i+2}\,\mathbf{p}_{i+1} + c_{i+2}\,\mathbf{p}_{i+2},$$

$$t \in [t_{i+2}, t_{i+3}].$$

If we set

$$N_i^2(t) = \begin{cases} \frac{t-t_i}{t_{i+1}-t_i}\,\frac{t-t_i}{t_{i+2}-t_i}, & t \in [t_i, t_{i+1}), \\[2mm] \frac{t_{i+2}-t}{t_{i+2}-t_{i+1}}\,\frac{t-t_i}{t_{i+2}-t_i} + \frac{t-t_{i+1}}{t_{i+2}-t_{i+1}}\,\frac{t_{i+3}-t}{t_{i+3}-t_{i+1}}, & t \in [t_{i+1}, t_{i+2}), \\[2mm] \frac{t_{i+3}-t}{t_{i+3}-t_{i+2}}\,\frac{t_{i+3}-t}{t_{i+3}-t_{i+1}}, & t \in [t_{i+2}, t_{i+3}), \\[2mm] 0, & \text{everywhere else,} \end{cases} \quad (7.28)$$

then[2] the effect of control point $\mathbf{p}_i$ on the whole curve is $N_i^2(t)\mathbf{p}_i$ and, summing the effects of all control points, the quadratic B-spline curve can be written as

$$\mathbf{Q}(t) = \sum_{i=0}^{n} N_i^2(t)\mathbf{p}_i. \tag{7.29}$$

We are now able to determine the necessary number of knots for the quadratic B-spline curve. Given control points $\mathbf{p}_0, \mathbf{p}_1, \ldots, \mathbf{p}_n$, using the above notation the first segment of the curve is $\mathbf{Q}_2(t)$ that uses $\mathbf{p}_0, \mathbf{p}_1, \mathbf{p}_2$ and requires knots t_1, t_2, t_3, t_4; the last segment of the curve is $\mathbf{Q}_n(t)$ that uses control points $\mathbf{p}_{n-2}, \mathbf{p}_{n-1}$, $\mathbf{p}_n$ and requires knots $t_{n-1}, t_n, t_{n+1}, t_{n+2}$. Therefore, a quadratic B-spline curve with $(n+1)$ control points $\mathbf{p}_0, \mathbf{p}_1, \ldots, \mathbf{p}_n$ requires $(n+2)$ knots $t_1, t_2, \ldots, t_{n+2}$; the domain of the curve is the union of the domains $[t_i, t_{i+1}]$ of its segments $\mathbf{Q}_i(t)$, $i = 2, 3, \ldots, n$, that is the parametric interval $[t_2, t_{n+1}]$. We note that relations (7.28) and (7.29) indicate that two more knots, t_0 and t_{n+3}, are required so that $N_0^2(t)$ and $N_n^2(t)$ are defined correctly. However, our previous analysis suggests that these knots do not contribute to the shape of the curve; they are simply "dummy" knots needed only for the mathematics of (7.28). Their values are of no interest, and they are only used if relation (7.29) is employed to compute points on the B-spline curve.

7.3.2 kth-Degree B-Spline Curves

The process outlined above for the generation of a quadratic B-spline curve can be generalized for higher-degree curves in a straightforward manner.

The construction of a segment $\mathbf{Q}_i(t)$, $t \in [t_i, t_{i+1}]$ of a kth-degree B-spline curve[3] requires k consecutive linear interpolation steps. In the first step, $(k+1)$ control points $\mathbf{p}_{i-k}, \mathbf{p}_{i-k+1}, \ldots, \mathbf{p}_i$ will be interpolated in pairs, producing points $\mathbf{q}_j^1(t)$, $j = i-k+1, i-k+2, \ldots, i$ on linear segments defined in the parametric intervals $[t_j, t_{j+k}]$, respectively. In each subsequent interpolation step $r = 2, 3, \ldots, k$, the points of the previous step will be interpolated to produce points $\mathbf{q}_j^r(t)$, $j = i-k+r, \ldots, i$ on segments of degree r defined in shrinking parametric intervals $[t_j, t_{j+k-r+1}]$. After k such steps, a single kth-degree segment $\mathbf{q}_i^k(t) = \mathbf{Q}_i(t)$ will be constructed, defined in $[t_i, t_{i+1}]$. It can be shown that the consecutive segments $\mathbf{Q}_i(t)$ join with C^{k-1} continuity, therefore they form a kth-degree B-spline curve.

---

[2]Whereas previous relations used closed intervals for $\mathbf{Q}_i(t)$, relation (7.28) uses half-open intervals for the branches of the function, in order to ensure that the value of the function at the common knots is computed by a single branch; this is just a formality, since consecutive branches give the same value at the common knots.

[3]Some sources refer to the *order* $(k+1)$ of a kth-degree B-spline curve; we use the degree k of the curve throughout, as it is the degree of its constituting polynomial segments.

In order to express the whole curve in terms of its control points and its knots, we can proceed similarly to the quadratic B-spline curve above. We notice that each control point $\mathbf{p}_i$ affects $(k+1)$ consecutive segments $\mathbf{Q}_j(t)$, $j = i, i+1, \ldots, i+k$, and we can construct a function $N_i^k(t)$ that expresses its contribution to the curve. These functions are called kth-*degree B-spline functions,* and we will discuss them thoroughly below; using them, the B-spline curve may be written as

$$\mathbf{Q}(t) = \sum_{i=0}^{n} N_i^k(t)\mathbf{p}_i. \tag{7.30}$$

The curve is comprised of $(n-k+1)$ polynomial segments of degree k, each defined over the parametric interval $[t_i, t_{i+1}]$ for $i = k, k+1, \ldots, n$. Therefore, the domain of the curve is the union of all these intervals, that is, the interval $[t_k, t_{n+1}]$. In total $(n+k)$ knots $t_1, t_2, \ldots, t_{n+k}$ are required (and, as for quadratic B-splines, two more "dummy" knots t_0 and t_{n+k+1} that are necessary to correctly define $N_i^k(t)$ but do not contribute to the shape of the curve).[4] The knots must be in ascending order, $t_i \leq t_{i+1}$, since they are the endpoints of the parametric intervals on which the segments of the curves are defined. Knots may be repeated, as we shall see below, with interesting effect on the properties of the curve; however, at most k consecutive knots may be equal, $t_i < t_{i+k}$. More details on the knot sequence of a B-spline curve are given in Section 7.3.5.

7.3.3   B-Spline Functions

The functions $N_i^k(t)$ that we referred to in the definition of B-spline curves above are called kth-degree *B-spline functions.* They are defined recursively by setting

$$N_i^0(t) = \begin{cases} 1, & t \in [t_i, t_{i+1}), \\ 0, & \text{everywhere else,} \end{cases} \tag{7.31a}$$

and then for $r = 1, 2, \ldots, k$ and $i = 0, 1, \ldots, n+k-r$,

$$N_i^r(t) = \frac{t - t_i}{t_{i+r} - t_i} N_i^{r-1}(t) + \frac{t_{i+r+1} - t}{t_{i+r+1} - t_{i+1}} N_{i+1}^{r-1}(t). \tag{7.31b}$$

One can observe that these relations give (7.28) for $k = 2$.

B-spline functions $N_i^r(t)$ are rth-degree polynomials of t with *local support* on the interval $[t_i, t_{i+r+1})$; in other words, they are non-zero only on this interval. Moreover, they are *spline functions,* since they consist of $(r+1)$ polynomial segments of degree r joined with C^{r-1} continuity at the knots.

---

[4]Most other sources include these "dummy" knots to the knot sequence of the B-spline curve. We shall not follow this practice here, but only refer to the knots $t_1, \ldots, t_{n+k}$.

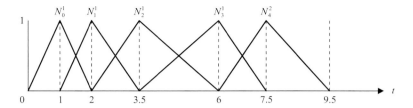

Figure 7.5. Linear B-spline functions ($k = 1$, $n = 4$).

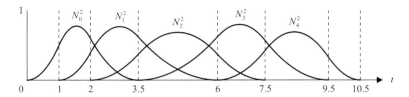

Figure 7.6. Quadratic B-spline functions ($k = 2$, $n = 4$).

Figures 7.5 and 7.6 show the first- and second-degree B-spline functions for an illustrative knot sequence. It can be observed that each first-degree B-spline function $N_i^1(t)$ consists of two linear segments joined at t_{i+1} (C^0 continuity). Similarly, each second-degree B-spline function $N_i^2(t)$ consists of three quadratic segments joined with C^1 continuity at t_{i+1} and t_{i+2}, respectively.

Given a degree k and a knot sequence $t_0, t_1, \ldots, t_{n+k}, t_{n+k+1}$, all the spline functions defined over this knot sequence constitute a vector space. It can be shown that the $(n + 1)$ B-spline functions of degree k defined over this knot sequence form a basis of this vector space. This is what the "B" in B-spline functions stands for: basis splines.

7.3.4 The de Boor Algorithm

Similarly to the de Casteljau algorithm for computing points on a Bézier curve, the *de Boor algorithm* [dB72, Cox72] provides an iterative scheme for computing points on a B-spline curve. This algorithm summarizes the linear interpolation steps involved in the generation of a kth-degree B-spline curve.

Due to the local support of B-spline functions, in order to compute a point $\mathbf{Q}(t)$ on a B-spline curve, we must know the interval to which the requested parametric value t belongs. Therefore the steps of the algorithm are the following:

1. For the required value of t, find the parametric interval $[t_i, t_{i+1})$ to which t belongs. Note that i will satisfy $k \leq i \leq n$, since the domain of the curve is $[t_k, t_{n+1}]$.

2. Set

$$\mathbf{q}_j^0(t) = \mathbf{p}_j, \quad j = i-k, i-k+1, \ldots, i. \tag{7.32a}$$

3. Perform the linear interpolation steps

$$\mathbf{q}_j^r(t) = \frac{t_{k-r+1+j} - t}{t_{k-r+1+j} - t_j} \mathbf{q}_{j-1}^{r-1}(t) + \frac{t - t_j}{t_{k-r+1+j} - t_j} \mathbf{q}_j^{r-1}(t),$$
$$r = 1, 2, \ldots, k$$
$$i = i-k+r, i-k+r+1, \ldots, i. \tag{7.32b}$$

4. Then the point on the curve corresponding to parametric value t is

$$\mathbf{Q}(t) = \mathbf{q}_i^k(t).$$

All the intermediate points involved in the de Boor algorithm can be written in a triangular arrangement, similar to the de Casteljau triangle. For the case of a cubic B-spline curve, the triangle is (omitting the parameter t)

$$
\begin{array}{llll}
\mathbf{p}_{i-3} = \mathbf{q}_{i-3}^0 & & & \\
\mathbf{p}_{i-2} = \mathbf{q}_{i-2}^0 & \mathbf{q}_{i-2}^1 & & \\
\mathbf{p}_{i-1} = \mathbf{q}_{i-1}^0 & \mathbf{q}_{i-1}^1 & \mathbf{q}_{i-1}^2 & \\
\mathbf{p}_i = \mathbf{q}_i^0 & \mathbf{q}_i^1 & \mathbf{q}_i^2 & \mathbf{q}_i^3 = \mathbf{Q}(t)
\end{array}
$$

This triangle has two notable differences compared to the de Casteljau triangle. First, the coefficients involved in the linear interpolation steps are not constant $(1 - t$ and $t)$ as in the de Casteljau triangle but depend on the specific row and column. Second, when implementing this algorithm using a one-dimensional array, the intermediate points must be computed from bottom to top so that any required points are not overwritten. Note that the de Boor algorithm never uses the "dummy" knots t_0 and t_{n+k+1}, as expected.

The pseudocode in Listing 7.2 presents a sample implementation of the de Boor algorithm. Since most modern programming languages impose that the array indices start from 0, we make a change of variable $m = j - i + k$ so that $m = 0, 1, \ldots, k - r$.

```
for (j = i-k; j <= i; j++)  {
    m = j-i+k;
    deBoorPt[m] = controlPt[j];
}
for (r = 1; r <= k; r++)  {
    for (j = i; j >= i-k+r; j--)  {
        m = j-i+k;
        coeff = (t-knots[j]) / (knots[k-r+1+j] - knots[j]);
        deBoorPt[m] = (1-coeff)*deBoorPt[m-1]
                                    + coeff*deBoorPt[m];
    }
}
```

Listing 7.2: The de Boor algorithm.

This algorithm allows us to draw a B-spline curve by computing successive points on the curve, for t from t_k to t_{n+1} in small increments Δt, depending on the required accuracy, and joining them with line segments. If we run through the domain of the curve in this way, it is easy to know at each step the subinterval $[t_i, t_{i+1})$ to which the current parametric value t belongs.

7.3.5   Knots and Parameterizations

The knot sequence of a B-spline curve directly affects its shape; using the same control points and different knot sequences, the shape of the resulting curves can vary considerably. In this section we shall examine the knot sequence and its properties more closely.

Properties of the knots of a B-spline curve. Suppose, first, that for a kth-degree B-spline curve the first knot has *multiplicity* k; in other words, it is repeated k times ($t_1 = t_2 = \cdots = t_{k-1} = t_k$). Then, by performing the relevant computations, we can show that $\mathbf{Q}(t_1) = \mathbf{Q}(t_k) = \mathbf{p}_0$; therefore, the curve interpolates its first control point. Similarly, if the last knot has multiplicity k, the curve interpolates its last control point $\mathbf{p}_n$. A knot sequence such that the first and last k knots are equal is called *open* or *clamped*. We observe that unlike Bézier curves, which always interpolate their extreme control points, B-spline curves have this property only when a clamped knot sequence is used.

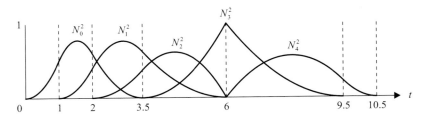

Figure 7.7. Quadratic B-spline functions ($k = 2$, $n = 4$) with $t_4 = t_5 = 6$.

More generally, if a knot of a B-spline curve is repeated, $t_i = t_{i+1}$, it can be shown that the curve loses one degree of continuity at the respective point $\mathbf{Q}(t_i)$. Consequently, if a knot has multiplicity r, the curve is C^{k-r} at the respective point. An illustration of this property is provided in Figure 7.7. The quadratic B-spline functions of Figure 7.6 are shown again, the only difference being that two knots are equal. It can be seen that the B-spline functions are no longer C^1 continuous everywhere but only C^0 continuous at the double knot. A quadratic B-spline curve that uses this knot sequence is therefore only C^0 continuous at that point, since it is a sum of terms $N_i^k(t)\mathbf{p}_i$.

Figure 7.8 shows a cubic B-spline curve having a knot with multiplicity one, two, and three. It can be seen that as the multiplicity of the knot increases, the curve on the neighborhood of this knot approaches its control polygon; when the multiplicity of the knot becomes equal to the degree of the curve, a cusp is formed at the control point that corresponds to this knot since the curve is only C^0 continuous at this point. This property can be exploited when using B-spline curves in practice, in order to better control the shape of the curve.

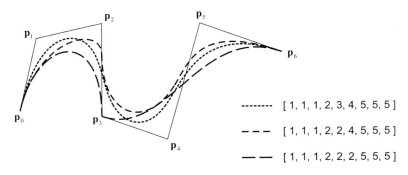

Figure 7.8. Effect of multiple knots on the shape of a B-spline curve.

Finally, we can now justify the restriction mentioned in Section 7.3.2 that no knot may be repeated more than k times: this would result in lower than C^0 continuity and would create a discontinuity on the curve.

Parameterizations. Our previous presentation of B-spline curves implied that the knot sequence is supplied by the user along with the control points of the curve. In practice, however, the user should mostly care about the control points of the curve, which provide an approximation of its shape. The knot sequence can be generated automatically, using specific algorithms (*parameterizations*) that try to produce a well-shaped curve.

The simplest parameterization is the *uniform* one, in which the knots are equidistant. This can be realized by setting

$$t_i = i - 1, \quad i = 1, 2, \dots, n + k. \tag{7.33}$$

If the curve should interpolate its first and last endpoints, a clamped uniform parameterization should be used, given by

$$t_i = \begin{cases} 0, & i = 1, \dots, k, \\ i - k, & i = k + 1, \dots, n, \\ n - k + 1, & i = n + 1, \dots, n + k. \end{cases} \tag{7.34}$$

Uniform knot sequences generate visually acceptable curves in most cases. However, their disadvantage is that they do not take into account the shape of the curve in any way, and so in some cases they may not produce well-shaped, "smooth" curves, for instance if control points are close to each other in areas where the curvature of the curve changes abruptly. Such cases are better handled by parameterizations that take into account the geometry of the control polygon of the curve.

One such parameterization often used in practice is the *chord-length* parameterization, in which the distances between the knots are proportional to the distances between corresponding control points. A clamped chord-length parameterization is

$$t_i = \begin{cases} 0, & i = 1, \dots, k, \\ t_{i-1} + |\mathbf{p}_{i-k} - \mathbf{p}_{i-k-1}|, & i = k + 1, \dots, n, \\ \sum_{j=0}^{n-k} |\mathbf{p}_{j+1} - \mathbf{p}_j|, & i = n + 1, \dots, n + k. \end{cases} \tag{7.35}$$

Different chord-length parameterizations can be produced by changing the extreme knots and/or by not requiring that the curve interpolates its first and last control points.

Another similar parameterization is the *centripetal* parameterization, in which the distances between the knots are proportional to the square root of the distances between corresponding control points. A clamped centripetal parameterization is

$$
t_i = \begin{cases}
0, & i = 1, \ldots, k, \\
t_{i-1} + \sqrt{|\mathbf{p}_{i-k} - \mathbf{p}_{i-k-1}|}, & i = k+1, \ldots, n, \\
\sum_{j=0}^{n-k} \sqrt{|\mathbf{p}_{j+1} - \mathbf{p}_j|}, & i = n+1, \ldots, n+k.
\end{cases}
\tag{7.36}
$$

Different centripetal parameterizations can be produced by changing the end conditions imposed. The name of this parameterization comes from the fact that if a particle moves on the curve at constant speed between successive knots, then its motion will counterbalance the centripetal force exercised on it.

Several other parameterizations have appeared in the literature, usually suited to specific applications. These are even better adapted to the geometry of the control polygon of the curve, but their complexity renders them unsuitable for general use. Drawing applications that require precision may use a simple initial parameterization such as the ones described above, and then let the user modify it interactively in order to generate the desired shape.

Knot insertion. An important operation on B-spline curves is *knot insertion*, the addition of a knot to the knot sequence of the curve while maintaining its shape. When inserting a knot, either the degree of the curve or the number of its control points must be increased by one so that the correlation between the degree, the number of control points, and the number of knots is maintained. In most cases it is not desirable to increase the degree of the curve, as high-degree curves become difficult to compute and manipulate. Therefore, during knot insertion a new control point is added—and some others are moved in order to maintain the shape of the curve.

The new knot and control point provide greater flexibility to the shape of the curve. In addition, it can be shown that as knots are inserted in the knot sequence of a B-spline curve, its control polygon comes closer to the curve; this result may be useful for drawing a B-spline curve, since after several knot insertions the control polygon will constitute a good enough approximation of the curve itself.

Suppose, then, that we wish to insert a new knot s between knots t_i and t_{i+1}; the new knot sequence will be $t_1, \ldots, t_i, s, t_{i+1}, \ldots, t_{n+k}$. Let $\mathbf{r}_j$, $j = 0, 1, \ldots, n+1$

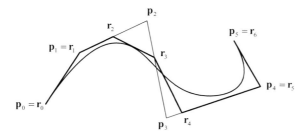

Figure 7.9. Knot insertion in a cubic B-spline curve.

be the new control points of the curve. Since a control point $\mathbf{p}_i$ only affects the curve on the interval $[t_i, t_{i+k+1}]$ where the corresponding B-spline function $N_i^k(t)$ is non-zero, only k of the new control points will be different from the original ones. The control points that are not affected are

$$\begin{aligned} \mathbf{r}_j &= \mathbf{p}_j, && j = 0, \ldots, i-k, \\ \mathbf{r}_j &= \mathbf{p}_{j-1}, && j = i+1, \ldots, n+1, \end{aligned} \qquad (7.37a)$$

and we need only determine $\mathbf{r}_j$ for $j = i - k + 1, \ldots, i$. It can be shown that these are given by

$$\mathbf{r}_j = \frac{t_{j+k} - s}{t_{j+k} - t_j} \mathbf{p}_{j-1} + \frac{s - t_j}{t_{j+k} - t_j} \mathbf{p}_j, \quad j = i-k+1, \ldots, i, \qquad (7.37b)$$

so they consist of linear interpolations of the original control points in suitable parametric intervals. This formula is called *Boehm's knot-insertion formula* [Boeh80]. The indices used in the above relations impose some restrictions on the interval where the knot insertion occurs; specifically, i must be between k and n (inclusive); in other words, a knot may be inserted only in the domain of the curve $[t_k, t_{n+1}]$.

Figure 7.9 demonstrates the insertion of the knot in a cubic B-spline curve. It is apparent that the control polygon approaches the curve, as already mentioned.

7.3.6 Properties of B-Spline Curves

The above discussion of B-spline curves reveals that they constitute a very flexible design tool, since they are formed by low-degree segments with guaranteed continuity. Here we summarize their most important properties.

Figure 7.10. Strong convex hull property of a quadratic B-spline curve.

- *Local control.* Unlike Bézier curves, which possess only pseudo-local control (see Section 7.2.5), B-spline curves exhibit full local control, so that changing the position of a control point affects the shape of the curve only on a restricted segment of the curve. Specifically, control point $\mathbf{p}_i$ affects only the part of the curve corresponding to the parametric interval $[t_i, t_{i+k+1})$ in which the respective B-spline function $N_i^k(t)$ has local support (is non-zero).

- *Strong convex-hull property.* All the interpolation steps performed for the generation of a B-spline curve are convex combinations of its control points (provided that the knot sequence is non-decreasing). It is evident, then, that the B-spline curve lies inside the convex hull of its control points.

  Additionally, any B-spline curve satisfies this property in an even stronger form: every point on the curve lies inside the convex hull of the $(k+1)$ control points that contribute to its computation (see relation (7.32a) of the de Boor algorithm), and, therefore, the whole curve lies inside the union of these convex hulls. Figure 7.10 demonstrates this property for a quadratic curve.

- *Invariance under affine transformations.* The B-spline curve is an affine combination of its control points, and, therefore, it is invariant under affine combinations. As a practical consequence, in order to apply an affine transformation to a B-spline curve, it is sufficient to transform its control points.

  We note that, in general, parameterizations are not maintained under affine transformations, so, for instance, if a curve that was parameterized with a chord-length parameterization is transformed, then distances between the knots will no longer be proportional to the distances of the control points. The only parameterization of those mentioned in Section 7.3.5 that is maintained is the uniform one.

- *Invariance under affine transformations of its parameter.* The B-spline curve remains invariant if its parameter is transformed affinely to $u = a + (b - a)t$. Just as in the previous property, the chord-length and centripetal parameterizations are not maintained under such parameter transformations.

- *Strong linear precision.* If the control points of a B-spline curve lie on a straight line, then the curve degenerates to a straight line.

  Additionally, if $(k + 1)$ control points of the curve are collinear, the corresponding segment of the curve is a straight line segment, due to the strong convex-hull property.

- *Strong variation-diminishing property.* B-spline curves enjoy the variation-diminishing property, so a planar B-spline curve may not be intersected by an arbitrary straight line more times than its control polygon, and a non-planar B-spline curve may not be intersected by a straight line or plane more times than its control polygon.

  B-spline curves satisfy this property in an even stronger form: it holds for the polygon formed by the $(k + 1)$ control points that contribute to any specific point on the curve.

- *Endpoint interpolation.* As we have shown, a B-spline curve interpolates its extreme control points only if a clamped knot sequence, in which the first and last knots are repeated k times, is used. This setting is often used in practice.

- *Derivative.* It can be shown that the tangent (first derivative) of a kth-degree B-spline curve is

$$\frac{d}{dt}\mathbf{Q}(t) = k \sum_{i=0}^{n-1} N_i^{k-1}(t) \, \frac{1}{t_{i+k+1} - t_{i+1}} (\mathbf{p}_{i+1} - \mathbf{p}_i). \qquad (7.38)$$

- *Generalization of Bézier curves.* A B-spline curve of degree k with $(k + 1)$ control points $\mathbf{p}_0, \mathbf{p}_1, \ldots, \mathbf{p}_k$ and knot sequence $(0^{<k>}, 1^{<k>})$, where $x^{<k>}$ denotes a knot with multiplicity k, is a Bézier curve of degree k with control points $\mathbf{p}_0, \mathbf{p}_1, \ldots, \mathbf{p}_k$. This can be verified by computing the B-spline functions $N_i^k(t)$ for this special knot sequence and noticing that they are equivalent to the Bernstein polynomials $B_i^k(t)$.

The above properties suggest that low-degree B-spline curves are easier to manipulate: the convex hull of the parts of the curve is closer to them, local control is better since the part of the curve affected by moving any control point is smaller, and the computations involved are more efficient. In practice, cubic B-spline curves are used most often since they provide satisfactory flexibility with rather low complexity.

7.3.7   B-Spline Curves in Bézier Form

As we saw, a kth-degree B-spline curve is composed of several kth-degree polynomial segments defined over parametric intervals $[t_i, t_{i+1}]$. Each of these segments may be written as a kth-degree Bézier curve for suitable (Bézier) control points. In this way we obtain a piecewise Bézier form of the B-spline curve. This form of the curve can be useful both theoretically, since Bézier curves are considerably simpler and well studied, and practically, for example by using an efficient method for drawing Bézier curves in order to draw the B-spline curve.

We shall present the Bézier form of quadratic ($k = 2$) and cubic ($k = 3$) B-splines which, as already mentioned, are the ones most often used in practice. The respective formulas for higher-degree curves are much more complicated.

Consider first a quadratic B-spline $\mathbf{Q}(t)$ and a specific segment $\mathbf{Q}_i(t)$ defined from (B-spline) control points $\mathbf{p}_{i-2}$, $\mathbf{p}_{i-1}$ and $\mathbf{p}_i$ over the parametric interval $[t_i, t_{i+1}]$. In Bézier form, this segment is defined by three (Bézier) control points which we denote $\mathbf{r}_0$, $\mathbf{r}_1$, and $\mathbf{r}_2$. Since any Bézier curve interpolates its first and last control points, $\mathbf{r}_0$ and $\mathbf{r}_2$ are exactly the endpoints of this segment, $\mathbf{Q}_i(t_i)$ and $\mathbf{Q}_i(t_{i+1})$, respectively. To determine $\mathbf{r}_1$, we can compare the B-spline and Bézier forms of this segment and conclude that it coincides with the B-spline control point $\mathbf{p}_{i-1}$. Overall, using the notation of the de Boor algorithm, we have

$$\mathbf{r}_0 = \mathbf{Q}_i(t_i) = \frac{t_{i+1}-t_i}{t_{i+1}-t_{i-1}}\mathbf{p}_{i-2} + \frac{t_i-t_{i-1}}{t_{i+1}-t_{i-1}}\mathbf{p}_{i-1} = \mathbf{q}_{i-1}^1(t_i),$$

$$\mathbf{r}_1 = \mathbf{p}_{i-1}, \tag{7.39}$$

$$\mathbf{r}_2 = \mathbf{Q}_i(t_{i+1}) = \frac{t_{i+2}-t_{i+1}}{t_{i+2}-t_i}\mathbf{p}_{i-1} + \frac{t_{i+1}-t_i}{t_{i+2}-t_i}\mathbf{p}_i = \mathbf{q}_i^1(t_{i+1}).$$

Consider now a cubic B-spline $\mathbf{Q}(t)$ and a specific segment $\mathbf{Q}_i(t)$ defined from (B-spline) control points $\mathbf{p}_{i-3}$, $\mathbf{p}_{i-2}$, $\mathbf{p}_{i-1}$ and $\mathbf{p}_i$ over the parametric interval $[t_i, t_{i+1}]$. In Bézier form, this segment is defined by four (Bézier) control points, which we denote $\mathbf{r}_0$, $\mathbf{r}_1$, $\mathbf{r}_2$, and $\mathbf{r}_3$. Again, the first and last control points $\mathbf{r}_0$ and $\mathbf{r}_3$ are exactly the endpoints of this segment, $\mathbf{Q}_i(t_i)$ and $\mathbf{Q}_i(t_{i+1})$, respectively.

The middle control points are now some of the intermediate points generated during the interpolation steps of the B-spline. Using the notation of the de Boor algorithm, we have

$$\mathbf{r}_0 = \frac{t_{i+1}-t_i}{t_{i+1}-t_{i-1}}\left(\frac{t_{i+1}-t_i}{t_{i+1}-t_{i-2}}\mathbf{p}_{i-3} + \frac{t_i-t_{i-2}}{t_{i+1}-t_{i-2}}\mathbf{p}_{i-2}\right) + \frac{t_i-t_{i-1}}{t_{i+1}-t_{i-1}}\mathbf{r}_1,$$

$$\mathbf{r}_1 = \mathbf{q}_{i-1}^1(t_i) = \frac{t_{i+2}-t_i}{t_{i+2}-t_{i-1}}\mathbf{p}_{i-2} + \frac{t_i-t_{i-1}}{t_{i+2}-t_{i-1}}\mathbf{p}_{i-1},$$

$$\mathbf{r}_2 = \mathbf{q}_{i-1}^1(t_{i+1}) = \frac{t_{i+2}-t_{i+1}}{t_{i+2}-t_{i-1}}\mathbf{p}_{i-2} + \frac{t_{i+1}-t_{i-1}}{t_{i+2}-t_{i-1}}\mathbf{p}_{i-1},$$

$$\mathbf{r}_3 = \frac{t_{i+2}-t_{i+1}}{t_{i+2}-t_i}\mathbf{r}_2 + \frac{t_{i+1}-t_i}{t_{i+2}-t_i}\left(\frac{t_{i+3}-t_{i+1}}{t_{i+3}-t_i}\mathbf{p}_{i-1} + \frac{t_{i+1}-t_i}{t_{i+3}-t_i}\mathbf{p}_i\right).$$

$$(7.40)$$

7.4   Rational Bézier and B-Spline Curves

Bézier and B-spline curves presented above are the most basic free-form parametric curves used in computer-aided geometric design. Bézier curves provide a useful expression of arbitrary degree single-segment curves, and B-spline curves generalize them to express smooth, flexible, multi-segment curves.

Unfortunately, these curve representations have two disadvantages that can potentially limit their usefulness in practical environments. First, they are not invariant to projections, which are not affine transformations; consequently, they may not be handled easily (or even correctly!) in a 3D graphics scene. Second, they cannot represent conic sections (circles, ellipses, parabolas, and hyperbolas) exactly, except for parabolas; however, conic sections are common modeling objects, and in a drawing program it would be convenient to have a common representation for all objects used.

These two problems are overcome by *rational* Bézier and B-spline curves. Rational curves, in general, are polynomial parametric curves that use homogeneous coordinates (see Section 3.4.1). Given a (usual) polynomial curve

$$\mathbf{X}(t) = \begin{bmatrix} x(t) \\ y(t) \\ z(t) \end{bmatrix}$$

$(z(t)$ would be zero everywhere for a planar curve), we can construct a family of rational curves

$$\mathbf{X}^h(t) = \begin{bmatrix} w(t)x(t) \\ w(t)y(t) \\ w(t)z(t) \\ w(t) \end{bmatrix}.$$

If $w(t)$ is constant for all t in the domain of the curve, we get the original curve $\mathbf{X}(t)$.

The definition of rational Bézier and B-spline curves is straightforward, since the coordinates in parametric form are independent of each other; therefore, the addition of the homogeneous coordinate simply requires extending the equations with one more coordinate. Still, this addition lends interesting properties to the curves, which we shall present in the following.

7.4.1 Rational Bézier Curves

Consider a sequence of homogeneous control points

$$\mathbf{p}_i^h = [w_i\mathbf{p}_i, w_i]^{\mathrm{T}} = [w_ix_i, w_iy_i, w_iz_i, w_i]^{\mathrm{T}},$$

$i = 0, 1, \ldots, n$. A homogeneous Bézier curve can be defined as

$$\mathbf{P}^h(t) = \sum_{i=0}^{n} B_i^n(t)\mathbf{p}_i^h = \begin{bmatrix} \sum_{i=0}^{n} B_i^n(t)w_i\mathbf{p}_i \\ \sum_{i=0}^{n} B_i^n(t)w_i \end{bmatrix}.$$

To get to the usual Cartesian form of the curve, we divide all coordinates by the homogeneous one, and we have (omitting the homogeneous coordinate that becomes equal to 1),

$$\mathbf{P}^r(t) = \frac{1}{\sum_{i=0}^{n} B_i^n(t)w_i} \sum_{i=0}^{n} B_i^n(t)w_i\mathbf{p}_i. \tag{7.41}$$

This is an nth-degree *rational Bézier curve*. The (Cartesian) points $\mathbf{p}_i$ are the *control points* of the curve and the w_i are the respective *weights*.

The weights are thus called because the value of each w_i affects the contribution of the corresponding control point to the curve. If a weight w_i is zero, then the control point $\mathbf{p}_i$ does not affect the curve at all. As w_i increases, the curve is pulled towards $\mathbf{p}_i$; however, it is only the ratio of the various w_i that matters and not their absolute values, since common factors are ruled out due to the division performed. As expected, if all weights are equal, the rational Bézier curve

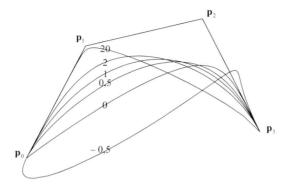

Figure 7.11. The effects of different weights to the shape of a rational Bézier curve. The control polygon is the same as the one in Figure 7.2. The weights used are $[1, w_1, 1, 1]$ where w_1 is shown on each curve.

reduces to a normal Bézier curve. Weights are chosen to be positive, because negative values have unpredictable and undesirable effect on the shape of the curve: first, the convex-hull property is not maintained, since the curve is no longer a convex combination of its control points, and second, poles may be created that would make the curve go to infinity. Overall, the weights of a rational Bézier curve offer an additional level of local control on the shape of the curve.

These properties are demonstrated in Figure 7.11, where the effect of w_1 on a cubic rational Bézier curve is shown. For $w_1 > 0$, as w_1 increases the curve is pulled towards $\mathbf{p}_1$. For $w_1 = 1$, all the weights are equal and the curve is a simple Bézier curve (compare to Figure 7.2). For $w_1 = 0$, the control point $\mathbf{p}_1$ does not affect the curve. Finally, for $w_1 < 0$, the curve is pushed away from $\mathbf{p}_1$ in a mostly unpredictable manner.

The procedure outlined above implies that a rational Bézier curve $\mathbf{P}^r(t)$ is actually the perspective projection of a higher-dimension regular Bézier curve, the homogeneous one $\mathbf{P}^h(t)$, onto the plane $w = 1$ (refer back to Figure 3.6 for a visualization of homogeneous coordinates).

Rational Bézier curves retain most of the properties of normal Bézier curves. A notable difference concerns the convex-hull and variation-diminishing properties, which hold only if the weights are non-negative. Furthermore, rational Bézier curves are invariant not only under affine transformations but also under projective transformations; this property stems from the fact that they are themselves projections of the respective homogeneous curves. Therefore, in order to project a rational Bézier curve it suffices to project its control points.

Rational Bézier curves can be evaluated using the familiar de Casteljau algorithm for the homogeneous control points $\mathbf{p}_i^h$ and performing the homogeneous division at the end. An alternative formulation, which may provide higher numerical accuracy at the cost of increased computational complexity, is to perform the division at each step, thus working effectively with the basic homogeneous representation of the intermediate points anew at each step of the algorithm.

Conic sections as rational Bézier curves. Conic sections (circles, ellipses, parabolas and hyperbolas) are the various curves resulting from the intersection of a plane and a cone at different angles [Weis04]. Their algebraic equations have a common form,

$$Ax^2 + Bxy + Cy^2 + Dx + Ey + F = 0, \tag{7.42}$$

with the following constraints for each kind of curve:

- If $B^2 - 4AC < 0$, the curve is an ellipse. If, in addition, $B = 0$ and $A = C$, the curve is a circle.

- If $B^2 - 4AC = 0$, the curve is a parabola.

- If $B^2 - 4AC > 0$, the curve is a hyperbola.

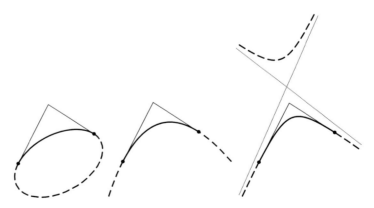

Figure 7.12. Conics as rational quadratic Bézier curves: ellipse ($|w_1| < 1$), parabola ($|w_1| = 1$), hyperbola ($|w_1| > 1$). The solid segment of each curve corresponds to $w_1 > 0$ and the dashed ("complementary") segment corresponds to $w_1 < 0$. It can be seen that the "infinite" segments of the parabola and the hyperbola correspond to $w_1 < 0$.

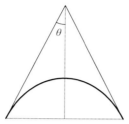

Figure 7.13. A circular arc constructed as a rational quadratic Bézier curve. The weight for the middle control point is $w_1 = \sin\theta$.

The only conic section that can be represented by a non-rational polynomial parametric equation is the parabola; in fact, any quadratic Bézier curve is a parabolic segment. The other conic sections can only be represented by rational curves, specifically by rational quadratic Bézier curves. It can be shown (see also Exercise 8) that a rational quadratic Bézier curve with (non-collinear) control points $\mathbf{p}_0$, $\mathbf{p}_1$, $\mathbf{p}_2$ and corresponding weights 1, w_1, 1, is

- an elliptical segment, if $|w_1| < 1$,

- a parabolic segment, if $|w_1| = 1$ (then the curve is a normal Bézier curve),

- a hyperbolic segment, if $|w_1| > 1$.

Figure 7.12 shows all the possibilities.

Circular arcs deserve special attention. Figure 7.13 shows the control polygon of a rational Bézier curve representing a circular arc. It can be shown that in this case the control polygon must be an isosceles triangle, $|\mathbf{p}_0\mathbf{p}_1| = |\mathbf{p}_1\mathbf{p}_2|$, and the weight of $\mathbf{p}_1$ is $w_1 = \sin\theta$, where θ is the half-angle between $\mathbf{p}_0\mathbf{p}_1$ and $\mathbf{p}_1\mathbf{p}_2$.

7.4.2 Rational B-Spline Curves—NURBS

Having presented rational Bézier curves, the construction of rational B-spline curves is straightforward. Given a sequence of control points $\mathbf{p}_i$, $i = 0, 1, \ldots, n$, a sequence of corresponding weights w_i, $i = 0, 1, \ldots, n$, and a knot sequence t_i, $i = 1, 2, \ldots, n + k$, a *rational B-spline curve* of degree k is given by

$$\mathbf{Q}^r(t) = \frac{1}{\sum_{i=0}^{n} N_i^n(t) w_i} \sum_{i=0}^{n} N_i^n(t) w_i \mathbf{p}_i. \tag{7.43}$$

Rational B-spline curves with arbitrary (not necessarily uniform) knot sequence are usually referred to as *NURBS*, non-uniform rational B-splines.

NURBS retain most of the properties of B-spline curves, with the strong convex-hull and strong variation-diminishing properties holding only if the weights are non-negative; also NURBS are invariant under projective transformations. The weights have the same properties mentioned for rational Bézier curves, thus offering additional flexibility to the designer.

NURBS are the most general of all curve representations examined up to this point: under suitable conditions they can represent simple B-spline curves (if all the weights are equal), simple and rational Bézier curves (see the last property of B-splines in Section 7.3.6), and conic sections (see also Exercise 9). Moreover, they possess all the desirable properties of the other types of curves, notably local control, and they are invariant under both affine and projective transformations. For all these reasons, NURBS are the standard tool for representing freeform curves in CAGD applications.

7.5 Interpolation Curves

Bézier and B-spline curves that we analyzed in the previous sections are *approximation* curves, since in general they do not pass through their control points, which only provide a good indication of their shape. However, there is often the need to construct *interpolation* curves that pass through given points.

This problem can be formulated as follows: given a set of points $\mathbf{p}_0, \mathbf{p}_1, \ldots, \mathbf{p}_n$ and corresponding parametric values (knots) $t_0, t_1, \ldots, t_n$, find a parametric curve $\mathbf{P}(t)$ that satisfies

$$\mathbf{P}(t_i) = \mathbf{p}_i, \quad i = 0, 1, \ldots, n. \tag{7.44}$$

Simple interpolation methods construct $\mathbf{P}(t)$ as a single polynomial curve of degree n. We note that this curve is unique: it is determined by the $(n+1)$ coefficients of the respective polynomial, which may be computed as the single solution of a linear system of $(n+1)$ equations formed by (7.44). This way of determining the interpolation curve by solving the linear system is not practical at all. Below we present two other methods for generating this curve, directly using Lagrange polynomials and recursively using Aitken's algorithm.

In spite of the virtues of these methods, the use of a single polynomial segment to interpolate a set of points has several drawbacks. First, the interpolation of several points requires a high-degree polynomial and, consequently, the computations involved are complex and numerically unstable. Second, the generated curve exhibits *oscillations* (Figure 7.14) and does not follow its control polygon in a predictable way; this defect compromises the usefulness of these methods.

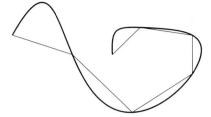

Figure 7.14. Oscillations of a high-degree interpolation curve.

To overcome these drawbacks, interpolation is usually performed using curves comprised of several low-degree segments, joined together with continuity constraints. In the following, we examine interpolation with cubic Hermite curves and cubic B-splines.

7.5.1 Simple Polynomial Interpolation

A simple way to construct an interpolation curve that satisfies the conditions set above is by using the nth-degree *Lagrange polynomials*,

$$L_i^n(t) = \prod_{\substack{j=0 \\ j \neq i}}^{n} \frac{t - t_j}{t_i - t_j}, \quad i = 0, 1, \ldots, n. \tag{7.45}$$

Then, the interpolation curve is

$$\mathbf{P}(t) = \sum_{i=0}^{n} L_i^n(t)\mathbf{p}_i(t). \tag{7.46}$$

Regarding the Lagrange polynomials, we observe that the ith polynomial $L_i^n(t)$ is zero on every knot t_j except for the ith knot t_i on which its value is 1; as a result, the curve satisfies condition (7.44). Further characteristics of the Lagrange polynomials reveal properties of the interpolation curve:

- *Invariance under affine transformations.* This holds since the Lagrange polynomials sum to 1; therefore, the interpolation curve is a barycentric combination of its control points.

- *No convex-hull property.* The Lagrange polynomials are neither always positive nor less than 1; therefore, the curve is not contained in the convex hull of its control points.

- *Linear precision.* If all control points lie on a straight line then the curve also has the shape of a straight line.

- *No variation-diminishing property.* The same argument that supports the absence of the convex-hull property indicates that the interpolation curve does not satisfy the variation-diminishing property; in other words, as already mentioned, the curve may demonstrate oscillations.

Aitken's algorithm provides a recursive evaluation of the interpolation curve, similar to the de Casteljau and the de Boor algorithms:

1. For the required value of t, set

$$\mathbf{p}_i^0(t) = \mathbf{p}_i, \quad i = 0, 1, \ldots, n. \tag{7.47a}$$

2. Perform the linear interpolation steps

$$\mathbf{p}_i^r(t) = \frac{t_{i+r} - t}{t_{i+r} - t_i} \mathbf{p}_i^{r-1}(t) + \frac{t - t_i}{t_{i+r} - t_i} \mathbf{p}_{i+1}^{r-1}(t), \quad \begin{array}{l} r = 1, 2, \ldots, n, \\ i = 0, 1, \ldots, n - r. \end{array} \tag{7.47b}$$

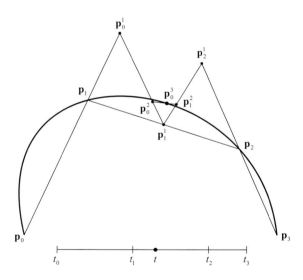

Figure 7.15. Aitken's algorithm for the construction of the interpolation curve (adapted from [Fari01]).

3. Then, the point on the curve corresponding to parametric value t is

$$\mathbf{P}(t) = \mathbf{p}_0^n(t).$$

It can be observed that in the linear interpolation steps performed, the parameter t does not always lie between t_i and t_{i+r}, and, consequently, the intermediate points generated are not convex combinations of the points in the previous step (Figure 7.15).

7.5.2 Hermite Curves

The interpolation problem, as stated above, concerns finding a curve that passes through given points. We may, however, seek a curve that interpolates other elements, such as tangents. In this section, we present interpolation with (cubic) Hermite curves that are required to interpolate given points and to have given tangents at these points.

Cubic Hermite interpolation. Suppose, initially, that we are given two points $\mathbf{p}_0$ and $\mathbf{p}_1$ and corresponding tangent vectors $\overrightarrow{\mathbf{m}}_0$ and $\overrightarrow{\mathbf{m}}_1$. In the simplest case, we are seeking a cubic curve $\mathbf{H}(t), t \in [0,1]$ (the *cubic Hermite curve*), that satisfies the following relations:

$$\begin{aligned} \mathbf{H}(0) &= \mathbf{p}_0, & \mathbf{H}'(0) &= \overrightarrow{\mathbf{m}}_0, \\ \mathbf{H}(1) &= \mathbf{p}_1, & \mathbf{H}'(1) &= \overrightarrow{\mathbf{m}}_1. \end{aligned} \qquad (7.48)$$

Notice that the four elements provided are adequate to determine a cubic curve.

In our analysis of Bézier curves, we showed that every cubic polynomial curve may be written in the form of a Bézier curve; so we express the Hermite curve as

$$\mathbf{H}(t) = \sum_{i=0}^{n} B_i^n(t)\mathbf{q}_i, \quad t \in [0,1] \qquad (7.49)$$

for some unknown Bézier control points $\mathbf{q}_i$. Using further properties of Bézier curves, we have

$$\begin{aligned} \mathbf{p}_0 &= \mathbf{H}(0) = \mathbf{q}_0, \\ \mathbf{p}_1 &= \mathbf{H}(1) = \mathbf{q}_3, \end{aligned}$$

and

$$\begin{aligned} \overrightarrow{\mathbf{m}}_0 &= \mathbf{H}'(0) = 3(\mathbf{q}_1 - \mathbf{q}_0) & \Leftrightarrow & \quad \mathbf{q}_1 = \mathbf{p}_0 + \tfrac{1}{3}\overrightarrow{\mathbf{m}}_0, \\ \overrightarrow{\mathbf{m}}_1 &= \mathbf{H}'(1) = 3(\mathbf{q}_3 - \mathbf{q}_2) & \Leftrightarrow & \quad \mathbf{q}_2 = \mathbf{p}_1 - \tfrac{1}{3}\overrightarrow{\mathbf{m}}_1. \end{aligned}$$

Therefore, the curve is

$$\mathbf{H}(t) = (1-t)^3 \mathbf{p}_0 + 3t(1-t)^2 \left(\mathbf{p}_0 + \tfrac{1}{3}\overrightarrow{\mathbf{m}}_0\right) + 3t^2(1-t)\left(\mathbf{p}_1 - \tfrac{1}{3}\overrightarrow{\mathbf{m}}_1\right) + t^3 \mathbf{p}_1$$

or, expressing it with respect to its defining elements,

$$\mathbf{H}(t) = H_0^3(t)\mathbf{p}_0 + H_1^3(t)\mathbf{p}_1 + H_2^3(t)\overrightarrow{\mathbf{m}}_0 + H_3^3(t)\overrightarrow{\mathbf{m}}_1, \quad t \in [0,1], \qquad (7.50)$$

where $H_i^3(t)$ are the *cubic Hermite polynomials*

$$\begin{aligned}
H_0^3(t) &= 2t^3 - 3t^2 + 1, \\
H_1^3(t) &= -2t^3 + 3t^2, \\
H_2^3(t) &= t^3 - 2t^2 + t, \\
H_3^3(t) &= t^3 - t^2.
\end{aligned} \qquad (7.51)$$

In case the curve is defined over an arbitrary parametric interval $[a,b]$, these relations must be modified. Unlike Bézier curves, Hermite curves are *not* invariant to affine transformations of their parameter; in other words, their defining elements (specifically $\overrightarrow{\mathbf{m}}_0$ and $\overrightarrow{\mathbf{m}}_1$) must be altered for the curve to remain the same when the parameter $t \in [0,1]$ is changed to $u \in [a,b]$ by setting $u = (1-t)a + tb$. Recalling relations (7.18), the tangents at the endpoints are now

$$\overrightarrow{\mathbf{m}}_0 = \mathbf{H}'(a) = \frac{1}{b-a}3(\mathbf{q}_1 - \mathbf{q}_0),$$

$$\overrightarrow{\mathbf{m}}_1 = \mathbf{H}'(b) = \frac{1}{b-a}3(\mathbf{q}_3 - \mathbf{q}_2),$$

and working as above we deduce that

$$\mathbf{H}(u) = H_0^3(u)\mathbf{p}_0 + H_1^3(u)\mathbf{p}_1 + H_2^3(u)(b-a)\overrightarrow{\mathbf{m}}_0 + H_3^3(u)(b-a)\overrightarrow{\mathbf{m}}_1,$$
$$u \in [a,b], \quad (7.52)$$

so the tangent vectors should be divided by $(b-a)$ in order to obtain the curve in the form (7.50). The physical explanation of this fact is rather straightforward: using $\mathbf{H}(t)$ we traverse the curve in one time unit (the length of the interval $[0,1]$); if we would like to traverse it in $(b-a)$ time units (the length of the new interval $[a,b]$), our speed, represented by the tangent vectors, must be smaller by a factor of $(b-a)$.

Piecewise cubic Hermite interpolation. The practical interest of interpolating only two points and the respective tangent vectors is limited. It would be more interesting to construct a smooth curve that interpolates a sequence of points $\mathbf{p}_0$, $\mathbf{p}_1, \ldots, \mathbf{p}_n$ and respective tangent vectors $\vec{\mathbf{m}}_0, \vec{\mathbf{m}}_1, \ldots, \vec{\mathbf{m}}_n$ at parametric values t_0, $t_1, \ldots, t_n$.

It is possible to construct this curve as a piecewise cubic Hermite curve. In fact, independent Hermite segments, one for each parametric interval $[t_i, t_{i+1}]$, may be constructed, and they will constitute a C^1-continuous curve since they share the tangent vectors $\vec{\mathbf{m}}_i$ at their endpoints. Each segment will be given by

$$\mathbf{H}_i(u) = H_0^3(u)\mathbf{p}_i + H_1^3(u)\mathbf{p}_{i+1} + H_2^3(u)(t_{i+1} - t_i)\vec{\mathbf{m}}_i + H_3^3(u)(t_{i+1} - t_i)\vec{\mathbf{m}}_{i+1},$$
$$u \in [t_i, t_{i+1}].$$

This construction of an interpolating curve provides great flexibility to a potential designer, since it allows her to modify the shape of the curve by altering the tangent vectors at the interpolated points. Even greater flexibility is easily achievable by requiring only G^1 geometric continuity at the joins, allowing the tangent vectors at the end of a segment and at the beginning of the next segment to be a multiple of each other instead of being equal.

Automatic generation of tangents. Nonetheless, in some situations, it might not be desirable to specify the tangent vectors at the knots explicitly, or it might not be easy to determine tangent vectors that produce a well-shaped curve. In such cases, an automated method for computing tangent vectors is needed. The simplest methods seek a curve that is C^1 continuous at the joins, whereas more complicated methods produce a C^2 continuous curve.

A natural approach for the computation of tangent vectors is to set $\vec{\mathbf{m}}_i$ parallel to the line through the two neighboring control points $\mathbf{p}_{i-1}$ and $\mathbf{p}_{i+1}$:

$$\vec{\mathbf{m}}_i = \tfrac{1}{2}(1-c)(\mathbf{p}_{i+1} - \mathbf{p}_{i-1}), \quad i = 1, 2, \ldots, n-1. \tag{7.53}$$

The constant c is a *tension parameter* that affects the norm of the tangent vectors. The curves generated using these tangent vectors are called *cardinal splines*. If $c = 0$ then $\vec{\mathbf{m}}_i = \tfrac{1}{2}(\mathbf{p}_{i+1} - \mathbf{p}_{i-1})$, and the curves are called *Catmull–Rom splines*. This procedure cannot determine the tangents $\vec{\mathbf{m}}_0$ and $\vec{\mathbf{m}}_n$ at the first and last control points.

A second approach is to use *Bessel tangents*: the tangent vector $\vec{\mathbf{m}}_i$ is set equal to the tangent of the parabola that interpolates the three neighboring points $\mathbf{p}_{i-1}$, $\mathbf{p}_i$, and $\mathbf{p}_{i+1}$. If $\mathbf{Q}_i(u), u \in [t_{i-1}, t_{i+1}]$ is this parabola, which may be computed using Lagrange polynomials or Aitken's algorithm, then

$$\vec{\mathbf{m}}_i = \frac{d}{du}\mathbf{Q}_i(t_i), \quad i = 1, 2, \ldots, n-1. \tag{7.54a}$$

For the first and last tangent vectors, we may use the tangents of the first and last parabolas, respectively,

$$\vec{\mathbf{m}}_0 = \frac{d}{du}\mathbf{Q}_1(t_0) \quad \text{and} \quad \vec{\mathbf{m}}_n = \frac{d}{du}\mathbf{Q}_{n-1}(t_n). \tag{7.54b}$$

Performing the necessary computations, we reach the following formulas for the tangent vectors in terms of the elements of the curve:

$$\vec{\mathbf{m}}_0 = \frac{-t_2 - t_1 + 2t_0}{(t_2 - t_0)(t_1 - t_0)}\mathbf{p}_0 + \frac{t_2 - t_0}{(t_2 - t_1)(t_1 - t_0)}\mathbf{p}_1$$
$$+ \frac{t_1 - t_0}{(t_2 - t_1)(t_2 - t_0)}\mathbf{p}_2,$$

$$\vec{\mathbf{m}}_i = -\frac{t_{i+1} - t_i}{(t_{i+1} - t_{i-1})(t_i - t_{i-1})}\mathbf{p}_{i-1} + \frac{t_{i+1} - 2t_i + t_{i-1}}{(t_{i+1} - t_i)(t_i - t_{i-1})}\mathbf{p}_i \tag{7.55}$$
$$+ \frac{t_i - t_{i-1}}{(t_{i+1} - t_i)(t_{i+1} - t_{i-1})}\mathbf{p}_{i+1},$$

$$\vec{\mathbf{m}}_n = \frac{t_n - t_{n-1}}{(t_n - t_{n-2})(t_{n-1} - t_{n-2})}\mathbf{p}_{n-2} - \frac{t_n - t_{n-2}}{(t_n - t_{n-1})(t_{n-1} - t_{n-2})}\mathbf{p}_{n-1}$$
$$+ \frac{2t_n - t_{n-1} - t_{n-2}}{(t_n - t_{n-1})(t_n - t_{n-2})}\mathbf{p}_n.$$

We notice that the Bessel tangents $\vec{\mathbf{m}}_0$ and $\vec{\mathbf{m}}_n$ at the ends of the curve can be used independently, in order to complement the tangents of cardinal splines mentioned above.

The two previous methods for computing the tangent vectors generate C^1 continuous curves. In order to create a curve that has C^2 continuity at the joins of its constituting cubic segments, we must require that the second derivatives of each pair of successive segments are equal at the joins. If $\mathbf{H}_i(u)$, $u \in [t_i, t_{i+1}]$ is the segment that interpolates $\mathbf{p}_i$ and $\mathbf{p}_{i+1}$, the following relation must hold:

$$\frac{d^2}{du^2}\mathbf{H}_{i-1}(t_i) = \frac{d^2}{du^2}\mathbf{H}_i(t_i).$$

Using (7.52), we differentiate the Hermite curve segments twice and get

$$(t_{i+1} - t_i)\vec{\mathbf{m}}_{i-1} + 2(t_{i+1} - t_{i-1})\vec{\mathbf{m}}_i + (t_i - t_{i-1})\vec{\mathbf{m}}_{i+1} =$$
$$3\frac{t_{i+1} - t_i}{t_i - t_{i-1}}(\mathbf{p}_i - \mathbf{p}_{i-1}) + 3\frac{t_i - t_{i-1}}{t_{i+1} - t_i}(\mathbf{p}_{i+1} - \mathbf{p}_i). \tag{7.56}$$

This relation holds for $i = 1, 2, \ldots, n - 1$, thus providing $(n - 1)$ equations for the computation of the $(n + 1)$ tangent vectors m_i, $i = 0, 1, \ldots, n$.

Since we have used all the available elements of the curve, we must impose two additional conditions on the interpolation curve, in order to create two more relations that will allow us to compute the tangent vectors. This situation may be unfortunate, but on the other hand, it offers some flexibility to the shape of the curve. It is customary to apply conditions referring to the ends of the curve, from which the values of $\vec{\mathbf{m}}_0$ and $\vec{\mathbf{m}}_n$ are computed. The easiest approach would be to allow the user to supply arbitrary values for these two tangent vectors; alternatively, geometric conditions that take into account the shape of the curve near its ends are applied. We will present such conditions below, for now we suppose that $\vec{\mathbf{m}}_0$ and $\vec{\mathbf{m}}_n$ are known. By combining equations (7.56) for all i, we construct the following linear system:

$$
\begin{bmatrix}
1 & 0 & \ldots & 0 & 0 \\
\alpha_1 & \beta_1 & \gamma_1 & & 0 \\
\vdots & \ddots & \ddots & \ddots & \vdots \\
0 & & \alpha_{n-1} & \beta_{n-1} & \gamma_{n-1} \\
0 & 0 & \ldots & 0 & 1
\end{bmatrix}
\cdot
\begin{bmatrix}
\vec{\mathbf{m}}_0 \\
\vec{\mathbf{m}}_1 \\
\vdots \\
\vec{\mathbf{m}}_{n-1} \\
\vec{\mathbf{m}}_n
\end{bmatrix}
=
\begin{bmatrix}
\vec{\mathbf{c}}_0 \\
\vec{\mathbf{c}}_1 \\
\vdots \\
\vec{\mathbf{c}}_{n-1} \\
\vec{\mathbf{c}}_n
\end{bmatrix},
\qquad (7.57)
$$

where we set

$$
\alpha_i = (t_{i+1} - t_i), \qquad \vec{\mathbf{c}}_0 = \vec{\mathbf{m}}_0,
$$
$$
\beta_i = 2(t_{i+1} - t_{i-1}), \qquad \vec{\mathbf{c}}_i = 3\frac{t_{i+1} - t_i}{t_i - t_{i-1}}(\mathbf{p}_i - \mathbf{p}_{i-1}) + 3\frac{t_i - t_{i-1}}{t_{i+1} - t_i}(\mathbf{p}_{i+1} - \mathbf{p}_i),
$$
$$
\gamma_i = (t_i - t_{i-1}), \qquad \vec{\mathbf{c}}_n = \vec{\mathbf{m}}_n.
$$

Solving this system will provide the tangent vectors $\vec{\mathbf{m}}_i$ so that the interpolating curve is C^2 continuous. It can be proven that this system always has a unique solution. Moreover, it is a tridiagonal system, and it may be solved efficiently using a direct method such as LU decomposition.

End conditions for C^2 piecewise Hermite interpolation. The additional conditions necessary to determine the tangents for a C^2 piecewise Hermite curve are called *end conditions* (or *boundary conditions*), since they involve the tangent vectors $\vec{\mathbf{m}}_0$ and $\vec{\mathbf{m}}_n$ at the ends of the curve.

One such condition is the *Bessel end condition*. The Bessel tangents computed in (7.55) for $\vec{\mathbf{m}}_0$ and $\vec{\mathbf{m}}_n$ are used so that the tangents at the ends are those of the parabolas that interpolate the first and last three control points. It suffices, then, to replace $\vec{\mathbf{c}}_0$ and $\vec{\mathbf{c}}_n$ in the system (7.57) with these expressions.

Another condition is the *quadratic end condition*, which requires that the second derivatives of the interpolation curve at the first two knots are equal (and similarly for the last two knots). Using our previous notation the following relations must hold:

$$\frac{d^2}{du^2}\mathbf{H}_0(t_0) = \frac{d^2}{du^2}\mathbf{H}_0(t_1) \quad \text{and} \quad \frac{d^2}{du^2}\mathbf{H}_{n-1}(t_{n-1}) = \frac{d^2}{du^2}\mathbf{H}_{n-1}(t_n).$$

By differentiating the Hermite curve twice, we can deduce that under this assumption

$$\overrightarrow{\mathbf{m}}_0 + \overrightarrow{\mathbf{m}}_1 = 2\frac{\mathbf{p}_1 - \mathbf{p}_0}{t_1 - t_0} \quad \text{and} \quad \overrightarrow{\mathbf{m}}_{n-1} + \overrightarrow{\mathbf{m}}_n = 2\frac{\mathbf{p}_n - \mathbf{p}_{n-1}}{t_n - t_{n-1}}.$$

These relations must be plugged into the system (7.57), replacing its first and last lines in full; fortunately, even after this change, the system remains tridiagonal and can be solved efficiently.

The last condition that we shall analyze is the *physical end condition*, which requires that the second derivatives vanish (are equal to zero) at the ends of the curve. If this condition is applied, the interpolating curve becomes a straight line near its ends, an effect which might or might not be desirable depending on the application. The name of this condition comes from the fact that the generated curve resembles the mechanical (or *physical*) spline, which is pinned at its ends so that its curvature vanishes. Working similarly to the quadratic end condition, we get

$$2\overrightarrow{\mathbf{m}}_0 + \overrightarrow{\mathbf{m}}_1 = 3\frac{\mathbf{p}_1 - \mathbf{p}_0}{t_1 - t_0} \quad \text{and} \quad \overrightarrow{\mathbf{m}}_{n-1} + 2\overrightarrow{\mathbf{m}}_n = 3\frac{\mathbf{p}_n - \mathbf{p}_{n-1}}{t_n - t_{n-1}},$$

and, again, we should replace the first and last equation of the system (7.57) with these equations.

7.5.3   Cubic B-Spline Interpolation⊛

B-spline curves, as studied above, approximate a given set of control points. In this section we show how to construct a cubic B-spline curve that interpolates a given set of points.

We shall denote the interpolating B-spline curve as $\mathbf{Q}(t)$; we require that the given parametric values t_i at which the curve interpolates points $\mathbf{p}_i$,

$$\mathbf{Q}(t_i) = \mathbf{p}_i, \quad i = 0, 1, \ldots, n, \tag{7.58}$$

are also used as the knots of the B-spline curve. Our aim is to find the control points $\mathbf{q}_i$ of this B-spline curve.

Supposing that the given points $\mathbf{p}_i$ are all different from each other, the values of t_i should also be different from each other. The first and the last points are easy to interpolate, if a clamped knot sequence is used. Therefore, we add knots t_{-2}, t_{-1} and t_{n+1}, t_{n+2} such that

$$t_{-2} = t_{-1} = t_0,$$

$$t_n = t_{n+1} = t_{n+2}.$$

Given this knot sequence, the control points are $\mathbf{q}_i$, $i = -3, -2, \ldots, n-1$ (the range of indices for the control points is imposed by the range of the indices of the knots). The first and the last control points are already known,

$$\mathbf{q}_{-3} = \mathbf{p}_0,$$
$$\mathbf{q}_{n-1} = \mathbf{p}_n. \tag{7.59}$$

For the remaining control points, the definition of the cubic B-spline curve and (7.58) give

$$\mathbf{p}_j = \mathbf{Q}(t_j) = \sum_{i=-3}^{n-1} N_i^3(t_j)\mathbf{q}_i, \quad j = 1, 2, \ldots, n-1. \tag{7.60}$$

The value of the cubic B-spline basis functions $N_i^3(t)$ at the knots t_j can be computed as follows: We start by evaluating the quadratic B-spline basis functions (7.28) at the knots, to get the simplified representation:

$$N_i^2(t_j) = \begin{cases} 0, & j = i, \\ \frac{t_{i+1}-t_i}{t_{i+2}-t_i}, & j = i+1, \\ \frac{t_{i+3}-t_{i+2}}{t_{i+3}-t_{i+1}}, & j = i+2, \\ 0, & \text{otherwise.} \end{cases}$$

Then, we apply the B-spline basis definition (7.31b) to get

$$N_i^3(t_j) = \begin{cases} \frac{t_{i+1}-t_i}{t_{i+3}-t_i}\frac{t_{i+1}-t_i}{t_{i+2}-t_i}, & j = i+1, \\ \frac{t_{i+2}-t_i}{t_{i+3}-t_i}\frac{t_{i+3}-t_{i+2}}{t_{i+3}-t_{i+1}} + \frac{t_{i+4}-t_{i+2}}{t_{i+4}-t_{i+1}}\frac{t_{i+2}-t_{i+1}}{t_{i+3}-t_{i+1}}, & j = i+2, \\ \frac{t_{i+4}-t_{i+3}}{t_{i+4}-t_{i+1}}\frac{t_{i+4}-t_{i+3}}{t_{i+4}-t_{i+2}}, & j = i+3, \\ 0, & \text{otherwise.} \end{cases}$$

Finally, we change the indices in order to get the $N_i^3(t_j)$ for a constant j and for all suitable i,

$$N_{j-1}^3(t_j) = \frac{t_j - t_{j-1}}{t_{j+2} - t_{j-1}} \frac{t_j - t_{j-1}}{t_{j+1} - t_{j-1}},$$

$$N_{j-2}^3(t_j) = \frac{t_j - t_{j-2}}{t_{j+1} - t_{j-2}} \frac{t_{j+1} - t_j}{t_{j+1} - t_{j-1}} + \frac{t_{j+2} - t_j}{t_{j+2} - t_{j-1}} \frac{t_j - t_{j-1}}{t_{j+1} - t_{j-1}}, \tag{7.61}$$

$$N_{j-3}^3(t_j) = \frac{t_{j+1} - t_j}{t_{j+1} - t_{j-2}} \frac{t_{j+1} - t_j}{t_{j+1} - t_{j-1}}.$$

Therefore (7.60) becomes

$$\mathbf{p}_j = N_{j-3}^3(t_j)\mathbf{q}_{j-3} + N_{j-2}^3(t_j)\mathbf{q}_{j-2} + N_{j-1}^3(t_j)\mathbf{q}_{j-1}.$$

Substituting $N_i^3(t_j)$ from (7.61), we get

$$\frac{(t_{j+1} - t_j)^2}{t_{j+1} - t_{j-2}} \mathbf{q}_{j-3}$$

$$+ \left[\frac{(t_j - t_{j-2})(t_{j+1} - t_j)}{t_{j+1} - t_{j-2}} + \frac{(t_{j+2} - t_j)(t_j - t_{j-1})}{t_{j+2} - t_{j-1}} \right] \mathbf{q}_{j-2}$$

$$+ \frac{(t_j - t_{j-1})^2}{t_{j+2} - t_{j-1}} \mathbf{q}_{j-1} = (t_{j+1} - t_{j-1})\mathbf{p}_j. \tag{7.62}$$

Relations (7.59) and (7.62) provide $(n+1)$ linear equations for the determination of the $(n+3)$ unknown control points $\mathbf{q}_i$, and, therefore, two more equations are needed in order to create a soluble system. The situation is very similar to the one that occured when we required that a Hermite interpolation curve be C^2 at the joins of its segments. This coincidence is not accidental, since in both cases we seek a piecewise cubic curve that is C^2 continuous and interpolates $(n+1)$ given points; the only difference is that in the former case the curve was expressed as a piecewise Hermite curve whereas in the latter it is given as a B-spline curve. Actually it can be proven that any expression of such a curve would require two additional conditions apart from the given interpolated points.

For the B-spline curve examined, it is customary to specify conditions for the two extreme unknown control points $\mathbf{q}_{-2}$ and $\mathbf{q}_{-1}$. We will present such conditions later; for now, we assume that $\mathbf{q}_{-2}$ and $\mathbf{q}_{-1}$ are known.

The linear system of (7.59) and (7.62) can be written as

$$
\begin{bmatrix}
1 & 0 & 0 & \cdots & 0 & 0 & 0 \\
0 & 1 & 0 & 0 & \cdots & 0 & 0 \\
0 & \alpha_1 & \beta_1 & \gamma_1 & 0 & \cdots & 0 \\
\vdots & & \ddots & \ddots & \ddots & & \vdots \\
0 & \cdots & 0 & \alpha_{n-1} & \beta_{n-1} & \gamma_{n-1} & 0 \\
0 & 0 & \cdots & 0 & 0 & 1 & 0 \\
0 & 0 & 0 & \cdots & 0 & 0 & 1
\end{bmatrix}
\cdot
\begin{bmatrix}
\mathbf{q}_{-3} \\
\mathbf{q}_{-2} \\
\mathbf{q}_{-1} \\
\vdots \\
\mathbf{q}_{n-3} \\
\mathbf{q}_{n-2} \\
\mathbf{q}_{n-1}
\end{bmatrix}
=
\begin{bmatrix}
\mathbf{p}_0 \\
\mathbf{r}_1 \\
(t_2 - t_0)\mathbf{p}_1 \\
\vdots \\
(t_n - t_{n-2})\mathbf{p}_{n-1} \\
\mathbf{r}_2 \\
\mathbf{p}_n
\end{bmatrix}, \quad (7.63)
$$

where we set α_j, β_j, γ_j the coefficients of $\mathbf{q}_{j-3}$, $\mathbf{q}_{j-2}$, $\mathbf{q}_{j-1}$ from (7.62), respectively, and also $\mathbf{r}_1 = \mathbf{q}_{-2}$ and $\mathbf{r}_2 = \mathbf{q}_{n-2}$. This is a tridiagonal system that can be solved efficiently using a direct method such as LU decomposition.

End conditions. In the case of B-spline interpolation, the end conditions required to complete the system (7.63) refer to the second and the penultimate control points, $\mathbf{q}_{-2}$ and $\mathbf{q}_{n-2}$. We shall examine the same end conditions as for cubic Hermite interpolation, the only difference being that now the equations will be expressed in terms of the given points $\mathbf{p}_i$ instead of the tangent vectors.

For the *Bessel end condition* the equations can be computed as follows. At the start of the curve, the tangent is

$$
\mathbf{Q}'(t_0) = \frac{3}{t_1 - t_0}(\mathbf{q}_{-2} - \mathbf{q}_{-3}) = \frac{3}{t_1 - t_0}(\mathbf{q}_{-2} - \mathbf{p}_0),
$$

and equating this with the expression of $\overrightarrow{\mathbf{m}}_0$, which is the required tangent, derived in (7.55), we have

$$
\mathbf{q}_{-2} = \frac{1}{3}\left(\frac{2t_2 - t_1 - t_0}{t_2 - t_0}\mathbf{p}_0 - \frac{t_2 - t_0}{t_2 - t_1}\mathbf{p}_1 - \frac{(t_1 - t_0)^2}{(t_2 - t_1)(t_2 - t_0)}\mathbf{p}_2 \right).
$$

Working similarly for the end of the curve, we reach

$$
\mathbf{q}_{n-2} = \frac{1}{3}\left(-\frac{(t_{n-1} - t_n)^2}{(t_{n-2} - t_{n-1})(t_{n-2} - t_n)}\mathbf{p}_{n-2} + \frac{t_{n-2} - t_n}{t_{n-2} - t_{n-1}}\mathbf{p}_{n-1} \right.
$$
$$
\left. + \frac{2t_{n-2} - t_{n-1} - t_n}{t_{n-2} - t_n)}\mathbf{p}_n \right).
$$

These two expressions for $\mathbf{q}_{-2}$ and $\mathbf{q}_{n-2}$ must replace $\mathbf{r}_1$ and $\mathbf{r}_2$ in system (7.63).

In order to apply the *quadratic end condition*, we may write the first (and similarly the last) segment of the B-spline curve, defined over the parametric interval

$[t_0, t_1]$ as a cubic Bézier curve (see Section 7.3.7) and differentiate this form of the curve twice. In this way we end up with the relations

$$\mathbf{q}_{-2} - \mathbf{q}_{-1} = \frac{t_2 - t_0}{3(t_1 - t_0)}(\mathbf{p}_0 - \mathbf{p}_1),$$

$$\mathbf{q}_{n-3} - \mathbf{q}_{n-2} = \frac{t_n - t_{n-2}}{3(t_n - t_{n-1})}(\mathbf{p}_{n-1} - \mathbf{p}_n),$$

which must replace the second and the penultimate equations of system (7.63) in full; the system remains tridiagonal even after this change.

Finally, the *natural end condition* can be applied similarly. The respective equations are

$$(t_2 + t_1 - 2t_0)\mathbf{q}_{-2} - (t_1 - t_0)\mathbf{q}_{-1} = (t_2 - t_0)\mathbf{p}_0,$$

$$(t_n - t_{n-1})\mathbf{q}_{n-3} - (2t_n - t_{n-1} - t_{n-2})\mathbf{q}_{n-2} = -(t_n - t_{n-2})\mathbf{p}_n.$$

7.5.4 Parameterizations of Piecewise Interpolation Curves

In all our discussion of piecewise parametric interpolation curves, we assumed that the knots of the curve (the parametric values at which the curve interpolates the given points) are given by the user. However, this is seldom the case, as the user is interested only in providing the points that the curve interpolates. In such cases, the required knots may be computed algorithmically, possibly using the given points in order to generate better-shaped curves. The parameterization methods that we have presented for general B-spline curves (see Section 7.3.5) can be applied here as well.

The simplest parameterization is the uniform one, in which the knots are equidistant. This parameterization is used in practice in spite of the fact that other methods may produce better curves, since it greatly simplifies the linear systems (7.57) and (7.63) that must be solved to produce C^2 cubic interpolating curves.

More complex parameterizations, which usually generate smoother curves, can be constructed by taking into account the given interpolated points $\mathbf{p}_i$. A chord-length parameterization can be computed from the relation

$$\frac{t_{i+2} - t_{i+1}}{t_{i+1} - t_i} = \frac{|\mathbf{p}_{i+2} - \mathbf{p}_{i+1}|}{|\mathbf{p}_{i+1} - \mathbf{p}_i|}$$

and a centripetal parameterization can be computed from

$$\frac{t_{i+2} - t_{i+1}}{t_{i+1} - t_i} = \sqrt{\frac{|\mathbf{p}_{i+2} - \mathbf{p}_{i+1}|}{|\mathbf{p}_{i+1} - \mathbf{p}_i|}}.$$

In both of these cases, the value of the initial knot t_0 can be specified arbitrarily. We notice that in contrast to B-spline parameterizations, which use the control points of the curve, parameterizations of interpolating curves use the points being interpolated since the shape of the curve should be adapted to them.

7.6 Surfaces

Bézier and B-spline curves can be used to generate parametric surfaces in several ways. The most straightforward and intuitive type of surfaces are *tensor product* Bézier and B-spline surfaces. It will be seen that these forms of parametric surfaces are simple generalizations of the respective curves, thus inheriting most of their properties.

7.6.1 Tensor Product Bézier Surfaces

Consider a Bézier curve of degree m with control points $\mathbf{p}_i$, $i = 0, 1, \ldots, m$, given in terms of a parameter u,

$$\mathbf{P}^m(u) = \sum_{i=0}^{m} B_i^m(u)\mathbf{p}_i, \quad u \in [0,1].$$

Consider further that each control point $\mathbf{p}_i$ traces a Bézier curve of degree n (constant for all control points) with control points $\mathbf{p}_{i,j}$, $j = 0, 1, \ldots, n$, in terms of a parameter v,

$$\mathbf{P}_i^n(v) = \sum_{j=0}^{n} B_j^n(v)\mathbf{p}_{i,j}, \quad v \in [0,1].$$

Then *every* point of the initial curve will trace a Bézier curve of degree n, and all these curves will generate a *tensor product Bézier surface*. The equation of this surface can be formed if we replace the points $\mathbf{p}_i$ in the first of the above equations with the curve $\mathbf{P}_i^n(v)$ that it traces. Thus, the equation of a tensor product Bézier surface $\mathbf{P}^{m,n}(u,v)$ of degree m in u and degree n in v is

$$\begin{aligned}
\mathbf{P}^{m,n}(u,v) &= \sum_{i=0}^{m} B_i^m(u) \left(\sum_{j=0}^{n} B_j^n(v)\mathbf{p}_{i,j} \right) \\
&= \sum_{i=0}^{m} \sum_{j=0}^{n} B_i^m(u)B_j^n(v)\mathbf{p}_{i,j}, \quad u \in [0,1], \, v \in [0,1].
\end{aligned} \tag{7.64}$$

The Bézier curves that were used for the definition of the surface have $(m+1) \times (n+1)$ control points, which are the *control points* (also called the *control net*)

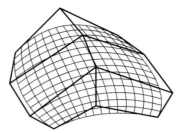

Figure 7.16. A tensor product Bézier surface of degrees 2 and 3.

of the tensor product Bézier surface. These points can be shown in a rectangular arrangement:

$$
\begin{array}{c|cccc}
 & v \longrightarrow & & & \\
\hline
u & \mathbf{p}_{0,0} & \mathbf{p}_{0,1} & \cdots & \mathbf{p}_{0,n} \\
\downarrow & \mathbf{p}_{1,0} & \mathbf{p}_{1,1} & \cdots & \mathbf{p}_{1,n} \\
 & \vdots & \vdots & & \vdots \\
 & \mathbf{p}_{m,0} & \mathbf{p}_{m,1} & \cdots & \mathbf{p}_{m,n}
\end{array}
\tag{7.65}
$$

The isoparametric curves that correspond to $u = 0$, $u = 1$, $v = 0$, and $v = 1$ are called *boundary curves* of the Bézier surface. Notice that the control points $\mathbf{p}_i$ of the boundary curve $\mathbf{P}^m(u)$ corresponding to $v = 0$ that we used initially are $\mathbf{p}_i = \mathbf{p}_{i,0}$ using the current notation.

The construction of a tensor product Bézier surface is symmetric: we may start off from the boundary curve $u = 0$ and trace a curve with each of its control points to construct the same surface as above; this can be verified by interchanging the two summations in (7.64). Generally, the same surface is constructed by starting with any of the boundary curves.

The de Casteljau algorithm for tensor product Bézier surfaces. The de Casteljau algorithm is very important for the processing of Bézier curves, since it is applied to the efficient computation of points on the curve as well as to the subdivision of the curve into two segments of the same type; subdivision has interesting applications as well, an important one being the drawing of the Bézier curve. The same algorithm can be used for tensor product Bézier surfaces, with similar applications; this should be expected since surfaces were defined exclusively in terms of Bézier curves.

Specifically, in order to compute a point $\mathbf{P}^{m,n}(u, v)$ of a Bézier surface, we first apply the de Casteljau algorithm to each of the rows of the table in (7.65) (in other

```
point bezierSurfacePoint ( int m, int n,
                           point[][] controlPt,
                           float u, float v )
{
    point tmpPt[n+1];
    point curvePt[n+1];

    for (i=0; i <= m; i++)  {
        for (j=0; j <= n; j++)  {
            tempPt[j] = controlPt[i][j];
        }
        curvePt[i] = bezierPoint(n, tempPt, v);
    }

    return bezierPoint(m, curvePt, u);
}
```

Listing 7.3: The de Casteljau algorithm for surfaces.

words, to each of the curves traced by $\mathbf{p}_{i,0}$); in this way $m+1$ points are computed, which correspond to the given value of the parameter v on these curves. These are the control points of the isoparametric curve corresponding to this value of v. The required point $\mathbf{P}^{m,n}(u,v)$ of the surface is the point on this curve that corresponds to the value of u, and it can be computed by another application of the de Casteljau algorithm.

The pseudocode in Listing 7.3 implements the de Casteljau algorithm for a tensor product Bézier surface. It uses the de Casteljau algorithm for curves provided in Section 7.2.3.

Properties of tensor product Bézier surfaces. The properties of tensor product Bézier surfaces are generalizations of the respective properties of Bézier curves. Bézier surfaces enjoy the convex-hull property, invariance under affine transformations, invariance under affine transformations of their parameters, symmetry with respect to their control points, planar precision, boundary control points interpolation, and pseudo-local control. The only property that does not generalize to surfaces is the variation-diminishing property.

Concerning the derivatives of a tensor product Bézier surface, we note that the most interesting ones are the partial derivatives with respect to each of the parameters; they are the tangents of isoparametric curves of the surface. In the case of a tensor product Bézier surface, these derivatives can be computed easily, since the parameters u and v are separated. The partial derivative with respect to u is

$$\frac{\partial}{\partial u}\mathbf{P}^{m,n}(u,v) = \sum_{j=0}^{n} B_j^n(v) \left(\frac{\partial}{\partial u} \sum_{i=0}^{m} B_i^m(u)\mathbf{p}_{i,j} \right),$$

where the term in parentheses is only dependent on u; therefore, it may be computed as the derivative of a Bézier curve, see relation (7.16). To apply this formula, one must differentiate all the mth-degree Bézier curves formed by the columns of the control net for the requested value of u; then these derivatives are considered as control points of a Bézier curve, which must be evaluated at the requested value of v to give the value of the surface derivative.

Bézier surface subdivision. Subdivision of a tensor product Bézier surface is a simple generalization of Bézier curve subdivision. In this case, a pair of parametric values (u_0, v_0) is chosen, and the surface is subdivided into *four* sub-surfaces of the same type, whose control points are produced during the evaluation of the surface point $\mathbf{P}^{m,n}(u_0, v_0)$ using the de Casteljau algorithm.

The process can be outlined as follows: The de Casteljau algorithm is applied to every line of the control point table (7.65), thus subdividing each of the corresponding curves into a "left" and a "right" segment, yielding two sets of $(m+1) \times (n+1)$ control points. Then the de Casteljau algorithm is applied to all the $2 \times (m+1) \times (n+1)$ columns of control points, subdividing each into a "top" and a "bottom" segment, thus producing in total four sets of $(m+1) \times (n+1)$ control points that define respective Bézier surfaces.

This subdivision process can be used in several applications involving tensor product Bézier surfaces, such as drawing a Bézier surface and finding intersections between a Bézier surface and a line or plane.

In order to draw a tensor product Bézier surface, we take into account that if its control points are coplanar, then the surface degenerates into a planar polygon defined by the four extreme control points. Therefore, to draw a Bézier surface we check whether its control points are coplanar (up to a given tolerance level); if this holds, we simply draw the aforementioned polygon; otherwise we subdivide the surface into four subsurfaces, for an arbitrary pair of parametric values (u_0, v_0), and perform the same procedure recursively for each of the subsurfaces.

The other applications of Bézier surface subdivision can be adapted similarly from their counterparts involving Bézier curves.

7.6.2 Tensor Product B-Spline Surfaces

Tensor product Bézier surfaces have, as we saw, common properties with Bézier curves; inevitably, they also have common disadvantages, the most important one being the need to use high-degree surfaces in order to describe complex shapes. For such surfaces, it is preferable to utilize techniques similar to the ones employed in curves and to construct smooth surfaces by joining together low-degree surfaces with suitable continuity constraints.

Tensor product B-spline surfaces are an instance of such surfaces. They are constructed by parametric surfaces of degree k with respect to u and degree ℓ with respect to v, joined together with continuity C^{k-1} with respect to u and $C^{\ell-1}$ with respect to v. They are generated from B-spline curves, in a manner similar to the generation of tensor product Bézier surfaces from Bézier curves: we start off with a kth-degree B-spline curve given in terms of the parameter u and consider that its points trace ℓth-degree B-spline curves in terms of the parameter v; the generated surface is a tensor product B-spline surface.

A tensor product B-spline surface has a set of $(m+1) \times (n+1)$ control points $\mathbf{p}_{i,j}$, where m and n are independent of the degrees k and ℓ of the surface; it has also two sets of knots, $u_1, u_2, \ldots, u_{m+k}$ for the parameter u and $v_1, v_2, \ldots, v_{n+\ell}$ for the parameter v. It is given by the formula

$$\mathbf{Q}(u,v) = \sum_{i=0}^{m} \sum_{j=0}^{n} N_i^k(u) N_j^\ell(v) \mathbf{p}_{i,j}. \tag{7.66}$$

(Four additional "dummy" knots u_0, u_{m+k+1}, v_0, and $v_{n+\ell+1}$ are needed for the proper definition of the B-spline basis functions $N_i^k(u)$ and $N_j^\ell(v)$, but these do not affect the shape of the curve.) The two knot sequences, for u and for v, are totally independent of each other. The domain of the surface is the parametric interval $[u_k, u_{m+1}] \times [v_\ell, v_{n+1}]$. The following arrangement depicts the control elements of a B-spline surface:

		v_1	$\cdots$	v_n	$\cdots$	$v_{n+\ell}$
	$\mathbf{p}_{0,0}$	$\mathbf{p}_{0,1}$	$\cdots$	$\mathbf{p}_{0,n}$		
u_1	$\mathbf{p}_{1,0}$	$\mathbf{p}_{1,1}$	$\cdots$	$\mathbf{p}_{1,n}$		
$\vdots$	$\vdots$	$\vdots$		$\vdots$		
u_m	$\mathbf{p}_{m,0}$	$\mathbf{p}_{m,1}$	$\cdots$	$\mathbf{p}_{m,n}$		
$\vdots$						
u_{m+k}						

The de Boor algorithm for tensor product B-spline surfaces. The de Boor algorithm, used to compute points on a B-spline curve, can be readily adapted to tensor product surfaces. This is similar to the adaptation of the de Casteljau algorithm for Bézier surfaces.

In order to compute a point $\mathbf{Q}(u,v)$ on a tensor product B-spline surface, we must first find the parametric interval $[u_i, u_{i+1}] \times [v_j, v_{j+1}]$ into which the parametric value (u,v) belongs. Then we can apply the familiar de Boor algorithm for B-spline curves to each of the rows of the control net for the parametric value $v \in [v_j, v_{j+1}]$; this produces $(m+1)$ points, to which we apply the de Boor algorithm once more, for the parametric value $u \in [u_i, u_{i+1}]$. The computed point on the latter curve is the point on the B-spline surface. Just as with Bézier surfaces, the procedure can be carried out first for u (to the columns of the control net) and then for v.

Knots and parameterizations. The two knot sequences, for u and for v, of a tensor product B-spline surface maintain all the properties of the knot sequence of a B-spline curve (see Section 7.3.5). So, for instance, when the first k knots for u are equal, the surface interpolates its isoparametric curve that corresponds to $u = u_1 = u_k$; similar properties hold when the first or last knots of the sequences for u or for v are equal. Furthermore, when any internal knot is repeated, the surface loses degrees of continuity accordingly, along the corresponding isoparametric curves.

Just like for B-spline curves, it would be beneficial to determine "good" *parameterizations* automatically, so that the user need not supply the knot sequences. Unfortunately, it is far more difficult to find such knot sequences in the case of tensor product surfaces than it is for curves. Contrary to all other forms of processing tensor product surfaces that we have examined, it is impossible to apply the methods mentioned in Section 7.3.5 to rows and columns of the control net of a B-spline surface in order to generate a parameterization that satisfies one of the properties mentioned (chord length, centripetal). The reason is that all the isoparametric curves of the surface use the same knot sequences for u (and, respectively, for v); therefore, it is not possible to construct a knot sequence that satisfies, for instance, the chord-length property, for all rows of the control net simultaneously. If a chord-length knot sequence is constructed based on the control points of a row, it will probably not produce satisfactory results when used in the other rows. One solution would seemingly be to combine knot sequences constructed for all rows, for instance by averaging the respective knot values; however, this approach would likely not produce good results for any of the rows, unless the geometry of the control points is uniform across the rows of the control net.

Methods to generate parameterizations based on all the control points of the surface have been presented only for surfaces of degree four or higher that demonstrate geometric and not parametric continuity. In other cases, the use of a uniform parameterization, which does not take into account the geometry of the control net, is the safest choice.

Knot insertion for tensor product B-spline surfaces is no more difficult than it is for curves, and the Boehm algorithm can be applied here as well. For a surface, a knot may be inserted independently in any of the two knot sequences, for u and for v. If a knot is inserted in the knot sequence $u_1, u_2, \ldots, u_{m+k}$ (in a permissible position, according to the restrictions mentioned for curves), a full row of control points must be added to the control net of the surface in order to maintain the relationship between the number of control points, the degree of the curve, and the number of knots; each of these points can be computed by applying the Boehm algorithm for curves to the respective column of the control net. The procedure is similar for knot insertion in $v_1, v_2, \ldots, v_{n+\ell}$, by applying the Boehm algorithm to the rows of the control net of the surface.

Properties of tensor product B-spline surfaces.

Most of the properties of B-spline curves generalize for surfaces. Tensor product B-spline surfaces enjoy local control, the strong convex-hull property, invariance under affine transformations, invariance under affine transformations of their parameters, planar precision, boundary control point interpolation if the extreme knots have suitable multiplicity, and are a generalization of tensor product Bézier surfaces under suitable conditions. The only property that is not carried over from curves is the variation-diminishing property.

Interpolation with tensor product B-spline surfaces.

Tensor product B-spline surfaces are, in general, approximating their control points. Analogously to B-spline curves, they can be adapted so as to interpolate a given set of points. The most interesting and practical case are *bi-cubic* tensor product B-spline surfaces, in other words surfaces of degree three for both u and v.

The problem can be stated as follows: given $(m+1) \times (n+1)$ points $\mathbf{p}_{i,j}$, $i = 0, 1, \ldots, m$, $j = 0, 1, \ldots, n$ and two knot sequences u_i, $i = 0, 1, \ldots, m$ and v_j, $j = 0, 1, \ldots, n$, determine the $(m+3) \times (n+3)$ control points $\mathbf{q}_{i,j}$ of a bi-cubic tensor product B-spline surface $\mathbf{Q}(u, v)$ that satisfies

$$\mathbf{Q}(u_i, v_j) = \mathbf{p}_{i,j}, \quad \begin{aligned} i &= 0, 1, \ldots, m, \\ j &= 0, 1, \ldots, n. \end{aligned}$$

The computation can be performed as follows: First we interpolate each column of the array of given points $\mathbf{p}_{i,j}$ in terms of u, computing the control points $\mathbf{s}_{i,j}$ of the respective interpolation curves. We recall that each of these curves has $(m+3)$ control points and requires two additional points to be specified, which we call $\mathbf{r}_{0,j}$ and $\mathbf{r}_{1,j}$, $j = 0, 1, \ldots, n$. Then we interpolate each row of these control points $\mathbf{s}_{i,j}$ in terms of v, computing the control points $\mathbf{q}_{i,j}$ of the respective interpolation curves. Each of these $(m+3)$ curves has $(n+3)$ control points and requires two additional points to be specified, which we call $\mathbf{c}_{i,0}$ and $\mathbf{c}_{i,1}$, $i = 0, 1, \ldots, m+2$. The control points $\mathbf{q}_{i,j}$ constitute the control points of the interpolating B-spline surface.

In conclusion, tensor product surfaces have a relatively simple mathematical form and interesting properties, which make them useful practical tools for the representation of surfaces. Their main drawback is that the set of points used as control or interpolation points must necessarily form a rectangular arrangement, otherwise this class of surfaces cannot be used. Specifically for B-spline surfaces, additional problems may arise if the points are not distributed relatively "uniformly," due to the fact that a constant parameterization is applied to all rows or columns of the control net. In the case of triangular topology, barycentric coordinates can be used to define surfaces in a manner analogous to tensor product surfaces. Subdivision surfaces, examined in Chapter 8, overcome these limitations and offer a more general description of surfaces.

7.7 Exercises

1. Construct the Bernstein polynomials for $n = 4$ and $n = 5$. Verify their properties mentioned in Section 7.2.4.

2. Create a program to draw Bézier curves. Implement two methods for drawing them:

    (a) Using the de Casteljau algorithm, compute points at equally spaced parametric values on the curve and join them with line segments.

    (b) Using Bézier curve subdivision, as described in Section 7.2.6.

    Compare the two implementations in terms of speed, visual quality, and ease of use (additional parameters or assumptions needed in each case).

3. (Degree elevation.) Given a Bézier curve $\mathbf{P}^n(t)$ of degree n with control points $\mathbf{p}_0, \mathbf{p}_1, \ldots \mathbf{p}_n$, determine the control points $\mathbf{q}_0, \mathbf{q}_1, \ldots \mathbf{q}_{n+1}$ of a new curve $\mathbf{Q}^{n+1}(t)$ of degree $n+1$ that has the same shape as $\mathbf{P}^n(t)$.

4. (Multiple knot insertion.) Construct an algorithm to insert the same knot s times to the knot sequence of a B-spline curve. You may reuse formula (7.37) for each step, renumbering the elements of the curve before proceeding to the next iteration. The resulting formula should be similar the the one of the de Boor algorithm; explain why this holds.

5. (Closed B-spline curves.) Investigate closed B-spline curves, whose two endpoints coincide. Find conditions under which the closed curve is smooth at the point it closes.

6. Prove that the first derivatives of Bézier and B-spline curves are given by (7.16) and (7.38), respectively.

7. Construct a program to visualize rational Bézier and B-spline curves. The user must have interactive control over all the parameters of the curves (control points, knot sequence, weights). Also explore the parameterizations presented in Section 7.3.5.

8. Verify that a planar rational quadratic Bézier curve represents a conic section under the assumptions of Section 7.4.1. You may eliminate the parameter t from the two coordinate parametric equations, construct the algebraic equation, and verify that the constraints of Equation (7.42) hold.

9. Given that a circular arc can be represented using a rational Bézier curve, a complete circle can be represented using a number of consecutive rational Bézier curves (with positive weights), as shown in Figure 7.17.

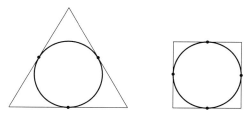

Figure 7.17. A circle represented as three and four consecutive rational Bézier curves. The control polygons of the curves are also shown.

Equivalently, the circle can be represented by a rational B-Spline curve with the same $\mathbf{p}_i$ as control points. Find the remaining elements of this NURBS curve (weights and knot sequence) for the two cases depicted. Can you see a pattern?

10. Construct a program to draw piecewise cubic interpolation curves. Verify that cubic Hermite interpolation with C^2 continuity yields the same curve as cubic B-spline interpolation. Experiment with various end conditions.

11. Construct a program to render the various types of tensor product surfaces presented. Integrate illumination and texturing algorithms (Chapters 12 and 14).

Subdivision for Graphics and Visualization

A. Nasri, F. A. Salem, and G. Turkiyyah

One reason my paintings have become realistic has to do
with my interest in what things really look like.
—Robert Bechtle

8.1 Introduction

Subdivision surfaces are now well established in the graphics community. They
provide simple techniques to generate a smooth surface from a given polygonal
mesh, often referred to as *polyhedron*. One of their major advantages over traditional B-spline surfaces and NURBS is the ability to handle meshes of arbitrary
topology. As such, complex shapes can be obtained, rendered, and edited at various levels of the refinement process. In this chapter, we present the basic ideas
about these surfaces and provide the algorithms of some of the well-known subdivision schemes. We also describe how to manipulate such surfaces and give an
overview of continuity analysis at extraordinary points. Finally, the application
of subdivision surfaces in the domain of finite elements is outlined. The discussion is far from complete, and more information on these topics can be found in
the cited references [Zori00, Warr01, Sabi04, Velh01a, Nasr02c, Nasr02b, Sede98,
Stam03, Stam98, Zhan02, Pakd05, Ivri03].

Tensor product B-spline surfaces restrict the defining control mesh to a rect-angular topology. Such a restriction tremendously limits the complexity of shapes that can be represented. This limitation motivated the search for a general solution that can handle arbitrary topology, yet still produce regular B-spline surfaces in the normal way. The concept of subdivision surfaces was initiated by two papers that appeared in the same journal in 1978. They were both extensions of B-spline surfaces over such a topology. The first paper presented the Doo–Sabin [Doo78] subdivision algorithm that produces standard quadratic B-splines and the second paper introduced the Catmull–Clark algorithm [Catm78] that produces cubic B-splines. Following these results, subdivision surfaces became a central issue for the graphics and geometric modeling community.

Since subdivision surfaces were initiated by knot insertion [Boeh80, Cohe80, Fari01], it is assumed that the reader is familiar with this topic in the context of curves and surfaces (see Chapter 7).

8.2   Notation

In this section, we introduce some basic notation to be used throughout this chapter.

Mask. A *mask* is generally defined by a set of scalars $(m_i)_{1 \leq i \leq n}$ which can be applied to a set of n vertices $\mathbf{v}_i$ to generate a new vertex $\mathbf{w}$ as follows:

$$\mathbf{w} = \frac{\sum_{i=1}^{n} m_i \mathbf{v_i}}{\sum_{i=1}^{n} m_i}.$$

Interior/boundary vertex. For a closed polyhedron all vertices are called *interior* vertices. Typically, an *interior* vertex corresponds to a point on the limit surface with an epsilon neighborhood homeomorphic to a closed disk. For an open polyhedron, a set of vertices fall on the boundary. The vertices that make up the *skirt* of the polyhedron are called *boundary* vertices. An edge linking two boundary vertices is always shared by one face of the polyhedron.

Valence of a vertex. The *valence* of a vertex is the number of edges incident on it. Accordingly, an interior vertex is at least three-valent whereas a boundary vertex could be two-valent.

Ordinary vertex/face. An ordinary vertex depends on the subdivision scheme used. For surfaces based on tensor products, an interior (boundary) vertex that is four-valent (three-valent) is called an *ordinary* vertex. An *ordinary* face is a face that has four ordinary vertices. For triangular meshes, an ordinary vertex is usually six-valent.

Extraordinary vertex/face. A vertex that is not an ordinary vertex is typically called an extraordinary vertex. A face with n ($n \neq 4$) vertices is called an *extraordinary* face.

1-ring. A *1-ring* of an interior vertex $\mathbf{v}_i$ is the set of vertices ($\mathbf{v}_j$), where $\mathbf{v}_i\mathbf{v}_j$ is an edge incident to $\mathbf{v}_i$.

Regular/irregular setting. When all vertices are ordinary vertices, the configuration is called *regular*. In irregular settings, the configuration contains at least one extraordinary vertex or one extraordinary face.

Tensor product. Given two masks $(m_i)_{1 \leq i \leq r}$ and $(n_i)_{1 \leq i \leq p}$, the *tensor product* of these two masks is another mask of $r \times p$ elements $(m_i \times n_j)_{1 \leq i \leq r, 1 \leq j \leq p}$.

8.3 Subdivision Curves

In this section, we present three popular subdivision curves: quadratic subdivision (Chaikin), cubic subdivision, and four-point schemes. We assume that the initial control-polygon vertices are indicated by $\mathbf{v}_i$ and the vertices of its refined polygon by $\mathbf{v}_i^j$, where the subscript j indicates the level of refinement; as such, $\mathbf{v}_i = \mathbf{v}_i^0$.

8.3.1 Quadratic Curve Subdivision

The first curve-subdivision algorithm was published in 1974 by Chaikin [Chai74]. The algorithm was mainly intended for hardware acceleration. The algorithm consists of the following steps:

1. For each edge e_i^j connecting two vertices $\mathbf{v}_{i-1}^j$ and $\mathbf{v}_i^j$, compute two new vertices using the masks $(1,3)$, and $(3,1)$ as follows:

$$\mathbf{v}_{2i-1}^{j+1} = \frac{3}{4}\mathbf{v}_i^j + \frac{1}{4}\mathbf{v}_{i-1}^j, \tag{8.1}$$

$$\mathbf{v}_{2i}^{j+1} = \frac{3}{4}\mathbf{v}_i^j + \frac{1}{4}\mathbf{v}_{i+1}^j. \tag{8.2}$$

2. Construct a new polygon as follows:

    (a) For each vertex $\mathbf{v}_i^j$, connect its two new vertices $\mathbf{v}_{2i-2}^{j+1}$ and $\mathbf{v}_{2i-1}^{j+1}$ forming a V-edge (corresponding to a vertex) of the new control polygon.

    (b) For each edge $\mathbf{e}_i^j$, connect its two new vertices $\mathbf{v}_{2i-1}^{j+1}, \mathbf{v}_{2i}^{j+1}$ forming an E-edge (corresponding to an edge) of the new control polygon.

The above steps can be repeated a number of times until the refined control polygon converges to a smooth limit curve. Figure 8.1 shows the corresponding masks and one step of refinement.

After the method was presented at a conference, it was shown that the resulting curve is simply a uniform quadratic B-spline [Ries75] and that the above construction can be obtained by inserting a knot at the middle of every interval defining the quadratic B-spline curve of the initial control polygon.

8.3.2 Cubic Curve Subdivision

Similar to the quadratic case, a cubic subdivision algorithm can be formulated by inserting a knot at the middle of each interval. The algorithm consists of the following steps:

1. For each vertex $\mathbf{v}_i^j$, compute a new vertex $\mathbf{v}_{2i}^{j+1}$, called V-vertex, using the mask $(1,6,1)$ as follows:

$$\mathbf{v}_{2i}^{j+1} = \frac{\mathbf{v}_{i-1}^j + 6\mathbf{v}_i^j + \mathbf{v}_{i+1}^j}{8}. \tag{8.3}$$

2. For each edge $\mathbf{v}_{i-1}^j\mathbf{v}_i^j$, compute a new vertex, called E-vertex, using the mask $(1,1)$ as follows:

$$\mathbf{v}_{2i-1}^{j+1} = \frac{\mathbf{v}_{i-1}^j + \mathbf{v}_i^j}{2}. \tag{8.4}$$

3. Construct a new refined polygon by connecting the E- and V-vertices generated as above.

If the algorithm is repeated recursively, then the subsequently refined control polygon will converge to the uniform cubic B-spline defined by the original control polygon. Figure 8.2 shows the corresponding masks and one step of refinement.

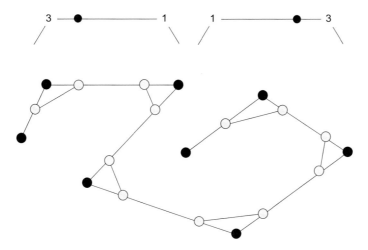

Figure 8.1. The quadratic curve subdivision masks (top) and one example of Chaikin's subdivision. The original vertices are shown as black disks and the refined ones as hollow disks.

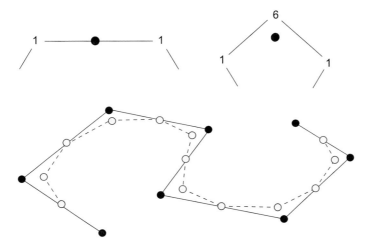

Figure 8.2. The cubic subdivision mask (top) and one refinement step (bottom). The original vertices are shown as black disks and the refined ones as hollow disks.

8.3.3 Four-Point Subdivision

In contrast to the previous two algorithms, the four-point subdivision is an interpolating scheme, where the limit curve interpolates the given control vertices.

The algorithm consists of the following steps:

1. For each vertex $\mathbf{v}_i$, denote the new corresponding vertex $\mathbf{v}_{2i}^{j+1}$, called V-vertex; $\mathbf{v}_{2i}^{j+1} = \mathbf{v}_i^j$.

2. For each edge $\mathbf{v}_{i-1}^j \mathbf{v}_i^j$, compute a new E-vertex using the mask $(-1, 9, 9, -1)$ as follows:

$$\mathbf{v}_{2i-1}^{j+1} = \frac{-\mathbf{v}_{i-2}^j + 9\mathbf{v}_{i-1}^j + 9\mathbf{v}_i^j - \mathbf{v}_{i+1}^j}{16}. \tag{8.5}$$

3. Construct a refined control polygon by connecting each V-vertex to its neighboring E-vertices.

Repeating this algorithm results in a limit curve that interpolates the vertices of the given control polygon. Figure 8.3 shows the corresponding masks and one step of refinement.

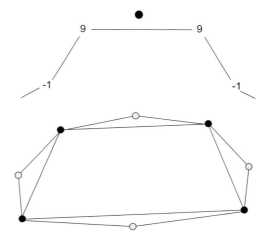

Figure 8.3. The four-point subdivision masks (top) and one step of refinement (bottom). The original vertices are shown as black disks and the refined ones as hollow disks.

8.4 Subdivision Surfaces

The extension of the quadratic and cubic curve subdivision algorithms to tensor product surfaces is straightforward. These surfaces have rectangular topology. However, the challenging task is how to extend such surface definitions to control meshes with arbitrary topology. We begin first by addressing the extension in the regular setting and then discuss its applications to irregular topology. In the former case, the subdivision coefficients, or the masks, are obtained by inserting knots at the middle of each interval in both parameter directions. As such, the coefficients can be easily obtained using the tensor-product formulation.

8.4.1 Quadratic Tensor Product Subdivision

Consider the rectangular mesh in Figure 8.4, which is used to illustrate the quadratic tensor product refinement rules. Let us assume that the surface is parameterized by the two parameters s and t. Along the s-direction, the quadratic curve subdivision generates two vertices on each edge using the mask $(1,3)$ and $(3,1)$, respectively. These vertices are indicated by solid squares in the figure. Using the same masks, we apply the refinement in the t-direction, generating two vertices (indicated by solid disks) on each edge joining two square vertices. Comparing the original and refined meshes, it is easy to notice the following (see Figure 8.4):

1. For each face $\mathbf{f}$ of the initial mesh, a new face (called F-face) is generated from its refined vertices.

2. For each edge $\mathbf{e}$ of the initial mesh, a new face (called E-face) is generated from the refined vertices of that edge on the faces common to it.

3. For each vertex $\mathbf{v}$ of the initial mesh, a new face (called V-face) is generated from the refined vertices of that vertex on the faces sharing it.

4. The refined polyhedron is actually obtained by connecting the refined vertices to form all of these faces.

It can be shown easily that the new vertices are then computed by the tensor product of the mask $(3,1)$. For example, the vertex $\mathbf{A}'$ is obtained by the tensor product $(3,1) \times (3,1)$, which is equivalent to $(9,3,1,3)$ applied to the vertices $\mathbf{A}, \mathbf{B}, \mathbf{C}, \mathbf{D}$ in that order. The other vertices are obtained by a rotation of this mask.

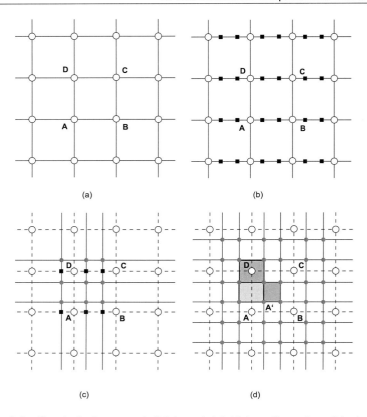

Figure 8.4. Quadratic tensor subdivision. (a) Initial configuration; (b) along the *s*-direction; (c) along the *t* direction; (d) one level of refinement, where the three types of faces, the F-face of **ABCD**, the E-face of **AD**, and the V-face of **D** are shown.

8.4.2 Cubic Tensor Product Subdivision

Similar to the quadratic case, the cubic subdivision rules can be obtained by the tensor product of the masks used in cubic curve subdivision. Applying these masks in the *s*-direction will generate a V-vertex corresponding to each old vertex and an E-vertex corresponding to each edge vertex (see Figure 8.5). The refined vertices are indicated by solid squares on this figure. Next, the same masks are applied to the square vertices in the *t*-direction, giving the final refined vertices. These are indicated by solid disks on the same figure.

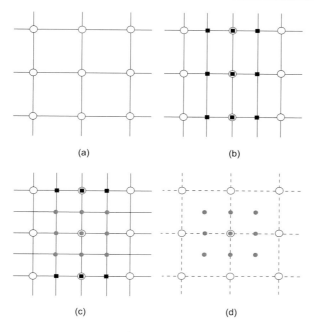

Figure 8.5. Cubic tensor subdivision. (a) Initial configuration; (b) refinement along the s-direction; (c) refinement along the t-direction; (d) the three types of vertices.

After comparing the old and the new mesh, it is easy to notice the following:

1. For each face **f** of the initial mesh, a new vertex (called F-vertex) is generated as the centroid of that face.

2. For each edge **e** of the initial mesh, a new vertex (called E-vertex) is generated from the vertices of that edge and the two F-vertices of its shared faces.

3. For each vertex **v** of the initial mesh, a new vertex (called V-vertex) is generated as a linear combination of that vertex, the E-vertices of the edges incident to it, and the F-vertices of the faces sharing it.

4. The refined mesh is similarly obtained by connecting the refined vertices to form all these faces.

Again, the new vertices can be computed using the tensor product of the masks used in cubic curve subdivision. For example, the F-vertex can be computed by the tensor product of the masks $(1,1) \times (1,1)$, the E-vertex can be computed by the masks $(1,1) \times (1,6,1)$ and finally the V-vertex is computed using the mask $(1,6,1) \times (1,6,1)$.

8.4.3 Subdivision Schemes

The above formulation led to the generalization of B-spline surfaces over arbitrary topology and, later, to the establishment of subdivision surfaces.

A *subdivision surface* is typically defined by a tuple (P_0, R), where P_0 is an initial mesh of arbitrary topology, called a polyhedron, and R is a set of rules, called a *refinement procedure*. By a polyhedron, we mean a set of vertices, edges, and faces in 3D space, where the faces do not have to be planar. The refinement procedure (often referred to as a *scheme*) is applied to the polyhedron P_0 to generate another polyhedron P_1, which in turn is taken as an input to the refinement procedure to generate another polyhedron P_2, and so on. If R satisfies the conditions stated in [Pete04] then the sequence of polyhedra $P_0, P_1, P_2, \cdots, P_i, \cdots$ will converge to a smooth surface.

The first two pioneering refinement procedures were developed by Doo–Sabin [Doo78] and Catmull–Clark [Catm78]. They are both extensions of B-spline surfaces over arbitrary topology. The Doo–Sabin scheme is an extension of quadratic tensor product subdivision, whereas the Catmull–Clark scheme is an extension of cubic tensor product subdivision. Since then, many subdivisions schemes have been devised. In this section, we only describe some of these schemes; other schemes can be found in the cited references.

In the following, we assume that P^j is the refined polyhedron at level j and that its vertices, edges, and faces are indicated by $\mathbf{v}_i^j$, $\mathbf{e}_i^j$, and $\mathbf{f}_i^j$, respectively.

The Doo–Sabin scheme. The Doo–Sabin scheme extends the quadratic tensor product to arbitrary topology. For regular meshes, where all faces are simply quads, the scheme generates biquadratic B-spline surfaces. The challenging task is to compute the refined vertices of an n-sided face $\mathbf{f}_i^j$, where n is not equal to 4. The following is an extended version of the algorithm given in Section 8.4.1.

1. For each n-sided face $\mathbf{f}_i^j$, compute n refined vertices $\mathbf{v}_i^{j+1}$ as a linear combination of the vertices of that face:

$$\mathbf{v}_i^{j+1} = \sum_{k=1}^{n} \alpha_{ik} \mathbf{v}_k^j, \qquad (8.6)$$

with

$$\alpha_{ii} = \frac{n+5}{4},$$

$$\alpha_{ik} = \frac{3+2\cos(2\pi(i-k))/n}{4n}, \quad \text{for } k \neq i. \qquad (8.7)$$

2. Construct a refined polygon P^{i+1} as follows:

   (a) For each n-sided face $\mathbf{f}_i^j$, generate a new face (called F-face) from its refined vertices.

   (b) For each edge $\mathbf{e}_i^j$, generate a new face (called an E-face) from the refined vertices of that edge on the faces common to it.

   (c) For each vertex $\mathbf{v}_i^j$, generate a new face (called V-face) from the refined vertices of that vertex on the faces sharing it.

Computing the refined vertices is achieved by applying the mask depicted in Figure 8.6 to the vertices of a given face. Figure 8.7 shows an example of a polyhedron, the first two refinements, and its corresponding limit surface.

For Doo–Sabin surfaces, the following observations can be made:

1. An n-sided face always generates an F-face with the same number of sides, i.e., an n-sided face remains n-sided after refinement. If $n \neq 4$, then such a face is called an extraordinary face, whereas a four-sided face is called an ordinary face.

2. An n-valent vertex generates an n-sided face. As such, all four-valent vertices generate ordinary faces.

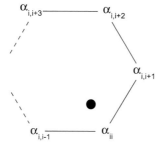

Figure 8.6. Masks for computing the vertices of an F-face.

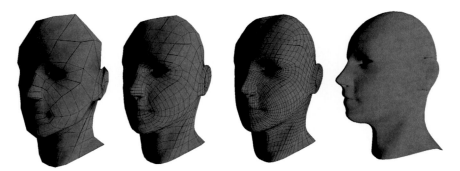

Figure 8.7. Doo–Sabin subdivision. From left to right: an initial configuration, its first and second refinements, and limit surface.

3. After the first refinement, all vertices are four-valent.

4. All E-faces are ordinary faces.

5. After a few steps of refinement, almost all the faces of the polyhedron are four-sided except for $ef + ev$ extraordinary faces, where ef and ev are the number of the extraordinary faces and vertices, respectively, of the initial polyhedron.

6. Similar to the curve subdivision, every vertex shared by four quads corresponds to a quadratic B-spline patch. Doo–Sabin surfaces are therefore biquadratic B-spline surfaces, except at small areas that correspond to the extraordinary vertices and faces.

7. The centroid of every face is a point on the limit surface, and a planar face is actually tangent to the limit surface at this point.

The Catmull–Clark scheme. The Catmull–Clark algorithm is basically an extension of the tensor cubic subdivision. Over arbitrary topology, the E-vertices and the F-vertices are computed using the same formulas adopted in the rectangular topology case. The major challenge is how to compute the V-vertices of the n-valent ($n \neq 4$) vertices. The full algorithm follows:

1. For each face $\mathbf{f}_i^j$ of the input polyhedron, generate a new vertex $\mathbf{v}f_i^{j+1}$ (called F-vertex) as the centroid of that face.

2. For each edge $\mathbf{e}_i^j = \mathbf{v}_i^j \mathbf{v}_{i+1}^j$ of the input polyhedron, generate a new vertex $\mathbf{v}e_i^{j+1}$ (called E-vertex) as a linear combination of $\mathbf{v}_i^j$, $\mathbf{v}_{i+1}^j$, and their four adjacent vertices on the two faces shared by that edge (see the masks in Figure 8.8).

3. For each vertex $\mathbf{v}_i^j$ of the input polyhedron, generate a new vertex (called V-vertex) $\mathbf{v}_i^{j+1}$ as a linear combination of $\mathbf{v}_i^j$ itself, the E-vertices of the edges sharing it, and the F-vertices of the faces sharing it. As such, the V-vertex $\mathbf{v}_i^{j+1}$ is then given by

$$\mathbf{v}_i^{j+1} = \alpha_n \sum_{k=1}^{n} \mathbf{v}f_k^j + \beta_n \sum_{k=1}^{n} \mathbf{v}e_k^j + \gamma_n \mathbf{v}_i^j, \tag{8.8}$$

where the original values of α_n, β_n, and γ_n are given by

$$\alpha_n = \beta_n = \frac{1}{n^2},$$

$$\gamma_n = \frac{n-2}{n}. \tag{8.9}$$

These values can be modified to improve the smoothness of the limit surface as suggested by Sabin [Sabi91].

4. Construct a refined polygon P^{i+1} as follows:

   (a) For each face $\mathbf{f}_i^j$ of P^i, connect its F-vertex to the E-vertices of the edges of $\mathbf{f}_i^j$.

   (b) For each vertex $\mathbf{v}_i^j$ of P^i, connect its V-vertex to E-vertices of the edge incident to $\mathbf{v}_i^j$.

Figure 8.8 depicts the various Catmull–Clark masks. The following observations can be made about Catmull–Clark refinement:

1. An n-valent vertex always generates a V-vertex of the same valency. For $n \neq 4$, the vertex is called an extraordinary vertex; otherwise, it is an ordinary vertex.

2. After the first refinement, every initial n-sided face generates an F-vertex with valence n. As such, all faces of the subsequently refined polyhedra will become four-sided. Accordingly, the Catmull–Clark algorithm is generally described for quad meshes, as one refinement step will get rid of the n-sided faces.

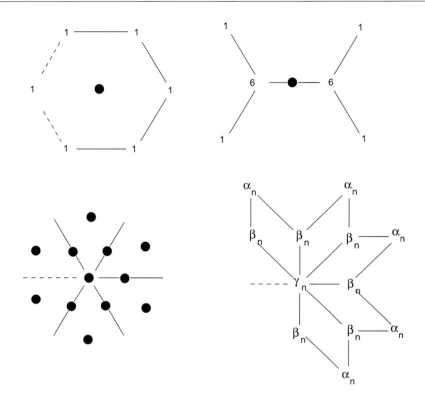

Figure 8.8. The Catmull–Clark masks. Top left: mask for F-vertex; Top right: mask for E-vertex; Bottom left: refined vertices (solid disks) around an extraordinary vertex; Bottom right: mask for V-vertex in the case of quad meshes.

3. All E-vertices are four-valent.

4. After one step of refinement, all vertices of the refined polyhedron become four-valent, except for $ev + ef$ extraordinary vertices, where ev and ef are the numbers of extraordinary vertices and faces, respectively, of the initial polyhedron.

5. Every quad surrounded by eight other quads corresponds to a bicubic B-spline patch. Accordingly, Catmull–Clark subdivision surfaces are mainly cubic B-spline surfaces except around a small number of extraordinary vertices.

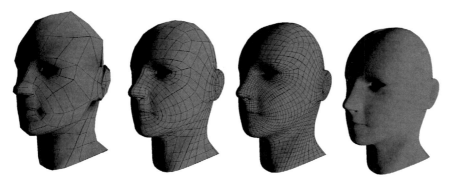

Figure 8.9. Catmull–Clark subdivision. From left to right: an initial configuration, first and second refinements, and limit surface

6. Every n-valent vertex $\mathbf{v}_i^1$ of the polyhedron P^1, i.e., first refinement, converges to a point on the limit surface given by

$$\mathbf{v}_i^\infty = \frac{n^2\mathbf{v}_i^1 + 4\sum_{j=1}^{n}\mathbf{v}e_j^1 + \sum_{j=1}^{n}\mathbf{v}f_j^1}{n(n+5)}, \qquad (8.10)$$

where $\mathbf{v}e_j^1$ are the E-vertices of the edges incident to the vertex $\mathbf{v}_i^1$, and $\mathbf{v}f_j^1$ are F-vertices of the faces sharing it.

The Loop scheme. While both the Catmull–Clark and Doo–Sabin schemes are quad-based schemes, the first subdivision algorithm that is mainly devoted to triangular meshes was developed by Loop [Loop87]. The algorithm takes as input a polyhedron P^j (at level j) with triangular faces and uses the following set of rules to generate another polyhedron P^{j+1}:

1. For each edge $\mathbf{e}_i^j$, do the following:

    (a) Let t_1 and t_2 be the two triangles sharing that edge.

    (b) Let $\mathbf{c}_1$ and $\mathbf{c}_2$ be the vertices of that edge and $\mathbf{c}_3$ and $\mathbf{c}_4$ be the other two vertices of t_1 and t_2.

    (c) Generate an E-vertex $\mathbf{v}e_i^{j+1}$ using the mask indicated in Figure 8.10 as follows:

    $$\mathbf{v}e_i^{j+1} = \frac{3\mathbf{c}_1 + \mathbf{c}_3 + 3\mathbf{c}_2 + \mathbf{c}_4}{8}. \qquad (8.11)$$

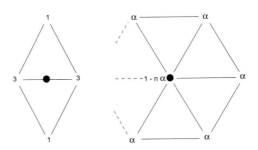

Figure 8.10. Loop masks. From left to right: E-vertex mask and V-vertex mask.

2. For each n-valent vertex $\mathbf{v}_i^j$, do the following:

   (a) Let $\mathbf{c}_1, \mathbf{c}_2, \cdots, \mathbf{c}_n$ be the vertices of the 1-ring around $\mathbf{v}_i^j$ (see Figure 8.10).

   (b) Generate a V-vertex $\mathbf{v}_{i+1}^j$ using a linear combination of the vertex $\mathbf{v}_i^j$ and its 1-ring vertices as follows:

$$\mathbf{v}_{i+1}^j = (1 - n\alpha_n)\mathbf{v}_i^j + \alpha_n \sum_{j=1}^n \mathbf{c}_j, \qquad (8.12)$$

where α_n is given by

$$\alpha_3 = \frac{3}{16},$$

$$\alpha_n = \frac{1}{n}\left(\frac{5}{8} - \left(\frac{3}{8} + \frac{1}{4}\cos\frac{2\pi}{n}\right)^2\right) \quad \text{for} \quad n > 3. \quad (8.13)$$

   (c) Generate a refined polyhedron P^{j+1} as follows:

   i. For each triangle of the polyhedron P^j, connect the E-vertices of its three edges to form a triangle of P^{j+1}.

   ii. For each n-valent vertex of the polyhedron P^j, connect its V-vertex to the E-vertices of all edges incident to it. As such, n triangles are added to the refined polyhedron P^{j+1}.

The above set of rules generate a sequence of polyhedra that converges to a smooth limit surface that is an extension of the three-direction quartic box-spline. The following are some observations about this scheme:

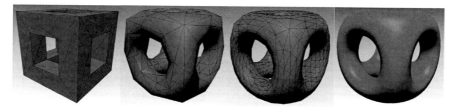

Figure 8.11. Loop subdivision: From left to right: an initial configuration, its first and second refinements, and limit surface. (See also Color Plate I.)

1. An ordinary point in this scheme is a six-valent vertex; otherwise, it is called an extraordinary vertex.

2. The limit surface is C^2, except at the extraordinary points where it is C^1.

3. A n-valent $\mathbf{v}_i^0$ vertex on the initial mesh converges to a limit point given by

$$\mathbf{v}_i^\infty = \frac{3 + 8\alpha(n-1)}{3 + 8n\alpha} \mathbf{v}_i^0 + \frac{8\alpha}{3 + 8n\alpha} \sum_{j=1}^{n} \mathbf{v}_j^0, \qquad (8.14)$$

where $\mathbf{v}_j^0$ are the one-ring vertices around $\mathbf{v}_i^0$.

Figure 8.11 (see also Color Plate I) shows an example of Loop surfaces.

The modified butterfly scheme. This scheme was initially developed as an extension of the four-point scheme by Dyn et al. [Dyn90] and later modified by Zorin [Zori96] to improve its smoothness. It is a triangle-based algorithm that consists of one main rule, i.e., how to compute the E-vertices. For practical applications, we provide the modified version of this algorithm:

1. For each vertex $\mathbf{v}_i^j$, let its V-vertex be the same as the original vertex, i.e., $\mathbf{v}_{i+1}^j = \mathbf{v}_i^j$.

2. For each edge $\mathbf{e}_i^j$:

    (a) If both vertices of that edge are 6-valent, then do the following:

        i. Let t_1 and t_2 be the two triangles sharing that edge.

        ii. Let t_3 and t_4 be the two other triangles sharing an edge with t_1, and let t_5 and t_6 be the triangles sharing an edge with t_2

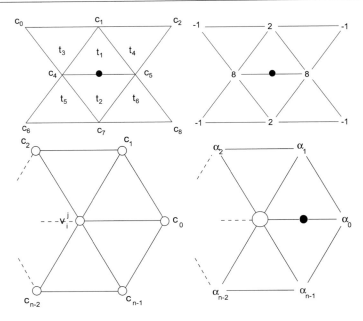

Figure 8.12. Butterfly masks and corresponding configurations. Regular E-vertex (top) and E-vertex near extraordinary point (bottom).

iii. Compute an E-vertex of that edge as a linear combination of the vertices of the above triangles as follows (see Figure 8.12):

$$\mathbf{v}e_{i+1}^{j} = \sum_{k=1}^{8} \alpha_i \mathbf{c}_i, \tag{8.15}$$

where

$$
\begin{aligned}
\alpha_i &= -1 &&\text{for} \quad i = 1,3,6,7,\\
\alpha_i &= 2 &&\text{for} \quad i = 2,8,\\
\alpha_i &= 8 &&\text{for} \quad i = 4,5.
\end{aligned}
$$

$$\tag{8.16}$$

(b) Else, if one of the vertices of the edge is an n-valent vertex, where $n \neq 6$, i.e., an extraordinary vertex (say $\mathbf{v}_i^{j}$), then do the following:

i. Let $(\mathbf{c}_i)_{(0 \leq i \leq n-1)}$ be the one-ring vertices around $\mathbf{v}_i^{j}$.

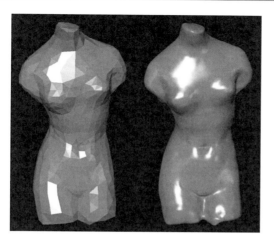

Figure 8.13. Butterfly subdivision. An initial configuration (left) and its limit surface (right). (Courtesy of D. Zorin.) (See also Color Plate II.)

 ii. Compute the E-vertex of the edge as a linear combination of the 1-ring vertices as follows:

$$\mathbf{v}e_{i+1}^{j} = \sum_{k=0}^{n-1} \alpha_i \mathbf{c}_i, \qquad (8.17)$$

where the α_i depend on the valency n as follows:

$$\alpha_i = \frac{1}{n}\left(\frac{1}{4} + \cos\frac{2\pi i}{n} + \frac{1}{2} + \cos\frac{4\pi i}{n}\right) \qquad \text{for} \quad n > 5,$$

$$\alpha_0 = \frac{5}{12}, \alpha_1 = \alpha_2 = -\frac{1}{12} \qquad \text{for} \quad n = 3,$$

$$\alpha_0 = \frac{3}{8}, \alpha_2 = -\frac{1}{8}, \alpha_1 = \alpha_3 = 0 \qquad \text{for} \quad n = 4.$$

 (c) Else, compute an average of the coefficients obtained by treating each vertex as extraordinary vertex and use the resulting mask to compute the E-vertex of that edge.

Figure 8.13 (see also Color Plate II) shows an example of butterfly surfaces. Some observations about this scheme follow:

 1. Since all initial vertices are part of the refined polyhedra, the scheme is an interpolating scheme.

2. The refinement can be done adaptively.

3. For regular meshes, the scheme is only C^1.

4. For irregular topology, the modified version produces smooth C^1 surfaces compared to the original version that exhibits undesirable creases.

The midpoint subdivision scheme. The midpoint subdivision scheme is known as the simplest subdivision scheme; it was developed by Peters and Reif [Pete97]. The algorithm consists of the following:

1. For each edge $\mathbf{e}_i^j$, compute its E-vertex as the midpoint of that edge.

2. Construct a new polyhedron as follows:

   (a) For each face $\mathbf{f}_i^j$, construct an F-face by connecting the E-vertices of its edges.

   (b) For each vertex $\mathbf{v}_i^j$, construct a V-face by connecting the E-vertices of the edges incident to it.

Looking at this scheme carefully, the following observations can be made:

1. Two steps of this algorithm resemble one step of Doo–Sabin with different coefficients for computing the new vertices. The steps become as follows:

   (a) On each n-sided face $\mathbf{f}_i^j$, generate n vertices $\mathbf{v}_i^{j+1}$ as linear combinations of the old vertices $\mathbf{v}_i^j$ as follows:

   $$\mathbf{v}_i^{j+1} = \sum_{k=1}^n \alpha_r \mathbf{v}_k^j, \tag{8.18}$$

   where $r = (k - j + n) \bmod n$ and the coefficients α_i are given by

   $$\alpha_i = 2 \sum_{j=0}^{\bar{n}} 2^{-j} \cos \frac{2\pi i j}{n}, \tag{8.19}$$

   and

   $$\bar{n} = \lfloor \frac{n-1}{2} \rfloor.$$

2. The limit surface is C^1.

3. The algorithm initially converges slowly for large n-sided faces. To overcome this problem, modified subdivision coefficients were reported in [Pete97].

The $\sqrt{3}$ subdivision scheme. The $\sqrt{3}$ subdivision scheme is a triangular-based scheme developed by Kobbelt [Kobb00]. Given a polyhedron whose faces are all triangles, the algorithm consists of the following:

1. For each face $\mathbf{f}_i^j$, generate an F-vertex as the centroid of that face.

2. For each n-valent vertex $\mathbf{v}_i^j$, do the following:

   (a) Let $(\mathbf{b}_i)$ be the 1-ring vertices around $\mathbf{v}_i^j$.

   (b) Generate a V-vertex $\mathbf{v}_i^{j+1}$ as follows:

   $$\mathbf{v}_i^{j+1} = (1 - \alpha_n)\mathbf{v}_i^j + \frac{\alpha_n}{n} \sum_{i=1}^{n} \mathbf{b}_i, \qquad (8.20)$$

   where α_n is given by

   $$\alpha_n = \frac{1}{9}\left(4 - 2\cos\left(\frac{2\pi}{n}\right)\right). \qquad (8.21)$$

3. Construct a new polyhedron as follows:

   (a) For each old edge, connect the F-vertices (centroid) of the two faces common to that edge.

   (b) For each old face, connect its F-vertex to the V-vertices of its corresponding vertices.

Figure 8.14 shows an example of $\sqrt{3}$ subdivision surfaces. The following observations can be made about this scheme:

1. It is an interpolating scheme.

2. One major advantage of this algorithm is the ability to accommodate adaptive subdivision; however, two neighboring triangles can only differ by one level of refinement.

3. The limit surface is C^2 except at the extraordinary vertices where it is C^1.

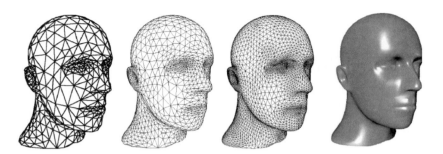

Figure 8.14. $\sqrt{3}$ subdivision. From left to right: an initial configuration, its first and second refinements, and limit surface. (Courtesy of L. Kobbelt.)

8.5   Manipulation of Subdivision Surfaces

Most subdivision algorithms are considered as smoothing operators. Given a coarse mesh, they generate a smooth surface at the limit. This is not needed at all times. For computer-graphics applications, often one needs to generate a surface with a crease or with a sharp edge. A criticism concerning this general smoothness was reported in the early 1980s. In response to this criticism, an example of generating subdivision surfaces with deliberate discontinuity along a common boundary curve (similar to creases) was originally suggested by Nasri [Nasr87]. This issue was rigourously addressed in the literature and later led to the generation of subdivision surfaces with sharp features; a necessity in modeling and animation [Hopp94, DeRo98].

In addition to sharp features, subdivision surfaces can be manipulated using interpolation constraints. We generally distinguish between two types of subdivision algorithms: interpolating and approximating; the latter approximate an initial given polyhedron whereas the former interpolate some or all of its vertices. For example, the Catmull–Clark, Doo–Sabin, midpoint, and Loop schemes are all approximating, whereas the butterfly and $\sqrt{3}$ schemes are interpolating. Typically, approximating schemes can be made interpolating as reported in [Nasr87, Hals93].

In this section, we briefly summarize some of the issues used in the manipulation of subdivision surfaces.

8.5.1   Sharp Features

The smoothness of a subdivision surface at a vertex can be deliberately reduced to C^0 by modifying appropriate masks of the subdivision process. Such a vertex,

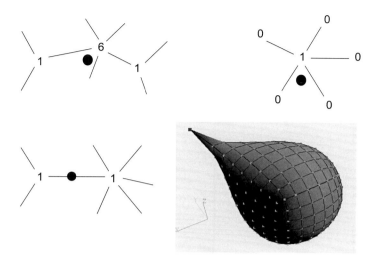

Figure 8.15. Subdivision surfaces with sharp features. Mask for crease vertex (top left), mask for a dart vertex (top right), mask for E-vertex incident to any sharp vertex (bottom left), and an example of a Catmull–Clark subdivision surface with a dart (bottom right).

often referred to as a *sharp vertex*, is labeled according to the number of tagged sharp edges incident to it. If the number of tagged edges is greater than two, it is called a *dart* vertex whereas if the number is equal to two, it is called a *crease* vertex. Otherwise, it is simply called a *corner* vertex. For example, in the Catmull–Clark scheme, if we modify the V-vertex coefficients of a tagged vertex $\mathbf{v}_i^0$ and its adjacent E-vertices as indicated in Figure 8.15, then that vertex will generate a dart. Similarly, the Loop scheme can be modified so that a tagged vertex can become a sharp vertex as indicated in [Hopp94].

For even-degree subdivision schemes, such as the Doo–Sabin or the midpoint scheme, generating sharp vertices requires some special treatment. Figure 8.15 shows an example of a Catmull–Clark surface with a dart vertex.

8.5.2 Open Polyhedra

Most of the subdivision schemes discussed so far work nicely for closed polyhedra. However, they suffer from the lack of control of the boundary curves of the limit surfaces generated from open polyhedra. This is due to the fact that a limit surface from an open polyhedron actually shrinks to its interior, making it hard to control its boundary curves. This problem was initially addressed by Nasri [Nasr87], and a solution was proposed for Doo–Sabin surfaces. It was revisited later in [Nasr95, Nasr97].

The idea consists of modifying the boundary faces to have some specific structure so that a limit surface has its boundary curves controlled by the boundary vertices of the initial configuration. These vertices form the boundary control polygon[1] of the surface. Naturally, the curve of this control polygon is considered to be its corresponding piecewise B-spline curve where pieces meet at two-valent boundary vertices. For example, consider the simple case of a Doo–Sabin surface where all boundary vertices are three-valent. The boundary faces can be modified by extending every edge $\mathbf{v}_i\mathbf{v}_j$ by reflecting its interior vertex $\mathbf{v}_j$ symmetrically about the boundary $\mathbf{v}_i$. However, more complicated boundary situations exist that can be addressed by introducing the notion of *n-reflected* faces [Nasr03a]. This method has the advantage of maintaining the same subdivision coefficients so (1) no specialized analysis of the limit surface is necessary, and (2) two subdivision surfaces can be joined with smoothness across their boundary curves. This work led later to the introduction of polygonal complexes and their applications in curve interpolation; these topics will be discussed in Section 8.5.4.

Another method for controlling the boundary curves consists simply of modifying the subdivision coefficients along the boundary [Zori00]. The idea is to refine the boundary control polygon using one of the basic curve subdivision algorithms. In the Catmull–Clark scheme, for example, the following steps are used:

1. For each boundary edge, generate an E-vertex at its midpoint.

2. For each boundary vertex, generate a V-vertex as indicated in Equation (8.3).

A similar algorithm could be devised for Doo–Sabin surfaces.

8.5.3   Interpolation in Approximating Schemes

For approximating schemes, the interpolation idea was first presented in [Nasr87], in which the generation of interpolating Doo–Sabin surfaces was established. This was later extended to Catmull–Clark surfaces by Halstead et al. [Hals93]. The problem can be stated as follows: Given a polyhedron[2] P with a set of tagged vertices $\mathbf{v}_k$ to be interpolated, find another polyhedron Q with a set of vertices $\mathbf{w}_k$, whose limit surface interpolates the tagged vertices $\mathbf{v}_k$.

---

[1]Note that a surface could well have many boundary control polygons.
[2]This can be the initial or a subsequently refined one.

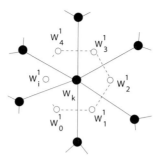

Figure 8.16. C^1 interpolation of one vertex.

Let us assume that the polyhedron Q has a similar topology to P. One solution consists of treating every tagged vertex $\mathbf{v}_k$ as a limit vertex $\mathbf{w}_k^\infty$ to which a face (in the Doo–Sabin scheme) or a vertex (in the Catmull–Clark or the Loop scheme) converges. Once this is identified, we can express $\mathbf{v}_k$ as a linear combination of a number of vertices ($\mathbf{w}_k$) and set up a system of linear equations whose solution gives the unknown $\mathbf{w}_k$. The major tasks involved are then to define the corresponding limit point or face, and then to set up the system of equations.

For Doo–Sabin surfaces, a centroid of a face is a limit point on the surface. We then need to associate every tagged vertex $\mathbf{v}_k$ with a centroid of a certain face, which leads to the following algorithm for computing the matrix $\mathbf{M}$ of the linear system (see Figure 8.16):

1. Initialize all elements of the $l \times l$ matrix $\mathbf{M}$ to zero, where l is the total number of vertices of the original polyhedron.

2. For each n-valent vertex $\mathbf{w}_k$ do the following:
   If $\mathbf{w}_k$ is to be interpolated then

   (a) let VF_k be the V-face generated from that vertex.

   (b) Let $(\mathbf{w}_i^1)_{1 \le i \le n}$ be the vertices of VF_k. The superscript indicates that these vertices belong to the first subdivision.

   (c) Form the equation
   $$\mathbf{v}_k = \frac{1}{n}\left(\sum_{i=1}^{n} \mathbf{w}_i^1\right).$$

   (d) Replace every vertex $\mathbf{w}_i^1$ by the linear combination of the vertices $(\mathbf{w}_k)$ of the face to which it belongs. Assuming that this face is m-sided, then

$$\mathbf{w}_i^1 = \sum_{r=1}^{m} \alpha_{ri} \mathbf{w}_r,$$

which gives

$$\mathbf{v}_k = \frac{1}{n} \left(\sum_{i=1}^{n} \sum_{r=1}^{m} \alpha_{ri} \mathbf{w}_r \right).$$

(e) Form the row k of the matrix $\mathbf{M}$ using the coefficients

$$\frac{1}{n} \alpha_{ri}.$$

This will define the $m \times n$ elements of this row. The remaining $l - m \times n$ elements are set to zero.

Else, set $\mathbf{w}_k = \mathbf{v}_k$ so the corresponding row of matrix $\mathbf{M}$ is 0 everywhere except at position k where it is 1.

3. Set up the system of equations:

$$\begin{pmatrix} \mathbf{v}_1 \\ \mathbf{v}_2 \\ \mathbf{v}_3 \\ . \\ . \\ . \\ \mathbf{v}_n \end{pmatrix} = \mathbf{M} \cdot \begin{pmatrix} \mathbf{w}_1 \\ \mathbf{w}_2 \\ \mathbf{w}_3 \\ . \\ . \\ . \\ \mathbf{w}_n \end{pmatrix}.$$

4. Solve the system for the unknown vertices $\mathbf{w}_k$.

5. Construct a new polyhedron Q from a copy of P but with new vertices given by the solution of the above system.

Figure 8.17 (left) shows an example of an interpolating Doo–Sabin surface.

For Catmull–Clark interpolating surfaces, a similar algorithm can be devised [Hals93]. Here, every vertex to be interpolated will be associated with the limit of its V-vertex given by Equation (8.10). It is true that a limit vertex is given in terms of vertices of the first refinement, but each of these can be replaced by their combinations of the vertices $\mathbf{w}_k$. As such, each vertex will correspond to a row of the matrix needed to solve the underlying linear system. Figure 8.17 (right) shows an example of an interpolating Catmull–Clark surface.

Other schemes can also follow the same strategy. For example, using the Loop scheme, every vertex to be interpolated is associated with the limit vertex given in Equation (8.14).

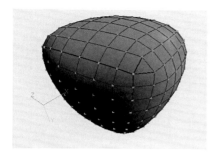 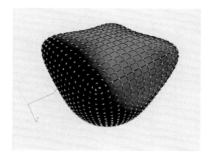

Figure 8.17. Interpolating subdivision surfaces. Left: A Doo–Sabin surface interpolating the top four vertices of a cube. Right: A Catmull–Clark surface with the
same interpolation conditions.

It is noteworthy to mention that for closed polyhedra, the matrix $\mathbf{M}$ is a square
matrix, since we have one equation for every unknown vertex. A solution exists
as long as $\mathbf{M}$ is not singular. For open polyhedra, boundary conditions must be
taken into consideration as suggested in [Nasr87, Nasr91].

8.5.4 Interpolation of Curves by Subdivision Surfaces

In this section, we consider the issue of interpolating curves by subdivision surfaces, which is related to both interpolating and approximating schemes.

Given a tagged control polygon cp on a polyhedron P^0, we need to force the
limit surface of P^0 to interpolate the B-spline curve defined by cp. To solve this
problem, we distinguish between two types of curves: a curve with C^0 continuity
(known as *crease*) and a curve with C^1 continuity. We first consider curves of the
first type.

Generating a crease can be achieved in two ways. The first approach is to treat
the control polygon cp as a boundary of two subdivision surfaces where they join
with C^0 continuity as discussed in [Nasr87]. Typically, each surface will have to
undergo the procedure of boundary modification as indicated in the open polyhedron case (Section 8.5.2). The second approach is to modify the subdivision coefficients such that each refinement of the polyhedron will refine the tagged control
polygon to generate the desired curve. In general, this can break the smoothness across the interpolated curve. For Catmull–Clark and Doo–Sabin surfaces,
a crease is typically the B-spline curve of the tagged control polygon. This polygon should then be refined by employing the same masks used in the subdivision
curve algorithms that are described in Section 8.3. For example, in Catmull–Clark

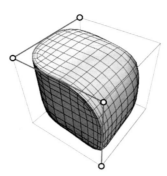 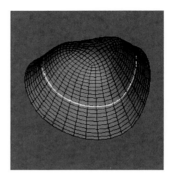

Figure 8.18. Interpolating curves by subdivision surfaces. Left: a Doo–Sabin surface interpolating a crease. Right: a Catmull–Clark surface interpolating a C^1-continuous curve. (See also Color Plate IV.)

surfaces, the following algorithm, which is similar to the curve subdivision case, is used (assume that the control polygon cp is given by vertices $(\mathbf{c}_i)$:

1. For each edge $\mathbf{v}_{i-1}\mathbf{v}_i$ of the control polygon cp, make its E-vertex the midpoint of that edge.

2. For each vertex $\mathbf{c}_i$ of the control polygon, make its V-vertex

$$\frac{\mathbf{v}_{i-1} + 6\mathbf{v}_i + \mathbf{v}_{i+1}}{8}.$$

3. For all other edges and vertices, generate the E- and V-vertices as indicated by the Catmull–Clark subdivision scheme.

Figure 8.18 (left) (see also Color Plate IV) shows an example of a Doo–Sabin surface interpolating a crease.

For the interpolation of curve with C^1 continuity, the notion of polygonal complexes was first introduced by Nasri in [Nasr00]. A polygonal complex is simply a polyhedron C that converges to a curve under a given subdivision scheme S. Embedding such a complex in a polyhedron P will generate a limit surface that interpolates the curve defined by C. If S is considered to be the Doo–Sabin scheme, then the simplest of these complexes is a strip of quads that converges to a quadratic B-spline curve. The control vertices of this curve are the midpoints of the shared edges between the adjacent quads. If two such complexes share one quad q, then the resulting two curves will intersect at the centroid of q. If

Figure 8.19. Lofted Catmull–Clark subdivision surfaces. Left: A set of control polygons defining cubic B-spline curves. Right: A Catmull–Clark subdivision surface interpolating these curves. (See also Color Plate V.)

more than two curves are to be interpolated through an extraordinary vertex, then an *n*-reflected face can be used as the shared face between the two corresponding complexes. More details can be found in [Nasr03a]. Figure 8.18 (right) (see also Color Plate IV) shows an example of a Catmull–Clark surface interpolating a curve with C^1 across.

For the Catmull–Clark scheme, a polygonal complex can be defined by two adjacent rows of faces. As discussed in [Nasr02a], such a complex converges to its corresponding cubic B-spline curve. The control vertices of this curve are also computed from the vertices of the shared edges between the faces of the complex. Curve interpolation was also considered by Levin using the combined subdivision schemes [Levi99].

Based on curve interpolation, lofted subdivision surfaces can be generated [Nasr03b]. Given a set of cross-section curves, we first construct a polygonal complex for each of these curves. After that, we connect these complexes into one polyhedron whose limit surface interpolates these curves. A Catmull–Clark lofted surface is shown in Figure 8.19 (see also Color Plate V). The generation of subdivision surfaces through a net of curves was also discussed in [Scha04].

For more information, a taxonomy of interpolation conditions on subdivision curves and surfaces is provided in [Nasr02c, Nasr02b].

8.6 Analysis of Subdivision Surfaces⊛

Since subdivision surfaces are generated from arbitrary topology, typical smoothness violations occur at and in the vicinity of extraordinary points. They involve the order of continuity there as well as curvature behavior. Avoiding such violations is essential to producing good quality surfaces. Analyzing, and then tuning, subdivision algorithms have thus emerged as an integral task in handling most of the current schemes. Initial attempts date back to the late 1970s where the role of *eigenanalysis* was first illustrated, i.e., that the spectrum of the subdivision operator can be used to analyze smoothness properties at and around extraordinary points [Doo78].

Since subdivision algorithms generalize the subdivision rules of biquadratic and bicubic tensor product B-spline surfaces, subdivision surfaces inherit the smoothness properties of their underlying polynomial splines at all but the extraordinary points, where regular subdivision rules no longer apply. While lower-order smoothness at extraordinary points was a well-known observation, it was only first formally verified in [Pete98, Umla00] and is now known to be a result of the low polynomial degree of subdivision surfaces [Reif96, Prau99, Pete00]. Although the goal of achieving C^2 continuity at extraordinary points has been shown to be unattainable [Reif96], the general understanding remains that high-quality surfaces must conform to conditions governing normal continuity, bounded, yet non-zero, curvature, and minimal curvature fluctuations at all points of the surface.

Analysis of many of the current schemes is now well established. The Catmull–Clark scheme [Catm78] generates piecewise bicubic C^2-continuous surfaces everywhere except at the extraordinary points, where the surface maintains C^1 continuity but exhibits unbounded curvature. The 4-8 approximating scheme [Velh01a, Velh01b] generalizing the four-directional box spline is C^4 continuous everywhere but only C^1 at extraordinary vertices. Loop's binary scheme [Loop87] achieves C^2 continuity everywhere, C^1 continuity at the extraordinary points, and bounded curvature only when the valence is equal to 4, 5, and 6. The Doo–Sabin [Doo78] and 4-3 [Pete03] schemes are C^2 continuous everywhere but only C^1 continuous at the extraordinary points. Since many of the standard algorithms fail to produce good quality surfaces at the extraordinary points, they have to be modified via *tuning*, i.e., modifying the masks around the extraordinary point to improve curvature behavior there. General analysis tools revolve mainly around three different approaches: z-transformation methods using difference schemes [Cava91, Dyn92], Fourier analysis techniques [Cohe92, Daub99, Dyn02, Pete98, Karc04, Pete04], and methods bounding the joint spectral radius of local subdivision operators [Han03, Jia95, Riou92]. We dedicate the remainder of this section to a brief outline of Fourier analysis tools and refer the reader to a comprehensive summary in [Reif06].

8.6.1 Fourier Analysis Techniques

Fourier analysis techniques apply in the context of subdivision surfaces that are generated by stationary,[3] linear, and symmetric subdivision algorithms generalizing box-splines or B-splines, and whose subdivision matrix is known to be nondefective. In the vicinity of an extraordinary point $\mathbf{m}$, the subdivision surface $\mathbf{x}$ can be viewed as the union of $\mathbf{m}$ and a nested sequence of spline rings $\mathbf{x}_m$. Each spline ring $\mathbf{x}_m$ is a function

$$\mathbf{x}_m : S_n \to \mathbb{R}^3, \quad S_n = \Sigma \times \mathbb{Z}_n, \ \Sigma = [0,2]^2 \setminus [0,1)^2,$$

where n is the valence of $\mathbf{m}$. We thus view each of the spline rings $\mathbf{x}_m$ as the exclusive union of segments of rings $\mathbf{x}_m^j$, $j \in \mathbb{Z}_n$, associated with every edge e_j emanating from the extraordinary point. Let m denote the index of an arbitrary spline ring in the entire union comprising $\mathbf{x}_m$. We consider a positive integer L, control points $\mathbf{B}_m^0, \ldots, \mathbf{B}_m^L$ in $\mathbb{R}^3$, and real-valued functions $\varphi_0, \ldots, \varphi_L$ that form a partition of unity, and are, at least piecewise, twice differentiable (thus, the spline ring can be generated by a C^2 interpolating subdivision [Pete04, Reif06]). The spline ring is then viewed as a linear combination of the φ^i defined on S_n with respective weights given by the $\mathbf{B}_m^i$, for $i = 0, \ldots, L$. We collect the functions in a row vector φ and the respective control points in a column vector $\mathbf{B}_m$, so that the spline rings can be expressed as

$$\mathbf{x}_m = \varphi \mathbf{B}_m. \tag{8.22}$$

The sequence of control points $\mathbf{B}_m$ is obtained via repeated application of an $(L+1) \times (L+1)$ subdivision matrix $\mathbf{A}$ onto the initial data $\mathbf{B}_0$, so that

$$\mathbf{B}_m = \mathbf{A}^m \mathbf{B}_0. \tag{8.23}$$

Combining (8.22) and (8.23) above, we have

$$\mathbf{x}_m = \varphi \mathbf{A}^m \mathbf{B}_0. \tag{8.24}$$

Let $\lambda_0, \ldots, \lambda_L$ denote the eigenvalues of $\mathbf{A}$ ordered by modulus and corresponding to right eigenvectors $\overrightarrow{\mathbf{v}}_0, \ldots, \overrightarrow{\mathbf{v}}_L$. For $\overrightarrow{\mathbf{v}}_i \neq 0$, define the eigenfunction

$$\Psi_i = \varphi \overrightarrow{\mathbf{v}}_i. \tag{8.25}$$

---

[3] A subdivision algorithm is stationary if the subdivision scheme is constant across all subdivision levels.

Let $\mathbf{d}_i \in \mathbb{R}^3$ represent eigen coefficients in $\mathbb{R}^3$ scaling the right eigenvectors such that

$$\mathbf{B}_0 = \sum_{i=0}^{L} \overrightarrow{\mathbf{v}}_i \mathbf{d}_i.$$

Then, $\mathbf{x}_m$ is represented by

$$\mathbf{x}_m = \sum_{i=0}^{L} \lambda_i^m \Psi_i \mathbf{d}_i. \tag{8.26}$$

Equation (8.26) is reminiscent of a local Taylor expansion whose first components indexed by $i = 0, \ldots, 5$ have geometric interpretations. In particular, the components corresponding to $i = 0$ affect the position of the extraordinary point $\mathbf{m}$, the components for $i = 1, 2$ affect the tangent plane configuration, and the components for $i = 3, 4, 5$ affect the curvature: $i = 3$ for the cup configuration and $i = 4, 5$ for the saddle configurations [Bart05].

Many numerical algorithms exist for computing the eigenstructure of the subdivision matrix $\mathbf{A}$, but these do not always return the correct eigenstructure (sometimes, complex eigenvalues are returned). One seeks to compute the eigenstructure explicitly, which becomes computationally infeasible with growing valence. Symmetry of the scheme, however, implies that the subdivision matrix is block-circulant, so that its (similar) image $\widehat{\mathbf{A}}$ under the discrete Fourier transformation $\mathbf{F}$ is a block diagonal matrix given by

$$\widehat{\mathbf{A}} = \mathbf{F}^{-1} \mathbf{A} \mathbf{F} = \operatorname{diag}\left(\widehat{\mathbf{A}}_0, \ldots, \widehat{\mathbf{A}}_{n-1}\right).$$

By similarity of the two matrices, $\mathbf{A}$ and $\widehat{\mathbf{A}}$ possess the same eigenvalues, which, owing to the block diagonal structure of $\widehat{\mathbf{A}}$, are then obtained as the union of the eigenvalues of the blocks $\widehat{\mathbf{A}}^k$, $k \in \mathbb{Z}_n$. Moreover, all these blocks are of the same fixed dimension for all integers $n \geq 3$, so that an explicit computation of the eigenstructure of $\mathbf{A}$ becomes feasible. In this context, the Fourier index of a given eigenvalue τ of $\mathbf{A}$ is defined as

$$\mathscr{F}(\tau) = \{k \in \mathbb{Z}_n \mid \tau \text{ is an eigenvalue of } \widehat{\mathbf{A}}^k\}.$$

8.6.2 Eigenspectrum Analysis

The eigencomponents in the expansion of Equation (8.26) contribute to a number of necessary conditions governing the subdivision scheme's smoothness around the extraordinary point and its curvature behavior there. Particularly, the following standard conditions are of primary importance so that C^1 and C^2 continuity are at least not violated [Doo78, Reif06]:

1. All rows of the subdivision matrix $\mathbf{A}$ sum to one, so that $\lambda_0 = 1$. This ensures the convergence of the scheme.

2. The subdominant eigenvalue λ is positive, is of algebraic and geometric multiplicity equal to 2:

$$1 > \lambda = \lambda_1 = \lambda_2 > |\lambda_3| \geq \ldots$$

and has Fourier index $\mathscr{F}(\lambda) = \{1, n-1\}$. If this fails, the scheme is not C^1.

3. The subsubdominant eigenvalue μ is positive and is of algebraic and geometric multiplicity equal to 3:

$$1 > \lambda > \mu = \lambda_3 = \lambda_4 = \lambda_5 > |\lambda_6|$$

and has Fourier index $\mathscr{F}(\mu) = \{0, 2, n-2\}$. If this fails, the scheme is not C^2.

4. The subsubdominant eigenvalue μ is equal to λ^2. If this fails, the scheme is not C^2; otherwise, this ensures bounded curvature.

5. Elements of the eigenvectors associated with λ and μ are in a quadratic configuration. If this condition, known as the *local quadratic precision*, fails, the scheme is not C^2. Otherwise, one obtains a configuration which avoids oscillations around the extraordinary point [Gero05, Sabi02].

8.6.3 The Characteristic Map

We now turn to sufficient conditions for establishing C^1 continuity at the extraordinary point. The eigenvectors corresponding to the subdominant eigenvalues induce the *characteristic map*, a local parameterization of the surface in the vicinity of the extraordinary point, by which the surface can be written as a differentiable function of two variables. Because of stationarity, the spline rings of the characteristic map coincide at different subdivision levels, and so it suffices to analyze one such spline ring around an extraordinary point in order to establish results about the smoothness of the subdivision surface itself [Pete98, Pete04, Reif06]. To illustrate, let Ψ_1 and Ψ_2 denote the eigenfunctions associated with the two-fold subdominant eigenvalue λ. The characteristic map is defined as

$$\Psi := (\Psi_1, \Psi_2) : S_n \to \mathbb{R}^2,$$

where Ψ_1 and Ψ_2 are the eigenfunctions corresponding to the subdominant eigenvalue. We denote by Ψ^j the restriction of Ψ to $\Sigma \times j$, for some $j \in \mathbb{Z}_n$. We further have that $\Psi^0 = \left(\Psi_1^0, \Psi_2^0\right)$ is regular if the Jacobian $\mathbf{J}^0 = \det D\Psi^0$ for

$$D\Psi^0 = \left(\begin{array}{cc} \Psi_{1,u}^0 & \Psi_{1,v}^0 \\ \Psi_{2,u}^0 & \Psi_{2,v}^0 \end{array} \right)$$

is not equal to zero, for any u and v. Peters and Reif [Pete98] establish a sufficient condition for the limit subdivision surface to achieve C^1 continuity everywhere, including the extraordinary point. In particular, if one assumes Conditions (1) and (2) above, and if the characteristic map is regular and injective, then the limit surface attains C^1 continuity everywhere for almost any choice of initial data $\mathbf{B}_0$. Simplified tests for regularity and injectivity appear later in [Pete98, Reif06, Umla05], but they follow mostly as a consequence of the crucial result of [Pete98] that restricts testing of injectivity and regularity to a single segment of the characteristic map. In particular, if the characteristic map segment Ψ^0 is regular and $\Psi_{1,v}^0(1,t)$, $\Psi_{2,v}^0(1,t)$ are strictly positive for all $t \in [0,1]$, then the characteristic map is regular and injective.

In [Pete04], a closed form for the spline ring of the characteristic map, also known as the *central surface*, is derived, and results relating this to the curvature behavior at the extraordinary point are proven. In particular, given generic initial control nets $\mathbf{B}_0$, the shape at the extraordinary point $\mathbf{m}$ is governed by the sign of the Gaussian curvature of the central surface, denoted by K_c. In particular,

- the shape is elliptic in the limit, if $K_c > 0$;

- the shape is hyperbolic in the limit, if $K_c < 0$;

- the shape is hybrid, if K_c changes sign.

8.6.4 Good Quality Surface Construction

Subdivision analysis tools establish the properties of a given subdivision scheme in a straightforward manner. Mathematical progress on this front, however, reveals shortcomings with most of the standard subdivision algorithms. Standard subdivision methods do not produce "good quality" surfaces in the limit, and this has been the motivation behind subdivision tuning, i.e., reformulating the subdivision rules at and around the extraordinary points so that many of the sought criteria are maintained. Although C^1 schemes turn out to be relatively easy to construct, achieving higher-order continuity is much more difficult, as can be seen by inspection of the necessary and sufficient conditions for C^2 continuity proven in [Reif06]. Yet, arranging for good curvature behavior rather than a desired mathematical property, such as C^2 continuity, may be of prime importance, if for instance, the scheme achieves the necessary C^2 condition of bounded curvature but exhibits flatness or oscillations around the extraordinary points, both of which are considered to be artifacts [Prau98, Sabi03]. One can also gather from the degree estimates of C^k piecewise polynomial subdivision surfaces obtained in [Prau99] that tuning a subdivision scheme in order to achieve C^2-continuity without flat points will likely introduce relatively large supports. Artifacts can also be introduced if the absolute value of the difference between the subdominant eigenvalue and the shrinking factor (1/2 for binary schemes and 1/3 for ternary ones) is relatively large [Bart04]. Also, of particular concern is the immediate ease by which one may sacrifice the convex hull property in the process of tuning [Levi06]. Thus, common current tuning techniques aim for as many of the following goals simultaneously:

- preserving the convex hull property;

- achieving C^1 continuity at extraordinary points;

- achieving bounded curvature at extraordinary points;

- avoiding flatness at extraordinary points;

- minimizing Gaussian curvature fluctuations;

- maintaining a small support;

- maintaining a small deviation of the subdominant eigenvalue from the shrinking factor.

See recent papers on subdivision tuning in [Augs06, Bart04, Gink06, Levi06, Loop98, Umla05, Zult06].

8.7 Subdivision Finite Elements⊛

This section introduces the formulation and use of subdivision-based (and/or spline-based) geometric modeling techniques in finite-element modeling and simulation. We describe the principles and specific numerical algorithms for constructing finite-element models that are directly coupled to the underlying geometric representations. Finite element models are a basic component of a very long list of simulation applications, see for example [Grin02, Tera05, Guen05, Thom06]. Some common graphics and simulation applications of subdivision models based on finite-element include:

- *Deformation of geometric models.* Geometric models augmented with material properties can deform when subjected to loads and to interpolation constraints on position and tangents. They can thus provide a natural framework for a mechanical metaphor for modeling organic shapes. By pushing, pulling, shearing, twisting, bending, holding, squeezing, etc., a user can model and edit freeform shapes using intuitive tools. A finite-element model directly coupled to the geometry allows such editors to be readily built.

- *Animation of graphical models.* Elastically deformable characters and models are powerful tools for creating realistic animations in game, film, and virtual reality environments. Physically-based models can automate a significant chunk of the animation tasks that would otherwise have to be performed manually. Character animations, cloth simulations, and a whole host of animations can be supported by finite-element models directly tied to the geometric representation. These models can be developed at varying levels of resolution to support different animation needs—from highly detailed and realistic simulations that are generally done off-line, to interactive, real-time approximate, visually-plausible animations.

- *Haptic interaction with solid models.* In recent years, user-interface hardware devices that incorporate the sense of touch have become widely available. Touch-enabled hardware interfaces render forces and pressures and allow users to manipulate virtual objects and directly sense their stiffness, compliance, yielding, and related mechanical characteristics. Applications in games/entertainment, virtual sculpting, and engineering design can be enhanced by haptic interaction. In order to support such interfaces, underlying finite-element models that are directly tied to the geometry are built and used to compute the forces and pressures that can be fed to the haptic devices at interactive rates.

- *Simulation of physical phenomena in engineering and science.* Many problems arising in engineering and science are described by partial differential field equations on general geometric two- and three-dimensional domains and solved by finite-element simulations. Heat flow, fluid flow, and electromagnetic field computations are common examples of such simulations that are performed routinely in design practice. The need for higher fidelity and higher resolution in these simulations continues to push the need for improved numerical discretization methods for their solution. One such improvement can be obtained by using the same basis functions of the geometry (e.g., subdivision basis functions) to represent the fields in the discretized finite elements, allowing an exact representation of the geometry being simulated. Although we will not cover these topics in this section, the reader can use methods similar to the ones described here for building these finite element simulations.

In this section, we introduce the key ideas for building finite-element simulation models in the context of curves. Section 8.7.1 describes the formulations and algorithms in a simple setting: the bending of a bar that is initially straight. This simple geometry serves to introduce the models without cluttering the discussion with the algebraic expressions that involve the curvature of general curves. Section 8.7.2 describes the framework for a finite-element deformation model of general 2D curves. Finite-element deformation models for surfaces in 3D, while similar in nature, are more complicated mathematically. We briefly describe their formulation in Section 8.7.3 and point the advanced readers to references for more complete derivations.

8.7.1 Bending of Initially Straight Shapes

Formulation. Consider an initially straight shape (a one-dimensional bar) defined by a single spatial coordinate $x(t)$, where t is the parametric coordinate. The geometry may be expressed as $x = \sum_i x_i \phi_i(t)$ where the ϕ_i are n basis functions associated with a knot vector. Let the spatial domain we are interested in simulating be defined in the region $a \leq x \leq b$ corresponding to a parametric domain $t_a \leq t \leq t_b$, and let $u(x)$ be the vertical displacement of the bar at any point due to the application of a distributed vertical loading $f(x)$ along the length of the bar. The objective of this section is to develop the techniques for finding $u(x)$ given $f(x)$. Figure 8.20 shows the set-up of the problem.

From basic principles of mechanics, which will not be described here, the equilibrium position of the bar is the function $u(x)$ that minimizes the following functional known as potential energy:

$$\Pi[u(x)] = \frac{1}{2}\int_a^b c\kappa^2 dx - \int_a^b fu\,dx = \frac{1}{2}\int_a^b c\left(\frac{d^2u}{dx^2}\right)^2 dx - \int_a^b fu\,dx,$$

where $\kappa = \kappa(x)$ is the curvature of the deformed shape and $\frac{d^2u}{dx^2}$ is its linearized

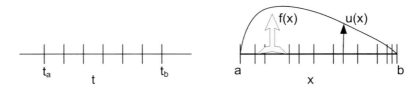

Figure 8.20. Bending of initially straight shapes. Problem set-up in one dimension.

approximation that we will use here. The variable c is a material parameter that may vary along the length of the rod. Larger values of c model stiffer shapes, while smaller values model more flexible ones. The first term in the potential energy is called the elastic strain energy and represents the energy stored in the bar as a result of deformation and change in curvature.

This minimization is subject to a set of constraints on the position and slope of the deformed shape of the bar. These constraints may be expressed at the end points of the spatial domain ($x = a$ and $x = b$) and are then known as "boundary conditions" on the problem. There may also be arbitrary interpolation constraints on position and slope at any point in the domain, or general relationships between the positions and slopes at a number of points. We will describe these conditions and how to incorporate them in the minimization in Section 8.7.1.

In order to find the function $u(x)$ that represents the position of equilibrium, geometry-based finite-element methods use the same knot discretization of the spatial domain to represent the solution $u(x)$ as $\sum_i u_i \phi_i(x)$, where the ϕ_i are the same basis functions used to define the geometry. This allows us to write a discretized expression for the potential energy as

$$\Pi(u_i) = \frac{1}{2} \int_a^b c \left(\sum_i u_i \frac{d^2 \phi_i}{dx^2} \right)^2 dx - \int_a^b f \left(\sum_i u_i \phi_i(x) \right) dx,$$

and the problem is now reduced to finding the vector $\mathbf{u}$ that minimizes Π. Setting the first derivatives to zero, we obtain the set of n equations that define the equilibrium position:

$$\frac{\partial \Pi}{\partial u_i} = \int_a^b c \frac{d^2 \phi_i}{dx^2} \left(\sum_j u_j \frac{d^2 \phi_j}{dx^2} \right) dx - \int_a^b f \phi_i dx = 0,$$

which can be written as

$$\sum_j \left[\int_a^b c \frac{d^2\phi_i}{dx^2} \frac{d^2\phi_j}{dx^2} dx \right] u_j = \int_a^b f\phi_i dx, \qquad i = 1\ldots n,$$

$$\sum_j K_{ij} u_j = f_i \qquad\qquad i = 1\ldots n,$$

$$\mathbf{Ku} = \mathbf{f},$$

where K_{ij} is the (i,j)th entry in the coefficient matrix $\mathbf{K}$ known as the stiffness matrix, and f_i is the ith entry in the vector $\mathbf{f}$ known as the force vector. The first task in a finite-element simulation is to compute these values.

Numerical computation of the stiffness matrix. In order to perform the integrals involved in K_{ij} and f_i conveniently, we express their integrands in parametric space and perform all integrations in that space. The second derivative with respect to the spatial coordinate x may be written in terms of the derivatives with respect to the parametric coordinate t, and the Jacobian a of the mapping, $a = \frac{dx}{dt} = x'$.[4] Using the chain rule, we can express $\frac{d^2\phi}{dt^2}$ in terms of the derivatives with respect to x and perform simple algebraic manipulations to obtain

$$\frac{d^2\phi}{dx^2} = \frac{1}{a^2}\left(\phi'' - \frac{1}{a}\phi'a'\right),$$

where a and a' are readily computed from the spatial mapping defining the geometry: $a = \sum_i x_i \phi'$ and $a' = \sum_i x_i \phi''$.

The coefficients K_{ij} have then the following form:

$$K_{ij} = \int_{t_a}^{t_b} c \frac{1}{a^4}\left(\phi_i'' - \frac{1}{a}\phi_i'a'\right)\left(\phi_j'' - \frac{1}{a}\phi_j'a'\right) a\, dt, \qquad (8.27)$$

where t_a and t_b are the parameter values that define the boundaries of the spatial domain $a \le x \le b$ (Figure 8.20).

For specificity, we consider cubic subdivision basis functions in this section, but similar ideas can be used for lower- or higher-order bases. Cubic basis functions are piecewise polynomials of degree 3; they have support over four adjacent knot-intervals (when knots are not repeated) in the parametric space, and can be analytically expressed as four cubic polynomials defined over these intervals. Therefore if $|i - j| \ge 4$, K_{ij} is 0 since the integrand vanishes identically. Only when the functions ϕ_i and ϕ_j overlap, non-zero values for the corresponding

---

[4]We will denote by $'$ the derivatives with respect to the parametric coordinate t.

coefficient K_{ij} are obtained. Because the integrands are rational functions, it is generally easier to perform the integration numerically. To do so, we can use a quadrature formula over each of the overlap segments. The segments between knots (knot intervals) in the region $t_a \leq t \leq t_b$ are referred to as *finite elements*.

Let r_{ij} be the number of overlap segments (elements) between two basis functions ϕ_i and ϕ_j. A numerical quadrature rule, such as Gauss quadrature, approximates the integral above by an expression of the form

$$
\begin{aligned}
k_{ij} &= \sum_{e=1}^{r_{ij}} \sum_{g=1}^{ng} \left[c \frac{1}{a^4} \left(\phi_i'' - \frac{1}{a} \phi_i' a' \right) \left(\phi_j'' - \frac{1}{a} \phi_j' a' \right) a \right]_{t_g} w_g \Delta t_e \\
&= \sum_{e=1}^{r_{ij}} \sum_{g=1}^{ng} I(t_g) \, w_g \, \Delta t_e,
\end{aligned}
\tag{8.28}
$$

where all the quantities in the bracketed expression are evaluated at t_g. The parametric coordinate of the gth Gauss point, w_g is a coefficient associated with the gth Gauss point, ng is the number of points used in the integration over each segment,[5] and Δt_e is the size of the segment in parametric space. This reduces the integral computation of k_{ij} to the evaluation of the integrand at $r_{ij} \cdot ng$ points.

There are two common ways of structuring the computations for generating the coefficients of the stiffness matrix:

- *Generating the coefficients of* **K** *one at a time.* This is a direct application of Equation (8.28) where a nested loop produces all the non-zero coefficients. The matrix **K** is banded. For cubic basis functions its semi-bandwidth is 3.

  > **for** $i \leftarrow 1..n$
  >   **for** $j \leftarrow 1..n$
  > $\triangleright$ Find the segments where the supports of ϕ overlap
  > $r \leftarrow overlap(i, j)$
  >   **for** e **in** r
  > $K_{ij} \leftarrow K_{ij} + \sum_g I(t_g) \, w_g \, \Delta t_e$

- *Generating the contributions to* **K** *one element at a time.* An alternative, and more popular way, of computing the entries of **K** is obtained by observing that every element is part of the support of four basis functions, and therefore there are 16 entries in **K** that involve contributions from integrals

---

[5]Values for Gauss integration of various orders of accuracy may be found in standard numerical methods texts.

over that element. We can then perform all the integrations that pertain to that element and assemble them in their corresponding four rows and four columns of **K**. The contributions that come from an element are stored in a small matrix (4×4 in this case) called the element stiffness matrix. This matrix, which we refer to as $\mathbf{k}_e$, represents the contributions coming from that element to the global matrix **K**. A typical coefficient K_{ij} gets contributions from multiple $\mathbf{k}_e$.

> **for** $e \leftarrow 1..m$
>   ▷ Generate the entries of the element stiffness matrix
>   **for** $i \leftarrow 1..4$
>   **for** $j \leftarrow 1..4$
> $k_e(i,j) = \sum_g I(t_g) \, w_g \, \Delta t_e$
>   ▷ Assemble the element stiffness matrix in **K**
> $s \leftarrow$ index set of basis functions with support over e
> $K(s,s) \leftarrow K(s,s) + \mathbf{k}_e$

In the simple one-dimensional context we are discussing in this section, both strategies for organizing the computations are equally convenient, but in two and three dimensions, and with adaptively changing discretizations, we may choose to use one or the other strategy for a variety of implementation and efficiency considerations.

Boundary conditions. The set of equations that describe the equilibrium position does not admit solutions without imposing appropriate constraints on **u**. Physically, these constraints are needed to restrain the shape from accelerating and moving as a rigid body when loads are applied to it. Mathematically, the co-efficient stiffness matrix **K** described above is singular: the additional constraints on admissible displacements are needed so that Π has a bounded minimum.

The constraints we may impose on the deformed curve are geometric constraints on its position and slope at various points. For example, we may want the deformed curve to interpolate a specified point at the left end of the domain: $\mathbf{u}(x = a) = u_o$, which in terms of the unknowns u_i, may be expressed as $\sum u_i \phi_i(t_a) = g$, where g is the imposed position of the constrained point. We can put this constraint in a canonical linear form $\mathbf{C}_i \mathbf{u} = \mathbf{g}$, where $\mathbf{C}_i$ is a $1 \times n$ row vector of the coefficients of u_i in the constraints:

$$\mathbf{C}_i = [\phi_1(t_a) \;\; \phi_2(t_a) \;\; \cdots \;\; \phi_i(t_a) \;\; \cdots \;\; \phi_n(t_a)].$$

For the example constraint above, $\mathbf{C}_i$ is very sparse as three basis functions only have non-zero value at the parameter $t = t_a$, the left end of the spatial domain (assuming t_a is one of the knots in the knot vector). However, not all constraints we may wish to impose on the deformation will have such sparse coefficient row vectors. For example, a constraint expressing that the average vertical displacement of the bar is zero, has a fully dense coefficient matrix. Constraints may also be imposed on the slopes of the deformed shape. For example, if we want the tangent at then right end of the interval ($x = b$) to be horizontal, then a constraint of the form $\sum u_i \phi_i'(t_b) = 0$, or

$$[\phi_1'(t_b) \ \phi_2'(t_b) \ \cdots \ \phi_i'(t_b) \ \cdots \ \phi_n'(t_b)] \, \mathbf{u} = \mathbf{0}$$

may be imposed. Again here, the row coefficient matrix for this constraint is extremely sparse. Algebraic constraints on the deformed shape represent a powerful tool for editing and expressing user specification on the final deformed curve. In the context of free-form deformation, both the applied "forces" and these constraints on position and slope allow the user to control the shape of the curve.

Assuming we have r linear constraints on the deformation, these constraints may be expressed in the form

$$\mathbf{Cu} = \mathbf{g}, \tag{8.29}$$

where $\mathbf{C}$ is a $r \times n$ coefficient matrix (involving the values of basis functions and their derivatives at various parameter values) and $\mathbf{g}$ is an $r \times 1$ column vector that represents the right-hand side of the constraint equations. In order to prevent rigid-body motion, we must have at least two constraints and one of them must involve displacements, not just slopes, for the problem to be well posed.

The complete formulation of the problem of finding the deformed shape can then be expressed as the problem to find $\mathbf{u}$ that minimizes $\Pi(\mathbf{u})$ subject to $\mathbf{Cu} = \mathbf{g}$.

The solution of this constrained minimization problem is obtained as the solution of the following set of equations:

$$\begin{bmatrix} \mathbf{K} & \mathbf{C}^{\mathrm{T}} \\ \mathbf{C} & \mathbf{0} \end{bmatrix} \begin{bmatrix} \mathbf{u} \\ \mathbf{v} \end{bmatrix} = \begin{bmatrix} \mathbf{f} \\ \mathbf{g} \end{bmatrix}, \tag{8.30}$$

where $\mathbf{v}$ is known as the vector of Lagrange multipliers and is obtained as part of the solution. Even though many techniques are available for solving this set of equations, when the problem size is relatively small, a method such as Gaussian elimination is likely to be good enough to obtain almost-interactive solution rates.

Examples. Figure 8.21 shows some examples of deformation of a bar under a variety of loading and constraint conditions. The bar is modeled by five cubic

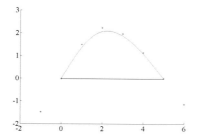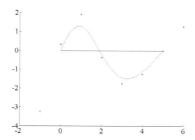

Figure 8.21. Deformation of an initially straight curve under forces (left) and interpolation constraints (right). Control point locations of deformed shape are shown.

segments and is initially horizontal. The left figure shows the deformation under an upward vertical load acting at $x = 1.5$ and interpolation constraints at the two ends. The right figure shows the deformed shape under interpolation constraints only: two at the ends and two at $x = 0.5$ (vertical displacement is $+1$) and $x = 2.5$ (vertical displacement is -1). The positions of the control points are shown. Note that the control points undergo only vertical displacements. This is because we have only taken into account bending deformations due to transversely applied loads and corresponding constraints. The addition of axial deformations in the problem formulation allow the control points to move horizontally. This is described next and developed more generally in Section 8.7.2.

Axial deformations. So far, we have only considered vertical displacements of the bar where the only unknown in the solution was the vertical displacement. We have further assumed that the "strain energy" consisted only of the bending energy due to linearized curvature ($\kappa = \frac{d^2u}{dx^2}$). In this section we consider the effect of axial deformations.

Material points on the bar can undergo displacements in the axial direction if horizontal loads $f_x(x)$ are applied. These displacements introduce changes in the length in the bar with corresponding axial strains. We will assume, for the moment, that the axial strains are due to a displacement in the x-direction only, which we will denote by $u_x(x)$. The formulation follows similar lines to the earlier one, except that axial strains (changes in length), which we will denote by $\varepsilon = \frac{du_x}{dx}$, replace the bending strains in the expression for potential energy. Upon discretization, $u_x(x) = \sum_i u_{xi} \phi_i(x)$, the potential energy can be expressed in terms of the unknown vector $\mathbf{u}_x$ as

$$\Pi_a[u_{xi}] = \frac{1}{2}\int_a^b c_a \varepsilon(x)^2 dx - \int_a^b f_x u_x dx \qquad (8.31)$$

$$= \frac{1}{2}\int_a^b c_a \left(\sum_i u_{xi}\frac{d\phi_i}{dx}\right)^2 dx - \int_a^b f\left(\sum_i u_{xi}\phi_i\right) dx, \quad (8.32)$$

where c_a is a material parameter that represents the axial stiffness of the bar, that may vary spatially. Assuming we have appropriate constraints imposed on the horizontal displacements to prevent rigid-body movement (at least one is needed), the solution for the axially-deformed bar may be obtained from the constrained minimization problem. Minimize Π_a subject to $\mathbf{C}_a \mathbf{u}_x = \mathbf{g}_a$, whose solution is obtained as

$$\begin{bmatrix} \mathbf{K}_a & \mathbf{C}_a^T \\ \mathbf{C}_a & \mathbf{0} \end{bmatrix}\begin{bmatrix} \mathbf{u}_x \\ \mathbf{v}_x \end{bmatrix} = \begin{bmatrix} \mathbf{f} \\ \mathbf{g} \end{bmatrix}, \qquad (8.33)$$

where $\mathbf{K}_a$ is the stiffness matrix associated with the axial deformations. Its entries K_{aij} are obtained by evaluating the integral

$$\int_a^b c_a \frac{d\phi_i}{dx}\frac{d\phi_j}{dx}dx = \int_a^b c_a \frac{1}{a^2}\phi_i'\phi_j'a\,dt$$

using the techniques discussed in Section 8.7.1

When both vertical and horizontal loads are applied, the deformed shape of the bar is due to displacements in both these directions. For the case of an initially straight bar and under our linearized approximations of curvature and elongation, the displacements are uncoupled, and we can simply solve both sets of equations, (8.30) and (8.33) independently:[6]

$$\left[\begin{array}{cc|cc} \mathbf{K}_a & \mathbf{C}_a^T & & \\ \mathbf{C}_a & \mathbf{0} & & \\ \hline & & \mathbf{K}_b & \mathbf{C}_b^T \\ & & \mathbf{C}_b & \mathbf{0} \end{array}\right]\begin{bmatrix} \mathbf{u}_x \\ \mathbf{v}_x \\ \mathbf{u}_y \\ \mathbf{v}_y \end{bmatrix} = \begin{bmatrix} \mathbf{f}_x \\ \mathbf{g}_x \\ \mathbf{f}_y \\ \mathbf{g}_y \end{bmatrix}.$$

By grouping the Lagrange multipliers, the equations may be expressed in the form

$$\left[\begin{array}{cc|cc} \mathbf{K}_a & & \mathbf{C}_a^T & \\ & \mathbf{K}_b & & \mathbf{C}_b^T \\ \hline \mathbf{C}_a & & & \\ & \mathbf{C}_b & & \end{array}\right]\begin{bmatrix} \mathbf{u}_x \\ \mathbf{u}_y \\ \mathbf{v}_x \\ \mathbf{v}_y \end{bmatrix} = \begin{bmatrix} \mathbf{f}_x \\ \mathbf{f}_y \\ \mathbf{g}_x \\ \mathbf{g}_y \end{bmatrix}.$$

---

[6]The subscript b correspond to the coefficient matrices and vectors related to bending deformations.

Perhaps the most important characteristic of the coefficient matrix of this set of equations is that its upper-left block, consisting of the stiffness matrices due to axial and bending deformations, is block-diagonal. Axial deformations are strictly due to $\mathbf{u}_x$, bending deformations are strictly due to $\mathbf{u}_y$, and there is no interaction between them. This will no longer be true when the initial shape of the bar is not straight. We discuss the curved case next.

8.7.2 Stretching and Bending of Curves

The formulation described above can be readily extended to shapes that are initially curved. The main change from the initially straight bar of the previous sections is that it is no longer reasonable to assume that axial elongations are due solely to displacements in a longitudinal direction, nor that bending is due solely to displacements in a transverse direction. In the case of curved geometries, both x- and y-components of the displacement (in any coordinate system) produce axial as well as bending deformations. The displacements are coupled and cannot be found independently.

Differential geometry of curves. The axial and bending strains are functions of the change in length and change in curvature along the bar. Length and curvature are differential geometric concepts, and we review them briefly here. The reader is encouraged to consult [Malv69, Fari01, Gray97] for additional details on the geometric aspects of deformation.

The initial geometry of the curved bar is defined by

$$\mathbf{x}(t) = \begin{bmatrix} x(t) \\ y(t) \end{bmatrix} \quad \text{with tangent vector} \quad \mathbf{a} = \mathbf{x}'(t) = \begin{bmatrix} x'(t) \\ y'(t) \end{bmatrix}$$

and curvature

$$\kappa_o = \frac{d\alpha}{ds} = \left| \frac{d^2\mathbf{x}}{ds^2} \right| = \frac{|\mathbf{x}' \times \mathbf{x}''|}{|\mathbf{x}'|^3} = \frac{|\mathbf{a} \times \mathbf{a}'|}{|\mathbf{a}|^3},$$

where $\times$ is the vector cross product, s is the arc length of the middle axis of the bar, and α is the angle the tangent vector $\mathbf{a}$ makes with the horizontal. These different forms of the curvature expression are useful in different contexts.

Let h measure the distance along the thickness from the middle axis of the bar. A differential parametric distance dt corresponds to a differential arc length $ds = |\mathbf{x}'|dt = |\mathbf{a}|dt = a\,dt$. This length may be also be written as $ds = \rho_o d\alpha$ where ρ_o is the radius of curvature ($\rho_o = 1/\kappa_o$). Because of the initially curved geometry of the bar, the corresponding length of a segment at a distance h from the middle axis is $ds_h = (\rho_o - h)d\alpha$.

Axial strains: Change in elongation. After the curve deforms, its new position is defined by

$$X(t) = x(t) + u(t) = \begin{bmatrix} x(t) + u_x(t) \\ y(t) + u_y(t) \end{bmatrix}.$$

The arc length along the middle axis is now $dS = |\mathbf{x}' + \mathbf{u}'|dt$. A common scalar measure to describe the change in length between the original and the deformed shape (an elongation strain measure) is known as the Green strain and is defined as

$$\varepsilon = \frac{1}{2}\frac{dS^2 - ds^2}{ds^2} = \frac{1}{2}\frac{(\mathbf{x}' + \mathbf{u}')^{\mathrm{T}}(\mathbf{x}' + \mathbf{u}') - \mathbf{x}'^{\mathrm{T}}\mathbf{x}'}{\mathbf{x}'^{\mathrm{T}}\mathbf{x}'},$$

which can be linearized to

$$\varepsilon = \frac{1}{a^2}\mathbf{a}^{\mathrm{T}}\mathbf{u}', \tag{8.34}$$

where

$$a^2 = |\mathbf{a}|^2 = \mathbf{a}^{\mathrm{T}}\mathbf{a}.$$

Bending strains: Change in curvature. Along the thickness of the bar the change in length, at a distance h from the middle axis, may be similarly written as

$$\varepsilon_h = \frac{1}{2}\frac{dS_h^2 - ds_h^2}{ds_h^2} = \frac{1}{2}\frac{(\rho_d - h)^2(\kappa_d dS)^2 - (\rho_o - h)^2(\kappa_o ds)^2}{ds_h^2}.$$

Assuming the thickness of the bar is small relative to other dimensions ($h/\rho << 1$), the $O(h^2)$ terms may be neglected to give

$$\varepsilon_h = \varepsilon - h\frac{(\kappa_d dS)^2 - (\kappa_o ds)^2}{ds^2} + O(h^2) \approx \varepsilon + \kappa h.$$

The change in length at a distance h is due to both the axial strain along the middle axis and to the change in curvature between the original and deformed shapes. The quantity κ is known as the *bending strain* and may be linearized to

$$\kappa = \frac{-1}{a^3}\left(\mathbf{a} \times \mathbf{u}'' - \mathbf{a}' \times \mathbf{u}' - \frac{1}{a^2}(\mathbf{a} \times \mathbf{a}')\mathbf{a} \cdot \mathbf{u}'\right). \tag{8.35}$$

Finite-element formulation. The finite-element discretization of the problem expresses the continuous quantities above in terms of discrete values that multiply basis functions. The initial geometry is written as

$$x(t) = \begin{bmatrix} \sum_i \phi_i(t)x_i \\ \sum_i \phi_i(t)y_i \end{bmatrix} = \begin{bmatrix} \Phi\mathbf{x} \\ \Phi\mathbf{y} \end{bmatrix},$$

where $\Phi = [\phi_1(t) \; \phi_2(t) \; \cdots \; \phi_n(t)]$ is a row vector of n basis functions. Similarly, the displacement vector is expressed as

$$u(t) = \begin{bmatrix} u_x(t) \\ u_y(t) \end{bmatrix} = \begin{bmatrix} \Phi \mathbf{u}_x \\ \Phi \mathbf{u}_y \end{bmatrix} = \Phi \mathbf{u} \qquad (8.36)$$

and the derivatives of $\mathbf{u}$ can then be written as

$$u'(t) = \begin{bmatrix} \Phi' \mathbf{u}_x \\ \Phi' \mathbf{u}_y \end{bmatrix} \qquad u''(t) = \begin{bmatrix} \Phi'' \mathbf{u}_x \\ \Phi'' \mathbf{u}_y \end{bmatrix}. \qquad (8.37)$$

The vectors Φ' and Φ'' are row vectors consisting of the first and second derivatives of the basis functions, respectively.

Let $\mathbf{f}$ be the force vector along the length of the bar:

$$f(t) = \begin{bmatrix} f_x(t) \\ f_y(t) \end{bmatrix}.$$

We seek to find the displacement vector $\mathbf{u} = [\mathbf{u}_x \; \mathbf{u}_y]^{\mathrm{T}}$ that is in equilibrium with the applied forces. This is found by discretizing and then minimizing the potential energy defined by

$$\Pi(\mathbf{u}) \;=\; \frac{1}{2} \int_0^l c_a \varepsilon^2 ds + \frac{1}{2} \int_0^l c_b \kappa^2 ds - \int_0^l (f_x u_x + f_y u_y) \, ds. \qquad (8.38)$$

Using the discretization introduced in Equation (8.37), the axial strain ε (Equation (8.34)) may be written in terms of $\mathbf{u}$ as

$$\varepsilon = \frac{1}{a^2} \left[a_x \Phi' \;\; a_y \Phi' \right] \begin{bmatrix} \mathbf{u}_x \\ \mathbf{u}_y \end{bmatrix} = \left[\mathbf{A}_{x\phi} \;\; \mathbf{A}_{y\phi} \right] \begin{bmatrix} \mathbf{u}_x \\ \mathbf{u}_y \end{bmatrix},$$

while the bending strain κ (Equation (8.35)) may be written as

$$\kappa \;=\; \frac{1}{a^2} \left[\frac{a_y}{a} \Phi'' - \frac{a_y'}{a} \Phi' + d\frac{a_x}{a} \Phi' \quad \frac{-a_x}{a} \Phi'' + \frac{a_x'}{a} \Phi' + d\frac{a_y}{a} \Phi' \right] \begin{bmatrix} \mathbf{u}_x \\ \mathbf{u}_y \end{bmatrix}$$

$$=\; \left[\mathbf{B}_{x\phi} \;\; \mathbf{B}_{y\phi} \right] \begin{bmatrix} \mathbf{u}_x \\ \mathbf{u}_y \end{bmatrix}, \qquad (8.39)$$

where $d = \frac{|\mathbf{a} \times \mathbf{a}'|}{a^2}$. The vectors $\mathbf{A}_{x\phi}$ and $\mathbf{A}_{y\phi}$ are row vectors consisting of derivatives of basis functions scaled by geometric data of the bar. They allow us to represent the axial strain along the bar as linear combinations of the $\mathbf{u}_x$ and $\mathbf{u}_y$ displacement vectors. The vectors $\mathbf{B}_{x\phi}$ and $\mathbf{B}_{y\phi}$ are also row vectors that perform a similar function with respect to the bending strain.

Substituting Equation (8.36) in the potential energy expression Equation (8.39), we obtain, after some algebraic manipulations,

$$\Pi(\mathbf{u}) = \frac{1}{2}\mathbf{u}^T \left[\int_0^l c_a \begin{bmatrix} \mathbf{A}_{x\phi}^T \\ \mathbf{A}_{y\phi}^T \end{bmatrix} [\mathbf{A}_{x\phi}\mathbf{A}_{y\phi}]\,ds + \int_0^l c_b \begin{bmatrix} \mathbf{B}_{x\phi}^T \\ \mathbf{B}_{y\phi}^T \end{bmatrix} [\mathbf{B}_{x\phi}\mathbf{B}_{y\phi}]\,ds \right] \mathbf{u}$$
$$- \left[\int_0^l f_x \Phi\,ds \quad \int_0^l f_y \Phi\,ds \right] \mathbf{u}, \quad (8.40)$$

or more compactly,

$$\Pi(\mathbf{u}) = \frac{1}{2}\mathbf{u}^T [\mathbf{K}_a + \mathbf{K}_b] \mathbf{u} - \begin{bmatrix} \mathbf{f}_x^T & \mathbf{f}_y^T \end{bmatrix} \mathbf{u} = \frac{1}{2}\mathbf{u}^T \mathbf{K}\mathbf{u} - \mathbf{f}^T\mathbf{u}. \quad (8.41)$$

The function Π is a quadratic form in which $\mathbf{K}_a$ and $\mathbf{K}_b$ are the stiffness matrices corresponding to axial and bending deformations, respectively. The vectors $\mathbf{f}_x$ and $\mathbf{f}_y$ may be interpreted as horizontal and vertical force vectors along the n degrees of freedom of the discretization.

Numerical solution. There are three remaining tasks we need to attend to in order to obtain the displacement vector:

1. Apply displacement/tangent constraints;

2. Evaluate the coefficient stiffness matrices and force vectors;

3. Solve the resulting system.

Displacement and tangent constraints. In order to find a unique solution to the displacement vector, we need to properly constrain the bar to prevent rigid-body displacements and rotations. Position and tangent constraints may be imposed at any point along the bar. The algebraic expressions for specifying the position interpolation constraints and slope constraints may be expressed in terms of the basis functions and their derivatives in the same fashion as we did in Section 8.7.1. Details are left as an exercise to reader.

Numerical evaluations of coefficients. As was the case with the straight bar, the solution of the constrained minimization problem may be obtained by solving the following set of algebraic equations, where $\mathbf{v}$ is the vector of Lagrange multipliers corresponding to the constraints $\mathbf{Cu} = \mathbf{g}$:

$$\left[\begin{array}{c|c} \mathbf{K}_a + \mathbf{K}_b & \mathbf{C}^T \\ \hline \mathbf{C} & \end{array} \right] \begin{bmatrix} \mathbf{u}_x \\ \mathbf{u}_y \\ \mathbf{v} \end{bmatrix} = \begin{bmatrix} \mathbf{f}_x \\ \mathbf{f}_y \\ \mathbf{g} \end{bmatrix}.$$

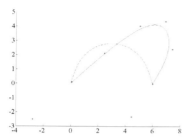 

Figure 8.22. Global deformation of a curve under forces (left) and position interpolation constraints (right). Control point locations of deformed shape are shown.

Notice here that, unlike the straight-geometry case, the stiffness block of the
above set of equation is not block-diagonal. The matrices $\mathbf{K}_a$ and $\mathbf{K}_b$ are both of
size $2n \times 2n$ as both the horizontal ($\mathbf{u}_x$) and vertical ($\mathbf{u}_y$) displacement components
contribute to axial as well as bending deformations.

As described in detail in Section 8.7.1, there are two strategies for computing
the entries in $\mathbf{K}_a$ and $\mathbf{K}_b$: entry-by-entry or element-by-element. In the more
common element-by-element approach, the effect of all of the basis functions with
partial support over a given segment (element) are computed and then assembled
in the right locations in the global stiffness matrix.

In order to evaluate the stiffness contributions from every element, the integrals for computing $\mathbf{K}$ and $\mathbf{f}$ in expression (8.40) need to be evaluated. The
analytical expressions of the integrands in these matrices and force vectors are
sufficiently cumbersome that we generally rely on numerical integration schemes
for their evaluation. A Gauss integration scheme is a convenient numerical integration strategy, and its use in finite-element computations is widespread.

Figure 8.22 shows the global deformation of a curve under the application
of loads and/or imposed interpolation constraints. The left diagram shows the
resulting shape due to a load acting at midpoint and pulling to the top right. The
right diagram shows the shape obtained by adding an interpolation constraint that
forces the curve to go through the point (3.5, 1). We note here that these deformed
shapes were generated by using the linearized kinematics expressions described
earlier, and they do not necessarily correspond to the physical deformations of
a real material. To get the physically correct deformed shapes, we can apply
the loads (or postion/slope constraints) incrementally, generating a new stiffness
matrix at each increment.

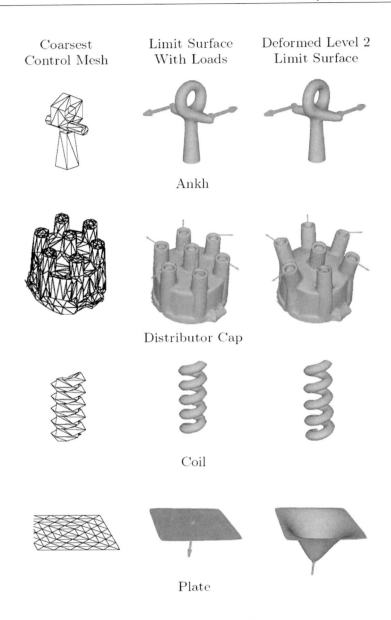

Figure 8.23. Examples of deformable subdivision surfaces. Green arrows are forces acting on the geometry to produce the shapes in the right column.

8.7.3 Stretching and Bending of Subdivision Surfaces

The formulation above may be generalized to surfaces, which is the case of more practical interest. As with curves, there are two types of deformations that the surface can undergo under the effect of forces and constraints on displacements/slopes.

- *In-plane deformations.* In-plane deformations involve stretching and shearing in the tangent space at every point of the surface. Theycorrespond to changes in the first fundamental form of the surface.

- *Out-of-plane deformations.* These deformations involve bending and twisting in the normal direction to the surface. Out-of plane deformations correspond to changes in the second fundamental form of the surface.

The force field that can act on the surface is a three-dimensional vector field, and the displacements sought are the displacement vector fields for every surface point. The formulations follow the same principles used in the curved bar case of the previous section, but naturally involve more detailed algebraic expressions. Details may be found in [Cira00, Gree04, Gree05]. By way of example, Figure 8.23 shows the deformation of a number of subdivision surfaces under various loads and interpolation constraints. The left column in the figure shows the control meshes used in the computations. The middle column and right column show the initial surfaces and the deformed surfaces, respectively.

8.8 Exercises

1. Apply Chaikin's subdivision algorithm to a square and prove that the limit curve is a periodic quadratic B-spline curve.

2. Find the subdivision masks for the quartic B-spline curve.

3. Consider a quadratic curve subdivision algorithm that inserts two knots in each interval. Find the subdivision masks for generating its refined vertices. Explain how to extend this algorithm to tensor product quadratic B-spline surfaces.

4. Repeat Exercise 3 for cubic B-spline.

5. Consider a modification of the Doo–Sabin algorithm that generates the refined vertices as follows. For each face, join the centroid with each of its vertices and take the midpoint of these edges as refined vertices.

    (a) Compare this algorithm with the Doo–Sabin algorithm.

    (b) Does it lead to a smooth surface?

    (c) Compare two steps of this algorithm to the midpoint subdivision algorithm.

6. Consider a variation of Chaikin's subdivision that splits each edge into three equal segments.

    (a) What is the mask(s) of this algorithm?

    (b) How can it be extended to tensor product surfaces?

    (c) Does it lead to smooth curves/surfaces?

7. Implement a subdivision system that handles most of the described schemes with interpolating and sharp features. In particular, provide a solution to the generation of Doo–Sabin surfaces with creases.

8. Let $\mathbf{A}$ denote the subdivision matrix of the Doo–Sabin algorithm. Derive the corresponding Fourier image $\widehat{\mathbf{A}}$ of $\mathbf{A}$ and determine its eigenvalues and corresponding multiplicities. Given the original weights,

$$\alpha^j = \frac{\delta_{j,0}}{4} + \frac{3 + 2\cos(2\pi j/n)}{4n}, \quad j = 0, \ldots, n-1, \qquad (8.42)$$

where $\delta_{j,0}$ denotes the Kronecker delta symbol, show that the subdominant eigenvalue $\lambda = 1/2$.

9. Let $\mathbf{A}$ denote the subdivision matrix of the Catmull–Clark algorithm. Derive the corresponding Fourier image $\widehat{\mathbf{A}}$ of $\mathbf{A}$ and determine its eigenvalues and corresponding multiplicities.

10. In your favorite programming language, implement the stiffness matrix generation algorithm described in Section 8.7.1.

11. Write the constraint matrix for position and slope interpolation constraints at a parametric location t_o for the curved bar (See Section 8.7.2).

9

Scene Management

No matter what the illusion created, it is a flat canvas
and it has to be organized into shapes.
—David Hockney

9.1 Introduction

In Chapter 5, we saw that in order to avoid clogging the graphics-rendering pipeline with data, polygons that are never meant to get displayed in the visible area
of the viewing frustum are discarded early using various culling techniques. In
order to efficiently perform the visibility tests, primitives are grouped together in
clusters and spatial hierarchies so that tests are performed only on the bounding
volumes of the clusters or their aggregations and not on the geometry elements
themselves. Of course, this results in far fewer calculations and, therefore, less
impact of the size of the dataset on the performance. Obviously, gathering polygons or other primitives in spatially coherent clusters and then grouping those
clusters in larger spatial aggregations in a hierarchical manner implies a scene
organization that is built bottom-up (primary element is the leaf primitive) and
queried top-down. This way, all primitives are arranged in a tree and can be efficiently accessed, removed early from operations such as viewport frustum culling,
and easily managed as memory objects (dynamic loading, caching, etc.). This
type of data organization is called *spatial partitioning*, and, as we have already
seen in Chapter 5, there are many interesting schemes to perform it.

Actually, this is only the data-driven side of scene management. When people
design a virtual world, a three-dimensional *scene*, they tend to think in ontological terms and group entities according to logical relationships rather than purely

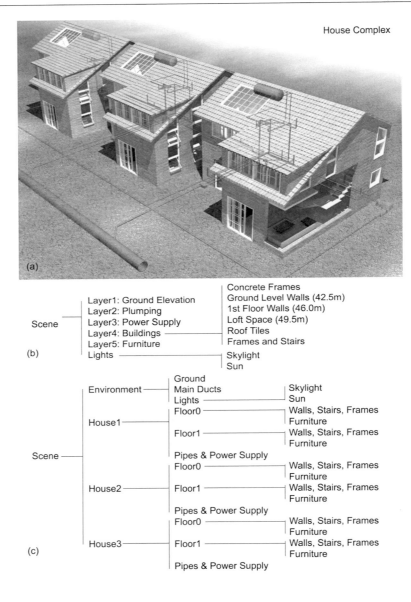

Figure 9.1. (a) Example of different scene organizations for the same scene. (b) Architectural plan layers—no spatial coherency. (c) Spatially coherent scene partitioning for real-time walkthrough.

spatial ones. Sometimes, ontological hierarchies tend to resemble spatial organizations, but not always. This can be demonstrated in the example of Figure 9.1 where the same scene—a house complex—is partitioned in an ontological manner to form a hierarchy of elements. In the architectural version of a scene organization (Figure 9.1(b)), elements are grouped according to function, material, and consistency with traditional floor plans. Obviously, the spatial organization of this scene does not facilitate culling and efficient traversal of the hierarchy for rendering but better serves the specific application in terms of clarity of entity decomposition.

On the other hand, intentionally breaking down the scene into spatially coherent hierarchies (e.g., House1, House2, etc.) provides a significant performance boost in most cases, because invisible geometry can be culled early in the process at a high hierarchy level. In our example, if an entire house is outside the view, then its (precomputed) extents can be checked against the viewing frustum, and the whole subtree of the scene can be rejected with a single operation.

For real-time graphics applications, the common practice is to build scenes as ontological hierarchies with spatial-coherency priority. Indoor environments are constructed with portal culling and BSP trees in mind and open, outdoor scenes are usually designed to provide hierarchies with a large branching factor for efficient frustum culling. Apart from culling efficiency, they offer better asset management, as one builds self-contained environments (e.g, a house) that can be easily replicated to form larger aggregations (e.g., a small town). As will be shown later, this has also a significant impact in memory conservation via the mechanism of geometry instancing.

Excessive decomposition of a scene into hierarchical elements can sometimes lead to the undesired effect of slowing down the rendering operation because of two main reasons: First, the application tends to spend too much time in the traversal of the scene hierarchy, while it would be faster to render some redundant elements. Second, in hardware-accelerated graphics, a fine partitioning can lead to poor geometry streams (e.g., short triangle strips or vertex arrays) and frequent state changes (e.g., color or texture switching), problems which have a direct impact on the number of instructions executed and the data transferred to, from, and within the graphics system.

9.2 Scene Graphs

A hierarchy of geometric elements that are related in an ontological manner and are spatially dependent is called a *scene graph*. Although an all-encompassing definition of a scene graph is hard to derive, the above statement at least covers the most common aspects of scene-graph implementations. A scene graph consists of nodes that represent aggregations of geometric elements (2D or 3D), transformations, conditional selections, other renderable entities (e.g., sounds), processes (calculation/simulation/trigger nodes), or other scene graphs.

A scene graph is a directed, non-cyclic graph (tree) of nodes, whose arcs define the geometrical or functional dependence of a child node to its parent node. One important point about scene graphs is that they are not only data structures for the efficient storage of geometrical information; the nodes encapsulate all the functionality that is required to define a behavior, and thus adhere to the object-oriented programming model (see Section 9.2.4). The root node is commonly the abstract scene node, whose purpose is to provide a single entry traversal point in the data organization of the application and propagate to the hierarchy any operations that need to be performed on the elements. In this sense, an operation performed on a node, affects all of its children. For instance, a transformation node applies a calculated transformation matrix to all of its children, which in turn may be transformation nodes as well. If a switch node is switched off, the entire subtree, whose root is the switch node, is excluded from rendering (and possibly processing).

The ability to group geometrical entities together and operate on them as if they were a single object, completely abstracting the internal operation of this part of the scene, makes modeling of complex environments and their animation easy and provides the means for the construction of self-contained and reusable elements.

Take, for instance, the case of a speedboat (Figure 9.2). It is very difficult to directly describe the movement of each individual mechanical part relative to the global coordinate system. For example, the propeller rotates around its axis, which in turn is shifted left or right following the steering mechanism, while the boat moves forward and oscillates (heaves, pitches, rolls, etc.) as it travels in the choppy sea. Well, what is the apparent motion of the propeller with respect to an observer sitting on a nearby dock (Figure 9.2, Viewer1)? How does one describe the propeller's motion if one is seated inside the boat (Figure 9.2, Viewer2)?

To actually answer these questions, we need to build a hierarchy of relations between objects, and this is what a scene graph is used for. The propeller is attached to an outboard motor with an offset $\vec{t}_{prop}$ relative to the motor's local coordinate system and is allowed to spin on the end of the transmission shaft (local z-axis) with a rotation transformation $\mathbf{R}_{z,\theta}$. The motor swings left and right around the mounting point on the hull of the boat ($\mathbf{R}_{y,\varphi}$), which also represents the

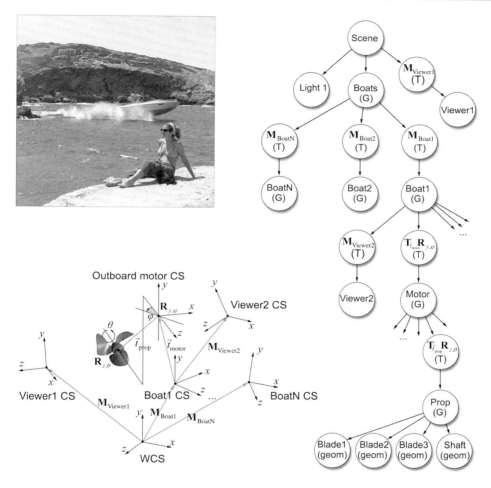

Figure 9.2. Example of spatial relationships in a scene-graph organization. (T) are transformation nodes, (G) are group nodes, and (geom) nodes represent actual geometric data. CS stands for coordinate system.

coordinate system origin of the outboard motor (See angle φ in Figure 9.2). The motor is translated by $\vec{t}_{\text{motor}}$ relative to the boat's coordinate center origin. The second observer is considered fixed with respect to the vessel coordinate system (seated/attached somewhere aboard—transformation $\mathbf{M}_{\text{Viewer2}}$ relative to the boat reference frame). The apparent motion of the propeller perceived by this second observer is the composite geometric transformation $\mathbf{M}_{\text{prop(Viewer2)}}$ that includes the offset of the motor mounting shaft with respect to the observer, the rotation of the outboard motor, the offset of the propeller, and the rotation of the latter:

$$\mathbf{M}_{\text{prop(Viewer2)}} = \mathbf{M}_{\text{Viewer2}}^{-1} \mathbf{T}_{\vec{t}_{\text{motor}}} \mathbf{R}_{y,\varphi} \mathbf{T}_{\vec{t}_{\text{prop}}} \mathbf{R}_{z,\theta}. \tag{9.1}$$

The observer is transformed away from the local coordinate system of the boat by $\mathbf{M}_{\text{Viewer2}}$, so the boat's reference frame is transformed with respect to the viewing coordinate system of Viewer2 by $\mathbf{M}_{\text{Viewer2}}^{-1}$. The cumulative effect of the translation of the outboard motor, followed by the rotation around its mounting point, and the offset and spin of the propeller is the composite transformation matrix that defines the motion of the propeller with regard to the boat's coordinate system.

In Equation (9.1), as we seek to express one node of the scene graph relative to another, we perform an upward traversal of the tree from the target node (here the propeller) to the common parent node of the target and reference nodes, and then we descend to the node whose reference system we use by inversely applying all transformations of this branch (here, $\mathbf{M}_{\text{Viewer2}}^{-1}$; see hierarchy in Figure 9.2).

Instead of using the common parent as a point of traversal-direction switching, one could blindly go all the way up the hierarchy and down again since the common path transformations would cancel one another. Of course, it is cheaper to spot the common root first and avoid unnecessary traversals (and matrix multiplications). In general, the transformation of a node at level k on a branch A relative to another node at level m on a branch B with a common root (connecting branch A and B) at level r is given by the following formula:

$$\mathbf{M}_{A \to B} = \prod_{j=m}^{r+1} \mathbf{M}_{Bj}^{-1} \prod_{i=r+1}^{k} \mathbf{M}_{Ai}. \tag{9.2}$$

Equation (9.2) is a direct consequence of the duality between transformations and change of reference frame. Here, we move the reference frame from the common node at level r to that of the reference node (level m on branch B). As the reference node is transformed by $\mathbf{M}_{Br+1} \cdot \mathbf{M}_{Br+2} \cdot \ldots \cdot \mathbf{M}_{Bm}$ with regard to the common root at level r, node r and everything that depends on it are inversely transformed to reflect this change of basis.

The speedboat is a self-contained entity, with animated parts and a complete geometric description. One can consider it a black box and completely disregard its internal workings when thinking of the speedboat as one of 200 different vessels in a marina. As the first observer (the one sitting on the dock) captures the image of the boat passing by, he/she also sees the *results* of the propulsion and steering procedure as the *visible* parts of the boat are animated and *revealed* to him/her. As will be discussed later in Section 9.2.4, these three keywords represent the major duty-cycle elements of a scene graph and of each individual node.

9.2.1 Data Organization

The majority of a scene graph describes relations between ontological entities and aggregations of nodes. Naturally, all actual geometric data are essentially leaves of the hierarchical structure. Geometry nodes may contain unordered, indexed, or raw polygonal data or other primitive data information, such as NURBS surfaces or volume data. Alternatively, the geometry nodes may be part of (or self-contained) space-partitioning structures, such as axis-aligned bounding box trees (AABB trees).

The above scheme of data organization is encountered frequently in applications that deal with large datasets. The scene graph represents the ontological hierarchy of the data and potentially encapsulates the functionality of each entity, while a space-partitioning system operates on the leaves for further accelerating rendering and search operations at a fine level. Since efficient space partitioning requires that the data are pre-processed and stored in the appropriate structure, the combined scene graph–space partitioning approach is effective for static data, i.e., geometric information that has a fixed representation relative to a local coordinate system and is not dynamically changed or animated. In some real-time applications, a scene graph is decoupled from the space-partitioning scheme and is used for animated objects only, while all static environment information is isolated in a high-performance spatial-partitioning system like a BSP tree.

9.2.2 Instancing

In the example of Section 9.2, the speedboat was modeled according to a local reference frame, and the whole subtree of the corresponding aggregation (or group) node was considered a black box. The speedboat node could be placed anywhere in the scene graph and replicated to create other moving boats in the scene. An important question to ask is why one should actually replicate the node to create separate copies of the same entity when the latter are identical? A common mechanism, which is directly associated with the underlying data structures that store the hierarchical information of the scene graph, is *node instancing*. Instead of making a copy of all the geometric information, transformations, and other data that are attached to a node, a reference is created to the original node wherever an identical node needs to be inserted into the scene graph (Figure 9.3). The tree-

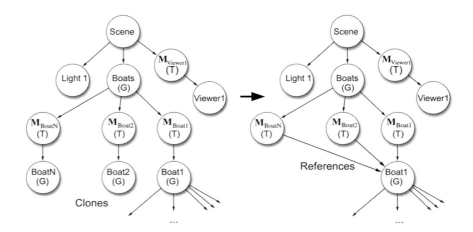

Figure 9.3. Node instancing.

like structure of the scene graph is transformed into a directed cyclic graph when instancing is used.

Creating instances of nodes instead of actual copies obviously saves substantial storage space in memory. It can also speed up the calculations in the case where certain simulation steps take place between subsequent frames. The processing step is performed once for the original node and all other instances reuse the new data. For example, the update to the rotation $\mathbf{R}_{\bar{v},\theta(k+1)}$ of the propeller in frame $k+1$,

$$\mathbf{R}_{\bar{v},\theta(k+1)} : \theta(k+1) = \theta(k) + 2\pi \cdot \Delta t \cdot \text{rpm}/60$$

can be done the first time the node is visited (from any one of the referencing super-nodes), and then the node can be marked as "processed" for the current time stamp. Future visits to the propeller transformation node would skip the matrix calculation and proceed to displaying the results. In fact, the whole speedboat would be traversed the first time it was visited for the current frame and "flattened," i.e., all calculations made and data transformed with respect to the reference frame of the top-level node of the aggregation. In OpenGL [Seg04], this would be equivalent to calculating the matrices and performing the corresponding matrix multiplications to create a display list for the current frame that would remain untouched by subsequent processing requests in the same cycle and would only be rendered multiple times, once per instance.

The above scheme for instancing "freezes" the internal operations of the instanced node and makes both calculations and storage more efficient. However, this is not always desired. In our example, as each boat follows a different path, its outboard engine should be able to turn according to the motion of the vessel in order for the latter to look convincing. If all instances used the same simulation data, then this result could never be obtained. This could also happen in the case where the instanced node contained a switch that should be independently triggered for each identical node. In situations similar to the above, instancing can only reflect the storage of the data in memory and no other operation. This also affects the order in which traversal operations are done; a processing step for one of the instances of a node must be immediately followed by a rendering call to display the results. Simulation and rendering cannot be done as separate passes for the entire scene graph, due to the dependency of the first on the common instanced data.

9.2.3 Scene Graph Traversal and Culling

In terms of application functionality and programming, the main advantage of building a scene-graph representation of a 3D world is that every operation can be applied to the root node of the hierarchy and propagated to the rest of the entities via the mechanism of scene-graph traversal. The four major operations performed on a scene graph are *initialization*, *simulation*, *culling*, and *drawing*, each one of them corresponding to respective procedures applied hierarchically on the nodes.

The simulation procedure is responsible for determining all the internal node parameters and performing all variable updates according to a node-specific behavior. Sometimes this operation is referred to as the animation or application stage, emphasizing either the visual impact of the node's change of state or the fact that this procedure is decoupled from the rendering algorithms.

Culling in scene graphs is tightly coupled with the node dependencies. Typically, each node is assumed to "contain" all of its children in the sense that, if a subtree root node is marked as completely hidden, then every child node is also invisible and the whole subtree is pruned. On the other hand, if an aggregate node passes the visibility test, its children may be individually tested, as in the case of partial parent-node occlusion, some children may be invisible. The result of the culling process is usually determined by testing the bounding volume of a node with the chosen criterion (e.g., frustum containment in the case of frustum or occlusion culling). For an aggregate node, the bounding volume is adjusted to reflect the collective extents of its children.

If a node contains an animated branch of the hierarchy, its extents need to be dynamically adjusted each time the extents of one of its children change. Recalculation of a geometry node's exact extents requires the iteration through all of its vertices to determine minimum and maximum values, or sometimes moments and principal axes. For animated subtrees that need to iterate through the raw data anyway (e.g., skeletal animation), this imposes no additional overhead. On the other hand, for rigid-body animation, this reevaluation involves substantial processing time and may be prohibitive for large models. A common practice that is adopted instead when speed is a more important factor than exact visibility is to adjust the bounding volume of an aggregate node based on the transformed, object-aligned bounding volumes of its children. For example, if a geometry node is bound by a local axis-aligned box and is indirectly connected to a group node via a transformation node, then the extents of the group node can be evaluated using the transformed eight corners of the box (Figure 9.4). This solution is suboptimal in terms of culling efficiency (bounding volume tightness) as the extents of the transformed bounding volumes are in general larger than the extents of the

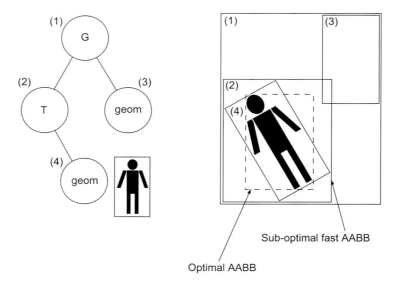

Figure 9.4. Aggregate node extent evaluation for real-time applications. The resulting axis-aligned bounding box (AABB) is non-optimal but can be rapidly calculated.

contained geometry. Culling at a fine level can be handled by the spatial subdivision scheme of the geometry nodes, if present.

The drawing operation recursively moves down the hierarchy and applies the rendering algorithms to each visible renderable node. In direct rendering and first-level ray-casting (see Chapter 15) the pruned subtrees are not traversed.

During rendering, regardless of the display method (direct or ray-casting), each time a transformation node is encountered, the state of the rendering elements is altered to reflect the transformation. For instance, if OpenGL direct rendering is used, when a draw operation is called on a transformation node as we traverse down the hierarchy, the transformation state is pushed in the matrix stack and the local transformation of the visited node is post-multiplied with the matrix of the parent node (current state). As the depth-first traversal returns to a higher level, child transformations are popped from the stack.

9.2.4 Programming with Scene Graphs

Remember that in a scene graph, most nodes tend to be self-managed, meaning that they provide their own drawing functionality and behavior. For instance, consider a rotor node, i.e., a specialized transformation node for rotating all its children around a certain axis with respect to its local coordinate system. The node needs to calculate the angle of rotation for the current frame based on the absolute time, the time the rotation started and its current state (active, stopped, disabled etc). This functionality can be implemented in a simulation operation of the node. Being an aggregate node, although it is not a renderable entity, it needs to propagate a draw command to its children; therefore, the node should provide a draw operation, whose task is to perform the operation on all dependent nodes. Similarly, the node is responsible for checking its boundaries against any culling criterion. This distributed operation of a scene graph facilitates an object-oriented design of the nodes and takes advantage of polymorphism and abstraction.

Typically, all nodes of a scene graph are derived from a common generic node class and mutate their behavior as one node inherits common attributes and overrides the behavior of another node. A top-level node interface would look like this:

```
class Node
{
protected:
    bool active;
    bool culled;
public:
```

```
    Node();
    virtual void init();
    virtual void simulate();
    virtual void cull();
    virtual void draw();
    virtual void reset();
};

class Group : Node
{
protected:
    vector<Node*> children;
    Bvolume extents;
public:
    Group();
    void add(Node *n);
    void remove(int i);
    Node * getChild(int i);
    int  getNumChildren();
    virtual void init();
    virtual void simulate();
    virtual void cull();
    virtual void draw();
};
```

Any node that extends the abstract class Node inherits the four basic operations. Aggregate nodes are derived from the Group class and all share a common
functionality: they provide a list of children and basic operations on them. More
elaborate Group subclasses may need to extend this behavior by adding more
specific methods, as in the case of a Transformation node or a Selector (ac-
tivates one child at a time). An essential common feature of all Group nodes is
the traversal of their children, which is manifested as an iterative call to all available Node objects in the list. Due to polymorphism, a Group object can invoke
the method init(), draw(), cull(), or simulate() without caring what subclass the
particular object is instantiated from. This way, all scene-graph node type classes
share a common interface:

```
void Group::draw()
{
    vector <Node>::size_type i,sz;
    sz = children.size();
    for (i=0; i<sz; i++)
        children[i]->draw();
}
```

```
void Geometry::draw() // Geometry is a subclass of Node
{
    if (!enabled || culled)
        return;
    // ... render the geometry
}
```

Culling, initialization, and simulation steps are similarly defined.

The order of the invocation of each method at runtime is defined by the traversal pattern of the scene graph. Usually, the initialization and the three repetitive steps are executed in a scene-graph basis and not at a node level. After initialization, the typical duty cycle of a scene graph involves the invocation of the simulation, the culling and the drawing methods of the root node (in our case, a subclass of Group). Therefore, three distinct traversals occur before the scene graph is visualized:

```
// Scene is a subclass of Group
Scene *myScene = new Scene();
myScene->load("village.scn");
myScene->init();
while (notTerminating)
{
    // ... other operations such as user input
    myScene->simulate() ;
    myScene->cull() ;
    myScene->draw() ;
}
```

This helps keep all nodes in pace with each other in terms of status and parameter values and leads to the more efficient *deferred update* strategy. In this strategy, changes in the state of an entity do not produce an immediate result. Instead, all attributes are evaluated once to produce a simulation, culling, or drawing result. Deferred updates are particularly useful when a computationally heavy operation needs to be repeated whenever a variable changes. Practical examples in the scene-graph paradigm are various geometry-dependent culling techniques (such as occlusion culling), physically based animation, and the estimation of shadow volumes.

As scene graphs become more complex and nodes represent autonomous entities, the need arises to exceed the limitations of strict hierarchical control. As part of the simulation process, nodes may communicate with each other either by direct method invocation or by *message passing*. In the latter (and more elegant)

case, each node primitive needs to be extended to support a message queue and
possibly an event map:

```
class NodeMessage
{
    Node *from, *to;
    int ID;
    void * params;
};
typedef EventID int;

class Node
{
protected:
...
    vector<NodeMessage *> msgQueue;
    multimap<EventID,NodeMessage *> eventMap;
    // Remove all pending messages and invoke appropriate
    // methods
    void processMessages();
    // Notify other nodes according to events registered in
    // the event map
    void dispatchMessages();
public:
...
    message( NodeMessage *msg ); // add msg to the queue
    registerEvent( EventID evt, Node* target,
                   int msgID, void* params );
};
```

The message queue is necessary because a node may receive multiple command messages from an unknown number of other nodes. An event map helps
create an interface for user-defined responses to state changes of a node (especially useful for trigger nodes). For instance, consider a room full of furniture.
The light is initially turned off, and, therefore, there is no need for the furniture
to cast shadows, so they can be also initially disabled for these geometry nodes.
When the light is turned on via a message, or because of an intrinsic behavior, the
furniture geometry needs to start casting shadows. We may also want to make a
halo object visible around the bulb to make the scene more realistic.

```
Light * bulb; // Light extends Node
Geometry *furniture, *halo;
...
```

```
bulb->registerEvent( EVENT_ON, furniture, MSG_SHADOWS_ON,
                     NULL);
bulb->registerEvent( EVENT_ON, halo, MSG_ENABLE, NULL);
```

In the extended `Node class` we have added two new protected member functions, `processMessages()` and `dispatchMessages()`. In order to correctly time the message-pumping procedure among the nodes of the scene graph, these operations have to be executed before and after the simulation step, respectively, for the whole scene graph. Therefore, we need to introduce additional *pre/post*-simulation methods, which will be invoked via a corresponding pre/post simulation step for the whole scene:

```
void Scene::simulate()
{
    preSimulate();
    Group::simulate();
    postSimulate();
}
...
void Group::preSimulate()
{
    vector <Node>::size_type i,sz;
    sz = children.size();
    for (i=0; i<sz; i++)
        children[i]->preSimulate();
}
```

Similar pre/post operation function calls can be implemented for the draw and culling stages, either locally for each node (they are invoked right before and after the corresponding operation on each node) or globally, as in the case of the pre- and post-simulation stages. For example, when rendering with OpenGL, a `Transformation` node needs to implement a pre-draw and a post-draw function to push and pop the current matrix state in the stack. A global post-draw function may trigger a buffer swap.

9.3   Distributed Scene Rendering

9.3.1   Introduction

The constant pursuit for detail and realism in both real-time and offline rendering, as well as for inherently concurrent applications such as multiplayer online games and multi-projection virtual reality installations, have necessitated the distribution of the scene-graph data and the rendering workload to multiple processing units. A processing unit is not necessarily a separate computer, like a cluster node or a personal computer connected to the Internet. It can also be a specialized co-processor for ray tracing, one or more parallel system processors, or a scalable graphics subsystem. Therefore, we shall consider the problem of managing a distributed rendering environment with parallel processes rendering the same three-dimensional world. The scene is not necessarily resident in a common space in memory (e.g., as in the case of an application-level cluster configuration), and data transfers between processing units occur at a wide range of bandwidth limitations.

A drawing operation of a scene can be split in three major ways: in the spatial domain, in the time domain, and in the image domain. The procedure for rendering a single frame of the synthetic imagery consists of four stages: splitting, distribution, rendering, and compositing.

9.3.2   Distributed Rendering Schemes

When distributing the rendering of a scene among processing units in the spatial domain, a portion of the scene is transferred to each unit, it is rendered independently and then composited to form a unified, final result. Typically, the scene is divided according to the hierarchy of a scene graph or a spatial subdivision scheme, and then the tokens are distributed among the available units according to a load-balancing mechanism. Each unit renders a partial result, which then needs to be combined with the output from its siblings.

In the case of direct rendering, the resulting partial images are unordered and overlap in the image domain (Figure 9.5). The resulting frame buffers alone cannot be combined, and the usual practice is to maintain and transmit the depth buffer of each partial rendering as well [Theo89a]. A unit (or process) plays the role of the *compositing engine*, i.e., gathers the results and combines the partial color information based on the fragment-by-fragment depth-buffer comparison of the incoming images and the transparency stored in the alpha buffer. Distributed rendering schemes such as this are called *sort-last* [Moln94] because the decision for which part of the image is attributed to which node occurs at the end of the frame generation [Muel95, Whit92].

A *data-parallel* rendering approach is also possible for ray tracing. The scene database is distributed among the units and a server node[1] casts rays, which are

---

[1]Here, a server signifies the node that spawned a ray. Secondary rays are cast by other nodes that act as gathering points, i.e., servers for the next level of ray casting.

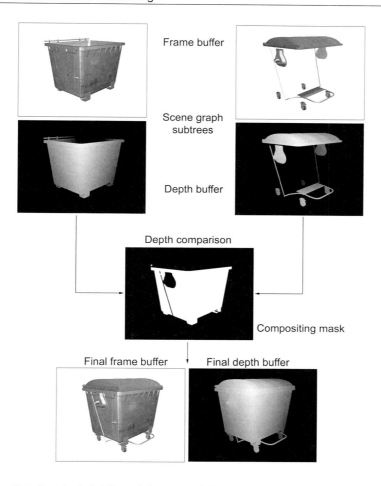

Figure 9.5. Sort-last distributed direct-rendering example on two rendering units.

then redirected to the appropriate rendering node(s) to calculate the ray-geometry intersection [Chal98, Lin91]. As the server maintains the hierarchical relationship among the data tokens that have been distributed, it can accumulate rays entering a particular bounding volume associated with a rendering unit and pass the whole bunch to it for intersection-test processing, as long as the previous package has been calculated and returned to the server. This is also a *sort-last* approach, because the resulting intersection tests from all rendering units need to be sorted according to distance from the starting point of a ray; this, of course, can happen when all results are reported back to the server unit. Because the distribution of rays among rendering units is a parallel task at a very fine level, this architecture is suitable for tightly-coupled parallel systems.

Sort-first schemes perform a pre-partitioning of the target output space (image domain or timeline), and each rendering unit is assigned one or more chunks [Fuch77, Muel95]. The composition of the rendered pieces is quite trivial in this genre of algorithms, as the gathered image chunks have no overlap.

In the case of offline rendering of animations, a flexible and easy-to-implement sort-first parallel rendering strategy is to split the sequence (time domain) into individual frames and assign them to separate units for rendering. Each processing unit maintains a full copy of the scene database as well as external assets, such as textures, and independently draws a complete frame image. This type of distributed rendering is trivially parallel in the sense that no communication occurs except from the initial batch copy of the scene material and the transfer of the result back to the server of the *render farm* (computer cluster). This scheme is usually further extended to also split each frame into chunks and assign the image blocks to different machines or processors in the same machine (demand-driven first-level parallel ray tracing).

Image-domain sort-first strategies are very common in both real-time and offline rendering. The scene database is replicated among the rendering units, or in the case of a multiprocessor and/or multi-GPU machine, it is shared by multiple processes that perform the rendering. Each unit is assigned one or more "windows" of the final image, and the results are easily composited by copying the prepared image segments into a common buffer. Direct distributed rendering in multiple graphics systems on the same machine can be handled by the hardware of the graphics display boards. This transparently splits the workload among the rasterizers using a master-slave architecture.

Partitioning strategies in image domain play a significant role in efficient load balancing. Common split methods are interlaced scan-line, tiled (rectangular regions, strips or columns), and offset full-image. The larger the segments, the higher the probability that the workload will not be balanced evenly among the rendering units. This is easy to grasp if you consider a simple example of a scene with a blank sky above and a landscape occupied by a large city. Assuming a split of the image into two strips: the top tile will have almost zero processing to perform, while the bottom tile will need to rasterize almost every triangle of the scene. A partitioning that splits the image in even and odd scan-lines (or columns) would ensure the best load balancing. On the other hand, if the image is split into too many individual segments, block memory transfers become less efficient.

For real-time rendering, another important factor for choosing a partitioning scheme is the incremental nature of the rasterization process. Spatial coherence and sampling in a regular pattern is beneficial for the rendering stages of the graphics subsystem. For example, rendering in even and odd fields (interlaced) does not significantly modify the scan-conversion procedure, as the scanline counter needs to advance by two units instead of one (See Chapter 5).

When using the post-filtering (multisampled) antialiasing technique to render an image, an interesting strategy is to distribute the sampling kernel among the rendering units. This is done by rendering the full frame on each unit but with a fragment center offset that corresponds to the sample offset of the multisampling matrix. The resulting fragments are then weighted to produce the final image.

Multi-display systems also perform a sort-first image-space split strategy, although the partitioning is done in a view level (e.g., different view frusta) and no image composition is required. Typical virtual reality computer clusters share a common (replicated) scene graph and render on each node a different "window" to the three-dimensional environment. On a master-slave architecture [Zuff02], the data transactions are kept to a minimum as only synchronization signaling and input data from the user(s) are communicated among the nodes.

9.4   Exercises

1. Build an optimal scene graph for a chessboard in the case of: (a) a static arrangement of the pawns; (b) pawns animated by supplying their transformations; (c) pawns animated by internal simulation methods.

2. How can a spatial partitioning scheme be beneficial to a scene graph organization? What factors affect the efficiency of the combined solution?

3. Implement a scene-graph node for geometry level-of-detail (LOD) switching. Describe in detail what data should be provided in the case of screen-space projection area and distance metrics.

4. Implement a proximity trigger scene-graph node. The node should issue a message to a specific node in the following cases: (a) any node has entered its area of effect; (b) any node has exited its area; (c) all nodes have exited its area; (d) a specific node has entered/exited its area of effect.

5. Implement a logical trigger (AND, OR, XOR, NOT) that is activated according to the activation state of other triggers. The other triggers should be passed by reference to the logical trigger, and they are not necessarily its children in the scene-graph hierarchy.

10

Visualization Principles

The man who can't visualize a horse galloping
on a tomato is an idiot.
—André Breton

10.1 Introduction

Suppose you unexpectedly see a picture of a person you care about. Suddenly, you feel the love you have for that person. Information flows from your visual system through your brain to the point of the experience of love. The net result in working memory is the feeling of love [Ledo02]. Proper artificial stimuli can produce the same effect as natural objects, with visual stimuli being extremely effective.

Modern scientific experiments and simulations often produce vast amounts of data; they are aided by the continuous gains in computing performance and reductions in storage costs. However, the nature of the data produced by experiments and simulations is usually symbolic, and it becomes harder and harder for humans to comprehend such data sets directly, due to their increasing size. Figure 10.1 illustrates the point with an example. On the left-hand side, we have a numeric matrix, and on the right-hand side, we have the mapping of the numbers onto grayscale values, with a specific range coding. Once again, a picture is worth a thousand words!

The applications of visualization can be categorized into two broad categories:

- Exploration of large *acquired* data sets, e.g.,

  - medical data (Color Plate XXIX (left));

23	24	25	27	26	25	25	24	24
24	26	28	30	29	27	26	28	31
26	28	29	31	32	29	30	32	36
26	27	30	32	33	34	35	38	41
27	28	28	32	34	35	37	41	42
27	28	31	33	36	38	40	42	43
28	29	32	32	35	37	41	43	44
30	33	33	34	36	38	41	42	44
32	34	27	29	40	42	43	44	45

23	24	25	27	26	25	25	24	24
24	26	28	30	29	27	26	28	31
26	28	29	31	32	29	30	32	36
26	27	30	32	33	34	35	38	41
27	28	28	32	34	35	37	41	42
27	28	31	33	36	38	40	42	43
28	29	32	32	35	37	41	43	44
30	33	33	34	36	38	41	42	44
32	34	27	29	40	42	43	44	45

22-25	26-29	30-33
34-37	38-41	42-45

Figure 10.1. Numeric versus grayscale-mapped data.

  – oil and gas data;

  – weather data;

• Exploration of large data sets that are the result of a *simulation*, e.g.,

  – engineering simulations;

  – meteorological forecasts (Color Plate XXIX (right));

  – computational fluid dynamics;

  – finance.

Of course, in some cases we merge the above categories as, for example, in the case of meteorology where we have actual weather and ground data from sensors and forecast weather data from weather-model simulations.

The goal of visualization is quite practical. Visualization aims to increase human understanding of complex data by taking advantage of the high-bandwidth human visual channel, using techniques mainly from the field of computer graphics to visually display the data. For a visualization to be useful, it must become the medium that enables information to be effectively communicated to the user [Hanr05]. The goal of visualization is to transform data into information and to bring data to life.

A number of definitions of visualization exist. Let us start with the definition of the verb *visualize* from the *Oxford Concise Dictionary* [Oxf04]: "*make visible esp. to the mind (thing not visible to the eye); make visible to the eye.*" Notice the emphasis placed on understanding in this definition.

The definition given by a 1987 NSF panel [NSF87] captures the essence of visualization well: "*Visualization* is a method of computing. It transforms the symbolic into the geometric, enabling researchers to observe their simulations and computations. Visualization offers a method for seeing the unseen. It enriches the process of scientific discovery and fosters profound and unexpected insights." Of course, not all data sets contain spatial information. But, more often than not, experiments and simulations are carried out on multidimensional grids that represent a discretization of space. These grids then become the vehicle for the visual display of the data, since grid points can generally be easily mapped onto a coordinate system.

A very descriptive definition is given in a modern visualization course [Edi05]: "*Visualization* is a cognitive process using the powerful information processing and analytical functions of the human vision system. It has always been a major factor in scientific progress, and now, with the assistance of computer graphics, it extends our vision system from sub-atomic to interstellar dimensions and allows geometric representations and simulations of any multidimensional data set. The fundamental objective is to acquire *new* knowledge rather than generating pictures." The important elements here are the flexibility in visualizing any scale of a data set and the aim of acquiring new knowledge.

And a nice short definition from [Hanr05]: "conveying information using graphical techniques."

Despite its strong growth since the middle 1980s, visualization is not new. Since ancient times, scientists used 2D plots to visualize measured or computed data in order to understand the behavior of phenomena and classify them into known mathematical entities (e.g., lines and curves). Currently, visualization refers to a body of knowledge that encompasses techniques and algorithms for the visual representation of generic types of data.

10.2   Methods of Scientific Exploration

Over the past few thousand years, scientists have been trying to explain the real world. The common objective has been to gain an understanding of how things work. Sufficient understanding of a certain phenomenon allows the construction

Figure 10.2. Exploration steps.

of a *model* of the phenomenon, i.e., a description, for example, in a mathematical framework. The model can then be used to make *predictions* (Figure 10.2).

Let us use gravity as a simple example. People had been observing falling objects for thousands of years before Newton systematically explained their behavior. He constructed a model, which was nothing less than the law of universal gravitation:

$$F = G\frac{m_1 \cdot m_2}{r^2},$$

where F is the gravitational force exerted between two objects, G the gravitational constant, m_1 and m_2 the masses of the two objects (e.g., apple and Earth), and r the distance between the two objects. Based on the astronomical observations of Copernicus (observation stage) and Kepler's third law for the period of rotation of the planets, Newton proposed this generalized model for the gravitational force between two objects (model-creation stage). His model was verified by the astronomical observations of his time and later by Cavendish for small objects (model-testing stage). Newton's ingenuity lies in the fact that he unified the force that attracts planets and sets them in orbital motion with the force that makes an apple fall to the ground and, in general, the force that is exerted between all objects (prediction stage).

The creation of a model is an iterative process. Having sufficiently observed a phenomenon, a scientist proposes an initial model. In attempting to validate it with real data, discrepancies often arise; these lead to corrections in the parameters of the model or even to the model itself. A number of simplifying assumptions are often made in order to make the model computationally tractable, but better hardware and more efficient algorithms allow us to introduce more complicated (and more accurate) models. Weather prediction is a good example. The initial computational models used a sparse computational grid. This was understandable given the complexity of weather models and the absolute necessity to finish predictive computations for a given time t, well before t arrived! However, the rapid increase in processing speed and the introduction of parallel algorithms allowed significant increases in the density of the grid used, which resulted in higher predictive accuracy and a longer prediction time frame.

Depending on the requirements, different types of models can be constructed. Mathematical models, consisting of systems of equations and computational models, describing phenomena algorithmically, are common. A mix of the two is often used.

An example of an evolving model from computer graphics is the illumination model (see Chapter 12). Initial illumination models consisted of simple depth cuing [Warn69]. Then came the Phong model [Phon75], which encompassed diffuse and specular reflections but took no account of the interactions of light between objects, assuming a constant ambient illumination value. Later, the ray-tracing model [Whit80] and then the radiosity model [Kaji86] included light-interaction computations, producing more photorealistic images at the cost of increased computations.

10.3   Data Aspects and Transformations

Visualization data arises from two main sources: *experiments* and *simulations*. Experimental data is often *external*, as it is produced externally to the visualization system, while simulated data is usually *internal*. This is not always the case, however, as, for example, simulated data may be acquired from other sources (externally). Another common classification is *original* (or *raw*) versus *derived* (or *processed*) data; the latter have been processed in some way, e.g., normalized or filtered.

Regardless of the source and processing applied, data is characterized by a large number of properties, such as data type, sampling domain and sampling pattern, dimensionality, format, etc. Visualization systems thus need to provide the user with powerful data-import modules. The type of data items largely determines the kind of visualization algorithm that can be applied (e.g., vector or scalar). The predominant algorithms for common data types is the main topic of Chapter 18.

Experimental or simulated data can assume arbitrary ranges. Visualization packages, on the other hand, may require a standard input range, e.g., [0.0, 1.0]. One reason for this standard range is the existence of a standard color map. The process of converting a given data range into a standard input range is called *normalization*. Normalization functions are usually linear, but other forms, such as logarithmic, may also be used. For example, if i_{min} and i_{max} represent the minimum and maximum input data values, respectively, we can linearly normalize an arbitrary input data value i into the normalized range $[n_{min}, n_{max}]$ using the formula

$$i_{norm} = \frac{i - i_{min}}{i_{max} - i_{min}} \cdot (n_{max} - n_{min}) + n_{min}.$$

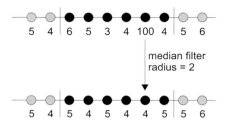

Figure 10.3. Application of 1D median filter with radius 2 (area of application indicated by vertical lines).

Experimental data acquired by electronic, optical, magnetic, or other physical means invariably contain a certain amount of noise or other data degradation. *Filtering techniques* are typically used to remove this noise, smooth, sharpen, or otherwise improve the quality of the data. A typical noise-removal filter that preserves detail is the *median filter*. The median filter replaces each data value (on a grid) with the median of the values of itself and its neighbors within a certain radius. Figure 10.3 shows a 1D example of the application of a median filter with radius 2; as can be seen from the figure, it removes the "noise spike" value 100.

Different data sources may produce data in different coordinate systems (e.g., Cartesian or polar coordinates, linear or logarithmic scales, etc.). Coordinate transformations must be applied to the data to ensure compatibility between the source and the visualization system, or between various sources when codisplaying data from multiple sources. The process of unifying coordinate systems is called *coregistration*, and it generally uses affine transformations (see Chapter 3).

10.3.1 Coregistration Case Study: MEG Signals within a Generic Model Brain

Suppose that we must display, in 3D, *magnetoencephalographic* (MEG) patient-specific signals within a transparent model of a generic brain [Kats05]. The generic brain and the MEG signals constitute two separate data sets, which must be codisplayed after coregistration (Figure 10.4; see also Color Plate XXX). The MEG signals have position, direction, and magnitude, so it seems natural to display them using arrow glyphs (see Section 10.7).

For the coregistration, we must first establish two coordinate systems in the two data sets and then convert one of the data sets to the coordinate system of the

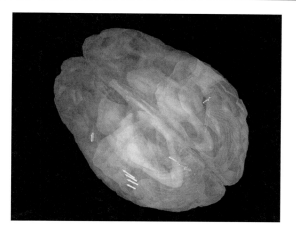

Figure 10.4. Coregistration of generic brain model with MEG signals. (See also Color Plate XXX.)

other. Let the coordinate systems of the generic brain model and the MEG signals be CS_B and CS_M, respectively. Three non-collinear points are sufficient to define a coordinate system (assume right-handed systems). The coordinate systems can thus be established by identifying the same three physiological points in the two data sets. Let these points be $\mathbf{a}_B$, $\mathbf{b}_B$, $\mathbf{f}_B$ and $\mathbf{a}_M$, $\mathbf{p}_M$, $\mathbf{f}_M$, respectively, and suppose that we are transforming the MEG data to the generic brain model. We shall take the $\mathbf{a}$ points to mark the origin of the two coordinate systems, the $\overrightarrow{\mathbf{ap}}$ vectors to mark the $+x$-axis, and the $\mathbf{f}$ points to indicate the "up" direction, from which the $+z$-axis is derived. The z-axis is not given explicitly in order to avoid numerical inaccuracies and to simplify the user interface (see Section 4.4.1).The directions of the three axes in each coordinate system are computed as follows (Figure 10.5):

$$\overrightarrow{\mathbf{f}} = \mathbf{f} - \mathbf{a},$$
$$\overrightarrow{\mathbf{x}} = \mathbf{p} - \mathbf{a},$$
$$\overrightarrow{\mathbf{y}} = \overrightarrow{\mathbf{x}} \times \overrightarrow{\mathbf{f}},$$
$$\overrightarrow{\mathbf{z}} = \overrightarrow{\mathbf{y}} \times \overrightarrow{\mathbf{x}}.$$

The first transformation step translates the MEG data set so that the origins of the two coordinate systems (the $\mathbf{a}$ points) coincide:

$$\mathbf{MEG}' = \mathbf{T}(\mathbf{a}_B - \mathbf{a}_M) \cdot \mathbf{MEG}.$$

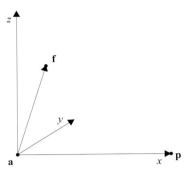

Figure 10.5. Coordinate system using three points.

The next transformation aligns the $+x$-axes. This requires two rotations, about the z- and y-axes (see Example 3.12 for details):

$$\mathbf{MEG}'' = \mathbf{R_z}(\theta_2) \cdot \mathbf{R_y}(\theta_1) \cdot \mathbf{MEG}'.$$

Another rotation about the x-axis aligns the other two axes of the two coordinate systems:

$$\mathbf{MEG}''' = \mathbf{R_x}(\theta_3) \cdot \mathbf{MEG}''.$$

Finally, since the size of the model and patient brains may differ, we can scale the MEG vectors according to the ratios of the respective measurements, assuming correspondence of the internal structures:

$$\mathbf{MEG}'''' = \mathbf{S}\left(\frac{\mathrm{XSIZE}_B}{\mathrm{XSIZE}_M}, \frac{\mathrm{YSIZE}_B}{\mathrm{YSIZE}_M}, \frac{\mathrm{ZSIZE}_B}{\mathrm{ZSIZE}_M}\right) \cdot \mathbf{MEG}'''.$$

The composite transformation

$$\mathbf{S}\left(\frac{\mathrm{XSIZE}_B}{\mathrm{XSIZE}_M}, \frac{\mathrm{YSIZE}_B}{\mathrm{YSIZE}_M}, \frac{\mathrm{ZSIZE}_B}{\mathrm{ZSIZE}_M}\right) \cdot \mathbf{R_x}(\theta_3) \cdot \mathbf{R_z}(\theta_2) \cdot \mathbf{R_y}(\theta_1) \cdot \mathbf{T}(\mathbf{a}_B - \mathbf{a}_M)$$

thus coregisters the MEG data onto the generic brain model, and the two data sets can now be correctly displayed together.

10.4 Time-Tested Principles for Good Visual Plots

The visual display of data was around long before the advent of visualization techniques in computer science. A number of simple but important rules of thumb

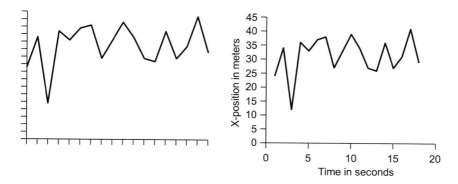

Figure 10.6. Visualization without (left) and with (right) proper axis labeling and legends

exist that are as applicable to visualization techniques today as they have been to graphs for a long time.

If a visualization includes *coordinate axes*, then these should be clearly marked and labeled with the quantities that they represent and their units (Figure 10.6). Legends should never be omitted, even when obvious. Even with a good legend, however, an *overloaded* visualization is hard to comprehend. If a large number of variables must be presented, overloading should be avoided by splitting a visualization into multiple units. As with traditional graphs, authors tend to be too optimistic about a graphical presentation; their mindset is very rarely shared by the audience, resulting in misinterpretations.

Of critical importance to a visualization is the issue of *scale* and the coordinate-axis origins. The wrong scale relative to the data values can result in large data fluctuations appearing small and vice versa; this is a well-known trick used in presentations to convey misinformation. On the same note, setting axis origins at a non-zero value can result in an apparent reduction in data values; while this may be useful when the data have small variations at high values, it should be used with caution, and the initial value of the axis should be clearly indicated (Figure 10.7).

Another source of misleading information in visual presentations is the comparison of *unlike quantities*; in other words, presenting side-by-side quantities with different properties. An example is a bar chart whose bars refer to sales volumes (vertical axis) by year (horizontal bar axis) except the last bar, which refers to the current year so far; the last bar thus has different properties than the rest of

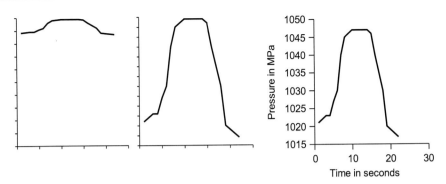

Figure 10.7. Left: Too large scale. Middle: Unlabeled non-zero axis origin. Right: Correct scale and origin labeling.

the bars since it refers to a period less than a year (Figure 10.8). Another example is a multiple line (or multiple surface) graph, where different lines plot different variables, without separate axis markings for each variable.

The transition from quantitative to visual information is another critical factor of a visualization. Visual information includes all visual aspects of a

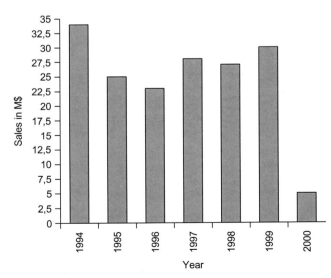

Figure 10.8. Comparing unlike quantities. Year 2000 measurements are not complete.

presentation, such as color and transparency. A well-chosen *color mapping* can bring out information that would otherwise be uncapturable. For example, mapping body organs to their physical colors helps understanding in medical visualizations. Also, choosing colors with sufficient disparity to display different variables avoids clutter. Color maps are discussed in detail in Section 10.5.2.

10.5   Tone Mapping

Scalar data come from various input sources, and so their range varies significantly. Furthermore, the scale that the raw data are represented in is not necessarily compatible with the sensory response curve of human photoreceptors, and therefore a direct linear mapping of the input data to light intensity does not have the desired visual effect. There are also times when we need to display linearly spaced sample data, but the domain is so large that we can only obtain a very poor discretization and scaling of the input range to the available intensity that the human eye can perceive. In these cases, we need to accentuate certain important value transitions in the scalar domain and compress the rest of the input scale.

In general, the raw input data domain scale needs to be converted to a meaningful range of intensity and color values that can be more effortlessly perceived by the human eye so that the desired information is pinpointed and extracted intuitively. This is achieved by transforming the data with the help of transfer functions to compress, accentuate, and shape the input signal into a more convenient scalar gradient and then visually enhance the result by encoding the intensity information with color. Color mapping results in a more easily distinguishable and recognizable relation between the visualized image and the underlying data. One example of this is the use of decibels in representing the power of sound signals. They are defined as $10\log_{10} S$, where S is the ratio of the power of a sound signal over a reference value.

10.5.1   Transfer Functions

Consider the example of Figure 10.9. The original signal (Figure 10.9(a)) is a thermal sensor capture with the sensor temperature-sensitivity range mapped to a linear 8-bit grayscale gradient. The visualization of the input data provides nothing but a general idea of the heat distribution, and the original source is not easily spotted. The useful information resides in a narrow intensity window within the full range of 256 different grayscale values, resulting in low contrast. Apart from that, the smooth shade transition makes it almost impossible to classify the heat

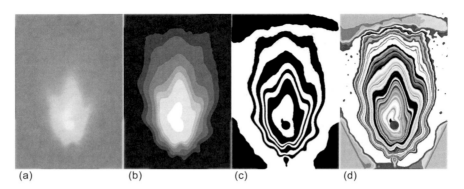

Figure 10.9. Transfer functions. (a) Original data: low contrast, no shape is discernible. (b) Normalized range and 4-bit quantization: intensity zones. (c) Clamped sinusoidal transfer function: zone measurements are possible. (d) Noisy transfer function: enhancement of subtle transitions reveals otherwise undetectable globules.

into temperature zones and measure the extent of the temperature zones. In Figure 10.9(b), the original signal was modified by a transfer function that enhanced its contrast and then quantized the grayscale levels into zones. In general, a transfer function is of the form

$$i_{\text{out}} = f_{\text{transfer}}(i_{\text{in}}). \tag{10.1}$$

The function f_{transfer} is not necessarily linear or even continuous. In our example, we have

$$i_{\text{out}} = f_{\text{quant}}\left(f_{\text{contrast}}\left(i_{\text{in}}\right)\right),$$

$$f_{\text{contrast}}(x) = \frac{x - x_{\text{min}}}{x_{\text{max}} - x_{\text{min}}} \cdot v_{\text{max}},$$

$$f_{\text{quant}}(x) = x_{\text{min}} + \frac{(x_{\text{max}} - x_{\text{min}})}{N} \cdot \left\lfloor N \cdot \frac{x - x_{\text{min}}}{x_{\text{max}} - x_{\text{min}}} + \frac{1}{2} \right\rfloor, \tag{10.2}$$

where x_{min} and x_{max} refer to the minimum and maximum input signal values, v_{max} is the maximum allowed range value, and N is the number of quantization steps.

We can increase the number of discrete intervals for the data representation without losing the contrast by allowing the use of non-monotonic transfer functions, such as the clamped sinusoidal function illustrated in Figure 10.9(c). Some other useful transfer functions are the sigmoid function, which non-linearly enhances the contrast across a predefined threshold and the binary transfer function (thresholding). Figure 10.10 presents some transfer functions.

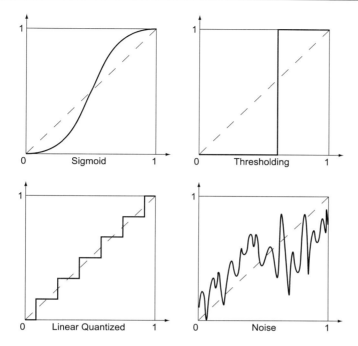

Figure 10.10. Some commonly used transfer functions. The horizontal axis represents the input values, and the vertical axis represents the output values.

10.5.2 Color Maps

Intensity alone cannot always convey an intuitive idea about the displayed data. As explained earlier in this chapter, human beings attribute certain colors to particular states of mind or recognize quantities and qualities by them. For example, when we look at a map, land mass is colored in brown for high altitudes and green for low flatlands, while the sea is rendered in blue hues. Such metaphors are encountered every day. Another example is the indication of critical levels on meters using a color gradient from green (low/safe) to yellow and then red (very high/critical).

However, apart from the conscious or subconscious connection between colors and attributes, there is another important reason for visualizing data in color grades rather than in intensity plots: colors have a better separation than grayscale values and can clearly highlight important value ranges. Combined color/intensity plots can help visualize dual parameter quantities. An example is the visualization

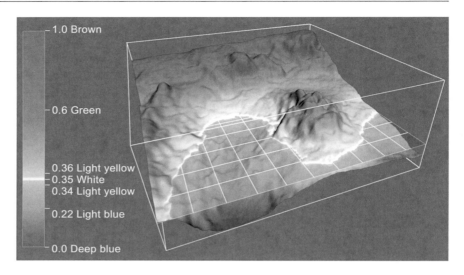

Figure 10.11. Color coding of height and sea depth using a color map that maps relative height information onto interpolated color values. (See also Color Plate XXVI.)

of density/temperature of air. Colors, represented as scalar triplets, may also be used to visualize vectors, although the resulting image may not be very intuitive (Color Plate XXII).

In order to move from a grayscale to an arbitrary color gradient, we use a *color map*, which is a look-up table of colors corresponding to specific sorted intensity values. An input intensity that matches one of the table records is directly mapped to the associated color, while other values are interpolated from the closest table entries (Figure 10.11; see also Color Plate XXVI).

Let N_C be the number of color entries c_i, $i = 0..N_C - 1$, in a color map, which are sorted in ascending order according to the associated input value s_i. The output color **c** for a given intensity s is easily calculated via interpolation (not necessarily linear) with the following algorithm.

```
if (Nc < 2)
    c = colormap[0].col;
i=Nc-2;
while ( colormap[i].val > s && i > 0 )
    i--;
s1 = colormap[i].val;
s2 = colormap[i+1].val;
```

```
if ( s1 == s )
    c = colormap[i].col;
else
    {
    t = (s - s1) / (s2  - s1);
    c = interp(colormap[i].col, colormap[i+1].col, t);
    }
```

10.6   Matters of Perception

In designing a visualization, one must take into account not only technical issues
relating to the presentation of information but also the characteristics of the *hu-*
man visual system [Greg97]. After all, the "customer" of any visualization output
is the human eye. The eye consists of the *pupil,* the entry point for light, which
is then focused by the *lens* onto the *retina.* The retina can be thought of as a
projection wall, and it is made up of nerve cells called *photoreceptors,* which
capture and transmit visual information to the brain. The center of the retina is
the *fovea.* There are two types of photoreceptors: *rods* and *cones* (Figure 10.12).
Rods are sensitive to variations in *intensity,* while cones are sensitive to variations
in *chromaticity* (see also Chapter 11). The rods outnumber the cones by more
than an order of magnitude. The cones are located close to the fovea, while the
rods are spread more evenly over the retina. Cones in a typical human eye have
the ability to separately sense three different portions of the spectrum. They are
maximally sensitive to either long wavelengths of light (red light), medium wave-

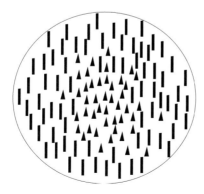

Figure 10.12. Rods and cones.

lengths (green light), or short wavelengths (blue light). Green cones constitute approximately 64% of the total number of cones, red cones 32%, and blue cones 4% [Ahne87,Marc77]. Red and green cones are mainly located close to the fovea, while blue cones form a ring around them.

Different color wavelengths require the lens to assume different focal lengths. For example, pure blue and pure red objects (at the same distance from the eye) require significantly different lens focusing, since red and blue are at opposite ends of the visible wavelength spectrum. A non-negligible percentage of people have some type of color blindness, a deficiency in distinguishing certain colors. This is usually between red and green, and it is related to the functioning of their red and green photoreceptors.

The above facts of the human visual system have a number of important consequences for visualization (see also [Murc84]):

- Since cones are located close to the fovea, we have better color vision near the center of the viewing direction.

- Since the rods significantly outnumber the cones, variations in intensity are more effective in a visualization than variations in chromaticity, especially when linked to variations in value; on the other hand, chromaticity variations are more useful for area segmentation.

- Colors with significantly different wavelengths should not be displayed close to each other, since they require different focusing and the eye gets tired (Color Plate XXXI).

- Pure blue is unsuitable for text and other detail that must be closely examined, because the area of the fovea has no blue cones. On the other hand, blue is excellent for backgrounds.

- Red and green should be avoided in peripheral areas, since there are no red or green cones on the periphery of the retina.

- Avoid colors that differ only in their red-green ratio to cater to color-blind individuals. For example, colors that differ in their blue-yellow ratio are a better choice.

Care should be taken when working with intensity variations. The perceived effect of intensity variations is logarithmic; thus, the apparent difference between the intensity pairs (0.2, 0.4) and (0.4, 0.8) is the same. Also, the perception of

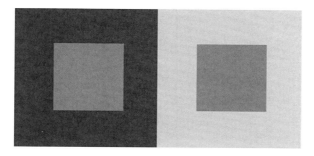

Figure 10.13. Perceived intensity levels depend on relative intensity. The inner square has the same intensity value in both images; however, on the right it appears darker (outer-region intensity on left is 50, outer-region intensity on right is 200, and inner-square intensity is 125 in both cases).

intensity levels is not absolute but instead relates to the relative intensity of their neighborhood. Thus, an object of the same intensity will appear darker in a light background and lighter in a dark background (Figure 10.13).

The perception of visual stimuli can be divided into conscious and preconscious processing [Frie91]. Preconscious visual processing takes place involuntarily, is extremely fast, and precedes conscious visual processing. One must therefore take advantage of preconscious processing when mapping values into visuals. This can be done in a number of ways, which include

- the use of intensity rather than chromaticity as a *value discriminator*—we can perceive the relative scale of multiple values much better when they are mapped onto an intensity scale instead of a chromaticity scale;

- the use of change to attract attention to detail—this change can affect object attributes such as position (movement), size, color, etc;

- the mapping of large values to nearer (and therefore larger) objects—the value of an object is perceived to be analogous to the area of its retinal projection.

Finally, since visual perception is not a mere physical but rather a psychophysical phenomenon, one must also consider the emotional response that different colors have on humans. The following list, taken from [Owen99], gives details on the significance of certain colors. Since the response to color is partly conscious processing, one must be aware that the same color can provoke different responses in different people (e.g., in different cultures):

- red—danger, stop, negative, excitement, hot;

- dark blue—stable, calming, trustworthy, mature;

- light blue—youthful, masculine, cool;

- green—growth, positive, organic, go, comforting;

- white—pure, clean, honest;

- black—serious, heavy, death;

- gray—integrity, neutral, cool, mature;

- brown—wholesome, organic, unpretentious;

- yellow—emotional, positive, caution;

- gold—conservative, stable, elegant;

- orange—emotional, positive, organic;

- purple—youthful, contemporary, royal;

- pink—youthful, feminine, warm;

- pastels—youthful, soft, feminine, sensitive;

- metallic—elegant, lasting, wealthy.

10.7   Visualizing Multidimensional Data

In traditional graph plotting, each variable is assigned a separate coordinate axis (dimension). However, in complex problems or database applications, we need to visualize many variables simultaneously, and these cannot easily be accommodated in the few dimensions that we can handle. Most displays are two-dimensional, and visualizations based on them can therefore display up to two variables at a time. Virtual-reality systems have made the visualization of the third dimension possible by simulating the 3D experience of the space that we live in. This extends the visualization capabilities by one extra simultaneously displayable variable, but even three variables is limiting for many data sets.

Given a data set of d variables $\{v_1, v_2, \ldots, v_d\}$, the straightforward mathematical method of reducing the problem is to project onto a subset of the dimensions (see also Chapter 4). A simple way to achieve such a projection is by assigning a constant value to some of the variables (orthogonal projection). For example, we can project d variables onto the first two by assigning constant values to the rest of them $\{v_1, v_2, v_3 = c_3, v_4 = c_4, \ldots, v_d = c_d\}$, thus achieving a two-variable data set, which can easily be displayed on a 2D display device. To explore such a multidimensional data set, the constant values must be updated manually (based on the user's intuition). The commonly used technique of *slicing* is an example of a 2D projection. Color Plate XXXII shows a 2D slice of a 3D volumetric data set.

One extra variable can be visually accommodated by exploiting the time dimension. It is obviously preferable to map onto the time dimension a variable that is itself related to time. Animation techniques (see Chapter 17) are very relevant (Color Plate XXXIII).

Color, grayscale, or *fill patterns* can also be used to map the value of a variable. In Color Plate XXX, two MEG data sets (different stimuli) are displayed in different colors; color thus identifies the stimulus variable in this example.

Glyphs can be used to display more variables in a visualization. A glyph is a visual object onto which variable values may be mapped, each onto a different visual attribute [Past02]. The type of glyph used should be chosen so as to invoke the desired human perception of the data being represented. For example, for vector data, the obvious glyph to use is the arrow. Spheres, disks, crosses, and

Figure 10.14. Mapping two variables onto glyph scale and color.

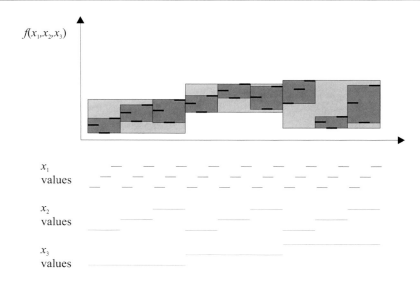

Figure 10.15. Hierarchical visualization of a multivariate function on a 2D graph.

cylinders are also commonly used glyphs. Up to three positional variables can be mapped onto the position of the glyph. A number of extra variables can be mapped onto other glyph attributes. In practice, this number can be no more than two, otherwise the glyphs get overloaded with information. A common way is to map one variable onto the scale of the glyph and the other onto its color/texture (Figure 10.14).

Mihalisin et al. [Miha91] proposed a hierarchical method for visualizing functions of N independent variables $f(x_1, x_2, \ldots, x_N)$ as 2D graphs. Each independent variable takes values from a finite, discrete, contiguous range. The vertical axis displays the function value while the independent variables are assigned a unique priority and are hierarchically mapped onto the horizontal axis. The variable with the highest priority, say x_1, varies the fastest, while the variable with the lowest priority, say x_N, the slowest. Thus for each value of x_N, which maps onto a line segment on the horizontal axis, all other variables cycle through their values like a *nested for-loop*, with x_1 cycling most frequently. The value of f is plotted for each set of values that the independent variables take. Figure 10.15 shows an example of a function with three independent variables. Note that the function values for each cycle of the variables can be hierarchically nested in bounding boxes, which help to visualize it better.

10.8 Exercises

1. (Hermann's Grid) Create a regular 2D grid of 4×4 black squares on a white background. For example, on a 512×512 white image, you can place black squares of size 70×70. Observe this image closely. Do you see something peculiar at the intersections (white crosses)? Most people see dark blobs that disappear when you concentrate on them individually.

2. Using your word processor, create a document with a few pages of blue text on a red background. Cut and paste the same text into another document with the usual black text on white background. Try reading a couple of pages from the two documents and compare the strain in your eyes.

3. Create a 512×256 window to hold two 256×256 images. The left half of the window should hold a yellow square; the right half should hold a blue square. Each half should contain a 100×100 orange square, centered within the larger square. How do the perceived colors of the inner squares compare?

11

Color in Graphics and Visualization

We need to investigate the fourth type of sense (vision), which must be subdivided, for it encompasses many varieties; we have jointly named these varieties colors...

—Plato: Timaios

11.1   Introduction

Color has always intrigued people and has been studied for millennia. Today the study of color, and the way humans perceive it, is an important branch of physics, physiology, psychology, and art as well as computer graphics and visualization.

The result of applying all the wonderful algorithms presented elsewhere in this book is a color or a grayscale image, which will eventually be viewed on an output device such as a computer monitor or a printer. The use of color or grayscale tones requires that the graphics programmer be aware of the fundamental principles behind color and its digital representation.

11.2   Grayscale

If we remove the color characteristics of light, we are left with *achromatic* light which is solely characterized by its *intensity*.[1] "Black and white" televisions and monitors display intensity only. Intensity can be represented by a real number between 0 (black) and 1 (white); values between these two extremes define different shades of gray, or *grayscales*.

---

[1] Intensity is formally defined as power per solid angle (see Chapter 12).

Suppose that we devote d bits for the representation of the intensity of each pixel in a digital image, allowing for $n = 2^d$ different intensity values per pixel. The question is, which intensity values shall we represent? The obvious answer, a linear scale of intensities between the minimum and maximum values, is not a good solution. It is known from physiology that the human eye perceives *intensity ratios* rather than absolute intensity values. For example the eye regards the absolute intensity pairs $(0.1, 0.2)$ and $(0.3, 0.6)$ as having the same internal difference. This fact can easily be verified experimentally by observing 3 light bulbs of, say, 20, 40, and 60 watts power. The difference between the first and second bulbs appears much greater than the difference between the second and the third. We should therefore opt for a logarithmic distribution of intensity values. Let the minimum intensity value[2] be Φ_0. For a typical monitor, Φ_0 is about $1/300$ of the maximum intensity value 1 (white); we say that such a monitor has a *dynamic range* of $300 : 1$ (see also Section 11.5). If λ is the ratio between successive intensity values, then

$$\Phi_1 = \lambda \cdot \Phi_0$$
$$\Phi_2 = \lambda \cdot \Phi_1 = \lambda^2 \cdot \Phi_0$$
$$\dots$$
$$\Phi_{n-1} = \lambda^{n-1} \cdot \Phi_0 = 1. \tag{11.1}$$

The ratio λ can be estimated from (11.1) if we know the Φ_0 of a particular output device, i.e.,

$$\lambda = (1/\Phi_0)^{1/(n-1)}.$$

How many intensity values do we need, or in other words, how many intensity values would allow us to make the difference between successive steps imperceivable to humans? This is an important question in digital images, if we want to ensure that they are not inferior compared to real photographs with respect to grayscale resolution. Fortunately, physiologists have addressed this question: If λ is smaller than 1.01 (i.e., successive levels differ by less than 1%) then the human eye can not distinguish between successive intensity values [Wysz00]. We can thus compute the minimum number of necessary intensity values by setting $\lambda = 1.01$ in (11.1) and solving for n:

$$1.01^{n-1} \cdot \Phi_0 = 1,$$
$$n = \log_{1.01}(1/\Phi_0) + 1.$$

---

[2]If the output device is a monitor, absolute black cannot be generated because of phosphor reflections.

Figure 11.1. Representation of an image with $n = 2, 4, 8, 16, 32, 64, 128, 256$ grayscale intensity values.

Since typical monitors have $\Phi_0 \sim 1/300$, n should be around 500. Figure 11.1 shows the representation of an image with varying numbers of intensity values.

11.2.1 Halftoning: Trading Spatial for Grayscale Resolution

Anti-aliasing methods trade grayscale (or color) resolution for spatial resolution (see Chapter 2). In certain situations, where we have abundant spatial resolution and can trade it for grayscale resolution, the reverse process is useful. *Halftoning*[3] techniques have this aim, and their roots are in the printing industry. In certain print media, it is preferable to use as few grayscale levels as possible (for economic reasons mainly); halftoning techniques are useful in other situations [Cho03]. Their effect can be observed in black and white newspaper photographs which, at a distance seem to possess a number of grayscale values, but upon closer observation one can spot the little black spots of varying sizes that

---

[3] Also known as *dithering*.

Figure 11.2. Left: initial photograph. Right: halftoning representation.

constitute the images. The size of the black spots are proportional to the grayscale value that they represent (Figure 11.2).

A common approach to halftoning in digital images is to simulate the spot size by the density of "black" pixels. The image is divided into small regions of $m \times m$ pixels, and the spatial resolution of these regions is traded for grayscale resolution. The spatial resolution is thus decreased m times in each image dimension, but the number of available grayscale values is increased by m^2. As an example, let us use the case of a bi-level image (black and white). Taking 2×2 pixel regions ($m = 2$) gives five possible final grayscale values (Figure 11.3). In general, for $m \times m$ regions and two initial grayscale values, we get $m^2 + 1$ final grayscale values.

The above assignment of pixel patterns to grayscale values can be represented concisely by the matrix

$$\begin{bmatrix} 3 & 1 \\ 0 & 2 \end{bmatrix},$$

where a particular grayscale level k ($0 \leq k \leq 4$) is represented by turning "on" the pixel positions of the 2×2 region for which the respective matrix element has a value less than k. For example, grayscale level 2 is represented by turning "on" the bottom-left and the top-right elements since their values are less than 2.

There are limits to the application of the halftoning technique; taking an ex-

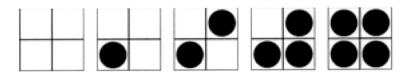

Figure 11.3. Five grayscale levels from two grayscale levels (black and white) using 2×2 pixel regions.

Figure 11.4. A bad selection for grayscale level 2.

treme case, it would make no sense to trade the full spatial resolution for a great
number of grayscale levels (by making m equal to the image resolution). These
limits depend on factors such as the original spatial image resolution and the distance of observation.

The sequence of patterns that define the grayscale levels must be carefully selected. For example, assigning the pixels of Figure 11.4 to grayscale level 2 would
make a constant image of this value appear to possess vertical stripes. Another
good rule is that the sequence of pixel patterns that represent successive grayscale
levels should be strictly incremental; in other words, the pixel positions selected
for grayscale level i should be a subset of the positions for level j for all $j > i$.
This rule is observed by the patterns of Figure 11.3.

A sequence of patterns that satisfies the quality criteria for 2×2 regions
is [Limb69]

$$\mathbf{H_2} = \begin{bmatrix} 0 & 2 \\ 3 & 1 \end{bmatrix}.$$

It is possible to recursively construct larger matrices, e.g., 4×4, 8×8 [Jarv76],
as follows:

$$\mathbf{H_m} = \begin{bmatrix} 4 \cdot \mathbf{H_{m/2}} & 4 \cdot \mathbf{H_{m/2}} + 2 \cdot \mathbf{U_{m/2}} \\ 4 \cdot \mathbf{H_{m/2}} + 3 \cdot \mathbf{U_{m/2}} & 4 \cdot \mathbf{H_{m/2}} + \mathbf{U_{m/2}} \end{bmatrix}, \quad m \geq 4 \quad m = 2^k,$$

where $\mathbf{U_m}$ is the $m \times m$ matrix with all elements equal to 1. The halftoning technique can be straightforwardly extended to media which can display multiple
grayscale levels per pixel. For example, if we can display four grayscale values per pixel (2 bits/pixel), we can increase the number of displayable grayscale
values to thirteen using 2×2 pixel regions as shown in Figure 11.5. In general, we
can use $m \times m$ pixel regions to increase the number of available grayscale levels
from k to $(k-1)m^2 + 1$, while reducing the available spatial resolution by m in
both the x- and the y-axes.

The halftoning technique assumes that we have an abundance of spatial resolution, (i.e., that the resolution of the display medium is significantly greater than

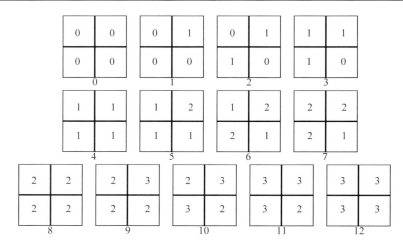

Figure 11.5. Thirteen grayscale levels from four grayscale levels using 2×2 pixel regions.

that of the image) and can thus be traded for grayscale resolution. What happens if the image and display medium have the same spatial resolutions but the image has a greater grayscale resolution than the display medium? Simple rounding gives poor results as a significant amount of image information is lost (Figure 11.6 (left)).

Floyd and Steinberg [Floy75] proposed a method that limits information loss by propagating the rounding error from a pixel to its neighbors. The technique is similar to the carrying of overflow units in the addition process. The difference ε between the image value $E_{x,y}$ and the nearest displayable value $O_{x,y}$ at pixel (x, y)

Figure 11.6. Left: simple rounding. Right: the Floyd-Steinberg method. Both images have two intensity levels.

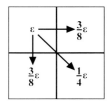

Figure 11.7. Error propagation in the Floyd-Steinberg method.

is computed as

$$\varepsilon = E_{x,y} - O_{x,y}.$$

The pixel is displayed as $O_{x,y}$ and the error ε is propagated to neighboring pixels in scan-line order, i.e., $(x+1,y), (x,y-1)$ and $(x+1,y-1)$, as follows (see also Figure 11.7):

$$E_{x+1,y} = E_{x+1,y} + 3 \cdot \varepsilon/8,$$
$$E_{x,y-1} = E_{x,y-1} + 3 \cdot \varepsilon/8,$$
$$E_{x+1,y-1} = E_{x+1,y-1} + \varepsilon/4.$$

The result represents a significant improvement over simple rounding, see Figure 11.6 (right).

The following table outlines the prerequisites for and benefits of antialiasing, halftoning, and the Floyd-Steinberg technique:

	Anti-aliasing	Halftoning	Floyd-Steinberg
Prerequisites	$I_G < D_G$	$I_S < D_S$	$I_S = D_S \,\&\, I_G > D_G$
Resolution gain	Spatial	Grayscale	Grayscale

where D_G and I_G are the grayscale resolutions of the display medium and image, respectively, and D_S and I_S are the spatial resolutions of the display medium and image, respectively.

11.2.2 Gamma Correction

Most monitors have a non-linear relationship between the voltage applied to them (i.e., the *input* pixel intensity) and the displayed or *output* intensity. This relationship follows a power law,

$$\text{output} = \text{input}^{\gamma}, \tag{11.2}$$

where γ is monitor-dependent and is usually in the range $[1.5, 3.0]$. As input voltage values are usually normalized in the range $[0,1]$, images that are not corrected

Figure 11.8. Left: gamma-corrected image. Right: non-gamma-corrected image.

for γ will appear too dark (Figure 11.8 (right)). Gamma correction is conceptually simple; we need to pre-adjust our input values to ensure a linear relationship between input and displayed values:

$$\text{input}' = \text{input}^{1/\gamma}. \tag{11.3}$$

Giving the input′ values to the monitor displays the gamma-corrected image (Figure 11.8 (left)).

In practice, of course, difficulties arise. First, some display systems[4] will perform gamma correction, some will perform partial gamma correction, and some none at all. It is thus necessary to know what a display system does before performing gamma correction. Second, most current image formats do not store gamma-correction information, making it hard to deal with gamma correction across platforms.

Gamma correction is relevant to both grayscale and color images; in the latter case the main effect of the gamma correction is on the intensity of the color image.

11.3   Color Models

In a world so rich in colors, there are actually no colors. Our perception of color stems from the reaction of our brain to the wavelengths of light that enter our eyes. Colors do not simply exist as "deeds of light," as Johann Wolfgang von Goethe put it, but are the product of a process that involves self-perception.

Given the overwhelming number of different colors that can be observed in nature, man has had a long-standing desire to communicate and use color in a

---

[4]By display system, we mean the combination of the graphics hardware (card), the monitor, and any display software.

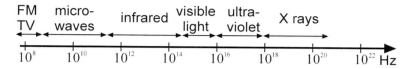

Figure 11.9. Electromagnetic spectrum.

consistent manner. He has thus been striving to invent a model for systematically describing, comparing, classifying, and ordering colors; such a model is referred to as a *color model*. Naturally the simplest approach was tried first, the linear model of Aristotle (Color Plate VI). Aristotle was inspired from the cyclical succession of colors that form the continuum of day and night. Unfortunately, this simple color model is a long way from reality. Plato and Pythagoras invented more elaborate color models and some of their ideas persisted until the Renaissance.

Actually, visible colors correspond to *frequencies* of light that cover a small fraction of the electromagnetic spectrum (Figure 11.9). Different frequencies within this small region represent the different colors, from about $4.3 \cdot 10^{14}$ Hz (red) to about $7.5 \cdot 10^{14}$ Hz (violet).[5]

An important classification of modern color models is based on whether they are *device-independent*. In a device-independent color model the coordinates[6] of a color will represent a unique color value, according to human perception. In contrast, in a device-dependent color model the same color coordinates will produce a slightly different visible color value on different display devices. The Commission Internationale d'Eclairage (CIE) has worked on producing device-independent color models; such models are useful, among other things, for the consistent conversion between device-dependent color models. For example, the red-green-blue (RGB) and cyan-magenta-yellow (CMY) models are device-dependent while CIE XYZ is device-independent.

Some device-dependent color models also follow the respective devices' philosophy of producing arbitrary color from primary colors; we can distinguish between *additive* and *subtractive* color models. An additive model encapsulates the way color is produced on a computer display by *adding* the contributions of the primaries while a *subtractive* model resembles the working of a painter or a printer, where color mixing is achieved through a *subtractive* (painting) process.

---

[5]*Frequency v* and *wavelength λ* are interchangeable since $\lambda \cdot v = c$, where c is the speed of light; red corresponds to a wavelength of about 780 nm and violet to 380 nm.

[6]See Section 11.3.1.

Another important characteristic of color models is *perceptual linearity*. If the perceived difference between two colors is proportional to the difference of their color values across the entire color model, then the color model is perceptually linear and offers the same perceptual color precision throughout its range. Finally, it is desirable that a color model is *intuitive* in its use.

In this section, a small selection of color models are presented, based on their relevance to computer graphics and visualization. A large number of additional color models exist [Wysz00], including models that were developed for television (such as YUV, YIQ, YCbCr and YPbPr) and proprietary models (such as Kodak's YCC).

11.3.1   The CIE XYZ Color Model

In color science, Grassman's first law states that any color can be created as a linear combination of *three basic colors*, provided that no combination of any subset of the basic colors can produce another. This is analogous to the linear-independence requirement for the basis vectors in a coordinate system.

Aiming to provide a standard way to describe all colors, the CIE defined the XYZ color model in 1931. This is now considered as the mother of all color models. Colors are represented in a three-dimensional color space whose axes are defined by the basic colors $\vec{X}$, $\vec{Y}$, and $\vec{Z}$. Mixing the basic colors in suitable proportions X, Y, and Z produces all visible colors (Figure 11.10); $\vec{X}$, $\vec{Y}$ and $\vec{Z}$ are actually not visible colors themselves but must be simply regarded as computational quantities. In fact, X and Z provide *chromaticity* information (what the color is) while Y corresponds to the level of *intensity*.[7]

The basic colors thus form a *color basis* and other colors $\vec{F}$ are expressed as linear combinations of the basis,

$$\vec{F} = X \cdot \vec{X} + Y \cdot \vec{Y} + Z \cdot \vec{Z},$$

where X, Y, Z are the *color coordinates* of $\vec{F}$.

Grassman's second law provides for color mixing in a system of three basic colors. If $\vec{F_1} = X_1 \cdot \vec{X} + Y_1 \cdot \vec{Y} + Z_1 \cdot \vec{Z}$ and $\vec{F_2} = X_2 \cdot \vec{X} + Y_2 \cdot \vec{Y} + Z_2 \cdot \vec{Z}$ are two given colors, then the color that represents their mixture is

$$\vec{F_M} = (X_1 + X_2) \cdot \vec{X} + (Y_1 + Y_2) \cdot \vec{Y} + (Z_1 + Z_2) \cdot \vec{Z}.$$

Color interpolation by a factor t $(0 \leq t \leq 1)$ between colors $\vec{F_1}$ and $\vec{F_2}$ can

---

[7]Note that, in this context, intensity is often referred to as *brightness*.

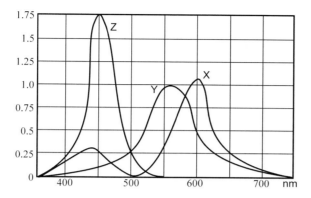

Figure 11.10. The XYZ mixing curves to produce the visible colors.

similarly be defined as

$$\overrightarrow{\mathbf{F_I}} = (t \cdot X_1 + (1-t) \cdot X_2) \cdot \overrightarrow{\mathbf{X}} + (t \cdot Y_1 + (1-t) \cdot Y_2) \cdot \overrightarrow{\mathbf{Y}} + (t \cdot Z_1 + (1-t) \cdot Z_2) \cdot \overrightarrow{\mathbf{Z}}.$$

If we project the CIE XYZ model colors onto the plane $X + Y + Z = 1$, we get the XYZ color triangle. An arbitrary color vector (X,Y,Z) corresponds to the point (x,y,z) of the XYZ triangle given by

$$x = \frac{X}{(X+Y+Z)}, \qquad y = \frac{Y}{(X+Y+Z)}, \qquad z = \frac{Z}{(X+Y+Z)}.$$

Point (x,y,z) is the intersection of the vector (X,Y,Z) and the XYZ triangle. Since $x + y + z = 1$, we can define all colors of the triangle by giving just two of their coordinates, say x and y; we thus take the projection of the XYZ triangle onto the xy-plane, which is the XY triangle (Figure 11.11). Therefore, an alternative way to specify a color is to give its x and y values (or any other pair from the (x,y,z) triplet) plus its intensity value Y. This color specification is referred to as Yxy.

To return to CIE XYZ from CIE Yxy, we use

$$X = x \cdot \frac{Y}{y}, \qquad Y = Y, \qquad Z = (1-x-y) \cdot \frac{Y}{y} = z \cdot \frac{Y}{y}.$$

Figure 11.12 shows a curve that encompasses all visible colors (a subset of the XY triangle colors) and a shaded area which represents the colors found in nature (a subset of the visible colors).

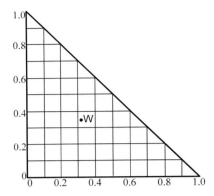

Figure 11.11. XY triangle.

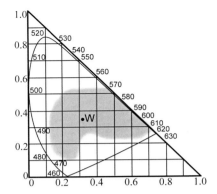

Figure 11.12. Visible colors in the XY triangle.

The XYZ model is perceptually non-linear and definitely not intuitive in its use.

11.3.2   The CIE Yu′v′ Color Model

This is a transformation of the CIE XYZ model which attempts to provide perceptual linearity. The u' and v' components of this system are defined in terms of the x and y components of CIE XYZ as follows:

$$u' = \frac{4x}{-2x + 12y + 3},$$
$$v' = \frac{9y}{-2x + 12y + 3}.$$

The above transformation is easily reversible. Again a third component could be specified but is redundant. A complete color specification in CIE Yu′v′ can be given as a triplet (Y, u', v'), where Y is the same intensity value as in CIE XYZ.

11.3.3   The CIE L*a*b* Color Model

This is another transformation of CIE XYZ which aims at perceptual linearity. Its parameters are defined relative to the *white point* of a display device (any display device, as it is device-independent). The white point is the color that is displayed when all color components are set to their maximum value[8] and is expressed in the

---

[8]Since display devices usually employ the RGB model (see Section 11.3.4), the white point is obtained by setting $r = g = b = 1$.

CIE XYZ model as (X_n, Y_n, Z_n). The CIE L*a*b* model defines three parameters $L*$ (for intensity[9]) and $a*, b*$ (for chromaticity) in terms of a CIE XYZ color specification X, Y, Z and the white point (X_n, Y_n, Z_n) (Color Plate VII):

$$L* = \begin{cases} 116\sqrt[3]{Y_r} - 16, & \text{if } Y_r > 0.008856, \\ 903.3 Y_r, & \text{if } Y_r \leq 0.008856, \end{cases}$$

$$a* = 500(f(X_r) - f(Y_r)),$$

$$b* = 200(f(Y_r) - f(Z_r)),$$

where

$$X_r = \tfrac{X}{X_n}, \quad Y_r = \tfrac{Y}{Y_n}, \quad Z_r = \tfrac{Z}{Z_n},$$

$$f(t) = \begin{cases} \sqrt[3]{t}, & \text{if } t > 0.008856, \\ 7.787t + 16/116, & \text{if } t \leq 0.008856. \end{cases}$$

The above transformation is reversible.

11.3.4 The RGB Color Model

As its name implies, the basic colors in the RGB additive color model are *red*, *green*, and *blue*. These basic colors were chosen, because our own vision is based on red, green, and blue color-sensitive cells (cones) (see Chapter 10). Again, other colors $\overrightarrow{\mathbf{F}}$ are expressed as linear combinations of the basis

$$\overrightarrow{\mathbf{F}} = r \cdot \overrightarrow{\mathbf{R}} + g \cdot \overrightarrow{\mathbf{G}} + b \cdot \overrightarrow{\mathbf{B}},$$

where $\overrightarrow{\mathbf{R}}, \overrightarrow{\mathbf{G}}, \overrightarrow{\mathbf{B}}$ are the red, green, and blue basis vectors and r, g, b are the color coordinates of $\overrightarrow{\mathbf{F}}$.

On most computer displays, colors are created using an additive method. Additive color mixing begins with black (no light present, the display phosphor is not illuminated) and ends with white (the sum of all basic colors). As more color is added, the result is lighter and tends to white (Color Plate VIII). Color scanners work in a similar way; they read the amounts of basic colors that are reflected from, or transmitted through, an object and convert these readings into digital values. The RGB model is useful for such devices due to its additive nature and its use of the red, green, and blue basis which consists of visible colors rather than theoretical computational quantities.

Color mixing and interpolation can be defined in a manner similar to the XYZ model. The RGB cube is the unit cube in RGB space (Figure 11.13; see also Color Plate IX).

---

[9]The actual term used was *luminance*, but, for simplicity and consistency, we shall take it to be synonymous to intensity here.

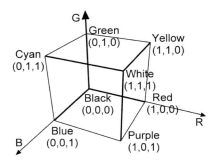

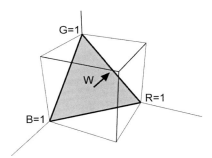

Figure 11.13. RGB cube diagram. (See also Color Plate IX.)

Figure 11.14. RGB triangle. (See also Color Plate X.)

Within the space of the RGB cube, colors correspond to vectors from the origin $(0,0,0)$, which is the black point. White is then $(1,1,1)$, green is $(0,1,0)$, etc. In this representation the direction of a color vector defines chromaticity and its length is the intensity. The main diagonal of the RGB cube consists of shades of gray only (from black to white). If we disregard intensity, it is possible to represent the RGB system with a triangle which is the intersection of the RGB cube with the plane defined by the points red $(1,0,0)$, green $(0,1,0)$, and blue $(0,0,1)$ (Figure 11.14; see also Color Plate X). All RGB colors are mapped onto this triangle, since all RGB vectors intersect it. The only information lost is intensity.

Using the RGB triangle it is possible to refine the notion of chromaticity by splitting it into *hue* and *saturation*. Hue is the dominant wavelength which gives a color its identity and saturation is the amount of white that is present in it. All hues are found on the perimeter of the RGB triangle; saturation is maximum at the center of the triangle and minimum at its perimeter. Colors of the same hue, but varying saturation, can be found on a line segment that connects a point on the perimeter with the triangle center. (In the RGB cube, saturation corresponds to the angle that a color vector forms with the cube diagonal.)

The correspondence between visible colors and the RGB model can be defined by giving the portions of red, green, and blue required to produce the visible colors (Figure 11.15).[10] The RGB model is not perceptually linear and, in terms of use, rather un-intuitive since it is not easy to come up with the mix of the three primaries required to produce an arbitrary color.

---

[10] Note the negative values required for red in a certain range, indicating the inability of this additive color model to produce *all* visible colors.

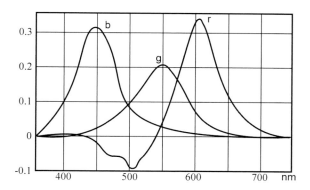

Figure 11.15. RGB mixing curves for visible colors.

Due to its device-dependent nature, the same RGB color triplet (r, g, b) will potentially produce perceptually different colors on different display devices. To ensure perceptual color equality when transferring color images across RGB display devices, it is necessary to convert from one to the other via an intermediate device-independent color model. Such devices often provide a matrix $\mathbf{M}$ for the conversion of their RGB color model to CIE XYZ:[11]

$$\begin{bmatrix} X \\ Y \\ Z \end{bmatrix} = \mathbf{M} \cdot \begin{bmatrix} r \\ g \\ b \end{bmatrix}, \tag{11.4}$$

where

$$\mathbf{M} = \begin{bmatrix} X_R & X_G & X_B \\ Y_R & Y_G & Y_B \\ Z_R & Z_G & Z_B \end{bmatrix}.$$

Given the RGB to CIE XYZ conversion matrices $\mathbf{M_1}$ and $\mathbf{M_2}$ of two display devices, we can convert RGB colors between them in a perceptually equivalent manner as

$$\begin{bmatrix} r_2 \\ g_2 \\ b_2 \end{bmatrix} = \mathbf{M_2}^{-1} \cdot \mathbf{M_1} \cdot \begin{bmatrix} r_1 \\ g_1 \\ b_1 \end{bmatrix}. \tag{11.5}$$

---

[11]Some display devices provide instead the CIE XYZ specifications for red, green, blue, and the white point, from which the matrix $\mathbf{M}$ can be derived.

Alpha color and RGB compressed modes. The number of bits assigned for the storage of the color of a pixel, the bits per pixel (bpp), determines the maximum number of colors that can be simultaneously present in an image as well as the size of the image. With the exception of high dynamic range images (Section 11.5), 8 bits per color component are typically used, giving 24 bpp. As computer words are commonly 32 bits wide, the remaining 8 bits are often allocated to represent the *alpha* value.

An *alpha color* is a quadruple $[r, g, b, \alpha]^T$, $\alpha \neq 0$ and corresponds to $[r/\alpha, g/\alpha, b/\alpha]^T$; α represents the area (or volume) in which the energy of the color is held [Will06]. An alpha color can thus be seen as $[C, \alpha]^T = [energy\_contribution, area\_contribution]^T$ where C is short for the RGB color components. Transparency or partial pixel coverage can be mimicked by reducing the α value of a color.

The alpha color representation very much resembles homogeneous coordinates used in projective geometry, where a homogeneous point $[x, y, z, w]^T$, $w \neq 0$, has the basic representation $[x/w, y/w, z/w]^T$ (see Section 3.4.1). In fact, Willis shows that alpha colors form a projective space, valid for any color computation [Will06].

For example, looking at transparency, let transparent object A of alpha color $[C_A, 1]^T$ be in front of transparent object B of alpha color $[C_B, 1]^T$. Since the front object is transparent, its color only contributes a fraction α_A so we have to reduce its area coverage; in projective terms its contribution is $[\alpha_A C_A, \alpha_A]^T$. The back object contribution is the fragment α_B of its own transparency times the portion of color energy $(1 - \alpha_A)$ that object A allows to pass through it, i.e., $[\alpha_B(1 - \alpha_A)C_B, \alpha_B(1 - \alpha_A)]^T$. Thus the total contribution of the two objects is

$$[\alpha_A C_A + \alpha_B(1 - \alpha_A)C_B, \alpha_A + \alpha_B(1 - \alpha_A)]^T,$$

which is also known as the *over* operator [Port84].

The size of an image can be reduced by decreasing the bpp and this is referred to as *compressed mode*. This is achieved by re-sampling the range of each color component. The bit allocation of the bpp into the red, green, blue, and alpha components is denoted by r:g:b:a; if 3 numbers are given then the alpha value is not used. Common compressed modes include 4:4:4:4, 5:5:5:1, 5:6:5[12] and 3:3:2.

---

[12]A larger number of bits is allocated to green, as the eye is more sensitive to variations in this color component.

11.3.5 The HSV Color Model

The amounts of red, green, and blue present in a color *indirectly* control its hue, saturation, and intensity characteristics. It is often simpler for humans to specify a color based on such characteristics, rather than proportions of red, green, and blue. One of the first modern attempts to systematically organize a color model was made by artist A. H. Munsell [Muns41]. Munsell sought a conceptually simple way to universally describe color and proposed the hue-value-chroma system, known today as the hue-saturation-value (HSV) system, which geometrically represents colors on a cone.[13]

Munsell started by arranging colors on a circle, like a color wheel, encapsulating the hue characteristic. Hue is described by an angle with respect to an initial position on the circle (Color Plate XI). For example, red is found at $0°$, green at $120°$, and blue at $240°$. This hue circle corresponds to a cross section of the cone. Saturation is maximum on the surface of the cone (minus the base), which represents pure colors with maximum "colorfulness"; the axis of the cone represents minimum saturation (shades of gray). The *value* component corresponds to intensity; the minimum value 0 indicates the absence of light (black) while the maximum value indicates that the color has its peak intensity. This component is represented by a position along the axis of the cone: 0 corresponds to the cone's apex, and the maximum value corresponds to the center of the cone's base.

A relatively simple linear transformation converts RGB values to HSV and vice versa; HSV can be used in place of a device's RGB model as a more intuitive color interface.

11.3.6 The CMY(K) Color Model

When colors are mixed during the painting or printing process, the subtractive color method is used. Subtractive color mixing starts with white (the color of the canvas or paper); as one adds color, the result gets darker and tends to black. For example, if we drop cyan paint on a piece of paper, it absorbs the red component of incident light; if the paper is illuminated with white light (white = red + green + blue), the reflected (visible) light from the painted area will be (red + green + blue) − red = (green + blue) = cyan.

The CMY model is defined as the complement of RGB. Its three basic colors are cyan ($\vec{C}$), magenta ($\vec{M}$), and yellow ($\vec{Y}$). The CMY cube is the unit cube in CMY space (Figure 11.16; see also Color Plate XII). White appears at $(0,0,0)$

---

[13]Note that, in this context, *value* refers to *intensity*.

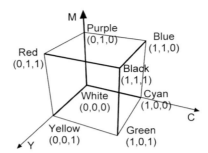

Figure 11.16. CMY cube diagram. (See also Color Plate XII.)

and black at the opposite vertex $(1,1,1)$; other colors are also in opposite vertices with respect to the RGB cube. A color $\overrightarrow{\mathbf{F}}$ is expressed as a linear combinations of the basic colors

$$\overrightarrow{\mathbf{F}} = c \cdot \overrightarrow{\mathbf{C}} + m \cdot \overrightarrow{\mathbf{M}} + y \cdot \overrightarrow{\mathbf{Y}},$$

where c, m, and y are the color coordinates of $\overrightarrow{\mathbf{F}}$.

Being a complement of RGB, it is perceptually nonlinear and rather non-intuitive, since it is not straightforward to specify a certain color as a mixture of $\overrightarrow{\mathbf{C}}$, $\overrightarrow{\mathbf{M}}$, and $\overrightarrow{\mathbf{Y}}$. The conversions between CMY and RGB are

$$\begin{bmatrix} c \\ m \\ y \end{bmatrix} = \begin{bmatrix} 1 \\ 1 \\ 1 \end{bmatrix} - \begin{bmatrix} r \\ g \\ b \end{bmatrix},$$

$$\begin{bmatrix} r \\ g \\ b \end{bmatrix} = \begin{bmatrix} 1 \\ 1 \\ 1 \end{bmatrix} - \begin{bmatrix} c \\ m \\ y \end{bmatrix}.$$

Some printing devices include black ink in addition to cyan, magenta, and yellow in order to avoid synthesizing black, which appears often in text and some diagrams; they thus economize on the use of ink and provide better quality black. In terms of the color model, black can be used to offset the color composition process by the minimum component of a color $\overrightarrow{\mathbf{F}}$. The CMYK color model is a derivative of CMY that includes black, and the (reversible) conversion from CMY to CMYK (with components c', m', y', b) is

$$b = \min(c, m, y),$$
$$c' = \frac{c - b}{1 - b},$$
$$m' = \frac{m - b}{1 - b},$$
$$y' = \frac{y - b}{1 - b}.$$

Caution should be exercised when converting from the RGB space of a display device to the CMY space of a printing device, since they are both device-dependent models. The above simple transforms are unlikely to result in accurate color reproduction. Ideally, one should convert from RGB to a device-independent system, such as CIE XYZ, and then to CMY using the transformation matrices of the respective devices, if known:

$$\begin{bmatrix} c \\ m \\ y \end{bmatrix} = \begin{bmatrix} XYZ \rightarrow \\ CMY \\ \text{of printer} \end{bmatrix} \cdot \begin{bmatrix} RGB \rightarrow \\ XYZ \\ \text{of display} \end{bmatrix} \cdot \begin{bmatrix} r \\ g \\ b \end{bmatrix}$$

The following table summarizes the main characteristics of the color models presented above, where Y and N denote yes and no.

	Device-independent?	Perceptually linear?	intuitive?
CIE XYZ	Y	N	N
CIE Yu′v′	Y	Y	$\sim$ N
CIE L*a*b*	Y	Y	$\sim$ N
RGB	N	N	$\sim$ N
HSV	N	N	Y
CMY	N	N	$\sim$ N

11.4 Web Issues

When making images for the Web, a prime consideration is that they will be potentially viewed by a large audience with various display systems. The same digital image can appear quite different on different display systems, if care is not taken.

The first consideration is *difference in gamma correction*. An image stored with different gamma correction than that of the actual display system will either appear too bright or too dark. If no particular audience can be assumed, it makes sense to use an "average" gamma-correction value for images, e.g., 2.2.

The second consideration is *difference in the color model.* It is quite common to store images in the device-dependent RGB model. As such, when the actual display device is different than the display device used for the creation of the image, the colors will most likely be perceptually different. This is particularly annoying in Web applications where the image creator is not even aware of the type of display device that will be used for viewing.

A logical possibility would be to consider one of the CIE device-independent models for the transfer of images; this has a number of drawbacks however. First, it imposes an extra step of calibration, as some models require the specification of the white point for the conversion. Second, if a semi-intuitive model such as L*a*b* is used, an expensive conversion involving cube roots is required. Finally, RGB models are widely accepted for display devices.

sRGB. Standard RGB or *sRGB* is a device-independent color model that is easier to handle for device manufacturers in the consumer market due to its similarity to RGB. The color model sRGB achieves its device-independence by providing

- colorimetric definition of the red, green, and blue basic colors in terms of the device-independent standard CIE XYZ;

- a gamma of 2.2;

- precisely defined viewing conditions.

In addition to Web applications, sRGB is useful in consumer electronics (e.g., digital cameras) as a standard format for the exchange of images.

11.5   High Dynamic Range Images

When we consider the future, we may wonder how likely it is that images created today, either natural or synthetic, will be useful to coming generations. With the advent of cheap digital capture and storage media, we have the tendency to think that our images are potentially immortal. We should ask ourselves how appealing our images will be at future times, assuming significant technological advances in display technology. The question then is, do we record our images in a format that is potentially immortal?

While it is virtually impossible to predict future technology, it is reasonable to assume that the human visual system will remain as it is today. The use of a format that can capture all that the human eye can see is significant insurance against the mortality of our images. Let us define the *dynamic range* of an image as the ratio of its highest to its lowest intensity value. The human eye has tremendous dynamic range capabilities; physiological experiments have shown that it can perceive about five orders of magnitude (10,000 : 1) of dynamic range simultaneously. If the eye is given a few minutes for adaptation, this range increases to over nine orders of magnitude. A good example of the use of this capability is driving a car into oncoming traffic at night; the contrast between the oncoming cars' headlights and the surrounding area is huge, but the eye can perceive both.

Conventional displays (such as cathode ray tubes or liquid crystal displays) do not even come close to the dynamic range of the eye; their typical dynamic range is 300 : 1. Even worse, conventional 24-bit RGB encoding has a useful dynamic range of only 90 : 1 [Ward01]. Thus, although 24-bit RGB encoding does a relatively good job of representing what a monitor can display (at least by orders of magnitude) it does a poor job of representing what the human eye can perceive [Ward01]. In fact the dynamic range of conventional camera film is significantly higher than that of 24-bit RGB, making film-captured images more likely to stand the test of time.

High dynamic range (HDR) images can be produced by specialized photography equipment (including high dynamic range CCDs), by combining multiple images of a scene taken at different brightness levels or synthetically (e.g., by global illumination techniques [Rein05]). *Tone-mapping*[14] methods have been developed [Dura02, Lars97, Tumb99] that compress HDR images into the dynamic ranges of conventional monitors according to specific preservation *intents* (Figure 11.17; see also Color Plate XIII). However recognizable such tone mapped images may be, no-one would confuse them with the visual experience of watching oncoming traffic lights at night, simply because the dynamic range does not exist. Note that the difference is not the maximum displayable intensity; increasing the brightness on a conventional display would simply turn dark pixels into medium gray [Rein05]. What is missing is the capability to display a wide dynamic range simultaneously. There are two advantages to creating HDR images:

1. The images can be saved for posterity at the dynamic range perceivable by human beings, thus accounting for future HDR displays.[15]

2. It is possible to subsequently apply *different* tone-mapping techniques to HDR images.

---

[14]For a general discussion of tone mapping, see Chapter 10.
[15]Current research in HDR displays is promising [Seet04].

(a)   (b)

(c)   (d)

Figure 11.17. Images of a scene with high dynamic range. (a) Obtaining a dark image loses information on the interior of the arch. (b) A bright image loses information on the clouds. (c, d) An HDR image created from several simple images (images (a) and (b) being the two extremes) and tone-mapped using histogram tone mapping (c) or Reinhard's global photographic tone mapping (d) is closer to what the human eye can see. (Images courtesy of Greg Ward.) (See also Color Plate XIII.)

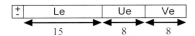

Figure 11.18. Bit assignments in 32-bit LogLuv.

It is possible to record HDR images by drastically increasing the bits per pixel (e.g., by assigning a 32-bit float for every color component for a total of 96 bpp). However HDR formats make clever use of the notion of just noticeable difference (JND) [Seet04]. A JND is the smallest intensity difference detectable by the human eye at a given intensity level. There is a logarithmic relationship between JNDs and intensity levels [Bart92,Bart93]; it therefore makes sense to separate the intensity component of a pixel from its chromatic content and store it separately, encoded at a logarithmic scale. This is the approach followed by HDR formats, such as RGBE of Radiance [Ward91, Ward94] and LogLuv [Lars98a, Lars98b]. Here we shall focus on 32-bit LogLuv.

The 32-bit LogLuv format assigns 32 bits to each pixel. The bit assignments are shown in Figure 11.18. Fifteen bits are used for the intensity value, 1 bit is used for the intensity sign (negative intensity is allowed), and 16 bits are assigned to chromaticity.[16] The logarithmic conversion between the (captured or computed) real intensity value L and its (integer) stored value L_e is of the form

$$L_e = \lfloor c_1(\log_2 L + c_2) \rfloor,$$
$$L = 2^{[L_e/c_1 - c_2]}.$$

The above encompasses the full range of perceivable intensity in imperceptible steps [Lars98a].

The chromaticity values are converted from CIE XYZ to Yxy, as shown in Section 11.3.1, and then to Yu'v' for perceptual linearity, as shown in Section 11.3.2 [Wysz00]; the visible u'v' range is then scaled to eight bits for each of u' and v', which gives enough precision to cover the visible chromatic spectrum.

11.6   Exercises

1. Implement the halftoning algorithm and use it to represent an image with five grayscale levels using two grayscale levels by employing the **H₂** matrix of Section 11.2.1.

---

[16]As stated earlier, chromaticity refers to two of the three color characteristics in the HSV model (hue and saturation); intensity (or "value" in HSV) is the third.

2. Design and implement an algorithm which takes a grayscale image as input and computes the number of intensity levels Q, in a format of your choice. The algorithm should then create the halftoning matrix $\mathbf{H_m}$ that provides at least Q grayscale levels (see Section 11.2.1) and convert the original image into a bi-level (black and white) image using $\mathbf{H_m}$.

3. Implement the Floyd-Steinberg algorithm and test it on grayscale images of your choice.

4. Generalize the Floyd-Steinberg algorithm so that it works for color images. Assuming an RGB representation, you will need to process each of the red, green, and blue components separately. Use it to convert a 24-bit image (8 bits for each color component) to a 6-bit image (2 bits per color component) and compare the result to the image obtained by simple rounding of each color component to 2 bits.

5. Check if your monitor provides an RGB to CIE XYZ conversion matrix $\mathbf{M_1}$. Find the equivalent matrix $\mathbf{M_2}$ for another monitor and convert images from the first monitor to the second monitor using Equation (11.5). Compare the result to the simple transfer of RGB images across the monitors.

   Note: Use a simple encoding format, such as raw RGB.

6. Write a small program to display and step through grayscale levels. The program must also allow jumps within the range that your monitor can display (e.g., by assigning 0 to the minimum level (black) and 1 to the maximum level (white) and then picking numbers within that range). Use this program to confirm the logarithmic relationship between JNDs and intensity levels by tabulating the absolute grayscale difference for a JND at different intensity levels (see Section 11.5).

   Note: you will have to ensure that your monitor performs reasonable gamma correction (see Section 11.2.2.)

Plate I. Loop subdivision: From left to right: an initial configuration, its first and second refinements, and limit surface. (See also Figure 8.11.)

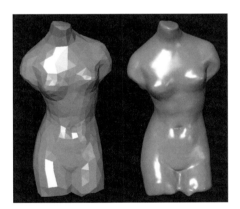

Plate II. Butterfly subdivision. An initial configuration (left) and its limit surface (right). (Courtesy of D. Zorin.) (See also Figure 8.13.)

Plate III. Procedure mapping example.

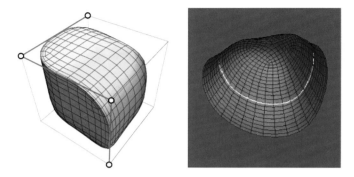

Plate IV. Interpolating curves by subdivision surfaces. Left: a Doo–Sabin surface interpolating a crease. Right: a Catmull–Clark surface interpolating a C^1-continuous curve. (See also Figure 8.18.)

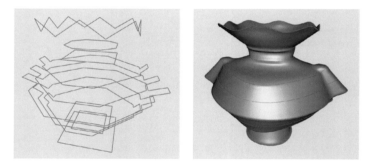

Plate V. Lofted Catmull–Clark subdivision surfaces. Left: A set of control polygons defining cubic B-spline curves. Right: A Catmull–Clark subdivision surface interpolating these curves. (See also Figure 8.19.)

Plate VI. Aristotle's linear color model.

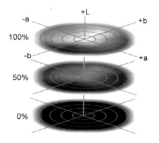

Plate VII. The L*a*b* color model.

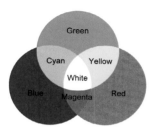

Plate VIII. RGB additive colors.

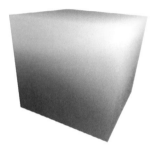

Plate IX. RGB cube. (See also Figure 11.13.)

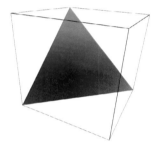

Plate X. RGB triangle. (See also Figure 11.14.)

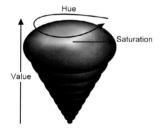

Plate XI. The hue-saturation-value color model.

Plate XII. CMY cube. (See also Figure 11.16.)

(a)   (b)

(c)   (d)

Plate XIII. Images of a scene with high dynamic range. Obtaining a dark image (a) loses information on the interior of the arch; a bright image (b) loses information on the clouds. An HDR image created from several simple images (images (a) and (b) being the two extremes) and tone-mapped using histogram tone mapping (c) or Reinhard's global photographic tone mapping (d) is closer to what the human eye can see. (Images courtesy of Greg Ward.) (See also Figure 11.17.)

(a)   (b)

Plate XIV. (a) Forward scattering (light source opposite observer). (b) Back scattering (light source behind observer).

Plate XV. The effect of the three components of the Phong model: (left) ambient only; (middle) ambient + diffuse; (right) ambient + diffuse + specular.

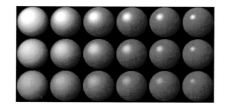

Plate XVI. The effect of the specular parameters in the Phong model: n increases to the right, k_s increases upwards. (See also Figure 12.10.)

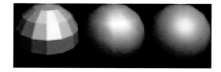

Plate XVII. Constant shading (left), Gouraud shading (middle), and Phong shading (right).

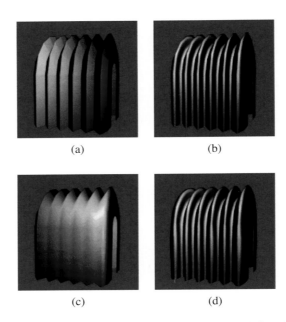

(a)   (b)

(c)   (d)

Plate XVIII. (a) Flat shaded polygons on a zigzag profile. (b) Quadratic interpolation of vertex normals on a zigzag profile. (c) Linear interpolation of vertex normals on a zigzag profile. (d) Reduction of straight silhouettes using a dense polygon mesh approximation of a curved patch model of the same object and linear approximation (polygon count increased by a factor of 4). (Color plate by permission from C.W.A.M. van Overveld [Over97].)

Plate XIX. Anisotropic reflectance. (See also Figure 12.30.)

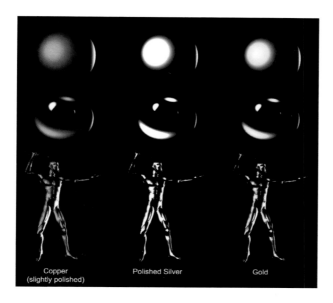

Plate XX. The Cook–Torrance Model for various materials. (See also Figure 12.25.)

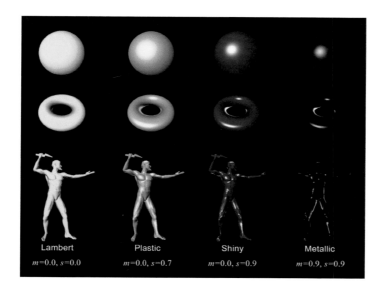

Plate XXI. Results using the Strauss model. (See also Figure 12.29.)

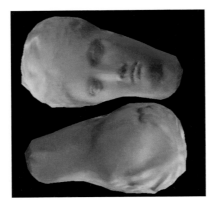

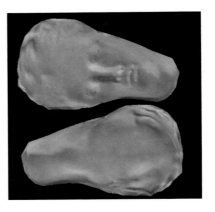

Plate XXII. The normal map applied to the low resolution model of Plate XXIII (left) to imitate the geometric complexity of the high resolution model of the same plate (right).

Plate XXIII. Tangent space version of the normal map of Plate XXII.

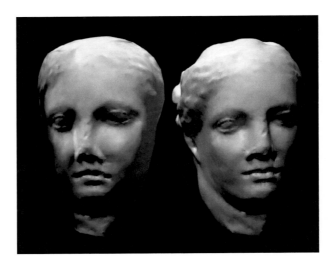

Plate XXIV. Detail transfer via normal mapping. A low resolution proxy surface (left) is rendered using the normal vector information of the corresponding high detail surface it represents.

Plate XXV. Texture Hierarchies. Complex surface finishes can be achieved by hierarchically combining textures to model material attributes. (See also Figure 14.35.)

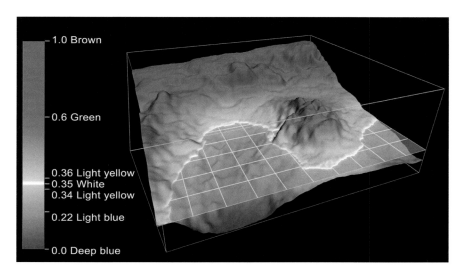

1.0 Brown

0.6 Green

0.36 Light yellow
0.35 White
0.34 Light yellow

0.22 Light blue

0.0 Deep blue

Plate XXVI. Color coding of height and sea depth using a color map that maps relative height information onto interpolated color values. (See also Figure 10.11.)

1 random shadow ray

9 random shadow rays

36 random shadow rays

100 random shadow rays

Plate XXVII. Direct illumination due to a single light source. Note the difference in quality of the image when the number of samples (shadow rays) is increased. (See also Figure 16.3.)

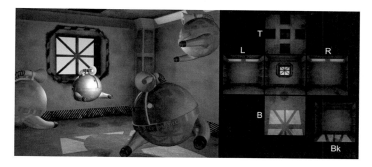

Plate XXVIII. Reflection mapping using a pre-rendered cube-map.

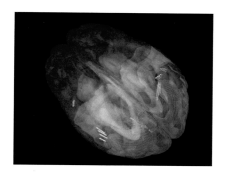

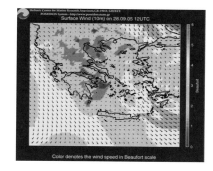

Plate XXIX. Left: brain visualization. Right: wind-data visualization. (Courtesy of L. Perivoliotis, Hellenic Centre for Marine Research.)

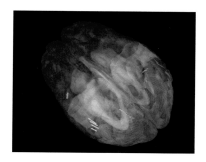

Plate XXX. Coregistration of generic brain model with MEG signals. (See also Figure 10.4.)

Plate XXXI. Colors with different wavelengths cause differential focusing and tire the eye.

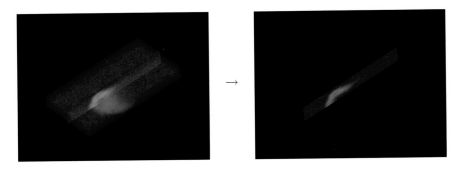

Plate XXXII. Slicing. Image created using OpenDX.

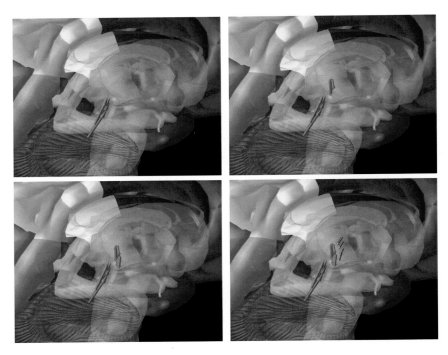

Plate XXXIII. Mapping a variable onto time. Four frames from the display of MEG activation records (arrows represent MEG activation vectors). (Images created using OpenDX/ViewMEG [Kats05].)

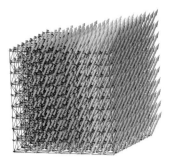

Plate XXXIV. An $O_{X \times Y \times Z}^{\text{vector3}}$.

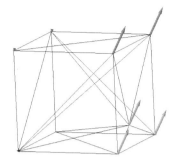

Plate XXXV. Tetrahedral grid.

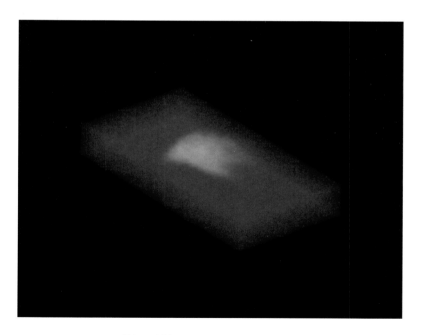

Plate XXXVI. Volume rendering.

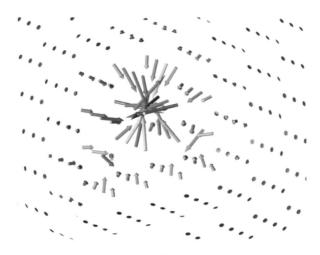

Plate XXXVII. Arrow plot for $O_{X \times Y \times Z}^{\text{vector3}}$. (Image created using OpenDX.)

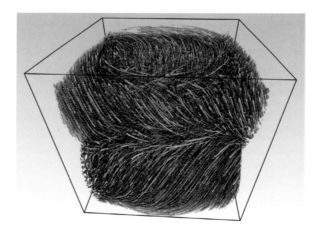

Plate XXXVIII. LIC on $O_{X \times Y \times Z}^{\text{vector3}}$ using ROI. (Image courtesy of Anders Helgeland [Helg04].)

Plate XXXIX. Streamlines (left) and ribbons (right) for static vector fields. (Images created using OpenDX.)

Plate XL. Effect of L on the LIC function ($L = 0, 5, 10, 20$ left to right, top to bottom).

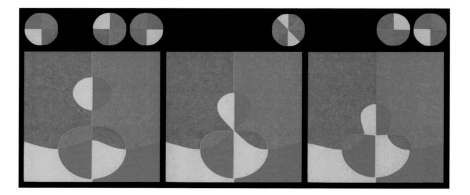

Plate XLI. Color quantization helps understanding. (Courtesy of Peter Hall [Hall93].)

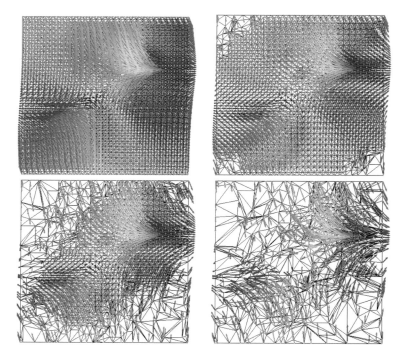

Plate XLII. Simplification of a vector field over a tetrahedral mesh. Initial field and simplification to 50%, 25%, and 10% of the original number of tetrahedra.

12

Illumination Models and Algorithms

Light is a thing that cannot be reproduced,
but must be represented by something else—by color.
—Paul Cézanne

12.1   Introduction

The realistic representation of illumination phenomena in computer graphics is based on the relevant laws of optics. These laws are the result of extensive physical investigations over centuries, and the relevant body of knowledge is extensive. In computer graphics we seek to implement those laws that make the most difference in practice, while at the same time considering the computational cost.

Let us make clear what the role of an *illumination model* is. When light illuminates a point $\mathbf{p}$ of an object (directly or indirectly via reflections) it changes the object's color at $\mathbf{p}$ according to such parameters as the direction of the incident light, the direction of observation, the surface normal at $\mathbf{p}$, the reflectivity of the material, etc. The illumination process should be contrasted to texture mapping algorithms which select the color of the object at $\mathbf{p}$. Texture mapping conceptually precedes illumination and is investigated separately in Chapter 14. The effects of illumination and texturing are often confused by newcomers to computer graphics; Figure 12.1 should help to make the distinction clear.

At this point we must distinguish between two trends in computer graphics. The first uses practical illumination models to produce acceptable illumination effects at a low computational cost, suitable for real-time applications and is explored in the present chapter. The second implements a large part of the available

367

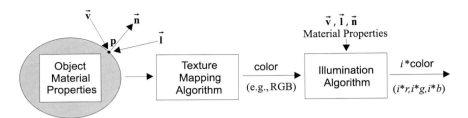

Figure 12.1. Texture-mapping and illumination algorithms.

illumination theory in order to produce the most convincing illumination effects, which come at a high computational cost, suitable only for very demanding and non-real-time applications and is explored in Chapter 16. An essential difference between the two approaches is that the latter considers the interaction of light between objects, or how objects are indirectly illuminated by light reflected from other objects. For this reason illumination models of the first type are usually referred to as *local* and of the second type as *global*.

Finally, we have to make the distinction between an illumination model and algorithm: An illumination model encapsulates a set of physical illumination laws. An illumination algorithm implements an illumination model efficiently.

12.2   The Physics of Light-Object Interaction I

Light energy that reaches an object breaks down into four components:

Incident light = reflected light + scattered light + absorbed light + transmitted light

Depending on the structure (roughness) of the object's surface as well as other secondary parameters, a portion of the incident light energy will be reflected in the "mirror" of the incident direction (*specular* reflection) and another portion will be scattered in all directions (*diffuse* reflection), adding to the ambient light energy. Yet another part will be absorbed, increasing the object's temperature, and a final part will be transmitted through the object, depending on the object's transparency (Figure 12.2).

In order to introduce the basic concepts of light-object interaction, we need to possess a basic understanding of *radiometric* quantities, as defined by international standards [Illi00, Shor05]. We shall use the International System of Units (SI). Radiometry is the measurement of optical radiation, that is, electromagnetic

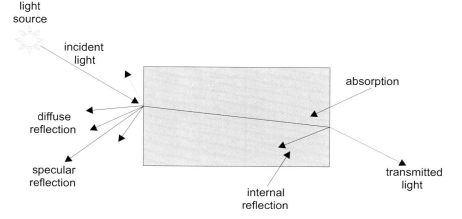

Figure 12.2. Incident light analysis.

radiation within the frequency range 3×10^{11} Hz and 3×10^{15} Hz, which includes the ultraviolet, the visible, and the infrared ranges [Palm05]. Before proceeding, please ensure that you have a sufficient grasp of *solid angle* calculations (see Appendix D).

Radiant energy (Q) is emitted from a light source or reflected from a surface and is transferred through space as photons. Radiant energy is the total energy emitted as radiation of all wavelengths in a defined period of time and is measured in joules. The rate at which radiant energy passes a spatial reference is called *radiant power* (or *flux* Φ) and is measured in watts (watts = joules/sec):

$$\Phi = dQ/dt. \tag{12.1}$$

The energy emitted or reflected from a point may be restricted to certain directions or it may be spreading equally in all directions. The *radiant intensity* (I_r) is defined as the radiant power per unit of solid angle ω_r in a certain direction:

$$I_r = d\Phi_r/d\omega_r. \tag{12.2}$$

The SI defines a special unit, the *candela*, as the luminous intensity in a given direction of a source that emits monochromatic radiation of frequency 540×10^{12} Hz and that has a radiant intensity in that direction of 1/683 watts per steradian. We shall adopt the watts/steradian as the unit for intensity. Notice that *intensity* is an overloaded term [Palm95] and by adopting the definition of power per solid

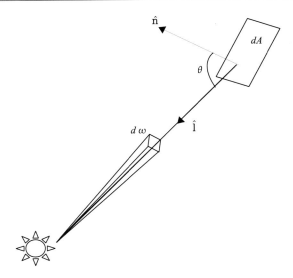

Figure 12.3. Radiance.

angle in a certain direction we side with the most widely accepted convention that conforms with the SI units.

We thus arrive at the concept of *radiance* (L). Assume an infinitesimal surface dA with normal vector $\hat{\mathbf{n}}$ forming an angle θ with the direction of incident or outgoing illumination $\hat{\mathbf{l}}$ (Figure 12.3). Radiance is defined as the radiant power per unit solid angle leaving or entering the infinitesimal area dA from a certain direction per unit projected surface area in that direction:

$$L = d\Phi/(d\omega dA \cos\theta) = d\Phi/(d\omega dA(\hat{\mathbf{n}} \cdot \hat{\mathbf{l}})). \qquad (12.3)$$

Due to the solid angle, radiance is inversely proportional to the square of the distance from the light source and is measured in watts/(steradians · m^2).

The *albedo* ρ of a material is the ratio of scattered to incident electromagnetic radiation across the spectrum; the albedo practically defines the color of a material without the effect of illumination.

The *irradiance* E_i of a surface point is the incident flux per unit area in the vicinity of the point. Irradiance can be visualized as the power per unit area incident from all directions within a hemisphere onto an elementary surface located at the center of the base of that hemisphere:

$$E_i = d\Phi_i/dA \qquad (12.4)$$

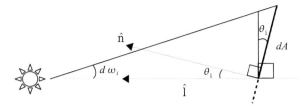

Figure 12.4. Defining $d\omega_i$.

and is measured in watts/m^2. Similarly the *radiosity B* is the flux per unit area exiting a surface

$$E_r = B = d\Phi_r/dA \tag{12.5}$$

and is also measured in watts/m^2.

For a point on an illuminated surface, we can define the *incident intensity* I_i in a manner equivalent to the radiant intensity, as the incident flux per unit solid angle,

$$I_i = d\Phi_i/d\omega_i. \tag{12.6}$$

We can relate incident intensity to irradiance by combining Equations (12.4) and (12.6):

$$E_i = I_i d\omega_i/dA. \tag{12.7}$$

From the definition of solid angle,

$$d\omega_i = \frac{dA\cos\theta_i}{d^2},$$

where $dA \cdot \cos\theta_i$ is the projection of the elementary surface dA onto a plane normal to the direction of illumination (giving an elementary spherical region) and d is the distance from the light source to the elementary surface (see Figure 12.4 and Appendix D).

We thus obtain the photometry law:

$$E_i = I_i \frac{\cos\theta_i}{d^2} = I_i \frac{(\hat{\mathbf{n}} \cdot \hat{\mathbf{l}})}{d^2}. \tag{12.8}$$

In computer graphics, we are interested in the relationship between the incident light from a certain direction onto a surface and the reflected light in another direction as well as the transmitted light through the object. This relationship is captured by the *bidirectional reflectance distribution function* (BRDF) [Nico77].

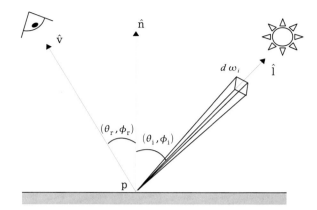

Figure 12.5. Determining the intensity at a point on a surface.

The BRDF depends on many parameters—lighting and observation directions, wavelength, shadow casting, the optical properties of the object, reflectivity, absorption, emission, etc. In practice, it can only be approximated and is also well known to the remote-sensing and modern painting communities. The BRDF associates the outgoing radiance dL_r in direction (θ_r, ϕ_r) to the irradiance dE_i from the incident direction (θ_i, ϕ_i) (see Figure 12.5):

$$\text{BRDF} = \frac{dL_r}{dE_i}. \tag{12.9}$$

Essentially the BRDF captures the fact that objects look differently when seen from different angles or when illuminated from different directions. A classic example from remote sensing is the difference that arises from forward scattering and back scattering [Rouj04] where the light source is opposite and behind the observer, respectively. Color Plate XIV illustrates the point with two grass scenes.

12.3   The Lambert Illumination Model⊛

The simplest illumination model for body reflection assumes that the incident light at the vicinity of a point **p** on a surface is equally diffused in all directions on the incident hemisphere (perfectly diffuse reflection). This means that the BRDF of the body surface is constant for all directions and invariant with respect to wavelength and polarization. A perfectly diffuse surface is called *Lambertian*. *Diffuse illumination* mostly accounts for the reflected light due to *body*

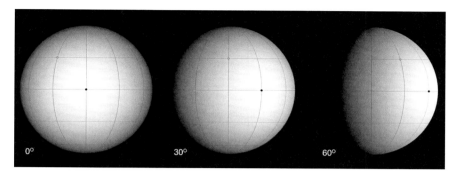

Figure 12.6. Lambert illumination model. The light reflected off a point on the surface is invariant with respect to the viewing direction. The sphere in this example is lit by a single distant point light source and viewed from three different directions.

reflectance: the shallow sub-surface propagation of light and exit through the interface of the surface. (In contrast, *specular illumination* corresponds to the light reflected off the surface, i.e., the interface between two media with different indices of refraction).

In 1760, Lambert published his work *Photometria* (in Latin) [Lamb60], which states what is known today as *Lambert's cosine law* or Lambert's emission law: The total radiant power observed from a Lambertian surface is directly proportional to the cosine of the angle θ_r between the observer's line of sight and the surface normal. A consequence of this law is that, when an elementary surface dA is viewed from an arbitrary direction within the hemisphere Ω surrounding dA, it exhibits the same radiance (Figure 12.6). An intuitive explanation of this phenomenon is the following: As the radiant power $d\Phi_r$ observed at a direction (θ_r, φ_r) diminishes according to Lambert's cosine law, so does the solid angle $d\xi$ subtended by the surface patch dA and viewed from a distant patch dS around the observer location (Figure 12.7). This leads to an equal decrease of both terms, which eventually cancel out.

Imagine that the receiving patch dS were positioned directly above dA,[1] perpendicular to the normal vector of dA (and therefore here the outgoing light direction). Since $\theta_r = 0$, from the definition of radiance (Equation 12.3) the observed radiance is

$$L_0 = \frac{d\Phi_0}{dS d\xi}. \tag{12.10}$$

---

[1]The terms dS and dA denote the areas of the respective patches.

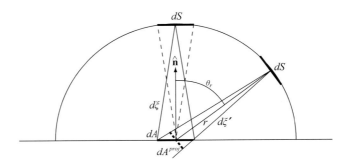

Figure 12.7. Solid angle of a differential patch as "seen" from locations equidistant to the surface patch dA.

Now, let us position dS at a different viewing angle, away from the normal direction of dA, but always perpendicular to the corresponding viewing direction vector, that is, lower on the hemisphere surrounding dA (Figure 12.7). According to Lambert's cosine law, the new radiance at this arbitrary outbound direction is

$$L = \frac{d(\Phi_0 \cos \theta_r)}{dS d\xi'} = \frac{\cos \theta_r d\Phi_0}{dS d\xi'}. \tag{12.11}$$

Furthermore, as dA is very small, the new solid angle $d\xi'$ is directly proportional to the projection of dA on the light transfer direction ($d\xi' = dA \cos \theta_r / r^2$), and therefore

$$d\xi' = \cos \theta_r d\xi. \tag{12.12}$$

Replacing the new solid angle in (12.11) yields

$$L = \frac{\cos \theta_r d\Phi_0}{dS d\xi'} = \frac{\cos \theta_r d\Phi_0}{\cos \theta_r dS d\xi} = \frac{d\Phi_0}{dS d\xi} = L_0. \tag{12.13}$$

We shall next derive the constant BRDF f_d for the Lambertian surface [Glas95]. Although the outgoing (radiant) flux is evenly distributed over the hemisphere subtended by the surface patch at the vicinity of **p**, f_d is not equal to $1/2\pi$ (hemisphere solid angle equals 2π steradians) as will be shown below.

The outgoing radiance is constant and, therefore, does not depend on the reflected light direction on the hemisphere $L_r(\theta_r, \varphi_r) = L_r$. Furthermore, irradiance is not attenuated by the material and is equally spread to every outgoing differential solid angle. The latter implies that the reflectance factor[2] $\rho(\vec{\omega}_i \rightarrow \Omega)$, i.e., the

---

[2]This is actually called the conical-hemispherical reflectance factor in photometry terminology; there are eight more types of reflectance factors (see [Nico77]).

ratio of total reflected light to incident light from $d\vec{\omega}_i$, equals one. From the definition of irradiance, radiosity, and radiance (Equations (12.4), (12.5), and (12.3)) as well as from the relation between the solid angle and the projected solid angle on the surface (Appendix D), we get

$$d\Phi_i = E_i dA, \tag{12.14}$$

$$L_r(\theta_r, \varphi_r) = \frac{dE_r(\theta_r, \varphi_r)}{d\vec{\omega}_r \cos\theta_r} = \frac{dE_r(\theta_r, \varphi_r)}{d\vec{\omega}_r^{\text{proj}}} \quad \Rightarrow \tag{12.15}$$

$$dE_r = L_r d\vec{\omega}_r^{\text{proj}} \Rightarrow E_r = \int_\Omega L_r d\vec{\omega}_r^{\text{proj}}.$$

Using the results from Equations (12.14) and (12.15), the unit reflectance becomes

$$\rho(\vec{\omega}_i \to \Omega) = 1 = \frac{d\Phi_r}{d\Phi_i} = \frac{dA \int_\Omega L_r d\vec{\omega}_r^{\text{proj}}}{E_i dA} = \frac{L_r dA \int_\Omega d\vec{\omega}_r^{\text{proj}}}{E_i dA}. \tag{12.16}$$

From the definition of the BRDF and taking into account that the BRDF for the Lambertian surface is constant, we have

$$f_d = \frac{dL_r}{L_i \cos\theta_i d\vec{\omega}_i} \quad \Rightarrow \quad dL_r = f_d L_i d\vec{\omega}_i^{\text{proj}} \quad \Rightarrow$$

$$L_r = \int_\Omega f_d L_i d\vec{\omega}_i^{\text{proj}} = f_d \int_\Omega L_i d\vec{\omega}_i^{\text{proj}} = f_d E_i. \tag{12.17}$$

Now we can return to Equation (12.16) and substitute L_r from Equation (12.17):

$$1 = \frac{L_r dA \int_\Omega d\vec{\omega}_r^{\text{proj}}}{E_i dA} = \frac{f_d E_i dA \int_\Omega d\vec{\omega}_r^{\text{proj}}}{E_i dA}$$

$$= f_d \int_\Omega d\vec{\omega}_r^{\text{proj}} = f_d \pi \Leftrightarrow f_d = \frac{1}{\pi}. \tag{12.18}$$

In the above derivation we have seen that the radiance associated with an infinitesimal surface patch of area dA around point **p** is proportional to the cosine of the angle θ_i between the normal vector at **p** and the incident direction. This is due to the flow of energy that passes through the (projected) area dA of the patch with respect to the incident light direction. For a more detailed description of the photometric principles, the interested reader is referred to [Glas95].

12.4   The Phong Illumination Model

Phong's classic illumination model [Phon75] is a local empirical model; it does not take into account the interaction of light between objects and some of the terms used do not directly derive from physical laws. However, it gives a reasonable approximation of reality at a modest computational cost, which explains its widespread adoption.

The Phong model proposes a simplified BRDF that relates incoming light intensity from direction (θ_i, ϕ_i) to reflected light intensity in direction (θ_r, ϕ_r) for an object point $\mathbf{p}$ (Figure 12.5). It estimates the visible intensity as the sum of four components: emission, ambient reflection, diffuse reflection, and specular reflection:

$$I = I_e + I_g + I_d + I_s. \tag{12.19}$$

The effect of the components of the Phong model can be seen in Color Plate XV. The emission component I_e caters to objects with self illumination. The ambient component I_g compensates for the fact that the Phong model takes no account of the interaction of light between objects; a surface that is not directly illuminated by a light source would appear completely un-illuminated (e.g., black) if it were not for this component. A constant value of ambient light I_a is assumed for the scene, and each object reflects this ambient light according to its ambient reflectance coefficient k_a:

$$I_g = I_a k_a \quad (0 \le k_a \le 1). \tag{12.20}$$

The light that hits an object directly from a light source is split into two reflected components: diffusely reflected light, which is uniformly scattered in all directions and specularly reflected light, which has its maximum value in the "mirror" of the lighting direction. The diffuse and specular reflection coefficients k_d and k_s depend mainly on the object's surface properties. In general, the rougher the surface the more light is diffusely reflected, while the shinier the surface the more light is specularly reflected. As all incident light must be accounted for: $0 \le k_d, k_s \le 1$ and $k_d + k_s \le 1$. The sum of k_d and k_s may be slightly smaller than 1 to account for light that is transmitted or absorbed by the object.

The diffuse component assumes a Lambertian surface (see Section 12.3) and distributes incident light evenly in all directions. It therefore does not depend on the viewing direction. Its value is proportional to the irradiance E_i which is replaced by intensity I_i according to the photometry law (Equation (12.8)); the

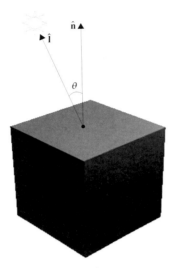

Figure 12.8. The $\hat{\mathbf{l}}$ and $\hat{\mathbf{n}}$ vectors.

distance d is ignored by assuming the light source is at infinity:

$$I_d = I_i k_d \cos\theta = I_i k_d(\hat{\mathbf{n}} \cdot \hat{\mathbf{l}}), \quad (0 \le \theta \le \pi/2, \quad 0 \le k_d \le 1) \qquad (12.21)$$

where I_i the intensity of a point light source, θ the angle between the direction of light incidence ($\hat{\mathbf{l}}$) and the normal vector to the surface ($\hat{\mathbf{n}}$) (Figure 12.8), and k_d is the object's diffuse reflection coefficient. Apart from the object's roughness, k_d also depends on the wavelength of the incident light. The vectors $\hat{\mathbf{l}}$ and $\hat{\mathbf{n}}$ should be unit vectors. The value of I_d is constant over a planar surface since both the $\hat{\mathbf{n}}$ and $\hat{\mathbf{l}}$ vectors are constant (light source at infinity). In practice, we do not accept negative values for $\cos\theta$:

$$I_d = I_i k_d \max(0, \hat{\mathbf{n}} \cdot \hat{\mathbf{l}}).$$

The diffuse component alone gives objects a totally matte appearance. The specular component follows the rule of the mirror. A perfect mirror will only specularly reflect in the direction of reflection $\hat{\mathbf{r}}$ (Figure 12.9). Most surfaces will have a diminishing function of specular reflection that attains its maximum value when the viewing direction $\hat{\mathbf{v}}$ coincides with $\hat{\mathbf{r}}$:

$$I_s = I_i k_s \cos^n \alpha = I_i k_s (\hat{\mathbf{r}} \cdot \hat{\mathbf{v}})^n, \qquad (12.22)$$

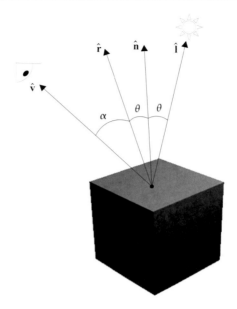

Figure 12.9. The $\hat{\mathbf{v}}$, $\hat{\mathbf{r}}$, $\hat{\mathbf{n}}$, and $\hat{\mathbf{l}}$ vectors.

where $\hat{\mathbf{r}}$ and $\hat{\mathbf{v}}$ are unit vectors and n is an empirical value that corresponds to surface shininess.

A better approximation to the specular reflection coefficient k_s is to make it a function $w(\theta, \lambda)$ of the angle of incidence θ and wavelength λ. Considering a piece of glass, when $\theta = 0$ we get no reflection, while at $\theta = 90$ we get total reflection.

Specular reflection is responsible for the *highlights* that are visible in shiny objects. The $\cos^n \alpha$ term intuitively approximates the spatial distribution of the specularly reflected light. The effect of the material exponent n and the specular reflection coefficient k_s can be seen in Figure 12.10 and Color Plate XVI. Small values of n correspond to coarse materials where the size of the highlight is relatively large and scattered. Conversely, large values of n correspond to shiny objects with a small and crisp highlight. The specular reflection takes the color of the light source. For example, if a blue object is illuminated by a white light source, the color of the diffuse reflection will be blue but that of the specular reflection will be white. Finally, the value of the specular factor $\cos^n \alpha$ should not take on negative values, so we can replace it by $\max(0, \cos^n \alpha)$.

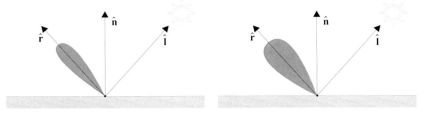

Figure 12.10. The Phong highlight (appears for $\hat{\mathbf{v}}$ in the shaded area) for large n (left) and small n (right).

Thus, the Phong model computes the illumination value as

$$I = I_e + I_a k_a + I_i (k_d (\hat{\mathbf{n}} \cdot \hat{\mathbf{l}}) + k_s (\hat{\mathbf{r}} \cdot \hat{\mathbf{v}})^n). \tag{12.23}$$

To simplify computations, the light source and the observation point are often assumed to be at infinity, giving constant values for the $\hat{\mathbf{l}}$ and $\hat{\mathbf{v}}$ vectors over the area of planar objects. An efficient variant of the specular reflection calculation [Blin77] uses the *halfway* vector $\hat{\mathbf{h}}$ which is the average of $\hat{\mathbf{l}}$ and $\hat{\mathbf{v}}$ (Figure 12.11):

$$\hat{\mathbf{h}} = \frac{(\hat{\mathbf{l}} + \hat{\mathbf{v}})/2}{|(\hat{\mathbf{l}} + \hat{\mathbf{v}})/2|}. \tag{12.24}$$

As can be seen in Figure 12.11, angle $\widehat{\mathbf{nh}} = \varphi + \alpha$, angle $\widehat{\mathbf{rv}} = \theta + \alpha$, and since $\theta = 2\varphi + \alpha$, we deduce that $\widehat{\mathbf{rv}} = 2\widehat{\mathbf{nh}}$, i.e., the angle formed by $\hat{\mathbf{r}}$ and $\hat{\mathbf{v}}$ is

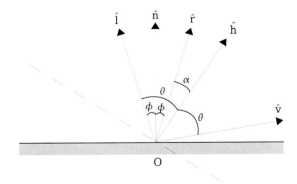

Figure 12.11. The halfway vector $\hat{\mathbf{h}}$.

double the angle formed by $\hat{\mathbf{n}}$ and $\hat{\mathbf{h}}$. We can thus replace the $\hat{\mathbf{r}} \cdot \hat{\mathbf{v}}$ product by $\hat{\mathbf{n}} \cdot \hat{\mathbf{h}}$, and suitably adjust the value of n:

$$I = I_e + I_a k_a + I_i(k_d(\hat{\mathbf{n}} \cdot \hat{\mathbf{l}}) + k_s(\hat{\mathbf{n}} \cdot \hat{\mathbf{h}})^n). \qquad (12.25)$$

The $\hat{\mathbf{h}}$ vector is much cheaper to compute than $\hat{\mathbf{r}}$ and, if $\hat{\mathbf{l}}$ and $\hat{\mathbf{v}}$ are constant (e.g., for planar objects with light source and observer at infinity), then the $\hat{\mathbf{h}}$ vector is also constant. Vector $\hat{\mathbf{h}}$ can be thought of as the normal vector to the plane for which the observer at $\hat{\mathbf{v}}$ would see the maximum value of the specular reflection from the light source at $\hat{\mathbf{l}}$ (this plane corresponds to the dashed line in Figure 12.11).

So far, having assumed the light source at infinity, the contribution of the specular and diffuse terms depend on the intensity of the light source and the ambient term is constant. Objects with the same properties and orientation but different distances from the light source would thus (wrongly) have the same intensity of illumination. This can be corrected by including a factor dependent on the distance of the object point from the light source. The physically correct calculation involves attenuation by the square of the distance d between light source and object, but we usually take a more flexible approach that also includes a linear and a constant term, often useful for special effects:

$$f(d) = 1/(c_1 + c_2 d + c_3 d^2).$$

The model thus becomes

$$I = I_e + I_a k_a + f(d)I_i(k_d(\hat{\mathbf{n}} \cdot \hat{\mathbf{l}}) + k_s(\hat{\mathbf{n}} \cdot \hat{\mathbf{h}})^n). \qquad (12.26)$$

Multiple point light sources can be handled by summing their individual contributions:

$$I = I_e + I_a k_a + \sum_j (f(d)I_{i,j}(k_d(\hat{\mathbf{n}} \cdot \hat{\mathbf{l}}_j) + k_s(\hat{\mathbf{n}} \cdot \hat{\mathbf{h}}_j)^n)). \qquad (12.27)$$

For monochromatic light, the original gray level value v of an object point $\mathbf{p}$ is thus modified by the result I of the intensity computation: $v' = vI$.

Color can be handled by giving the color of the light source to the specular reflection; the color of the ambient and diffuse components depends on the color coefficients of the object material. Three intensity values, one for each of the three primary colors, are then computed:

$$I_r = I_{er} + I_a k_{ar} + (f(d)I_i(k_{dr}(\hat{\mathbf{n}} \cdot \hat{\mathbf{l}}) + k_s(\hat{\mathbf{n}} \cdot \hat{\mathbf{h}})^n)),$$

$$I_g = I_{eg} + I_a k_{ag} + (f(d)I_i(k_{dg}(\hat{\mathbf{n}} \cdot \hat{\mathbf{l}}) + k_s(\hat{\mathbf{n}} \cdot \hat{\mathbf{h}})^n)), \qquad (12.28)$$

$$I_b = I_{eb} + I_a k_{ab} + (f(d)I_i(k_{db}(\hat{\mathbf{n}} \cdot \hat{\mathbf{l}}) + k_s(\hat{\mathbf{n}} \cdot \hat{\mathbf{h}})^n)).$$

Notice that the specular reflection contributes equally to the three equations, simulating a white light source. Thus if (r, g, b) is the original color of an object at point $\mathbf{p}$ (usually given by a texture mapping algorithm), this is modified by the result of the color intensity computation as $(r', g', b') = (rI_r, gI_g, bI_b)$.

Numerical Example. We shall base our example on the basic Phong model with the halfway vector (Equation (12.25)). Let us assume that we want to estimate the intensity value for a point $\mathbf{p}$ which, for ease of calculations, lies at the origin of the coordinate system $\mathbf{p} = [0,0,0]^T$ as shown in Figure 12.12. Also let the normal to the object at $\mathbf{p}$, the light and the viewing vectors, respectively, be

$$\overrightarrow{\mathbf{n}} = [0,2,0]^T, \quad \overrightarrow{\mathbf{l}} = [1,1,0]^T, \quad \overrightarrow{\mathbf{v}} = [0,1,1]^T.$$

The values of the emitted, ambient and incident intensity from the light source are

$$I_e = 2, \quad I_a = 1, \quad I_i = 12,$$

and the constant values are

$$k_a = 0.3, \quad k_d = 0.3, \quad k_s = 0.6, \quad n = 3.$$

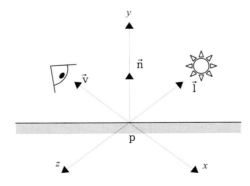

Figure 12.12. Simple Phong example.

In other words, the light source is twelve times more intense than the ambient light, and the object is self-illuminated and emits twice the ambient intensity. Also since $k_d + k_s = 0.9$, 10% of the incident light is absorbed by the object. Before we apply the Phong formula, we must compute the halfway vector and normalize all the vectors involved:

$$\hat{\mathbf{l}} = \frac{\vec{\mathbf{l}}}{|\vec{\mathbf{l}}|} = \frac{[1,1,0]^T}{\sqrt{1^2 + 1^2}} = \left[\frac{1}{\sqrt{2}}, \frac{1}{\sqrt{2}}, 0 \right]^T,$$

$$\hat{\mathbf{v}} = \frac{\vec{\mathbf{v}}}{|\vec{\mathbf{v}}|} = \frac{[0,1,1]^T}{\sqrt{1^2 + 1^2}} = \left[0, \frac{1}{\sqrt{2}}, \frac{1}{\sqrt{2}} \right]^T,$$

$$\vec{\mathbf{h}} = (\hat{\mathbf{l}} + \hat{\mathbf{v}})/2 = \left[\frac{1}{2\sqrt{2}}, \frac{1}{\sqrt{2}}, \frac{1}{2\sqrt{2}} \right]^T,$$

$$\hat{\mathbf{h}} = \frac{\vec{\mathbf{h}}}{|\vec{\mathbf{h}}|} = \frac{[\frac{1}{2\sqrt{2}}, \frac{1}{\sqrt{2}}, \frac{1}{2\sqrt{2}}]^T}{\sqrt{3}/2} = \left[\frac{1}{\sqrt{2}\sqrt{3}}, \frac{\sqrt{2}}{\sqrt{3}}, \frac{1}{\sqrt{2}\sqrt{3}} \right]^T,$$

$$\hat{\mathbf{n}} = \frac{[0,2,0]^T}{\sqrt{2^2}} = [0,1,0]^T.$$

We can now apply Equation (12.25):

$$I = 2 + 1 \cdot 0.3 + 12 \cdot \left(0.3 \cdot (\frac{1}{\sqrt{2}}) + 0.6 \cdot (\frac{\sqrt{2}}{\sqrt{3}})^3 \right) = 8.76.$$

This final intensity value corresponds to the specified viewing angle and is related to the input intensities. Notice that the angle between the directions of reflection and viewing is $\widehat{\mathbf{r}\mathbf{v}} = 2\widehat{\mathbf{n}\mathbf{h}} = 2\arccos(\frac{\sqrt{2}}{\sqrt{3}}) = 70°$. If the viewing direction coincided with the direction of reflection i.e.,

$$\hat{\mathbf{v}} = \left[-\frac{1}{\sqrt{2}}, \frac{1}{\sqrt{2}}, 0 \right]^T,$$

then the specular reflection would attain its maximum value since $\widehat{\mathbf{r}\mathbf{v}} = 2\widehat{\mathbf{n}\mathbf{h}} = 2\arccos(1) = 0°$:

$$\hat{\mathbf{h}} = [0,1,0]^T,$$

$$I = 2 + 1 \cdot 0.3 + 12 \cdot \left(0.3 \cdot (\frac{1}{\sqrt{2}}) + 0.6 \cdot 1^3 \right) = 12.05.$$

12.5 Phong Model Vectors

The Phong model requires a number of vectors for the computation of the illumination value at a surface point, namely $\overrightarrow{\mathbf{n}}$, $\overrightarrow{\mathbf{l}}$, $\overrightarrow{\mathbf{v}}$, and $\overrightarrow{\mathbf{r}}$ or $\overrightarrow{\mathbf{h}}$. It is important to use efficient formulae for the computation of these vectors, since such computation is repeated for every point where the model is applied.

12.5.1 The Normal Vector

The *normal vector* $\overrightarrow{\mathbf{n}}$ is defined as a vector perpendicular to a surface at a certain point. The direction of the normal vector defines the orientation of the surface and is extremely useful in computer graphics: two examples of its use are in illumination calculations and in back-face removal (see Chapter 5).

Normal vector for implicit surfaces. Implicit surfaces are defined by an equation of the form

$$f(x,y,z) = 0.$$

The normal vector at a point $\mathbf{p} = [a,b,c]^{\mathrm{T}}$ of such a surface is given by the gradient vector in the vicinity of $\mathbf{p}$:

$$\overrightarrow{\mathbf{n}} = \begin{bmatrix} \partial f/\partial x \\ \partial f/\partial y \\ \partial f/\partial z \end{bmatrix}.$$

In the case of a planar surface defined by

$$f(x,y,z) = ax + by + cz + d = 0,$$

the normal vector, which is constant over the entire planar surface, is

$$\overrightarrow{\mathbf{n}} = [a,b,c]^{\mathrm{T}}.$$

Normal vector for parametric surfaces. Surfaces are often represented parametrically (see Chapter 7). In three dimensions, a surface is represented by three parametric equations in terms of two parameters u and v:

$$x = f_x(u,v),$$

$$y = f_y(u,v),$$

$$z = f_z(u,v).$$

The normal vector is then

$$\vec{\mathbf{n}} = \frac{\partial \vec{\mathbf{f}}}{\partial \mathbf{u}} \times \frac{\partial \vec{\mathbf{f}}}{\partial \mathbf{v}},$$ (12.29)

where

$$\vec{\mathbf{f}} = \begin{bmatrix} f_x \\ f_y \\ f_z \end{bmatrix}, \quad \frac{\partial \vec{\mathbf{f}}}{\partial \mathbf{u}} = \begin{bmatrix} \partial f_x/\partial u \\ \partial f_y/\partial u \\ \partial f_z/\partial u \end{bmatrix}, \quad \frac{\partial \vec{\mathbf{f}}}{\partial \mathbf{v}} = \begin{bmatrix} \partial f_x/\partial v \\ \partial f_y/\partial v \\ \partial f_z/\partial v \end{bmatrix}.$$

Normal vector for polygons. Polygons, and in particular triangles, are the usual building element for model composition. In practice the equation of a polygon's plane is not known and the polygon is given in terms of a list of its vertices. There are a number of ways to compute the normal vector in this case.

Given three consecutive, non-collinear vertices of a polygon $\mathbf{v_{i-1}}$, $\mathbf{v_i}$, and $\mathbf{v_{i+1}}$, we can compute the normal vector to the polygon's plane by taking the cross product of the two vectors defined by the three points:

$$\vec{\mathbf{n}} = (\mathbf{v_{i+1}} - \mathbf{v_i}) \times (\mathbf{v_{i-1}} - \mathbf{v_i}).$$

Care should be taken as the cross product is not associative. The above computation follows the right-hand rule: if the first vector is the thumb and the second the index finger, then the normal is the middle finger of the right hand (Figure 12.13). As graphics APIs usually allow the definition of polygon perimeters to be either clockwise or counter-clockwise (when looking from the "outside"), it is essential to select the correct definition, otherwise all normal computations will be reversed and objects will take an "inside-out" look.

For polygons with more than three vertices, it is possible in practice that not all vertices are exactly coplanar; this can be due to errors in digitization, for example. We may then compute the polygon normal as the average of the normal vectors given by each pair of consecutive polygon edges. Another technique suitable for non-planar polygons is due to Martin-Newell [Suth74b]; if $[x_i, y_i, z_i]^T, i = 1, 2, ..., n$ are the n vertices of a polygon, then the coefficients a, b, c of an approximating plane are computed as

$$a = \sum_{i=1}^{n} (y_i - y_{i\oplus 1})(z_i + z_{i\oplus 1}),$$
$$b = \sum_{i=1}^{n} (z_i - z_{i\oplus 1})(x_i + x_{i\oplus 1}),$$ (12.30)
$$c = \sum_{i=1}^{n} (x_i - x_{i\oplus 1})(y_i + y_{i\oplus 1}),$$

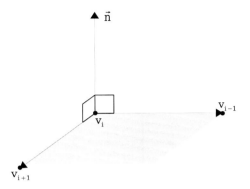

Figure 12.13. Right-hand rule.

where $\oplus$ represents addition modulo n. The d (constant) coefficient of the plane equation can be computed (if required) using the coordinates of one of the polygon's vertices:

$$d = -(ax_1 + by_1 + cz_1).$$

Another way of computing the normal vector uses three known non-colinear vertices of a polygon. If $[x_1, y_1, z_1]^T$, $[x_2, y_2, z_2]^T$, and $[x_3, y_3, z_3]^T$ are three such points, then they must satisfy the plane equation

$$ax_1 + by_1 + cz_1 = -1,$$
$$ax_2 + by_2 + cz_2 = -1,$$
$$ax_3 + by_3 + cz_3 = -1,$$

or

$$\begin{bmatrix} x_1 & y_1 & z_1 \\ x_2 & y_2 & z_2 \\ x_3 & y_3 & z_3 \end{bmatrix} \begin{bmatrix} a \\ b \\ c \end{bmatrix} = \begin{bmatrix} -1 \\ -1 \\ -1 \end{bmatrix},$$

or

$$\mathbf{XC} = \mathbf{D}.$$

So

$$\mathbf{C} = \mathbf{X}^{-1}\mathbf{D}.$$

Numerical Example. Given a polygon with vertices $\mathbf{v_1} = [0,0,0]^T$, $\mathbf{v_2} = [1,0,0]^T$, $\mathbf{v_3} = [1,1,0]^T$, and $\mathbf{v_4} = [0,1,0.5]^T$ (Figure 12.14), we are required to compute its normal vector. Notice that the polygon is slightly non-planar. We

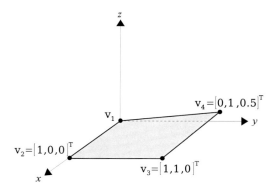

Figure 12.14. Example of normal calculation.

shall consider two suitable methods: the average of the normals for each pair of successive edges and Martin-Newell's technique.

We first compute four normal vectors (one for each pair of successive edges); these normals are indexed by the vertex onto which both edges are incident:

$$\vec{\mathbf{n}}_{v_1} = [1,0,0]^{\mathrm{T}} \times [0,1,0.5]^{\mathrm{T}} = [0,-0.5,1]^{\mathrm{T}},$$
$$\vec{\mathbf{n}}_{v_2} = [0,1,0]^{\mathrm{T}} \times [-1,0,0]^{\mathrm{T}} = [0,0,1]^{\mathrm{T}},$$
$$\vec{\mathbf{n}}_{v_3} = [-1,0,0.5]^{\mathrm{T}} \times [0,-1,0]^{\mathrm{T}} = [0.5,0,1]^{\mathrm{T}},$$
$$\vec{\mathbf{n}}_{v_4} = [0,-1,-0.5]^{\mathrm{T}} \times [1,0,-0.5]^{\mathrm{T}} = [0.25,-0.5,1]^{\mathrm{T}}.$$

We can next compute the polygon normal by averaging the above. To give equal weight to all edges, we normalize the vectors before summation:

$$\vec{\mathbf{n}} = \frac{\hat{\mathbf{n}}_{v_1} + \hat{\mathbf{n}}_{v_2} + \hat{\mathbf{n}}_{v_3} + \hat{\mathbf{n}}_{v_4}}{4} = [0.17, -0.22, 0.91]^{\mathrm{T}}$$

and

$$\hat{\mathbf{n}} = [0.18, -0.23, 0.96]^{\mathrm{T}}.$$

Using Martin-Newell's technique ,we get

$$a = 0 \cdot 0 + (-1) \cdot 0 + 0 \cdot 0.5 + 1 \cdot 0.5 = 0.5,$$
$$b = 0 \cdot 1 + 0 \cdot 2 + (-0.5) \cdot 1 + 0.5 \cdot 0 = -0.5,$$
$$c = (-1) \cdot 0 + 0 \cdot 1 + 1 \cdot 2 + 0 \cdot 0.5 = 2.$$

Thus, $\vec{\mathbf{n}} = [0.5, -0.5, 2]^{\mathrm{T}}$ and

$$\hat{\mathbf{n}} = [0.24, -0.24, 0.94]^{\mathrm{T}}.$$

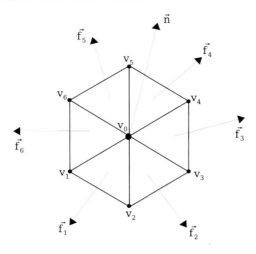

Figure 12.15. The star of a vertex.

Vertex normal vector for polygonal meshes. Polygonal meshes are often used to approximate objects with smooth change of their surface normal vector, i.e., without discontinuities (e.g., a sphere). We shall assume objects that consist of a single manifold surface (i.e., each edge is shared by precisely two polygons).

In illumination (and also for other algorithms), we need the normal vector to an object's surface at a discrete set of points covered by the surface (e.g., the pixel grid). To this end, it is common to determine the normal at the vertices of the polygonal mesh as a weighted average of the normals to the adjacent faces to the vertex [Meye03], and then use this normal to perform bilinear interpolation along edges and finally across edges, on points of the underlying grid. The polygons that are adjacent to a vertex are often called the *1-ring neighbors* or the *star* of the vertex (Figure 12.15). Thus, the paradoxical term *vertex normal* refers to a weighted average of the normals to the faces of the vertex's star.

There are a number of approaches for computing the unit vertex normal $\hat{\mathbf{n}}$, and we shall outline three of the most common [Jirk02]. First, the weights can be taken to be equal. This amounts to normalizing (to unit length) the normals of the faces of the star $\vec{\mathbf{f_i}}$ before averaging:

$$\hat{\mathbf{n}} = \frac{\sum_{i=1}^{m} \hat{\mathbf{f_i}}}{|\sum_{i=1}^{m} \hat{\mathbf{f_i}}|},$$
(12.31)

where $\hat{\mathbf{f_i}} = \vec{\mathbf{f_i}} / |\vec{\mathbf{f_i}}|$ and m is the number of faces in the star. A second approach observes that larger polygons should contribute more than smaller ones; the face normals are thus weighted by the area of the corresponding polygons. In the case of triangular faces, this simply amounts to taking the face normals as computed by the outer product of the vectors represented by two of the triangle's edges. This is because the outer product is equal to twice the area of the triangle:

$$\hat{\mathbf{n}} = \frac{\sum_{i=1}^{m} \vec{\mathbf{f_i}}}{|\sum_{i=1}^{m} \vec{\mathbf{f_i}}|}. \tag{12.32}$$

Third, Thuermer and Wuthrich [Thue98] observed that in order to ensure that vertex normals are invariant to mesh restructuring, a good weight is the incident angle θ of the faces of the star. For example, in Figure 12.15, the incident angle for the first face is $\theta_1 = \widehat{\mathbf{v_1}\mathbf{v_0}\mathbf{v_2}}$. The angle θ can be computed by taking the arccos of the dot product of the vectors defined by the incident edges that form it:

$$\hat{\mathbf{n}} = \frac{\sum_{i=1}^{m} \theta_i \hat{\mathbf{f}}_i}{|\sum_{i=1}^{m} \theta_i \hat{\mathbf{f}}_i|}. \tag{12.33}$$

Note that vertex normals should be computed before the perspective division (projection).

Symbolic Example.   We shall give a symbolic example to simply illustrate the computations of the vertex normal. Take the situation depicted in Figure 12.15; m is 6 as there are six polygons in the star. In order to evaluate all the vertex normal expressions above, we need to compute the $\vec{\mathbf{f_i}}$, the $\hat{\mathbf{f}}_i$, and the θ_i. Take the first triangle $\mathbf{v_0}\mathbf{v_1}\mathbf{v_2}$,

$$\vec{\mathbf{f_1}} = \vec{\mathbf{v_0}\mathbf{v_1}} \times \vec{\mathbf{v_0}\mathbf{v_2}},$$

$$\hat{\mathbf{f}}_1 = \frac{\vec{\mathbf{f_1}}}{|\vec{\mathbf{f_1}}|},$$

$$\theta_1 = \arccos(\frac{\vec{\mathbf{v_0}\mathbf{v_1}}}{|\vec{\mathbf{v_0}\mathbf{v_1}}|} \cdot \frac{\vec{\mathbf{v_0}\mathbf{v_2}}}{|\vec{\mathbf{v_0}\mathbf{v_2}}|}).$$

Similar computations are performed for the other five triangles in the star and expressions (12.31)–(12.33) can then be evaluated.

12.5.2 The Reflection Vector

The *reflection vector* $\overrightarrow{\mathbf{r}}$ is computed by noticing that the angles between the pairs of vectors $(\hat{\mathbf{l}}, \hat{\mathbf{n}})$ and $(\hat{\mathbf{n}}, \overrightarrow{\mathbf{r}})$ are equal and that $\hat{\mathbf{l}}$, $\hat{\mathbf{n}}$, and $\overrightarrow{\mathbf{r}}$ are coplanar (Figure 12.16).

Let $\overrightarrow{\mathbf{r_1}}$ be the vector defined by the projection of $\hat{\mathbf{l}}$ onto the axis of $\hat{\mathbf{n}}$. We have

$$|\overrightarrow{\mathbf{r_1}}| = |\hat{\mathbf{l}}| \cos\theta = |\hat{\mathbf{l}}|(\hat{\mathbf{n}} \cdot \hat{\mathbf{l}}) = \hat{\mathbf{n}} \cdot \hat{\mathbf{l}},$$

since $\hat{\mathbf{l}}$ is a unit vector, so

$$\overrightarrow{\mathbf{r_1}} = \hat{\mathbf{n}}|\overrightarrow{\mathbf{r_1}}| = \hat{\mathbf{n}}(\hat{\mathbf{n}} \cdot \hat{\mathbf{l}}).$$

We also have

$$\overrightarrow{\mathbf{r}} = \overrightarrow{\mathbf{r_1}} + \overrightarrow{\mathbf{t}} \qquad \overrightarrow{\mathbf{t}} = \overrightarrow{\mathbf{r_1}} - \hat{\mathbf{l}}.$$

Thus,

$$\overrightarrow{\mathbf{r}} = 2\overrightarrow{\mathbf{r_1}} - \hat{\mathbf{l}} = 2\hat{\mathbf{n}}(\hat{\mathbf{n}} \cdot \hat{\mathbf{l}}) - \hat{\mathbf{l}}, \qquad (12.34)$$

which requires six multiplications and five additions. There are special cases in which $\overrightarrow{\mathbf{r}}$ can be computed more cheaply, but we shall not consider them since, when performance is an issue, the reflection vector is replaced by the halfway vector as shown in Equation 12.25.

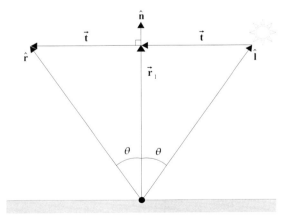

Figure 12.16. Computation of the reflection vector.

12.5.3   The Light, View, and Halfway Vectors

The *light* and *view vectors* $\overrightarrow{\mathbf{l}}$ and $\overrightarrow{\mathbf{v}}$ are either given constant vectors, if the light and view points are placed at infinity, or they are simply computed as

$$\overrightarrow{\mathbf{l}} = \mathbf{l} - \mathbf{p}, \tag{12.35}$$

$$\overrightarrow{\mathbf{v}} = \mathbf{v} - \mathbf{p}, \tag{12.36}$$

where $\mathbf{p}$ is the object point and $\mathbf{l}$ and $\mathbf{v}$ are the given light and view points, respectively. The halfway vector $\overrightarrow{\mathbf{h}}$, which is useful for the specular reflection, is then computed as the average of the unit $\overrightarrow{\mathbf{l}}$ and $\overrightarrow{\mathbf{v}}$ vectors:

$$\overrightarrow{\mathbf{h}} = (\hat{\mathbf{l}} + \hat{\mathbf{v}})/2, \tag{12.37}$$

with its normalized form being Equation (12.24).

12.6   Illumination Algorithms Based on the Phong Model

Historically, illumination has been increasingly applied to produce realistic synthetic images. In 1969 Warnock introduced the concept of diminishing intensity according to depth [Warn69]; objects were illuminated according to their distance from the light source (which usually coincided with the view point). In 1971 Gouraud suggested the interpolation of intensity values within polygons from intensity values computed at the vertices [Gour71]. Phong then proposed the computation of intensity values at every pixel by linearly interpolating vertex normals and using the model he introduced in 1975 [Phon75]. There are instances where the linear interpolation of the vertex normals does not work well; Overveld [Over97] proposed a quadratic interpolation scheme in 1997. We shall next describe some algorithms for the computation of illumination values within a polygon; they progressively provide higher realism at increasing computational complexity. Complexity however is becoming less of an issue as operations are implemented on graphics hardware.

12.6.1   Constant Shading

The simplest illumination algorithm for polygonal objects applies a constant illumination value to each polygonal facet. There is no specular reflection and no reduction of illumination values with distance. Only constant ambient lighting and diffuse reflection are incorporated into this algorithm. The light and view points coincide and are both placed at infinity ($\overrightarrow{\mathbf{l}} = \overrightarrow{\mathbf{v}}$), which eliminates shadows and makes the $(\hat{\mathbf{n}} \cdot \hat{\mathbf{l}})$ term constant for each polygon. If the light and view points are on the positive z-axis then $\hat{\mathbf{l}} = \hat{\mathbf{v}} = [0,0,1]^T$, and $(\hat{\mathbf{n}} \cdot \hat{\mathbf{l}}) = n_z$ for $\hat{\mathbf{n}} = [n_x, n_y, n_z]^T$. The illumination equation (12.26) then becomes

$$I = I_e + I_a k_a + I_i k_d n_z. \tag{12.38}$$

The intensity value I is computed once for each polygon and is used for all pixels covered by the polygon (Color Plate XVII (left)).

Unfortunately the human eye is quite sensitive to intensity discontinuities (Mach-band phenomenon) and polygon silhouettes stand out with this algorithm, giving objects a "polygonal" look. This problem arises from the fact that a polygon mesh that is supposed to approximate a curved surface is actually discretely sampling this surface. By using a sufficiently high sample density (polygon count), the shape difference between the curved surface and the mesh could be made arbitrary small. However, high sampling density implies large data volumes and requires large processing capacity; it is therefore advantageous to compensate for the illumination artifacts (i.e., the under-sampling artifacts) by some form of illumination interpolation.

12.6.2 Gouraud Shading

Gouraud shading is a simple illumination interpolation algorithm and, if the sampling density is sufficiently high, it can capture local maxima (highlights) and minima of the shading distribution over the polygon mesh.

The Gouraud algorithm computes intensity values for pixels inside a polygon by interpolating the intensity values at its vertices. Intensity values at the vertices are estimated using the Phong model. Since intensity is a scalar value, simple scalar interpolation is performed within the polygon. Vertex normals are computed (see Section 12.5.1) and used to evaluate the Phong equation at the vertices. The vertex intensities are then bi-linearly interpolated along the polygon edges and between the edges (along the scanlines). In Figure 12.17, intensities I_1, I_2, and I_3 are computed using the Phong model while I_a, I_b and I_s are computed by interpolation:

$$I_{\mathbf{a}} = I_1 \frac{y_{\mathbf{s}} - y_2}{y_1 - y_2} + I_2 \frac{y_1 - y_{\mathbf{s}}}{y_1 - y_2} = \frac{1}{y_1 - y_2}(I_1(y_{\mathbf{s}} - y_2) + I_2(y_1 - y_{\mathbf{s}})),$$

$$I_{\mathbf{b}} = \frac{1}{y_1 - y_3}(I_1(y_{\mathbf{s}} - y_3) + I_3(y_1 - y_{\mathbf{s}})),$$

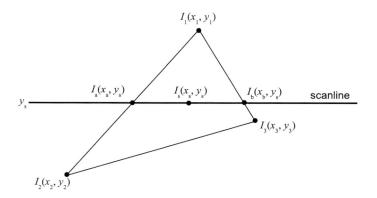

Figure 12.17. Gouraud algorithm computations.

$$I_s = \frac{1}{x_b - x_a}(I_a(x_b - x_s) + I_b(x_s - x_a)). \qquad (12.39)$$

Intensity values are computed incrementally within a scanline. If s_1 and s_2 are the indices of two pixels on the same scanline, then

$$I_{s_1} = \frac{1}{x_b - x_a}(I_a(x_b - x_{s_1}) + I_b(x_{s_1} - x_a)),$$

$$I_{s_2} = \frac{1}{x_b - x_a}(I_a(x_b - x_{s_2}) + I_b(x_{s_2} - x_a)),$$

and, by subtracting the above equations,

$$\Delta I_s = I_{s_2} - I_{s_1} = \frac{x_{s_2} - x_{s_1}}{x_b - x_a}(I_b - I_a) = \frac{\Delta x}{x_b - x_a}(I_b - I_a),$$

which, in the case of neighboring pixels ($\Delta x = 1$), becomes

$$\Delta I_s = \frac{I_b - I_a}{x_b - x_a}.$$

Thus, the intensity of neighboring pixels can be computed incrementally:

$$I_{s,n} = I_{s,n-1} + \Delta I_s.$$

The visual effect of Gouraud shading is significantly better than constant shading (Color Plate XVII (middle)).

12.6.3 Phong Shading

Unfortunately the sampling density (polygon count) is rarely sufficient to capture highlights with the Gouraud algorithm. These only arise when the reflection vector $\vec{\mathbf{r}}$ (almost) equals the view vector $\vec{\mathbf{v}}$. In Gouraud shading the vectors are not interpolated within the polygon but are only used to compute intensities at the vertices (Figure 12.18). Also the Gouraud algorithm does not eliminate mach-bands; the linear intensity interpolation leaves second-order intensity discontinuities that are often visible.

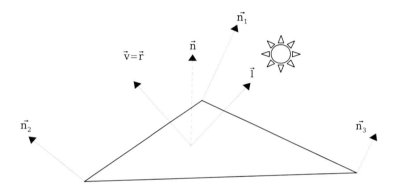

Figure 12.18. Vector set-up for highlight.

The Phong algorithm solves the above problems by applying the Phong model to each pixel. The required unit normal vectors are computed by bi-linear interpolation from the unit vertex normals (Figure 12.19).

We have

$$\vec{\mathbf{n}}_a = \frac{1}{y_1 - y_2}\left(\hat{\mathbf{n}}_1(y_s - y_2) + \hat{\mathbf{n}}_2(y_1 - y_s)\right),$$

$$\vec{\mathbf{n}}_b = \frac{1}{y_1 - y_3}\left(\hat{\mathbf{n}}_1(y_s - y_3) + \hat{\mathbf{n}}_3(y_1 - y_s)\right),$$

$$\hat{\mathbf{n}}_s = \frac{1}{x_b - x_a}\left(\hat{\mathbf{n}}_a(x_b - x_s) + \hat{\mathbf{n}}_b(x_s - x_a)\right). \qquad (12.40)$$

The following relations hold for neighboring pixels on the same scanline, and they can be used to facilitate incremental computation:[3]

---

[3] $\hat{\mathbf{n}}_s = [n_{sx}, n_{sy}, n_{sz}]^T$, $\hat{\mathbf{n}}_a = [n_{ax}, n_{ay}, n_{az}]^T$, and $\hat{\mathbf{n}}_b = [n_{bx}, n_{by}, n_{bz}]^T$.

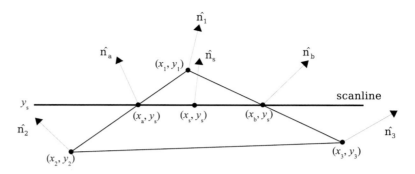

Figure 12.19. Phong algorithm computations.

$$n_{sx,n} = n_{sx,n-1} + \Delta n_{sx},$$

$$n_{sy,n} = n_{sy,n-1} + \Delta n_{sy},$$

$$n_{sz,n} = n_{sz,n-1} + \Delta n_{sz},$$

where

$$\Delta n_{sx} = \frac{n_{bx} - n_{ax}}{x_b - x_a},$$

$$\Delta n_{sy} = \frac{n_{by} - n_{ay}}{x_b - x_a},$$

$$\Delta n_{sz} = \frac{n_{bz} - n_{az}}{x_b - x_a}.$$

The result of the Phong algorithm is a significant improvement over Gouraud (Color Plate XVII (right)) but also requires considerably more computation since the illumination equation is evaluated at every pixel. This is no longer a major concern, however, as the Phong algorithm can now be found implemented on graphics accelerators.

12.6.4   Quadratic Interpolation of Vertex Normals

Images generated by means of the Phong shading algorithm are of acceptable quality, provided the polygonal mesh is sufficiently dense. For larger polygons, where the rate of change of the normal vectors over the surface can be high, shading artifacts can arise. The *silhouette edge problem* is probably the most notorious one. In Figure 12.20, the normal vectors (computed by linear interpolation from the vertex normals) do not vary at all over the surface, resulting in a completely

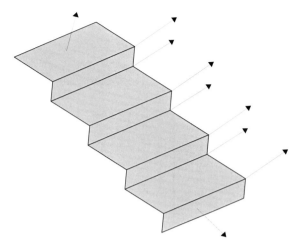

Figure 12.20. Silhouette edge problem.

flat illumination appearance which is at odds with the appearance of the silhouette.

The vertex normal interpolation essentially aims to reconstruct a surface from
a discretely sampled version. Reconstruction cannot add information, but at least
we can try to come up with a reconstructed surface that is consistent with the
sampled data, that is, that both interpolates the normal data at the vertices of the
polygon mesh and is perpendicular to the normal vectors. The linear interpolation
of vertex normals in Phong shading is not consistent in this sense, as can be seen
in Figure 12.20.

Overveld and Wyvill [Over97] showed that the quadratic interpolation of nor-
mals achieves better results. If $\hat{\mathbf{n}}_0$ and $\hat{\mathbf{n}}_1$ are the normal vectors to be interpolated
and $\overrightarrow{\delta}$ is the vector defined by the subtraction of the first from the last interpolation point ($\overrightarrow{\delta}$ corresponds to a polygon edge or part of a scanline), then the
interpolated vector $\overrightarrow{\mathbf{n}}(s)$ is given as

$$\overrightarrow{\mathbf{n}}(s) = \hat{\mathbf{n}}_0 + s\,\overrightarrow{\mathbf{a}} + s^2\,\overrightarrow{\mathbf{b}}, \qquad (12.41)$$

with $s \in [0,1]$ and

$$\overrightarrow{\mathbf{a}} = \hat{\mathbf{n}}_1 - \hat{\mathbf{n}}_0 - \overrightarrow{\mathbf{b}},$$

$$\overrightarrow{\mathbf{b}} = 3\left(\frac{(\hat{\mathbf{n}}_0 + \hat{\mathbf{n}}_1) \cdot \overrightarrow{\delta}}{\overrightarrow{\delta}^{\,2}}\right)\overrightarrow{\delta}.$$

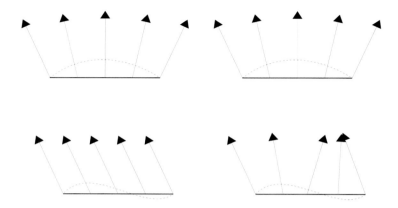

Figure 12.21. Linear (left) versus quadratic (right) vector interpolation; the dashed line shows the surface being reconstructed (from [Over97]).

As expected, $\vec{\mathbf{n}}(0) = \hat{\mathbf{n}}_0$ and $\vec{\mathbf{n}}(1) = \hat{\mathbf{n}}_1$. This quadratic interpolation scheme can be efficiently implemented by taking the forward differences of the quadratic function at a cost two vector additions per pixel (as opposed to one vector addition per pixel for linear interpolation).

Figure 12.21 shows the effect of the above quadratic interpolation scheme, and Color Plate XVIII demonstrates the benefit of the scheme, especially in cases where the sampling density (polygon count) is relatively low.

Numerical Example.   Suppose that we are given the triangle mesh shown in Figure 12.22.

$$\mathbf{v_0} = [2, 2, 1]^T, \qquad \mathbf{v_1} = [6, 2, 1]^T, \qquad \mathbf{v_2} = [4, 5, 1]^T,$$
$$\overrightarrow{\mathbf{n_{v_0}}} = [-1, -1, 1]^T, \qquad \overrightarrow{\mathbf{n_{v_1}}} = [1, 0, 0]^T, \qquad \overrightarrow{\mathbf{n_{v_2}}} = [0, 1, 1]^T,$$
$$\mathbf{a} = [2.66, 3, 1]^T, \qquad \mathbf{b} = [5.33, 3, 1]^T, \qquad \mathbf{s} = [4, 3, 1]^T.$$

Let us assume, as in the numerical example in Section 12.4, that the values of the emitted, ambient, and incident intensity from the light source are

$$I_e = 2, \quad I_a = 1, \quad I_i = 12,$$

and the constant values are

$$k_a = 0.3, \quad k_d = 0.3, \quad k_s = 0.6, \quad n = 3.$$

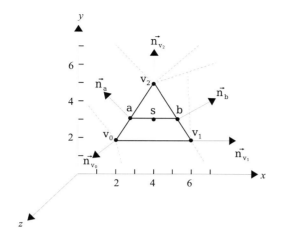

Figure 12.22. Simple triangle mesh.

In addition, to simplify calculations, let the light and view point be positioned at infinity on the positive z-axis:

$$\hat{\mathbf{l}} = \hat{\mathbf{v}} = [0,0,1]^{\text{T}}.$$

Constant shading. We compute the polygon normal as

$$\overrightarrow{\mathbf{n}} = (\mathbf{v_1} - \mathbf{v_0}) \times (\mathbf{v_2} - \mathbf{v_0}) = [0,0,12]^{\text{T}}$$

or

$$\hat{\mathbf{n}} = [0,0,1]^{\text{T}},$$

and from Equation (12.38),

$$I = 2 + 1 \cdot 0.3 + 12 \cdot 0.3 \cdot 1 = \mathbf{5.9}.$$

Gouraud shading. We first normalize the vertex normals

$$\hat{\mathbf{n}}_{\mathbf{v_0}} = [-\tfrac{1}{\sqrt{3}}, -\tfrac{1}{\sqrt{3}}, \tfrac{1}{\sqrt{3}}]^{\text{T}}, \quad \hat{\mathbf{n}}_{\mathbf{v_1}} = [1,0,0]^{\text{T}}, \quad \hat{\mathbf{n}}_{\mathbf{v_2}} = [0, \tfrac{1}{\sqrt{2}}, \tfrac{1}{\sqrt{2}}]^{\text{T}}.$$

We then use the Phong model to compute the intensities at the vertices:

$$I_{\mathbf{v_0}} = 2 + 1 \cdot 0.3 + 12(0.3(\hat{\mathbf{n}}_{\mathbf{v_0}} \cdot \hat{\mathbf{l}}) + 0.6(\hat{\mathbf{n}}_{\mathbf{v_0}} \cdot \hat{\mathbf{h}})^3) = 5.76,$$
$$I_{\mathbf{v_1}} = 2 + 1 \cdot 0.3 + 12(0.3(\hat{\mathbf{n}}_{\mathbf{v_1}} \cdot \hat{\mathbf{l}}) + 0.6(\hat{\mathbf{n}}_{\mathbf{v_1}} \cdot \hat{\mathbf{h}})^3) = 2.3,$$
$$I_{\mathbf{v_2}} = 2 + 1 \cdot 0.3 + 12(0.3(\hat{\mathbf{n}}_{\mathbf{v_2}} \cdot \hat{\mathbf{l}}) + 0.6(\hat{\mathbf{n}}_{\mathbf{v_2}} \cdot \hat{\mathbf{h}})^3) = 7.39,$$

and using Equation (12.39),

$$I_{\mathbf{a}} = \frac{1}{3}(1 \cdot I_{\mathbf{v}_2} + 2 \cdot I_{\mathbf{v}_0}) = 6.3,$$

$$I_{\mathbf{b}} = \frac{1}{3}(1 \cdot I_{\mathbf{v}_2} + 2 \cdot I_{\mathbf{v}_1}) = 4.0,$$

$$I_{\mathbf{s}} = \frac{1}{2.67}(1.33 \cdot I_{\mathbf{a}} + 1.33 \cdot I_{\mathbf{b}}) = \mathbf{5.13}.$$

Phong shading. We use linear interpolation to compute the normals at the edge points **a** and **b** from the unit vertex normals:

$$\vec{\mathbf{n}_{\mathbf{a}}} = \frac{1}{3}(1 \cdot \hat{\mathbf{n}}_{\mathbf{v}_2} + 2 \cdot \hat{\mathbf{n}}_{\mathbf{v}_0}) = [-0.39, 0.15, 0.62]^{\mathrm{T}},$$

$$\vec{\mathbf{n}_{\mathbf{b}}} = \frac{1}{3}(1 \cdot \hat{\mathbf{n}}_{\mathbf{v}_2} + 2 \cdot \hat{\mathbf{n}}_{\mathbf{v}_1}) = [0.67, 0.71, 0.71]^{\mathrm{T}}.$$

We then convert them to unit vectors

$$\hat{\mathbf{n}}_{\mathbf{a}} = [-0.52, 0.2, 0.83]^{\mathrm{T}},$$

$$\hat{\mathbf{n}}_{\mathbf{b}} = [0.55, 0.59, 0.59]^{\mathrm{T}},$$

and compute the unit normal vector at the scanline point **s**:

$$\vec{\mathbf{n}_{\mathbf{s}}} = \frac{1}{2.67}(1.33 \cdot \hat{\mathbf{n}}_{\mathbf{a}} + 1.33 \cdot \hat{\mathbf{n}}_{\mathbf{b}}) = [0.02, 0.4, 0.71]^{\mathrm{T}},$$

$$\hat{\mathbf{n}}_{\mathbf{s}} = [0.02, 0.49, 0.87]^{\mathrm{T}}.$$

The intensity at **s** is finally computed by applying the Phong model using the unit normal vector $\hat{\mathbf{n}}_{\mathbf{s}}$:

$$I_{\mathbf{s}} = 2 + 1 \cdot 0.3 + 12(0.3(\hat{\mathbf{n}}_{\mathbf{s}} \cdot \hat{\mathbf{I}}) + 0.6(\hat{\mathbf{n}}_{\mathbf{s}} \cdot \hat{\mathbf{h}})^3) = \mathbf{10.25}.$$

Notice the considerably higher intensity value computed by Phong shading when compared to constant or Gouraud shading. This is easily explained by the existence of a highlight at **s**.

The quadratic interpolation scheme computes the intensity $I_{\mathbf{s}}$ in a manner similar to Phong shading; the only difference being the quadratic formulae used for the computation of $\hat{\mathbf{n}}_{\mathbf{a}}$, $\hat{\mathbf{n}}_{\mathbf{b}}$, and $\hat{\mathbf{n}}_{\mathbf{s}}$.

12.7   The Cook–Torrance Illumination Model⊛

Although the Phong model produces convincing results for various types of glossy materials or dull but not particularly rough surfaces, objects rendered with the

Phong reflectance model often appear too plastic. The metallic shine or the off-specular-direction highlights are not captured correctly for many shiny materials. Also the reflected light-scattering distribution due to the geometric variation of a rough surface cannot be captured by the Phong model.

Cook and Torrance [Cook82] extended the Phong model as well as the model suggested by Blinn [Blin77], to build a general illumination model for rough surfaces that takes into account the directional distribution and the wavelength dependence of the reflected light.

Like the Phong model, Cook and Torrance distinguished the reflected light in three components: the ambient term, the diffuse scattering, and the specular highlight, but instead of using a simple approximate cosine rule for the specular and diffuse components, they provide a modeling and parameterization of the BRDF f_r of a material.[4] More specifically, f_r is assumed to be linearly composed of two distinct terms, a pure diffuse and a pure specular one:

$$f_r = k_d f_d + k_s f_s, \qquad k_d + k_s = 1. \tag{12.42}$$

The above assumption may not hold, of course, for some complex materials [Glas95]. The Cook–Torrance reflectance model for N_L light sources is described by

$$I_r = I_a f_a + \sum_{l=1}^{N_L} I_i^{(l)} (\hat{\mathbf{n}} \cdot \hat{\mathbf{l}}^{(l)}) \ [k_s f_s + k_d f_d] \ d\vec{\omega}_i^{(l)}, \tag{12.43}$$

where $I_i^{(l)}$ is the incident light intensity from light source l located at a direction $\hat{\mathbf{l}}^{(l)}$ through a solid angle $\vec{\omega}_i^{(l)}$, and $\hat{\mathbf{n}}$ is the normal vector at the given surface location.

The quantity $I_a f_a$ is the ambient term and I_a can be regarded as constant, as in the Phong model. In the original paper, this term was multiplied by a visibility factor f that represented the amount of incoming ambient light that was not blocked by the surrounding environment. A distant uniformly luminous hemisphere (that represents the indirect lighting from other reflecting surfaces) radiates light toward the inspected surface point $\mathbf{p}$. The portion of this light that finally reaches the surface depends on the amount of the unblocked solid angle around the point. If we introduce a binary visibility function $V(\mathbf{p}, \hat{\mathbf{l}})$ that takes its maximum value 1 when there is a clear line of sight between point $\mathbf{p}$ and the surrounding distant hemisphere in the direction $\hat{\mathbf{l}}$, this factor becomes

---

[4]The BRDF f_r represents here the transfer of energy between a differential incoming and a differential outgoing solid angle $d\vec{\omega}_i \rightarrow d\vec{\omega}_r$.

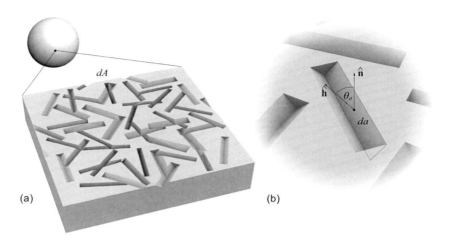

Figure 12.23. The Torrance–Sparrow modeling of rough surfaces. (a) A surface consists of arbitrarily oriented V-shaped grooves. (b) Close-up on a groove.

$$f = \int_{\text{unblocked } \Omega} (\hat{\mathbf{n}} \cdot \hat{\mathbf{l}}) d\vec{\omega} = \int_{\Omega} (\hat{\mathbf{n}} \cdot \hat{\mathbf{l}}) V(\mathbf{p}, \hat{\mathbf{l}}) d\vec{\omega}. \qquad (12.44)$$

This concept was also exploited in the work of Zhukov et al. [Zhuk98b] to derive an empirical model to simulate diffuse global illumination—more on this in Chapter 16.

In the reflectance model of Equation (12.43), f_d is the diffuse BRDF of a Lambertian surface (see Equation (12.18)); f_a uses the same distribution as f_d. The specular part of the BRDF depends on the relative location of the observer and the properties of the material.

For the derivation of f_s, Cook and Torrance rely on the micro-facet model of Torrance and Sparrow [Torr67]. In this widely adopted modeling of rough materials, a surface is assumed to be composed of long symmetric V-shaped grooves, each consisting of two planar facets (Figure 12.23(a)) tilted at equal but opposite angles to the surface normal at dA. In order to estimate the specular reflectivity of the surface, the facets are considered perfect mirrors and, therefore, reflect light only in the direction of perfect reflection. The slope of the facets (polar angle) θ_a as well as the orientation of the cavities (azimuth) φ_a are determined by a statistical distribution that characterizes the material (Figure 12.23(b)).

In order for the Torrance–Sparrow model to work, the area da of the micro-facets is small compared to the inspected area dA, where the reflectance is calculated. Also, the wavelength λ of the incident light is supposed to be significantly smaller than the dimensions of the facets in order to avoid interference phenomena and be able to work with geometrical optics and dispense with wave theory.

According to the modification of Blinn to the Phong model [Blin77], we achieve perfect reflection when a face's normal is equal to the halfway vector $\hat{\mathbf{h}}$ (see Equation (12.24)). The shape and angular dependence of the specular highlight is determined by the aggregation of the contributions of the perfectly reflected light from all facets. Due to the fact that the micro-facets are perfect mirrors, the contribution of each one of them is binary, i.e., full reflected light from direction $\hat{\mathbf{l}}$ to $\hat{\mathbf{v}}$ or no light at all. Therefore, the fraction D of micro-facets facing in the direction of $\hat{\mathbf{h}}$ determines the fraction of incident light that can be reflected back to the environment in the view direction. Many formulations for the micro-facet distribution have been proposed and Cook and Torrance singled out two of them, the Gaussian distribution model found in [Blin77] (Torrance–Sparrow) and the Beckmann [Beck63] distribution. The first is easier to compute and the second one is more physically correct, as it does not depend on any arbitrary constants and results in absolute reflectance values. The two distributions are

$$
\begin{aligned}
D_{(\text{Gaussian})} &= c \cdot e^{-(\theta_a/m)^2}, \\
D_{(\text{Beckmann})} &= \frac{1}{m^2 \cos^4 \theta_a} \cdot e^{-(\tan \theta_a/m)^2},
\end{aligned}
\tag{12.45}
$$

where m is the RMS slope of the surface and θ_a is the angle between the normal $\hat{\mathbf{n}}$ of the surface dA and the vector $\hat{\mathbf{h}}$ (micro-facet normal vector). The higher the mean slope m, the more rough the surface becomes, and the specular highlight is spread out. Small values of m imply micro-facets with normal vectors closer to the average normal vector $\hat{\mathbf{n}}$ of the surface, giving the material a more polished look and a tighter specular highlight.

But D is not the only term that affects the specularly reflected light off the small patch dA. As the micro-facets are arranged in V-shaped grooves, some of the outgoing light in the direction of $\overrightarrow{\mathbf{v}}$ is attenuated due to the interception of the energy leaving the surface of a micro-facet by the opposite facet of the groove (Figure 12.24). The amount of blocking depends on the outgoing direction and the slope (hence the facet normal, or half-way vector $\hat{\mathbf{h}}$) relative to the overall normal $\hat{\mathbf{n}}$ of the face. Blinn [Blin77] has calculated the amount of light that is blocked due to light interception $G_{\text{intercept}} \in [0, 1]$ as

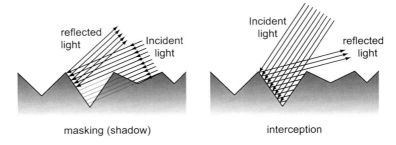

masking (shadow)   interception

Figure 12.24. Attenuation of the light in the Cook–Torrance model due to the interception of incident and reflected light by the micro-facets.

$$G_{\text{intercept}} = \frac{2(\hat{\mathbf{n}} \cdot \hat{\mathbf{h}})(\hat{\mathbf{n}} \cdot \hat{\mathbf{v}})}{\hat{\mathbf{v}} \cdot \hat{\mathbf{h}}}. \tag{12.46}$$

As illustrated in Figure 12.24, some of the light radiating from a direction $\hat{\mathbf{l}}$ on a facet da is also blocked by the opposite facet of the groove, leaving the lower part of the micro-facet in shadow. Geometrically, this is the inverse of the incoming light interception, and the attenuation factor G_{shadow} can be derived by exchanging the roles of $\hat{\mathbf{l}}$ and $\hat{\mathbf{v}}$ in Equation (12.46) and using the definition of $\hat{\mathbf{h}}$:

$$G_{\text{shadow}} = \frac{2(\hat{\mathbf{n}} \cdot \hat{\mathbf{h}})(\hat{\mathbf{n}} \cdot \hat{\mathbf{l}})}{\hat{\mathbf{l}} \cdot \hat{\mathbf{h}}} = \frac{2(\hat{\mathbf{n}} \cdot \hat{\mathbf{h}})(\hat{\mathbf{n}} \cdot \hat{\mathbf{l}})}{\hat{\mathbf{v}} \cdot \hat{\mathbf{h}}}. \tag{12.47}$$

Combining Equations (12.46) and (12.47) in a single *geometric attenuation factor* G, and bearing in mind that there are cases where there is no interception of either incident or reflected light (zero attenuation), G can be calculated by

$$G = \min \left\{ 1, \frac{2(\hat{\mathbf{n}} \cdot \hat{\mathbf{h}})(\hat{\mathbf{n}} \cdot \hat{\mathbf{v}})}{\hat{\mathbf{v}} \cdot \hat{\mathbf{h}}}, \frac{2(\hat{\mathbf{n}} \cdot \hat{\mathbf{h}})(\hat{\mathbf{n}} \cdot \hat{\mathbf{l}})}{\hat{\mathbf{v}} \cdot \hat{\mathbf{h}}} \right\}. \tag{12.48}$$

In general, the ambient, diffuse, and specular reflectance of a material depends on the wavelength of the incident light, altering both the amount and color of the reflected light. To obtain the spectral composition of the reflected light, one needs to multiply the incident spectral energy with the transfer function of the material (reflectance spectrum), i.e., the measured reflectance at each wavelength. The reflectance spectrum also depends on the angle of incidence of the incoming light. This makes the measurement and modeling of the reflectance quite complex; in most cases the reflectance of materials with respect to wavelength is measured only for normal incidence ($\theta_a = 0$).

The Cook–Torrance model simplifies the spectral dependence of the reflectance distribution function terms by allowing the diffuse BRDF to be constant and equal to the reflectance at normal incidence, because the later varies only slightly for incidence angles within $70°$ of the surface normal. The specular part of the BRDF, however, is associated with the angle of incidence, as it leads to a color shift when the direction of incidence and reflection are at about grazing angles (see below). This effect is particularly evident in metals.

The spectral transfer function of the material depends on the relative index of refraction of the material n_{12}, or simply n and the extinction coefficient k, which is associated with the depth an incident wave of wavelength λ may penetrate the material until it is extinct. In the Cook–Torrance model, the dependence on n and k is introduced through the Fresnel term F (the third factor, along with D and G) that describes how a single micro-facet reflects light. Note that, in general, both n and k vary with the wavelength of the incident light. For $k = 0$ and unpolarized light, the Fresnel equation is

$$F = \frac{1}{2} \frac{(g-c)^2}{(g+c)^2} \left(1 + \frac{[c(g+c) - 1]^2}{[c(g-c) + 1]^2} \right), \tag{12.49}$$

where

$$c = \hat{\mathbf{v}} \cdot \hat{\mathbf{h}},$$

$$g = \sqrt{n^2 + c^2 - 1}.$$

From Equation (12.49), we can see that when we look at the direction of the light source from a very low position with respect to the surface (grazing angle), the angle between $\hat{\mathbf{v}}$ and $\hat{\mathbf{h}}$ tends to $\pi/2$ and therefore $F \to 1$ regardless of the wavelength-dependent values of n and k. This means that at a grazing angle, the spectral composition of the reflected light is the same as that of the light source. In the general case, $F \neq 1$ for other angles.

The assumption that $k = 0$ is also true for non-metals. Still, Equation (12.49) produces a good approximation of the angular dependence of F for metals too, as the Fresnel term is only weakly dependent on k.

Gathering the micro-facet distribution D, the geometric attenuation factor G, and the Fresnel term F in a single equation, the specular part of the BRDF is

$$f_s = \frac{1}{\pi} \frac{DGF}{(\hat{\mathbf{n}} \cdot \hat{\mathbf{l}})(\hat{\mathbf{n}} \cdot \hat{\mathbf{v}})}. \tag{12.50}$$

The term $(\hat{\mathbf{n}} \cdot \hat{\mathbf{l}})(\hat{\mathbf{n}} \cdot \hat{\mathbf{v}})$ maximizes the specular highlight when viewing the light at a grazing angle. Because the estimation of the wavelength-dependent Fresnel

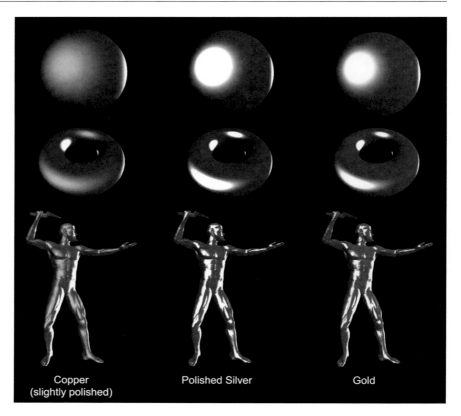

Figure 12.25. Various materials simulated with the Cook–Torrance illumination model using the OpenGL Shading Language. All surfaces are illuminated by two sources, one a little off the normal incidence direction and one near the grazing angle. (See also Color Plate XX.)

term is an expensive calculation, Cook and Torrance suggest an approximation: First, one can measure or estimate via the Fresnel equation (if $n(\lambda)$, $k(\lambda)$ are known) the reflected color at normal incidence F_0. Second, as F at grazing angle is always 1 for all wavelengths ($F_{\frac{\pi}{2}} = 1$), the color components (R, G, and B) of the reflected light are equal to the respective components of the incident light. Then, the reflected specular color component at an intermediate angle $\theta = \widehat{\mathbf{v}\hat{\mathbf{h}}}$, may be roughly interpolated from the two extreme values:

$$c_i = c_{i,0} + (c_{i,\frac{\pi}{2}} - c_{i,0}) \frac{\max(0, F_\theta(\lambda) - F_0(\lambda))}{F_{\frac{\pi}{2}} - F_0(\lambda)}, \qquad (12.51)$$

where c_i, $c_{i,\frac{\pi}{2}}$, $c_{i,0}$ are the color components (i=red, green, blue) of the resulting color, the material color at normal incidence, and the incident light color, respectively. The functional form of F, $F(\lambda)$, signifies its indirect dependence on the wavelength λ through the index of refraction. The final color c_i is obtained by multiplying Equation (12.50) with Equation (12.51):

$$c_i = \frac{1}{\pi} [c_{i,0} + (c_{i,\frac{\pi}{2}} - c_{i,0}) \frac{\max(0, F_\theta(\lambda) - F_0(\lambda))}{F_{\frac{\pi}{2}} - F_0(\lambda)}] \frac{DGF_\theta(\lambda)}{(\hat{\mathbf{n}} \cdot \hat{\mathbf{l}})(\hat{\mathbf{n}} \cdot \hat{\mathbf{v}})}. \qquad (12.52)$$

Figure 12.25 (see also Color Plate XX) demonstrates the behavior of the Cook–Torrance model for various materials. The images were generated with the OpenGL Shading Language real-time shader provided in Section 12.12.

12.8   The Oren–Nayar Illumination Model ⊛

In all the illumination models examined so far, the diffuse component of the outgoing light from a surface was considered to adhere to the Lambert model, which assumes that surfaces appear equally bright from all viewing directions (see Section 12.2). In nature however, there exist many common cases of rough surfaces whose reflectance cannot be explained by the Lambert model. A very interesting example to demonstrate this is the full Moon. The Moon, being a spherical body and reflecting light from a distant yet wide emitter (area light), the Sun, should look very bright at the center while the reflected light should diminish gradually toward the rim of the visible disk. However, this is not the case, as the reflected light perceived by a viewer on the Earth's surface gives the impression of a more even illumination across the entire disk. Clearly, at a macroscopic level, the rough, craggy surface of the moon is not Lambertian. Other rough surfaces made of materials such as clay, cement, and sand also deviate from the Lambertian model. But how is this divergence justified?

The Lambert model works well for smooth surfaces. A rough surface exhibits phenomena such as light masking and shadows like those addressed in the Torrance–Sparrow model (see Section 12.3), but also secondary reflections of light on the walls of the irregular microscopic structures. This leads to an apparent brightness of the reflected light that increases as the viewing direction approaches

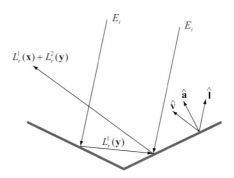

Figure 12.26. First- and second-order reflections in Lambertian micro-facets comprise the output radiance in the Oren–Nayar model.

the light direction. Oren and Nayar studied these phenomena and proposed an alternative detailed model that incorporates these factors and closely predicts the behavior of rough materials [Oren92, Oren94]. While a complete analysis of the derivation of the Oren–Nayar model is quite complex and extends beyond the scope of this book, in the following paragraphs we will present the principles and the practical, simplified model.

In the Oren–Nayar diffuse illumination model, the micro-facet model of the Torrance–Sparrow theory is also adopted. A rough surface consists of long—relative to their width—V-shaped grooves. Unlike the Blinn and Cook–Torrance models where the micro-facets are perfect mirrors (the two models estimate the specular component), in the Oren–Nayar model the facets are Lambertian surfaces. What makes this model interesting is that although it relies on the same surface modeling as the Cook–Torrance and Blinn models, the assumption that the micro-facets are not perfect mirrors but Lambertian surfaces, completely changes the mechanisms of light interaction. The reflected light in direction (θ_r, ϕ_r) given an incident direction $\hat{\mathbf{l}}$ is computed as a two-part contribution: the first-order and the second-order reflected radiance $L_r^1(\theta_r, \phi_r, \theta_i, \phi_i)$ and $L_r^2(\theta_r, \phi_r, \theta_i, \phi_i)$. These correspond to light directly reflected in a direction $\hat{\mathbf{v}}$ from a micro-facet and to light reflected in the same direction after having bounced off the opposite facet of the groove (Figure 12.26).

The Torrance–Sparrow model used a distribution D of facets facing in the same direction $\hat{\mathbf{h}}$, the direction a facet should have to perfectly reflect light from the incident direction $\hat{\mathbf{l}}$ to the viewing direction $\hat{\mathbf{v}}$. As we are interested in the calculation of radiance reflected to the environment from a small area dA in the vicinity of the rendered point, a more intuitive and convenient distribution to consider is the portion of this area that consists of facets facing in a particular direction $\hat{\mathbf{a}}$ (not necessarily the halfway vector $\hat{\mathbf{h}}$) $P(\theta_a, \phi_a)$. Oren and Nayar have considered a simple single-slope distribution (directional identical grooves) and an isotropic Gaussian distribution.

Let us now compute the contribution of a facet with slope θ_a (relative to the surface tangent plane) to the radiance perceived by the viewer. We need to consider the area of the facet projected on the actual surface of the patch dA, $da \cos \theta_a$, rather than the original facet area da. The corresponding contribution of the micro-facet to the total radiance of the patch dA is the *projected radiance* $L_{rp}(\theta_a, \phi_a)$:

$$L_{rp}(\theta_a, \phi_a) = \frac{d\Phi_r(\theta_a, \phi_a)}{(da \cos \theta_a) \cos \theta_r d\overrightarrow{\omega}_r}. \tag{12.53}$$

From the relation between radiance and irradiance and the definition of radiant flux, we have

$$\left. \begin{aligned} dE_r(\theta_r, \phi_r) &= L_r(\theta_r, \phi_r) \cos \theta_r d\overrightarrow{\omega}_r = L_r(\theta_r, \phi_r)(\hat{\mathbf{a}} \cdot \hat{\mathbf{v}}) d\overrightarrow{\omega}_r \\ d\Phi_r(\theta_r, \phi_r) &= dE_r(\theta_r, \phi_r) da \end{aligned} \right\} \Leftrightarrow$$

$$d\Phi_r(\theta_r, \phi_r) = L_r(\theta_r, \phi_r)(\hat{\mathbf{a}} \cdot \hat{\mathbf{v}}) d\overrightarrow{\omega}_r da. \tag{12.54}$$

Substituting the radiant flux in Equation (12.53), the projected radiance becomes

$$L_{rp}(\theta_a, \phi_a) = \frac{L_r(\theta_r, \phi_r)(\hat{\mathbf{a}} \cdot \hat{\mathbf{v}}) d\overrightarrow{\omega}_r da}{(da \cos \theta_a) \cos \theta_r d\overrightarrow{\omega}_r} = \frac{L_r(\theta_r, \phi_r)(\hat{\mathbf{a}} \cdot \hat{\mathbf{v}})}{(\hat{\mathbf{a}} \cdot \hat{\mathbf{n}})(\hat{\mathbf{v}} \cdot \hat{\mathbf{n}})}. \tag{12.55}$$

As we have assumed the micro-facets to be Lambertian, the BRDF of each one of them is constant and equal to $\frac{1}{\pi}$ (Equation (12.18)). Allowing for the absorption of some light according to the surface albedo ρ, from the definition of the BRDF we have

$$L_r(\theta_r, \phi_r) = \rho f_d E_i(\theta_i, \phi_i) = \rho f_d E_0 \cos \theta_i = \rho f_d E_0(\hat{\mathbf{l}} \cdot \hat{\mathbf{a}}) = \frac{\rho}{\pi} E_0(\hat{\mathbf{l}} \cdot \hat{\mathbf{a}}), \tag{12.56}$$

where E_0 is the irradiance from the source at normal incidence. Replacing the radiance in Equation (12.55),

$$L_{rp}(\theta_a, \phi_a) = \frac{\rho}{\pi} E_0 \frac{(\hat{\mathbf{l}} \cdot \hat{\mathbf{a}})(\hat{\mathbf{a}} \cdot \hat{\mathbf{v}})}{(\hat{\mathbf{a}} \cdot \hat{\mathbf{n}})(\hat{\mathbf{v}} \cdot \hat{\mathbf{n}})}. \tag{12.57}$$

The radiance that is directly returned towards the view direction, not accounting for any attenuation due to masking and shadowing, is calculated by integrating the contribution of the projected radiance of Equation (12.57) over every possible direction that the micro-facets may assume. The contribution of all facets facing in the direction of $\hat{\mathbf{a}}$ is determined by the fraction of the total area dA that this group of facets occupies, i.e., $P(\theta_a, \phi_a)$:

$$L_r^1(\theta_r, \phi_r, \theta_i, \phi_i) = \int_{\theta_a=0}^{\pi/2} \int_{\phi_a=0}^{2\pi} P(\theta_a, \phi_a) L_{rp}^1(\theta_a, \phi_a) \sin\theta_a d\phi_a d\theta_a. \quad (12.58)$$

The effect of masking and shadowing of the outgoing and incident light, respectively, due to the presence of the opposite facet of the groove is the attenuation of the perceived brightness by a certain factor. The geometric attenuation factor GAF chosen in the Oren–Nayar model is a generalization of the corresponding Cook–Torrance/Blinn factor G and works for any facet normal $\hat{\mathbf{a}}$ and not necessarily the halfway vector $\hat{\mathbf{h}}$ between the viewing and the incident direction:

$$GAF = \min\left\{1, \max\left\{0, \frac{2(\hat{\mathbf{l}}\cdot\hat{\mathbf{n}})(\hat{\mathbf{a}}\cdot\hat{\mathbf{n}})}{\hat{\mathbf{l}}\cdot\hat{\mathbf{a}}}, \frac{2(\hat{\mathbf{v}}\cdot\hat{\mathbf{n}})(\hat{\mathbf{a}}\cdot\hat{\mathbf{n}})}{\hat{\mathbf{v}}\cdot\hat{\mathbf{a}}}\right\}\right\}. \quad (12.59)$$

The projected outgoing radiance is scaled by GAF, for each group of facets in dA that face in the direction of $\hat{\mathbf{a}}$; therefore, taking into account also the blocked incident and reflected light, Equation (12.58) becomes

$$L_r^1(\theta_r, \phi_r, \theta_i, \phi_i) = \int_{\theta_a=0}^{\pi/2} \int_{\phi_a=0}^{2\pi} P(\theta_a, \phi_a) L_{rp}^1(\theta_a, \phi_a) GAF \sin\theta_a d\phi_a d\theta_a. \quad (12.60)$$

The calculation of the facet inter-reflection contribution is significantly more tedious and, thus, we will provide only some key elements of the concept and the results of the analysis. The interested reader may find more details in the original work of Oren and Nayar [Oren92] and in [Fors89].

As the micro-facets are Lambertian and thus do not reflect very intensely in a particular direction, energy transmitted via secondary reflection bounces rapidly diminishes. This energy exchange is further attenuated by the oblique relative positioning of the facets. This means that the cumulative contribution of any more than two bounces is not significant and can be ignored. The Oren–Nayar model ignores the third- and higher-order reflections.

The calculation of the radiance that comes from a direction (θ_i, ϕ_i), bounces off one facet (L_r^1), and is reflected by the opposite side to the view direction (L_r^2), involves the estimation of the visible portion of the second facet and the part of the first not in shadow (Figure 12.27(a)). Taking advantage of the translational symmetry of the V-shaped groove, the calculation of the total projected radiance can

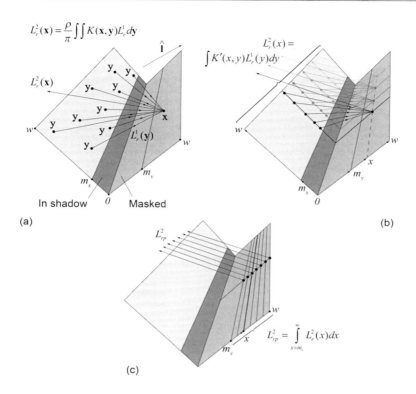

$$L_r^2(\mathbf{x}) = \frac{\rho}{\pi} \int\int K(\mathbf{x},\mathbf{y})L_r^1 d\mathbf{y}$$

$$L_r^2(x) = \int K'(x,y)L_r^1(y)dy$$

$$L_{rp}^2 = \int_{x=m_s}^{w} L_r^2(x)dx$$

Figure 12.27. Radiance from second-order reflections. (a) All points **y** on the opposite side not in shadow reflect light to a point **x** on the facet. K is a geometrical kernel that specifies the attenuation between the two points. (b) By expressing L_r in terms of the distance x from the bottom of the groove, translational symmetry helps treat all equidistant points from the bottom of the groove identically. (c) The total radiance leaving the facet is the sum of the contributions from all lines above the masking limit.

be split into two consecutive sums: For all points on a line parallel to the length of the groove, the first-bounce radiance from all points on the opposite side is summed. The translational symmetry helps treat this stage as a symmetrical sum over a cross-section extended both ways along the groove (Figure 12.27(b)). The total radiance leaving the cross section of the second surface toward the direction $\hat{\mathbf{v}}$ is found by integrating over all lines of surface points, the points which lie above the masking limit m_v (Figure 12.27(c)).

The overall radiance leaving patch dA in the direction $\hat{\mathbf{v}}(\theta_r, \phi_r)$ is the sum of the two contributions:

$$L_r(\theta_r, \phi_r, \theta_i, \phi_i) = L_r^1(\theta_r, \phi_r, \theta_i, \phi_i) + L_r^2(\theta_r, \phi_r, \theta_i, \phi_i). \qquad (12.61)$$

Based on the concepts described above, Oren and Nayar devised a detailed analytical model for the reflectance of rough surfaces, which is not provided here due to its complexity and dependence on unintuitive parameters. Fortunately, they were able to simplify the original model by specifying a functional approximation that depended only on the angles of incidence and reflection as well as the surface roughness. The final results for a Gaussian slope-area distribution $P(\theta_a, \phi_a)$ of facets with zero mean value and standard deviation σ are given below:

$$L_r^1(\theta_r, \phi_r, \theta_i, \phi_i) = \frac{\rho}{\pi} E_0 \cos\theta_i [C_1 + \cos(\phi_r - \phi_i) C_2 \tan\beta + (1 - |\cos(\phi_r - \phi_i)|) C_3 \tan(\frac{\alpha+\beta}{2})], \qquad (12.62)$$

$$L_r^2(\theta_r, \phi_r, \theta_i, \phi_i) = 0.17 \frac{\rho}{\pi} E_0 \frac{\sigma^2}{\sigma^2 + 0.13} \cos\theta_i [1 - (\frac{2\beta}{\pi})^2 \cos(\phi_r - \phi_i)], \quad (12.63)$$

where

$$C_1 = 1 - 0.5 \frac{\sigma^2}{\sigma^2 + 0.3},$$

$$C_2 = \begin{cases} 0.45 \frac{\sigma^2}{\sigma^2 + 0.09} \sin\alpha, & \cos(\phi_r - \phi_i) \geq 0, \\ 0.45 \frac{\sigma^2}{\sigma^2 + 0.09} (\sin\alpha - (\frac{2\beta}{\pi})^3), & \text{otherwise,} \end{cases}$$

$$C_3 = 0.125 \frac{\sigma^2}{\sigma^2 + 0.09} (\frac{4\alpha\beta}{\pi^2})^2,$$

$$\alpha = \max(\theta_r, \theta_i), \quad \beta = \min(\theta_r, \theta_i).$$

The BRDF of the Oren–Nayar model is easily acquired by applying the BRDF definition to Equation (12.61). The irradiance is dropped and the final formula depends on the constant parameters and the angles of incidence and reflection:

$$f_{\text{Oren–Nayar}} = \frac{L(\theta_r, \phi_r, \theta_i, \phi_i)}{E_i} = \frac{L(\theta_r, \phi_r, \theta_i, \phi_i)}{E_0 \cos\theta_i} = \frac{L_r^1(\theta_r, \phi_r, \theta_i, \phi_i) + L_r^2(\theta_r, \phi_r, \theta_i, \phi_i)}{E_0 \cos\theta_i} \qquad (12.64)$$

Figure 12.28. Comparison of the Phong and Oren–Nayar models on a clay pot and a sphere (inset).

Figure 12.28 presents a comparison of the Oren–Nayar and the Phong model. The same rough materials were rendered using both models. The characteristic Lambertian intensity fall-off of the Phong model does not provide a very convincing impression. The quick fall-off is very noticeable along the intersection of the walls and at the outline and grooves of the clay pot.

12.9 The Strauss Illumination Model⊛

Illumination models that are based on geometrical optics, such as the Blinn, Cook–Torrance, and Oren–Nayar models, produce very realistic shading but also have an inherent problem that makes them difficult to work with: they use actual physical parameters found in material science (expressed in real units), which tend to be very unintuitive for artists. The Phong model on the other hand, cannot effectively capture the appearance of metallic surfaces and also suffers from a small but sometimes frustrating issue: the specular exponent is specified as an unbounded positive number. Therefore, one cannot easily produce a balanced shininess between a dull surface and a fully reflective one by adjusting a value between two limits. The shininess adjustment is further made complex by the fact that two seemingly independent parameters (the exponent and the specular coefficient) control the same material attribute.

Strauss [Stra90] proposed an illumination model that borrows many lighting calculations from the Phong model but also incorporates features like metallic appearance, off-specular reflections, and unified shininess control, through intuitive normalized parameters. It is an empirical model that was designed with simplicity in mind, targeting animators and 3D modelers.

The basic normalized parameters that control the surface appearance are three: The material color $\mathbf{c} = (r, g, b)$, which represents the albedo of the surface, the smoothness s, ranging from 0 (dull surface) to 1 (perfect mirror), and the metalness m also ranging from 0 to 1 (1 corresponds to metallic surface). The smoothness controls both the specular/diffuse contribution ratio and the size of the highlight. The metalness parameter affects the color of the specularly reflected light, which, as seen in the Cook–Torrance model, is biased for metals toward the surface basic color, except when the light source is reflected to the eye at a grazing angle.

The intensity of the reflected light per color channel c_r is calculated as the corresponding incident light component c_i multiplied (filtered) by the diffuse, specular and ambient components of the Strauss model (Q_d, Q_s, and Q_a, respectively):

$$c_r = c_i(Q_d + Q_s + Q_a). \tag{12.65}$$

The amount of diffuse illumination Q_d that contributes to the final color depends on the shininess of the surface s. The more shiny the surface, the less it behaves as a Lambertian reflector. Also, the diffuse component is decreased as the surface adopts a metallic quality with the increase of the metalness variable m. Of course, the diffuse component also depends on the angle of incidence. The Strauss diffuse and ambient components are

$$\begin{aligned}
Q_d &= (\hat{\mathbf{n}} \cdot \hat{\mathbf{l}}) r_d d c, \\
Q_a &= r_d c, \\
r_d &= (1 - s^3)(1 - t), \\
d &= (1 - ms),
\end{aligned} \tag{12.66}$$

where t is the transparency of the surface and ranges between 0 and 1 (0 = fully opaque) and c is one of the red, green, or blue components of the surface color. The $(1 - s^3)$ factor is experimentally chosen to account for a linear perceptual transition from a dull surface to a perfect mirror with a corresponding linear change in the s parameter.

The specular component Q_s is a product of two terms, the specular reflectivity r_s, which defines the shape of the highlight and the specular color c_s, which is interpolated for metallic surfaces between the surface color and the light color as in the Cook–Torrance model (see Strauss shader implementation in Section 12.12):

$$Q_s = r_s c_s. \tag{12.67}$$

As in the Phong model, the specular reflectivity depends on the angle between the mirror reflection direction and the view vector, raised to a power to tighten the highlight:

$$r_s = (\hat{\mathbf{r}} \cdot \hat{\mathbf{v}})^h \, r_j,$$
$$h = \frac{3}{1-s}. \tag{12.68}$$

The value r_j is the adjusted reflectivity and encapsulates the specular attenuation due to the Fresnel term and the geometric attenuation factor (see also Section 12.7); r_j depends on the reflectivity of the surface at normal incidence, $r_n = 1 - t - r_d$, giving

$$r_j = \min[1, \, r_n + (r_n + k_j) F(\theta_i) G(\theta_i) G(\theta_r)]. \tag{12.69}$$

The function $F(x)$ is an empirical Fresnel-like function and $G(x)$ is a geometric attenuation function. They are defined as:

$$F(x) = \left[\frac{1}{(x-k_f)^2} - \frac{1}{k_f^2} \right] \Big/ \left[\frac{1}{(1-k_f)^2} - \frac{1}{k_f^2} \right],$$
$$G(x) = \left[\frac{1}{(1-k_g)^2} - \frac{1}{(x-k_g)^2} \right] \Big/ \left[\frac{1}{(1-k_g)^2} - \frac{1}{k_g^2} \right]. \tag{12.70}$$

The constants k_j, k_f, and k_g are experimentally chosen and Strauss suggests the values 0.1, 1.12, and 1.01, respectively. Essentially, the adjusted reflectivity creates an increase in the specular highlight near the grazing angle, while the geometric attenuation factor counteracts this increase when the incident angle or the viewing angle comes too close to $\pi/2$.

An OpenGL shader implementation of the Strauss model is given in Section 12.12. Some results for various values of m, s, and c can be seen in Figure 12.29 (see also Color Plate XXI). Note that the shader uses the conventions

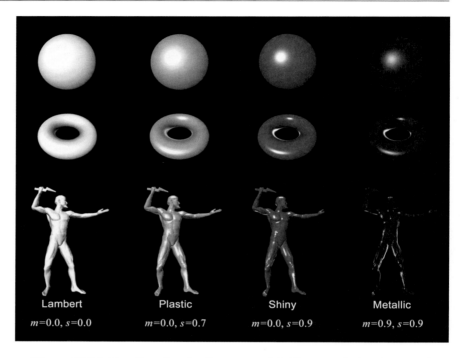

Figure 12.29. Results using the Strauss model. (See also Color Plate XXI.)

found in the original work of Strauss, who defines the $\hat{\mathbf{v}}$ and $\hat{\mathbf{l}}$ vectors to point to the surface point $\mathbf{p}$.[5]

12.10   Anisotropic Reflectance

All of the models that have been discussed so far possessed an isotropic BRDF, meaning that the reflected light did not depend on the azimuth angle of incidence ϕ_i. However, many real materials and treated surfaces exhibit a distinctive directional bias, i.e., the highlight appears brighter or wider at particular incident directions. Anisotropic specular reflection is caused by the microscopic geometric structures of the surface. Most anisotropic reflective materials possess a char-

---

[5]For the Fresnel term, $F(x)$ is used with the angle between the bisector of $\widehat{\hat{\mathbf{v}}\hat{\mathbf{l}}}$ and $\hat{\mathbf{l}}$: $F((\theta_i + \theta_r)/2)$. Note that this is necessary as the original paper assumes that $\hat{\mathbf{n}}$, $\hat{\mathbf{v}}$, and $\hat{\mathbf{l}}$ are expressed in normalized eye-space.

acteristic grain or a set of very small grooves that are roughly locally oriented in a specific direction. The grooves appear parallel within a magnified surface area. Good examples of anisotropic reflectors are brushed metals (for example, brushed aluminum (Figure 12.30; see also Color Plate XIX)), varnished wood, or vinyl music records.

Figure 12.30 shows a simulated experiment with a geometry consisting of parallel grooves illuminated from two directions: one is parallel and the other is

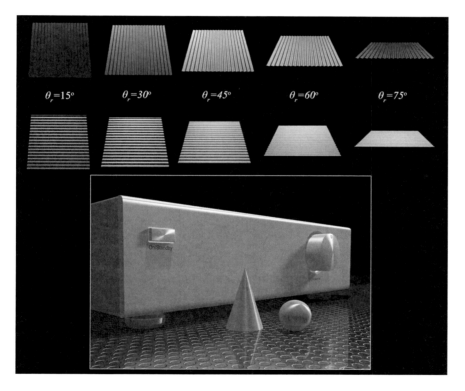

Figure 12.30. Anisotropic reflectance. Microscopic parallel grooves on specularly reflective surfaces reflect light differently according to the relative angle between the plane of incidence and the grain direction. Above: Magnification of a brushed metal. Reflected light is calculated for various viewing directions and for grooves parallel or vertical to the plane of incidence. Below: Rendering of brushed aluminum (amplifier front panel, volume knob, power switch, cone and sphere). (See also Color Plate XIX.)

perpendicular to the surface grain. Both cases are examined from the same view directions with θ_r ranging from 15 to 75 degrees. Observe that the average reflectivity in the case of the vertical grooves is different from that of the horizontal ones.

Let us model the surface according to the micro-facet approach and assume that the surface grain lays on a longitude direction ϕ_g. The distribution of the facets da with respect to their normal direction $\hat{\mathbf{a}} = (\theta_a, \phi_a)$ is clearly directional, with θ_a being zero for $\phi_a = \phi_g, \phi_g + \pi$ and ranging from $-\theta_s$ to θ_s for $\phi_a = \phi_g \pm \pi/2$, where θ_s is the maximum slope. Let us now observe the surface from a macroscopic level with incident light coming from (θ_i, ϕ_i). In the extreme case where all grooves are ideally aligned with ϕ_g, the surface becomes a perfect mirror when $\phi_i = \phi_g, \phi_g + \pi$ and has a wider spread of the highlight as ϕ_i tends to $\phi_g \pm \pi/2$ (maximum anisotropy). If ϕ_a is allowed to vary according to some distribution, for instance a Gaussian with mean azimuth ϕ_g and standard deviation σ_g, the anisotropy becomes less pronounced as σ_g becomes larger.

Several models have been proposed in order to deal with anisotropy, like the Kajiya model [Kaji85] that uses Kirchoff's diffraction theory to simulate the effect, the Poulin-Fournier approach [Poul90] that models the surface as an aggregation of parallel cylinders embedded in it or cut out from a planar area, or the empirical, observation-based Ward model [Ward92].

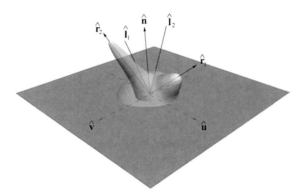

Figure 12.31. Specular reflectance distribution lobes for an anisotropic reflector. The directional dependence of the distribution with respect to the incident direction can be defined relative to the local tangent space.

One property that is difficult to represent for arbitrary geometry or polygonal meshes is the direction of maximum (and minimum) reflectance on the surface, which is dependent on the azimuth angle ϕ_g. This direction is a local attribute of the model and cannot in general be expressed relative to the object or world reference frame (e.g., parallel to the x-axis). Most implementations rely on the local tangent space and align ϕ_g relative to the tangent coordinate system $(\hat{\mathbf{n}}, \hat{\mathbf{u}}, \hat{\mathbf{v}})$ (Figure 12.31). A convenient way to define the tangent and bitangent vectors at any given surface point on an arbitrary surface is via texture mapping. Refer to Section 14.7.5 for the derivation of the tangent space from an arbitrary polygonal surface parameterization.

12.11 Ambient Occlusion

Most local illumination models regard the ambient illumination contribution as constant. The ambient term is the irradiance that reaches a surface as the summed contribution of the emitted or reflected light from the environment and accounts for the exchange of energy between the patch dA under consideration and all other possibly contributing patches in a scene. Having a constant value reflect this ambient illumination is clearly a very rough approximation. Even simple scenes, like an empty room or objects resting on one another, contain surfaces that exchange different amounts of energy according to the location and the relative orientation with their neighbors. The walls of a room are darker near corners and a lot of light coming from the environment is blocked underneath a table or under a car. Normally, the exchange of energy in a closed environment is simulated via a *global illumination* method, which is the subject of Chapter 16. But one aspect of the global energy exchange that affects the ambient term, the darkening effect in obscured parts of a scene, i.e., patches where incident light from the environment is blocked due to the presence of other geometry, can be simulated in a more efficient manner.

Zhukov et al. [Zhuk98b, Zhuk98a, Ione03] proposed an ambient illumination model that, assuming a uniform (ambient) distant environment irradiance from every direction, estimates the portion of it that finally reaches a small patch dA. The situation is equivalent to calculating the visibility of a patch due to the presence of the rest of the geometry, that is, the portion of the solid angle around the patch, from where dA is visible. Inversely, the *obscurance* of a patch dA is the portion of the hemispherical solid angle around the patch that is blocked by other geometry (Figure 12.32). The higher the obscurance, the darker the patch,

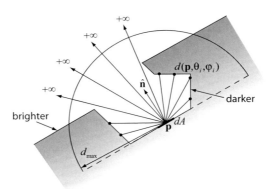

Figure 12.32. Evaluation of the obscurance function in ambient occlusion.

because dA is blocked at many incident directions from other patches and, therefore, less light from the environment can hit the surface. In the original paper by Zhukov et al. [Zhuk98b], the term "obscurance" $w(\mathbf{p})$ was used to refer to the visibility of the surface patch and from hereafter this term will reflect the "openness" of a patch dA centered at a point $\mathbf{p}$.

An important benefit of linking the ambient illumination on a surface patch to its obscurance is that the latter is a purely geometric property and does not depend on any particular lighting conditions or viewing direction. The obscurance is usually pre-calculated and stored on a polygonal mesh as vertex color information or in a texture image, which is subsequently applied at render time to the surface (see also texture mapping and texture atlases in Chapter 14). The obscurance $w(\mathbf{p})$ can be multiplied with a constant ambient term and provides a convincing estimate of the incident light from the environment. It should be noted, however, that obscurance shading or *ambient occlusion* is not a physical simulation model and was not conceived to provide an accurate global illumination calculation; it misses the high-order bounces of energy that eventually hit the surface and regards irradiance due to ambient illumination to be constant in all incident directions.

Let us assume that there are no specific light sources in the environment. The (uniform) incident ambient illumination can be modeled as a perfectly diffuse light that radiates from all directions towards dA. Another important assumption is that light is not emitted from some infinite medium far from the scene itself, but that the geometry is immersed in a radiating, non-absorbing, gaseous medium. Why should this be so? Due to the exchange of energy among surface patches, even if light is blocked from a particular direction, a portion of the original radiance hits dA, due to inter-reflections. Having open space subtended by the hemispherical solid angle above the patch behave as an emitter approximately accounts for the diffusely reflected energy on nearby patches.

Let $d(\mathbf{p}, \theta_i, \phi_i)$ be the distance between $\mathbf{p}$ and the closest surface point to $\mathbf{p}$ in the direction (θ_i, ϕ_i) (Figure 12.32). If there is no surface point in this direction, $d(\mathbf{p}, \theta_i, \phi_i)$ is infinite:

$$d(\mathbf{p}, \theta_i, \phi_i) = \begin{cases} |\mathbf{c} - \mathbf{p}|, & \mathbf{c}: \text{ first intersection point in direction } (\theta_i, \phi_i), \\ +\infty, & \text{no intersections in direction } (\theta_i, \phi_i). \end{cases}$$

$$(12.71)$$

According to this model, the farther from $\mathbf{p}$ an intersection point is, the more light reaches the surface of the patch dA. If the hemispherical solid angle above the patch is completely open up to a distance $d_{\max}$ (which is seldom the case), the obscurance $w(\mathbf{p})$ equals 1. Obscurance can become exactly zero only in degenerate cases or where two surfaces firmly touch each other. The value $d_{\max}$ is the maximum distance at which the contribution of the surrounding geometry is non-negligible and is empirically set per scene, according to the scale of the environment.

The intensity of the reflected light from patch dA centered at $\mathbf{p}$, due to ambient illumination coming from the hemisphere Ω above dA can thus be approximated as

$$I_a(\mathbf{p}) = k_a I_a w(\mathbf{p}),$$
$$w(\mathbf{p}) = \frac{1}{\pi} \int_{\Omega} \mu(d(\mathbf{p}, \theta_i, \phi_i)) \cos \theta_i d\vec{\omega},$$

$$(12.72)$$

where $\mu(x)$ is a function that maps the distance $x = d(\mathbf{p}, \theta_i, \phi_i)$ to a normalized obscurance factor and represents the energy emitted by the gaseous medium in the line of sight from $\mathbf{p}$ to the closest surface in the direction (θ_i, ϕ_i). The function $\mu(x)$ is required to meet the following requirements: monotonically increasing and smooth (the larger the distance to the intersection point, the greater the contribution of ambient light), zero for zero distance and 1 at infinity with a decreasing slope (Figure 12.33). These constraints are

$$\mu(x) = \begin{cases} 0, & x = 0, \\ 1, & x = +\infty \end{cases} \qquad \frac{d\mu(x)}{dx} = \begin{cases} 0, & x = +\infty, \\ > 0, & \text{otherwise,} \end{cases} \qquad \frac{d^2\mu(x)}{dx^2} < 0.$$

$$(12.73)$$

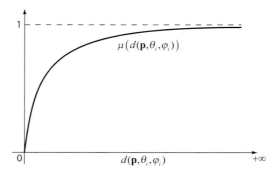

Figure 12.33. Mapping function from distance to visibility (openness) in a particular direction.

A common family of functions that conforms to the requirements is

$$\mu(x) = 1 - e^{-\tau x}. \tag{12.74}$$

The parameter τ regulates the spread of the shadowed area. In the original paper, τ is experimentally set to 1. As d_{max} defines a range of distance from **p** beyond which no patch is taken into account, $\mu(x)$ has to be modified to normalize this input range.

Let us now introduce N_L light sources with intensity $I_L(j), j = 1 \ldots N_L$, at distance d_j from the patch dA and direction of incidence $\hat{\mathbf{l}}_j$. Assuming Lambertian surfaces, these light sources contribute to the illumination of the patch both in the ambient and in the diffuse term. The resulting illumination for a point **p** of the patch has the form

$$I(\mathbf{p}) = [k_a I_a + k_d I_d(\mathbf{p})] w(\mathbf{p}) + I_d(\mathbf{p}),$$
$$I_d(\mathbf{p}) = \sum_{j=1}^{N_L} \delta(\mathbf{p}, j) \frac{I_L(j)}{d_j^2} (\hat{\mathbf{l}}_j \cdot \hat{\mathbf{n}}), \tag{12.75}$$

where $\delta(\mathbf{p}, j)$ is a visibility factor that becomes 1 if the jth light source is visible from the patch and 0 if the patch is in shadow for the specific light source.

Figure 12.34 shows an example of the application of the ambient occlusion model, for various values of τ and d_{max}, as well as the final results of combining the obscurance function with the diffuse and ambient terms of Equation (12.75).

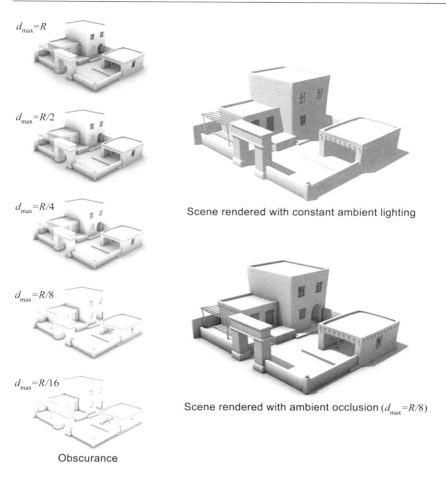

$d_{\mathrm{max}}=R$

$d_{\mathrm{max}}=R/2$

$d_{\mathrm{max}}=R/4$

$d_{\mathrm{max}}=R/8$

$d_{\mathrm{max}}=R/16$

Obscurance

Scene rendered with constant ambient lighting

Scene rendered with ambient occlusion ($d_{\mathrm{max}}=R/8$)

Figure 12.34. Example of obscurance estimation for various values of the distance limit (left). R is the scene radius. The same scene is rendered with constant ambient illumination (top right) and with obscurance-weighted ambient and diffuse illumination (bottom right).

12.12   Shader Source Code

12.12.1   Cook–Torrance Shader

```
//################### Cook-Torrance Model ####################//
//################### Vertex program #########################//
varying vec3 N,P;

void main() {
    gl_Position = gl_ModelViewProjectionMatrix * gl_Vertex;
    N = normalize ( gl_NormalMatrix * gl_Normal );
    P = vec3 (gl_Position) / gl_Position.w;
}


//################### Cook-Torrance Model ####################//
//################### Fragment program #######################//

varying vec3 N, P; const float pi = 3.1415936; const float e
=2.718282; const int numLights = 2;

uniform float Ka, Kd, Ks, // ambient, diffuse, specular coefs.
              m;          // RMS micro-facet slope
uniform vec3  n;          // n(630nm) n(530nm) n(465nm)
                          // at normal incidence
uniform vec3  color;      // The material color

// The Beckmann distribution function
float Beckmann ( in float a ) {
    float tana = tan(a)/m;
    float cosa = cos(a);
    cosa *= cosa;
    return pow ( e, -tana*tana ) / (m*m*cosa*cosa);
}



// The Fresnel term
float Fresnel( in float n, in float c ) {
    float g, gc, F;
    g = clamp ( n*n+c*c-1, 0.000001, 1.0);
    g = sqrt(g);
    gc = g+c;
    F = (g-c)*(g-c)/(2*gc*gc);
    return F * ( 1 + (c*gc-1)*(c*gc-1)/( (c*gc+1)*(c*gc+1) ) );
}
```

```
// The Cook-Torrance model for the specular reflectance
void CookTorrance ( in vec3 L,        // light direction
                    in vec3 V,        // view direction
                    in vec3 H,        // half-way vector
                    in float a,       // angle ( N, H )
                    in vec3 Il,       // incident illumination
                    in vec3 C0,       // material color
                    out vec3 Is_I     // resulting specular color
                  )
{
    float NL, NV, VH, NH; // dot products
    float D, G;           // D and G scalar terms
    vec3 F0, F;           // The tri-chromatic Fresnel terms
                          // for normal & arbitrary incidence

    NL = dot(N,L);
    NV = dot(N,V);
    VH = dot(V,H);
    NH = dot(N,H);

    D = Beckmann(a);

    G = min ( 1, min( 2*NH*NV/VH, 2*NH*NL/VH ) );

    F0.r = Fresnel(n.r,1);
    F0.g = Fresnel(n.g,1);
    F0.b = Fresnel(n.b,1);
    F.r = Fresnel(n.r,VH);
    F.g = Fresnel(n.g,VH);
    F.b = Fresnel(n.b,VH);

    Is_i = (C0 + (Il-C0)*(max(F-F0,0)/(1.0-F0)) ) *
           ( (F.r+F.g+F.b)/3 )*D*G/(pi*NL*NV);
}

void main() {
    vec3 Pl;                     // Light position
    vec3 L, H, V;                // directions (unit vectors)
    vec3 Ia, Id, Is, Is_i, Il;   // Intensity values
    int i;
    float NL, a;

    V = vec3 (0.0, 0.0, 1.0);  // View direction
```

```
      Ia = vec3 (0.0, 0.0, 0.0); // Init. amb/dif/spec values
      Id = vec3 (0.0, 0.0, 0.0);
      Is = vec3 (0.0, 0.0, 0.0);

      // Add the contribution of all light sources
      for ( i = 0; i< numLights; i++ )
      {
          Pl = vec3 (gl_LightSource[i].position);
          L = normalize( Pl - P );
          H = normalize( L + V );
          NL = dot (N,L);
          // Diffuse
      Id +=  gl_LightSource[i].diffuse * NL;

          a = acos( dot(N,H) );
          Il = vec3 (gl_LightSource[i].diffuse);
          CookTorrance ( L, V, H, a, Il, color, Is_i );
          // Specular
          Is += Is_i;
      }

      // Ambient
      Ia = Ka * gl_FrontLightModelProduct.sceneColor;

      gl_FragColor = vec4(Ia,1) +
                     Kd * vec4(Id,1) * vec4(color,1) +
                     Ks * vec4(Is,1);
}
```

12.12.2 Strauss Shader

```
//################### Strauss Model #########################//
//################### Vertex program ########################//

varying vec3 N; varying vec3 P;

void main() {
    gl_Position = gl_ModelViewProjectionMatrix * gl_Vertex;
    N = normalize ( gl_NormalMatrix * gl_Normal );
    P = vec3 (gl_Position) / gl_Position.w;
}


//################### Strauss Model #########################//
//################### Fragment program ######################//
```

```glsl
varying vec3 N; varying vec3 P; const float pi = 3.1415936; const
int numLights = 2; uniform float m;           // metalness uniform
float s;            // shininess uniform float t;          //
transparency uniform vec3 C;              // surface color

//------------------------ Fresnel term ---------------
float F ( in float x ) {
    const float kf = 1.12f;
    const float kf2 = kf*kf;
    const float denom = ( 1.0/((1.0-kf)*(1.0-kf)) - 1.0/kf2 );
    return ( ( 1.0/((x-kf)*(x-kf)) - 1.0/kf2 ) / denom);
}

//------------------------ Geometric Attenuation------
float G ( in float x ) {
    const float kg = 1.01f;
    const float kg2 = kg*kg;
    const float denom = ( 1.0/((1.0-kg)*(1.0-kg)) - 1.0/kg2 );
    return ( 1.0/((1.0-kg)*(1.0-kg)) - 1.0/((x-kg)*(x-kg)) )
            / denom;
}

void main() {
    vec3 Pl, L, V, H;
    vec3 Qa, Qd, Qs, Ir, Cs;
    int i;
    float NL, NV, f;
    float theta_i, theta_r;
    float rn, rj, rd, rs, d;
    const float kj = 0.1;

    // Note that conventions in the original paper
    // differ from standard normalized vector definitions:
    // L and V face towards the local point P

    // View direction
    V = -normalize(P);
    NV = dot(N,V);

    Ir = vec3 (0.0, 0.0, 0.0);

    for ( i = 0; i< numLights; i++ )
    {
        Pl = vec3 (gl_LightSource[i].position);
```

```
L = normalize( P - Pl );
NL = dot(N,L);
H = normalize( L-2*NL*N );
theta_i = 2*acos(abs(NL))/pi;
theta_r = 2*acos(abs(NV))/pi;
rd = (1-s*s*s)*(1-t);
d  = 1-m*s;
rn = 1-t-rd;
f = F((theta_i+theta_r)/2);
rj = min (1, rn+(rn+kj)*f*G(theta_i)*G(theta_r));
rs = pow(-dot(H,V),3/(1.0001-s))*rj;
Cs = 1 + m*(1-f)*(C-1);

Qd = clamp (-NL*d*rd*C,0,1);
Qs = clamp (rs*Cs,0,1);

Ir +=  gl_LightSource[i].diffuse * (Qd+Qs) +
       gl_LightSource[i].ambient * Qa;
}

gl_FragColor = vec4(Ir,1-t);

}
```

12.13   Exercises

1. Based on the derivation of the Lambert BRDF, explain in your own words why a Lambertian surface appears equally bright from all viewing directions.

2. Consider a polygonal model of a sphere which is illuminated by a point light source in the viewing direction ($\hat{v} = \hat{l}$). Write a program to illuminate the sphere using the Phong model and algorithm (Equation (12.26)) and allow the user to vary the values of the various parameters of the model (k_a, k_d, k_s, d, n) and inspect the result on the sphere.

3. The same as Exercise 2, but use the Gouraud algorithm instead.

4. Extend Exercise 2 to include multiple point light sources (Equation (12.27)) and allow the user to move them individually.

5. Extend Exercise 2 to allow the user to vary the color components of the light source (you will need to break down the incident light intensity I_i in Equation (12.28) into its color components).

6. Implement the quadratic interpolation of vertex normals (Section 12.6.4) and compare it to linear interpolation on a polygonal model that has the "staircase" structure, using the Phong shading model and algorithm.

7. In what ways do the modeling of the surfaces in the Cook–Torrance and Oren–Nayar models differ? How do these differences affect the estimated light that is propagated to the viewer?

8. Write an OpenGL Shading Language shader that implements the Oren–Nayar model.

9. Using the Strauss model, provide the appropriate parameters to simulate glossy, plastic material. Compare the resulting formula to the Phong model.

10. Compare the results of the ambient occlusion technique with those of a global illumination method, assuming uniform hemispherical illumination (skylight). More specifically, address the following cases in terms of visual result similarity and credibility:

    • surfaces on the exterior of tightly packed buildings in an outdoor scene with an infinite ground object;

    • surfaces inside sparse individual buildings with openings;

    • surfaces inside a single concave object with a small aperture.

13

Shadows

There is strong shadow where there is much light.
—Johann Wolfgang von Goethe

13.1   Introduction

Wherever there is light, there is shadow and this is exactly what we expect to see when observing a three-dimensional environment. But shadows are not just another type of photorealistic element adding credibility to a synthetic image. Shadows help the eyes register the objects relative to their surroundings, they define the direction of the incident light and provide clues for the shape and depth of three-dimensional objects. The latter is more important in the case of monoscopic imaging. The human visual system is equipped with stereoscopic viewing, which extracts depth information from the slightly different images that are registered by the left and the right eye. When rendering in a single image, this piece of information is lost, but shadows help resolve part of the depth ambiguities that may arise. Perspective alone cannot always give us enough clues about the perceived objects, especially when their relative scale is not known.

Consider the example of Figure 13.1. In Figure 13.1(a), a staircase is lit by a single light source that casts no shadows. A ball is visible in the foreground. Although the ball is not occluded by any other object, it is impossible to determine whether the ball is resting on a step or if it is airborne. We have no clue on its relative position with respect to the staircase, even though we can judge from a priori knowledge that the ball is not too small to be closer to the viewer than to the staircase. Figure 13.1(b) shows three possible position/size combinations that could have produced the same version of the ball raster from the same viewpoint.

429

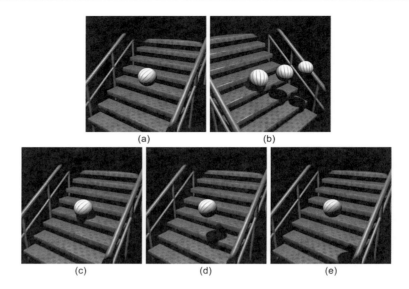

Figure 13.1. Size and depth clues from shadow. (a) A lit scene showing a ball in front of a staircase. (b) Size/distance ambiguity, when scene is perceived from the viewpoint of (a). (c)–(e) The three different positions/sizes of the ball. Images are rendered from the same viewpoint as (a) and the ball looks identical. Shadows help us define the object relative to its surroundings.

Figure 13.2. Shadows add a complex look to an otherwise simple geometry.

Now, if we add shadows, the set of visible constraints that the eye needs to extract the relative distance of the objects is complete. Figure 13.1(c)–(e) show the result of the three different ball positions of Figure 13.1(b) when shadows are applied to the scene.

In real-time graphics applications, such as games, shadow-generation algorithms can be utilized to enhance the apparent complexity of an otherwise low-polygon surface by casting dramatic, high-contrast shadows (see, for instance, the scene in Figure 13.2). The sharp illumination transitions help our vision system justify the lack of detail-related contrast and help us better detect movement as well as place the objects in three-dimensional space.

13.2 Shadows and Light Sources

Shadows are formed on surfaces due to the blocking of direct illumination caused by parts of objects that are placed between the light source(s) and the surface (blockers/shadow casters). Although indirect illumination (see Chapter 16) contributes to the diffuse color of the areas in shadow, the outgoing intensity of the

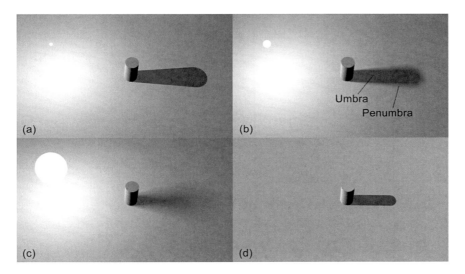

Figure 13.3. The sharpness and shape of a shadow depend on the size and distance of the light source(s). (a) Point light source. (b) Small non-infinitesimal light source (area light). (c) Large area light. (d) Infinite (directional) light source.

diffuse illumination of these areas is generally low, unless the surface is directly lit by other light sources.

The exact shape of the shadow is influenced by the proximity of the light source to the shadow casters, as well as the size of the light emitter. A shadow consists of two zones: the *umbra*, which is the surface area where the shadow is cast with full light-source occlusion, and the *penumbra*, which is partially lit by the light-emitting source. In order for a surface to be partially in shadow, the light source needs to be of non-negligible volume compared to the size of the objects. To be more precise, as distance affects the apparent size of objects, the apparent projection of the light emitter on the surface needs to be non-negligible to create a penumbra. The shadows that are caused by non-infinitesimal light sources and have both an umbra and a penumbra are called *soft shadows* (Figure 13.3(b) and (c)). *Hard shadows* only consist of an umbra and are caused by point-sized light sources and infinitely far light emitters (Figure 13.3(a) and (d)).

The interaction of a point light source and a shadow caster produces, in general, a pyramidal shadow shaft (part of the space where the light of the source cannot reach) clipped at the caster surface (Figure 13.4). The volume that represents the unlit space is called a *shadow volume*. Normally a shadow volume is infinite, meaning that it extends away from the light source to infinity, unless the light source has a local effect and a finite range. In the latter case, the shadow volume extends up to the range of influence of the light source. Directional lights, i.e., lights that are placed at infinity are considered to be casting light in parallel rays toward the scene. Thus, the shadow shafts produced by directional lights are

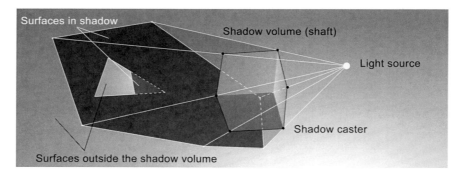

Figure 13.4. Shadow volume. Light is blocked inside the shadow volume. Every surface part that intersects the shaft formed by the shadow caster and the light position is in shadow.

prismatic volumes with parallel sides and the resulting shadows neither converge nor diverge (Figure 13.3(d)).

There are several approaches to shadow generation, but they are mostly distinguished according to the requirement for real-time rendering. For offline photorealistic rendering, shadow generation is usually an integral part of the ray-tracing or global illumination procedure that is used for shading and image synthesis (see Chapters 15 and 16). In real-time computer graphics, there are two algorithms most commonly employed for shadow casting. The first technique, *shadow volumes*, works in object space and is ideal for casting hard, precise shadows on polygonal objects. The second, *shadow mapping*, works in image/texture space, and although it is applicable in a wide range of geometric entity representations and can be adapted to handle semi-transparent and partially occluding media, it is not effective in producing sharp-edged shadows. We will first explain the shadow-volume algorithm, as it is closely related to the geometric aspects of shadow casting and is therefore more intuitive. Then, we will proceed to the shadow-map method.

13.3   Shadow Volumes

The *shadow-volume algorithm*, which first appeared in the late seventies [Crow77], has been through many optimizations and improvements since its inception. As the name implies, it attempts to construct in object space the frusta that are formed for each combination of light source and light-blocking piece of geometry (*occluder*). Then, each pixel to be drawn that lies on the visible geometry is tested for containment in the shadow volumes, and its shading is determined according to this query. The shadow-volume algorithm requires that the occluders are polygonal and assumes that connectivity information is available (or can be determined as a pre-processing step) for these meshes.

13.3.1   Stenciled Shadow Volumes

The shadow-volume containment query for each visible fragment can be mapped to a simple counter check, if the following observation is made (Figure 13.5): Consider a ray that is shot from the eye toward the surface of the object to be drawn. Each time the ray crosses into a shadow frustum, a counter is increased, and when the ray exits the frustum,the counter is decreased. If the surface point is between the eye point and the shadow volume, i.e., evidently not in shadow, the shadow frustum is not visible from the eye location and the first hit occurs

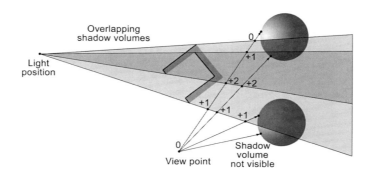

Figure 13.5. Surface-in-shadow test in the basic shadow-volume algorithm. A counter is incremented each time the eye-to-fragment line enters a shadow volume and decremented when it exits. The surface is in shadow when the counter is other than zero.

on the rendered surface. Therefore, no attempt to generate shadow should be made in this case. When the surface fragment is beyond the shadow frustum, the ray enters and exits the shadow volumes an equal number of times before hitting the surface. This means that whenever the counter is zero (n entries meaning n counter increases and n exits resulting in n counter decreases), the surface is not in shadow. If the rendered point lies within the shadow volume, the surface will be hit before the ray exits one or more of the overlapping shadow volumes, leaving the counter with a value greater than zero. This procedure can be supported by graphics hardware if the counter is implemented via the stencil buffer.

The *stencil buffer* is an auxiliary buffer that is allocated in the graphics hardware or the system memory (depending on implementation and application) and implements a counter and comparator unit per image pixel. The stencil buffer is equal in dimension to the frame buffer and usually has a resolution of 8 bits per pixel (values in the range [0, 255]). Similar to the stencil-painting technique, the result stored in the stencil buffer can work as a mask. The most common procedure using this special buffer is to perform one or more rendering passes that fill the buffer with the appropriate values and then use these results to prevent areas of the final rendering pass to be drawn in the frame buffer. The contents of the stencil buffer are compared to a reference value and depending on the *stencil test*, the incoming fragments are eliminated or propagated to the frame buffer. The stencil test is a comparison operator (always/never pass, $\neq, =, \geq, \leq, >, <$).

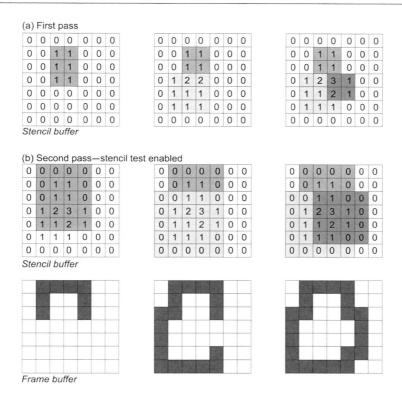

Figure 13.6. Example of stencil-buffer use. (a) Stencil buffer update pass: writing to the frame buffer is disabled and the operation on the stencil values is set to always increase. (b) Conditional rendering pass in the frame buffer: fragments are rendered only if the corresponding stencil values are equal to zero.

Not unlike the depth buffer, the stencil buffer can be conditionally updated; one can specify what operation should be performed on the existing data in the case of a failed or successful Z-buffer test or a comparison of the stencil buffer contents with a reference value. The conditionals are the same as in the case of the stencil mask comparison (see above). Operations on the stencil buffer include replacing, setting, maintaining, incrementing, decrementing, and inverting the current values. Figure 13.6 shows an example of using the stencil buffer to draw the silhouette of a group of primitives in the frame buffer, using an unconditional increment operator (increment always) on the stencil values and an equality test as the stencil-masking operator.

The basic *stenciled shadow-volume* algorithm proposed in [Heid91] and further refined in [Kilg00] generates shadows in hardware-accelerated real-time applications according to the following steps (Figure 13.7):

1. Begin the rendering: Clear the depth and frame buffers and ignore the stencil operations.

2. Render the geometry using only the indirect illumination components (Figure 13.7, Step 1). Surfaces are only affected by ambient light, emissive effects (self-illumination), and additive blending of lightmaps that represent static, indirect illumination (see Chapter 14). The most common practice is to simply draw the objects with the predetermined ambient component of the surface's material while all light sources are switched off.

3. For each occluder (shadow caster), prepare and render the shadow volume:

   (a) Construct a closed (watertight) shadow volume by extruding the faces of the caster that face in the direction of the light source away from the light position according to the light source range. Proper capping of the far end of the frustum is accomplished by inverting the extruded polygons and using them as caps. Further details and optimizations of the shadow-volume construction are presented in Section 13.3.2.

   (b) Render the (eye-space) front-facing polygons of the shadow volumes without actually updating either the frame or the depth buffer (Figure 13.7, Step 2). This is the so-called *Z-pass* test, because it only accepts fragments for further manipulation that are drawn in front of the geometry already rendered. This is only a test and the shadow volumes do not affect the rendered result, as nothing is written into the depth and frame buffers. On the other hand, each time a fragment successfully passes the depth test, the stencil buffer is incremented.

   (c) Now render the (eye-space) back-facing polygons of the shadow volumes and again only update the stencil buffer when a shadow-volume fragment passes the depth test. This time, though, decrement the corresponding stencil values instead of incrementing them (Figure 13.7, Step 3). Steps (b) and (c) together implement the eye-to-surface ray and shadow-volume intersections counter.

4. Render the lit geometry: Enable all diffuse and specular illumination components, enable light sources, and render the geometry over the first pass

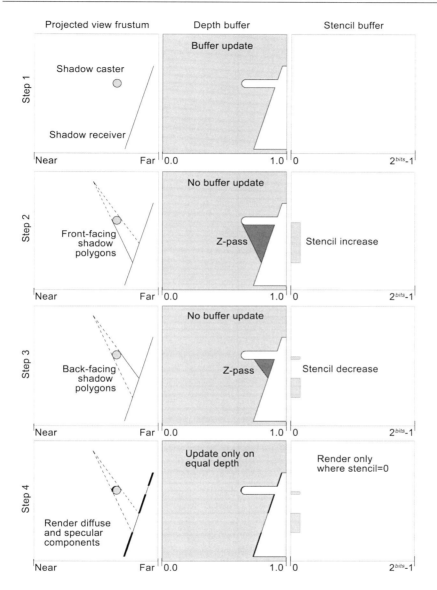

Figure 13.7. Successive steps of the stenciled shadow-volume algorithm. For one light source, two passes are required to render the visible geometry (shadow and diffuse/specular—passes 1 and 4) plus two shadow-volume geometry passes (front and back faces—passes 2 and 3).

(only render where depth values in the Z-buffer are equal to the current pass fragments). The method involves checking the stencil buffer and discarding all fragments that correspond to stencil values not equal to zero (Figure 13.7, Step 4).

Shadows from multiple light sources are handled by repeating Steps 3 and 4 for each light source. In order to properly mix the illumination of the shadowed areas and avoid overshooting the lit surfaces, Step 4 should use additive blending when writing to the frame buffer and completely disable the ambient component of the light sources (as it has already been rendered in Step 2) [Ever02].

13.3.2   Shadow-Volume Construction

The easiest way to construct the shadow volumes for an occluder is to select all the polygons that face the light source and extrude them away from the light position. This will create a shadow shaft for every polygon, and the shadow volume of the entire object is then the union of these polygonal (triangular) frusta (Figure 13.8(d) and (f)). In the case of the stenciled shadow-volume algorithm, these are rendered into the stencil buffer, and all of the common interior shaft faces eventually cancel out.

Let $\mathbf{p}_1\mathbf{p}_2\mathbf{p}_3$ be a polygon that is visible from the position of the light source. The shadow frustum should extend away from this polygon toward the direction of the incident light. Let $\mathbf{p}_L$ be the position of a light source with attenuation range r_L. In the case of a non-attenuating (infinite) light source, r_L is chosen so that it is significantly larger than the scene extents. For each polygon point $\mathbf{p}_i$, the extruded point $\mathbf{p}'_i$ is given by

$$\mathbf{p}'_i = \mathbf{p}_i + (r_L - |\mathbf{p}_i - \mathbf{p}_L|) \cdot (\mathbf{p}_i - \mathbf{p}_L)/|\mathbf{p}_i - \mathbf{p}_L|. \qquad (13.1)$$

Usually, the light sources are considered infinite with respect to the size of the scene, therefore the shadow-volume sides are very long and need not be sized according to the caster position relative to the light source, as is the case in (13.1). This of course simplifies the calculation of the extruded point, considering that $r_L >> |\mathbf{p}_i - \mathbf{p}_L|$:

$$\mathbf{p}'_i = \mathbf{p}_i + r_L \cdot (\mathbf{p}_i - \mathbf{p}_L)/|\mathbf{p}_i - \mathbf{p}_L|. \qquad (13.2)$$

Obviously, for infinite (directional) light sources, where rays are always parallel to a direction $\hat{\mathbf{l}}$, Equation (13.2) is simplified to $\mathbf{p}'_i = \mathbf{p}_i + r_L \cdot \hat{\mathbf{l}}$ for every point of all casters.

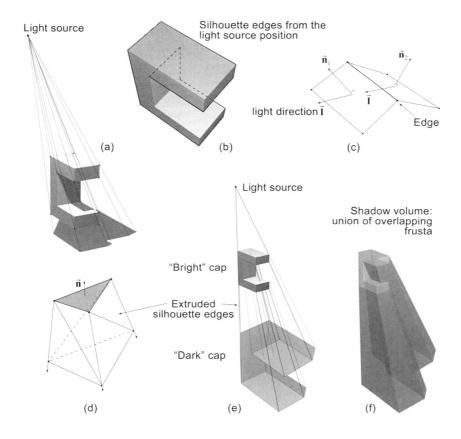

Figure 13.8. Shadow-volume creation using triangle and silhouette extrusion. (a) Casters do not need to be convex and may be self-shadowed. (b) Silhouette edges as seen from the point of view of the light. (c) Silhouette edge determination. (d) 2-triangle shaft-sides are formed by extruding the triangle or silhouette edges. (e) The "bright" and "dark" caps are the polygons facing toward and away from the light source, respectively. (f). The final closed shadow volume.

This technique is very straightforward and adds no computational cost apart from the one required to build the geometry for the shafts. However, it takes no advantage of the fact that triangles on the occluder surface share edges, which, when extruded, will create triangles that share all vertices and eventually cancel each other. These shadow-shaft polygons, although invisible, are transformed and rasterized, slowing down the rendering procedure. Even worse, if we use the stenciled shadow-volume algorithm, we have to render all front-facing shadow-volume polygons in one pass and all back-facing polygons in another pass, leading to a very likely situation that the stencil buffer gets saturated. An alternative methodology can be adopted, which involves a more complex shadow-frustum generation stage but results in far fewer polygons. The extra computations needed can significantly slow down performance in case of highly tessellated models in dynamically lit scenes, so this variation is recommended either for low polygon models or for static light-object relationships (the shadow-frustum generation is performed as a pre-processing step).

The pairs of sides that form the frusta for the occluder triangles can be efficiently removed if, instead of extruding the silhouette of each individual triangle, one extrudes the *silhouette* of the union of the faces visible from the light source. This union of triangles also forms the "near" cap, relative to the light source (also called the "bright cap").

The above consideration leads to the breakup of the shadow-volume construction into a silhouette-determination stage and an edge-extrusion stage, similar to the one used for the triangular shafts.

The silhouette of a polygonal surface relative to a viewpoint in space (here the light position) is the set of all visible polygon edges that are shared by at least one back-facing and one front-facing polygon with respect to the particular point of view (Figure 13.8(b)). For open (non-watertight) 3D shapes, this set is extended to include all open edges.

As objects or light sources move, polygons leave or enter the shadow, i.e., face toward or away from a light, and therefore, the silhouette needs to be dynamically modified for these meshes. The search for the edges that comprise the object silhouette poly-lines requires that all polygons are compared and the common edges between polygon i and j are identified. First, as a preprocessing step, assuming a *polygon soup* (unstructured set of polygons), we have to determine all neighboring polygons and mark the common edges. For a manifold triangulated surface, the basic structure that holds the information about the polygon points and normals (indexed or not) has to be enriched with connectivity information, which can be filled according to the following code fragment:

```
typedef struct
{ Point3f v[3]; Vector3f n[3];
  Vector3f facenormal;
  long neighbor[3]; // <-- initialize to -1;
} Triangle;
```

```
int CommonEdge(Point3f a1, Point3f a2, Point3f b1, Point3f b2)
{
  extern float weld_thres_squared; // avoid sqr. root
  Vector3f d1 = PointSubtract(a1-b1);
  Vector3f d2 = PointSubtract(a2-b2);
  return ( DotProduct(d1,d1)<weld_thres_squared &&
           DotProduct(d2,d2)<weld_thres_squared )
}


void FindConnectivity(Triangle *tri, long numOfTris)
{
  long i,j; int k,n;
  for (i=0;i<numOfTris-1;i++)
    for (j=i+1;j<numOfTris;j++)
      for (k=0;k<3;k++)
        for (n=0;n<3;n++)
          if ( CommonEdge(tri[i].v[k], tri[i].v[(k+1)%3]
                          tri[j].v[n], tri[j].v[(n+1)%3])
          {
            tri[i].neighbor[k] = j;
            // edge v[k]-v[k+1] is shared with tr. j
            tri[j].neighbor[n] = -1;
            // mark adjacency only on one triangle to
            // avoid double edges during sil. detection
            break;
          }
}
```

Whenever the silhouette needs to be updated, the connectivity information of the mesh is used and if $\left[\hat{\mathbf{n}}_i \cdot (\mathbf{p}_L - \mathbf{p}_{i0})\right] \cdot \left[\hat{\mathbf{n}}_j \cdot (\mathbf{p}_L - \mathbf{p}_{j0})\right] < 0$ for two polygons i and j, their common edge belongs to the edge list of the silhouette (Figure 13.8(c)). In our code example this is translated to the following silhouette determination routine:

```
typedef struct
{ Point3f * edgeVertex;
  int numOfEdges;
} edgeList;

edgeList* FindSilhouette( Triangle * tri, long numOfTris, Vector3f
                          light, boolean infinite)
{
  long i,j, edges=0;
  int k;
```

```
Vector3f L, ni, nj;
float visi, visj;
Point3f * endpts = // Allocate a large edge buffer:
    (Point3f*)malloc(sizeof(Point3f)*numOfTris*3*2);
for (i=0; i<numOfTris; i++)
  for (k=0; k<3; k++)
  {
    j = tri[i].neighbor[k];
    if (j!=-1) // if neighbor is marked:
    {
      ni = tri[i].facenormal;
      L = infinite? VectorInvert(light):
          VectorNorm(PointSubtract(light,tri[i].v[0]));
      visi = DotProduct(ni,L);
      nj = tri[j].facenormal;
      L = infinite? VectorInvert(light):
          VectorNorm(PointSubtract(light,tri[j].v[0]));
      visj = DotProduct(nj,L);
      if (visi*visj<0)
      {
        PointCopy(endpts[2*edges+0],tri[i].v[k];
        PointCopy(endpts[2*edges+1],tri[i].v[(k+1)%3];
        edges++;
      }
    }
  }
edgeList * list = (edgeList*)malloc(sizeof(edgeList));
list->numOfEdges = edges;
list->edgeVertex = (Point3f*)malloc(sizeof(Point3f)*2*edges);
for (i=0;i<2*edges;i++)
  PointCopy(list->edgeVertex[i],endpts[i]);
free(endpts);
return(list);
}
```

The shadow volumes from silhouette edges are created in a manner identical to the simple, triangle-based-shaft case. An interesting observation for watertight meshes is that the near (bright) cap of the shadow volume consists of all the triangles that face towards the light source. The far (dark) cap is made of the rest of the mesh's faces, after extruding their vertices according to Equations (13.1) and (13.2) (Figure 13.9). The shadow-volume sides are the extruded silhouette edges.

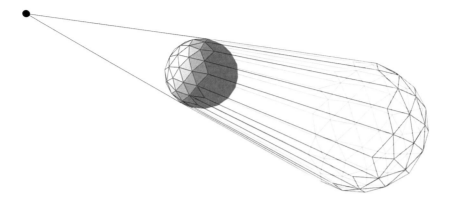

Figure 13.9. Shadow volume using the shadow caster's back- and front-facing triangles as caps and the extruded silhouette edges.

A small problem that is associated with the geometry of the shadow volume is the *self-shadowing* of polygons at the bright cap. In practice, due to the fact that the polygons that comprise the cap belong to the occluder and therefore coincide with the actual rendered polygons lit by the light source, the "bright" side of the occluder may exhibit shadow artifacts during the second pass, as depth-test accuracy may be inadequate. The shadow-volume triangles generated have the same coordinates as the renderable geometry of the occluder, and this is prone to cause the erroneous update of the stencil buffer due to incorrect depth comparison during the scan conversion (*Z-fighting*). An easy way to overcome this problem is to push the near cap a little further away from the light source, using the same extrusion direction as the far-cap vertices.

13.3.3 Pitfalls and Improvements

The Z-pass stenciled shadow-volume algorithm is a robust, low-complexity method for rendering shadows, but unfortunately it demands that the near clipping plane of the viewing frustum does not intersect the shadow volume, and this also includes the case when the viewpoint lies inside the shadow volume. As stated in [Horn05], the problem is not as simple as determining whether the viewpoint is inside the shadow frustum. Cases may occur where the view plane is entirely in shadow while the viewer is outside the shadow frustum. To this end, some solutions have been proposed that try to clamp the shadow volume at the near clipping plane or fill in the missing geometry of the volume [Bata99, Dief96]. However, it has been proven that such an approach cannot guarantee an accurate result in all view-frustum and shadow-frustum configurations [Ever02].

Carmack [Carm00] and Bilodeau and Songy [Bilo99] independently proposed a solution to the Z-pass algorithm problem by introducing two similar approaches that reverse the counting tests. The popular *Z-fail* algorithm by John Carmack (also called *Carmack's Reverse*) removes the near clipping problem but raises the same problem at the far clipping plane. Fortunately, it is easier to ensure that the far clipping plane does not intersect the shadow volumes, either by consistently preparing the far caps of the shadow volume or by pushing the clipping plane to infinity. Let us first see how the stenciled shadow-volume algorithm is modified according to the Z-fail test:

1. Begin the rendering: Clear the depth and frame buffers and ignore the stencil operations.

2. Render the geometry using only indirect illumination and emissive components (Figure 13.10, Step 1).

3. For each occluder (shadow caster), prepare and render the shadow volume:

    (a) Construct a closed (watertight) shadow volume by extruding the faces of the caster that face in the direction of the light source away from the light position, according to the light-source range. Proper capping of the far end of the frustum is accomplished by inverting the extruded polygons and using them as caps or, for watertight models, by using the extruded back-facing polygons.

    (b) Render the (eye-space) back-facing polygons of the shadow volumes without actually updating either the frame or the depth buffer (Figure 13.10, Step 2). This is the Z-fail test. If the shadow-volume fragments fail the depth test (i.e., they are hidden), the stencil buffer is incremented. The shadow volumes do not affect the rendered result, as nothing is written into the depth and frame buffers.

    (c) Now render the (eye-space) front-facing polygons of the shadow volumes and again only update the stencil buffer when a shadow-volume fragment fails the depth test. This time though, decrement the corresponding stencil values instead of incrementing them (Figure 13.10, Step 3).

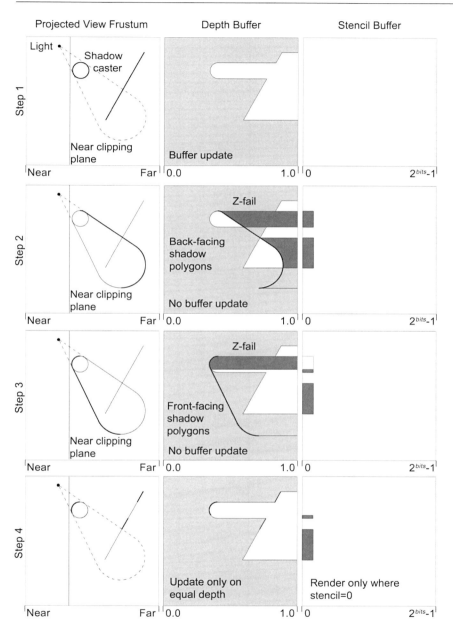

Figure 13.10. Successive steps of the Z-fail stenciled shadow-volume algorithm.

(d) Render the lit geometry: Enable all diffuse and specular illumination components, enable the light source and render the geometry over the first pass wherever the stencil values are equal to zero (Figure 13.10, Step 4).

As already mentioned, the Z-fail stenciled shadow-volume algorithm transposes the problem of the intersection of the near clipping plane with the shadow volume to the far clipping plane. Instead of counting shadow volume enters and exits along the eye-pixel ray starting from the eye and ending at the first visible fragment, the Z-fail algorithm counts ray intersections starting from infinity and ending at the nearest visible fragment. This means that a failure to render a front-facing shadow-volume fragment due to the fact that it is discarded by the near clipping plane has the same impact as suggesting that the shadow volume is closer to the viewer than the nearest fragment. Therefore, near-plane clipping of the shadow volume causes no problems.

On the other hand, as counting starts from back (infinity) to front, all back-facing shadow-volume fragments should be closer than or at "infinity" of the view frustum in order to be taken into account. Otherwise, the resulting stencil mask may be incorrect. By capping the open far end of the shadow volume at or before the far clipping plane, one makes sure that infinity is always outside the shadow volume. To solve the capping problem, one may create a far (dark) cap by selecting the back-facing polygons of the caster relative to the light direction and extruding them to a safe distance that ensures that they are not clipped by the far plane.

Although the capping of the shadow volume solves the far clipping problem, the extrusion of the faces to a fixed distance may still produce errors if the light source moves close relative to the expanse of a caster (Figure 13.11). As the light position approaches the geometry of the caster, the solid angle subtended by the silhouette increases while the radial distance (extrusion distance) remains fixed. This means that the far cap moves closer to the light and possibly leaves parts of the scene outside the shadow volume. A unified solution, which takes this situation into account, was given by Everitt and Kilgard [Ever02]. They suggested using the Z-fail variation of the stenciled shadow-volume algorithm but proposed setting the far clipping plane at "infinity" and constructing an infinite closed shadow volume.

Setting the far clipping plane at infinity can be achieved by changing the standard projection matrix used to render the scene (see Chapter 4) and, more specifically, by estimating the limit of the matrix as the far clipping plane distance tends

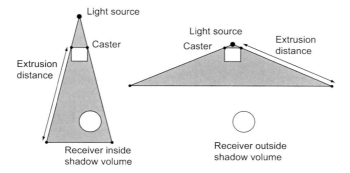

Figure 13.11. Finite shadow-frustum deficiency. When the light source is close to the shadow-casting geometry, the distance between the bright and dark caps is shortened, leaving potentially shadowed geometry outside the shadow volume.

to infinity. For instance, consider the transformation matrix specified in OpenGL:

$$\mathbf{P} = \begin{bmatrix} \frac{2n}{r-l} & 0 & \frac{r+l}{r-l} & 0 \\ 0 & \frac{2n}{t-b} & \frac{t+b}{t-b} & 0 \\ 0 & 0 & -\frac{f+n}{f-n} & -\frac{2nf}{f-n} \\ 0 & 0 & -1 & 0 \end{bmatrix}. \tag{13.3}$$

In the well-known form of the above projection matrix definition, n is the near clipping plane distance, f is the far clipping plane range, and l, r, t, and b are the extents of the frustum at the near (view plane) distance. In order to acquire a matrix formulation for the perspective projection when f moves to infinity, we need to evaluate the limit of the matrix in Equation (13.3). Considering that only the third row of the matrix is affected by the limit operation and the fact that $\lim_{x \to \infty} (x \pm a / x \pm b) = 1$, we get

$$\mathbf{P}_{\text{inf}} = \lim_{f \to \infty} (\mathbf{P}) = \begin{bmatrix} \frac{2n}{r-l} & 0 & \frac{r+l}{r-l} & 0 \\ 0 & \frac{2n}{t-b} & \frac{t+b}{t-b} & 0 \\ 0 & 0 & -1 & -2n \\ 0 & 0 & -1 & 0 \end{bmatrix}. \tag{13.4}$$

The Z-fail approach is slower than the Z-pass one, depending on the scene's depth complexity. However, the two methods can be used interchangeably, according to whether the viewport intersects the shadow volume or not. Therefore, the Z-fail method may be applied only when necessary.

Another issue that may sometimes arise is that successive stencil increases or decreases can saturate the stencil buffer. This can happen when the depth complexity of the overlapping shadow frusta exceeds the stencil-buffer accuracy [McGu03]. In simple terms, for an 8-bit stencil buffer, there is room for only 255 overlapping shadow volumes, because the stencil-buffer values can only be incremented that many times. A solution that may partially alleviate the problem is to utilize wrap-around stencil operations, supported by modern graphics hardware. When the stencil count reaches the maximum integer value allowed, it wraps to zero and keeps increasing. Similarly, when decrementing the stencil buffer, values below zero are wrapped to 2^{bits}-1 where *bits* denotes the number of available stencil-buffer bits.

Many optimizations of the basic shadow-volume algorithm can be devised to increase the performance of the real-time execution of the algorithm. For static lights and casters, the shadow volumes need only be calculated once. After the shadow frusta have been determined and the corresponding geometry set, the shadow volumes for light sources that do not move and light-blocking static geometry are valid as long as both conditions hold. This knowledge can greatly improve the speed of the algorithm, because much of its computational cost lies in the determination of the silhouettes and the set-up of the shadow-volume frusta.

13.4   Shadow Maps

In contrast to the shadow-volume method for shadow generation, which is geometry-based, shadow maps operate in image space and use the depth buffer to sort surfaces with respect to the light source line of sight. This shadow-generation technique was first introduced by Williams in 1978 [Will78], and its variations are still widely used in rendering software and real-time applications, such as computer games.

The main concept of the algorithm is that the geometry is projected once from the viewpoint of the light source to determine which parts of the objects have a clear line of sight to the light-source location (i.e., are visible/lit by the source). Then, the scene is normally projected in the eye-space coordinate system and each fragment produced is transformed to the light-space reference frame, where its (new, transformed) depth value is compared with the visibility information stored in the light-space depth buffer. If the fragment's depth in light-space coordinates is greater than the stored one, then the fragment is hidden from the light source's point of view and, therefore, in shadow.

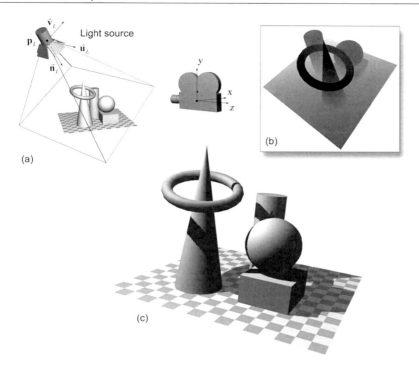

Figure 13.12. The shadow-map algorithm. (a) Spotlight set-up. (b) Depth-buffer capture of the scene from the point of view of the light source. (c) Final pass. Each fragment is tested for visibility against the light-space depth map.

Let a directional spotlight with a lighting range r_L be placed at a location $\mathbf{p}_L$ in the scene and point along the direction $\hat{\mathbf{n}}_L$ (Figure 13.12(a)). We can define a local (right-handed) coordinate system for this light source by arbitrarily selecting a pair of up- and right-directional vectors, which comprise along with the light direction an orthonormal basis of mutually perpendicular unit vectors $(\hat{\mathbf{u}}_L, \hat{\mathbf{v}}_L, -\hat{\mathbf{n}}_L)$. Also let $\mathbf{M}_L$ and $\mathbf{P}_L$ be the geometric transformation and projection matrices, respectively, of the light source. The projection matrix can be defined by the symmetrical frustum formed along the spotlight central axis $\hat{\mathbf{n}}_L$ with a near plane distance set to a small positive number n and the far clipping plane adjusted to r_L. The top, bottom, right and left extents of the frustum should depend on the spotlight-beam aperture θ_a: $l = r = t = b = n \cdot \tan(\theta_a/2)$. The shadow test itself is very simple and is divided into the following two steps:

- Render the scene from the light-source's reference frame $(\mathbf{p}_L, \hat{\mathbf{u}}_L, \hat{\mathbf{v}}_L, -\hat{\mathbf{n}}_L)$ by first transforming every object according to $\mathbf{M}_L^{-1}$ and projecting it using $\mathbf{P}_L$ (Figure 13.12(b)). Store the corresponding depth map Z_L (*shadow map*).

- Revert to the normal camera view and render the scene (Figure 13.12(c)). A point $\mathbf{p} = (x, y, z)$ on a surface is shadowed if it is located at a greater distance than the value stored in Z_L, when $\mathbf{p}$ is expressed in the light source's viewport coordinates: $\mathbf{p}' = (x', y', z') = \mathbf{P}_L \cdot \mathbf{M}_L^{-1} \cdot \mathbf{p}$, that is, if $z' > Z_L(x', y')$. If z' is outside the range $[n, r_L]$, $\mathbf{p}$ is considered to be in shadow (beyond the limits of the light beam).

In order to apply this method to non-directional lights, multiple shadow maps must be combined to hold the visibility information around the point light source so that any direction on the unit sphere centered at $\mathbf{p}_L$ is addressable. If multiple light sources participate in the scene, the above procedure is duplicated for each one of them.

Note that, as is the case with the shadow volumes, the shadow information (here, the shadow map) need not be recalculated at every frame in the basic algorithm but only whenever the lit environment changes or the light source moves. A change in the viewpoint of the camera has no impact on the calculation of the shadow map.

Today's graphics hardware can take advantage of projective texture-coordinate transformations [Sega92] and complex texture-component manipulations [Seg04] to provide good quality shadows in real time [Jr.04], even with a high polygon count.

Rendering shadows with the shadow-map algorithm using hardware acceleration and standard APIs normally requires a number of simple steps, but first, we need to realize that we are operating on screen-order, scan-converted fragments. We have to transform these eye-clip-space coordinates back to world space coordinates and then to light-clip space (Figure 13.13):

$$\mathbf{p}'_{\text{frag}} = (x'_{\text{frag}}, y'_{\text{frag}}, z'_{\text{frag}}) = \mathbf{P}_L \cdot \mathbf{M}_L^{-1} \cdot \mathbf{M}_C \mathbf{P}_C^{-1} \cdot \mathbf{p}_{\text{frag}}, \qquad (13.5)$$

where $\mathbf{M}_C$ is the rigid transformation that places the virtual camera in the world and $\mathbf{P}_C$ is the camera-projection matrix. The three steps required are the following (Figure 13.13):

- If necessary, compute the shadow map of one or more lights by rendering the world from the light source's point of view. Maintain the affine- and projection-transformation matrices used for the light-space frustum set-up.

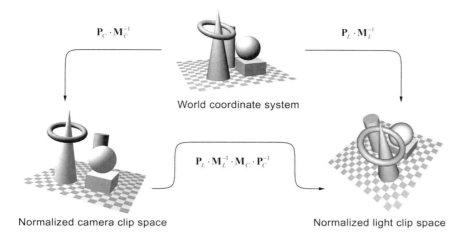

Figure 13.13. Fragment transformation from eye space to light space for comparison with the shadow-map depth values.

- Render the unlit world into the normal-view frame buffer. The lighting at this stage should simulate the illumination perceived at the areas that will be in shadow. The WCS-to-VCS transformation of this pass (modelview matrix in OpenGL) needs to be inverted and stored (see Equation (13.5)). Note that this is indirectly calculated by transforming the eye-space texture-generation coordinate plane along with the actual geometry [Jr.04].

- Perform the shadow-comparison pass and shade the lit parts of the surfaces. This step requires that all eye-clip-space fragments be transformed to the normalized texture space of the shadow map. We have pre-calculated and stored the necessary transformations, which can be applied to the fragments in the order described by Equation (13.5). To further convert the light-clip-space coordinates to shadow-map coordinates, the transformed fragments are scaled and translated so that the $(x'_{\text{frag}}, y'_{\text{frag}})$ pair may correspond to the (u, v) shadow-map texture coordinates and z'_{frag} can be compared to the stored, normalized depth map. Graphics hardware often allows the comparison of the third texture coordinate (normalized z'_{frag}) with the stored texture depth. The result can be used as a mask for the current rendering pass, which draws the scene with the particular light source turned on (Figure 13.14). The comparison outcome is treated as a transparency com-

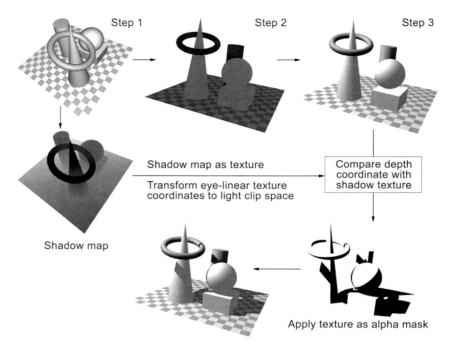

Step 1   Step 2   Step 3

Shadow map as texture

Transform eye-linear texture
coordinates to light clip space

Compare depth
coordinate with
shadow texture

Shadow map

Apply texture as alpha mask

Figure 13.14. Hardware shadow maps. Shadowed geometry is rendered in three passes. Step 1: Shadow-map generation. Step 2: Shadowed illumination. Step 3: Lit surface illumination.

ponent in a texture map (alpha channel), which modulates the overlay of the current pass over the darkened surface (first camera pass).

13.4.1 Advantages of and Problems with Shadow Maps

The biggest advantage of the shadow-map algorithm is its simplicity and utilization of a well-established hardware-accelerated algorithm. The method does not directly depend on the scene complexity and is only affected by the image-level depth comparisons and depth-map rendering time.

For complex, dynamic environments, shadow maps are regarded as the most attractive choice. Relying on the very generic Z-buffer algorithm, shadow maps can be used with any type of rendering primitive, from polygons to volumetric data and implicit surfaces, provided that a depth buffer can be prepared from the rendered fragments of the geometry.

Apart from this, shadow maps allow the generation of shadows from transparent geometry because they operate at fragment level. If a fragment is alpha-culled (fragment is rejected due to opacity dropping below a predefined threshold) in the light-space rendering pass, it will not produce a shadow in the eye-space pass. This fact can be exploited to produce elaborate shadows from simple geometry, such as planes with texture maps depicting foliage or netting with transparency.

On the other hand, the main shadow-map algorithm suffers from aliasing, which comes in various forms. A depth map, being an image itself, has a limited resolution and, therefore, the shadow-map rendering pass samples the space subtended by the light frustum at a finite spatial resolution. Since each shadow-map cell represents a sheared pyramidal ray that is projected through the shadow frustum's near clip plane toward the world, the footprint size s_{shadow} of the corresponding shadow texel varies according to the distance from and the angle at which a surface is encountered. If s_{shadow} is larger than the footprint of a pixel projected on the same surface point, the shadow map is oversampled, leading to magnification aliasing manifested as jagged shadow boundaries (Figure 13.15). If s_{shadow} is significantly smaller than the corresponding image-pixel footprint, the shadow map is undersampled and may cause noise artifacts. Stamminger and Drettakis call this class of aliasing problems *perspective aliasing* [Stam02]. See Section 13.4.2 for ways to address this problem.

Another form of aliasing, *projection aliasing*, occurs when the projected light from the light source—and therefore the shadow-map texel footprint—becomes almost parallel to the surface. This type of aliasing can only be partially alleviated by increasing the resolution of the shadow buffer at the expense, of course, of rendering time and texture memory.

Depth-value quantization can cause serious aliasing problems, especially when the extents of the clipping volume of the light source are too large, or the light cone is very wide. Placing the near clipping plane of the light source frustum near the light position relative to the far-light volume plane can dramatically decrease the depth resolution at the far end of the frustum. When the eye-space fragments are transformed to light space, depth comparisons are prone to numerical errors due to insufficient quantization of the stored z-values, resulting in poor and misplaced shadow boundaries. The problem is most noticeable in self-shadowing cases, where the same surface region is rendered in both the shadow map and the eye-space buffers. This problem can be observed in Figure 13.15, where dark spots appear on the surfaces of the objects due to erroneous self-shadowing depth comparisons. A solution to this problem is to offset the depth values a little further away from the near depth value (0), according to the expected "worse" resolution

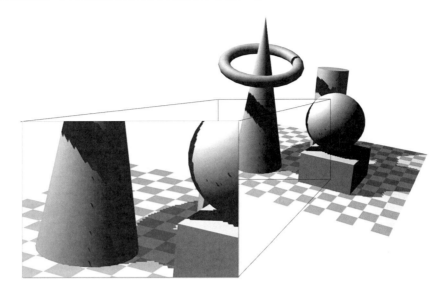

Figure 13.15. Aliasing in the shadow-map algorithm due to shadow-map resolution and depth comparison inaccuracy.

of the shadow-map depth quantization. This depth bias introduces a safety margin in the self-shadowing depth comparisons but also moves the shadows a little further away from the light source, making them appear detached from the shadow casters in some cases.

In shadow-mapped light sources, there is always the trade-off between range and shadow accuracy and, therefore, smart ways to adjust the light frustum near and far planes are sought, mostly in the form of detecting the nearest and furthest casters and receivers subtended by the light cone. Bounding volumes and scene graph management can help in this sorting/culling problem, but they introduce a CPU overhead nevertheless.

The shadow-map algorithm works for directional light sources with a light cone of less than 180 degrees. In order to use the method with point lights, multiple shadow maps have to be used to cover all directions around the light source. These maps are usually organized in a cubical configuration with the light source at the center of the cube, because it allows a straightforward implementation in conventional hardware-accelerated APIs and a reasonable depth distortion due to the 90-degree aperture of the resulting frusta. Of course, producing the full range of shadow maps means that the scene has to be rendered up to six times just to prepare the shadow information.

Finally, as part of treating their aliasing problems, shadow maps can produce smooth shadow boundaries. In fact, with shadow maps, it is almost impossible not to produce soft shadows at high image resolutions, if jagged boundaries are to be avoided.

13.4.2 Dealing with Shadow-Map Aliasing⊛

As will be explained in Chapter 14, texture maps can be accessed by filtering the texture values over some region of the texture image instead of finding the closest value that corresponds to the current fragment. The problem is that filtering the depth information of the shadow map with this scheme would not effectively remove the aliasing; after all, the resulting filtered light-space depth image value of the shadow map would then be compared with the transformed eye-space fragment depth, and thus, we would again end up with a binary outcome.

This, of course, makes the rendering of soft shadow boundaries impossible and, as stated in [Reev87], the (filtered) depth values along the edges of objects would not correspond to the depicted geometry, because near and far values on surface boundaries would be erroneously averaged. This is demonstrated in Figure 13.16, where a 3×3 filter kernel was applied to a shadow map before comparing the transformed fragments (shown as small circles) to the map depth values. Averaging has caused one of the texels to darken significantly. After comparing it with the incoming fragment, the binary outcome is no shadow, while the fragment should be in the shadow.

Swapping the order of filtering and depth comparisons results in what is called *percentage closer filtering* (PCF) [Reev87]. With PCF, the shadow value is no longer binary (shadow/no shadow). A number of depth samples distributed in the neighborhood of the final eye-space fragment to be rendered are compared to the unfiltered shadow-map depth values. The binary results are then averaged and the final shadow value is the percentage of the surface area corresponding to the fragment that is in shadow. Many sampling patterns, weighting functions, and interpolation schemes can be applied in the final stage to smooth out the shadow values. PCF has been implemented in most software renderers and has been adapted for modern GPUs [Bunn04]. The original algorithm by Reeves et al. [Reev87] rendered the surfaces using micro-polygons, i.e., a fine tessellation of a surface into small planar fragments. Point samples could be acquired over the micro-polygons using Monte Carlo techniques and then transformed into light

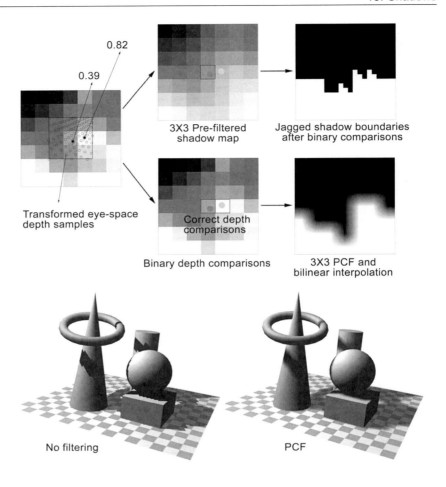

Figure 13.16. Percentage closer filtering (PCF) versus shadow-map pre-filtering. Averaged map samples may produce wrong depth-sort results and also cannot avoid jagged edges. PCF filters the binary results, producing smooth shadows.

space where the binary comparisons would take place. In scanline polygonal renderers, as in hardware rasterizers, the pixel fragments cannot be sampled with a varying size and shape pattern as in the case of the micro-polygons but instead, a fixed kernel has to be used. Still, practical implementations of the algorithm give good visual results.

The post-filtering of the shadow samples produces smooth shadow boundaries by default. Although this may be a desirable feature in some cases, the jagged pattern samples can still be noticeable, especially in a real-time implementation of the algorithm, where PCF is sub-optimal, if applicable at all. Another way to deal with aliasing and at the same time avoid the significant loss of shadow-boundary crispness is to try to sample the object space over a grid that more closely matches the eye-space sample distribution of the world. Up to now, we have regarded shadow maps as a view-independent method for shadow generation. Although this is essentially true, the quality of the shadow depends on the relation between the view frustum and the shadow frustum.

Stamminger and Drettakis [Stam02] proposed a modification of the shadow-map algorithm that adapts the map resolution to the current view angle. Instead of transforming and projecting the geometry expressed in the world coordinate system as the original algorithm does, their method, *perspective shadow maps* (PSM), creates the shadow maps after transforming the world and the light source into the camera-view clip-space (post-perspective space—CSS). As the authors explain, because the captured shadow map "sees" the scene *after* the camera perspective projection, perspective aliasing is significantly reduced. But let us see why this is true.

When the geometry of the scene is subjected to the perspective projection in order to render it into the viewport, the view frustum—and consequently the geometry—is distorted into a cube, which is then orthogonally mapped onto the viewport (see Section 4.4.2). This projective mapping enlarges elements near the viewpoint, while it shrinks objects far from it. However, the same effect applies to the footprints of the shadow map onto the surfaces (Figure 13.17). The depth samples stored in the shadow map correspond to evenly placed cells (pixels) on the light source projection plane. If the light coordinate system is rigidly transformed relative to the world coordinate system, the world is evenly sampled from the viewpoint of the light. But when these samples are projected onto the camera view plane, the same perspective distortion occurs as with the projected geometry, leading to the jagged artifacts described in Section 13.4.1. With PSM, the shadow map samples the geometry evenly, after it has been enlarged or shrunk by the perspective projection of the camera (Figure 13.17, bottom). Therefore, surfaces near the camera viewpoint are captured with finer detail in the shadow map because they appear larger in the post-perspective space. When the view fragments are transformed to the shadow-map space, the sampling of the shadow texture is more even, as the projective portion of the viewing transformation has already been taken into account.

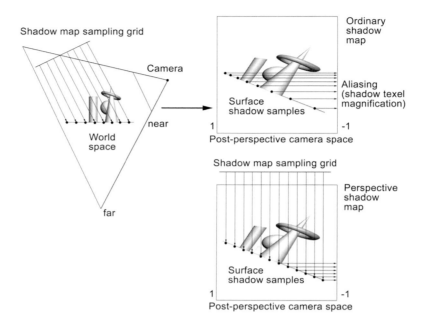

Figure 13.17. Perspective shadow maps capture the light depth buffer after both the geometry and the light source have been transformed to post-projective space (CSS). Aliasing due to perspective magnification of the shadow samples is substantially suppressed.

One obvious drawback of the PSM is the need to update the shadow volume when the view changes considerably, regardless of whether the world has changed or not. Of course, in practice, real-time applications seldom contain solely static environments and therefore the shadow maps need to be redrawn anyway.

The benefits of the perspective shadow-map algorithm do not come without a cost though. PSM is more complex as an algorithm than the generic shadow-map algorithm. The added complexity comes from the need to treat relative positions of the light source and projection method (point/infinite) as separate cases (Figure 13.18) [Stam02].

When transforming the light frustum from world coordinates to post-perspective space, parallel rays from infinite light sources become convergent or divergent. The rays diverge from a point on the infinity plane in post-perspective space (where a new point source replaces the infinite light) when the directional light faces toward the camera (Figure 13.18(a)). When the directional light faces

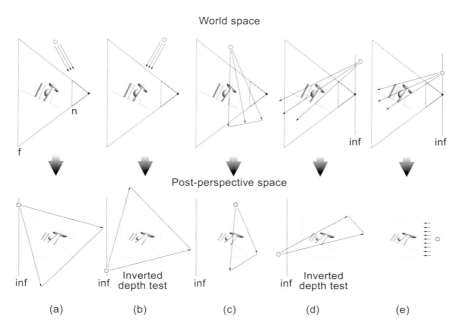

Figure 13.18. Light set-up cases in post-perspective space for the PSM algorithm. (a) Infinite light facing toward the viewpoint. (b) Infinite light facing away from the viewpoint. (c) Point light in front of the viewpoint. (d) Point light behind the viewpoint. (e) Point light on the infinity plane (plane $z = 0$ in the camera-coordinate system).

away from the viewpoint, light rays converge to a point on the infinity plane in post-perspective space (Figure 13.18(b)). Technically, this case is treated as a point source placed at the point of convergence and an inversion of the depth range in the shadow map.

A similar distinction in separate cases happens when dealing with point light sources in world space. Point light sources in front of the viewer remain point lights (Figure 13.18(c)), while lights behind the view plane are inverted and mapped to the infinity plane (Figure 13.18(d)). Finally, light sources exactly on the camera plane become infinite lights in post-perspective space (Figure 13.18(e)).

The projective transformation of the world according to the camera-view frustum before the recording of the shadow map has a small side effect. Objects that act as shadow casters (present in the shadow frustum) but are on the back side of the viewpoint frustum, will move "beyond infinity" (Figure 13.19). In post-

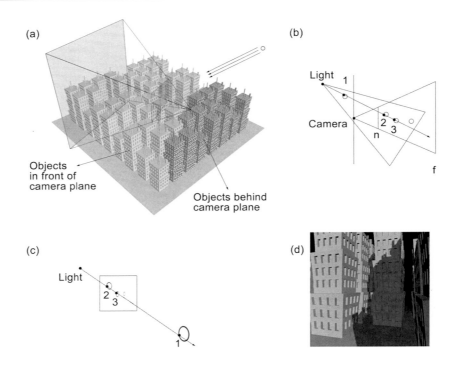

Figure 13.19. Post-perspective space problems. (a) Some shadow casters may by behind the camera plane. (b) The desired depth sorting of casters and receivers, including objects behind the camera. (c) Objects behind the camera move beyond infinity in post-perspective space and are sorted at a wrong depth. (d) Missing shadows due to bad caster-depth sorting.

perspective space, these objects will appear beyond the object in front of the camera (Figure 13.19(c)), leading to wrong depth order and, of course, missing or misplaced shadows (Figure 13.19(d)).

In the original paper [Stam02], the author proposed to move back the camera point so that the view frustum includes all shadow casters (virtual camera) (Figure 13.20). The change in the camera frustum is of course done only for the post-projective space calculation for the shadow-map acquisition and not during the actual frame-buffer rendering. This operation has the added cost of identifying whether there are casters outside the frustum and then modifying the camera to accommodate them inside the clipping volume. Moving the camera away results

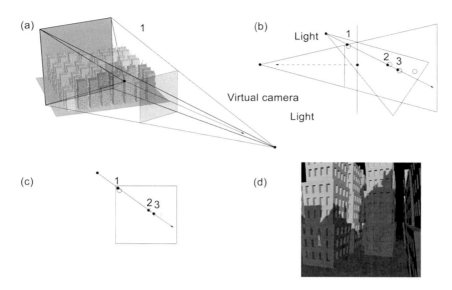

Figure 13.20. The virtual camera PSM modification. (a), (b) In post-perspective space, the camera moves back to include all casters in front of the viewpoint. (c) All objects are sorted correctly. (d) Correct shadows.

in decreased perspective foreshortening, which degrades the quality of the perspective shadow maps. Kozlov [Kozl04] proposes some interesting variations of the original method based on the original PSM algorithm, such as building a special projection matrix to dispense with the virtual camera. Figure 13.21 presents comparative results between a standard shadow map and the perspective shadow map.

13.5   Exercises

1. Using the Z-fail stenciled shadow-volume algorithm, implement an extended version to support area lights (spherical and quadrilateral sources). *Hint:* Choose appropriate sample points on the light source surface and use them as multiple point lights. How should their brightness be adjusted? How should the rendering passes be blended to create a penumbra?

2. Which shadow-generation algorithm would you use to render a dense forest and why? What optimizations can be done?

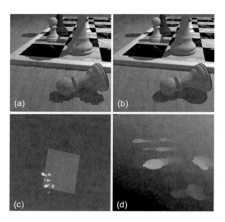

Figure 13.21. Comparison of the regular shadow map with the perspective shadow map. (a) Resulting image (regular shadow map). (b) Resulting image with PSM. (c) Regular shadow map. (d) PSM. (*Images courtesy of M. Stamminger and G. Drettakis.*)

3. If shadows were to be accompanied by volumetric light shafts (like sun rays passing through clouds), which algorithm would you use and how would you integrate both effects in one algorithm?

4. If, for a highly detailed scene, one could use low-polygon invisible proxy geometry (mattes) to cast shadows instead of using the high-resolution models, what problems could occur and how could one counter them? *Hint:* Consider shadow proxy–actual object intersection problems and self-shadowing.

5. Implement a shadow-map algorithm for point (omnidirectional) lights.

14

Texturing

The picture will have charm when each colour
is very unlike the one next to it.
—Leon Battista Alberti

14.1   Introduction

Up to this point, we have defined material properties for surfaces and explained how it is possible to assign color information per vertex to them. We have also presented a mechanism to modulate the resulting, interpolated color according to an illumination model and the visibility of the light sources in order to get a properly lit, solid look for the three-dimensional objects. Color and other material properties have been assigned to vertices and then interpolated during the scan conversion across the entire polygon surface. Unfortunately, this slow polygon-structured variation of the material properties over the surface of an object is very unlikely to occur in a real environment. In practice, on every surface, from the most dull and uninteresting real objects to the most intricate ones, one can detect small imperfections, geometric details, patterns, or variations in the material consistency. These variations are perceived by the human eye and help us identify objects and materials and determine the physical qualities of the various media.

It is often possible to represent the apparent discontinuities or transitions of the material properties as changes in the surface structure and vertex properties. This might even be an efficient modeling approach in the case of plain and well-defined patterns, as is the case in Figure 14.1(a). In this particular example, a planar polygon is split at the boundaries of an A-shaped embedded pattern of a different color than the rest of the surface (Figure 14.1(b)). But what if the

463

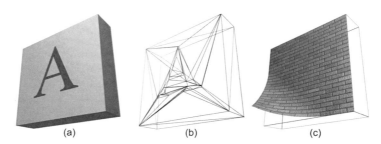

(a)   (b)   (c)

Figure 14.1. Appearance variation of a surface. A simple pattern (a) can be approximated via surface restructuring (b). Complex patterns cannot be efficiently represented this way. With texture mapping (c), an elaborate design can be imprinted on a surface without modifying the actual geometry.

desired pattern is more irregular and complex, as is the case of the material of the surface in Figure 14.1(c)? Clearly we need a different approach to modify the local material behavior across a polygonal or otherwise-defined surface.

Texturing deals with the mechanism of spatially varying one or more of the material attributes of a surface in a predefined manner without affecting the underlying topology of the geometry (Figure 14.1(c)). These attributes can be anything from the color and the transparency of the surface to the local normal and reflectivity at a given point. The association between a given surface point $\mathbf{p}$ (or one of its local properties, like the normal vector) and a material value in the texture space, where the desired pattern is defined, is done via a *texture-mapping function* $f_{\text{tex}}(\mathbf{p})$.

The pattern itself can be a one-, two-, or three-dimensional digital image (texture map) or a procedurally generated material. Depending on the attribute of the material that is affected by texture mapping, the result can be a scalar value, as in the case of a surface's specular coefficient or alpha value (transparency), or a vector, signifying an RGB color value, a new local normal vector, etc. Multiple textures can be applied to a single surface in order to modify one or more of its material properties. Different texture-mapping functions may be associated with a single attribute and combined under a texture hierarchy (texture tree). More about this subject can be found in Section 14.9.

14.2   Parametric Texture Mapping

When the material attribute is defined as a pre-computed, hand-drawn or digitized digital image, the texture-mapping process is called *texture* or *image mapping*.

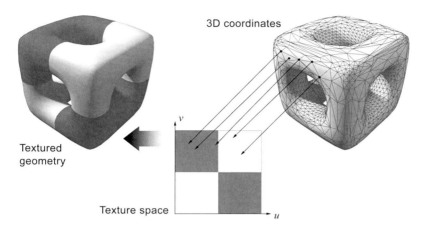

Figure 14.2. Parametric texture mapping. Cartesian coordinates are mapped to texture coordinates and then the material attributes are estimated from the discrete texel values and applied to the initial surface locations.

Texture images, or simply *textures*, can be one-, two-, or three-dimensional and are essentially buffers of pre-calculated data that the mapping function addresses to acquire material values.

In *parametric texture mapping*, the mapping function is split into two parts: one that associates the three-dimensional coordinates to the parametric domain of the digital image and one that defines the final material attribute values (scalar or vector) according to the color intensity of the pixels in the image that correspond to a particular set of parameters (Figure 14.2). The discrete texture elements (image pixels in the two-dimensional case) are generally called *texels*. The digital image is usually mapped to a normalized domain of the parametric space T^D, where D is the dimensionality of the pattern ($D = 2$ for the case of a conventional two-dimensional bitmap). The continuous normalized parameters are called *texture coordinates*. The mapping of the three-dimensional coordinates to the texture space produces parameters that are either wrapped or clamped to the [0,1] range. For sake of simplicity, in the rest of this section a texture map will refer to a two-dimensional pattern with corresponding texture parameters $u, v \in [0, 1]$.

One important aspect of texture mapping is that a texture-coordinate pair is not necessarily uniquely associated with a location on the three-dimensional surface. This provides a great economy when applying a periodic texture to an object as a pattern can be repeated by addressing a range of (u, v)-coordinates from multiple surface areas (*texture tiling*). The above notion is illustrated in Figure 14.3.

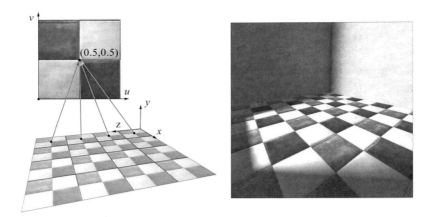

Figure 14.3. Texture-map tiling. Multiple points address the same texture co-ordinates in a periodic manner, resulting in a repeated, efficient coverage of the surface.

When there is a guaranteed 1-to-1 mapping between the entire surface covered by a single texture and the parametric space of the texture coordinates, the mapping and the respective image used are referred to as a *texture atlas*. This special condition, where the reverse mapping from texture space to object space is possible, has many useful applications which are discussed along with the principles of texture-atlas parameterization in Section 14.8.

The calculation of the material attributes from the texel values using the continuous set of texture coordinates is performed via standard sampling methods, like truncation, rounding, and interpolation, which are fully implemented in hardware by all modern graphics accelerators.

14.2.1 Texture Value Estimation

Let a texture map of $N_x \times N_y$ texels be sampled at an arbitrary point (u, v) in parametric space and $I(u, v)$ be the resulting intensity (monochromatic) at the specified texture coordinates. Using bilinear interpolation, $I(u, v)$ can be estimated as follows.

The intensity is extracted from the four neighboring texels of the arbitrary input point (Figure 14.4). The scalar texel locations x and y that correspond to the (u, v) parameters are given by

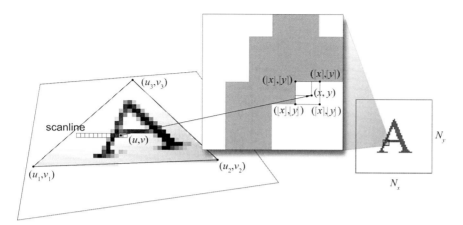

Figure 14.4. Texture value calculation for an arbitrary (u,v) pair. In polygon scan-conversion, texture coordinates are interpolated from the corresponding vertex parameters.

$$\begin{aligned} x &= u \cdot N_x, \\ y &= v \cdot N_y. \end{aligned} \qquad (14.1)$$

The intensity interpolation coefficients for the horizontal and vertical texel spans are, respectively,

$$\begin{aligned} u' &= x - \lfloor x \rfloor, \\ v' &= y - \lfloor y \rfloor, \end{aligned} \qquad (14.2)$$

where $(\lfloor x \rfloor, \lfloor y \rfloor)$ is the nearest lower-left texel center relative to the arbitrary point (x,y) on the image. The parameter u' goes to 0 or 1 as x approaches $\lfloor x \rfloor$ and $\lceil x \rceil$, repsectively. The same holds for the relation between v' and y.

The final intensity $I(u,v)$ is given by the row-column bilinear interpolation of the intensity at the four texel centers $(\lfloor x \rfloor, \lfloor y \rfloor)$, $(\lceil x \rceil, \lfloor y \rfloor)$, $(\lceil x \rceil, \lceil y \rceil)$, and $(\lfloor x \rfloor, \lceil y \rceil)$:

$$I_{\text{bot}} = I(\lfloor x \rfloor, \lfloor y \rfloor) \cdot (1 - u') + I(\lceil x \rceil, \lfloor y \rfloor) \cdot u',$$

$$I_{\text{top}} = I(\lfloor x \rfloor, \lceil y \rceil) \cdot (1 - u') + I(\lceil x \rceil, \lceil y \rceil) \cdot u',$$

$$I(u,v) = I_{\text{bot}} \cdot (1 - v') + I_{\text{top}} \cdot v'. \qquad (14.3)$$

14.2.2   Texture Mapping Polygonal Surfaces

The usual practice, at least for direct polygonal rendering, is that the determination of the (u, v)-coordinates, that is, the first stage of the texture-mapping procedure, is performed before the actual rendering of the surface. As mentioned earlier in this book, the various surface and material attributes are stored on a per-vertex basis. The texture coordinates for each vertex are assigned to them before the polygon rasterization. During the scan-conversion of triangles, the texture coordinates for each sample taken in the interior of the triangle are interpolated from the texture parameters stored in the vertex data, with the exception of procedural textures and dynamic texture effects. In the latter case, texture coordinates are determined from the local surface and rendering attributes, such as the normal vector and light direction, which are in turn interpolated from the vertex data.

The bilinear interpolation is done per scanline, in a manner similar to the per-fragment estimation of the local color and depth from the vertex colors or normalized vertex-space coordinates during the polygon rasterization (see Chapters 12 and 5). Unfortunately, directly interpolating the texture coordinates from the vertex texture parameters (bilinear mapping) does not account for the projective mapping that the vertex coordinates undergo. Texture parameters are assigned to vertices and are obviously not transformed when the polygons are perspectively projected. Then, during scan conversion, the perspectively correct vertices are linearly interpolated and so are the texture coordinates, but the latter have not been divided by the depth value, as the projective transformation dictates. This leads to an inconsistent mapping (bilinear-projective and bilinear) which results in visible stretching, bitmap tearing, and "texture floating" [Heck89].

One way to render perspectively correct textures is to interpolate the (u, v)-coordinates after dividing them with the z vertex value. The $1/z$ quantity is also interpolated from the projected vertex depth values. Then, the perspectively correct parameters are obtained by dividing the interpolated u/z and v/z parameters by the estimated $1/z$. The same practice can be applied to other quantities of a polygon that are not affected by the perspective transformation, such as the color and the normal vector, although the distortion is more visible in the case of texture-parameter interpolation.

After the (u, v) pair for the current scanline point has been defined, the texture value is determined according to the sampling method chosen. Figure 14.4 demonstrates the whole procedure of the texture-coordinate extraction during the scan-conversion and the bilinear interpolation of the texture value. In modern programmable GPUs, fragment programs can access and modify the texture coordinates produced by the progressive scan-conversion algorithm and thus perform a custom sampling of the texture space [Rost04].

Bilinear coordinate interpolation is only possible when progressively sampling the polygon surface in a regular manner, as in scan-conversion, or when the surface- and texture-coordinate parameterizations are coincident. If a single texture-coordinate sample is required at an arbitrary location on a triangle, which is the case when casting rays on geometry, this interpolation is not very convenient. We can use the *barycentric coordinate* representation of the triangle instead, which directly associates any point inside a triangle with its three vertices.

Let $\mathbf{p}_1$, $\mathbf{p}_2$ and $\mathbf{p}_3$ be the three vertices of the triangle $\mathbf{p}_1\mathbf{p}_2\mathbf{p}_3$. Any point $\mathbf{p}$ on the triangle plane can be represented as an affine combination of those three basis points:

$$\mathbf{p} = \lambda_1\mathbf{p}_1 + \lambda_2\mathbf{p}_2 + \lambda_3\mathbf{p}_3, \tag{14.4}$$

with the additional constraint,

$$\lambda_1 + \lambda_2 + \lambda_3 = 1. \tag{14.5}$$

According to (14.5), the parametric domain is a plane in $\mathbb{R}^3$, as one parameter depends on the other two. By restricting λ_1, λ_2, and λ_3 to $[0,1]$, the *barycentric triangle form* of Equation (14.4) becomes a function that maps an equilateral triangle in space to a range that is exactly the interior of the triangle $\mathbf{p}_1\mathbf{p}_2\mathbf{p}_3$ [Schn03].

By definition, the properties (14.4) and (14.5) imply that the three barycentric coordinates are directly associated with the ratios of the triangle areas formed by point $\mathbf{p}$ to the total triangle area (Figure 14.5):

$$\begin{aligned} \lambda_1 &= \frac{A_1}{A} = \frac{A(\mathbf{p}p_2\mathbf{p}_3)}{A(\mathbf{p}_1\mathbf{p}_2\mathbf{p}_3)}, \\ \lambda_2 &= \frac{A_2}{A} = \frac{A(\mathbf{p}_1\mathbf{p}p_3)}{A(\mathbf{p}_1\mathbf{p}_2\mathbf{p}_3)}, \\ \lambda_3 &= 1 - \lambda_1 - \lambda_2 = \frac{A_3}{A} = \frac{A(\mathbf{p}_1\mathbf{p}_2\mathbf{p})}{A(\mathbf{p}_1\mathbf{p}_2\mathbf{p}_3)}, \end{aligned} \tag{14.6}$$

where $A(\mathbf{v}_1\mathbf{v}_2\mathbf{v}_3)$ is the area of triangle $\mathbf{v}_1\mathbf{v}_2\mathbf{v}_3$.

This can be intuitively illustrated as follows. Consider all points $\mathbf{p}$ on one of the triangle's edges and let that edge be $\mathbf{p}_1\mathbf{p}_2$ without loss of generality. Point $\mathbf{p}$ is linearly interpolated from the two edge vertices $\mathbf{p}_1$ and $\mathbf{p}_2$, regardless of where $\mathbf{p}_3$ lies. This means that λ_3 should be zero. Indeed, as $\mathbf{p}_1$, $\mathbf{p}_2$, and $\mathbf{p}$ are

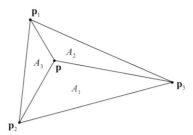

Figure 14.5. Calculation of the barycentric triangle coordinates from ratios of triangle areas.

collinear, $A(\mathbf{p}_1\mathbf{p}_2\mathbf{p})$ is zero. When $\mathbf{p}$ coincides with one of the vertices $\mathbf{p}_i$, then $A_i = A \Leftrightarrow \lambda_j = 0, j \neq i$.

Since the area of a triangle is proportional to the magnitude of the cross product of two of its edges and, in particular, $A(\mathbf{v}_1\mathbf{v}_2\mathbf{v}_3) = \left| \overrightarrow{\mathbf{v}_1\mathbf{v}_2} \times \overrightarrow{\mathbf{v}_1\mathbf{v}_3} \right|/2$, the barycentric coordinates can be more conveniently calculated by transforming Equation (14.6) to

$$\lambda_1 = \frac{\left| \overrightarrow{\mathbf{p}\mathbf{p}_2} \times \overrightarrow{\mathbf{p}\mathbf{p}_3} \right|}{\left| \overrightarrow{\mathbf{p}_1\mathbf{p}_2} \times \overrightarrow{\mathbf{p}_1\mathbf{p}_3} \right|}, \qquad \lambda_2 = \frac{\left| \overrightarrow{\mathbf{p}_1\mathbf{p}} \times \overrightarrow{\mathbf{p}_1\mathbf{p}_3} \right|}{\left| \overrightarrow{\mathbf{p}_1\mathbf{p}_2} \times \overrightarrow{\mathbf{p}_1\mathbf{p}_3} \right|}, \qquad \lambda_3 = 1 - \lambda_1 - \lambda_2. \quad (14.7)$$

After calculating the three barycentric coordinates for an arbitrary triangle point from Equation (14.7), its texture coordinates (u, v) can be easily interpolated from the texture coordinates $(u_i, v_i), i = 1 \ldots 3$ stored in the vertex data of $\mathbf{p}_1\mathbf{p}_2\mathbf{p}_3$:

$$\begin{aligned} u &= \lambda_1 u_1 + \lambda_2 u_2 + \lambda_3 u_3, \\ v &= \lambda_1 v_1 + \lambda_2 v_2 + \lambda_3 v_3. \end{aligned} \qquad (14.8)$$

The reader should keep in mind that although this parameter-interpolation method is more generic than the bilinear interpolation of the scan-conversion, it is more costly to perform and should only be used when selecting random points on a triangle and, in general, when a progressive scan is not possible.

14.3   Texture-Coordinate Generation

In the previous section, two sampling methods have been presented for estimating the texture parameters at a triangle location given the pre-calculated texture coordinates at the triangle vertices. The (u, v)-coordinate data can be dynamically calculated for each vertex or can be retrieved from a data structure along with the rest of the mesh information. In both cases, unless the texture coordinates have been explicitly assigned by the user, the u and v parameters have been deduced from the Cartesian coordinates of the vertices with the help of a *texture-coordinate generation function*.

A texture-coordinate generation function provides a simple mapping from the Cartesian domain to the bounded normalized domain in texture space. Most common functions perform the mapping in two steps. First the arbitrary Cartesian coordinates are mapped on a predetermined "auxiliary" surface embedded in space, whose shape can be represented parametrically. Then the auxiliary surface parameters themselves are normalized to represent the texture coordinates. Loosely speaking, the parametric surface determines the way that a planar textured sheet is wrapped around the original object in order to imprint the image on its surface.

One important issue that arises when generating texture coordinates for vertex data is the way tiling is implemented. Normally, a texture-coordinate generation transformation should map a point in space into the bounded domain of the image map: $(u,v) : u \in [0,1], v \in [0,1]$. The mathematical representation of the texture-coordinate generation functions presented here performs this wrapping step when using a tiling greater than 1 for any direction. When the mapping is intended for use with interpolated sampling of the surfaces, as is the case in polygon scan-

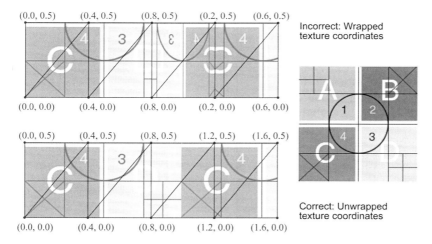

Figure 14.6. Improper texture tiling in polygon rendering. Wrapping the coordinates to the range [0,1] before the interpolation step causes texture mirroring in the transition from high to low coordinate values.

conversion, the wrapping to the bounded domain should be performed *after* the interpolation of the texture coordinates and not when assigning the (u, v) parameters to the polygon vertices. When a texture parameter is wrapped to the [0,1] range before it is assigned to a vertex, the interpolated values between two consecutive vertices can be accidentally reversed, as is demonstrated in Figure 14.6. The problem is corrected if the tiled u and v parameters are allowed to take values outside the [0,1] range. The tiling operation in this case is simply implemented by multiplying the resulting parameters of the mapping function by the tiling factor.

Next, we shall look in detail into some of the most frequently used texture-coordinate generation functions. The two most common local attributes that are used for texture-coordinate generation are the location in space of the fragment being rendered and the local surface normal vector. Of course, other local attributes such as the incident-light direction can be exploited in order to address the texture space. These are treated similarly to the point location Cartesian coordinates or the normal vector, depending on whether they are expressed as points or vectors, respectively.

14.3.1 Planar Mapping

This is the simplest (u, v)-coordinate generation function. Consider illuminating the surface of an object by shooting parallel rays from a video projector that displays the texture map but with the provision that rays pass through the surface and also illuminate the hidden sides. Planar mapping uses a plane as an intermediate parametric surface. The Cartesian coordinates are parallelly projected on the plane, and the parametric representation of the projected points is used as a set of texture-coordinate pairs. Although an arbitrary plane can be used, selecting one that is axis-aligned greatly simplifies the calculations. To achieve a planar projection from an arbitrary direction, it is more efficient and comprehensive to transform the Cartesian coordinates before projecting them to an axis-aligned plane instead of using an arbitrary plane from the beginning. More about texture-coordinate transformations will be discussed in Section 14.6.

For now, let us consider one of the three axis-aligned planar mappings and, in particular, the case of the xy-plane shown in Figure 14.7(a). The texture-coordinate generation function is in essence a linear transformation of the Cartesian coordinates, with the z-component being eliminated and the resulting values wrapped around to fall into the $[0, 1]$ range:

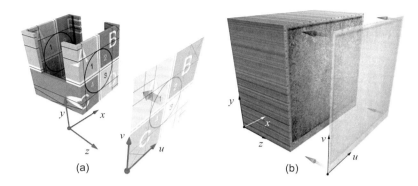

Figure 14.7. Planar mapping using the *xy*-plane. (a) The texture-coordinate parameterization. (b) Planar mapping of an axis-aligned box. All points with the same *x*- and *y*-coordinates are mapped on the same texture-map location.

$$
\begin{aligned}
u &= x' - \lfloor x' \rfloor & x' &= a \cdot x + \text{offset}_x \\
v &= y' - \lfloor y' \rfloor & y' &= b \cdot y + \text{offset}_y
\end{aligned}
\tag{14.9}
$$

In Equation (14.9), a and b are the horizontal and vertical *tiling factors*, and $(\text{offset}_x, \text{offset}_y)$ is the offset from the lower-left corner of the image in texture-coordinate space. The tiling factor determines how many repetitions of the texture image should fit in one world-coordinate-system unit, or, in other words, $(1/a, 1/b)$ are the dimensions of the quadrilateral texture tile in the Cartesian coordinate system. For the assignment of texture coordinates to polygon vertices, following the discussion regarding the coordinate wrap-around problems in polygon rendering, $(u, v) = (x', y')$.

Planar mapping is very useful for texturing relatively flat surface regions or geometry that can be represented in a functional manner, as in $z = f(x, y)$. The more parallel a surface region is to the projection plane, the less distorted the projected texture becomes. In Figure 14.7(b), the sides of the box are perpendicular to the projection plane, and therefore, all points with the same *x*- and *y*-coordinates are mapped to the same set of texture coordinates. In practice, when modeling complex objects, the artists break up the surfaces in nearly coplanar regions and apply a separate planar mapping to each one of them. This is also part of one of the techniques for automatically generating texture atlases as will be explained later in this chapter. Alternatively, one of the other texture-generation functions discussed below can be used.

14.3.2   Cylindrical Mapping

In this mapping, the texture coordinates are derived from the cylindrical coordinates of a point in space. One form of the cylindrical coordinates for a point $\mathbf{p} = (x, y, z)$ is

$$
\begin{aligned}
\theta &= \tan^{-1}(x/z), \\
h &= y, \\
r &= \sqrt{(x^2 + z^2)},
\end{aligned}
\tag{14.10}
$$

where θ is the right-handed angle from the z- to x-axis, with $-\pi < \theta \leq \pi$, h is the vertical offset from the xz-plane, and r is the radius or distance of $\mathbf{p}$ from the y-axis.

The (u, v)-coordinates can be associated with any two of the cylindrical coordinates of Equation (14.10), but usually u is derived from θ and v is calculated from the height h. The result of cylindrical mapping is similar to wrapping a photograph around an infinitely long tube (Figure 14.8). Note that all points with the same bearing and height are mapped to the same point in texture space for all $r \in [0, \infty)$. The cylindrical coordinates of Equation (14.10) can be easily transformed into texture coordinates according to the following formula (Figure 14.8(a)):

(a)   (b)

Figure 14.8. Cylindrical mapping around the y-axis. (a) The texture coordinate parameterization and image wrapping. (b) An example of cylindrical mapping.

$$u = \frac{1}{2} + \frac{\theta}{2\pi} = \frac{1}{2} + \frac{\tan^{-1}(x/z)}{2\pi},$$
$$v = h = y.$$

(14.11)

The above formulation of the (u,v)-coordinate pair can be augmented to include the tiling factors a and b around and along the y-axis, respectively:

$$u = \frac{a(\theta + \pi)}{2\pi} - \left\lfloor \frac{a(\theta + \pi)}{2\pi} \right\rfloor,$$
$$v = by - \lfloor by \rfloor .$$

(14.12)

14.3.3 Spherical Mapping

Similarly to the cylindrical mapping, the spherical texture-coordinate generation function depends on an alternative to the Cartesian coordinate representation and, in particular, on the spherical coordinates (θ, φ, r) of a point in space. As in the cylindrical coordinates of Equation (14.10), θ is the longitude of the point, and φ and r are, respectively, the latitude and distance from the coordinate system origin. The spherical coordinates of a point $\mathbf{p} = (x, y, z)$ are given by

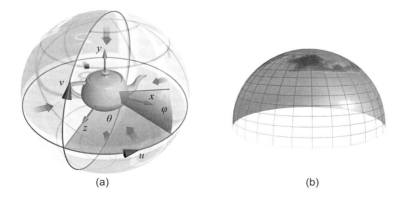

(a) (b)

Figure 14.9. Spherical mapping. (a) The texture-coordinate parameterization and image wrapping. (b) An evening-sky texture mapped to a dome using the spherical texture-coordinate generation function.

$$\theta = \tan^{-1}\left(\frac{x}{z}\right) \qquad\qquad -\pi < \theta \le \pi$$

$$\varphi = \tan^{-1}\left(\frac{y}{\sqrt{x^2+z^2}}\right) \qquad -\frac{\pi}{2} < \varphi \le \frac{\pi}{2}, \qquad (14.13)$$

$$r = \sqrt{x^2+y^2+z^2}.$$

The spherical texture-coordinate generation usually associates the u- and v-coordinates with the two angular components of the above representation (Figure 14.9):

$$u = \frac{\theta + \pi}{2\pi}, \qquad v = \frac{\varphi + \pi/2}{\pi}. \qquad (14.14)$$

Using a pair of tiling factors (a,b) for the u- and v-coordinates, respectively, the spherical mapping is given by

$$u = \frac{a\,(\theta + \pi)}{2\pi} - \left\lfloor \frac{a\,(\theta + \pi)}{2\pi} \right\rfloor,$$

$$v = \frac{b\,(\varphi + \pi/2)}{\pi} - \left\lfloor \frac{b\,(\varphi + \pi/2)}{\pi} \right\rfloor. \qquad (14.15)$$

This very common spherical mapping operation wraps an image around an object like a world atlas maps to the globe. This means that the spatial resolution of a texel when mapped to a surface varies according to the latitude of the point and results in heavy distortion of the displayed features at the poles, as a whole line of the texture is typically mapped onto a single point in space. This is demonstrated in Figure 14.10.

For the calculation of the texture parameters, the normal vector coordinates can be used instead of the point location. This is easily done by replacing the (x,y,z) point coordinates of Equation (14.13) with the normal vector components (n_x, n_y, n_z). This is a quite useful mapping when the surface normal vector is expressed in the world coordinate system, i.e., after the three-dimensional object has been transformed, because it allows for the rendering of complex-environment diffuse illumination on the object's surface. A spherical projection of the incoming diffuse illumination from distant light sources and ambient light is precalculated and stored in a texture map. Then, instead of applying the Phong or some other local illumination model for the modulation of the surface material, the diffuse illumination is sampled from the texture using the spherical mapping. Similarly, pseudo-color illumination and cartoon-style shading can be achieved, if light sources are considered to be infinitely far from the objects.

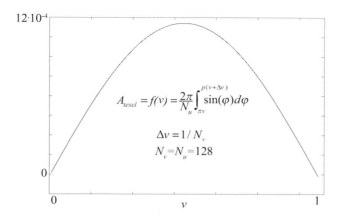

Figure 14.10. Inherent distortion in spherical mapping. The plot relates the texel area of a 128×128 texture to the v texture coordinate as it sweeps the sphere from pole to pole.

14.3.4 Cube Mapping

Cube mapping combines the local surface-direction information with the Cartesian coordinates of the point to derive the texture coordinates. Essentially, it works like planar mapping, but instead of using a single projection direction, like z, one out of the three primary axes is selected based on which axis the normal vector is more aligned with. This means that a point **p** is projected onto plane xy, yz, or xz, depending on whether the absolute value of the z-, x-, or y- coordinate, respectively, of the normal vector is the largest one (Figure 14.11(a)). The planar mapping for each one of the three cases is obtained by properly substituting the coordinates pairs in Equation (14.9).

Cube mapping is ideal for multifaceted geometry and especially for shapes with right angles, like rooms, buildings, or crates (Figure 14.11(b)). One very useful property of cube mapping is that the texture map is never projected on a surface from an angle of more than 45 degrees from the surface normal. This implies that we get no significant distortion from texel stretching. On the other hand, the transition from one projection plane to another is prone to causing discontinuities as it often does when this mapping is applied to smooth curved surfaces.

When cube mapping is directly associated with the local surface normal vector or when a surface location is treated as a vector, the calculations are different. The significance of using this mode of cube mapping must first be explained. In

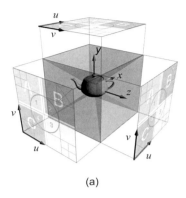 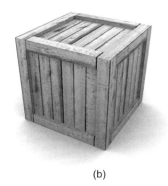

(a)   (b)

Figure 14.11.   Cube (box) mapping.   (a) Texture-coordinate generation.
(b) Texture-mapping example.

this section, we have seen how spherical mapping warps the projected image and causes significant distortion at the poles due to the inherent mapping singularity. Clearly, this can be very annoying, especially when texture mapping large surfaces like sky domes. Cube mapping avoids this pitfall by always selecting the side of a cube that is most perpendicular to the vector associated with the current point (Figure 14.12(a)). In order to achieve a similar result with the spherical mapping though, six different sides and the respective texture maps are used instead of three sides and a single bitmap (Figure 14.12(b)). This way, a 1-to-1 mapping between a specific direction (longitude/latitude pair) and an addressed texture location can be obtained, even though the u and v parameters generated are not unique.

The cube mapping formulation for the texture-coordinate generation from vectors is quite simple. If we consider a vector $\overrightarrow{\mathbf{v}} = (v_x, v_y, v_z)$, which defines a point $\mathbf{v} = \mathbf{o} + \overrightarrow{\mathbf{v}}$ or a direction in space, cube-mapping texture coordinates are calculated as the normalized coordinates of this vector in the range [0,1]. The appropriate cube texture is selected according to the largest-in-magnitude signed component of the vector provided, i.e., $-x$, $+x$, $-y$, $+y$, $-z$, $+z$. The selection of the correspondence rules between primary axes and texture-coordinate axes is not very restrictive and depends on the application or implementation. Cube mapping on vector coordinates is implemented in the major graphics application programming interfaces and both OpenGL and DirectX™ APIs implement a consistent mapping mechanism, which is summarized in the following formula [Seg04]:

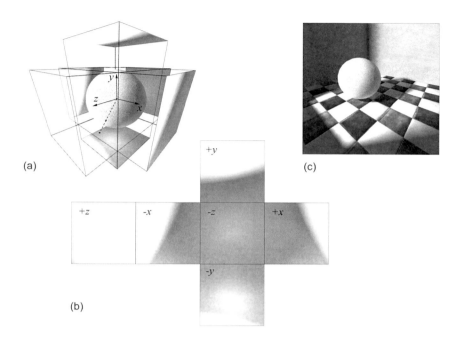

Figure 14.12. Cube mapping using vector coordinates to apply pre-calculated diffuse illumination to an object. (a) Cube mapping set-up. (b) The six cube maps. (c) The texture-shaded object in its final environment.

$$u = \frac{1}{2}\left(\frac{u_c}{|m_a|} + 1\right),$$
$$v = \frac{1}{2}\left(\frac{v_c}{|m_a|} + 1\right),$$

(14.16)

where

$$
\begin{aligned}
(u_c, v_c, m_a) &= (-v_z, -v_y, v_x) & v_x &= \max\{|v_x|, |v_y|, |v_z|\}, \\
(u_c, v_c, m_a) &= (v_z, -v_y, v_x) & -v_x &= \max\{|v_x|, |v_y|, |v_z|\}, \\
(u_c, v_c, m_a) &= (v_x, v_z, v_y) & v_y &= \max\{|v_x|, |v_y|, |v_z|\}, \\
(u_c, v_c, m_a) &= (v_x, -v_z, v_y) & -v_y &= \max\{|v_x|, |v_y|, |v_z|\}, \\
(u_c, v_c, m_a) &= (v_x, -v_y, v_z) & v_z &= \max\{|v_x|, |v_y|, |v_z|\}, \\
(u_c, v_c, m_a) &= (-v_x, -v_y, v_z) & -v_z &= \max\{|v_x|, |v_y|, |v_z|\}.
\end{aligned}
$$

(14.17)

Cube mapping is very frequently used for representing three-dimensional environment extents, such as distant landscapes, buildings in cityscapes, sky boxes, and sky domes. When the interpolated normal vector of a surface is used to generate the texture coordinates, cube mapping can be exploited to apply pre-computed diffuse illumination on a surface (Figure 14.12). In fact, as long as a calculation associated with a rendered fragment results in a vector, cube mapping can provide an indexing of a pre-calculated attribute map with this vector. Environment mapping, discussed in detail below, as well as various fragment shaders take advantage of cube maps to approximate reflected, refracted or specularly transmitted light on a surface.

14.3.5 Environment Mapping

The determination of the texture coordinates that correspond to a surface location as well as the selection of a texture image can be dynamically calculated at render time. For instance, in the case of the diffuse illumination presented in the example of Figure 14.12, the cube maps could be recalculated whenever a change in the surrounding scene could affect the diffuse light recorded on the textures. Additionally, as the diffuse light interaction measured is location-dependent, a significant pose change of the texture-mapped object would necessitate the recalculation of the incident diffuse light. Of course, a change in the object's orientation would also certainly affect the texture-coordinate calculation.

As mentioned in the previous section, cube maps or other kinds of texture-projection mechanisms can be used to simulate and store the various local illumination calculations or material properties of the surface in a texture map [Cabr99]. Recall that the physical or empirical models for specular light transmission and reflection depend on the viewing direction from the surface point to the eye and its relation to the local surface normal. This means that if we choose to pre-calculate any quantity that involves the above vectors and consequently the mirror-reflection direction, the texture coordinates need to be recalculated every time the view position or the object pose changes.

The general category of mapping-coordinate calculations that treats the texture map as a storage medium for directionally indexed incident light is called *environment mapping*, although the term is most frequently associated with the approximate representation of the light reflected on the surface when the object is a perfect mirror [Blin76].

Let $\hat{r}$ be the direction vector that results from reflecting an imaginary ray from the viewpoint to an arbitrary surface point with normal vector $\hat{n}$. We may recall from the shading model calculations that, if we denote the direction from the surface point to the viewpoint as $\hat{\mathbf{v}}$, the reflection direction is given by

$$\hat{\mathbf{r}} = 2\hat{\mathbf{n}}(\hat{\mathbf{n}} \cdot \hat{\mathbf{v}}) - \hat{\mathbf{v}} \qquad (14.18)$$

The vector $\hat{\mathbf{r}}$ essentially points to the direction from which the light from the environment comes, before being reflected toward the viewpoint. This property holds only for perfect mirrors, where the two direction vectors can be used interchangeably. The reflection direction is used for generating the (u, v)-coordinates according to the mapping function of preference. Equation (14.18), when combined with the cube-mapping formulas of (14.16) and (14.17), implements this idea, which is also demonstrated in Figure 14.13. Cube maps are ideal for en-

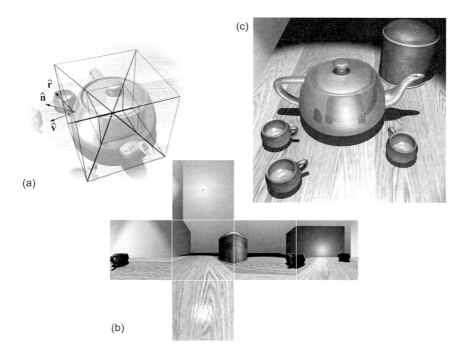

Figure 14.13. Environment (reflection) mapping using cube maps. (a) The reflection vector is used for indexing the maps and the (u, v)-coordinates. (b) The cube maps. Images were created by rendering six 90-degree views from the center of the teapot. (c) The final modulation of the teapot surface by the mapped environment enhances the metallic look of the surface.

vironment mapping due to their low distortion, although spherical mapping is an applicable alternative mapping, which has been used extensively in the past, before cube maps were natively supported by the prevailing APIs.

Note that in order for environment mapping to work effectively, the reflected environment elements are assumed to reside adequately far from the reflective object, so that object motion does not render the reflected environment inconsistently with the current object's location. Otherwise, different, location-dependent reflection maps should be made available during render time by pre-rendering the environment on the texture(s) for each location.

A common practice when representing the reflection map as a set of cube maps is to render the environment from the center of the object using a 90° square field of view into low-resolution textures six times (Figure 14.13). As the reflected image bending is usually large and the surfaces are not ideally smooth, even low-resolution reflection maps work extremely well. Using low-resolution environment textures has the added advantage of being able to frequently recalculate them, even in real time and thus facilitate the display of reflected moving objects or overcome the environment distance assumption mentioned above. Color Plate XXVIII displays a number of reflective metallic objects. All of them use the same static cube-map set captured from the center of the scene. This minimizes the map-capture overhead and, in this particular scene, provides quite convincing reflections. Capture of the cube maps from a location away from the object's center position may provide unrealistic results in other cases.

14.3.6   View-Dependent Texture Maps⊛

In cube mapping, we have seen that a cube texture, which is a *subtexture* of the whole environment map, is selected according to a direction vector. The notion of selecting a texture map according to a view direction goes way back before the introduction of cubical texture maps, to the first versions of the 3D game engines, when *sprite* bitmaps were being selected to represent a different visible side of an object in space, depending on the orientation of the object relative to the viewpoint. The sprite selection is the simplest form of *image-based rendering (IBR)*, where instead of actually rendering a three-dimensional entity, the appropriate view of the object is reconstructed from the interpolation or warping of pre-calculated or captured images, in many cases accompanied by depth or view-direction information, as, for example, in [Shad98, Levo96, Gort96]. The advantage of using image-based rendering is the decoupling of scene complexity from the rendering calculations, providing a constant frame rate, regardless of

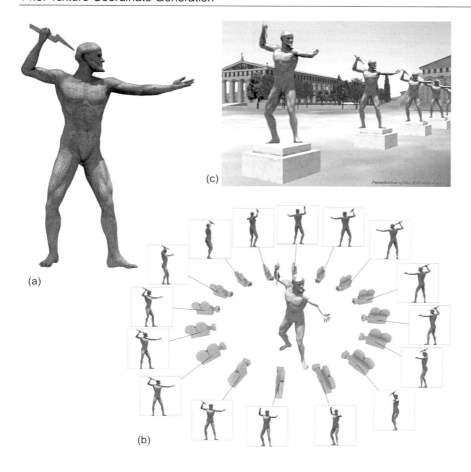

Figure 14.14. Simple image-based rendering using view-dependent textures. (a) The original statue of Zeus consisting of approximately 36,000 triangles. (b) Multiple views are rendered from a fixed distance around the object. (c) A simple polygon is texture-mapped with the nearest (or linearly interpolated) view in real time. The texture selection depends on the viewing direction from the eye point to the center of the object. (Screenshot from the VR production "A Walk through Ancient Olympia." Courtesy of the Foundation of the Hellenic World.)

the detail of the displayed geometry. A very complex object, like a detailed tree or a human figure, can be pre-rendered or captured from various angles, usually from equidistant locations around the object with the camera pointing at the object itself (Figure 14.14(b)). At render-time, the image of the object as seen from the viewpoint is approximated by the closest pre-calculated views. Image-based techniques may become very computationally intensive, especially when missing depth information or gaps need to be extrapolated.

Not surprisingly, the most popular IBR methods are the simplest ones, although the resulting images cannot stand scrutiny. In the easiest case of an IBR *impostor*, a three-dimensional placeholder or *geometry proxy*, like a plane or a simple aggregation of such, is texture-mapped with a view-dependent criterion for selecting the texture or mixing the textures that represent the closest available views to the current one (Figure 14.14). The subtextures used in this technique are usually pre-ordered and the views represented are regularly spaced, so the texture selection can be very straightforward and therefore fast. IBR impostors make good use of the hardware since the textures from the closest viewpoints can either be rendered in multiple passes or composed of the source subtextures using multiple texture units and/or vertex shaders. This method is very popular in computer games and virtual reality, especially for rendering complex flora and crowds [Tecc02].

The reverse approach to image-based rendering is QuickTime VR [Chen95], where instead of sampling a fixed area of 3D space from various locations around a point of interest, an environment map is constructed from a fixed point in space that represents the view of the three-dimensional world from that particular vantage point. This technique has been and still is very extensively used in multimedia applications and computer games to render complex environments when the user location is considered fixed in space or the displayed objects quite far away.

A hybrid compromise between simple IBR proxies and actual three-dimensional geometry is the use of *view-dependent texture maps* on three-dimensional objects that represent a simplified version of the displayed geometry [Debe96]. The need for alternative, view-dependent texture maps arises mostly when texturing low-polygon meshes for real-time applications where surface details are omitted on purpose to enhance rendering efficiency. To this end, other important techniques such as bump and normal mapping are also utilized to fake the apparent complexity of the actually missing geometric information, but even these work well to some extent.

Imagine the case of Figure 14.15. The high-detail duct displayed at the upper left of the figure consists of several polygons and is actually hollow and driven through the wall. The wall is also properly tessellated, with a hole cut out where the duct penetrates the building. In real-time rendering applications, it is crucial to keep the polygon count as low as possible and also maximize the object reuse for efficient environment modeling. A building element like a wall or a whole house

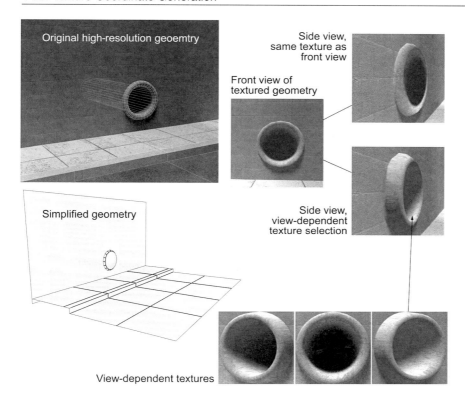

Figure 14.15. View-dependent texture maps. Here, pre-rendered views of a high-resolution model were applied as textures to a low polygon mesh, depending on the inspection direction in order to correctly simulate the appearance of the original model.

should be reusable and re-configurable. Therefore, decorations like the duct of Figure 14.15 should not alter the basic model and must be as inexpensive to render as possible. A less detailed version is shown in the lower left of Figure 14.15. Notice that the duct does not penetrate the wall.

Now, an obvious way to imprint the geometric detail of the high-resolution model onto the lower-resolution one is to render the object from a viewpoint that ensures maximum visibility and project the image as a texture on the low-detail model. The problem is that there are cases, such as Figure 14.15, where the eye cannot be tricked, primarily due to very intense parallax and illumination-information variations expected from alternative viewpoints. Bump mapping (see

Section 14.7) alleviates part of the problem (shading), but even this cannot provide the correct depth cue and shading/shadow information. If we use a couple of textures representing the object from different viewpoints instead of a single view and interpolate or switch through them as the inspection direction changes, a much more realistic appearance can be achieved at the expense of texture memory.

14.4   Texture Magnification and Minification

When a map is applied to a surface, its texels are stretched to occupy a certain area of the surface, according to the locally varying spacing of the texture parameters and the dimensions of the polygons. When the textured surface is projected on the viewing plane, a texel covers a certain portion of the image space. Obviously, apart from the textured-surface orientation and parameterization, the area occupied by a texel in image space depends on the projection-transformation parameters and viewport size, as well as in the case of a perspective projection, on the distance of the object from the viewpoint. In the case when the projected texel in image space covers an area of more than a pixel, it is locally *magnified*, whereas in the opposite case, when its footprint is less than a pixel, the texture is *minified* or *compressed* (Figure 14.16).

The effect of texture magnification is to make intensity discontinuities apparent in a semi-regular manner and generate a step-ladder effect when the slope of the texture parameter change in image space is not aligned with the sampling pattern of the image (Figure 14.16). The phenomenon is called texture pixelization and results in poor and unconvincing texturing. Fortunately, the interpolation methods used for extracting a texture value from the neighboring texels rectifies the blocky image by smoothing the texture. The bilinear interpolation implemented by hardware rasterizers and explained in Section 14.2.1 offers a good compromise between quality and speed, although higher-order filtering generates far better images that can be subjected to further texture magnification [Sigg05].

When a texture is minified, the visual problems are usually more serious as image space and time-varying sampling artifacts are produced. The texture patterns are erratically sampled, leading to a noisy result and a Moiré pattern at high frequencies. The problem is called *texture aliasing* and is explained below.

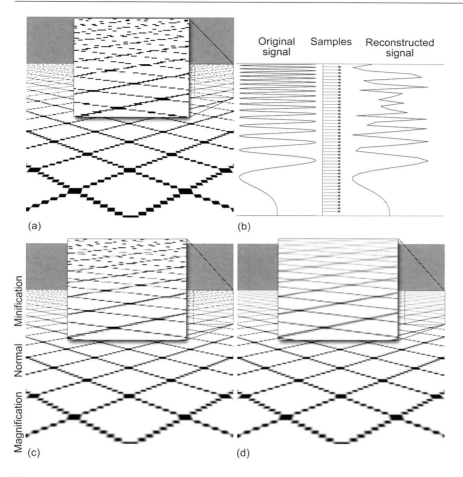

Original signal   Samples   Reconstructed signal

Figure 14.16. Texture magnification and minification. (a) Nearest-neighbor sampled texture values, no filtering. (b) Aliasing artifacts in texture mapping under perspective projection. (c) Bilinear filtering for the magnification case, aliasing in compressed texture portions. (d) Mip-mapped texture (pyramidal pre-filtering with trilinear interpolation).

14.4.1   Texture Antialiasing⊛

From a signal-theory perspective, the rendering procedure records samples of the textured surfaces at specific locations on the resulting image at a predefined spatial resolution, for example, once per pixel. In order for a signal to be correctly reconstructed from the samples taken, the original signal has to be band-limited and the highest frequency must be at most half the sampling rate (*uniform sampling theorem*) [Glas95]. To translate this into the texture-mapping paradigm, when a textured surface is subject to the various geometric transformations and is finally projected onto the view plane, the density of the texture-map texels in image space varies locally and is also anisotropic. The rate at which a transition from one projected texel on the image plane to the next occurs defines the apparent *spatial frequency* of the textured surface. In the case of texture compression, a texel corresponds to less than two pixel samples, and when a texture is severely minified, the sampling of the map skips many texels. This can be clearly observed in the example of Figure 14.16(b). A sinusoidal signal is perspectively distorted and then regularly sampled. The infinite transformed signal is no longer band-limited, and the regular sampling fails to correctly reconstruct the shape of the original signal above a frequency limit (which is half the sampling rate of course).

There are two solutions to this problem. One is to adequately super-sample the texture in image space in order to ensure that we sample the source signal above the Nyquist sampling rate and then band-limit the resulting signal to the image's actual spatial resolution by integration (*post-filtering*). This is illustrated in Figure 14.17. The other solution is to band-limit the original signal before rendering the geometry into the image buffer (*pre-filtering*).

The first solution, although it helps improve the final image quality and provides a means for global antialiasing (i.e., also for edges and lines; see Section 2.8), suffers from an obvious problem in the case of texture mapping; If we pick a larger number of samples for a pixel, we only transpose the aliasing problem higher in the spatial frequency domain. For instance, when we double the samples taken in each image direction (four samples per pixel), we increase the sampling rate of the projected texels. This may be adequate for many synthetic images but provides no guarantee for the correct reconstruction of the textured surface, simply because there is no association between the sampling rate and the density of the projected texels on the image plane. There are indeed cases where this approach fails, and the example in Figure 14.16 is one of them (infinite textured plane under perspective projection). Supersampling for texturing is also a poor solution in the case of real-time rendering algorithms because it is not easy to predict the required number of samples. Even if one can actually do that, the extra samples are limited by the multisampling capacity of the graphics system (hardware implementation) or the software renderer and can dramatically decrease the rendering performance. Nevertheless, as super-sampling is the most

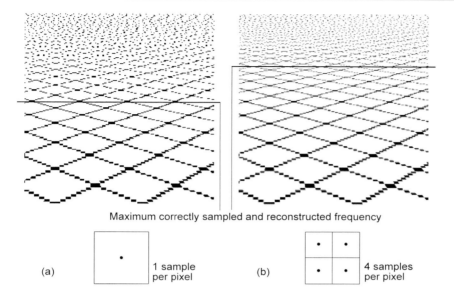

Figure 14.17. Texture antialiasing using post-filtering. (a) A perspectively projected surface with planar mapping. Without filtering, the final image is severely aliased. (b) The same surface rendered with a 2×2 supersampling pattern. The aliasing is transposed to higher spatial frequencies.

common method for global image antialiasing, it also contributes to the solution of the texture aliasing problem when combined with other techniques.

The second antialiasing option is the local pre-filtering of the texture before rendering the corresponding fragment into the frame buffer in order to limit the bandwidth of the texture when this is expressed in image-space coordinates. In essence, we try to predict how many texels are contributing to the intensity of each pixel when the textured surface is projected on the image plane. The contributing texels are first averaged (low-pass filtering) and then used for rendering the surface texture.

The filtering is performed in texture space by *convolution* of a filter kernel $f(s,t)$ (impulse response) of finite spatial support G with the texture values $i(u,v)$:

$$(f*i)(u,v) = \iint_G f(s,t) \cdot i(u-s,v-t)\,ds\,dt. \qquad (14.19)$$

Let us first discuss how the filtering of a signal works. Filtering in the frequency domain is transformed into a multiplication of the Fourier coefficients of the signal and the filter, i.e., the signal *spectrum* and the filter *frequency response*, respectively. To band-limit a signal in the frequency domain, all we have to do is to create a filter, whose frequency response is zero outside the band limits and then multiply it with the spectrum of the input signal. However, the matter is not so simple, due to the fact that a naïve box filter (1 inside the desired band and 0 outside the limits) has an infinite impulse response (IIR), i.e., it has an infinite support in the spatial domain. Since it is far more efficient and straightforward to filter a signal in the spatial domain in the case of rendering, an IIR filter could not be appropriately applied, because we would need an infinite filter kernel. There exist however many good practical finite impulse response (FIR) low-pass filters and their discrete counterparts, like the B-spline approximation to the Gaussian filter, but further discussion on filter construction is beyond the scope of this book. In practice, filtering in the texture domain is a weighted averaging in a finite area of non-zero filter kernel weights, centered at the sample point (u, v). For more details regarding the construction of filters and their application on discrete and continuous signals, please refer to a signal- or image-processing textbook.

Examining the relationship between an image-plane pixel and a texel, due to the cumulative effect of surface curvature and perspective projection, a pixel in image space is transformed in general into a curvilinear quadrilateral in texture space (*pixel pre-image*) [Heck89] (Figure 14.18). In order to correctly sample the texture at a specific pixel, the shape and area of its pre-image have to be estimated

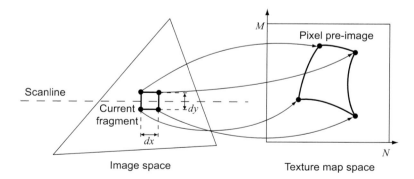

Figure 14.18. The "footprint" of an image-space fragment when projected into the texture space (pre-image). When a texture is minified (compressed), the pixel pre-image may cover an area of many texels.

by mapping its area from image space to texture space and have the texture values be integrated over it. The corresponding filter shape and size need to adapt to the pre-image for the texture spatial frequency to be appropriately limited, without unnecessarily blurring the texture. A larger pixel pre-image means that a larger number of texture samples need to be averaged and vice versa. Unfortunately, due to the nature of texture mapping and the pixel-dependent variance of the pixel pre-image shape, ideally, a filter kernel should be estimated for each pixel sampled. Another important issue that arises is that minification (compression) and magnification may occur at the same image location (in different directions, of course) since the pixel pre-image may be elongated. Various solutions to this filter kernel construction problem have been proposed, like the elliptical weighted average (EWA) filter, which is based on truncated (FIR) Gaussian filters properly scaled and aligned according to the pixel pre-image [Gree86].

14.4.2 Mip-Mapping⊛

Clearly, re-computing or dynamically selecting pre-constructed filter kernels and performing the texture filtering in real time is computationally expensive. If we make the assumption that the filter kernel has a constant aspect ratio and orientation but a variable size, then pre-filtered versions of the texture map can be a priori generated and efficiently stored. At render-time, all that is needed is to determine the proper kernel size and, consequently, the proper pre-filtered version of the texture for the specific fragment that is being rendered in image space. This idea was effectively captured in L. Williams' work on pyramidal parametric interpolation [Will83] that introduced the notion of *mip-mapping* for texturing surfaces. The acronym "mip" stands for the Latin phrase "*multum in parvo*," which means "many things in a small place" and mostly refers to the memory-storage format of the pre-filtered maps.

Mip-mapping works as follows: The original texture map (not necessarily square) is recursively filtered and down-sampled into successively smaller versions of the high-resolution image (*mip-maps*), each one-half the linear dimension of its parent (Figure 14.19(a)). A simple 2×2 box filter is used for averaging the parent texels to produce the next minified version of the map. This produces a hierarchy of mip-maps that represent the result of the convolution of the original image with a square filter. The filter is a power-of-two pixels in side length (Figure 14.19(a) and (b)). The initial image is the 0th level of the pyramidal texture representation and corresponds to a filter kernel of $2^0 = 1$. Successive levels are sequentially indexed and correspond to filter kernels of length 2^i, where i is the

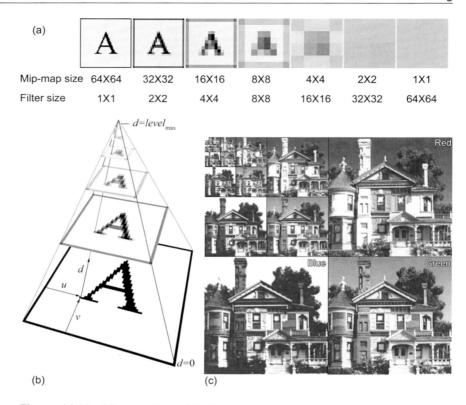

Mip-map size	64X64	32X32	16X16	8X8	4X4	2X2	1X1
Filter size	1X1	2X2	4X4	8X8	16X16	32X32	64X64

Figure 14.19. Mip-mapping. (a) The successively re-sampled mip-map levels. The leftmost map is the base level (level 0). (b) The pyramidal parametric representation of the mip-map. (c) Memory organization of a three-channel color texture.

mip-map level. Assuming that the original texture image has dimension $N \times M$, both powers of two, there are at most $\lfloor \log_2 (\max(N,M)) \rfloor + 1$ levels in the mip-map set. The i-th mip-map level has dimension given by

$$\max \left(\frac{N}{2^i}, 1 \right) \times \max \left(\frac{M}{2^i}, 1 \right). \qquad (14.20)$$

We have seen in Section 14.2.1 that in order to evaluate a two-dimensional texture map at an arbitrary continuous parameter pair (u, v), bilinear interpolation is used on the nearest discrete texels. To approximate an image pre-filtered with a filter kernel of arbitrary size, a third parameter d is introduced, $d \in [0, \text{level}_{\max}]$,

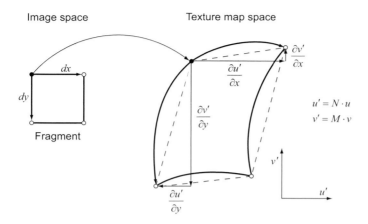

Figure 14.20. Pixel (fragment) pre-image and its corresponding partial derivatives with respect to the image-space parameters.

which moves up and down the hierarchy and interpolates between the nearest mip-map levels, according to the apparent minification measured at a given fragment. This means that all filters in the mip-mapping pre-filtering procedure are approximated by linearly blended square box filters. Although this is far from the ideal filtering and does not take into account any affine transformation of the kernel to counter the compression anisotropy, it usually works very well provided that an appropriate value for d is selected. The computation of the pyramidal interpolation parameter d is of critical importance to the resulting image quality. A poorly selected pyramidal filter parameter d results either in failure to antialias the texture or in excessive blurring.

Let us consider the rate of change of texels in relation to the pixels (fragments) in image space. For an $N \times M$ map, the partial derivatives of the applied texture image with respect to the horizontal and vertical image-buffer directions are $\partial u'/\partial x$, $\partial u'/\partial y$, $\partial v'/\partial x$, $\partial v'/\partial y$ (Figure 14.20), where

$$u' = u \cdot N, \qquad v' = v \cdot M, \qquad u, v \in [0, 1]. \qquad (14.21)$$

The pixel pre-image size and orientation is directly related to these quantities. In the simplified case of mip-mapping, in which we are only interested in square filter selection, the linear scaling ρ of the filter kernel is roughly equal to the maximum dimension of the pixel pre-image, which reflects the worst-case aliasing scenario [Will83]:

$$\rho = \max\left\{ \sqrt{\left(\frac{\partial u'}{\partial x}\right)^2 + \left(\frac{\partial v'}{\partial x}\right)^2}, \sqrt{\left(\frac{\partial u'}{\partial y}\right)^2 + \left(\frac{\partial v'}{\partial y}\right)^2} \right\}. \qquad (14.22)$$

Although the above definition of the scaling factor gives good results, in practical implementations a less computationally intensive approximation of the above formula is often sought [Seg04]. The desired value for the parameter d, which is essentially the continuous level of texture detail, is associated with the filter scaling factor and can be estimated with the following formula:

$$d = \begin{cases} \text{level}_{max} & \lambda > \text{level}_{max}, \\ \lambda & 0 \leq \lambda \leq \text{level}_{max}, \\ 0 & \lambda < 0, \end{cases} \qquad (14.23)$$

where $\lambda = \log_2 \rho$ and level_{max} is the maximum pre-calculated mip-map level.

Depending on the selection mechanism for the mip-maps, d can be used either as a nearest-neighbor decision variable or as a third interpolation parameter to perform tri-linear interpolation between adjacent levels, the latter case fully implementing the pyramidal parametrics paradigm and producing a smooth transition from one mip-map level to the next (Figure 14.16(d)).

The actual memory organization of the mip-maps is implementation-dependent and affected by the number of channels that the texture map consists of. For three-channel images, Williams suggested splitting the image into its red, green, and blue components and tiling them in the manner shown in Figure 14.19(c). Higher mip-map levels are stored above and to the left of their parent RGB triplets. The concept behind this memory organization is that once a (u,v) has been selected, the corresponding locations across the mip-maps can be indexed by a simple binary shift of the texture parameters.

Texture pre-filtering with mip-maps significantly speeds up rendering due to the fact that all filtering takes place when the texture is first loaded. The approximation of an arbitrary size filter kernel with a linear interpolation of discrete pre-calculated square box filters permits a robust and effective realization of pre-filtering in hardware for one-, two- or three-dimensional texture images in a unified manner. Today, all commodity graphics hardware systems implement the mip-mapping functionality in its full extent. However, the reader should keep in mind that mip-mapping performs sub-optimal filtering in the case where the pre-image deviates from a square shape. Finally, an important limitation of all algorithms that rely on measured quantities in image space is that they are screen driven and applicable only to incremental screen-order rendering tech-

niques. Clearly other rendering methods, such as ray-tracing cannot directly benefit from mip-mapping as there is no knowledge of a pre-image area for an arbitrary
isolated sample on a textured surface.

14.5 Procedural Textures

Up to this point, we have mainly dealt with texture mapping as a two-step process
from the Cartesian space to a parametric domain where the texture coordinates
are defined and finally to the texture values themselves, as indexed by the texture
coordinates, hence the name parametric texture mapping. As mentioned earlier
in this chapter, this kind of texture representation is the most comprehensive and
natural way to apply a texture that is stored in an array of pre-recorded or computed discrete values. There are many cases, however, when a surface (or volume)
attribute can be directly calculated from a mathematical model or can, in general,
be derived in a procedural algorithmic manner. *Procedural texturing* does not
make use of an intermediate parametric space. Instead, it directly and uniquely
associates an input set of coordinates with an output texture value. Procedural
textures can be considered as time-varying self-contained systems and are often
referred to as *procedural shaders*, i.e., black boxes that can be linked together to
process a set of input coordinates and modify a material attribute of a surface or
volume. A procedural texture can be used to calculate a color triplet, a normalized
set of coordinates, a vector direction, or a scalar value. Some of the forms that a
procedural texture with an attribute parameter vector **a** and an input point **p** may
take are listed below:

$$\begin{aligned}
\mathbf{v} &= \mathbf{f}_{\text{proc}}(\mathbf{p}, \mathbf{a}), \\
\overrightarrow{\mathbf{n}} &= \overrightarrow{\mathbf{f}}_{\text{proc}}(\mathbf{p}, \mathbf{a}), \\
t &= f_{\text{proc}}(\mathbf{p}, \mathbf{a}).
\end{aligned} \tag{14.24}$$

These output parameters can be used in turn as input to another procedural
texture or as a mapping function to index a parametric texture. Figure 14.21
demonstrates some examples of procedural texture utilization.

An important question to pose is why one should use procedural textures instead of parametric image maps. In order to explain this, we need to examine the
properties of a procedural texture. First, by definition, a procedural texturing system operates on continuous input parameters and generates a continuous output
of infinite resolution (constrained, of course, by the numerical precision). This
means that sampling a surface at a high resolution will not yield a blurred version

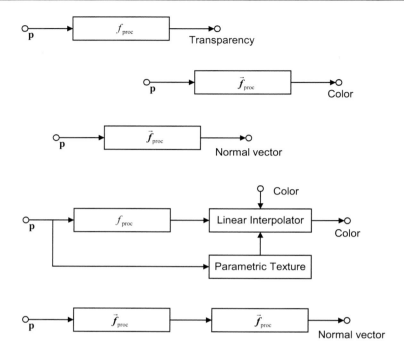

Figure 14.21. The use of procedural textures to perform various color and shading calculations.

of some interpolated discrete data, as is the case with the bitmap-based texturing, but rather a finer version of the output domain. Therefore, procedural textures do not suffer from magnification problems. Second, there is nothing that can cause distortion, since no intermediate parametric representation is involved, which may introduce mapping singularities. Last, the procedural textures can (and should be) defined in a way to ensure a meaningful mapping from the entire input domain to the output domain.

In nature, many periodic patterns, self-similar shapes, or chaotic and noisy signals can be very accurately modeled using procedural textures at an arbitrary sampling rate. The ability of procedural textures to mathematically control the appearance of the generated pattern with the proper selection of texture modeling parameters provides a useful visualization tool for artists and scientists alike. Refer to Color Plate III for an example of image synthesis using procedural textures.

Until recently, procedural texturing was practically applicable only to non-real-time rendering systems, because the graphics hardware could not provide support for shaders. All computations were performed in the CPU processing time, resulting in a waste of a critical resource, and produced results that were incompatible with the rest of the graphics pipeline. The only way to reasonably integrate parametric texture mapping and a procedural texture was to sample the latter into a texture map, which of course is a solution that suffers from the sampling problems discussed in Section 14.4 and completely fails to take advantage of the beneficial properties of procedural texture mapping. Since the invention of GPUs with support for vertex and fragment programs, procedural shaders have been extensively used for the creation of stunning surface materials and visual effects.

14.5.1 Noise Generation⊛

Very frequently in nature we come across materials and surfaces with irregular patterns or grainy textures. For instance, if we carefully inspect a rough wall covered with stucco, or painted with a non-glossy coating, we will discover that the diffuse, even illumination that is reflected off of the surface is caused by tiny, irregular bumps of the deposited material. A patch of sand and various minerals and stones consist of an uneven aggregation of small, irregular fragments of diverse materials. Granite and marble often exhibit intense and even abrupt color transitions in a noisy and turbulent manner. Clearly, one can think of many examples where a natural texture looks like or depends upon a noisy pattern. The design and implementation of a procedural texture, which acts like a pseudo-number generator but also exhibits some more convenient and controllable properties, is crucial for the domain of texture-generation algorithms. The reader should also keep in mind that superimposing a granular pattern on a parametric image texture or modulating it with a slow-varying noise function can make a tiled texture look more convincing and pleasant to the eye, as the repetitiveness of the pattern is substantially diminished.

A useful noise generator for image synthesis must adhere to a number of rules, in order to ensure a consistent output at an arbitrary input. The procedural noise should be all of the following:

- *Stateless.* The procedural noise model needs to be memory-less. The new output value or vector should not depend on previous states of the generator or past input values. This restriction is necessary if we want to have an uncorrelated train of output samples.

- *Time-invariant.* The output has to be deterministic. Dependence of the noise function on clock-based random generators should be avoided as the procedural noise produced would be different at consecutive samples of the same location in space.

- *Smooth.* The output signal of the noise generator should be continuous and smooth. First-order partial derivatives with respect to Cartesian coordinates should be computable at an arbitrary location in space as they are required by many effects and shading calculations.

- *Band-limited.* A white-noise generator (infinite support, constant power spectrum) is not very useful for computing image or spatial domain texture values, as the signal will never be correctly sampled, regardless of the density of the samples, thus leading to aliasing. The procedural noise model should provide the means to control the maximum (and minimum) variation rate of the pattern. Band-limited noise with a low cut-off frequency produces space-coherent slow-varying output values, which can even be used for the modulation of vertex locations in space.

The most widely used procedural noise generator for computer graphics is the one introduced by Perlin [Perl85]. *Perlin noise* encompasses all the properties listed above and relies on a common and efficient numerical hashing scheme on pre-calculated random values.

Assume a lattice in $\mathbb{R}^3$ formed by all the triplet combinations of integer values, so that node $\Omega_{i,j,k}$ lies on (i, j, k): $i, j, k \in \mathbb{N}$. Every lattice node is associated with a pre-generated pseudo-random number $\gamma_{i,j,k}$ in the range $[-1.0, 1.0]$, a triplet of pseudo-random numbers in the case of a random point, or a pseudo-random unit-length vector $\overrightarrow{\gamma}_{i,j,k}$ if a result is required in vector form. Without loss of generality, we will examine the scalar version of the noise generator unless stated otherwise. The procedural noise output is the weighted sum of the values on the eight nodes nearest to the input point $\mathbf{p}$. More specifically, Perlin uses the lattice nodes $\Omega_{i,j,k}$ as spline knots, which contribute to the sum according to the following weighting function [Perl89]:

$$\omega(t) = \begin{cases} 2|t|^3 - 3t^2 + 1 & |t| < 1, \\ 0 & |t| \geq 1. \end{cases} \qquad (14.25)$$

The above function has a support of 2, centered at 0, so for an integer i, $\omega(t - i)$ is maximized at i and drops off to 0 beyond $i \pm 1$. The final noise pattern $f_{\text{noise}}(\mathbf{p})$ for an arbitrary point $\mathbf{p} = (x, y, z)$ is given by trilinear interpolation of the values $\gamma_{i,j,k}$ of the eight lattice points $\Omega_{i,j,k}$ closest to $\mathbf{p}$ (Figure 14.22(a)) using $\omega(t - \lfloor t \rfloor)$ as the interpolation coefficient instead of $t - \lfloor t \rfloor$, $t \in \mathbb{R}$. The eight lattice nodes closest to $\mathbf{p}$ are of course $\Omega_{i,j,k}$, $\Omega_{i+1,j,k}$, $\Omega_{i,j+1,k}$, $\Omega_{i,j,k+1}$, $\Omega_{i+1,j+1,k}$, $\Omega_{i,j+1,k+1}$, $\Omega_{i+1,j,k+1}$, $\Omega_{i+1,j+1,k+1}$: $i = \lfloor x \rfloor, j = \lfloor y \rfloor, k = \lfloor z \rfloor$.

In order to be able to achieve repeatable, time-invariant results, without letting the results be repetitive in a perceivable manner, $\gamma_{i,j,k}$ is selected from a table G of N pre-computed uniformly distributed scalars in the desired output range, using a common modulo-based hashing mechanism:

$$\gamma_{i,j,k} = G\left[\text{hash}\left(i + \text{hash}\left(j + \text{hash}(k)\right)\right)\right],$$
$$\text{hash}(n) = P[n \bmod N]. \tag{14.26}$$

In the above formula, P is a table containing a pseudo-random permutation of the first N integers. Results of the three-dimensional Perlin noise function are shown in Figure 14.22(b). Many variations of the definition given here have been implemented, with slight changes in the weighting/interpolation of the lattice values or in the output response curve, which is assumed linear in this text.

14.5.2 Turbulence⊛

An extension of the noise procedural texture described in Section 14.5.1 is the 1/f noise or *turbulence* function, also introduced by Perlin [Perl85]. This is also a band-limited noise function, which is commonly encountered in various natural formations and processes. As the name suggests, $1/f$ noise, has a spectrum profile whose magnitude is inversely proportional to the corresponding frequency. An approximation to this stochastic signal is achieved by overlaying suitably scaled harmonics of a basic band-limited noise function like $f_{\text{noise}}(\mathbf{p})$. Based on the scale-uncertainty principle of the spatial/frequency domain relation, a contraction of the noise-pattern duration results in an expansion of the resulting spectrum. In order to create the required high-order harmonics, the input signal, i.e., the point upon which the noise function is evaluated, is suitably scaled by the central frequency of the shifted lobe. This leads to an expression for the $1/f$ noise of the form (Figure 14.23):

$$f_{\text{turb}}(\mathbf{p}) = f_{1/f}(\mathbf{p}) = \sum_{i=1}^{\text{octaves}} \frac{1}{2^i f} f_{\text{noise}}(2^i f \cdot \mathbf{p}), \tag{14.27}$$

where f is the base frequency of the noise in the spatial domain and *octaves* is the maximum number of overlaid noise signals. The visual result of the above noise function is that of Brownian motion. Equation (14.27) can be written in a

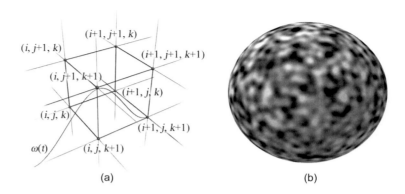

Figure 14.22. Perlin noise. (a) Texture values at arbitrary three-dimensional co-ordinates are calculated from pseudo-random values associated with the nearest integers. (b) The result of sampling Perlin procedural noise on a spherical surface.

more generalized form, allowing for an adjustment of the octave contribution that is unrelated to the noise frequency:

$$f_{1/f}(\mathbf{p}) = \sum_{i=1}^{\text{octaves}} \omega^i \cdot f_{\text{noise}}(\lambda^i \cdot \mathbf{p}), \tag{14.28}$$

where $\omega > 0$ regulates the contribution of higher frequencies to the final result and $\lambda > 1$ modulates the chaotic behavior of the noise. When $\lambda \to 1$, $f_{1/f}(\mathbf{p})$ appears as a scaled version of the $f_{\text{noise}}(\mathbf{p})$, while larger values give a more swirling look to the result. If we consider the vector form of the $1/f$ noise function, where $\vec{f}_{1/f}(\mathbf{p})$ can be regarded as the resulting offset of point $\mathbf{p}$ after performing a random walk, ω corresponds to the speed of motion and λ simulates the entropy of the system under Brownian motion.

A common variation of the turbulence function uses the absolute values of the $f_{\text{noise}}(\mathbf{p})$ octaves, resulting in a tighter and sharper pattern of fractal "wisps." This modification has, of course, no meaning in the vector form of the texture function.

Many interesting patterns can be generated by applying the scalar or vector turbulence function to simple mathematical formulas. The noise function can act as a bias to the input points or as part of a composite function:

$$f_{\text{proc}}(\mathbf{p}) = f_{\text{math}}\left(f_{\text{turb}}(\mathbf{p})\right), \tag{14.29}$$

$$f_{\text{proc}}(\mathbf{p}) = f_{\text{math}}(\mathbf{p} + a \cdot \vec{f}_{\text{turb}}(\mathbf{p})). \tag{14.30}$$

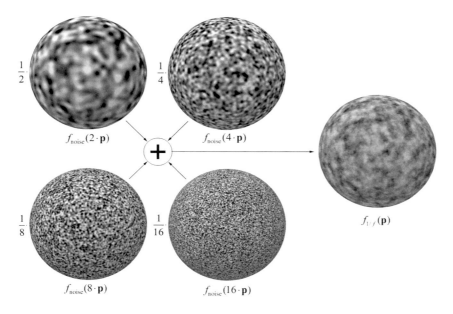

Figure 14.23. 1/f noise pattern composition.

14.5.3 Common 3D Procedural Textures

One of the most commonly used procedural textures is the solid checker pattern (Figure 14.24), which consists of interleaved solid blocks of two different colors (monochrome intensities here). This pattern is preferably rendered using a procedural texture due to the discontinuity in the transition from one color block to the next that cannot be represented correctly with a texture image at an arbitrary resolution, because it would be eventually pixelized or blurred at the checker limits. The simple mathematical expression behind this elegant pattern is

$$f_{\text{checker}}(\mathbf{p}) = (\lfloor x \rfloor + \lfloor y \rfloor + \lfloor z \rfloor) \bmod 2. \tag{14.31}$$

For quite the opposite reason, an extremely useful pattern is the linear gradient transition from one value to another. When performing color interpolation based on Cartesian coordinates or measured distances in the three-dimensional space, a procedural gradient produces a high quality smooth transition from one value to another, without the danger of generating perceivable bands. These bands are a result of color quantization when using texture maps with fixed-point arithmetic,

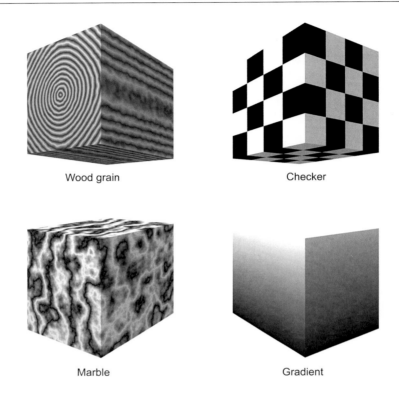

Figure 14.24. Solid procedural texture examples.

yielding discontinuity of the second-order derivatives of the linearly interpolated texture values. Linear gradients are easy to implement and can be defined in a meaningful way using many alternative input parameters, from single Cartesian coordinates to distances in space, or spherical parameters. A gradient procedural texture can be defined in its simplest form as a ramp along a primary coordinate-system axis:

$$f_{\text{gradient}}(\mathbf{p}) = y - \lfloor y \rfloor . \tag{14.32}$$

Natural formations can be effectively modeled by combining a base mathematical expression that provides the primary features of a material with the turbulence or noise function, as described in Equations (14.29) and (14.30).

Wood can be represented as an infinite succession of concentric cylindrical layers that can be modeled by a ramp function over the cylindrical coordinate r, i.e., the distance from an axis (Figure 14.24). By adding an amount of perturbation a to the input points and accenting the sharp transition between layers without a discontinuity in the texture values using an absolute sine or cosine function, we get the wood procedural texture:

$$f_{\text{wood}}(\mathbf{p}) = |\cos(2\pi(d - \lfloor d \rfloor))|,$$
$$d = \sqrt{y^2 + z^2} + a \cdot f_{\text{turb}}(\mathbf{p}). \tag{14.33}$$

Another natural pattern, which can be easily simulated by a procedural texture, is the shape of marble veins. We can use a smoothly varying function to generate the basic formation of compressed earth layers, such as a sine wave. If the input parameter is perturbed by the turbulence function, we can get a very realistic approximation of self-similar marble veins (Figure 14.24):

$$f_{\text{marble}}(\mathbf{p}) = \frac{1}{2} + \sin(2\pi(x + f_{\text{turb2}}(\mathbf{p}))),$$
$$f_{\text{turb2}} = \sum_{i=1}^{\text{octaves}} \frac{1}{2^i f} |f_{\text{noise}}(2^i f \cdot \mathbf{p})|. \tag{14.34}$$

14.6 Texture Transformations

In the previous section, in order to produce turbulence, successively higher frequencies of the texture were overlaid on each other. What we did, in fact, was to take a basic noise pattern, scale it down so that its frequency becomes higher by compressing the signal in the spatial domain, and then use it in the sum of noise octaves. But what mechanism was employed to shrink the texture output? Consider Equations (14.27) and (14.34). When an output signal of half the initial period was needed, the input signal was multiplied, i.e., it was stretched by a factor of two. This operation simply takes advantage of the duality between the transformations applied to the coordinates and the reference frame they depend on. Remember from Chapter 3 that when a point $\mathbf{p}$ in space is expressed as a set of coordinates (x, y, z) relative to a reference coordinate system $L = \{\mathbf{o}, \hat{e}_1, \hat{e}_2, \hat{e}_3\}$, the effect of transforming $\mathbf{p}$ can be achieved by inversely transforming the reference frame:

$$\mathbf{p}' = (x', y', z') = \mathbf{M}(\mathbf{p}) : \mathbf{p} = \mathbf{o} + x\hat{\mathbf{e}}_1 + y\hat{\mathbf{e}}_2 + z\hat{\mathbf{e}}_3 \quad \Leftrightarrow$$
$$\mathbf{p}' = \mathbf{o}' + x'\hat{\mathbf{e}}_1' + y'\hat{\mathbf{e}}_2' + z'\hat{\mathbf{e}}_3' : \{\mathbf{o}', \hat{\mathbf{e}}_1', \hat{\mathbf{e}}_2', \hat{\mathbf{e}}_3'\} = \mathbf{M}^{-1}(\{\mathbf{o}, \hat{\mathbf{e}}_1, \hat{\mathbf{e}}_2, \hat{\mathbf{e}}_3\}). \tag{14.35}$$

This simple principle is very useful, because it allows for the creation of procedural texture variations without requiring any modification of the pattern shader

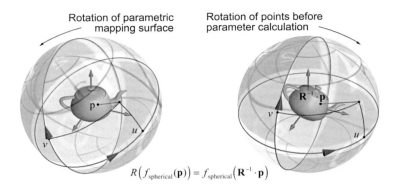

Rotation of parametric   Rotation of points before
mapping surface   parameter calculation

$$R\big(f_{\text{spherical}}(\mathbf{p})\big) = f_{\text{spherical}}\big(\mathbf{R}^{-1} \cdot \mathbf{p}\big)$$

Figure 14.25. Example of practical intermediate parametric surface transformation in image mapping.

itself. For example, a gradient along the x-axis can be achieved by reusing Equation (14.32) but instead of directly applying the formula to the input points, a transformed version can be used:

$$f_{\text{gradientX}}(\mathbf{p}) = \mathbf{R}_{-90,z}\big(f_{\text{gradient}}(\mathbf{p})\big) = f_{\text{gradient}}(\mathbf{R}_{90,z} \cdot \mathbf{p}). \qquad (14.36)$$

In the same manner, any transformation that needs to be applied to the texture pattern, can be implemented by applying the inverse transformation to the input domain:

$$M\big(f_{\text{proc}}(\mathbf{p})\big) = f_{\text{proc}}\big(\mathbf{M}^{-1} \cdot \mathbf{p}\big). \qquad (14.37)$$

The above transformation formulation is also applicable to the case of parametric texture mapping. When a transformed version of the intermediate parametric mapping surface is needed, it is easier to inversely transform the vertices for which the new (u, v)-coordinates are to be estimated, rather than produce a new parametric mapping function (Figure 14.25).

When working with parametric texture mapping, we have the flexibility to perform transformations in the texture parameter domain as well. Texture coordinates can be directly shifted, rotated, and translated using two-dimensional transformations (or three-dimensional ones in the case of volume textures). This is very helpful for tiling at modeling time, where an artist can use a graphical interface (commonly named as a "uv editor") to tweak the texture parameters by transforming the corresponding mapped locations of the polygon vertices in the texture domain.

14.7 Relief Representation

A texture map can be used, apart from altering the material characteristics of a surface, for modulating its geometry to create patterns in relief, or better, to imitate the apparent effect of a bumpy surface without generating the extra geometric detail required. There are two major approaches to building a bumpy surface using texturing (either parametric or procedural). The first approach, *displacement mapping*, distorts the geometry to create the relief pattern, while the second approach, *bump mapping*, or the similar *normal mapping*, tries to create the illusion of a bumpy surface without altering the actual surface in any way.

14.7.1 Displacement Mapping

Displacement mapping creates relief patterns on a surface by moving the vertices along the original surface normal direction or along a predefined vector according to the intensity of the texture evaluated at each point (see Figure 14.26). The

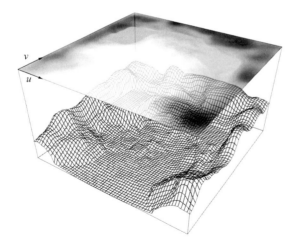

Figure 14.26. Displacement mapping. In this particular example, darker bump-map values represent higher elevation, for the sake of visual clarity.

elevation pattern used in both the displacement and the bump mapping is a scalar-valued map, called a *bump map*. This technique requires either that the surface is highly tessellated from the beginning or that an appropriate adaptive algorithm adds more surface elements at high slope areas. Displacement mapping cannot be applied on a per-pixel basis during rendering by pushing away from the original surface the fragment being drawn, because due to the different amount of elevation in neighboring fragments, holes are very likely to appear.

The big advantage of displacement mapping is that it truly generates a pattern in relief and not a shading illusion. This means that the textured surface exhibits the proper parallax effect from all viewing angles and at all surface locations, including the object's silhouette. On the downside, the highly detailed surface it requires makes the technique unfavorable for real-time rendering of relief patterns. Displacement mapping is used in real-time applications in conjunction with vertex shader programs as a surface deformation mechanism, e.g., for animating large waves.

14.7.2   Bump Mapping⊛

A visual trick devised in the late 1970s by Blinn for faking the appearance of detailed bumpy and wrinkled surfaces is called bump mapping, a method that since then has been extensively used to enhance the rendering of surfaces with relief details recorded in a texture map (or procedural texture).

Consider the two-dimensional simplified bump-mapping paradigm of Figure 14.27. Let $b(u)$ be the elevation pattern in the texture domain and $\mathbf{s} = \mathbf{s}(u)$ the surface location that corresponds to the same parameterization (in fact, multiple points may address the same parameter u, according to the mapping function). The displaced surface $\mathbf{s}' = \mathbf{s}'(u)$ is $\mathbf{s}'(u) = \mathbf{s}(u) + b(u)\hat{\mathbf{n}}(u)$. The new surface has a different normal vector $\hat{\mathbf{n}}'(u)$ than the original one, since the normal vector is by definition perpendicular to the new, wrinkled surface.

The important observation, which is the key idea to bump mapping, is how the relief pattern is finally perceived by the human eye. When we look at a bumpy surface, what we actually deduce the shape of the relief pattern from is the variation of the surface illumination, which is the result of the surface shading. Now, recall from the Phong shading model that the only local surface attribute that contributes to the shading calculation is the normal vector itself and no other "elevation" information. This has the amazing implication that we can have the same local visual effect of a geometrically wrinkled surface by directly calculating how the normal vector would be perturbed if the surface were elevated, but without

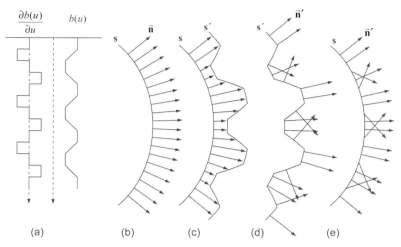

Figure 14.27. The principle of bump mapping. (a) An intensity pattern modulates an initial surface (b) by pushing it along the normal direction (c). The bump-mapping algorithm calculates the new normals (d) and, instead of actually changing the surface, it replaces the new normals on the original surface (e), to achieve the same visual result.

actually moving the surface points. This way, the eye is tricked to believe that the three-dimensional model is substantially elaborate in terms of geometry, whereas we only alter the normal vector in the shading calculation according to an elevation texture.

To better understand the workings of bump mapping in three-dimensional space, let us define the notion of *tangent space* (Figure 14.28). Given a surface parameterization (u,v): $\mathbf{s} = \mathbf{s}(u,v)$, the local unit-length normal vector $\hat{\mathbf{n}} = \hat{\mathbf{n}}(u,v)$ of the surface is given by

$$\hat{\mathbf{n}} = \hat{\mathbf{u}} \times \hat{\mathbf{v}}, \qquad \hat{\mathbf{u}} = \frac{\overrightarrow{\mathbf{t}}}{|\overrightarrow{\mathbf{t}}|},$$

$$\hat{\mathbf{v}} = \frac{\overrightarrow{\mathbf{b}}}{|\overrightarrow{\mathbf{b}}|}, \qquad \overrightarrow{\mathbf{t}} = \frac{\partial \mathbf{s}(u,v)}{\partial u}, \qquad (14.38)$$

$$\overrightarrow{\mathbf{b}} = \frac{\partial \mathbf{s}(u,v)}{\partial v}.$$

The two normalized vectors $\hat{\mathbf{u}}$ and $\hat{\mathbf{v}}$, as well as the corresponding unnormalized surface derivatives $\tilde{\mathbf{t}}$ and $\tilde{\mathbf{b}}$, lie on the tangent plane at $\mathbf{s}(u,v)$ and are called

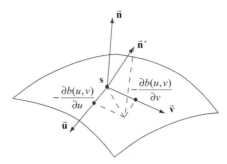

Figure 14.28. Tangent space and the new normal vector that results from the bump-mapping calculations.

the *tangent vector* and the *bitangent vector*, respectively. The bitangent vector is sometimes called the *binormal vector*, which is actually a misnomer, as binormal vectors are used in the description of curves and not surfaces. The two parameters that are used when the bump information is extracted from a texture map are the texture coordinates, i.e., the tangent vector corresponds to the u parameter in texture space and the bitangent vector corresponds to the v parameter. The reader should refer to Section 14.7.5 for the calculation of the tangent vectors at an arbitrary texture-mapped point in a polygon.

The elevated surface $\mathbf{s}'(u,v)$ is given by

$$\mathbf{s}'(u,v) = \mathbf{s}(u,v) + \hat{\mathbf{n}}(u,v) \cdot b(u,v), \qquad (14.39)$$

and the perturbed normal vector is perpendicular to the new tangent vectors:

$$\hat{\mathbf{n}}' = \hat{\mathbf{u}}' \times \hat{\mathbf{v}}' = \frac{\partial \mathbf{s}'(u,v)}{\partial u} \times \frac{\partial \mathbf{s}'(u,v)}{\partial v}. \qquad (14.40)$$

Evaluating the partial derivatives using the chain rule on Equation (14.39), we get

$$
\begin{aligned}
\frac{\partial \mathbf{s}'(u,v)}{\partial u} &= \frac{\partial \mathbf{s}(u,v)}{\partial u} + \frac{\partial \hat{\mathbf{n}}(u,v)}{\partial u} \cdot b(u,v) + \hat{\mathbf{n}}(u,v) \cdot \frac{\partial b(u,v)}{\partial u}, \\
\frac{\partial \mathbf{s}'(u,v)}{\partial v} &= \frac{\partial \mathbf{s}(u,v)}{\partial v} + \frac{\partial \hat{\mathbf{n}}(u,v)}{\partial v} \cdot b(u,v) + \hat{\mathbf{n}}(u,v) \cdot \frac{\partial b(u,v)}{\partial v}.
\end{aligned}
\qquad (14.41)
$$

For slow (smooth) normal vector variations relative to the extent of the surface, $\partial \hat{\mathbf{n}}/\partial u$ and $\partial \hat{\mathbf{n}}/\partial v$ are negligible, simplifying Equation (14.41) to

$$
\begin{aligned}
\frac{\partial \mathbf{s}'(u,v)}{\partial u} &= \frac{\partial \mathbf{s}(u,v)}{\partial u} + \hat{\mathbf{n}}(u,v) \cdot \frac{\partial b(u,v)}{\partial u} = \overrightarrow{\mathbf{t}} + \hat{\mathbf{n}}(u,v) \cdot \frac{\partial b(u,v)}{\partial u}, \\
\frac{\partial \mathbf{s}'(u,v)}{\partial v} &= \frac{\partial \mathbf{s}(u,v)}{\partial v} + \hat{\mathbf{n}}(u,v) \cdot \frac{\partial b(u,v)}{\partial v} = \overrightarrow{\mathbf{b}} + \hat{\mathbf{n}}(u,v) \cdot \frac{\partial b(u,v)}{\partial v}.
\end{aligned}
\tag{14.42}
$$

Substituting the partial derivatives of (14.42) into Equation (14.40), we get

$$
\begin{aligned}
\hat{\mathbf{n}}' &= \left(\overrightarrow{\mathbf{t}} + \hat{\mathbf{n}} \cdot \frac{\partial b(u,v)}{\partial u} \right) \times \left(\overrightarrow{\mathbf{b}} + \hat{\mathbf{n}} \cdot \frac{\partial b(u,v)}{\partial v} \right) \\
&= \overrightarrow{\mathbf{t}} \times \overrightarrow{\mathbf{b}} + \overrightarrow{\mathbf{t}} \times \hat{\mathbf{n}} \cdot \frac{\partial b(u,v)}{\partial v} + \hat{\mathbf{n}} \times \overrightarrow{\mathbf{b}} \cdot \frac{\partial b(u,v)}{\partial u} + \hat{\mathbf{n}} \times \hat{\mathbf{n}} \cdot \frac{\partial b(u,v)}{\partial u} \frac{\partial b(u,v)}{\partial v} \Rightarrow \\
\hat{\mathbf{n}}' &= \hat{\mathbf{n}} - \overrightarrow{\mathbf{b}} \cdot \frac{\partial b(u,v)}{\partial v} - \overrightarrow{\mathbf{t}} \cdot \frac{\partial b(u,v)}{\partial u}.
\end{aligned}
$$

$$
(14.43)
$$

The new perturbed normal vector of Equation (14.43), which is expressed relative to the object or world coordinate system, depends only on the tangent vectors and the partial derivatives of the bump map (Figure 14.28).

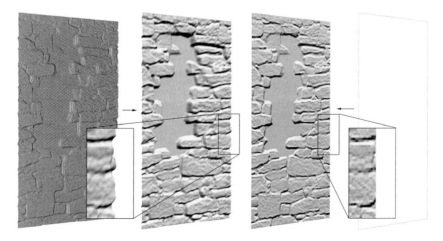

Figure 14.29. Displacement versus bump mapping. The first produces accurate elevation parallax and offset geometry at the edges in exchange for a high geometry tessellation. A bump-mapped surface can be very simple and still convey a convincing relief appearance, which nevertheless lacks in accuracy and fails to produce correct edges.

Figure 14.29 shows a comparison between a displaced surface and a bump-mapped surface. The displaced surface needs a fine tessellation in order for the vertices to be able to track the texture-space offset variations. The resulting, displaced mesh correctly captures the relief details and is accurately shaded and clipped across the whole surface. On the other hand, if the same texture information is applied as a bump map to the surface, there is no need for excessive tessellation of the polygons. A very simple geometric representation can be used and still produces a good approximation of the shading on the surface. However, this otherwise convincing shading trick (see also the normal mapping method below) has two disadvantages. First, the representation of relative offsets is poor when deep depressions are present in the elevation pattern. The other problem occurs at the surface edges, where due to the fact that the geometry is not actually bumpy, the shading conflicts with the clean, smooth surface extents. In some cases, this problem can be solved by clipping the low-resolution geometry at the silhouettes of the high-resolution version of the surface (here, the displaced, tessellated one) [Sand00].

14.7.3   Normal Maps⊛

The bump-mapping method presented so far, uses as input the same image map as the displacement mapping, i.e., a grayscale elevation image. An alternative relief-representation method is *normal mapping*, where instead of providing an elevation offset at each point, the normal vector that should be used in the shading calculations is directly supplied [Cohe98]. In procedural mapping, the normal vector for the given input point can be calculated using a predefined function. When parametric texturing is required to transfer a pre-calculated relief pattern onto a model, the normal vector $\hat{\mathbf{n}}(u,v)$ that corresponds to a texture coordinate pair is stored as a color-coded triplet in a bitmap file. The R, G, and B components of the image $\mathbf{c}(u,v)$ keep properly scaled and usually quantized (unless it is a floating-point-number format) Cartesian coordinate values of the unit-length vector:

$$\hat{\mathbf{n}}(u,v) = \mathbf{c}(u,v)/2^{\text{Nbits}} - (0.5, 0.5, 0.5), \qquad (14.44)$$

where Nbits is the number of bits used for storing each color channel.

The above mapping method is called *object-space normal mapping*. Object-space normal mapping has two advantages. First, in contrast to bump-mapping, the normals can be calculated intuitively from high resolution surfaces and stored in normal maps on simplified texture-mapped versions. Color Plate XXII shows

(a)   (b)

Figure 14.30. Normal mapping. (a) A low-resolution mesh has its normal vectors replaced per rendered fragment, according to the normal map of Color Plate XXII. (b) The original, high-resolution surface from which the normal map was extracted.

an example of an object-space normal map. Figure 14.30 and Color Plate XXIII demonstrate the use of the technique to render detail on a simplified version of a high-resolution model. The normal map has been constructed by sampling the high resolution model and storing its normal vectors in a normal atlas texture (see Section 14.8). This is a very useful technique in real-time rendering, where high resolution geometry is first created using a modeling tool and then the final application uses low-poly models coated with normal maps to display the intricate shapes of their high-fidelity cousins at an affordable frame rate. The second advantage of object-space normal maps is that they need significantly fewer calculations to derive the local normal and perform the shading calculations. On the other hand, because normals are expressed relative to an object or world reference frame, they need to be transformed along with the object. When the object undergoes any kind of distortion, such as skeletal animation or vertex morphing, the object-space normals are wrong and result in unconvincing images.

14.7.4   Tangent-Space Normal Maps⊛

To overcome the limitations of object-space normal mapping, the normal vectors can be defined using the tangent space as a reference frame. The normal maps produced by this variation are called *tangent-space normal maps* (Color Plate XXIV). Tangent-space-based normal maps may be less intuitive for a general purpose calculation or visualization, and they look a lot like edge-filtered versions of the relief patterns they represent (actually, they are directly related to the partial derivatives of the bump map). Since they have a local reference frame, tangent-space normals are immune to transformations and deformations, and the corresponding normal maps can be used as tiled textures on an arbitrary surface.

Unfortunately, tangent-space normal maps require some extra calculations to be performed in order to integrate them with a shading model. More specifically, originally defined in the world coordinate system, the light-direction ($\hat{\mathbf{n}}_L$) and view-direction ($\hat{\mathbf{n}}_V$) vectors have to be transformed to the local tangent-space coordinate system.

The tangent space is defined in such a way that the local z-direction points at the (unperturbed) interpolated normal vector, the x-direction coincides with the tangent vector, and the bitangent vector is parallel to the local y-axis. After replacing the normal direction according to the normal map values, we get a new normal vector $\tilde{\mathbf{n}}'(u,v)$. The resulting coordinate system is not necessarily orthonormal, but the tangent vectors lie in approximately the right direction, provided the bump effect is not too pronounced. There are two options. One is to leave the tangent vectors as they are and create an "almost-orthonormal" coordinate system if we are absolutely positive that we have small perturbations of the normal vector. The safest solution is to rectify the tangent and bitangent vectors by first performing an orthonormalization step before using them to express the light- and view-direction vectors in tangent space. Applying the Gram-Schmidt orthogonalization formula [Leng04] and then normalizing the tangent vectors we get

$$\begin{aligned} \overrightarrow{\mathbf{u}}' &= \hat{\mathbf{u}} - (\hat{\mathbf{n}}' \cdot \hat{\mathbf{u}}) \cdot \hat{\mathbf{n}}', \\ \overrightarrow{\mathbf{v}}' &= \hat{\mathbf{v}} - (\hat{\mathbf{n}}' \cdot \hat{\mathbf{v}}) \cdot \hat{\mathbf{n}}' - (\mathbf{u}' \cdot \hat{\mathbf{v}}) \cdot \overrightarrow{\mathbf{u}}'. \end{aligned} \qquad (14.45)$$

The rotation matrix that transforms the light- and view-direction vectors, initially expressed in world coordinates, to the local tangent coordinate system is the well-known change-of-basis matrix that is made up of the target coordinate system axes expressed in the source coordinate system, as rows of the rotational part of the homogeneous 4×4 transformation matrix:

$$\mathbf{R}_{\text{Tangent}} = \begin{bmatrix} u'_x & u'_y & u'_z & 0 \\ v'_x & v'_y & v'_z & 0 \\ n'_x & n'_y & n'_z & 0 \\ 0 & 0 & 0 & 1 \end{bmatrix}. \qquad (14.46)$$

14.7.5 Tangent-Space Calculation⊛

Given an arbitrary texture-mapped point $\mathbf{s}$ on a polygonal surface, regardless of the relief representation method chosen, we need to calculate the object-space

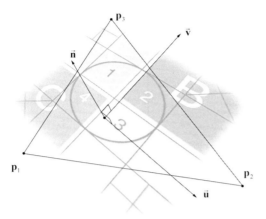

Figure 14.31. Texture-aligned tangent space of a triangle.

tangent vectors $\vec{t}$ and $\vec{b}$ and the respective normalized ones, $\hat{u}$ and $\hat{v}$. Let us consider the common case of a triangle containing the surface point **s**. We use here the derivation of $\vec{t}$ and $\vec{b}$ found in [Leng04].

Let the texture coordinate pairs of a triangle $\mathbf{p}_1\mathbf{p}_2\mathbf{p}_3$ be (u_1, v_1), (u_2, v_2), and (u_3, v_3). We require that the tangent and bitangent vectors be locally parallel to the texture isoparametric curves. This way, the tangent space is always aligned with the normal or bump map (Figure 14.31), and the texture parameters are local coordinates up to a scale factor on the xy-plane of the tangent space (remember local $z-$axis coincides with the normal vector). We will also assume for now that the tangent space remains constant across the polygon's surface. We can express an arbitrary point **p** in the interior of the triangle with respect to the tangent and bitangent vectors by

$$\mathbf{p} = \mathbf{p}_1 + (u - u_1)\tilde{\mathbf{u}} + (v - v_1)\hat{\mathbf{v}}. \qquad (14.47)$$

As all three triangle vertices share the same tangent coordinate system, they satisfy Equation (14.47) simultaneously:

$$\begin{aligned}
\mathbf{p}_2 - \mathbf{p}_1 &= (u_2 - u_1)\,\hat{\mathbf{u}} + (v_2 - v_1)\,\hat{\mathbf{v}}, \\
\mathbf{p}_3 - \mathbf{p}_1 &= (u_3 - u_1)\,\hat{\mathbf{u}} + (v_3 - v_1)\,\hat{\mathbf{v}},
\end{aligned} \qquad (14.48)$$

or in a more compact form,

$$\vec{q}_2 = u_{21}\hat{u} + v_{21}\hat{v},$$
$$\vec{q}_3 = u_{31}\hat{u} + v_{31}\hat{v}. \tag{14.49}$$

The above linear system of six equations (two vectors, three coordinates per vector) can be expressed in a matrix form with respect to the six unknown coordinates of $\tilde{t}$ and $\tilde{b}$:

$$\left[\begin{array}{cc} u_{21} & v_{21} \\ u_{31} & v_{31} \end{array}\right] \left[\begin{array}{ccc} t_x & t_y & t_z \\ b_x & b_y & b_z \end{array}\right] = \left[\begin{array}{ccc} q_{2x} & q_{2y} & q_{2z} \\ q_{3x} & q_{3y} & q_{3z} \end{array}\right]. \tag{14.50}$$

The six unknown vector coordinates are obtained by solving this trivial linear system. Using the determinant formula for the inversion of the coefficient matrix we get

$$\left[\begin{array}{ccc} t_x & t_y & t_z \\ b_x & b_y & b_z \end{array}\right] = \frac{1}{u_{21}v_{31} - u_{31}v_{21}} \left[\begin{array}{cc} v_{31} & -v_{21} \\ -u_{31} & u_{21} \end{array}\right] \left[\begin{array}{ccc} q_{2x} & q_{2y} & q_{2z} \\ q_{3x} & q_{3y} & q_{3z} \end{array}\right]. \tag{14.51}$$

The resulting coordinate system is not normalized and possibly not even orthogonal. The vectors should be adjusted according to Equation (14.45) and then normalized. The vectors $\vec{t}$ and $\vec{b}$ represent the triangle's tangent space. In order to assign a tangent coordinate system to each of the three vertices of a triangle in a mesh, the tangent and normal vectors of triangles that share a particular vertex have to be averaged and stored in the vertex information, along with the other vertex attributes. Then, for every point in the triangle, the three vectors are interpolated in the same manner as the other vertex values (i.e., bilinear interpolation or barycentric coordinates).

14.8   Texture Atlases⊛

In many practical applications of texture mapping, the need arises for a unique mapping between surface points on a three-dimensional object and the texture domain. The one-to-one surface parameterization is commonly used in situations where texture values are location-dependent, the texture map is used as a storage medium for surface data, or when we need to be able to bidirectionally address the texture space and the surface points. The most prominent examples of such a parameterization are the use of textures to store pre-calculated diffuse illumination (*light maps* or *illumination maps*), the *normal maps*, and the *geometry images*, where the Cartesian coordinates of the surface are themselves encoded in texture maps. More about these particular applications will be discussed later.

A *texture atlas* is a surface parameterization where connected parts of the object's surface, called *charts*, are each mapped onto contiguous regions of the texture domain. An object is first partitioned into charts, which are surface regions homeomorphic to discs [Levy02]. Then, each chart is parameterized so that the surface patch is unfolded on a two-dimensional domain to ensure a unique mapping for each point in the chart. At this stage, the texture-domain pieces that the charts are mapped to may overlap. Finally, the individual map pieces and the corresponding parameter ranges are packed in a single texture so that the charts do not overlap in texture space. This way the final atlas ensures the unique mapping between Cartesian coordinates on the surface and locations on the bounded texture domain of the image map (Figure 14.32).

Numerous algorithms have been proposed for addressing each one of the three stages of the texture-atlas-generation procedure as efficiently as possible. The parameterization stage depends on the constraints chosen for the surface segmentation. When cutting a surface patch and unfolding it into the two-dimensional parameter space, a set of implementation-dependent criteria must be satisfied in order to

- minimize texture distortion and artifacts;

- distribute the texels over the surface as evenly as possible;

- ensure continuity and conformity of the mapping among the charts, if possible;

- maximize the area coverage of the charts and minimize the number of separate charts.

The third stage, i.e., texture packing, is actually a variant of the classic NP-complete problem "bin packing," where a number of objects of different volumes need to be packed into a finite set of bins, while minimizing the vacant space. In the two-dimensional case of the texture-atlas packing, a finite number of atlas elements of known shape (concave in general) need to be arranged (moved, rotated, and scaled) in the final texture map so that the gaps are minimized and the coverage of the atlas texture is maximized. As the particular problem belongs to the NP-complete class of problems, only near-optimal approximate solutions have been proposed, from aggressive binary partitioning schemes to non-linear programming optimization implementations.

The "polypacks" approach is presented in Section 14.8.1 along with some modifications. This approach is a simple and relatively easy-to-implement solution for texture atlas parameterization [Zhuk98b]. Not surprisingly, it is one of the most common parameterization methods and has been extensively used for the creation of lightmaps, i.e., textures that hold diffuse illumination information. The algorithm is complemented with the kd-tree approach to texture packing. Some more complex yet elegant and efficient solutions to the 1-to-1 surface parameterization problem can be found in [Levy02, Purn04, Shef05].

14.8.1 Surface Segmentation⊛

The surface is segmented in such a way that each surface region (polygon cluster or *polypack*) is mapped to a plane with as little distortion as possible. The easiest

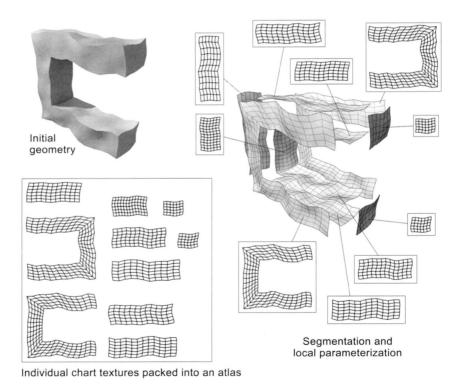

Initial geometry

Segmentation and local parameterization

Individual chart textures packed into an atlas

Figure 14.32. The parameterization of a surface as an atlas.

way to do this is to cut the surface into areas of connected polygons that face the same primary half-axis and use the corresponding plane (perpendicular to the primary axis) as the projection plane for the planar mapping (Figure 14.32).

The problem with this naïve segmentation method is that for relatively complex surfaces and models with creases or irregular curved regions, there are too many polypacks produced which are also relatively small. We seek to minimize the number of charts in the final atlas because first, the unused space in the atlas texture is increased with the number of atlas elements and second, the seams between adjacent textured patches tend to be noticeable as the texture parameterization changes in scaling or direction across the surface. If bilinear filtering or mip-mapping is also utilized on the texture atlas, this makes the need for fewer charts even more imperative due to the extra space that is required between the packed atlas elements to act as guard space and avoid averaging texels of different surface regions when interpolating or averaging texture values.

The planar mapping method can be modified to produce fewer polygon clusters and partly alleviate the problem. First, the clustering criterion can be changed so that adjacent polygons are clustered together if they have similar normal vectors, regardless of the primary half-axis that they are aligned with. This way, we can apply a region-growing algorithm on a number of seed polygons on the surface and create connected regions of polygons. The criteria for the assimilation of new polygons usually depend on the deviation of the new polygon's normal vector from that of the seed polygon or from the average normal vector of the expanding chart, as in [Sand01]. The planar mapping projection plane is chosen to be perpendicular to the normal vector. In some cases, depending on the chart growth or surface segmentation method, there are still small and disconnected patches, some of them even inside larger regions. If we relax the distortion constraint for the smaller patches, then we can assimilate them into larger regions, thus cleaning up the surface charts and producing far fewer final polygon clusters [Papa00].

The surface parameterization is straightforward in the case of the axis-aligned segmentation. The axis-aligned bounding rectangle of the chart on the projection plane is directly mapped onto the normalized parametric domain. Sander et al. [Sand01] perform the additional optimization step of finding the minimum-area bounding rectangle of the projected polygons (not necessarily axis-aligned) and mapping this to the parametric domain, thus effectively minimizing the unused space.

If the projection plane is aligned with the cluster normal, we need to project the points on the intermediate parameterization plane and normalize the texture coordinates to the range $[0, 1]$. Alternatively, we can transform the patch points so that the cluster normal becomes aligned with a primary axis and then proceed with mapping the transformed points as in the axis-aligned case.

14.8.2 Texture Allocation and Packing[®]

After splitting and parameterizing the surface, which is not assumed to be water-tight or manifold in general, each cluster is mapped to the normalized parametric domain ([0,1],[0,1]). In order for the texels of the final atlas texture to be uniformly distributed among the atlas charts and avoid stretching the texture, each chart needs to be assigned a bitmap, whose aspect ratio $r(i)$ matches the aspect ratio of the planar projection of the ith polygon cluster, prior to packing. This atlas element does not need to be a power-of-two sized bitmap. As the elements will be packed to fill up the atlas texture, we only need to worry about the size of the elements.

The size $N_{\text{texels}}(i)$ of each atlas element in texels is decided according to the ratio of the area coverage $A_{\text{proj}}(i)$ of the bounding rectangle of the projected polygons on the plane to the sum of all $A_{\text{proj}}(i)$ (total textured area, including unused space):

$$N_{\text{texels}}(i) = \alpha N_{\text{total}} \cdot \frac{A_{\text{proj}}(i)}{\sum\limits_{j=1}^{\text{Charts}} A_{\text{proj}}(j)}, \quad 0 < \alpha < 1. \qquad (14.52)$$

The dimensions of the ith atlas element are easily determined by the aspect ratio and the number of texels allocated to it:

$$\begin{cases} w_i \cdot h_i = N_{\text{texels}}(i) \\ r(i) = w_i/h_i \end{cases} \Leftrightarrow \begin{cases} h_i = \sqrt{N_{\text{texels}}(i)/r(i)} \\ w_i = r(i) \cdot h_i \end{cases}. \qquad (14.53)$$

When inversely projecting a texel onto a polygon of the polygon cluster, the resulting *patch* is a parallelogram and if there is small distortion in the texture parameterization phase, this patch is approximately square. Therefore, the surface is almost uniformly sampled and the texture atlas can be ideally used for surface resampling or the mapping of pre-calculated illumination (see Section 14.8.3).

The preparation of the individual atlas elements is not yet complete. In order to avoid using texture values from neighboring elements in the final packed atlas texture, the texture coordinates of the polygon clusters need to be pulled toward the inside of the area they occupy in texture space (Figure 14.33). Let us call "active texels" the texels actually mapped to the polygons after shrinking the texture coordinates. The unused pixels left in the atlas element outside the active

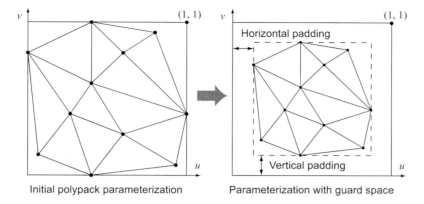

Figure 14.33. Transformation of the texture coordinates in an atlas element in order to leave some guard space around the parameterized polypack.

texels are flagged as "sand texels" and they act as a guard space. After calculating the texture values for the active texels, the sand texel values are iteratively extrapolated or copied from the nearest texels already evaluated (active texels or previously estimated sand texels).

If N_sand are the desired number of unused texels on each side of the atlas element, the corresponding transformation matrix for shrinking the ith polygon cluster texture coordinates is given by

$$\mathbf{M}_\text{sand} = \mathbf{T}\left(\frac{1}{w_i}N_\text{sand}, \frac{1}{h_i}N_\text{sand}\right) \cdot \mathbf{S}\left(\frac{w_i - 2N_\text{sand}}{w_i}, \frac{h_i - 2N_\text{sand}}{h_i}\right). \qquad (14.54)$$

In the work of Zhukov et al., the problem of intersecting polygons is also addressed [Zhuk98b]. When two surfaces intersect and part of one polygon goes beneath the other, the texture values on the atlas elements that correspond to the sunken patches will be incorrect. Furthermore, due to interpolation, the intersecting patches will draw color from the sunken patches, resulting in visible artifacts and discontinuities in the sampled function. The authors suggest flagging the texels of the sunken patches as sand texels and averaging the texel values of the intersecting patches to ensure a smooth transition from one intersecting surface to the other.

The texture packing is performed by recursively partitioning the final atlas texture, i.e., the placeholder for the individual atlas elements, into areas that will eventually host the atlas elements. The method presented here performs a non-uniform binary partitioning of the image space that results in an unbalanced *kd*-

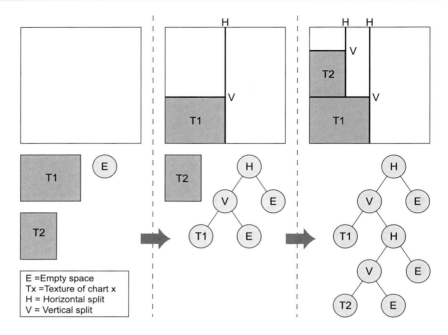

Figure 14.34. Construction of a texture atlas by packing individual chart textures with a kd-tree binary image subdivision.

tree with variable keys. (A kd-tree is a binary tree where sorting and searching is performed using a *k*-dimensional attribute key.) At each internal level *i* of the tree traversal, the *i* mod(*k*)-coordinate of the *k*-dimensional input value is compared with the corresponding threshold stored in the node to select the left or right branch. In the case of image partitioning, the internal nodes of the tree are decision nodes that correspond to the splitting lines of an image partitioned into two non-equal areas, either vertically or horizontally. The leaf nodes represent either an empty space or a region occupied by a texture map (Figure 14.34).

Normally, following the definition of a kd-tree, the splitting of the image alternates between horizontal and vertical. The variation that is described in detail below uses a variable key selection according to the best fitting of the atlas element to be inserted into the available space, thus taking care to utilize the texture as efficiently as possible. This means that as we traverse the tree, a horizontal split is not necessarily followed by a vertical split and vice versa.

Initially, there is one empty node, representing the entire atlas texture space. Before inserting any elements into the atlas tree, the elements are sorted by their

longest edge in order to insert the bulkiest subtextures first and avoid any unnecessary fragmentation of the available space.

When the first element is inserted in the lower-left corner of the atlas texture,
the latter is split horizontally into two cells, the left adopting the element's width,
the right becoming an empty node (Figure 14.34). Now, the left cell is not a
well-defined node and needs to be split further into two nodes, one that precisely
contains the inserted element and one representing the remaining empty space
above the element. Therefore, the left cell becomes a branching node that is
marked as a vertical split with the separating line at the height of the inserted
element. The element becomes one child of the vertical split (occupied leaf node)
and the remaining space becomes an empty node. New elements traverse the
tree in search of an empty space that can accommodate them. In this particular
example, a new element map can be inserted either at the second-level empty node
or at the first-level empty node, caused by the horizontal split. The procedure is
repeated until either all elements have been placed in the texture atlas or there is
an error encountered in fitting a map.

A reason why the packing may fail is that the size of the atlas texture is too
small to accommodate the atlas elements. Note that an element must be at least
1×1 texels in size. Furthermore, leaving some guard space requires chunks of
at least 3×3 pixels. If the final texture is too small, there is no way to fit the
subtextures into the atlas.

The insertion of an element into the tree structure as well as the basic node
definition are described in the following piece of code.

```
class TreeNode
{
    //DATA MEMBERS:
    //atlas texture area extents subtended by the node
    int width, height, xmin, ymin, xmax, ymax;
    //node type: branch (vert/horiz), empty, leaf (atlas element)
    int type;
    // In case of leaf node, pointer to allocated element bitmap
    TextureMap *map;

    //MEMBER FUNCTIONS:
    TreeNode(TreeNode *parent, int minx, int maxx,
            int miny, int maxy);
    bool isBranch();
    bool isLeaf();
    bool insert(Element * element);
    ...
}
```

```
bool TreeNode::insert (Element * element)
{
// CASE A. terminal, occupied node: cannot insert
if (isLeaf ())
    return false;

// CASE B. Branch node, try inserting in children nodes
if (isBranch())
{
    if (child[0]->insert (element)) // try to insert in left child
        return true;
    else
    if (child[1]->insert (element)) //  failed, try the right child
        return true;
    else                            //  failed, element cannot fit
        return false;
}


// CASE C. Unused node, try inserting element
    // 1) Check if the remaining space is adequate for this element
    if (width < element->width || height < element->height)
    {   // doesn't fit as is, try to fit it sideways:
        if (height < element->width || width < element->height)
        {
            // doesn't fit either way, insertion failed
            return false;
        }
        else
            // fits sideways, rotate the element by swapping params
            element->swapUVs ();
    }
    // 2)Choose splitting direction, split space and insert element
    if (width - element->width >= height - element->height)
    {
        //i. if the map leaves more space horizontally, split the
        //   cell horizontally, creating a left and a right child
        type = NODE_HORIZONTAL_SPLIT;
        child[CHILD_LEFT] = new TreeNode (this,
            xmin, xmin + element->width - 1, ymin, ymax);
        child[CHILD_RIGHT] =new TreeNode (this,
            xmin + element->width, xmax, ymin, ymax);
        // Now split the left child vertically into:
        //a leaf node (top)...
```

```
            child[CHILD_LEFT]->type = NODE_VERTICAL_SPLIT;
            child[CHILD_LEFT]->child[CHILD_TOP] =
            new TreeNode (child[CHILD_LEFT],
                xmin, xmin + element->width - 1, ymin,
                ymin + element->height - 1);
            child[CHILD_LEFT]->child[CHILD_TOP]->type = NODE_LEAF;
            child[CHILD_LEFT]->child[CHILD_TOP]->map = element->map;
            // ... and an empty node (bottom)
            child[CHILD_LEFT]->child[CHILD_BOTTOM] =
                new TreeNode (child[CHILD_LEFT],
                             xmin, xmin + element->width - 1,
                             ymin + element->height, ymax);
        }
        else
        {
            // ii. split the cell vertically, creating a top and
            // bottom child
            type = NODE_VERTICAL_SPLIT;
            child[CHILD_TOP] = new TreeNode (this,
                xmin, xmax, ymin, ymin + element->height - 1);
            child[CHILD_BOTTOM] = new TreeNode (this,
                xmin, xmax, ymin + element->height, ymax);
            // Now split the top child into a leaf node (left)...
            child[CHILD_TOP]->type = NODE_HORIZONTAL_SPLIT;
            child[CHILD_TOP]->child[CHILD_LEFT] =
                new TreeNode (child[CHILD_TOP],
                    xmin, xmin + element->width - 1,
                    ymin, ymin + element->height - 1);
            child[CHILD_TOP]->child[CHILD_LEFT]->type = NODE_LEAF;
            child[CHILD_TOP]->child[CHILD_LEFT]->map = element->map;
            // ... and an empty node (right)
            child[CHILD_TOP]->child[CHILD_RIGHT] =
                new TreeNode (child[CHILD_TOP],
                    xmin + element->width, xmax,
                    ymin,ymin + element->height - 1);
        }

    return true;
}
```

Lévy et al. proposed a slightly more complex packing approach [Levy02]. It is more suitable for large polygon charts with low compactness (highly irregular boundaries) than the binary subdivision method and operates in the discrete texture space. After rotating the charts so that their longest diameter is vertically aligned, they are sorted according to height and inserted into the atlas. The incoming charts are stacked on top of the existing clusters in the atlas, not unlike the well-known Tetris game. The topmost texels occupied by the charts already in the atlas form a "horizon," which the new chart's underside texels ("bottom horizon") cannot penetrate. The new chart's position is optimized so that the space left between the existing horizon and the bottom horizon is minimized. Then, the horizon is updated, taking into account the upper texels of the new chart.

14.8.3 Applications of Texture Atlases[⊛]

The most common application of texture atlases is for the storage of pre-calculated, view-independent illumination. A three-dimensional model is parameterized into a texture atlas, called a *light map* or *illumination map*, and the incident direct and indirect diffuse illumination is stored in the texels of the map. When the object is rendered, instead of performing complex shadow and global illumination calculations, the pre-recorded information on the light map can be used, provided that the geometry is part of a static environment and that the moving objects' contribution to the diffuse illumination of the model is negligible. This assumption is valid for most static three-dimensional environments often encountered in 3D games and other productions, and therefore, light-mapping is extensively used for the accelerated real-time rendering of realistic scenes [Watt01]. In practice, since illumination varies more slowly on a surface than a color or bump pattern that may be applied to it (with the exception of sharp shadow boundaries), the resolution of the light map does not need to be very high. Furthermore, for most cases, the surface already has at least one set of texture parameters, associated with the modulation of the surface material. This means that a separate set of parameters for light mapping is stored on the polygon vertices (calculated from the atlas parameterization). The light map is applied as a second pass to the surface, modulating the underlying high-detail color and bump shading. In contemporary hardware, where multiple texture units operate in parallel, the different textures are blended in one pass, making the rendering overhead of the pre-calculated illumination negligible.

In Section 14.7, we have seen how texture mapping is used to simulate the appearance of surfaces with a relief pattern and how normal mapping is exploited to transfer the shading of a complex surface onto a simplified version of the surface. If the object to be normal-mapped is not a trivial model case (e.g., a wall) or if it does not bear any repetitive geometric features, a texture atlas is necessary for its parameterization.

Extending further the idea behind the normal mapping, *geometry images* [Gu02, Sand03] store in the R, G, and B components of the texture the surface locations that correspond to each texel of the object's atlas. This efficient three-dimensional representation provides a regular sampling of the surface and can be used for three-dimensional pattern recognition (on 2D input data), easy multi-resolutional object representation, fast transmission, re-meshing and many other important applications.

14.9   Texture Hierarchies

Complex surface materials and finishes can be achieved by using parametric and procedural textures as building blocks in a hierarchical tree-like structure (a *texture tree*). Texture hierarchies were introduced by Cook in his work on shade trees, a generalized hierarchical shader design and implementation [Cook84]. The individual textures can be blended, multiplied, added, or combined in many ways to produce a new output. Furthermore, the output of one texture can be used as input to another or as a weighting function in an interpolated blending of textures (see Figure 14.35). Texture trees can contain texture transformations, transfer function filters (see Section 10.5.1), or output format converters, as well. A texture tree may be utilized to calculate any material attribute, provided the output of the root node is compatible with the attribute format (e.g., a grayscale value to modulate the transparency of a surface and not a unit-length vector).

In a texture tree, nodes can be instantiated (Figure 14.35). If a texture pattern is used multiple times in various locations of the hierarchy, there is no need to replicate the data or the computations associated with it. The texture is allocated once and referenced by the calling nodes multiple times. Nor does the referenced node need to be re-evaluated for the same point (fragment) each time its output is required. The shader is flagged as evaluated upon the first call to the node and subsequent texture evaluations reuse the cached value.

Hierarchical textures are heavily used in off-line rendering because they provide great freedom to artists. They allow the creation of material libraries consisting of basic, reusable building blocks that can be combined in an easy and reconfigurable manner to produce the desired final result. In real-time rendering, texture trees are implemented via the use of multiple texture units and hardware texture combiners, along with fragment shader programs that are executed in the GPUs' programmable cores.

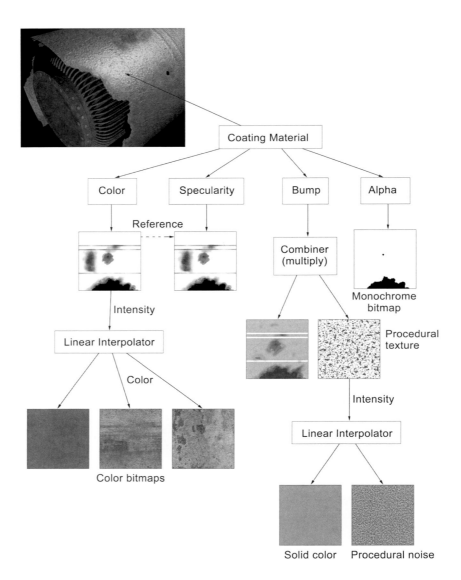

Figure 14.35. A practical example of texture hierarchies. (See also Color Plate XXV.)

14.10   Exercises

1. Derive a formula for calculating nested procedural textures, taking into account potential transformations: $\mathbf{M}_1 f_{\text{proc1}}(\mathbf{M}_2 f_{\text{proc2}}(\ldots \mathbf{M}_N f_{\text{procN}}(\mathbf{p})))$.

2. Write a program to calculate the mip-map levels of a texture image of dimension $2^M \times 2^N$, including the filtering and downsampling operations.

3. Implement the box-mapping selection and addressing mechanism as a procedural texture (shader). The input should be the direction vector and the output a pair of texture coordinates plus a map index. Comment on the use of texture transformations in this particular case. Remember that cube mapping can be used for capturing the incoming intensity from the surrounding environment. How can transformations help minimize the rendering of the individual cube maps when the user rotates the viewing direction of a reflective/refractive object that uses cube mapping?

4. What relief texturing method would be more appropriate for the rendering of (a) sand dunes, (b) a crater field? Consider rendering speed and image quality at ground level as the important factors to justify your choice.

5. Take the texture-hierarchy example of Figure 14.35. Assuming that the image maps use the same texture coordinates, can the tree be reduced further by pre-multiplying image maps and modifying the procedural texture attributes?

⊛6. Modify the bin-packing algorithm of Section 14.8 to resize the charts and then the final atlas before the final packing of the charts, in case of insufficient space. Keep in mind that a chart cannot occupy less than a texel-wide area (active texels) and that the sand texels also contribute to the minimum size of the charts.

7. Implement a normal map for pond ripples using a texture tree of combined wood procedural textures, properly adapted to produce normal vectors as output.

⊛8. Can cube maps be used for caching shadow-related information and help accelerate one or more of the shadow-generation methods? Justify your answer.

15

Ray Tracing

There are two ways of spreading light. . .
To be the candle, or the mirror that reflects it.
—Edith Wharton

15.1   Introduction

Direct-rendering (scan-line) algorithms operate on geometric primitives and fill arbitrary and overlapping locations in the frame buffer with color information. In a general sense, they are object-to-screen space image synthesizers. Sorting (hidden surface elimination) is also performed in image space using the Z-buffer algorithm. Ray tracing is a general and versatile algorithm that in fact operates in exactly the opposite manner, i.e., it is a screen-to-object space image synthesizer.

In *ray tracing*, the path (ray) along the line of sight starting from the camera focal point (center of projection) and passing through each pixel is followed as it travels through the three-dimensional scene, and it registers what the observer sees along this direction [Appe68]. As the ray encounters geometric entities, it is specularly reflected, refracted, or attenuated (and completely absorbed of course) depending on the material properties of the objects. Hidden surface elimination (in object space and not image space) happens as an integral part of this process because the ray encounters surface interfaces closer to the viewer first while it travels through the three-dimensional world.

The notion of following a path of light and calculating its behavior at the interface between materials has existed long before the beginning of the computer graphics era. Electromagnetic wave transmission theory, but most of all geometrical optics and the laws of reflection and refraction, provided the framework for the study of light-object interaction in the physics domain, a long time before the inception of ray tracing as a computer algorithm in the early 1980s.

Direct real-time rendering in its pure form disassociates the color and shading of a particular surface area from the existence of other objects in the same environment. Shadows and reflected/refracted light on surfaces need to be simulated or approximated separately and fused as color information in the local illumination model that is used during scan conversion. Ray tracing, on the other hand, integrates all calculations that involve the specular transmission of light in one single and elegant recursive algorithm, the *recursive ray tracing* algorithm (see Section 15.3).

15.2   Principles of Ray Tracing

Let us first look at how light that emanates from a single point light source is transmitted through space. In Figure 15.1, a glass cube resting on a checkered surface is lit by a single point light source. Light emanates from the location of the light source toward every direction, following an infinite number of straight paths until it hits a surface.

On the interface between two different solids,[1] light is diffusely scattered and specularly reflected or refracted. In this particular example, the checkered surface has no mirror-like qualities or transparency, so light leaving this surface is estimated by using a local illumination model, such as the Blinn model (see Chapter 12). According to the surface's BRDF, part of the specularly and diffusely reflected light is directly received by the observer, unless there is no clear line of sight between this point and the center of projection of the observer. However, light reaches the observer indirectly as well, after following secondary paths through transparent media or by being reflected off perfect mirrors. The surface of the glass cube is partially reflective, and thus some rays that are spawned after the direct illumination of the checkered surface hit the observer after being reflected on the cube. Light is also refracted through the cube, illuminates the interfaces it encounters (a local illumination model is applied each time), and is attenuated as it changes medium and is absorbed by the material it travels through. Finally, it reaches the observer.

---

[1]Parametric and polygonal surfaces are treated as watertight models that enclose a (not necessarily homogeneous) volume of space. The surfaces are assigned material properties such as an index of refraction or a reflectivity coefficient that characterize the body of the object. These attributes can be further modulated by texturing techniques (See Chapter 14).

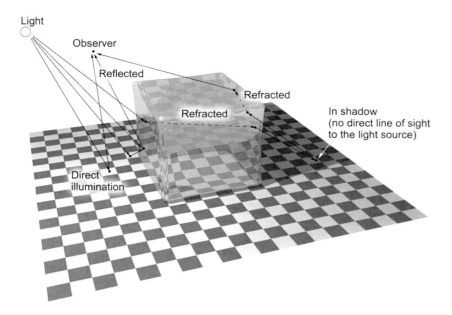

Figure 15.1. Light transmission. An infinite number of rays emanate from a light source, and a small number reach the eye after following complex paths within the scene.

Returning to the paradigm of ray tracing, the light that is seen through a pixel of the rendered image is the cumulative contribution of the rays that directly or indirectly hit the surface point visible in this direction and that travel toward the viewpoint (Figure 15.2). The nearest point encountered by looking at the scene though pixel (i, j) in general obstructs all other geometry behind it. This point may or may not be directly illuminated by the light source(s), depending on whether other geometry prevents the light from reaching it. If it is indeed directly lit by the light source, then a local illumination model can be applied to modulate the incoming light according to the material properties.

Rays that reach the intersection point from other directions (via reflection or refraction) and travel toward pixel (i, j) can be tracked and followed to discover what light has been reflected off the surface from which they spawned. This is possible due to the reciprocity of light propagation: Light follows the same path during refraction or perfect reflection on a material interface regardless of the direction of propagation (with the exception of total internal reflection; see

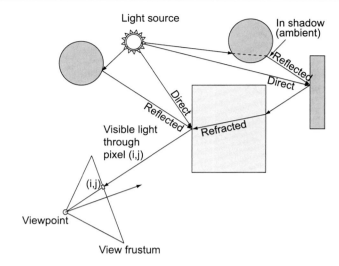

Figure 15.2. Cumulative illumination visible through a frame-buffer pixel (i,j) due to the contribution of direct and indirect rays.

Section 15.2.2). For each ray that we follow back to its source, we can evaluate the light that is propagated toward the viewer by applying a local illumination model and re-investigating for other secondary rays that reach that point. This is exactly the mechanism of ray tracing. Given that among all infinite rays that a light casts to the environment we are only interested in those that eventually reach the viewpoint through a viewport pixel, we can trace back the light contributions by following the rays in the opposite direction of their propagation toward the source. The notion of tracing back the rays to their source instead of following the light from the sources to the environment is what makes ray tracing a computationally manageable algorithm, applicable in many simulation applications apart from computer graphics.

Compared to direct-rendering algorithms, ray tracing has two significant advantages. First, ray-geometry intersections can be directly performed using non-polygonal surfaces, such as geometric solids, implicit or parametric surfaces, and fractals, without requiring any conversion to polygons first. Any mathematical surface that can be intersected by a ray can be rendered. Second, reflection and refraction phenomena can be accurately modeled.

In the next two sections, we shall briefly state the laws of reflection and refraction in a manner convenient for the ray-tracing model.

15.2.1 Reflection

In Chapter 12, in order to predict the direction of maximum specular highlight, we derived the reflection vector $\hat{\mathbf{r}}$ in terms of the normal vector $\hat{\mathbf{n}}$ of the surface at the point of incidence and the direction of the incoming light $\hat{\mathbf{l}}$. The reflected and incident directions lie on a plane perpendicular to the surface, and according to the law of reflection, the angle of incidence θ_i equals the angle of reflection θ_r; that is, the incident and reflected light-propagation directions are symmetrical with respect to the normal vector. Summarizing the calculations of Section 12.5.2, for an arbitrary ray of light from a direction $\hat{\mathbf{r}}_i$ incident on a perfectly reflecting interface between two bodies, the reflected ray in the perfect mirror-reflection direction $\hat{\mathbf{r}}_r$ is given by (Figure 15.3(a)):

$$\hat{\mathbf{r}}_r = \hat{\mathbf{r}}_i - 2\hat{\mathbf{n}}(\hat{\mathbf{n}} \cdot \hat{\mathbf{r}}_i). \tag{15.1}$$

Notice that here the incident direction is the opposite of the light direction vector $\hat{\mathbf{l}}$ of Section 12.5.2 since we need to emphasize the direction of propagation for clarity.

15.2.2 Refraction

When light crosses the boundary between two uniform dielectric media, its velocity in the direction of propagation changes, while its frequency remains unchanged. The *simple index of refraction n* (or *refractive index*) of a material is the ratio between the speed of light c in a vacuum and the phase velocity of light υ in this medium:

$$n = c/\upsilon. \tag{15.2}$$

The index of refraction n is greater than 1 for transparent materials and almost 1 for the air. The index of refraction also depends on the wavelength λ of the light, therefore $n = n(\lambda)$. In particular, for visible light, n decreases with increasing wavelength. In practice though, most implementations of ray-tracing simulations disregard the dependency of the index of refraction on the wavelength.

The phase velocity with which the light travels through different media is responsible for the bending of the propagation direction as the light crosses the interface between them (Figure 15.3(b)). According to *Snell's law*, the angle θ_t at which the incident light leaving a material with index of refraction n_1 is transmitted through a material with index of refraction n_2 is given by

$$\frac{\sin \theta_t}{\sin \theta_i} = \frac{n_1}{n_2}. \tag{15.3}$$

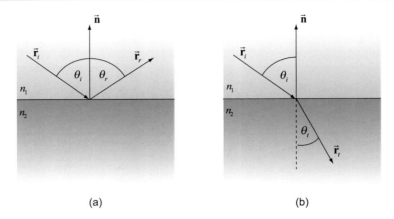

Figure 15.3. Ray diversion. (a) Reflection. (b) Refraction.

According to (15.3), light entering a medium with larger index of refraction ($n_2 > n_1$) is bent toward the normal direction of the optically denser medium.

When $n_2 < n_1$ (light enters a less optically dense material), the phenomenon of *total internal reflection* may occur, depending on the angle of incidence. In this situation, light is not transmitted through the boundary but is reflected instead back into the denser material. A case where total internal reflection can be easily observed is when diving underwater: at large viewing angles, the water surface acts as a mirror. The minimum angle of incidence at which total internal reflection occurs is called a *critical angle* θ_c:

$$\theta_c = \arcsin\left(\frac{n_2}{n_1}\right). \tag{15.4}$$

Let us now calculate the direction of the new, transmitted ray $\hat{\mathbf{r}}_t$ through the second body based on the incident ray direction $\hat{\mathbf{r}}_i$, the normal vector $\hat{\mathbf{n}}$ of the surface at the point of incidence, and the refractive indices n_1 and n_2 (Figure 15.4). Following the derivation in [Leng04], the transmitted-ray direction vector can be expressed as the sum of a component parallel to the normal vector and one parallel to the material interface (see Figure 15.4):

$$\hat{\mathbf{r}}_t = -\hat{\mathbf{n}}\cos\theta_t - \hat{\mathbf{g}}\sin\theta_t, \tag{15.5}$$

where $\hat{\mathbf{g}}$ is the unit length vector parallel to $\hat{\mathbf{r}}_p$ as in Figure 15.4. The vector $\hat{\mathbf{r}}_p$ can be calculated from the normal vector and the incident direction:

$$\hat{\mathbf{r}}_p = -\hat{\mathbf{r}}_i - \hat{\mathbf{n}}\cos\theta_i = -\hat{\mathbf{r}}_i - \hat{\mathbf{n}}\cdot(-\hat{\mathbf{r}}_i\cdot\hat{\mathbf{n}}) = -\hat{\mathbf{r}}_i + \hat{\mathbf{n}}(\hat{\mathbf{r}}_i\cdot\hat{\mathbf{n}}). \tag{15.6}$$

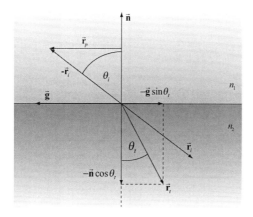

Figure 15.4. Refracted ray calculation

Due to the fact that $\hat{\mathbf{r}}_i$ is a unit vector, the length of $\hat{\mathbf{r}}_p$ equals $\sin \theta_i$. After normalizing it, we get:

$$\hat{\mathbf{g}} = \frac{\hat{\mathbf{r}}_p}{\sin \theta_i} = \frac{-\hat{\mathbf{r}}_i + \hat{\mathbf{n}}(\hat{\mathbf{n}} \cdot \hat{\mathbf{r}}_i)}{\sin \theta_i}. \tag{15.7}$$

Replacing $\hat{\mathbf{g}}$ from Equation (15.7) into Equation (15.5), we get

$$\hat{\mathbf{r}}_t = -\hat{\mathbf{n}} \cos \theta_t - (\hat{\mathbf{n}}(\hat{\mathbf{n}} \cdot \hat{\mathbf{r}}_i) - \hat{\mathbf{r}}_i) \frac{\sin \theta_t}{\sin \theta_i}. \tag{15.8}$$

From Snell's law (Equation (15.3)), we can replace the sines in the above relation with the indices of refraction. Also, from the Pythagorean trigonometric identity, $\cos \theta_t$ can be replaced by $\sqrt{1 - \sin^2 \theta_t}$. This step is necessary in order to relate the transmission vector with known variables. Reusing Snell's law on the identity, we get

$$\cos \theta_t = \sqrt{1 - \sin^2 \theta_t} = \sqrt{1 - \frac{n_1^2}{n_2^2} \sin^2 \theta_i} = \sqrt{1 - \frac{n_1^2}{n_2^2} (1 - \cos^2 \theta_i)}. \tag{15.9}$$

Introducing these relations in Equation (15.8) we end up with a relation that is free of variables on the transmission side of the interface:

$$\hat{\mathbf{r}}_t = -\hat{\mathbf{n}} \sqrt{1 - \frac{n_1^2}{n_2^2} (1 - \cos^2 \theta_i)} - (\hat{\mathbf{n}} (\hat{\mathbf{n}} \cdot \hat{\mathbf{r}}_i) - \hat{\mathbf{r}}_i) \frac{n_1}{n_2}. \tag{15.10}$$

As a final step, we replace the cosine with the corresponding inner product:

$$
\begin{aligned}
\hat{\mathbf{r}}_t &= -\hat{\mathbf{n}}\sqrt{1 - \frac{n_1^2}{n_2^2}\left(1 - (\hat{\mathbf{n}}\cdot\hat{\mathbf{r}}_i)^2\right)} - (\hat{\mathbf{n}}(\hat{\mathbf{n}}\cdot\hat{\mathbf{r}}_i) - \hat{\mathbf{r}}_i)\frac{n_1}{n_2} \\
&= \hat{\mathbf{r}}_i\frac{n_1}{n_2} - \hat{\mathbf{n}}\left((\hat{\mathbf{n}}\cdot\hat{\mathbf{r}}_i)\frac{n_1}{n_2} + \sqrt{1 - \frac{n_1^2}{n_2^2}\left(1 - (\hat{\mathbf{n}}\cdot\hat{\mathbf{r}}_i)^2\right)}\right)
\end{aligned}
\tag{15.11}
$$

Note that the quantity inside the radical of Equation (15.11) is positive (and therefore valid) only when $n_2^2/n_1^2 \geq 1 - (\hat{\mathbf{n}}\cdot\hat{\mathbf{r}}_i)^2 \Leftrightarrow n_2/n_1 \geq \sin\theta_i$. In the opposite case, we have the phenomenon of total internal refraction (see above) and the new ray is calculated according to the law of reflection (Equation (15.1)).

15.2.3 Reflectance and Transmittance[®]

We have seen that light that reaches the boundary between two different dielectric materials is split into a reflected wave and a refracted one. Snell's law and the law of reflection define the direction at which light is propagated, but they do not provide an insight into the intensity distribution between reflected and refracted waves. The amount of light that is reflected off an interface between materials with indices of refraction n_1 and n_2 is given by the *Fresnel equations*.

The Fresnel equations provide the reflection and refraction coefficients for light crossing the boundary between two dielectrics, which correspond to the ratio between the amplitude of the reflected or transmitted electric field and the amplitude of the incident electric field. Light is a transverse electromagnetic field, and therefore the electric and magnetic fields are oscillating in a direction perpendicular to the direction of propagation. At any given time, the electric field (or the magnetic field, which is perpendicular to the electric one) can be decomposed into one component parallel to and one component perpendicular to the plane of reflection. For non-magnetized, isotropic materials, A. J. Fresnel provided two equations for the reflection coefficient r_p and r_s as well for the transmission coefficient t_p and t_s for the case of parallel and perpendicular polarization, respectively:

$$
\begin{aligned}
r_s &= \frac{n_1\cos\theta_i - n_2\cos\theta_t}{n_1\cos\theta_i + n_2\cos\theta_t}, & r_p &= \frac{n_1\cos\theta_t - n_2\cos\theta_i}{n_1\cos\theta_t + n_2\cos\theta_i}; \\
t_s &= \frac{2n_1\cos\theta_i}{n_1\cos\theta_i + n_2\cos\theta_t}, & t_p &= \frac{2n_1\cos\theta_i}{n_1\cos\theta_t + n_2\cos\theta_i}.
\end{aligned}
\tag{15.12}
$$

Since the index of refraction depends on the wavelength of the light, the reflection and refraction coefficients depend on the incident angle and the wavelength of the incoming ray. The Fresnel formulas for wave intensity can be derived by squaring Equation (15.12):

$$R_s = r_s^2, \quad R_p = r_p^2, \quad T_s = t_s^2, \quad T_p = t_p^2. \tag{15.13}$$

Note that one should not expect that $T_s = 1 - R_s$ or $T_p = 1 - R_p$ (energy conservation) due to the fact that intensity is flux per unit area and the incoming beam is spread or shrunk according to the relation between the refractive indices.

As the exact oscillation direction and polarization of the incident wave is seldom considered in computer graphics applications, when the Fresnel reflection model is applied, the average reflection and refraction coefficients can be used:

$$R = (R_s + R_p)/2, \qquad T = (T_s + T_p)/2. \tag{15.14}$$

In a more simplified (yet common) paradigm, the transmission and reflection coefficients are user-selected constants, and the energy-conservation constraint is not always respected. One reason for this convention is that in order to make a rough approximation of the attenuation of the light as it is transmitted through the solid body, the transmission (or refraction) coefficient is significantly lower than the expected value. Another problem is that the contribution of the reflected and refracted light to the local reflection model also should be balanced to avoid saturating the cumulative intensity that is propagated to the eye or to exaggerate the resulting effect at will.

15.3 The Recursive Ray-Tracing Algorithm

Although the ray-casting mechanism to display a three-dimensional scene with hidden surface removal as an alternative to scan-conversion is attributed to Appel [Appe68] and Goldstein and Nagel [Gold71], an integrated approach to recursively tracing rays through a scene via reflection and refraction was proposed later by Whitted [Whit80]. It combined the previous algorithms that shot primary rays from the viewpoint toward the scene until they hit a surface and then illuminated the intersection points with the recursive re-spawning of new rays from these points.

The principle of the algorithm is quite simple: For each pixel, a *primary ray* is created starting from the viewpoint and passing through the center of the pixel. The ray is tested against the scene geometry to find the closest intersection with respect to the starting point (Figure 15.5). When a successful hit is detected, a

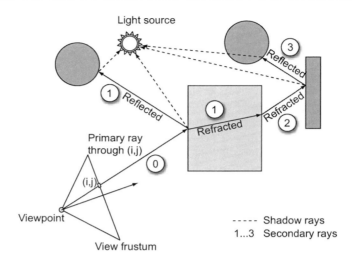

Figure 15.5. Recursive re-spawning of rays and their tracing through the scene.

local illumination model is applied to determine the color of the point according to which light sources are visible from this point. Otherwise, the color returned is the background color. If the material of the surface hit is transparent, a refracted ray is spawned. If the surface is reflective, a *secondary ray* is also spawned toward the mirror-reflection direction. Both secondary rays (reflected, refracted) are treated the same way as the primary ray; they are cast and intersected with the scene. When and if they hit a surface, a local illumination model is applied, new rays are potentially spawned, and so on (Figure 15.5).

Each time a ray hits a surface, a local color is estimated. This color is the sum of the illumination from the local shading model as well as the contributions of the refracted and reflected rays that were spawned at this point. Therefore, each time a recursion step returns, it conveys the cumulative color estimated from this level and below (Figure 15.6). This color is added to the local color according to the reflection and refraction coefficients and propagated to the higher (outer) recursion step. The color returned after exiting all recursion steps is the final pixel color.

The depth of the recursion, i.e., how many times new rays are spawned, is controlled primarily by three factors: First, if the ray hits a surface with no transparency or reflective quality, no new rays are generated. Second, if a ray's contribution drops significantly, there is no point in continuing to accumulate light

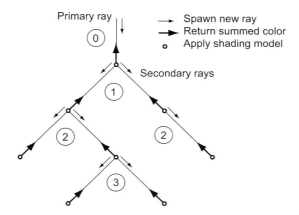

Figure 15.6. Schematic view of the recursive ray-tracing algorithm.

on this particular path through the scene as it will have very little impact on the resulting illumination registered on the pixel. Finally, to prevent an uncontrollable spawning of rays in highly reflective or elaborate transparent environments, a maximum ray-tracing depth is usually defined (typical values for most scenes are between 4 and 8, depending on object curvature and material transmission and reflection coefficients). For scenes with highly curved reflective or transparent objects, heavy distortion prevents the eye from registering the missing reflected/refracted information. Figure 15.7 shows a comparison between renderings with different maximum ray-tracing depth. Early ray pruning results in very wrong images for certain scenes. In this particular example, a polished sphere is placed inside a Plexiglas cube. If one recursive step is allowed, the transparent cube only acts as a reflector, as the transmitted ray does not penetrate the cube walls (another refracted ray at the inner boundary is required). From maximum depth of 4 and above, the image begins to convey the correct visual information, as multiple refracted and reflected rays penetrate the cube and hit the surface and the background beyond, signifying a see-through object.

The recursive ray-tracing algorithm can be summarized as follows:

```
Color raytrace( Ray r, int depth, Scene world,
                vector <Light*> lights )
{
  Ray   *refl, *tran;
  Color color_r, color_t, color_l;
```

```
// Terminate the procedure if the maximum recursion
// depth has been reached
if ( depth > MAX_DEPTH )
  return backgroundColor;

// Intersect ray with scene and keep nearest
// intersection point
int hits = findClosestIntersection(r, world);
if ( hits == 0 )
  return backgroundColor;

// Apply local illumination model, including shadows
color_l = calculateLocalColor(r, lights, world);

// Trace reflected and refracted rays according to
// material properties
if (r->isect->surface->material->k_refl > 0)
```

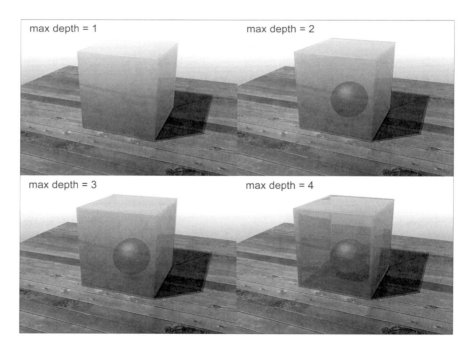

Figure 15.7. The impact of maximum ray-tracing depth on the rendered image accuracy.

```
  {
    refl = calculateReflection(r);
    color_r = raytrace(refl, depth+1, world, lights);
    delete refl;
  }
  if (r->isect->surface->material->k_refr > 0)
  {
    tran = calculateRefraction(r);
    color_t = raytrace(tran, depth+1, world, lights);
    delete tran;
  }

  return color_l + color_r + color_t;
}
```

15.3.1   Ray-Tracing Data Structures

To better understand the algorithm, we need to introduce a data structure for the rays and explain what data are propagated and when. As the light passes through transparent objects or bounces off reflective surfaces, it is attenuated because of the reflection and refraction coefficients and potential distance attenuation that we may apply to the rays. If volumetric effects are accounted for, the ray is also attenuated due to absorption and scattering as it travels through a dense body (this case is not covered here, see volume rendering in Chapter 18). These considerations imply that a ray needs to keep track of its "strength" in order to properly modulate the contributed local color at the intersection point and facilitate the ray-significance termination criterion for the recursion (see termination criteria above).

As a ray is tested for intersection with multiple surfaces, many intersection points are usually identified along the semi-infinite line that it defines. This means that the ray structure must keep track of the closest point to the ray origin in order to be able to compare it with the next intersection that may occur while an iterative ray-primitive intersection test is performed (see Section 15.3.2). To this end, we can also keep the distance between the currently closest hit and the ray origin, because we need to compare it with the distance to the next intersection point. The calculated distance is also useful in the case of distance or volumetric attenuation calculations.

In terms of data representation and storage, an intersection point is not a simple point in space in the case of ray tracing. It is used in calculations involving the normal vector at this location, the reflection and refraction coefficients, other material properties (for the local illumination model), etc. Therefore, when an intersection is identified, a number of parameters must be passed to the ray (or a special intersection point structure therein). We need to keep the local normal, the texture coordinates, and a reference to the material that is valid for this particular location. Furthermore, a reference to the primitive where the intersection point belongs is useful in order to be able to retrieve additional information. In the case of ray tracing in polygonal scenes, the ray could only keep the intersection point and distance, the reference to the polygon, and a set of barycentric coordinates to derive all required attributes from the vertex information when and if required (see Section 14.2.2). A potential data structure for a ray and intersection point could look like this:

```
class Ray
{
public:
  IsectPoint *isect;
  int level;
  Vector4f origin;
  Vector3f dir;
  float strength;


  // methods
  transform (Matrix4X4 mat);

}

class IsectPoint : Vector4f
{
public:
  Vector3f n;            // local normal
  Primitive *surface;    // intersected primitive
  double barycentric[3]; // for triangular meshes
  double t;              // parametric distance between
                         // origin and intersection point
}
```

15.3.2 Ray-World Intersection

As it may already be apparent, for normal primary and secondary rays (shadow rays are slightly different; see Section 15.3.3) the search for the closest intersection point is exhaustive with respect to the scene database. Distance sorting for hidden surface removal requires that all intersection points along the semi-infinite line of the ray be identified.

Without some form of intersection acceleration, rays have to be tested against the whole database of the scene at a primitive level. A primitive in ray tracing is any mathematically defined entity that can be tested for intersection with a line in space. Ray-primitive intersection tests are the most frequent operations in a ray tracer, and the exhaustive and repetitive nature of this search for intersection points is what makes ray tracing computationally expensive, but also trivially parallel. Highly optimized intersection tests for different types of primitives have been proposed and a number of them can be found in [Leng04] and [Schn03] as well as in Appendix C. A discussion on the subject of how the number and type of intersection tests performed can be optimized is discussed in Section 15.5.1. For the current discussion, we will assume a generic primitive class of type Primitive that provides a common intersection interface for all sub-classes of geometric primitives (e.g., Sphere, Box, Triangle, Plane, etc) through polymorphism.

The following code fragment provides the findClosestIntersection() function implementation of the basic recursive ray tracer, which is an exhaustive search mechanism for the detection of the intersection point (and corresponding distance). The results are stored in the ray instance and the number of intersection points encountered is returned.

```
int findClosestIntersection(Ray r, Scene world)
{
  int hits=0;
  r.isect = new IsectPoint();
  r.isect->t = 10000000; // a large intersection distance
  for ( j=0; j<world.numObjects(); j++ )
    for ( k=0; k<world.getObject(j)->numPrims(); k++ )
    {
      Primitive *prim = world.getObject(j)->getPrim(k);
      IsectPoint *Q = prim->isect(r);
      if (Q==NULL)
        continue;
      hits++;
      // if found closer intersection, copy it in r
      if ( r.isect->t > Q->t )
        r.isect->copy(Q);
    }
  return hits;
}
```

15.3.3   Local Illumination Model and Shadows

For every light source in the scene, we need to evaluate a local illumination model at the point of ray-surface intersection. To do this we must send a *shadow ray* (or *shadow feeler*) to each one of the light sources and determine their visibility. If we make the assumption that light is either completely blocked or completely visible from the intersection point, then the first time we encounter a blocking surface, the contribution of the particular light drops to zero. However, as objects are not always fully opaque, the color and intensity of the light is filtered through the objects that are blocking the direct path from the intersection point to the light-source position. Even in this case, when the contribution of the light drops below a threshold, we can consider it as negligible and terminate the search for further obstacles in the shadow ray's path. This is a major distinction between a normal ray and a shadow ray. Shadow rays can be computed faster because we do not have to sort the intersected points along their path, and we can therefore interrupt the intersection tests as soon as the attenuation from the obstacles becomes significant.

In the block of code that follows, a basic integrated shadow feeler and local illumination model algorithm is presented. For every light in the scene, its contribution is calculated (penetration variable) and a local illumination model produces a color according to the light direction, the normal vector, the material of the surface, and the ray direction (corresponding to the opposite of the view direction in the local illumination models of Chapter 12). The resulting cumulative color is the final output. Note that each time an intersection is found, the light penetration is diminished according to the transparency of the primitive. For closed polygonal surfaces, this results in a ray being attenuated both when the ray enters a mesh and exits its surface. If this is not desired, an extra step must be performed to check if the ray exits a polygon and disregard all such intersections.

```
Color calculateLocalColor( Ray r, Vector<Light*> lights,
                           Scene world )
{
  int i,j,k;
  // Initialize color to the minimum illumination
  Color col = ambientColor();

  // For all available lights, trace a ray toward them
  for ( i=0; i<lights.size(); i++ )
  {
    Ray *shadowRay = new Ray(r->isect,lights[i]->pos);
```

```
      // Measure how much light reaches the intersection
      float penetration=1.0f;
      // Filter the light as it passes through the scene
      for ( j=0; j<world.numObjects(); j++ )
        for ( k=0; k<world.getObject(j)->numPrims(); k++ )
        {
          Primitive *prim = world.getObject(j)->getPrim(k);
          IsectPoint *Q = prim->isect(r);
          // Case 1: ray not blocked by prim: no attenuation
          if (Q==NULL)
            continue;
          // Case 2: light contribution is filtered
          penetration *= 1 - prim->material->alpha;
          // Termination criterion: light almost cut off
          if ( penetration < 0.02 )
          {
            penetration=0;
            break;
          }
        }

      // check if light[i] contributes to local illumination
      if (penetration==0)
        continue;
      col+=localShadingModel( r, prim, lights[i]->pos,
                              penetration );
    } // light[i]
    return col;
  }
```

15.4 Shooting Rays

15.4.1 Primary Rays

There are many ways to determine the primary rays that are shot toward each pixel. We present here a calculation suitable for an arbitrary camera coordinate system $(\hat{\mathbf{n}}, \hat{\mathbf{u}}, \hat{\mathbf{v}})$ and a symmetrical view frustum centered at the optical axis. For now, let us also assume an ideal pinhole camera model with focal distance d and an aspect ratio $a = w/h$, where w and h are the width and the height of the image in pixels, respectively (Figure 15.8(b)). Pixels are regarded as square image areas (1 : 1 aspect ratio).

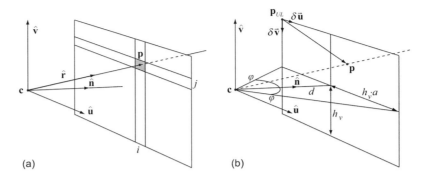

Figure 15.8. Primary ray calculation. (a) The ray passes through the center of the pixel. (b) Camera parameters.

The half-width w_v and height h_v of the view window at the near clipping distance (the focal length here) in world coordinates are, respectively (Figure 15.8(b)),

$$w_v = d \tan \varphi, \qquad h_v = w_v/a. \qquad (15.15)$$

The main loop in a ray tracer iterates through all image pixels (i, j) and casts (at least) one ray from each one of them (Figure 15.8(a)). Due to this iterative procedure, it is convenient to formulate the calculation of the ray starting point $\mathbf{p}$ and direction $\hat{\mathbf{r}}$ in an incremental manner. We can calculate the position of the point $\mathbf{p}_{UL}$ that corresponds to the upper-left corner of the image and the incremental offsets $\delta \overrightarrow{\mathbf{u}}$ and $\delta \overrightarrow{\mathbf{v}}$, between successive pixels in world coordinates. Then, the center of each pixel, which can then be used as the ray origin, is efficiently determined. The point $\mathbf{p}_{UL}$ is calculated by adding an offset along the view direction to the camera center $\mathbf{c}$ and moving across the view window plane to the upper-left corner:

$$\mathbf{p}_{UL} = \mathbf{c} + d \cdot \hat{\mathbf{n}} - w_v\hat{\mathbf{u}} + h_v\hat{\mathbf{v}}, \qquad (15.16)$$

or using Equation (15.15),

$$\mathbf{p}_{UL} = \mathbf{c} + d \left[\hat{\mathbf{n}} + \left(\frac{h}{w} \cdot \hat{\mathbf{v}} - \hat{\mathbf{u}} \right) \tan \varphi \right]. \qquad (15.17)$$

The incremental offsets $\delta \overrightarrow{\mathbf{u}}$ and $\delta \overrightarrow{\mathbf{v}}$ depend on the resolution of the image in each direction:

$$\delta \overrightarrow{\mathbf{u}} = \frac{2w_v}{w}\hat{\mathbf{u}}, \qquad \delta \overrightarrow{\mathbf{v}} = -\frac{2h_v}{h}\hat{\mathbf{v}}. \qquad (15.18)$$

As we have assumed square pixels, the image resolution only affects the aspect ratio of the horizontal versus the vertical view aperture and the pixel size, but not the pixel shape. Indeed,

$$\left| \delta \overrightarrow{\mathbf{u}} \right| = \frac{2w_v}{w} \left| \hat{\mathbf{u}} \right| = \frac{2ah_v}{w} = \frac{2h_v}{h} = \left| \delta \overrightarrow{\mathbf{v}} \right|. \tag{15.19}$$

If we use the center of the pixel as the origin $\mathbf{p}$ of the ray, then for $i = 0..w - 1$ and $j = 0..h - 1$,

$$\mathbf{p} = \mathbf{p}_{UL} + \left(i + \frac{1}{2} \right) \delta \overrightarrow{\mathbf{u}} + \left(j + \frac{1}{2} \right) \delta \overrightarrow{\mathbf{v}}. \tag{15.20}$$

The ray direction vector is simply the normalized difference between the origin and the camera focal point:

$$\hat{\mathbf{r}} = \frac{\mathbf{p} - \mathbf{c}}{|\mathbf{p} - \mathbf{c}|}. \tag{15.21}$$

15.4.2 Clipping

An interesting consequence of performing the hidden surface removal in object space and not in a post-projection step, as in the case of the Z-buffer algorithm, is that the near and far clipping planes can take arbitrary values (even negative), as they are essentially distances from the origin along the primary ray. In the Z-buffer, the ratio between the near and the far clipping distances has a significant impact on the accuracy of the depth sorting and a zero near-distance is not allowed. In ray tracing, the near clipping plane can be set to the origin (near clipping distance = 0) and the far clipping plane to infinity (practically to a very large number) without any kind of side effect.

As we have discussed in Section 15.3.1, distance sorting in ray-world intersection compares the last and current distance of the intersection point from the origin of the ray. Given a parametric representation of the semi-infinite ray, a point along its path is defined as

$$\mathbf{q} = \mathbf{q}(t) = \mathbf{p}_{\text{start}} + t \cdot \hat{\mathbf{r}}. \tag{15.22}$$

Due to the fact that the ray vector is considered normalized, t is the signed distance along the ray from its starting point. If $\mathbf{p}_{\text{start}}$ lies on the near clipping surface, intersections $\mathbf{q}(t)$ with t < 0 are disregarded as invisible. For the planar clipping surface model of Section 15.4.1, the focal length d: $d > 0$ defines the near clipping distance and $\mathbf{p}_{\text{start}} = \mathbf{p}$ (Equation (15.20)). For an arbitrary clipping

distance n from the focal point, we get ray starting points on a spherical clipping
surface,

$$\mathbf{p}_{start} = \mathbf{c} + n \cdot \hat{\mathbf{r}}. \tag{15.23}$$

15.4.3   Secondary Rays

Secondary rays are cast according to the direction of reflection, refraction or direct illumination depending on whether the ray path is followed due to reflection,
transmission, or shadow test, respectively. The starting point for those rays is
always the intersection point of the previous recursion step.

One important observation is that rays emanating from a surface point are
prone to intersect with it again, unless we find a way to exclude this point from
the procedure. Recall that due to the parameterization of the semi-infinite line of
the ray, any intersection point $\mathbf{q}$ along the path is associated with the distance t
from the origin. Consequently, an easy test to perform is to check whether t at
the intersection is greater than zero. If, however, surfaces are allowed to coincide
precisely, then this test has to be extended to check the surface to which the new
intersection point belongs:

```
class Ray
{
public:
  ...
  Primitive * startPrim;
  ...
}

int findClosestIntersection(Ray r, Scene world)
{
  ...
      if (Q==NULL)
        continue;
      if ( Q->t <0 || (nearZero(Q->t) && r.startPrim == prim) )
        continue;
      hits++;
      // if found closer intersection, copy it in r
      if ( r.isect->t > Q->t )
        r.isect->copy(Q);
  ...
}
```

15.5 Scene Intersection Traversal

15.5.1 Hierarchical Intersection Tests

Ray-primitive intersections can benefit from the fact that geometry is organized in object hierarchies (see Chapter 9). Instead of exhaustively searching for intersections with the primitives as a heap, we can significantly accelerate the intersection procedure by first testing the ray with the scene management hierarchy, regardless of whether the latter is a bounding volume hierarchy, a spatial subdivision hierarchy, or a combined scheme.

The idea to first perform a computationally efficient intersection test with a simple volume that bounds a cluster of primitives instead of attempting to blindly search for hits on the latter from the beginning was introduced many years ago [Clar76, Whit80]. Simple solids such as boxes and spheres were utilized for this purpose. The most common types of bounding volumes of objects used for ray-tracing acceleration are spheres, axis-aligned bounding boxes (AABBs), oriented bounding boxes (OBBs), and bounding slabs [Kay86] (Figure 15.9) (see also Section 5.6). As the alignment to the primary axes restriction of the AABBs does not apply to the OBBs, the latter can fit significantly more tightly to the original object with a careful selection of the box orientation. If the three mutually perpendicular pairs of parallel planes of the OBB are replaced by an arbitrary number of parallel planes, the object is enclosed in a set of *bounding slabs*, which ensures even less void space inside the bounding volume.

When the scene is organized as a scene graph, the bounding volume of each node can provide a first crude intersection rejection test for the geometry contained (Figure 15.10) [Rubi80]. On a positive bounding volume–ray hit, the test is recursively applied to children nodes. At leaf level, geometry primitives are exhaustively tested for intersection as the basic ray-tracing algorithm suggests, or the ray is passed to a space subdivision structure for further early primitive rejection processing (see below). Intersection tests with AABBs are quite inexpensive. Even in the case of object-aligned (oriented) bounding volumes, we may transform the rays to bring them to the local coordinate system of the bounding volume and perform the test as if they were AABB (see Section 15.5.2).

An important factor that affects the efficiency of the bounding volumes as a ray-pruning mechanism is the amount of void space that they occupy. A scene organization with large bounding volumes at high levels (bounding volumes for node aggregations) tends to leave a lot of unused space between the actual ge-

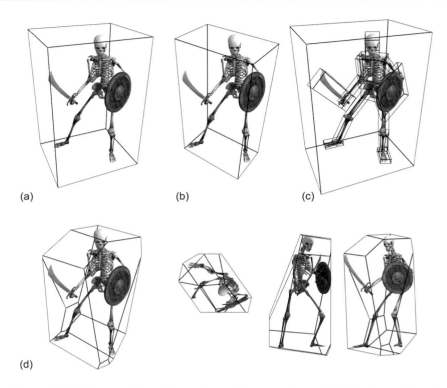

Figure 15.9. Common bounding volumes for ray tracing. (a) Axis-aligned bounding box (AABB). (b) Oriented bounding box (OBB). (c) Bounding volume hierarchy
(here, OBB hierarchy). (d) Bounding slabs.

ometry elements, resulting in many false hits. This is also the reason why a
tighter object-aligned bounding slab can be more efficient to use for ray-bounding
volume testing instead of a large axis-aligned bounding box. Goldsmith and
Salmon [Gold87] also showed that rays are hierarchically pruned most effectively
if the bounding volume has as small a surface area as possible. However, the number of rays hitting a bounding volume is not the sole criterion for the selection of
a particular type of container, as the computational complexity of intersecting the
ray with the solid plays a significant part due to the very large amount of rays shot
during a typical rendering.

A different approach to speed up ray tracing is space subdivision. The scene
space is decimated into a large number of simple cells, most often axis-aligned

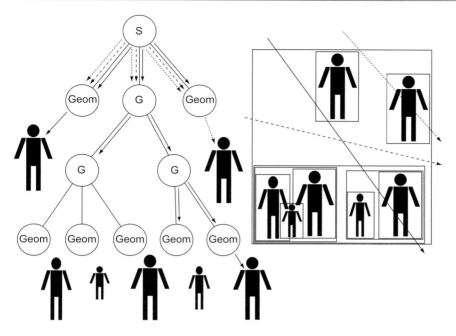

Figure 15.10. Intersection of a ray and a bounding volume hierarchy. Most primitive intersection tests are prevented by simple ray–bounding volume tests.

boxes, and each one of them references the primitives it intersects. When a ray is shot, the cells it intersects are determined and possible intersections with primitives are only examined for the contents of these volume elements. When a ray enters a cell, it is intersected with the primitives indexed by it or with a hierarchical space subdivision structure that further splits this cell into smaller ones. If no intersection is found, then the ray is tested against the contents of the next cell in the path. An important benefit from using non-overlapping regular partitioning grid cells is that if the later are visited in an ordered manner according to the direction of the ray, a preliminary sorting is performed at a container level. When the nearest intersection within a cell is found, the scene intersection traversal can be terminated. This is also the main advantage of using a spatial subdivision method instead of bounding volume hierarchies for spatial coherency ray-tracing acceleration. Note, though, that some extra preprocessing time is necessary in order to build and fill the data structures that represent the containers for the scene elements, and this should be taken into account when rendering frame sequences

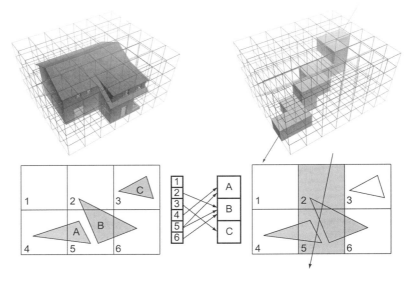

Figure 15.11. Uniform space subdivision for acceleration of ray-tracing intersection tests. A voxel space is generated around the scene (left) and the primitives are indexed according to which voxels they intersect (middle). A ray is tested against primitives indexed by the voxels it passes through (right).

where many objects are animated. Dynamic scenes require the recalculation and update of the acceleration data structures of the space-partitioning scheme.

The simplest form of space partitioning for ray tracing is a regular subdivision of the space occupied by the primitives into uniform volume elements (voxels) (Figure 15.11). First, all primitives are pre-processed to determine which voxels they intersect. A reference to a particular primitive is created in all cells intersected by it. Then, during ray casting, the voxels that the ray passes through are identified and their contents tested for intersections. The selection of voxels for each ray is done with an incremental algorithm similar to the 2D DDA, only for voxel space instead of image space [Kauf86, Fuji86, Aman87]. Amanatides and Woo [Aman87] also proposed an acceleration technique, *mailboxing*, to make the intersection tests for penetrating rays (rays that do not stop at the closest intersection) more efficient. A unique ray identifier is stored in each intersected primitive. So, if a primitive spans more than one voxel, it is intersected only once, since the ray identifier is compared to the one stored in the primitive before attempting to calculate the intersection.

The resolution of the voxel space (and, consequently, the size of each cell) plays an important role in the performance of the uniform spatial subdivision method. Large cells lead to fewer intersected voxels, a small probability of primitives intersecting more than one cell, and therefore to less redundant intersection tests. Smaller voxels reduce the number of primitives indexed by each one of them and therefore lead to faster intra-voxel intersection searches.

Voxels in a spatial subdivision scheme can be hierarchically refined. One reason to do this is to attempt to create cells with a balanced number of referenced primitives. In Figure 15.12, you can observe that too many cells (both in the two-dimensional case and the three-dimensional one) are empty, while others may contain too many primitives due to an uneven distribution of the latter into the space the models occupy. The most common hierarchical space-partitioning organization for ray tracing uses an *octree* [Glas84] (see Section 5.6 for the def-

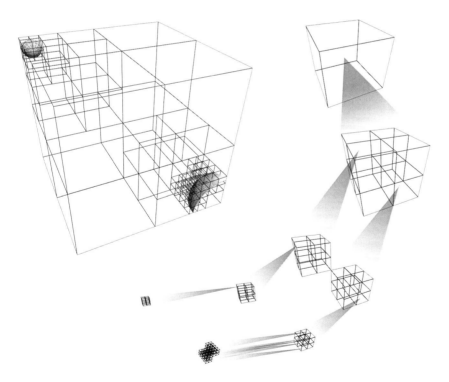

Figure 15.12. An octree.

inition of an octree). The space of a top-level cell (e.g., the AABB of the whole scene) is subdivided into eight equally-sized voxels. Those voxels that contain no primitives are not subdivided further, while the others are split in the same manner (Figure 15.12). The partitioning stops either when a maximum number of subdivisions is reached or when the number of primitives a cell contains is small enough to make further refinement unnecessary. The maximum number of subdivisions performed defines the depth of the tree. In contrast to the case of regular space partitioning, ray–octree data structure intersection tests are unbalanced, but intersection-test distribution at the leaf nodes is more even.

15.5.2   Ray Transformations

Ray-object intersections are frequently far more efficiently performed if both geometry and rays are expressed in a reference frame other than the common world coordinate system or the camera-space reference frame. This means that a ray may need to intersect an OBB volume, which is aligned with an arbitrary set of axes. We can perform this intersection test more efficiently if we compute a ray-AABB intersection instead, after expressing the ray in the local coordinate system of the oriented bounding box. Another important situation, where rays need to be transformed, is the case of object transformations. Recalculating the coordinates (or the parameters) of the transformed primitives is far more expensive than simply transforming the ray in the local reference frame of the object, especially when the transformations above the object in the scene hierarchy are animated. Transforming a ray instead of the object also facilitates the use of spatial partitioning (per object) for complex models, because rigid animation of the latter requires no recalculation of the acceleration structures. Finally, when rendering mathematical primitives such as solids or space functions, it can be very difficult to re-parameterize them to calculate a transformed version of the object. On the other hand, moving the ray in the local space of the original mathematical expression is straightforward.

If $\mathbf{M}$ is the composite transformation that has been applied to an object in a scene hierarchy (see Section 9.2), then we only need to apply the inverse transformation to the ray and perform the intersection test in the local space of the object:

$$\mathbf{q} = \mathbf{M} \cdot \mathbf{q}' = \mathbf{M} \cdot \text{Object.RayIntersection}(\mathbf{M}^{-1} \cdot \mathbf{p}, \mathbf{M}^{-1} \cdot \hat{\mathbf{r}}), \qquad (15.24)$$

where $\mathbf{q}$ is the resulting intersection point in the original reference frame of the ray (e.g., WCS) and $\mathbf{q}$ is the intersection point expressed in the local object coordinate system, $\mathbf{p}$ is the ray origin, and $\hat{\mathbf{r}}$ is the direction vector of the ray. Often, for static parts of a scene, or when a ray is first tested against a dynamic object in an animation frame, the inverse matrix is calculated and stored in the object to be reused as long as the current transformation of the geometry is valid.

For oriented bounding boxes or other solids, as they are frequently produced via principal component analysis on the geometry, we directly obtain the three local coordinate system axes $(\hat{\mathbf{a}}_1, \hat{\mathbf{a}}_2, \hat{\mathbf{a}}_3)$ and the corresponding dimensions of the container. We need to precompute and store in the oriented bounding volume the transformation that produces the resized and rigidly transformed solid from its normalized axis-aligned version (or its inverse):

$$\mathbf{M}_{\text{OBV}} = \mathbf{T}_{\text{OBV}} \begin{bmatrix} a_{1x} & a_{2x} & a_{3x} & 0 \\ a_{1y} & a_{2y} & a_{3y} & 0 \\ a_{1z} & a_{2z} & a_{3z} & 0 \\ 0 & 0 & 0 & 1 \end{bmatrix}^{-1} \mathbf{S}_{\text{OBV}}, \qquad (15.25)$$

where $\mathbf{T}_{\text{OBV}}$ is the translation according to the bounding volume origin offset and $\mathbf{S}_{\text{OBV}}$ scales the bounding volume to fit its new dimensions.

15.5.3   Constructive Solid Geometry

One of the strongest points of ray tracing is its ability to render very quickly objects that are modeled as set operations on solids. *Constructive solid geometry* (CSG) is a modeling method that uses Boolean operations on a binary hierarchy of simple solid primitives to generate new complex solids. The bounding surface of a CSG-generated solid can be calculated either during rendering or after the operations have been performed in object space and the solids have been converted to a boundary (surface) representation. In the latter case, operations on the geometry of the original surface models are required, which are both non-trivial and sensitive to numerical errors. In ray tracing, the union (A OR B), intersection (A AND B), and difference (A AND NOT B) operations are treated as classification tests of the ray-object intersection points. This means that the combined result of the Boolean operation between two solids is efficiently calculated at run time without modifying the original solids in any way. But let us first understand how constructive solid modeling works in principle.

In Figure 15.13, a complex solid model is created from a set of simple solids that are easy to define mathematically. The primitives are combined using pairwise logical operations to merge pieces together and/or cut out unwanted parts.

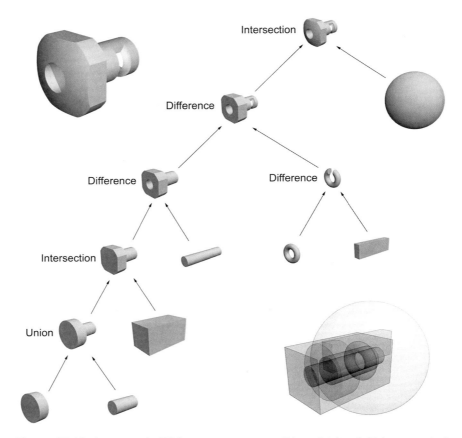

Figure 15.13. An example CSG tree to create a solid model (top left) from a set of simple solid primitives (bottom right).

In many cases, the priority of operations can be changed or optimized without affecting the final model, although this is not true in general. The combined and primitive solids that take part in a CSG model form a binary tree, the *CSG tree*. In a CSG tree, Boolean operations are expressed as CSG nodes. Each CSG node combines two sub-trees into one solid model. The left- and right-CSG children sub-trees may contain transformations or any other modifiers before encountering a solid model or another CSG node. From the modeler's point of view, the CSG tree is constructed bottom up, by continuously combining intersected, subtracted, or merged aggregations of solids with new ones.

In ray tracing, if the primitives of the CSG tree were treated separately, we would seek to find all the intersections with the boundaries of these solids and determine which one is the closest to the ray origin. As the solids are combined in pairs according to Boolean operations, the corresponding intersection points form segments that are inside or outside the resulting solid. If a ray segment is outside the combined solid, its endpoints (ray-primitive intersections) have to be discarded. If an intersection point lies inside the resulting volume, it is of no consequence to the ray-tracing paradigm and must also be discarded. What we need to keep from each Boolean operation is a set of boundary surface points. So, a CSG combination step is essentially an intersection point classification step:

- Find all intersection points between the ray and the left CSG node child.

- Find all intersection points between the ray and the right CSG node child.

- Merge all intersection points in one sorted list.

- Mark each point according to its containment in the left and right CSG children as IN (inside the solid model), OUT (outside the solid model), or SURFACE (on the boundary of the solid model).

- Classify each point as IN, OUT, or SURFACE for the combined solid according to a set of logical rules (see Table 15.1).

- Keep all SURFACE points as the resulting intersection points of the CSG node.

A CSG tree is recursively traversed from the root CSG node down to the leaves (solid primitives). If a node is a CSG operation node, the intersection points from its two children are requested, and the ray is propagated down and transformed according to the geometric transformations encountered (see Section 15.5.2). Then, the above steps are performed and a new set of intersection points is determined. If a node is a solid primitive, it is intersected with the transformed ray and all the resulting points are gathered and returned upwards.

The algorithm is illustrated in Figure 15.14. Beside each CSG node, the list of gathered intersection points is presented along with the corresponding classification results for the particular set operations. Refer to Table 15.1 for the classification of points.

The ray is passed to the root of the CSG tree (intersection) and is propagated recursively (depth-first) to the leaves. The first CSG node that can be computed

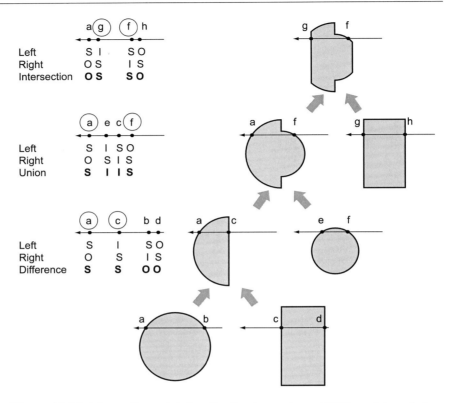

Figure 15.14. Intersection point classification for ray-traced CSG model rendering.

is the difference node. The intersection points of the ray **a**, **b** and **c**, **d** with the sphere and the box, respectively, are calculated from the left and right children of the difference node and returned to the CSG node for classification. In the subtraction of the two solids, all surface points of the first operand (sphere) that are not clipped by the second operand's volume (box) are maintained, because they continue to lie on the shell of the combined solid. All points of the second operand that reside outside the volume of the first operand are discarded because they are subtracted from void space. The surface points of the second operand form the boundary surface of the clipped region and so they are kept. The intersection points marked as SURFACE are then regarded as the intersection points of the combined solids and propagated upward.

At the next level, the CSG node is a union set operation. Here, we need to keep those points that define the largest combined ray segments (**a** and **f**). So we keep

Union			
Branch *Right* Left	IN	OUT	SURFACE
IN	IN	IN	IN
OUT	IN	OUT	SURFACE
SURFACE	IN	SURFACE	

Difference			
Branch *Right* Left	IN	OUT	SURFACE
IN	OUT	IN	SURFACE
OUT	OUT	OUT	OUT
SURFACE	OUT	SURFACE	

Intersection			
Branch *Right* Left	IN	OUT	SURFACE
IN	IN	OUT	SURFACE
OUT	OUT	OUT	OUT
SURFACE	SURFACE	OUT	

Table 15.1. Point classification for Boolean CSG operations. The table shows the resulting status of an intersection point in the combined left and right branch of a CSG node, according to the classification of the point in the two branches (adapted from [Wyvi95]).

only SURFACE points of one solid that are outside the volume of the other solid. The last operation is an intersection. Here we seek to keep intersection points that bound ray segments intersecting both solids simultaneously. We classify as SURFACE points the boundary points of the one solid that are inside the volume of the other and vice versa (**g** and **f**). All other points that are inside both volumes are valid ones but do not contribute to the outlier of the combined solid.

15.6   Deficiencies of Ray Tracing

Compared to direct-rendering methods, the major drawback of ray tracing is the rendering speed. Although the basic ray tracing algorithm is significantly accelerated by various optimization techniques and space-partitioning methods, it is still many times slower than hardware-accelerated scan-conversion algorithms, which rely on local, coherent data and can perform incremental computations in image space. Ray tracing is inherently easy to implement in parallel, both at an image-space level or in a ray distribution/spatial manner. Recently, there has been a lot of research in the effort to take advantage of the programmable pipeline of the graphics hardware to render or approximate the results of the first recursive steps of ray tracing using direct rendering (see, for instance, methods presented in [Wald01]). These hybrid methods, along with parallel implementations of ray tracers in software and hardware [Schm02, Wald02] provide a significant speed-up.

Apart from rendering speed, other deficiencies of ray tracing concern the quality and realism of the generated images. With the introduction of ray tracing to image synthesis, reflections, shadows, and refracted parts of the three-dimensional world appeared in the so-far uninteresting images only shaded with a local illumination model. The images obtained a fresh, startlingly clear look that boosted the credibility of the displayed subject significantly. Or were they too provocatively clear?

As we have discussed in Chapter 12, the surface of real solid objects possesses structural irregularities that scatter incident light to various directions, away from the ideal reflection direction, depending on the smoothness of the material. For the computation of specular highlights this principle is respected, but it should also apply to the reflected and refracted light during ray tracing. Images reflected on or transmitted through objects as calculated by a ray tracer appear extremely sharp, due to the fact that a single ray is spawned for each intersection point encountered (Figure 15.15(a)). The material interfaces are assumed perfectly smooth in the neighborhood of the intersection point. Therefore, incoming light from a slightly different direction than the perfect reflection or refraction direction that would normally reach our eyes from a non-ideal reflector or transparent object cannot appear in a ray-traced image. This super-realistic rendering of the reflected and refracted images is characteristic to ray tracing and gives the synthetic images a very "polished" look that is hardly encountered in real environments, natural or man-made.

Another implication of the fact that a single shadow ray is shot from an intersection point is that it is not possible to generate soft shadows, which are naturally produced by emitters of non-negligible size, such as area lights. Shadow rays may only hit or completely miss an occluding surface when cast toward the light source, and consequently only sharp shadows are produced (Figure 15.16(a)).

In ray tracing, similar to the direct-rendering case, the indirect illumination that reaches a small surface area via diffuse inter-reflection is considered constant and is still replaced by the ambient term. More advanced models that better approximate the rendering equation [Kaji86] also compute this term and simulate other phenomena, like caustics. See Chapter 16 for more details.

15.7   Distributed Ray Tracing⊛

A major improvement to the basic ray-tracing algorithm in terms of visual quality is *distributed* or *stochastic ray tracing* (see also Chapter 16 for more details). In distributed or stochastic ray tracing, instead of sampling the contributing energy from a single direction as in the basic algorithm, multiple rays randomly distributed over a solid angle centered at the principal ray direction are cast [Cook84, Cook86]. This is essentially a Monte Carlo approximation of the integral of all energy contributing to the path that was traced from the eye point to the scene. This method dramatically enhances the visual quality of the result at the expense of the rendering time (or hardware resources for parallel rendering) required to intersect the extra rays with the scene.

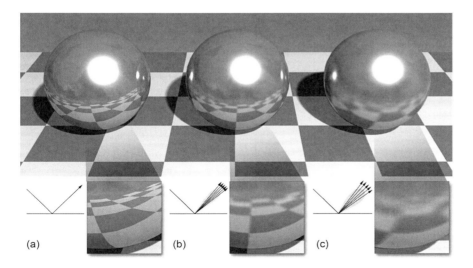

(a)   (b)   (c)

Figure 15.15. Distributed ray tracing. (a) Reflections in simple ray tracing look unrealistically sharp. (b) Shooting multiple jittered rays simulates the uneven surface of a reflective object and produces a realistic blurring of the reflected image. (c) Same as (b) but with a less polished surface.

Figure 15.16. Soft shadows using distributed shadow rays and a spherical emitter.

Distributed ray tracing enhances the appearance of the synthetic images in many ways. For reflected or refracted rays, the blurring effect of non-perfectly smooth surfaces is achieved by spawning multiple rays that diverge from the ideal reflection/transmission direction (Figure 15.15(a) and (b)). The deviation of the rays is determined by the roughness or the desired blurring of the material interface.

The shadow-generation stage of the basic algorithm is similarly extended in distributed ray tracing and can support area lights of arbitrary size and shape. Recall from Section 13.2 that shadow penumbrae appear where only a portion of the emitter is occluded by other geometry. Instead of mathematically calculating the exact visibility of the area light source from the shaded point, a number of rays are cast toward a set of randomly selected points over the surface or volume of the emitter (Figure 15.16), thus making a Monte Carlo approximation of the integral of a visibility function over the solid angle subtended by the emitter with respect to the illuminated point.

Distributed ray tracing can also improve the visual realism at the first ray-casting stage. Conventional ray tracing relies on the pinhole-camera model to

Figure 15.17. Focal blur using multiple rays per pixel and a camera model with non-zero aperture.

cast a single ray from the view plane though the center of each pixel. By shooting multiple rays, more elaborate camera models that simulate real lenses with single or multiple elements can be implemented [Cook84, Kolb95]. These advanced models produce images that exhibit focal blurring and distortions that resemble pictures taken with an actual photographic camera (Figure 15.17). For multi-element lens models, a number of points on the lens-element surface closer to the imaginary sensor (view) plane are selected and a ray is cast through each one of them. Using Snell's law, the ray is transmitted through the elements and finally traced through the scene. The averaged intensity of all rays is registered as the sampled color for this pixel.

Note that when averaging multiple rays per pixel, we also perform antialiasing on the resulting image. In the common pinhole-camera model, multiple samples are taken for each pixel by selecting random points inside a pixel instead of its center and shooting a new ray through these points. The resulting samples are averaged, usually using some importance function (smoothing kernel). Multi-sampled antialiasing in ray casting can be performed in an adaptive manner, either by comparing neighboring pixel intensities and shooting extra rays if the intensity difference exceeds a predefined threshold, or by comparing multiple samples within the same pixel and increasing the sampling rate when necessary.

As in every Monte Carlo integration method, the chosen distribution of the rays and importance sampling function play a significant role in the quality and the performance of distributed ray tracing [Glas95, Cook86]. For instance, when spawning multiple rays to trace reflections from a surface, the distribution of the rays depends on the specular model adopted for the reflector and the material parameters narrow or widen the strata of emitted rays.

15.8   Exercises

1. Comment on the efficiency of a regular grid-space subdivision algorithm for ray-tracing acceleration based on the factors of voxel space resolution and average element size. How does the mailboxing technique improve the performance of a spatial subdivision method?

2. Modify the basic ray tracing algorithm to support distributed ray tracing for transmitted/reflected and shadow rays. Isolate the multisampling algorithm and pass it a pointer to a generic probability distribution function as a parameter. Later, you should be able to experiment with different ray distributions by passing a reference to the corresponding randomizer.

3. Implement a simple CSG ray tracer for hierarchies of transformed spheres, boxes, infinite cylinders, cones, and planes (half-spaces).

16

Global Illumination
Algorithms

P. Dutré

*The secret to painting in shadow is the amount of
bounced light you see in the shadow itself.*
—William Hook

16.1   Introduction

Global illumination algorithms deal with the realistic computation of light transport in a 3D scene. Not only is direct illumination considered, but the indirect
light (light that reaches a point of interest through one or more reflections) is
computed as well. The resulting images are radiometrically accurate and thus
photorealistic.

In order for global illumination computations to reach a photorealistic level of
accuracy, it is necessary that all aspects of the image-generation pipeline are based
in fundamental physics. More precisely, this means that the reflection properties
of all materials are described by proper BRDFs[1], the light sources are radiometrically modeled, the transport of light through the scene is computed accurately,
and the display of the image uses accurate tone-mapping operators.

This chapter will focus on the underlying equations of the light transport and
the mathematical tools needed to compute a full global illumination solution.

---

[1]bidirectional reflectance distribution function

16.2   The Physics of Light-Object Interaction II

16.2.1   Rendering Equation

The *rendering equation* is the most fundamental equation for photorealistic synthesis algorithms. It expresses the equilibrium of the light distribution in a three-dimensional scene, taking into account the radiometric specification of the light sources and the BRDF specifications of all materials. In its basic form, the rendering equation is an energy balance that expresses how much exitant radiance is present at a given surface point in a certain direction, given a distribution of incident radiance values.

The rendering equation was first introduced by Kajiya [Kaji86]. However, current forms of the rendering equations are quite different from the original formulation of Kajiya.

Hemispherical integration. To derive the rendering equation, we can start from the definition of BRDF at a surface point $\mathbf{x}$ that expresses exitant radiance L_r in direction (ϕ_r, θ_r) versus incident irradiance E_i from direction (ϕ_i, θ_i):

$$
\begin{aligned}
f_r(\phi_r, \theta_r, \phi_i, \theta_i) &= \frac{dL_r(\phi_r, \theta_r)}{dE_i(\phi_i, \theta_i)} \\
&= \frac{dL_r(\phi_r, \theta_r)}{L_i(\phi_i, \theta_i)\cos(\theta_i)d\omega_i}.
\end{aligned}
\tag{16.1}
$$

Rewriting the previous equation and integrating over the hemisphere Ω_i of all possible differential solid angles $d\omega_i$ yields

$$
\begin{aligned}
dL_r(\phi_r, \theta_r) &= L_i(\phi_i, \theta_i) f_r(\phi_r, \theta_r, \phi_i, \theta_i)\cos(\theta_i)d\omega_i, \\
L_r(\phi_r, \theta_r) &= \int_{\Omega_i} L_i(\phi_i, \theta_i) f_r(\phi_r, \theta_r, \phi_i, \theta_i)\cos(\theta_i)d\omega_i.
\end{aligned}
\tag{16.2}
$$

The latter formulation is simply the equivalent integral equation of the definition of the BRDF, which is a differential equation. To complete the integration, a constant term has to be added, corresponding to the self-emitted radiance $L_e(\phi_r, \theta_r)$of point $\mathbf{x}$. This term will only be different from 0 if surface point $\mathbf{x}$ is located on a modeled light source in the scene.

Thus, the complete rendering equation, expressing the exitant radiance L_r is given by

$$
L_r(\phi_r, \theta_r) = L_e(\phi_r, \theta_r) + \int_{\Omega_i} L_i(\phi_i, \theta_i) f_r(\phi_r, \theta_r, \phi_i, \theta_i)\cos(\theta_i)d\omega_i.
\tag{16.3}
$$

This equation is known as a Fredholm equation of the second kind, since the unknown quantity, radiance, appears both on the left-hand side and on the right-hand side, where it is integrated with a kernel function.

Surface-area integration. It is possible to rewrite the rendering equation such that the integral is taken over all visible surfaces rather than over the hemisphere of incoming directions. This is accomplished by transforming the solid angle $d\omega_i$ to the corresponding differential surface dA. Let $\mathbf{y}$ be the first visible surface point seen from point $\mathbf{x}$ in direction (ϕ_i, θ_i); (ϕ_y, θ_y) is the direction pointing from $\mathbf{y}$ towards $\mathbf{x}$, and $r_{\mathbf{xy}}$ is the distance between $\mathbf{x}$ and $\mathbf{y}$, then

$$d\omega_i = \frac{\cos(\theta_y) dA}{r_{\mathbf{xy}}^2}, \tag{16.4}$$

and Equation (16.3) becomes

$$L_r(\phi_r, \theta_r) = L_e(\phi_r, \theta_r) + \int_{S_{\text{Visible}}} L_i(\phi_i, \theta_i) f_r(\phi_r, \theta_r, \phi_i, \theta_i) \frac{\cos(\theta_i)\cos(\theta_y)}{r_{\mathbf{xy}}^2} dA, \tag{16.5}$$

where S_{Visible} denotes the set of all visible surfaces as seen from $\mathbf{x}$.

Since the radiometric quantity radiance remains constant along a straight line, we can express the incoming radiance $L_i(\phi_i, \theta_i)$ at $\mathbf{x}$ (which we write as $L_i(\mathbf{x}, \phi_i, \theta_i)$) as an equivalent exitant radiance value $L_r(\mathbf{y}, \phi_y, \theta_y)$ leaving surface point $\mathbf{y}$ towards $\mathbf{x}$:

$$L_i(\phi_i, \theta_i) = L_i(\mathbf{x}, \phi_i, \theta_i) = L_r(\mathbf{y}, \phi_y, \theta_y). \tag{16.6}$$

In Equation (16.5), the product of both cosine terms divided by $r_{\mathbf{xy}}^2$ is a geometric coupling term only dependent on the geometrical relationship between $\mathbf{x}$ and $\mathbf{y}$, and independent of the actual radiance distribution or BRDFs defined on the surfaces:

$$G(\mathbf{x}, \mathbf{y}) = \frac{\cos(\theta_i)\cos(\theta_y)}{r_{\mathbf{xy}}^2}. \tag{16.7}$$

Substituting all of the above in (16.5) yields

$$L_r(\mathbf{x}, \phi_r, \theta_r) = L_e(\mathbf{x}, \phi_r, \theta_r) + \int_{S_{\text{Visible}}} L_r(\mathbf{y}, \phi_y, \theta_y) f_r(\phi_r, \theta_r, \phi_i, \theta_i) G(\mathbf{x}, \mathbf{y}) dA. \tag{16.8}$$

Equation (16.8) is an equivalent form of Equation (16.3). Instead of integrating over the hemisphere of incident directions, the integration is taken over the set of visible surface points. Both equations merely differ in a transformation of the integration domain.

However, we would like to write the equation as an integral over all surfaces, not just the visible surfaces seen from $\mathbf{x}$. This would offer the advantage of having a single integration domain, identical for all points $\mathbf{x}$ in which the rendering equation has to be evaluated. In order to expand the integration domain to all surface points, a visibility term $V(\mathbf{x}, \mathbf{y})$ needs to be introduced. This visibility term equals 1 when $\mathbf{x}$ and $\mathbf{y}$ are mutually visible and equals 0 otherwise.

The surface area integration formulation of the rendering equation then becomes

$$L_r(\mathbf{x}, \phi_r, \theta_r) = L_e(\mathbf{x}, \phi_r, \theta_r) + \int_S L_r(\mathbf{y}, \phi_y, \theta_y) f_r(\phi_r, \theta_r, \phi_i, \theta_i) G(\mathbf{x}, \mathbf{y}) V(\mathbf{x}, \mathbf{y}) dA,$$
(16.9)

where S is the integration domain indicating *all* surface points $\mathbf{y}$ in the scene.

A special case of the surface-area integration (16.9) occurs when we only want to consider direct illumination from one (or more) light sources. Suppose we want to compute $L_r(\mathbf{x}, \phi_r, \theta_r)$ due to the direct illumination of a single source only:

$$L_r(\mathbf{x}, \phi_r, \theta_r) = \int_{S_1} L_e(\mathbf{y}, \phi_y, \theta_y) f_r(\phi_r, \theta_r, \phi_i, \theta_i) G(\mathbf{x}, \mathbf{y}) V(\mathbf{x}, \mathbf{y}) dA,$$
(16.10)

where S_1 is the surface area domain of the light source (Figure 16.1).

If multiple light sources are present, and by splitting the integral over the combined light source area in a sum of integrals taken for each light source separately, the total direct illumination contribution due to L light sources is written as

$$L_r(\mathbf{x}, \phi_r, \theta_r) = \sum_{j=1}^{L} \int_{S_j} L_e(\mathbf{y}, \phi_y, \theta_y) f_r(\phi_r, \theta_r, \phi_i, \theta_i) G(\mathbf{x}, \mathbf{y}) V(\mathbf{x}, \mathbf{y}) dA.$$
(16.11)

Both Equations (16.10) and (16.11) are important when designing algorithms for computing the direct illumination due to one or more light sources. It allows for specialized numerical integration techniques to accurately determine the illumination caused by such light sources.

Environment map illumination. A last variant of direct illumination that is relevant and that has become important in recent years is the case in which the light source is encoded as a (hemi)-spherical environment map. An emitted radiance $L_e(\phi_i, \theta_i)$ is defined for each incoming direction, irrespective of the location of the point $\mathbf{x}$ to be shaded:

$$L_r(\phi_r, \theta_r) = \int_{\Omega_i} L_e(\phi_i, \theta_i) f_r(\phi_r, \theta_r, \phi_i, \theta_i) \cos(\theta_i) d\omega_i.$$
(16.12)

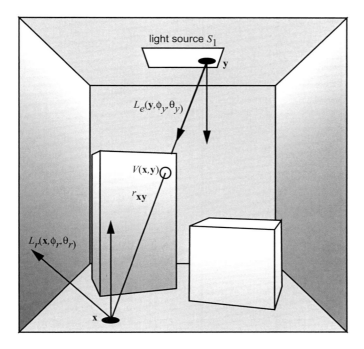

Figure 16.1. Direct illumination due to a single light source.

Usually, an environment map is given as a high dynamic range image and can contain more than a million pixels, each representing a different radiance value. Thus, numerical procedures that can evaluate an integral over an hemispherical image are necessary to evaluate the direct illumination in these scenes.

16.2.2 Discretized Form of the Rendering Equation

All variant formulations of the rendering equation described above express radiance in a single point and single direction. For some applications, it can be more useful to express light energy per surface patch (usually individual polygons) instead of a single point and for the hemisphere of all outgoing directions instead of a single direction. This can be achieved by discretizing the rendering equation, thus obtaining a finite element formulation of the energy equilibrium in a scene.

This equilibrium will be expressed as a linear system, each equation describing the energy balance for a single patch. The family of techniques describing this approach are known as *radiosity algorithms*. The name radiosity algorithm is mostly historical and covers a wide range of finite element methods that compute a global illumination solution for a given scene. Not all of these algorithms are using the radiometric quantity *radiosity* to express the energy equilibrium; many variants work directly with the radiometric *flux* per surface patch.

In this section, we will formally derive the discretized version of the rendering equation, by making a few assumptions about the nature of the scene. Techniques for solving these equations are discussed in Section 16.6.

The most common assumptions for formulating the radiosity equations are the following:

1. All surfaces in the scene are subdivided in surface patches. Usually, these patches are polygons of a given maximum size, but the patches could as well be curved subsets of a spline or quadric surface. For each patch it is assumed that the outgoing radiance is similar for all surface points on the patch, such that we can approximate the radiance for the patch by averaging over all surface points. For each patch, the algorithm will compute only this average radiance.

2. All surface patches have diffuse reflectance characteristics (i.e., the BRDF for each surface has a constant value, see Chapter 12). This implies that a surface point looks identical independent of the viewing direction. Together with the previous assumption, this leads to a global illumination in which each patch (polygon) has only one radiance value as a final solution, usable for all surface points on that patch. It is therefore practical to use any interactive polygon renderer to visualize the scene at interactive rates. This is the most useful advantage of radiosity algorithms.

3. Although not strictly necessary, the light sources are considered to be diffuse as well (equal exitant radiance in all directions). This simplifies the equations and solution methods.

The radiosity problem can be described by a simplification of the rendering equation for diffuse environments and a discretized version that will provide us with a linear system describing the energy equilibrium in the scene.

The *radiosity B* for a single point $\mathbf{x}$ is defined as flux per surface area, or equivalently, radiance integrated over the hemisphere of outgoing directions at $\mathbf{x}$. The *average* radiosity B_i emitted by a surface patch i with area A_i is therefore given by

$$B_i = \frac{1}{A_i} \int_{S_i} \int_{\Omega_{\mathbf{x}}} L_r(\mathbf{x}, \phi_r, \theta_r) \cos(\theta_r) d\omega_i dA, \qquad (16.13)$$

in which $L_r(\mathbf{x}, \phi_r, \theta_r)$ for a specific surface point $\mathbf{x}$ is given by the rendering equation (16.3).

On purely diffuse surfaces, self-emitted radiance L_e and the BRDF f_r do not depend on incoming or outgoing directions. The rendering equation for a surface point $\mathbf{x}$ can then be written as

$$L_r(\mathbf{x}) = L_e(\mathbf{x}) + \int_{\Omega_x} L_i(\mathbf{x}, \phi_i, \theta_i) f_r(\mathbf{x}) \cos(\theta_i) d\omega_i. \qquad (16.14)$$

Of course, the incident radiance $L_i(\mathbf{x}, \phi_i, \theta_i)$ still depends on incident direction. It corresponds to the exitant radiance $L_r(\mathbf{y})$ emitted towards $\mathbf{x}$ by the point $\mathbf{y}$ visible from $\mathbf{x}$ along the direction (ϕ_i, θ_i). As explained previously, the integral over the hemisphere Ω_x can be transformed into an integral over all surfaces S in the scene. The result is an integral equation without any directions present:

$$L_r(\mathbf{x}) = L_e(\mathbf{x}) + f_r(\mathbf{x}) \int_S G(\mathbf{x}, \mathbf{y}) V(\mathbf{x}, \mathbf{y}) L_r(\mathbf{y}) dA_{\mathbf{y}}. \qquad (16.15)$$

In a diffuse environment, radiosity and radiance are related since $B(\mathbf{x}) = \pi L_r(\mathbf{x})$ and $B_e(\mathbf{x}) = \pi L_e(\mathbf{x})$. Multiplication by π of the left- and right-hand side of the above equation yields the *radiosity integral equation*:

$$B(\mathbf{x}) = B_e(\mathbf{x}) + \frac{\rho(\mathbf{x})}{\pi} \int_S K(\mathbf{x}, \mathbf{y}) B(\mathbf{y}) dA_{\mathbf{y}}, \qquad (16.16)$$

where $\rho(\mathbf{x}) = \pi f_r(\mathbf{x})$ is the diffuse hemispherical reflectance bounded by $[0, 1]$, and the kernel $K(\mathbf{x}, \mathbf{y}) = G(\mathbf{x}, \mathbf{y}) V(\mathbf{x}, \mathbf{y})$.

Equation (16.13) now becomes

$$\begin{aligned}
B_i &= \frac{1}{A_i} \int_{S_i} L_r(\mathbf{x}) \int_{\Omega_{\mathbf{x}}} \cos(\theta_r) d\omega_i dA \\
&= \frac{1}{A_i} \int_{S_i} L_r(\mathbf{x}) \pi dA \\
&= \frac{1}{A_i} \int_{S_i} B(\mathbf{x}) dA. \qquad (16.17)
\end{aligned}$$

Often, integral equations such as Equation (16.16) are solved by reducing them to an approximate system of linear equations by means of a procedure known as *Galerkin* discretization [Delv85, Kres89, Cohe93, Sill94].

Assume the radiosity $B(\mathbf{x})$ is constant over each surface element i, i.e., $B(\mathbf{x}) = B'_i$ for all $\mathbf{x} \in S_i$. Equation (16.16) can be converted into a linear system as follows:

$$B(\mathbf{x}) = B_e(\mathbf{x}) + \frac{\rho(\mathbf{x})}{\pi} \int_S K(\mathbf{x}, \mathbf{y}) B(\mathbf{y}) dA_y$$

$$\Rightarrow \quad \frac{1}{A_i} \int_{S_i} B(\mathbf{x}) dA_x = \frac{1}{A_i} \int_{S_i} B_e(\mathbf{x}) dA_x$$

$$+ \frac{1}{A_i} \int_{S_i} \int_S \frac{\rho(\mathbf{x})}{\pi} K(\mathbf{x}, \mathbf{y}) B(\mathbf{y}) dA_y dA_x$$

$$\Leftrightarrow \quad \frac{1}{A_i} \int_{S_i} B(\mathbf{x}) dA_x = \frac{1}{A_i} \int_{S_i} B_e(\mathbf{x}) dA_x$$

$$+ \sum_j \frac{1}{A_i} \int_{S_i} \int_{S_j} \frac{\rho(\mathbf{x})}{\pi} K(\mathbf{x}, \mathbf{y}) B(\mathbf{y}) dA_y dA_x$$

$$\Leftrightarrow \quad B'_i = B_{ei} + \sum_j B'_j \frac{1}{A_i} \int_{S_i} \int_{S_j} \frac{\rho(\mathbf{x})}{\pi} K(\mathbf{x}, \mathbf{y}) dA_y dA_x.$$

If we also assume that the hemispherical diffuse reflectivity is constant over the surface patch, i.e., $\rho(\mathbf{x}) = \rho_i$ for all $\mathbf{x} \in S_i$, the following classical radiosity system of equations results:

$$B'_i = B_{ei} + \rho_i \sum_j F_{ij} B'_j. \tag{16.18}$$

The factors F_{ij} are called *patch-to-patch form factors*:

$$F_{ij} = \frac{1}{A_i} \int_{S_i} \int_{S_j} \frac{K(\mathbf{x}, \mathbf{y})}{\pi} dA_y dA_x. \tag{16.19}$$

The form factors represent the amount of energy transfer between two surface patches i and j; they are nontrivial four-dimensional integrals. They are only dependent on the geometry of the scene and not on any specific configuration of light sources in the scene.

Note that the radiosity values B'_i that result after solving the system of linear equations (Equation (16.18)) are only an approximation of the average radiosities B_i over a surface patch. The true radiosity value $B(\mathbf{y})$ that was replaced by B'_j in the above equations is in practice not piecewise constant, as we assumed in the above derivation. The difference between B_i and B'_i is, however, rarely visible in practice. For this reason, both the average radiosity (Equation (16.13)) and the radiosity coefficients in Equation (16.18) are used interchangeably.

16.3 Monte Carlo Integration

An important numerical tool for evaluating the global illumination equation is Monte Carlo integration, which evaluates integrals based on a selection of random samples drawn from the integration domain. Monte Carlo integration has a long history in numerical analysis, and a thorough description of various Monte Carlo methods can be found in [Kalo86, Hamm64].

The strength of Monte Carlo integration lies in its simplicity and robustness. An integral can be evaluated simply by generating random points in the integration domain, evaluating the integrand in this random sample, and averaging these evaluations. It is also robust, since the Monte Carlo method will work no matter how complex the function to be integrated is. For example, high-dimensional integrals, disjunct integration domains, or discontinuities in the integrand can all be handled by Monte Carlo integration.

The drawback is the relatively slow convergence rate of Monte Carlo integration. When drawing N samples from the integration domain, we can expect a convergence rate of $1/\sqrt{N}$. Consequently, many variance-reduction techniques have been developed, many specifically in the context of global illumination algorithms.

Suppose we want to evaluate the following one-dimensional integral, defined over the unit interval $[0,1]$:

$$I = \int_0^1 f(x)dx. \tag{16.20}$$

We will uniformly draw N samples $x_1, x_2, \ldots, x_N$ from the domain $[0,1]$. By averaging the function evaluations $f(x_i)$, we obtain an estimator for I:

$$\langle I \rangle = \frac{1}{N} \sum_{i=1}^{N} f(x_i). \tag{16.21}$$

It is easy to prove that the expected value $E[\langle I \rangle]$ of $\langle I \rangle$ equals the value of the integral I:

$$\begin{aligned}
E[\langle I \rangle] &= E\left[\frac{1}{N} \sum_{i=1}^{N} f(x_i) \right] = \frac{1}{N} \sum_{i=1}^{N} E\left[f(x_i) \right] \\
&= \frac{1}{N} \sum_{i=1}^{N} \int_0^1 f(x)dx = \frac{1}{N} \cdot N \cdot \int_0^1 f(x)dx \\
&= \int_0^1 f(x)dx = I.
\end{aligned} \tag{16.22}$$

Thus, we have defined a stochastic process whose expected outcome equals the integral value I that we would like to compute. Of course, every different computation of $\langle I \rangle$ will yield a different result, but, *on average*, we will get the right answer.

The variance σ^2 of this stochastic computation, indicating the spread of possible values of $\langle I \rangle$ around the expected outcome I, can be computed as follows:

$$
\begin{aligned}
\sigma^2[\langle I \rangle] &= \sigma^2 \left[\frac{1}{N} \sum_{i=1}^{N} f(x_i) \right] \\
&= \frac{1}{N^2} \sum_{i=1}^{N} \sigma^2 [f(x_i)] \\
&= \frac{1}{N^2} \cdot N \cdot \int_0^1 (f(x) - I)^2 dx \\
&= \frac{1}{N} \int_0^1 (f(x) - I)^2 dx.
\end{aligned}
\tag{16.23}
$$

Thus, as the number of samples N increases, the variance σ^2 decreases linearly with N. The standard deviation σ, which can be considered an approximation of the error we make when estimating the integral, therefore decreases with $1/\sqrt{N}$. This means that if we want to decrease the error by a factor of two, we need four times as many samples. This convergence speed is typically lower than that of many other integration techniques, but it is independent of the number of dimensions in the integral. Estimating the variance itself can be part of a separate Monte Carlo integration process, but can also be done using the same sample points x_i used for the estimation of I. However, in the latter case, care has to be taken about possible correlation effects.

Generalizing to the domain $[a, b]$, and using a non-uniform probability density $p(x)$ to draw the samples, we obtain the following expressions for the estimator $\langle I \rangle$ and variance σ^2:

$$
\begin{aligned}
\langle I \rangle &= \frac{1}{N} \sum_{i=1}^{N} \frac{f(x_i)}{p(x_i)}, \\
\sigma^2[\langle I \rangle] &= \frac{1}{N} \int_a^b (\frac{f(x)}{p(x)} - I)^2 dx.
\end{aligned}
\tag{16.24}
$$

Again, one can prove that the expected value of $\langle I \rangle$ equals the value of the integral, or $E(\langle I \rangle) = I$.

The probability density function (pdf) $p(x)$ has to satisfy two constraints:

1. The value of $p(x)$ must be strictly larger than 0 over the entire integration domain $[a,b]$.

2. The function $p(x)$ has to integrate to 1: $\int_a^b p(x)dx = 1$.

In order to draw samples distributed according to $p(x)$, several techniques are possible. Analytically, one has to compute the cumulative distribution function $P(x)$:

$$P(x) = \int_a^x p(y)dy. \qquad (16.25)$$

$P(x)$ is a monotonic increasing function over the interval $[a,b]$ with $P(a) = 0$ and $P(b) = 1$. If a random number t is generated uniformly over the interval $[0,1]$, then the distribution of the values $x = P^{-1}(t)$ is distributed according to $p(x)$. In practice, the inverse cumulative function is often computed numerically and stored as a table in which a binary search is possible to compute the inverse value quickly. The main advantage of using a non-uniform pdf is that the variance, and thus the error, of the integration can be decreased. As a rule of thumb , the more the shape of the pdf is similar to the function to be integrated, the lower the variance will be.

Other strategies for reducing variance usually involve distributing the sampling points over the interval using techniques such as stratified sampling, N-Rooks sampling, multiple importance sampling, or combinations of all methods. [Kalo86] and [Hamm64] contain more thorough reviews of these techniques.

Multidimensional Monte Carlo integration works in exactly the same way as one-dimensional integration. Thus, if the integral we want to compute is defined over a domain $[a,b] \times [c,d]$:

$$I = \int_a^b \int_c^d f(x,y)dxdy,$$
$$\langle I \rangle = \frac{1}{N} \sum_{i=1}^N \frac{f(x_i, y_i)}{p(x_i, y_i)}. \qquad (16.26)$$

The main advantage of Monte Carlo integration is that it is simple to implement and is very robust. It provides an answer independent of the complexity of the function to be integrated or the dimensions of the integration domain. The drawback is that the error is hard to control and often cannot be expressed by explicit lower and upper bounds.

16.4 Computing Direct Illumination

Computing the direct illumination based on various forms of the rendering equation usually involves applying Monte Carlo integration. In this section, various approaches are described that all assume that we want to compute the reflected radiance value in a surface point $\mathbf{x}$ and in a specific direction, usually the direction pointing towards the camera if $\mathbf{x}$ is the result of the intersection of the viewing ray with the scene geometry in a ray tracing algorithm (see Chapter 15).

16.4.1 Single Light Source

Let us first take a look at direct illumination from a single light source (Equation (16.10)). The integration domain is defined as the surface S_1 of the light source, thus we have to use a pdf $p(\mathbf{y})$ that is able to generate surface points $\mathbf{y}_j$ over the total light source area. This leads to the following estimator for the radiance value $L_r(\mathbf{x}, \phi_r, \theta_r)$ when using N sample points $\{\mathbf{y}_1, \mathbf{y}_2, \ldots, \mathbf{y}_N\}$:

$$\langle L_r(\mathbf{x}, \phi_r, \theta_r)\rangle = \frac{1}{N}\sum_{j=1}^{N} \frac{L_e(\mathbf{y}_j, \phi_{y_j}, \theta_{y_j}) f_r(\phi_r, \theta_r, \phi_i, \theta_i) G(\mathbf{x}, \mathbf{y_j}) V(\mathbf{x}, \mathbf{y_j})}{p(\mathbf{y}_j)}. \quad (16.27)$$

The pdf $p(\mathbf{y})$ is a two-dimensional pdf that has to generate two coordinates u and v, which can be transformed to a 3D point $\mathbf{y}$ on the surface of the light source using a proper mapping. This mapping is usually identical to the mapping used in texture-mapping procedures. Care has to be taken that each point on the light source has a non-zero value for the pdf, otherwise some parts of the light source will not be sampled and the estimated radiance will have a biased value.

The procedure for evaluating the direct illumination due to a single light source is shown in Figure 16.2, and the algorithmic overview is given in Listing 16.1. Algorithmically, evaluating the visibility term $V(\mathbf{x}, \mathbf{y}_j)$ involves shooting a shadow ray from $\mathbf{x}$ towards $\mathbf{y}_j$ and checking whether any objects are blocking the visibility.

As can be seen in Figure 16.3, there are quite some differences in pixel intensities that are visible as noise in the final image. Noise is unavoidable in a stochastic process such as Monte Carlo integration, but will decrease gradually if more samples are drawn.

Different factors contribute to the visible noise in the image:

- The visibility function $V(\mathbf{x}, \mathbf{y}_i)$ is usually the most important factor causing noise in direct illumination computations. When the light source is

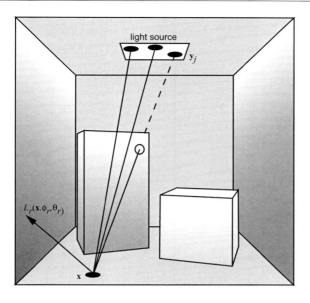

Figure 16.2. Sampling a single light source.

```
// direct illumination from a single light source
// for a surface point x, direction phi, theta
directIllumination (x, phi, theta)
    estimatedRadiance = 0;
    for all shadow rays
        generate point y on light source;
        estimatedRadiance +=
            Le(y,phi_y,theta_y)*BRDF*radianceTransfer(x,y)/pdf(y);
    estimatedRadiance = estimatedRadiance / #shadowRays;
    return(estimatedRadiance);

// transfer between x and y
// 2 cosines, distance and visibility taken into account
radianceTransfer(x,y)
    transfer = G(x,y)*V(x,y);
    return(transfer);
```

Listing 16.1: Computing direct illumination from a single light source.

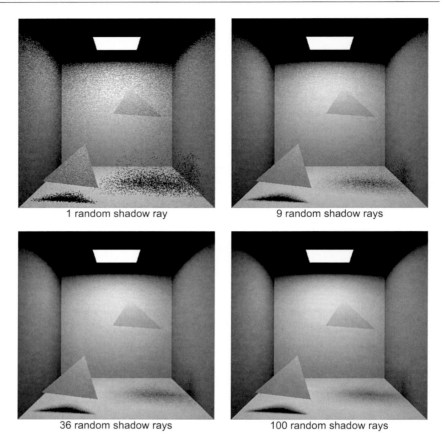

1 random shadow ray   9 random shadow rays

36 random shadow rays   100 random shadow rays

Figure 16.3. Direct illumination due to a single light source. Note the difference in quality of the image when the number of samples (shadow rays) is increased. (See also Color Plate XXVII.)

fully visible to the point $\mathbf{x}$ to be shaded (in other words, $V(\mathbf{x}, \mathbf{y}_i) = 1$ for all points $\mathbf{y}_i$), or fully occluded ($V(\mathbf{x}, \mathbf{y}_i) = 0$ for all points $\mathbf{y}_i$), there is no problem. However, when $\mathbf{x}$ is located in the penumbra or soft-shadow region due to a partial blocking of a light source by a shadow caster, artifacts will occur (see Chapter 13 for more details and definitions regarding shadow generation). In this case, some points $\mathbf{y}_i$ will be visible to $\mathbf{x}$, and some will not. If only one shadow ray per pixel will be drawn, this means the estimated radiance can become equal to 0, resulting in a black pixel in the final image. Increasing the number of samples will smoothen the soft shadow (Figure 16.3). In practice, the number of samples will be dependent on the size of the penumbra region.

- The geometric coupling term $G(\mathbf{x}, \mathbf{y}_i)$ (16.7) also can contribute significantly to the stochastic error visible in the image. Even if there are no visibility problems, variations in the cosine factors or the inverse distance can become significant. Especially when the light source is large, and for points $\mathbf{x}$ located close to the light source, $1/r_{\mathbf{x}\mathbf{y}_i}$ can take on arbitrarily large values, resulting in very bright pixels. The evaluation of $G(\mathbf{x}, \mathbf{y}_i)$ usually does not cause problems when the light source is small, since then this term tends to be near constant for the different $\mathbf{y}_i$.

- When using non-diffuse BRDFs, the direction of the shadow rays (see Chapter 15) might or might not coincide with the specular lobes of the BRDF model. If the BRDF values vary largely within the solid angle subtended by the light source, additional noise can be introduced into the picture.

- In principle, any valid pdf $p(\mathbf{y})$ can be chosen to compute the estimate $\langle L_r(\mathbf{x}, \phi_r, \theta_r) \rangle$. However, $p(\mathbf{y})$ is usually uniform over the area of the light source and, thus, will not affect the noise in the final image.

16.4.2 Multiple Light Sources

When dealing with direct illumination due to multiple light sources present in the scene, two approaches can be followed, each with distinct advantages. The first approach considers all light sources as individual contributors to the illumination of a single point, while the second approach groups all light sources in a single integration domain.

In global illumination algorithms, as in all of computer graphics, light is considered to be linearly additive. Therefore, the separate contributions of each individual light source to the illumination of surface point $\mathbf{x}$ can be added together. A number of shadow rays is generated for each light source and can be chosen independently (e.g., an equal number for all light sources or proportional to the power of each light source).

However, it is often better to consider all combined light sources as a single integration domain and apply Monte Carlo integration to the combined integral. As a result, when shadow rays are generated, they can be directed to any of the light sources, without explicitly attributing a fixed number of shadow rays to each

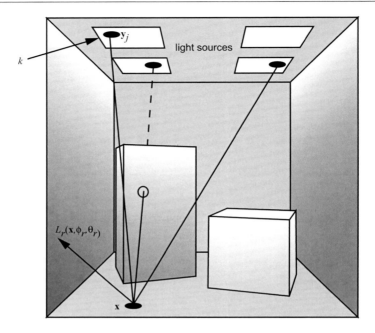

Figure 16.4. Direct illumination due to multiple light sources.

light source. When using this procedure, it is therefore possible to compute the direct illumination due to any number of light sources with just a single shadow ray for each point **x** to be shaded and still obtain an unbiased image. This approach works because we make a complete abstraction of the light sources as separate modeled entities, and instead we look at the combined integration domain. However, in order to have a working sampling algorithm, we still need access to any of the light sources separately, because any individual light source might require a separate sampling procedure for generating points over their respective surfaces.

A two-step sampling process is used for each shadow ray (Figure 16.4):

1. First, a discrete pdf $p_L(k)$ generates a randomly selected light source k_i. We assign each of the N_L light sources a probability value for it being chosen to send a shadow ray to. This probability function is usually the same for all different points **x**, but in principle, it can be chosen differently for different parts of the scene. This proves beneficial especially when the scene is subdivided in different sub-scenes, which have their own light sources, but which are also mutually hidden from each other.

```
// direct illumination from multiple light sources
// for surface point x, direction phi, theta
directIllumination (x, phi, theta)
    estimatedRadiance = 0;
    for all shadow rays
        select light source k;
        generate point y on light source k;
        estimatedRadiance +=
            Le(y, phi_y, theta_y) * BRDF * radianceTransfer(x,y) /
                (pdf(k) * pdf(y|k));
    estimatedRadiance = estimatedRadiance / #shadowRays;
    return(estimatedRadiance);

// transfer between x and y
// 2 cosines, distance and visibility taken into account
radianceTransfer(x,y)
    transfer = G(x,y)*V(x,y);
    return(transfer);
```

Listing 16.2: Computing direct illumination due to multiple light sources.

2. During the second step, a surface point $\mathbf{y}_i$ on the selected light source k is selected using a conditional pdf $p(\mathbf{y}|k_i)$. Any of the pdfs applicable to single light source illumination can be used.

The combined pdf for the sampled point y_i on the combined area of all light sources therefore equals $p_L(k)p(\mathbf{y}|k)$. The total estimator, using N shadow rays, is then expressed as

$$\langle L_r(\mathbf{x}, \phi_r, \theta_r)\rangle = \frac{1}{N}\sum_{i=1}^{N} \frac{L_e(\mathbf{y}_i, \phi_{y_j}, \theta_{y_j})f_r(\phi_r, \theta_r, \phi_i, \theta_i)G(\mathbf{x}, \mathbf{y}_i)V(\mathbf{x}, \mathbf{y}_i)}{p_L(k_i)p(\mathbf{y}_i|k_i)}. \quad (16.28)$$

Listing 16.2 shows the algorithm for computing the direct illumination due to multiple light sources.

Although any pdfs $p_L(k)$ and $p(\mathbf{y}|k)$ will produce unbiased images, the choice of specific pdfs will have an impact on the variance of the estimators and the noise in the final picture. Two of the more common choices are the following:

Uniform source selection with uniform sampling of light source area. Both pdfs are uniform, i.e., $p_L(k) = 1/N_L$ and $p(\mathbf{y}|k) = 1/S_{L_k}$. Every light source will receive, on average, an equal number of shadow rays, and these shadow rays are distributed uniformly over the area of each light source. This is easy to implement, but the disadvantages are that the illumination of both bright and weak light sources is computed with an equal number of shadow rays. Also, light sources that are far away or invisible receive an equal number of shadow rays as light sources that are nearby. Thus, the relative importance of each light source to the illumination of a single surface point source is not taken into account. Substituting the pdfs in Equation (16.28) provides the following estimator for the direct illumination:

$$\langle L_r(\mathbf{x}, \phi_r, \theta_r) \rangle = \frac{N_L}{N} \sum_{i=1}^{N} S_{L_k} L_e(\mathbf{y}_i, \phi_{y_j}, \theta_{y_j}) f_r(\phi_r, \theta_r, \phi_i, \theta_i) G(\mathbf{x}, \mathbf{y}_i) V(\mathbf{x}, \mathbf{y}_i).$$
(16.29)

Power-proportional source selection with uniform sampling of light source area. Here, the pdf $p_L(k) = P_k/P_{\text{total}}$ with P_k being the radiant power of light source k and P_{total} the total power emitted by all light sources. Bright sources receive more shadow rays, and very dim light sources receive very few. This is likely to reduce variance and noise in the picture. The estimator can be written as

$$\langle L_r(\mathbf{x}, \phi_r, \theta_r) \rangle =$$
$$\frac{P_{\text{total}}}{N} \sum_{i=1}^{N} \frac{S_{L_k} L_e(\mathbf{y}_i, \phi_{y_j}, \theta_{y_j}) f_r(\phi_r, \theta_r, \phi_i, \theta_i) G(\mathbf{x}, \mathbf{y}_i) V(\mathbf{x}, \mathbf{y}_i)}{P_k}.$$
(16.30)

If all light sources are diffuse, $P_k = \pi S_k L_{e,k}$, and thus

$$\langle L_r(\mathbf{x}, \phi_r, \theta_r) \rangle = \frac{P_{\text{total}}}{\pi N} \sum_{i=1}^{N} f_r(\phi_r, \theta_r, \phi_i, \theta_i) G(\mathbf{x}, \mathbf{y}_i) V(\mathbf{x}, \mathbf{y}_i).$$
(16.31)

This approach is typically superior since it gives a higher importance to bright sources, but it could result in slower convergence at pixels where the bright lights are invisible and illumination is dominated by less bright lights. This latter occurrence can only be solved by using sampling strategies that use some knowledge about the visibility of the light sources with respect to specific parts of the scene.

No matter what $p_L(k)$ is chosen, one has to be sure not to exclude any light sources that might contribute to $L_r(\mathbf{x}, \phi_r, \theta_r)$. Just dropping small, weak, or far-away light sources might result in bias, and for some portions of the image, this bias can be significant.

One of the drawbacks of the above two-step procedure is that three random numbers are needed to generate a shadow ray: one random number to select the light source k and two random numbers to select a specific surface point $\mathbf{y}_i$ within the area of the light source. This makes stratified sampling more difficult to implement. In [Shir00], a technique is described that makes it possible to use only two random numbers when generating shadow rays for a number of disjunct light sources. The two-dimensional integration domain covering all light sources is mapped on the standard two-dimensional unit square. Each light source corresponds to a small sub-domain of the unit square. When a point is generated in the unit square, we find out what sub-domain it belongs to and then transform the location of the point to the actual light source. Sampling in a three-dimensional domain has been reduced to sampling in a two-dimensional domain, which makes it easier to apply stratified sampling or other variance-reduction techniques.

16.4.3   Environment Map Illumination⊛

The computational techniques outlined in the previous sections are applicable to almost all types of light sources. It is sufficient to choose an appropriate pdf to select one light source from among all light sources in the scene and, subsequently, to choose a pdf to sample a random surface point on the selected light source. The total variance, and hence the stochastic noise in the image, will be highly dependent on the types of pdf chosen.

The use of environment maps (sometimes also called illumination maps or reflection maps—see Chapter 14) as a type of light source has received significant attention in recent years. An environment map encodes the total illumination present on the hemisphere of directions around a single point. Usually, environment maps for illumination purposes are captured in natural environments using digital cameras.

An environment map can be described mathematically as a stepwise continuous function, in which each pixel corresponds to a small solid angle $\Delta\Omega$ around the point $\mathbf{x}$ at which the environment map is centered. The intensity of each pixel then corresponds to an incident radiance value $L(\mathbf{x}, \phi_i, \theta_i)$, with $(\phi_i, \theta_i) \in \Delta\Omega$.

Capturing environment maps. Environment maps usually represent real-world illumination conditions. A *light probe* in conjunction with a digital camera, or a digital camera equipped with a fisheye lens are the most common techniques for capturing environment maps.

A practical way to acquire an environment map of a real environment is the use of a light probe. A light probe is nothing more than a specularly reflective ball

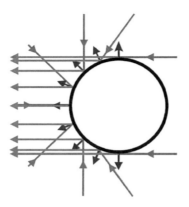 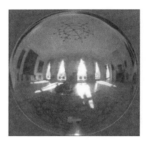

Figure 16.5. Photographing a light probe results in an environment map representing incident radiance from all directions.

that is positioned at the point where the incident illumination needs to be captured. The light probe is subsequently photographed using a camera equipped with an orthographic lens, or alternatively, a large zoom lens such that orthographic conditions are approximated as closely as possible.

The center point of a pixel in the recorded image of the light probe corresponds to a single incident direction. This direction can be computed rather easily, since the normal vector on the light probe is known, and a mapping from pixel coordinates to incident directions can be used. A photograph of the light probe therefore results in a set of integrated samples of the function $L(\mathbf{x}, \phi_i, \theta_i)$ (Figure 16.5).

Although the acquisition process is straightforward, there are a number of issues to be considered:

- The camera will be reflected in the light probe and will be present in the photograph, thereby blocking light coming from directions directly behind the camera.

- The use of a light probe does not result in a uniform sampling of directions over the hemisphere. Directions opposite the camera are sampled poorly, whereas directions on the same side of the camera are sampled densely.

- All directions sampled at the edge of the image of the light probe represent illumination from the same direction. Since the light probe has a small radius, these values may differ slightly.

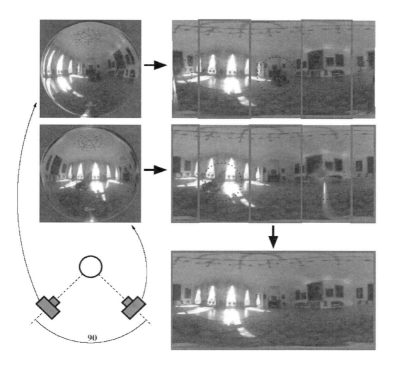

Figure 16.6. Photographing a light probe twice, 90 degrees apart. Combining both photographs produces a well-sampled environment map without the camera being visible.

- Since the camera cannot capture all illumination levels due to its non-linear response curve, a process of high dynamic range photography needs to be used to acquire an environment map that correctly represents radiance values.

Some of these problems can be alleviated by capturing two photographs of the light probe 90 degrees apart. The samples of both photographs can be combined into a single environment map as is shown in Figure 16.6.

An alternative for capturing an environment map is to make use of a camera equipped with a fisheye lens. Two photographs taken from opposite view directions result in a single environment map as well. However, good fisheye lenses can be very expensive and hard to calibrate. Both images need to be taken in perfect opposite view directions, otherwise a significant set of directions will not be present in the photograph. If only the incident illumination of directions in one hemisphere need to be known instead of the full sphere of directions, the use of a fisheye lens can be very practical.

Parameterizations. When using environment maps in global illumination algorithms, they need to be expressed in some parametric space. Various parameterizations can be used, and the effectiveness of how well environments maps can be sampled is dependent on the type of parameterization used. In essence, this is the same choice one has to make when computing the rendering equation as an integral over the hemisphere.

Various types of parameterizations are used in the context of environment maps, and we provide a brief overview here. A more in-depth analysis can be found in [Mass04].

Latitude-longitude parameterization. These are the classic hemispherical coordinates, but extended to the full sphere of directions. Advantages are an equal distribution of the tilt angle θ, but there is a singularity around both poles, which is represented as a line in the map. Additional problems are that the pixels in the map do not occupy equal solid angles, and that the $\phi = 0$ and $\phi = 2\pi$ angles are not mapped continuously next to each other (Figure 16.7(a)).

Projected-disk parameterization. This parameterization is also known as Nusselt embedding. The hemisphere of directions is projected on a disk of radius 1. The advantage is the continuous mapping of the azimuthal angle ϕ and the fact that the pole is a single point in the map. However, the tilt angle θ is non-uniformly distributed over the map (Figure 16.7(b)). A variant is the paraboloid parameterization, in which the tilt angle is distributed more evenly [Heid99] (Figure 16.7(c)).

Concentric-map parameterization. The concentric-map parameterization transforms the projected unit disk to a unit square [Shir97]. This makes sampling of directions in the map easier and keeps the continuity of the projected disk-parameterizations (Figure 16.7(d)).

Sampling environment maps. The direct illumination of a surface point due to an environment map can be expressed as follows:

$$L_r(\mathbf{x}, \phi_r, \theta_r) = \int_{\Omega_{\mathbf{x}}} L_{\text{map}}(\phi_i, \theta_i) f_r(\phi_r, \theta_r, \phi_i, \theta_i) \cos(\theta_i) d\omega_i. \qquad (16.32)$$

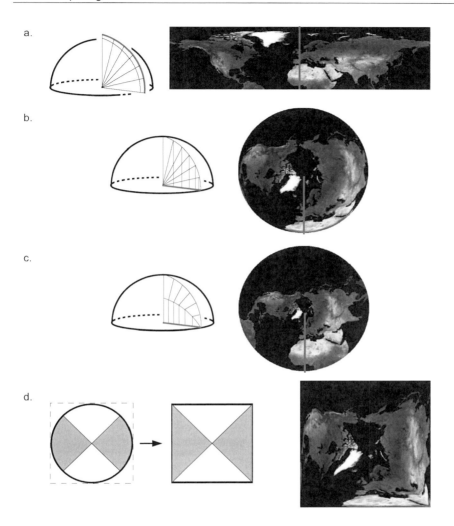

Figure 16.7. Different parameterizations for the hemisphere: (a) latitude-longitude parameterization; (b) projected-disk parameterization; (c) paraboloid parameterization; (d) concentric-map parameterization.

The integrand contains the incident illumination $L_{\mathrm{map}}(\phi_i, \theta_i)$ on point $\mathbf{x}$, coming from direction (ϕ_i, θ_i) in the environment map. Other surfaces present in the scene might prevent the light coming from this direction from reaching $\mathbf{x}$. These surfaces might belong to other objects, or the object to which $\mathbf{x}$ belongs can cast a self-shadow onto $\mathbf{x}$. In these cases, a visibility term $V(\mathbf{x}, \phi_i, \theta_i)$ has to be added:

$$L_r(\mathbf{x}, \phi_r, \theta_r) = \int_{\Omega_{\mathbf{x}}} L_{\mathrm{map}}(\phi_i, \theta_i) f_r(\phi_r, \theta_r, \phi_i, \theta_i) V(\mathbf{x}, \phi_i, \theta_i) \cos(\theta_i) d\omega_i. \quad (16.33)$$

A straightforward application of Monte Carlo integration results in the following estimator:

$$\langle L_r(\mathbf{x}, \phi_r, \theta_r) \rangle = \frac{1}{N} \sum_{j=1}^{N} \frac{L_{\mathrm{map}}(\mathbf{x}, \phi_{i,j}, \theta_{i,j}) f_r(\phi_r, \theta_r, \phi_{i,j}, \theta_{i,j}) V(\mathbf{x}, \phi_{i,j}, \theta_{i,j}) \cos(\theta_{i,j})}{p(\phi_{i,j}, \theta_{i,j})},$$
$$(16.34)$$

in which the different sampled directions $(\phi_{i,j}, \theta_{i,j})$ are generated directly in the parameterization of the environment map using a pdf $p(\phi_{i,j}, \theta_{i,j})$.

However, various problems present themselves when trying to approximate this integral using Monte Carlo integration:

Integration domain. The environment map acting as a light source occupies the complete solid angle around the point to be shaded, and, thus, the integration domain of the direct illumination equation has a large extent, usually increasing variance.

Textured light source. Each pixel in the environment map represents a small solid angle of incident light. The environment map can therefore be considered as a textured light source. The radiance distribution in the environment map can contain high frequencies or discontinuities, thereby again increasing variance and stochastic noise in the final image. Especially when capturing effects such as the sun or bright windows, very high peaks of illumination values can be present in the environment map.

Product of environment map and BRDF. As expressed in Equation (16.33), the integrand contains the product of the incident illumination $L_{\mathrm{map}}(\phi_i, \theta_i)$ and the BRDF $f_r(\phi_r, \theta_r, \phi_i, \theta_i)$. In addition to the discontinuities and high frequency effects present in the environment map, a glossy or specular BRDF also contains very sharp peaks. These peaks on the sphere or hemisphere of directions for both illumination values and BRDF values usually are not located in the same directions. This makes it very difficult to design a very efficient sample scheme that takes these features into account.

Visibility. If the visibility term is included, additional discontinuities are present
in the integrand. This is very similar to the handling of the visibility term
in standard direct illumination computations, but might complicate an efficient sampling process.

Practical approaches try to construct a pdf $p(\phi_{i,j}, \theta_{i,j})$ that addresses these
problems. Roughly, these can be divided into three categories: pdfs based on the
distribution of radiance values $L_{\mathrm{map}}(\phi_i, \theta_i)$ in the illumination map only, usually
including $\cos(\theta_i)$ that can be pre-multiplied into the illumination map; pdfs based
on the BRDF $f_r(\phi_r, \theta_r, \phi_i, \theta_i)$, which are especially useful if the BRDF is of a
glossy or specular nature; and pdfs based on the product of both functions, but
which are usually harder to construct.

Direct illumination map sampling. A first approach for constructing a pdf based
on the radiance values in the illumination map can be simply to transform
the piecewise constant pixel values into a pdf, by computing the cumulative
distribution in two dimensions and subsequently inverting it. This typically
results in a 2D look-up table, and the efficiency of the method is highly
dependent on how fast this look-up table can be queried.

A different approach is to simplify the environment map by transforming it
into a number of well-selected point light sources. This has the advantage
that there is a consistent sampling of the environment map for all surface
points to be shaded, but can possibly introduce aliasing artifacts, especially
when using a low number of light sources. In [Koll03] an approach is
presented in which a quadrature rule is generated automatically from a high
dynamic range environment map. Visibility is taken into account in the
structured importance sampling algorithm, in which the environment map
is subdivided in a number of cells [Agar03].

BRDF sampling. The main disadvantage of constructing a pdf based only on the
illumination map is that the BRDF is not included in the sampling process,
but is left to be evaluated after the sample directions have been chosen. This
is particularly problematic for specular and glossy BRDFs, and if this is the
case, a pdf based on the BRDF will produce better results.

This, of course, requires that the BRDF can be sampled analytically, which
is not always possible, except for a few well-constructed BRDFs (e.g., a
Phong BRDF or Lafortune BRDF). Otherwise, the inverse cumulative distribution technique will have to be used for the BRDF as well.

Sampling the product. The best approach is to construct a sampling scheme based on the product of both the illumination map and the BRDF, possibly including the cosine and some visibility information as well. In [Burk05], *bidirectional importance sampling* is introduced that constructs a sampling procedure based on rejection sampling. The disadvantage is that it is difficult to predict exactly how many samples will be rejected and, hence, the computation time. *Resampled importance sampling* is a variant of this approach [Talb05]. *Wavelet importance sampling* [Clar05] constructs a pdf based on the wavelet representation of both the illumination map and the BRDF, but this implies some restrictions on what type of map and BRDF can be used.

16.5   Indirect Illumination

16.5.1   Stochastic Ray Tracing

The stochastic ray tracing algorithm is a global illumination algorithm that does not limit itself to direct illumination only, but includes all possible indirect illumination effects. It can be derived by applying Monte Carlo integration directly to the hemispherical rendering equation (16.3).

Ray-tracing set-up. In order to compute a global illumination picture, we need to attribute a radiance value L_{pixel} to each pixel in the final image. This value is a weighted measure of radiance values incident on the image plane, along a ray coming from the scene, passing through the pixel, and pointing to the eye (see Chapter 15 and Figure 16.8). This is best described by a weighted integral over the image plane,

$$
\begin{aligned}
L_{pixel} &= \int_{\text{image plane}} L(\mathbf{p}) h(\mathbf{p}) d\mathbf{p} \\
&= \int_{\text{image plane}} L_r(\mathbf{x}, \phi_r, \theta_r) h(\mathbf{p}) d\mathbf{p},
\end{aligned}
\tag{16.35}
$$

where $\mathbf{p}$ is a point on the image plane, $h(\mathbf{p})$ is a weighting or filtering function (see Appendix E), and $\mathbf{x}$ is the visible point seen from the eye through $\mathbf{p}$. Often, $h(\mathbf{p})$ equals a simple box filter such that the final radiance value is computed by uniformly averaging the incident radiance values over the area of the pixel. A more complex camera model is described in [Kolb95]. To evaluate $L_r(\mathbf{x}, \phi_r, \theta_r)$,

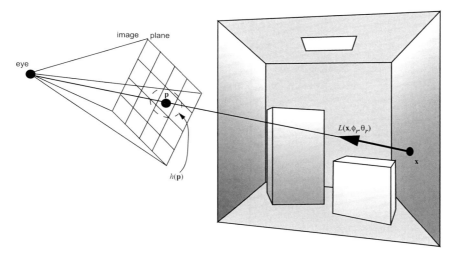

Figure 16.8. Ray-tracing set-up.

a ray is cast from the eye through **p** in order to find **x**. Then, $L_r(\mathbf{x}, \phi_r, \theta_r)$ is computed by evaluating the rendering equation.

The complete pixel-driven rendering algorithm (Listing 16.3) consists of a loop over all pixels, and, for each pixel, the integral in the image plane is computed using an appropriate integration rule (Equation (16.35)). A simple Monte Carlo sampling over the image plane where $h(\mathbf{p}) \neq 0$ can be used. For each sample point **p**, a primary ray needs to be constructed. The radiance along this primary ray is computed using a function rad(ray). This function finds the intersection point **x** and then computes the radiance leaving surface point x in the direction of the eye. The final radiance estimate for the pixel is obtained by averaging over the total number of viewing rays, and taking into account the normalizing factor of the uniform PDF over the integration domain ($h(\mathbf{p}) \neq 0$).

Truly random paths. The function compute_radiance(x, direction eye to p) in the pixel-driven rendering algorithm uses the rendering equation to evaluate the appropriate radiance value. The most simple algorithm to compute this radiance value is to apply a basic and straightforward Monte Carlo integration scheme to the standard form of the rendering equation (16.3). The integral can be evaluated using Monte Carlo integration, by generating N random directions (ϕ_i, θ_i) over the hemisphere $\Omega_\mathbf{x}$, distributed according to some probability density

```
// pixel-driven rendering algorithm
computeImage(eye)
    for each pixel
        radiance = 0;
        H = integral(h(p));
        for each viewing ray
            pick uniform sample point p such that h(p) <> 0;
            construct ray at origin eye, direction from eye to p;
            radiance = radiance + rad(ray)*h(p);
        radiance = radiance / (#viewingRays*H);

rad(ray)
    find closest intersection point x of ray with scene;
    computeRadiance(x, direction eye to p);
```

Listing 16.3: Pixel-driven rendering algorithm.

function $p(\phi_i, \theta_i)$. The estimator for $L_r(\mathbf{x}, \phi_r, \theta_r)$ is then given by

$$\langle L_r(\mathbf{x}, \phi_r, \theta_r) \rangle = \frac{1}{N} \sum_{j=1}^{N} \frac{L(\mathbf{x}, \phi_{i,j}, \theta_{i,j}) f_r(\phi_r, \theta_r, \phi_{i,j}, \theta_{i,j}) \cos(\theta_{i,j})}{p(\phi_{i,j}, \theta_{i,j})}. \qquad (16.36)$$

The cosine and BRDF terms in the integrand can be evaluated by accessing the scene description. However, $L(\mathbf{x}, \phi_{i,j}, \theta_{i,j})$, the incident radiance at $\mathbf{x}$, is unknown. Since radiance remains invariant along straight lines, we need to trace the ray leaving $\mathbf{x}$ in direction $(\phi_{i,j}, \theta_{i,j})$ through the environment to find the closest intersection point $\mathbf{y}$. At this point, another radiance evaluation is needed. Thus, we have a recursive procedure to evaluate $L(\mathbf{x}, \phi_{i,j}, \theta_{i,j})$, and a path, or a tree of paths, is traced through the scene.

Any of these radiance evaluations will only yield a non-zero value, if the path hits a surface for which L_e is different from 0. In other words, the recursive path needs to hit one of the light sources in the scene. Since the light sources usually are small compared to the other surfaces, this does not occur very often, and very few of the paths will yield a contribution to the radiance value to be computed. The resulting image will mostly be black. Only when a path hits a light source will the corresponding pixel be attributed a color. The algorithm generates paths in the scene, starting at the point of interest and slowly working toward the light sources in a very uncoordinated manner.

In theory, this algorithm could be improved somewhat by choosing $p(\phi_i, \theta_i)$ to be proportional to the cosine term or the BRDF, according to the principle of importance sampling. In practice, the disadvantage of picking up mostly zero-value terms is not changing the result considerably. Note however, that this simple approach will produce an unbiased image if a sufficient number of paths per pixel are generated.

Terminating the recursion. The recursive path generator described in the simple stochastic ray tracing algorithm needs a stopping condition. Otherwise, the generated paths are of infinite length and the algorithm does not come to a halt. When adding a stopping condition, one has to be careful not to introduce any bias to the final image. Theoretically, light reflects infinitely in the scene, and we cannot ignore those light paths of a long length that might be very important. Thus, we have to find a way to limit the length of the paths, but still be able to obtain a correct solution.

In classic ray-tracing implementations, two techniques are often used to prevent paths from growing too long. A first technique is cutting off the recursive evaluations after a fixed number of evaluations. In other words, the paths are generated up to a certain specified length. This puts an upper bound on the amount of rays that need to be traced, but important light transport might have been ignored. Thus, the image will be biased. A typical fixed path length is set at 4 or 5, but really should be dependent on the scene to be rendered. A scene with many specular surfaces will require a larger path length, while scenes with mostly diffuse surfaces can usually use a shorter path length.

Another approach is to use an adaptive cut-off length. When a path hits a light source, the radiance found at the light source still needs to be multiplied by all cosine factors and BRDF evaluations (and divided by all pdf values) at all previous intersection points, before it can be added to the final estimate of the radiance through the pixel. This accumulating multiplication factor can be stored along with the lengthening path. If this factor falls below a certain threshold, recursive path generation is stopped. This technique is more efficient compared to the fixed path length, because many paths are stopped sooner and fewer errors are made, but the final image will still be biased.

Russian roulette is a technique that addresses the problem of keeping the lengths of the paths manageable, but at the same time leaves room for exploring all possible paths of any length. Thus, an unbiased image can still be produced. To explain the Russian roulette principle, let us look at a simple example first.

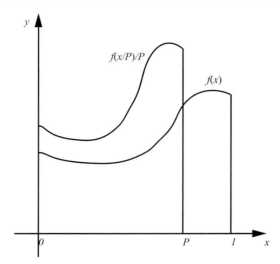

Figure 16.9. Principle of Russian roulette.

Suppose we want to compute the one-dimensional integral

$$I = \int_0^1 f(x)dx.$$

The standard Monte Carlo integration procedure generates random points x_i in the domain $[0, 1]$, and computes the weighted average of all function values $f(x_i)$. Assume that for some reason $f(x)$ is difficult or complex to evaluate (e.g., $f(x)$ might be expressed as another integral), and we would like to limit the number of evaluations of $f(x)$ necessary to estimate I. By scaling $f(x)$ by a factor P horizontally and a factor $1/P$ vertically, we can also express the quantity I as

$$I_{RR} = \int_0^P \frac{1}{P}f(\frac{x}{P})dx,$$

with $P \leq 1$ (Figure 16.9).

Applying Monte Carlo integration to compute the new integral, using a uniform pdf $p(x) = 1$ to generate the samples over $[0, 1]$, we get the following estimator for I_{RR}:

$$\langle I_{RR} \rangle = \begin{cases} \frac{1}{P}f(\frac{x}{P}) & \text{if } x \leq P, \\ 0 & \text{if } x > P. \end{cases}$$

```
// simple stochastic ray tracing
computeRadiance(x, dir)
    find closest intersection point x of ray with scene;
    estimatedRadiance = simpleStochasticRT(x, phi, theta);
    return(estimatedRadiance);

simpleStochasticRT (x, phi, theta)
    estimatedRadiance = 0;
    if (no absorption)          // Russian roulette
        for all paths           // N rays
            sample direction phi_i, theta_i on hemisphere;
            y = trace(x, phi_i, theta_i);
            estimatedRadiance +=
                simpleStochasticRT(y, phi_i, theta_i)*BRDF
                *cos(theta_i)/pdf(phi_i, theta_i);
        estimatedRadiance /= #paths;
        estimatedRadiance /= (1-absorption)
    estimatedRadiance += Le(x, phi_i, theta_i)
    return(estimatedRadiance);
```

Listing 16.4: Simple stochastic ray-tracing algorithm.

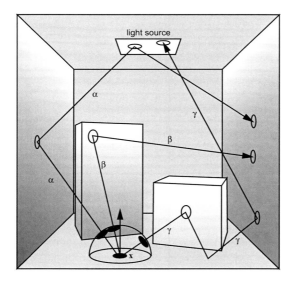

Figure 16.10. Tracing paths using simple stochastic ray tracing.

It is easy to verify that the expected value of $\langle I_{RR} \rangle$ equals I. If $f(x)$ is another recursive integral (as is the case in the rendering equation), the result of applying Russian roulette is that recursion stops with a probability equal to $\alpha = 1 - P$ for each evaluation point. The value α is called the absorption probability. Samples generated in the interval $[P, 1]$ will generate a function value equal to 0, but this is compensated by weighting the samples in $[0, P]$ with a factor $1/P$. Thus, the overall estimator still remains unbiased.

If α is small, the recursion will continue many times, and the final estimator will be more accurate. If α is large, the recursion will stop sooner, but the estimator will have a higher variance. For our simple path-tracing algorithm, this means that either we generate accurate paths having a long length or very short paths that provide a less accurate estimate. However, the final estimator will be unbiased.

In principle, we can pick any value for α, and we can control the execution time of the algorithm by picking an appropriate value. In global illumination algorithms, it is common for $1 - \alpha$ to be equal to the hemispherical reflectance of the material of the surface. Thus, dark surfaces will absorb the path more easily, while lighter surfaces have a higher chance of reflecting the path. This corresponds to the physical behavior of light incident on these surfaces.

Simple stochastic ray tracing. The complete algorithm for simple stochastic ray tracing is given in Listing 16.4, and is illustrated in Figure 16.10. Paths are traced starting at point $\mathbf{x}$. Path α contributes to the radiance estimate at $\mathbf{x}$, since it reflects off of the light source at the second reflection and is absorbed afterwards. Path γ also contributes, even though it is absorbed at the light source. Path β does not contribute, since it gets absorbed before reaching the light source.

16.5.2 Putting it All Together

We now have all the algorithms in place to build a full global illumination renderer using stochastic path tracing. The efficiency and accuracy of the complete algorithm will be determined by all of the following settings:

Number of viewing rays per pixel. The number of viewing rays N_p to be cast through the pixel, or more generally, the support of $h(\mathbf{p})$ (Equation (16.35)). A higher number of viewing rays eliminates aliasing and decreases noise.

Direct illumination. For direct illumination, a number of choices are necessary that will determine the overall efficiency:

- the total number of shadow rays N_d cast from each point $\mathbf{x}$;

- how a single light source is selected from among all the available light sources for each shadow ray;
- the distribution of the shadow rays over the area of a single light source.

Indirect illumination. The indirect illumination component is usually implemented using hemisphere sampling:

- number of indirect illumination rays N_i distributed over the hemisphere Ω_x;
- exact distribution of these rays over the hemisphere;
- absorption probabilities for Russian roulette in order to stop the recursion.

The complete algorithm for computing the global illumination for the entire image is given in schematic form in Listing 16.5.

It is obvious that the more rays we cast at each of the different choice points, the more accurate the solution will be. Also, the better we make use of importance sampling, the better the final image and the less objectionable noise there will be. The interesting question is, when given a total amount of rays one can cast per pixel, how should they best be distributed to reach a maximum level of accuracy for the full global illumination solution?

This is still very much an open problem in global illumination algorithms. There are some generally accepted "default" choices, but there are no hard and fast rules. It generally is accepted that branching out too much (i.e., recursively generating multiple rays at every surface point) at all levels of the tree is less efficient. Indeed, progressively more rays will be cast at each deeper level, while at the same time, the contribution of each of those individual rays to the final radiance value of the pixel will diminish. For indirect illumination, a branching factor of 1 is often used after the first level. Many implementations even limit the indirect rays to one per surface point, but then compensate by generating more rays through the area of the pixel. This approach is known as path tracing: many paths, without any branching (except for direct illumination), are cast. Each path by itself is a bad approximation of the total radiance, but many paths combined are able to produce a good estimate.

```
//stochastic ray tracing
computeImage(eye)
    for each pixel
        radiance = 0;
        H = integral(h(p));
        for each sample          // Np viewing rays
            pick sample point p within support of h;
            construct ray at eye, direction eye to p;
            radiance = radiance + rad(ray)*h(p);
        radiance = radiance/(#samples*H);

rad(ray)
    find closest intersection point x of ray with scene;
    return Le(x,dir) + computeRadiance(x, dir);

computeRadiance(x, dir)
    estimatedRadiance += directIllumination(x, dir);
    estimatedRadiance += indirectIllumination(x, dir);
    return(estimatedRadiance);

directIllumination (x, dir)
    estimatedRadiance = 0;
    for all shadow rays          // Nd shadow rays
        select light source k;
        sample point y on light source k;
        estimated radiance +=
            Le * BRDF * G(x,y) * V(x,y) /(pdf(k)pdf(y|k));
    estimatedRadiance = estimatedRadiance / #paths;
    return(estimatedRadiance);

indirectIllumination (x, dir)
    estimatedRadiance = 0;
    if (no absorption)           // Russian roulette
        for all indirect paths   // Ni indirect rays
            sample random direction on hemisphere;
            y = trace(x, random direction);
            estimatedRadiance +=
                compute_radiance(y, random direction) *
                BRDF * cos / pdf(random direction);
        estimatedRadiance = estimatedRadiance / #paths;
    return(estimatedRadiance/(1-absorption));
```

Listing 16.5: Complete global illumination algorithm.

16.5.3 Bidirectional Ray Tracing$^{\circledast}$

Stochastic ray tracing traces paths through the scene starting at the surface points that eventually end at the light sources (whether or not explicit light-source sampling is used). *Light tracing*, a variant path-tracing algorithm, does the opposite: paths are generated starting from the light sources, and contributions to relevant pixels are recorded. It is the dual algorithm of stochastic ray tracing.

Bidirectional ray tracing combines both approaches in a single algorithm and can be viewed as a two-pass algorithm in which both passes are tightly intertwined. Bidirectional ray tracing generates paths starting at the light sources and at the surface point simultaneously and connects both paths in the middle to find a contribution to the light transport between the light source and the point for which a radiance value needs to be computed. Bidirectional ray tracing was developed independently by both Lafortune [Lafo94] and Veach [Veac94].

The core idea of the algorithm is that one has the availability of two different path generators when computing a Monte Carlo estimate for the flux through a certain pixel:

- An eye path is traced starting at a sampled surface point $\mathbf{y}_0$ visible through the pixel. By generating a path of length k, the path consists of a series of surface points $\mathbf{y}_0, \mathbf{y}_1, \ldots, \mathbf{y}_k$. The length of the path is controlled by Russian roulette. The probability of generating this path can be composed of the individual pdf values of generating each successive point along the path.

- Similarly, a light path of length l is generated starting at the light source. This path, $\mathbf{x}_0, \mathbf{x}_1, \ldots, \mathbf{x}_l$, also has its own probability density distribution.

By connecting the endpoint $\mathbf{y}_k$ of the eye path with the endpoint $\mathbf{x}_l$ of the light path, a total path of length $k + l + 1$ between the pixel and the light sources is obtained. The probability density function for this path is the product of the individual pdfs of the light paths and eye paths.

Thus, an estimator for the flux Φ through the pixel using this single path is then given by

$$\Phi = \frac{K}{\text{pdf}(\mathbf{y}_0, \mathbf{y}_1, \ldots, \mathbf{y}_k, \mathbf{x}_l, \ldots, \mathbf{x}_1, \mathbf{x}_0)}, \qquad (16.37)$$

with

$$K = L_e(\mathbf{x}_0, \ldots) G(\mathbf{x}_0, \mathbf{x}_1) V(\mathbf{x}_0, \mathbf{x}_1) f_r(\mathbf{x}_1, \ldots) \ldots$$
$$G(\mathbf{x}_l, \mathbf{y}_k) V(\mathbf{x}_l, \mathbf{y}_k) f_r(\mathbf{y}_k, \ldots) \ldots$$
$$f_r(\mathbf{y}_1, \ldots) G(\mathbf{y}_1, \mathbf{y}_0) V(\mathbf{y}_1, \mathbf{y}_0) h(\mathbf{p}). \quad (16.38)$$

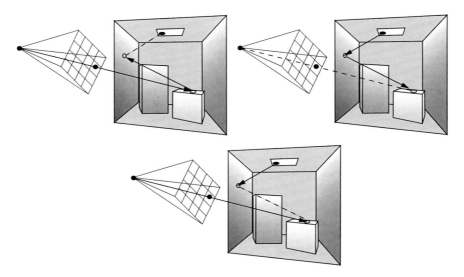

Figure 16.11. Different combinations for a path of length 3: eye path is of length 2, light path of length 0 (upper left); both eye path and light path of length 1 (middle); eye path is of length 0, light path of length 2 (upper right).

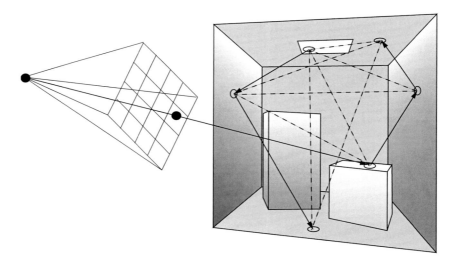

Figure 16.12. Reuse of all subpaths of both the eye path and the light path in a bidirectional ray-tracing algorithm.

Paths of a certain length can now be generated by using different combinations. For example, a path of length 3 could be generated by a light path of length 2 and an eye path of length 0; or by a light path of length 1 and an eye path of length 1; or by a light path of length 0 (a single point at the light source) and an eye path of length 2. These different combinations of generating a path of given length are shown in Figure 16.11.

Depending on the light transport mode, and the sequence of G, V, and f_r functions, some light distribution effects are better generated using either light paths or eye paths. For example, when rendering a specular reflection that is visible in the image, it is better to generate those specular bounces in the eye path. Similarly, the specular reflections in caustics are better generated in the light path. Generally, it is better to use the BRDF f_r to sample the next point or direction if f_r has sharp peaks. If f_r is mainly diffuse, the energy transport along the connection between the two paths will not be influenced by the value of the BRDF and, thus, will not possibly yield a low contribution to the overall estimator. Another advantage is that if light sources are concealed, it might be easier to generate light paths to distribute the light, rather than count on shadow rays to be able to reach the light source.

When implementing bidirectional path tracing, an eye path or light path of length $k - 1$ can be extended to a path of length k. Thus, we use the same subpath more than once. Intuitively, this means that if we have a light path and an eye path, we do not only connect the endpoints, but also all possible subpaths to each other (Figure 16.12). Care has to be taken that the Monte Carlo estimators are still correct. This can be achieved by optimally combining the sampling methods of each of the individual subpaths. More details and an extensive discussion can be found in [Veac97].

Figure 16.13. Left: Stochastic ray tracing; middle: bidirectional tracing using only light paths; right: full bidirectional ray tracing.

Figure 16.14. Bidirectional ray tracing. Note the extensive caustics, an effect difficult to achieve using stochastic ray tracing.

Figure 16.13 shows a simple scene, with a comparison of images generated by stochastic ray tracing, light tracing, and bidirectional ray tracing. In both images, the total number of paths is the same, so each image took an equal time to compute. Figure 16.14 shows a picture generated by bidirectional ray tracing, with a significant amount of caustics, which would have taken a long time to generate using stochastic ray tracing only.

16.5.4   Photon Mapping⊛

Photon mapping, introduced by Jensen [Jens01, Jens95, Jens96b, Jens96a], is a practical and robust two-pass algorithm that, like bidirectional path tracing, traces illumination paths both from the lights and from the viewpoint. However, unlike bidirectional path tracing, this approach caches and reuses illumination values in a scene for efficiency. In the first pass, *photons* are traced from the light sources into the scene. These photons, which carry flux information, are cached in a data structure, called the *photon map*. In the second pass, an image is rendered using the information stored in the photon map.

Photon mapping decouples photon storage from surface parameterization. This representation enables it to handle arbitrary geometry, including procedural geometry, thus increasing the practical utility of the algorithm. It is also not prone to meshing artifacts.

By tracing or storing only particular types of photons (i.e., those that follow specific types of light paths), it is possible to make specialized photon maps, just for that purpose. The best example of this is the caustic map, which is designed to capture photons that interact with one or more specular surfaces before reaching a diffuse surface. These light paths cause caustics. Traditional Monte Carlo sampling can be very slow at correctly producing good caustics. By explicitly capturing caustic paths in a caustic map, the photon-mapping technique can find accurate caustics efficiently.

One point to note is that photon mapping is a biased technique. Recall that in a biased technique, the bias is the potentially non-zero difference between the expected value of the estimator and the actual value of the integral being computed. However, since photon maps are typically not used directly, but are used to compute indirect illumination, increasing the photons eliminates most artifacts.

Pass 1: Tracing photons. The use of compact, point-based photons to propagate flux through the scene is key in making photon mapping efficient. In the first pass, photons are traced from the light sources and propagated through the scene just as rays are in ray tracing; i.e., they are reflected, transmitted, or absorbed. Russian roulette and the standard Monte Carlo sampling techniques described earlier are used to propagate photons. When the photons hit non-specular surfaces, they are stored in the photon map. To facilitate efficient searches for photons, a balanced kd-tree is used to implement this data structure.

As mentioned before, photon mapping can be efficient for computing caustics. A caustic is formed when light is reflected or transmitted through one or more specular surfaces before reaching a diffuse surface. To improve the rendering of scenes that include caustics, the algorithm separates out the computation of caustics from global illumination. Thus, two photon maps, a caustic photon map and a global photon map, are computed for each scene (Figure 16.15).

Caustic photon maps can be computed efficiently because caustics occur when light is focussed; therefore, not too many photons are needed to get a good estimate of caustics. Additionally, the number of surfaces resulting in caustics in typical scenes is often very small. Efficiency is achieved by shooting photons only towards this small set of specular surfaces.

The reflected radiance at each point in the scene can be computed from the photon map as follows. The photon map represents incoming flux at each point in the scene; therefore, the photon density at a point estimates the irradiance at that point. The reflected radiance at a point can then be computed by multiplying the irradiance by the surface BRDF.

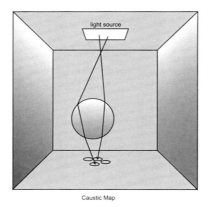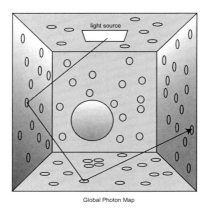

Caustic Map   Global Photon Map

Figure 16.15. Caustic map and global photon map. The caustic map captures photons which traverse through specular surfaces, while the global photon map represents all paths.

To compute the photon density at a point, the n closest photons to that point are found in the photon map. The photon density is then computed by adding the flux of these n photons and dividing by the projected area of the sphere in which these photons were located.

Pass 2: Computing images. The simplest use of the photon map would be to display the reflected radiance values computed above for each visible point in an image. However, unless the number of photons used is extremely large, this display approach can cause significant blurring of radiance, thus resulting in poor image quality. Instead, photon maps are more effective when integrated with a ray tracer that computes direct illumination and queries the photon map only after one diffuse or glossy bounce from the viewpoint is traced through the scene.

Thus, the final rendering of images could be done as follows. Rays are traced through each pixel to find the closest visible surface. The radiance for a visible point is split into direct illumination, specular or glossy illumination, illumination due to caustics, and the remaining indirect illumination. Each of these components is computed as follows:

- Direct illumination for visible surfaces is computed using regular Monte Carlo sampling.

- Specular reflections and transmissions are ray traced.

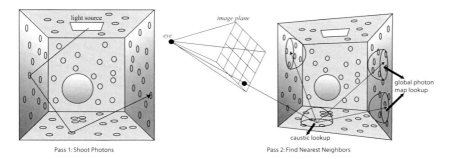

Pass 1: Shoot Photons Pass 2: Find Nearest Neighbors

Figure 16.16. Two passes of photon mapping in a Cornell box with a glass sphere. During pass 1, photons are traced and deposited on non-specular surfaces. During pass 2, global illumination is indirectly computed using the global photon map. For each indirect ray, the closest photons in the global photon map are found. Caustics are located by doing a similar look-up in the caustic map. Direct illumination and specular and glossy reflections are computed using ray tracing.

- Caustics are computed using the caustic photon map.

- The remaining indirect illumination is computed by sampling the hemisphere; the global photon map is used to compute radiance at the next recursion step.

Figure 16.16 shows a visualization of both passes of the photon-mapping algorithm.

16.6 Radiosity

Previously, we derived the radiosity linear system of equation to describe the energy equilibrium in a scene. This section will describe various solution strategies for solving the radiosity problem.

16.6.1 Classic Radiosity

The classic radiosity method consists of the following steps:

1. discretization of the input geometry in different patches i; for each resulting patch i, a radiosity value B_i will be computed;

2. computation of form factors F_{ij} (Equation (16.19)) for every pair of patches i and j;

3. numerical solution of the radiosity system of linear equations (Equation (16.18));

4. display of the solution, using any rendering algorithm that can display patches with a given color (radiosity) value B_i.

In practical implementations of the classic radiosity method, these steps are highly connected, e.g., form factors are only computed when they are needed when solving the system of equations; intermediate results can already be displayed during system solution; in adaptive or hierarchical radiosity algorithms [Cohe86, Hanr91], discretization is performed during system solution, etc.

Each of the above steps of the classic radiosity method is nontrivial. At first sight, one would expect that Step 3, solving the radiosity system, would be the main problem. Indeed, the size of the linear systems that need to be solved can be very large (one equation per patch; 100,000 patches or more is quite common). The system of linear equations is usually very well-behaved, such that simple iterative methods such as Jacobi or Gauss-Seidel iterations converge after relatively few iterations.

The main problems of the radiosity method are related to discretization of the scene into patches and the form factor computation. The patches should be small enough to capture illumination variations such as shadow boundaries. One of the basic assumptions of the radiosity method is that the radiosity $B(x)$ across each patch needs to be approximately constant. A higher number of patches usually solves for artifacts caused by discretization, but the number of patches shouldn't be too large, because this would result in exaggerated storage requirements and computation times. Between each pair of patches, a form factor needs to be computed. The number of form factors can thus be huge so that the mere storage of form factors in computer memory is a major problem. Each form factor also requires the solution of a nontrivial, four-dimensional integral (Equation (16.19)). The integral will be singular for adjacent patches, where the distance r_{xy} in the denominator of Equation (16.4) can possibly become 0. The integrand can also exhibit discontinuities of various degrees due to changing visibility (Figure 16.17).

Extensive research has been carried out in order to address these problems. Proposed solutions include specialized algorithms for form-factor integration such as the hemicube algorithm or shaft culling ray-tracing acceleration, discontinuity meshing, adaptive and hierarchical subdivision, clustering, form-factor caching strategies, the use of view importance, and higher-order radiosity approximations.

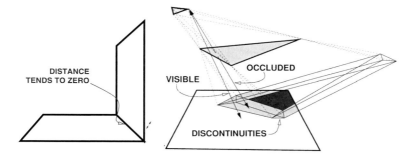

Figure 16.17. Form-factor difficulties: the form-factor integral contains the inverse square distance between points of both patches. This causes a singularity for adjacent patches. Changing visibility can also introduce discontinuities of various degrees in the form-factor integrand.

16.6.2 Form Factors

The radiosity of B_i of a single patch i is expressed as (see Equation (16.18))

$$B_i = B_{ei} + \rho_i \sum_j F_{ij} B_j. \tag{16.39}$$

The radiosity B_i at a patch i is the sum of two contributions. The first contribution consists of the self-emitted radiosity B_{ei}. The second contribution is the fraction of the (incident) irradiance $\sum_j F_{ij} B_j$ at i that is reflected. The form factor F_{ij} indicates the fraction of the irradiance on patch i that originates at patch j.

We can also rewrite the above equation by transforming radiosity values to flux values: $P_i = A_i B_i$ and $P_{ei} = A_i B_{ei}$. By multiplying both sides of the equation by A_i and using the symmetry between F_{ij} and F_{ji}, the following system of linear equations is obtained:

$$B_i = B_{ei} + \rho_i \sum_j F_{ij} B_j$$

$$\Leftrightarrow \quad A_i B_i = A_i B_{ei} + \rho_i \sum_j A_i F_{ij} B_j$$

$$\Leftrightarrow \quad A_i B_i = A_i B_{ei} + \rho_i \sum_j A_j F_{ji} B_j$$

$$\Leftrightarrow \quad P_i = P_{ei} + \sum_j P_j F_{ji} \rho_i. \tag{16.40}$$

This system of equation states that the total power P_i emitted by patch i consists of two parts: the self-emitted power P_{ei} and the power received and reflected from all other patches j. The form factor F_{ji} indicates the fraction of power emitted by j that arrives at i.

Since there is conservation of total energy in a scene, the total amount of power emitted by i and received on other patches j must equal P_i in a closed scene. Therefore, an important property of form factors is that they sum to 1:

$$\sum_j F_{ij} = 1. \tag{16.41}$$

The interpretation of the form factor F_{ij} being the fraction of power emitted by a patch i, that lands on a second patch j suggests that form factors can be estimated using a simple and straightforward simulation (Figure 16.18). Let i be the source of a number N_i of virtual particles (small energy packets) originating on a diffuse surface. The number N_{ij} of these particles that land on the second patch j yields an estimate for the form factor: $F_{ij} \approx F_{ij}N_{ij}/N_i$. Consider a particle originating at a uniformly chosen location $\mathbf{x}$ on S_i and being distributed over the hemisphere using a cosine-distributed direction with regard to the surface normal N_x at $\mathbf{x}$. The pdf $p(\mathbf{x}, \phi, \theta)$ is written as

$$p(\mathbf{x}, \phi, \theta) = \frac{\cos(\theta)}{\pi A_i}. \tag{16.42}$$

Let $\chi_j(\mathbf{x}, \phi, \theta)$ be a function that evaluates to 1 or 0 depending on whether or not the particle hits the patch j. The probability P_{ij} that the particle lands on patch

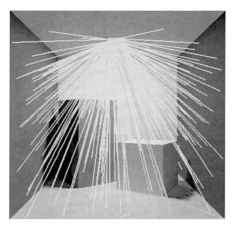

Figure 16.18. The fraction of local lines hitting a particular destination patch is an estimate for the form factor between source and destination.

j is then written as

$$P_{ij} = \int_{S_i} \int_{\Omega_x} \chi_j(\mathbf{x}, \phi, \theta) p(\mathbf{x}, \phi, \theta) dA_x d\omega \qquad (16.43)$$

$$= \frac{1}{A_i} \int_{S_i} \int_{S_j} \frac{\cos(\theta_i)\cos(\theta_j)}{\pi r_{xy}^2} V(\mathbf{x}, \mathbf{y}) dA_y dA_x \qquad (16.44)$$

$$= F_{ij}. \qquad (16.45)$$

Thus, when generating N_i particles from i, the expected number of hits on patch j equals $N_i F_{ij}$. The more particles used, the better the ratio N_{ij}/N_i will approximate F_{ij}. The variance of this estimator is $F_{ij}(1 - F_{ij})/N_i$. As mentioned before, however, we will not need to compute form factors explicitly. If we are given a patch i, we can select a subsequent patch j among all patches in the scene, with probability equal to the form factor F_{ij}, by shooting a ray from i.

16.6.3   The Jacobi Iterative Method for Radiosity[⊛]

We will outline one widely-used solving scheme for computing the radiosity so-lution in a scene, the so-called Jacobi iterative method, which is a method to solve systems of linear equations $\mathbf{x} = e + \mathbf{A}\mathbf{x}$ using a simple iteration scheme. Suppose a system with n equations and n unknowns is to be solved, where e, $\mathbf{x}$, and any approximation of $\mathbf{x}$ are n-dimensional vectors or points. The idea is to start with an arbitrary point $\mathbf{x}^{(0)}$. During each iteration, the current point $\mathbf{x}^{(k)}$ is transformed into the next point $\mathbf{x}^{(k+1)}$ by evaluating $\mathbf{x}^{(k+1)} = e + \mathbf{A}\mathbf{x}^{(k)}$. It can be shown that under certain conditions the sequence of points $\mathbf{x}^{(k)}$ will always converge to the same point $\mathbf{x}$, which is the solution of the system. The method will converge if the matrix norm of $\mathbf{A}$ is strictly less than 1.

The coefficient matrix in the radiosity or power system of equations fulfills this requirement. In the context of radiosity, vectors such as $\mathbf{x}$ and e correspond to a distribution of light power over the surfaces of a scene. Each Jacobi iteration consists of computing an additional single bounce of light interreflection, fol-lowed by re-adding self-emitted power. The equilibrium illumination distribution in a scene is the solution of this process.

We will now show three slightly different ways of how repeated single-bounce light interreflection steps can be used in order to solve the radiosity problem.

Regular gathering of radiosity. Let us first apply the above idea to the radios-ity system of equations. As the starting radiosity distribution, $B_i^{(0)} = B_{ei}$ can be chosen. The next approximation $B_i^{(k+1)}$ is then obtained by filling in the previous approximation $B^{(k)}$ in the right-hand side of Equation (16.18):

$$
\begin{aligned}
B_i^{(0)} &= B_{ei}, \\
B_i^{(k+1)} &= B_{ei} + \rho_i \sum_j F_{ij} B_j^{(k)}.
\end{aligned}
$$

(16.46)

The stochastic form-factor approximations described earlier can be used to compute all form factors F_{ij} for a fixed patch i simultaneously. The various iteration steps can be interpreted as gathering steps: In each step, the previous radiosity approximations $B_j^{(k)}$ for all patches j are *gathered* in order to obtain a new approximation for the radiosity $B^{(k+1)}$ at i.

Regular shooting of power. When applied to the power system, a *shooting* variant of the above iteration scheme follows:

$$
\begin{aligned}
P_i^{(0)} &= P_{ei}, \\
P_i^{(k+1)} &= P_{ei} + \sum_j P_j^{(k)} F_{ji} \rho_i.
\end{aligned}
$$

(16.47)

In each step of the resulting algorithm, the power approximation $P_i^{(k+1)}$ of all patches i, visible from j, will be updated based on $P_j^{(k)}$: j *shoots* its power towards all other patches i.

Incremental shooting of power. Each regular power-shooting iteration above replaces the previous approximation of power $P^{(k)}$ by a new approximation $P^{(k+1)}$. Similar to progressive refinement radiosity [Cohe88], it is possible to construct iterations in which *unshot* power is propagated rather than total power. An approximation for the total power is then obtained as the sum of increments $\Delta P^{(k)}$ computed in each iteration step:

$$
\begin{aligned}
\Delta P_i^{(0)} &= P_{ei}, \\
\Delta P_i^{(k+1)} &= \sum_j \Delta P_j^{(k)} F_{ji} \rho_i, \\
P_i^{(k)} &= \sum_{l=0}^{k} \Delta P_i^{(l)}.
\end{aligned}
$$

16.7 Conclusion

Global illumination algorithms have been in constant development since the publication of the first recursive ray-tracing algorithm in 1979. There has been a gradual evolution from simple algorithms, some of them deemed to be hacks by today's standards, to very advanced, fully physically based rendering algorithms.

It has become possible to generate an image that is indistinguishable from a photograph of a real scene. This has been achieved by carefully implementing and investigating the physical processes that form the basis of photorealistic rendering: light-material interaction and light transport. In each of these domains, extensive research literature is available. This chapter provides an overview of some of these aspects, mostly focusing on the light transport mechanism. As in most modern algorithms, it is strongly believed that a good understanding of all fundamental issues is the key to well-designed global illumination light transport algorithms.

Global illumination has not yet found its way into many mainstream applications, but some use has already been made in feature-animation films and, to a limited extent, in some computer games. High-quality rendering of architectural designs has become more common, and car manufacturers have become more aware of the possibilities of rendering cars in realistic virtual environments for glossy advertisements. It is therefore to be expected that global illumination will be used more frequently in future computer-graphics applications.

16.8 Exercises

1. Write a program to compute the integral of a one-dimensional function using Monte Carlo integration. Plot the absolute error versus the number of samples used. This requires that you do know the analytic answer to the integral, so use well-known functions such as polynomials.

2. Using the algorithm designed above, try to compute the integral for sine functions with increasing frequencies. How is the error influenced by the various frequencies over the same integration domain?

3. Implement an algorithm to generate uniform distributed points over a triangle in the 2D-plane. Start with a simple triangle first (connecting points $(0,0)$, $(1,0)$ and $(0,1)$), then try to generalize to a random triangle in the 2D plane.

How can such an algorithm be used to generate points on a triangle in 3D space?

4. Pick an interesting geometric solid in 3D: a sphere, cone, cylinder, ... Design and implement an algorithm to generate uniform distributed points on the surface of these solids. Visualize your results to make sure that the points are indeed distributed uniformly.

5. Study the original formulation of the rendering equation as introduced by Kajiya [Kaji86]. It is different from the radiance formulation as mostly used today. Explain the differences. Could these differences have an influence on the final algorithms?

6. Implement a simple stochastic ray tracer that is able to render scenes with direct illumination only. The type of geometric primitives that are included is not important, it can be limited to triangles and spheres only. Surfaces should have a diffuse BRDF, and area light sources should be included as well.

7. Add the computation of indirect illumination to your ray tracer. This requires the implementation of a sampling scheme over the hemisphere of directions around a surface point. Experiment with different values for the absorption value used in the Russian roulette termination scheme.

8. Add the direct and indirect illumination components together to render the full global illumination solution of a given scene. Design a user interface such that all different sampling parameters can be adjusted by the user before the rendering computation starts.

9. A glass sphere is resting on a diffuse surface. The transparent BRDF of the sphere is almost perfectly specular. A so-called caustic is formed on the diffuse floor, due to the focusing effect of the glass sphere. What problems will occur when rendering the caustic?

10. We want to render an outdoor scene at night, in which the only source of illumination is the full moon. The moon occupies a relatively small solid angle in the sky. However, being astronomy buffs, we have modeled the moon as a diffuse sphere without any self-emissive illumination, and the only real light source in our scene is the (non-visible) sun. In other words, all the light reaching our scene is light from the sun reflected at the moon.

Of course, our basic Monte Carlo path tracer does not know the concept of full moon.

11. Suppose we want to render a city at night, containing hundreds of different modeled light sources (street-lights, neon-signs, lit windows, . . .). Shooting a shadow ray to each of these light sources would mean a large amount of non-efficient work, since clearly not every light source contributes significantly to the illumination of every visible surface point. What optimization techniques would you use such that scenes like this can be rendered in a reasonable amount of time?

    A very similar problem can occur if the light source is textured (e.g. a stained glass window), effectively subdividing the light source into many different smaller light sources, each with uniform color and intensity.

12. We look at the same city, but from across the river next to the city. Now we see the entire city scene reflected in the water, including all different light sources. The water is modeled as a surface with many different little waves (e.g. using bump mapping) and as a perfect mirror-like surface with respect to reflection. For any given ray, the direction in which the ray will be reflected on the water can therefore not be predicted unless the intersection point and hence the surface normal is already known.

17

Basic Animation Techniques

A moving picture is worth a million words.
—Anonymous

17.1   Introduction

To *animate* literally means to give life. In motion pictures and computer animation, life is given by presenting a sequence of still images (or *frames*) in rapid succession. If this sequence of frames resembles our notion of movement and the frames are presented at a sufficiently high rate, then the human eye-brain duo perceives them as smooth motion, or *animation* (Figure 17.1). The minimum rate required to perceive smooth motion is around 12 frames per second (fps). Below that, the motion appears jerky as moving objects seem to jump from one point to another. In fact, the required fps is not constant but depends on the speed of movement of the objects as well as on illumination parameters. Modern theater films use 24 fps, and there are systems that use 48 or even 72 fps. Rates above 70 fps generally offer no improvement to a human observer.

The technology of animation goes back to the late nineteenth century. Technological inventions such as celluloid film (Goodwin, 1887), the Kinetoscope, which offered single-audience movie viewing (Edison, 1893), and the cinematograph which allowed multiple-audience movie viewing by projecting on a screen (Lumière, 1894) set the basis for what was to follow. The first attempts at creating serious animation content date back to the early twentieth century; early milestones are *The Enchanted Drawing* and *Humorous Phases of Funny Faces* (Black-

615

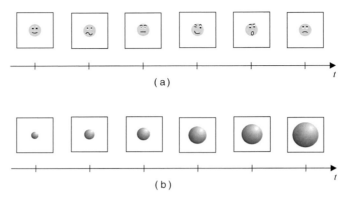

Figure 17.1. Examples of animation: (a) Sequence of frames of a face changing expressions; (b) frames of a moving observer sequence.

ton, 1900 and 1906), *Fantasmagorie* (Cohl, 1908), *Little Nemo* (McCay, 1911), and the well-known Disney cartoons from the 1920s. Since most cartoon animation was performed by *tweening*, the drawing of frames in between *keyframes*, it was only a matter of time before computers took up much of the tweening work using interpolation techniques (See Section 17.2.1). When computer graphics could produce realistic images, computer animation was introduced in feature films, with *Tron* and *Star Trek* (1982) being some of the first examples that contained significant computer-animated parts. Later on, entire films were made exclusively using computer animation; *Tin Toy* (1989) was one of the first.

Apart from films, animation is an integral part of interactive graphics applications, such as computer games. It also finds important applications in visualization, because it can be used to show the time-dependent behavior of a system.

Computer animation can be created by altering a multitude of parameters that can affect change between frames. Typical examples include the observer parameters that define the position and direction of view, the positions of objects within the scene, which can change dynamically between frames, as well as the characteristics of the objects themselves, such as color and size. These parameters are encoded in a large number of *animation variables*. As it is virtually impossible for an animator to explicitly define every animation variable for every frame, various *animation-control methods* have been developed which help the animator to work at a higher level. Examples include procedural and representational methods for animating rigid bodies and skeletal animation for animating human-like or animal-like characters. These methods use common low-level techniques such as interpolation, collision detection, and motion blur.

The rest of this chapter is organized as follows. First, common low-level techniques used in most animation-control methods are discussed. Then, higher-level animation-control methods are presented. These are grouped into *rigid-body animation, skeletal animation, deformable models,* and *particle systems,* and they are not mutually exclusive.

In addition to the above animation-control methods, the term *procedural animation* is used to refer to the encapsulation of the animation of an object in a procedure. Thus animation sequences can automatically be generated, often in real time. Particle systems (see Section 17.6) form the largest subclass of procedural animation. Rigid-body motion planning (see Section 17.3) and skeletal animation (see Section 17.4) can also be done procedurally. *Behavioral animation* is a subclass of procedural animation where the objects (characters) determine their own actions, taking into account their environment. Typical examples of behavioral animations include bird flocking [Reyn87], artificial fish [Tu94], and autonomous pedestrians [Shao06, Shao07]. Behavioral animation allows the production of animations automatically and perpetually.

Computer animation is a wide field, encompassing knowledge from computer science, film-making, physics, mathematics, and physiology. This chapter does not intend to provide an exhaustive coverage of the subject but rather to supply the essential reading for a computer graphics or visualization course. Interested readers may refer to specialized animation volumes.

17.2   Low-Level Animation Techniques

The techniques discussed in this section are useful in most animation-control methods and can thus be thought of as a common lower layer of tools. *Interpolation techniques*, for example, are the means by which the computer takes over the task of tweening. *Collision-detection* algorithms are essential in order to provide realism by detecting when moving objects collide so that appropriate action can be taken. Antialiasing in the time domain, or *motion blur*, is essential to most animations. *Morphing* allows the smooth transition from one graphical object to another (in a number of frames) and is the successor to the well-known effect of cross-fading in traditional motion pictures.

17.2.1   Interpolation, Keyframes, and Tweening

In the early 1900s, experienced artists were employed to produce *keyframes* of an animation sequence. At keyframes, there are significant changes in the animation

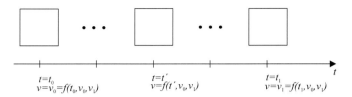

Figure 17.2. Tweening between keyframes at t_0 and t_1.

variables, such as the direction of motion. Then, less experienced (and less costly) artists would do the *tweening* work, i.e., fill the in-between frames to reach the desired frame rate (fps).

Today, animation-control methods use interpolation techniques to do the tweening work automatically. Extreme values of the animation variables are specified by the user. The values of animation variables are linked to frames of the animation and, since there is a one-to-one mapping between frames and time, they are ultimately linked to time. We can thus use parametric functions $f(t)$ to interpolate the animation variables between extreme values, e.g., v_0 and v_1, which are the interpolation control points (Figure 17.2).

Care must be taken in selecting the variables to be interpolated. A classic example is the movement of a stick that is fixed at one end (Figure 17.3). If the position of the free end of the stick is interpolated between two extreme points, then the stick will seem to shrink as it goes through the middle of its movement, regaining its original size as it approaches the end of the movement (Figure 17.3(a)). Instead, if the angle of rotation is interpolated, the desired result is obtained (Figure 17.3(b)).

Interpolation is based on the parameter t that represents time. Interpolation functions pass through the interpolation control points, so

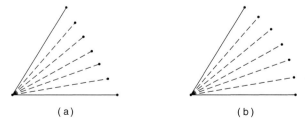

(a)   (b)

Figure 17.3. Importance of animation variable selection. Choosing the endpoint (a) and the rotation angle (b) as animation variable.

$$f(t_0) = v_0, \qquad f(t_1) = v_1,$$

for some t_0 and t_1. The simplest form of parametric interpolation function is the linear function

$$L(t) = (1-t)v_0 + tv_1, \qquad t \in [0,1]. \qquad (17.1)$$

Linear interpolation is used frequently but when more advanced change is required, we need to employ more complex forms. For example, the smooth path of an object that is not moving in a straight line could be described better by a function such as a Bézier function (see Chapter 7). The quadratic Bézier function interpolates between control values v_0 and v_2 using an extra value v_1 as an attractor:

$$B^2(t) = (1-t)^2 v_0 + 2t(1-t)v_1 + t^2 v_2, \qquad t \in [0,1]. \qquad (17.2)$$

The nth-degree Bézier function interpolates between v_0 and v_n using $n-1$ attractor values v_i, $i = 1, 2, \ldots, n-1$. These values attract the interpolation toward them, and they exert their maximum attraction at values i/n of the parameter t; for example, the quadratic Bézier function has the nearest value to v_1 at $t = 0.5$.

In general, the functions of parametric curves $\mathbf{X}(t)$ are good interpolation functions (see Appendix B). Their tangent vector $\mathbf{X}'(t)$ defines velocity, which is extremely useful if they describe motion. The arc length traveled along such a curve (see Section B.1.1) can be computed by integrating velocity (Equation (B.4)).

Unfortunately, the arc length traveled is not proportional to the time parameter t. Thus, for example, one cannot use constant differences of t to get constant arc lengths of travel on a general curve. The reparameterization of a curve by arc length s (see Section B.1.2) is therefore often required (Figure 17.4).

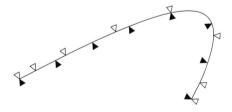

Figure 17.4. Points on a curve for constant differences of the parameter t ($\triangle$: not equidistant) and, after reparameterization, for constant differences of the parameter s ($\blacktriangle$: equidistant).

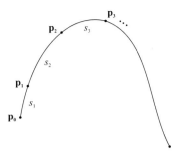

Figure 17.5. Arc lengths between points on a curve.

Point	Arc length
p_0	0
p_1	s_1
p_2	$s_1 + s_2$
p_3	$s_1 + s_2 + s_3$
...	...

Table 17.1.

However, reparameterization by arc length is not possible for every curve. In such cases a pre-computed set of arc lengths s_i for points on the curve can be used, as shown in Table 17.1 and Figure 17.5.

Then the point $\mathbf{p}'$ on the curve that corresponds to arc length s' can be approximated by linearly interpolating the points of the two nearest arc lengths s_i and s_{i+1} ($s_i \leq s' \leq s_{i+1}$):

$$\mathbf{p}' = \frac{s_{i+1} - s'}{s_{i+1} - s_i}\mathbf{p_i} + \frac{s' - s_i}{s_{i+1} - s_i}\mathbf{p_{i+1}}. \tag{17.3}$$

Interpolation of rotation.[⊛] Suppose that we express an arbitrary rotation as a synthesis of three basic rotations $\mathbf{R_x}(\theta_x) \rightarrow \mathbf{R_y}(\theta_y) \rightarrow \mathbf{R_z}(\theta_z)$. If we were to animate this by gradually incrementing θ_x, θ_y, and θ_z, we would encounter several problems. First, it is rather difficult to estimate the basic rotation angles that make up the required rotation about an arbitrary axis. Second, we would observe a "twisting" motion, since the rotations are applied sequentially and the object seems like it is rotating alternately about the three axes. And third, we may encounter a phenomenon known as *gimbal lock*. For example, suppose that in the first three rotation steps we rotate around x by θ_x, around y by $\frac{\pi}{2}$, and around z by θ_z. Then, as shown in Figure 17.6, the initial rotation around the x-axis by θ_x is obsolete since it could be replaced at the third step by rotating by $-\theta_x$ around z. One degree of freedom has thus been lost due to the fact that the middle rotation (by $\frac{\pi}{2}$ around y) made the positive x-axis coincide with the negative z-axis.

One solution is to use a composite rotation matrix about an arbitrary axis, such as the one proposed in Section 3.13. However a better solution is to use quaternions. Compared to the composite rotation matrix, quaternion rotation is

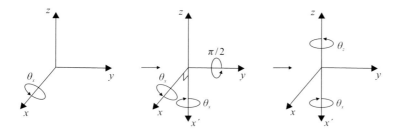

Figure 17.6. Gimbal lock.

more stable, requires fewer calculations, and consecutive rotations can be handled in a smooth way, as will be explained below.

The two extreme positions of the rotation can be represented by two unit quaternions, $q_0 = (1, \overrightarrow{\mathbf{0}})$ corresponding to the initial position (zero rotation) and $q_1 = (\sin\frac{\theta}{2}, \cos\frac{\theta}{2}\hat{\mathbf{n}})$ corresponding to the position after rotation by θ around the given axis with direction $\hat{\mathbf{n}}$. Unfortunately, linear interpolation between these two quaternions, of the form $q_L(t) = (1-t)q_0 + tq_1$, would not produce the expected smooth rotation between the two positions, but instead a motion that would accelerate towards the middle. This is due to the fact that quaternions representing rotations are unit quaternions, but the intermediate $q_L(t)$ generated by the linear interpolation formula are not unit quaternions and require normalization (division by their norm); therefore, equidistant time intervals correspond to non-equidistant rotations. Geometrically, all unit quaternions representing rotations lie on the surface of the four-dimensional unit hypersphere, but linear interpolation interpolates on the chord through them (see Figure 17.7(a) for the 2D analog).

The required smooth interpolation of the rotation can be achieved by performing *spherical linear interpolation* (*slerp*), that is, interpolation on the surface of the 4D unit hypersphere along the great arc (geodesic) between q_0 and q_1 (Figure 17.7(b) shows the 2D analog). The usual trigonometric rules hold on the 4D

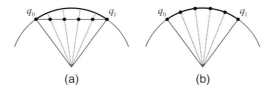

(a)   (b)

Figure 17.7. (a) Linear interpolation; (b) spherical linear interpolation.

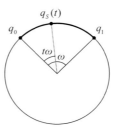

Figure 17.8. Interpolation of rotation using spherical linear interpolation

arc, and thus slerp is given by the formula (see Figure 17.8)

$$q_S(t) = q_0 \frac{\sin(1-t)\omega}{\sin \omega} + q_1 \frac{\sin t\omega}{\sin \omega}, \quad t \in [0,1], \qquad (17.4)$$

with $\omega = \frac{\theta}{2}$ the angle between the two quaternions.

Slerp solves the problem of smooth interpolation of rotation between two positions adequately. However, if a motion involves consecutive rotations around different axes (all passing through a common point), applying successive slerps between consecutive quaternions would produce a sharply changing motion, just as successive linear interpolations between consecutive points produce a polygonal line. This problem can be alleviated by using *smooth spherical curves* [Shoe85], which are similar to Bézier and spline curves (Chapter 7) but employ spherical linear interpolation instead of (simple) linear interpolation.

Interpolation of rotation using quaternions eliminates the problems of traditional animation of rotation mentioned earlier. Since any rotation is expressed directly using an axis and an angle, the intermediate angles are straightforward to compute (using slerp), and their application yields the expected result. Furthermore, the "twisting" motion and gimbal lock are not an issue since the rotation is performed in one step and not as a sequence of basic rotations.

17.2.2 Collision Detection

Collision detection[1] has received much attention as it finds applications in fields such as robotics and CAD/CAM, in addition to computer animation. However the requirements of each field are slightly different. In computer animation, an approximate solution is often preferred over a slow solution. Collision detection libraries exist that can save a lot of implementation time.

---

[1] Also known as *interference* or *contact* detection.

Both theoretical work from researchers in computational geometry and practical collision-detection algorithms are available. This section does not attempt to present the large body of work on collision detection (which is worth a book on its own right) but rather to explore alternative collision detection strategies for polyhedral objects. The interested reader is referred to surveys on the subject; Lin et al. classify collision detection approaches according to the object representation used [Lin98] while Jimenez et al. classify them according to their algorithmic characteristics [Jime01].

Collision detection between N objects requires solving the two-object problem $O(N^2)$ times, although optimizations are possible for special cases by exploiting *time coherence*, i.e., the property that most scene objects change little or predictably between frames. Here we shall consider the basic two-object collision detection problem.

A general way to handle the collision detection problem is to compute for each moving 3D object its 4D *extruded volume*, which consists of the spatiotemporal set of points occupied by the moving object [Came90]. Then, a collision between two objects exists if and only if their extruded volumes intersect; Figure 17.9 shows an example for 2D objects.

Unfortunately the computation of the extruded volume for a general object is not a simple task. Two simplification approaches have therefore been developed.

The first is to consider the *sweep volume* by disregarding the time parameter; Figure 17.9 shows an example for 2D objects. The sweep volume of a 3D object

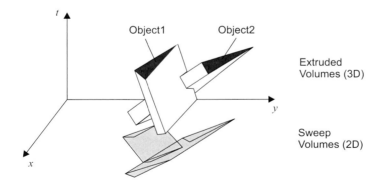

Figure 17.9. Intersection of extruded volumes (above) is necessary and sufficient for a collision. Intersection of sweep volumes (below) is necessary but not sufficient for a collision (example for 2D objects).

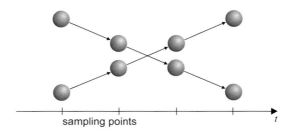

Figure 17.10. Collisions may be missed if the temporal sampling points are too sparse.

consists of the 3D spatial points defined by the motion of the object. Intersection of sweep volumes is necessary but not sufficient for a collision. To make it sufficient, the relative motion of the two objects must be considered, which may be quite complicated.

The second simplification approach is to *sample discrete points in time* and test for a collision between the two 3D objects themselves. If the sampling points are chosen too sparsely, a collision can be missed (Figure 17.10), while if they are chosen too densely, the computational cost rises sharply. A solution is to perform adaptive sampling, by selecting as the next temporal sampling point the one at which a collision can possibly occur. A simple adaptive sampling strategy is to relate a lower bound on the distance of the two objects to an upper bound in their relative velocities [Cull86].

Whichever method is used to capture motion, a basic intersection test between polyhedral objects must be used in the inner loop. For two convex polyhedral objects with m and n vertices, this costs $O(n+m)$ time [Lin91,Jime01], as the problem reduces to detecting if there is a plane that separates the convex hulls of two sets of points. For general polyhedral objects with convex faces, the collision test can be replaced by a check for intersection of the boundaries of the two objects.[2] To test for intersection of the boundaries, one can examine each edge of one object with every face of the other object for penetration. This costs $O(nm)$, but optimizations are possible. In the most general case of arbitrary polyhedra, which is rare in practice, few approaches exist; one way is to decompose the general polyhedra into their convex parts.

---

[2]Disregarding the case where one object is contained within the other, which can be easily detected by testing their bounding volumes.

Even for the simplest types of object, the collision tests are expensive since they have to be repeated for every object pair and for every frame. *Bounding volumes* are commonly used to quickly decide if two objects *A* and *B* potentially collide (see Section 5.6.1). In animation, the bounding volumes are often extended to enclose the extruded volume in 4D space or the sweep volume in 3D space.

17.2.3 Temporal Antialiasing

In feature films, it is common to observe the streaking effect produced by fast-moving objects. This is caused if the shutter speed[3] of the camera is slow relative to the speed of a moving object and, hence, captures it at a continuum of positions (Figure 17.11). It is known as *motion blur*. If a single frame of a film is observed, fast-moving objects appear "streaky" and blurred. Motion blur is usually not annoying because the human eye operates in a similar way.

In computer animation the situation is slightly different. Each frame is created for a point in time that corresponds to an infinitely high shutter speed, or infinitely small exposure time. The effect is that moving objects appear "jumpy," i.e., they seem to move from position to position in a discrete way across frames. This is known as *temporal aliasing*. It occurs because the frames of a computer animation represent a discretization of time, just like pixels of a frame represent a discretization of space in the generation of still images.

Figure 17.11. Motion blur.

---

[3]The slower the shutter speed the longer the period of exposure of each film frame.

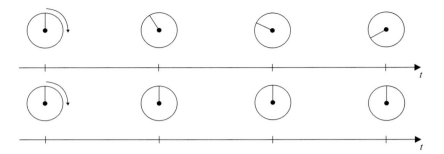

Figure 17.12. The wagon-wheel effect. Single-spoked wheel shown for simplicity.

Another classic occurrence of temporal aliasing, observable both in feature films and computer animation, is the wagon-wheel effect. A turning wheel whose image is sampled at a discrete rate, either by capturing it on film or by lighting it by a stroboscopic light, can appear to be rotating slower, backwards, or not at all. This is well known to Western fans (and takes its name from Western wagon wheels) but can be produced by any regularly spoked wheel, e.g., a helicopter blade. It happens because the brain merges successive positions of the spokes based on the minimum distance between them. Thus, if the wheel is rotating just below the fps rate, it appears to be rotating backwards (Figure 17.12 (top)); if it is rotating at exactly the fps rate, it appears to be in the same position at every frame (Figure 17.12 (bottom)); and if it is rotating just above the fps rate, it seems to be rotating much slower than it actually is.

One way to reduce temporal aliasing in pre-rendered computer animation[4] is to increase the sampling rate, i.e., the fps, but that is often fixed beyond the control of the animation producer. We therefore have to resort to *temporal antialiasing* techniques, which effectively introduce motion blur to computer animations.

Temporal antialiasing is handled in a manner similar to the post-filtering technique in spatial antialiasing (see Section 2.8.2). The main difference is that it is performed in the time dimension (Figure 17.13). The steps are as follows:

1. Sample at k times the desired fps rate creating virtual frames I_v.

2. Low-pass filter the virtual frames to eliminate high frequencies that cause temporal aliasing.

---

[4]In real-time animation, such as games, temporal antialiasing is considered a luxury, since it is hard enough to keep the fps rate sufficiently high to avoid flicker.

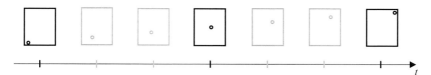

Figure 17.13. Virtual frames (all frames) and final frames (black frames only).

3. Re-sample the virtual frames at the desired fps rate to produce the final frame I_f.

The low-pass filtering is achieved by a one-dimensional convolution filter h (see Appendix E), for example

| 1 | 2 | 4 | 2 | 1 |

A typical convolution operation is performed. The filter weights are multiplied by the virtual frames and summed to produce the final frame:

$$I_f^i = \sum_{p=0}^{k-1} I_v^{i*k+p} \cdot h(p). \tag{17.5}$$

As in spatial antialiasing, k is chosen to be odd in order to have a middle sampling point *on* the final frame. The weights of the convolution filter must be normalized, i.e., $\sum_{p=0}^{k-1} h(p) = 1$.

17.2.4 Morphing

Morphing is a technique that transforms one *graphical object* into another. It has been extensively applied to images, often to morph facial images (Figure 17.14(a)). Morphing is, however, more general and the graphical objects to which it can be applied range from images to surface models to volumetric models. Morphing can be used on its own or as a component that facilitates the smooth transition between graphical objects in higher-level animation techniques.

Morphing is the successor to *cross-fading*, a traditional motion-picture technique that gradually fades one image into another. Morphing is more general as it involves the change of both the *shape* and the *visual attributes* (such as color and texture) and is applicable to various graphical objects, not just images. For images, morphing can produce more convincing results than cross-fading.

Morphing uses *warping*, a unary function that changes the shape of a graphical object. Given a graphical object G whose shape is represented by a set of points

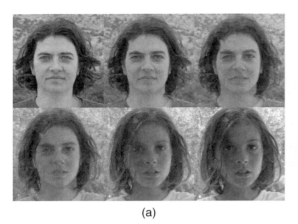
(a)

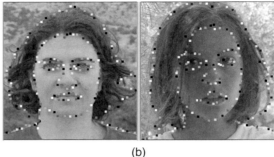
(b)

Figure 17.14. An example of a morph sequence between two facial images: (a) successive frames of the morph sequence; (b) using points to mark corresponding features on the two images.

s in n-dimensional space ($s \subseteq \mathbb{R}^n$), the warp function W produces a new set of points that define the transformed shape, $s' = W(s)$.

Morphing is a binary function that takes two graphical objects as input and produces another graphical object as output. Let $G_1 = (a_1, s_1)$ and $G_2 = (a_2, s_2)$ be two graphical objects whose shapes are represented by s_1 and s_2 and whose attributes by a_1 and a_2, respectively. Morphing between G_1 and G_2 can be split into four steps (Figure 17.15):

1. *Feature specification.* Corresponding features on G_1 and G_2 are determined, usually manually. Let f_1 and f_2 be the corresponding feature sets.

2. *Warp* the shapes s_1 and s_2 into s_1' and s_2' based on an interpolated set of features f'.

3. *Blend* s_1' and s_2', i.e., define an intermediate shape $s*$.

4. *Combine* a_1 and a_2 for $s*$, producing $a*$ and thus a new graphical object $G* = (a*, s*)$.

At the feature specification stage, corresponding features of the two graphical objects are established. This usually involves the user specifying pairs of corresponding points, lines, or curves on the two graphical objects (Figure 17.14(b)). Some automated methods for feature specification also exist.

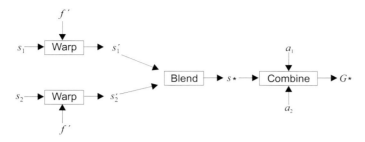

Figure 17.15. Morphing between two graphical objects $G_1 = (a_1, s_1)$ and $G_2 = (a_2, s_2)$ to produce a new graphical object $G* = (a*, s*)$.

The warp operation $W: s \rightarrow s'$ transforms a shape according to a transformed set of features f', which is the result of interpolating f_1 and f_2; the warp transforms s_1 and s_2 according to f'. There are many ways of defining W, including barycentric mapping, field-based mapping, or as a multi-pass spline mesh.

In barycentric mapping, f_1 and f_2 are corresponding point sets. A triangulation is computed on these point sets. Then a point $\mathbf{p}$ in s_1 maps to a point $\mathbf{p}'$ in s_1' with the same barycentric coordinates relative to the triangle that contains it. Let $\mathbf{p} = b_1\mathbf{v_1} + b_2\mathbf{v_2} + b_3\mathbf{v_3},^5$ where $\mathbf{v_1}$, $\mathbf{v_2}$, and $\mathbf{v_3}$ are the vertices of the triangle of f_1 feature points that contains $\mathbf{p}$ in s_1. Then $\mathbf{p}' = b_1\mathbf{v_1'} + b_2\mathbf{v_2'} + b_3\mathbf{v_3'}$, where $\mathbf{v_1'}$, $\mathbf{v_2'}$, and $\mathbf{v_3'}$ are the corresponding f' feature points. The situation is similar for s_2.

In field-based mapping, the features can be points, vectors, or more complex shapes. Each pair of corresponding features defines a different mapping for a point in s_1. The final mapping is computed by considering the fields of all feature pairs, which are weighted by such parameters as distance from the feature and size of the feature.

For example, if vectors are used as features, then field-based mapping can be defined as follows. Let $\overrightarrow{\mathbf{v_i}}$ be a feature vector in f_1 and $\overrightarrow{\mathbf{v_i'}}$ be the corresponding transformed vector in f' (i.e., the result of interpolation between $\overrightarrow{\mathbf{v_i}}$ and the corresponding vector in f_2). The mapping of a point $\mathbf{p}$ in s_1 defined by this feature vector is (see Figure 17.16)

$$W_i(\mathbf{p}) = \mathbf{a_i'} + u\overrightarrow{\mathbf{v_i'}} + v\bot\hat{\mathbf{v_i'}}, \qquad (17.6)$$

$^5 b_1 + b_2 + b_3 = 1.$

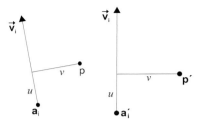

Figure 17.16. Warp mapping defined by a vector pair.

where $\mathbf{a_i'}$ is the base of $\overrightarrow{\mathbf{v_i'}}$, $\perp\hat{\mathbf{v_i'}}$ is the unit vector normal to $\overrightarrow{\mathbf{v_i'}}$, and u,v define $\mathbf{p}$ with respect to $\overrightarrow{\mathbf{v_i}}$ (in proportion to its magnitude). The final mapping for $\mathbf{p}$, taking all feature vectors into account, is then

$$W(\mathbf{p}) = \mathbf{p} + \frac{\sum_{i=1}^{n} b_i(W_i(\mathbf{p}) - \mathbf{p})}{\sum_{i=1}^{n} b_i}, \qquad (17.7)$$

where $W_i(\mathbf{p}) - \mathbf{p}$ is the displacement defined by feature i, n is the number of features, and b_i is the weight of feature i, which can be defined as

$$b_i = \frac{|\overrightarrow{\mathbf{v_i}}|^m}{d(\overrightarrow{\mathbf{v_i}}, \mathbf{p})^2}, \qquad (17.8)$$

where $d(\overrightarrow{\mathbf{v_i}}, \mathbf{p})$ is the distance from point $\mathbf{p}$ to vector $\overrightarrow{\mathbf{v_i}}$. The situation is similar for s_2. Note that field-based mapping is not one-to-one. It is therefore possible that some regions of the new graphical object $G*$ will be undefined; so it is common to use a *reverse mapping* from $G*$ onto G_1 and G_2. For example, in the case of images, the pixels of $G*$ are mapped onto pixels of G_1 and G_2.

Once s_1 has been warped to s_1' and s_2 has been warped to s_2', it is necessary to blend s_1' and s_2' in order to produce the intermediate shape $s*$. This is not always straightforward as the two shapes may differ in such characteristics as topology and genus, and these differences must be addressed by blending techniques. In the case of images, the blending step can be omitted.

Finally the attribute sets a_1 and a_2 are combined into $a*$ and assigned to regions of $s*$ (e.g., to vertices or pixels). The combination usually involves interpolation, and the attributes to be combined are determined from the established correspondences in the topologies of G_1 and G_2.

A static graphical object G_1 (such as an image) can be morphed into another static graphical object G_2 over time, by repeating the latter three steps of the mor-

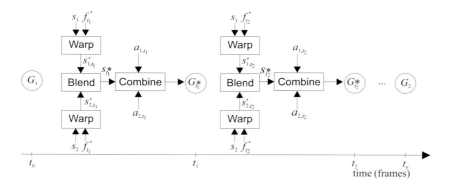

Figure 17.17. Morphing static graphical objects; the circled objects represent the morph sequence.

phing process for interpolated values of the features, thus generating an animation sequence $G_1, G*_{t_1}, G*_{t_2}, ..., G_2$ (Figure 17.17).

A dynamic graphical object $G_{1,t_0}, G_{1,t_1}, G_{1,t_2}, ..., G_{1,t_n}$ (such as an animation representing a talking face) can be morphed into another dynamic graphical object $G_{2,t_0}, G_{2,t_1}, G_{2,t_2}, ..., G_{2,t_n}$ by repeating all four morphing steps for corresponding (static) instances of the dynamic objects (e.g., corresponding frames) and generating a new dynamic graphical object $G_{1,t_0}, G*_{\frac{1}{n-1},t_1}, G*_{\frac{2}{n-2},t_2}, ..., G_{2,t_n}$ which progressively moves away from the first and approaches the second graphical object (Figure 17.18). The first index of $G*$ represents the morph distance from G_1 and G_2, which corresponds to the interpolation factor for the feature sets.

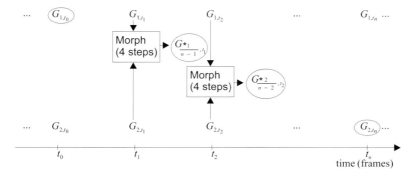

Figure 17.18. Morphing dynamic graphical objects; the circled objects represent the morph sequence.

Morphing has been extensively studied due to its many applications. These are not limited to animation special effects but include medical imaging, correction of lens distortion, and accelerated rendering. Several generalizations have also been proposed, such as morphing between more than two graphical objects. The interested reader is referred to a specialized source, such as [Gome99].

17.3   Rigid-Body Animation

Rigid-body animation techniques use only rigid transformations of objects to create animation sequences. Rigid transformations are a subclass of affine transformations and are made up of translation, rotation and combinations of the two (see Section 3.10). Rigid-body transformations do not deform objects.

A central issue in rigid-body animation is *motion planning*. Motion planning refers to the specification of the trajectory of an object and of such physical parameters as velocity and acceleration along the trajectory. It is related to *path planning*, a well-researched area in robotics for finding a collision-free path for the movement of a robot. This is a complex problem[6] and probabilistic approaches have been developed [Barr97, Plak05].

In basic motion planning, it is desirable to ensure *continuity* of motion and to be able to *specify physical parameters* along the trajectory. Continuity can be established by using a continuous parametric curve, such as a Bézier or B-spline, to define the trajectory. Unfortunately such curves are not parameterized by arc length, and it is therefore not directly possible to define physical parameters, such as velocity. If arc length reparameterization is not simple for a specific curve, we can resort to interpolations on a pre-computed table of arc lengths (see Section 17.2.1).

In order to reduce the tediousness of specifying trajectories but also to provide realistic motion, frameworks have been developed that allow the animator to specify the *what* of a motion (e.g., initial and final position), and they fill in the *how* of the motion (e.g., trajectory with plausible motion parameters) using a *physical model* [Witk88, Ngo93]. They employ a set of physical constraints that lead to the solution of a system of equations. Let $q(t)$ be a state vector that describes the characteristics of motion (e.g., position and velocity) of one or more

---

[6]It is known as the *mover's problem*, and its objective is to decide if there exists a collision-free path that moves a polyhedral object from an initial to a final position in an environment of static polyhedral obstacles. In the general case, where the object to be moved consists of a set of polyhedra linked together at certain vertices (see Section 17.4), the mover's problem is *PSPACE*-hard [Reif79].

objects at time t. The differential motion behavior can be described by

$$\frac{d}{dt}q(t) = F(t,q(t)), \qquad (17.9)$$

where F is the physical model. The motion characteristics at time t are obtained by integrating F:

$$q(t) = q_0 + \int_{t_0}^{t} F(t,q(t))dt, \qquad (17.10)$$

where q_0 is the initial state vector at t_0.

More recently, such systems have become interactive, allowing the animator to edit the parameters of motion at desirable points along the trajectory [Popo00]; the system then re-estimates a physically plausible motion.

17.4   Skeletal Animation

In Chapter 9, we saw how geometric entities can be linked in a hierarchical manner to form a scene-graph tree. Complex rigid-body animation can be achieved as the cumulative effect of many simple transformations applied to a geometry node as the hierarchy is traversed. In fact, geometry nodes need not necessarily be terminal nodes in a network of associations among scene entities. Objects can be linked in a chain of control to make the motion of one or more geometric elements dependent on the motion of a parent entity, thus creating a *kinematic chain*. In such an object configuration, child nodes are animated relative to their parent's local coordinate system. The actual motion of each node in a kinematic chain is determined by the transformations on all previous (higher) nodes in the hierarchy; this type of modeling can be very advantageous for the animation of articulated and linked or hinged objects.

The usefulness of a hierarchy of kinematic chains as a tool for directly modeling the animation-control layer of objects (*rigging*) is limited to discrete, rigid bodies (e.g., a robotic arm). Most articulated models that need to be animated are soft, deformable bodies with no discrete parts, as in the case of *character animation*, where humaniform or other models perform a complex motion by deforming a continuous mesh according to structural constraints imposed by their internal skeleton and soft-tissue behavior.

The primary animation method for characters or other deformable articulated structures is *skeletal animation*. A polygonal mesh that is the actual renderable deformable geometry (called *skin*), is animated by moving the individual vertices that it consists of according to the motion of a hierarchy of nodes linked in a kinematic chain that forms a *skeleton* for the body (Figure 17.19). These nodes are called *bones* and are rigidly transformed relative to each other, defining an articulated motion in time. The vertices of the skin are associated with one or more bones using weights that define how the motion of each bone affects a particular vertex. If vertex **v** follows the motion of bone J_i, then the weight w_j is 1 only

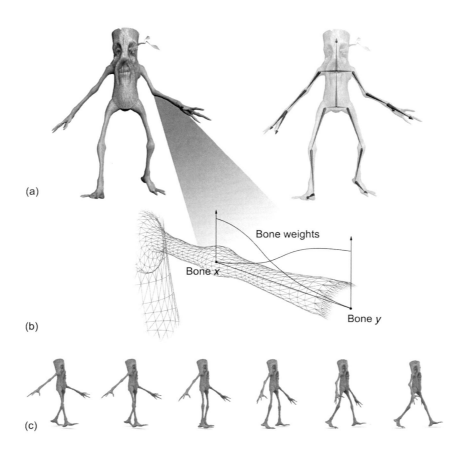

Figure 17.19. Skeletal animation. (a) Rigging of an animated character mesh (skin) with a bone system. (b) Weight variation of skin vertices between bone *x* and bone *y*. (c) The character skin in motion, under the influence of the bone kinematic chain transformations.

for $j = i$. When the skin vertices are associated with one bone each, the resulting animation of the skin resembles the motion of rigid connected bodies and creates unnatural-looking folds and stretched polygons. To achieve a realistic result with gradually bending surface patches at joint locations and smooth stretching of the skin between them, each vertex should depend on the motion of multiple adjacent bones and, therefore, needs to have more than one non-zero weight w_j. The sum of all weights w_j for a vertex $\mathbf{v}$ must be equal to 1.

In order to efficiently create a skeletal animation sequence, bones are placed inside the skin at the same reference frame and then connected to form the skeleton. During the construction of the skeleton and the assignment of weights, the polygonal mesh represents a *rest pose* of the model that is only used for the skinning procedure and is chosen in such a way as to facilitate the easy adjustment of weights. Usually, the initial assignment of vertex weights is done by choosing the closest bones to a vertex and taking the normalized distances of the vertex from them as the corresponding weight; all other dependencies are assigned a zero value. For bipeds, the most convenient pose to create a model for skinning is the crucifixion pose with the legs spread out, because it ensures minimum interference between different parts of the mesh. For example, if an arm is resting beside the torso, some of the vertices on it could be accidentally assigned non-zero weights from the torso bones and vice versa.

Let us now examine how the motion of a vertex $\mathbf{v}$ is derived from the corresponding animation of the kinematic chain (Figure 17.20). For the moment, we will focus on a single dependency between $\mathbf{v}$ and a bone J_i. The local coordinate system of a bone J_i in rest pose is defined relative to its parent bone J_{i-1} according to a rigid transformation (Figure 17.20):

$$\mathbf{M}(J_i) = \mathbf{T}_i \mathbf{R}_i. \tag{17.11}$$

By recursively applying all consecutive transformations up to the root bone J_0, we get the WCS coordinates of bone J_i in rest pose:

$$J_i = \left(\prod_{j=0}^{i} \mathbf{T}_j \mathbf{R}_j \right) \cdot \mathbf{o} = \mathbf{A}_i \cdot \mathbf{o}, \tag{17.12}$$

where $\mathbf{o}$ is the WCS origin. If the orientation of a bone does not participate in any calculation (e.g., bend limit check), the skeleton can be frozen in the rest pose, in which case only the offsets (T_i) are required in Equations (17.11) and (17.12).

If the length of the bones remains fixed during animation (which is a reasonable constraint in most character animations), the only part that differentiates the

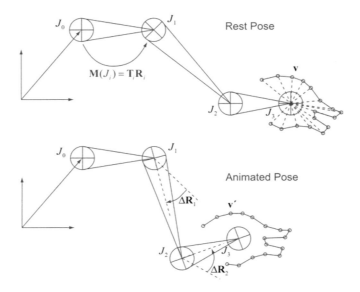

Figure 17.20. Rigid transformation calculation for an animated kinematic chain and skin vertices.

pose of a joint relative to its parent at an arbitrary time is an extra rotation $\Delta \mathbf{R}_i$ relative to the rest pose [Kava03]. The animated joint location J_i' is expressed with regard to its parent according to the following transformation:

$$\mathbf{M}'(J_i) = \mathbf{T}_i \mathbf{R}_i \Delta \mathbf{R}_i. \tag{17.13}$$

As in Equation (17.12), the animated bone J_i' is expressed relative to the origin of the WCS as (Figure 17.20)

$$J_i' = (\prod_{j=0}^{i} \mathbf{T}_j \mathbf{R}_j \Delta \mathbf{R}_j) \cdot \mathbf{o}. \tag{17.14}$$

In order to calculate the new position $\mathbf{v}'$ of a vertex $\mathbf{v}$ on the skin mesh in WCS coordinates after applying the animation to the kinematic chain, we first need to express the point in the local reference frame of the bone it depends on:

$$\mathbf{v}(J_i) = (\prod_{j=0}^{i} \mathbf{T}_j \mathbf{R}_j)^{-1} \cdot \mathbf{v} = (\prod_{j=i}^{0} \mathbf{R}_j^{-1} \mathbf{T}_j^{-1}) \cdot \mathbf{v} = \mathbf{A}_i^{-1} \cdot \mathbf{v}. \tag{17.15}$$

Then, we can apply the transformation of Equation (17.14) to the relative position and obtain the altered location of the dependent vertex at the given time:

$$\mathbf{v}' = (\prod_{j=0}^{i} \mathbf{T}_j \mathbf{R}_j \Delta \mathbf{R}_j) \cdot \mathbf{v}(J_i) = \mathbf{F}_i \mathbf{A}_i^{-1} \cdot \mathbf{v}. \qquad (17.16)$$

When a vertex depends on more than one bone of the skeleton, the matrices $\mathbf{F}_i \mathbf{A}_i^{-1}$ of the nodes are combined according to the assigned weights w_i to produce a single transformation that is then applied to the original point on the skin:

$$\mathbf{v}' = \sum_{i=0}^{N} (w_i \mathbf{F}_i \mathbf{A}_i^{-1}) \cdot \mathbf{v}, \qquad (17.17)$$

where $\sum_{i=0}^{N} w_i = 1$. Skeletal animation is an invaluable tool for both real-time animation and photo-realistic rendering. The incremental bone rotations $\Delta \mathbf{R}_i$ can be calculated either by forward or by inverse kinematics. Alternatively, they can be indirectly estimated from new locations of the joints, in the case where the end positions are available via *motion capture* of body markers on actual moving persons or animals. In *forward kinematics*, the local coordinate system of each bone of an articulated object is determined by the cumulative transformation of Equation (17.14) using as input the rotational parameters of the rotation transformations (angles or quaternions). In *inverse kinematics*, a terminal bone called end-effector is set to the desired pose relative to the WCS, and the parameters of the bone rotations are estimated by solving a system of equations of bone offsets and angular velocities. For more details see [Pare01].

17.5 Physically-Based Deformable Models

For modeling and animation of complex objects, one can use the deformation of B-spline curves and surface patches (see Sections 7.3 and 7.6) and their generalization to non-uniform rational B-spline curves and surface patches (see Section 7.4.2). These geometric entities are used extensively in the CAD industry and to some extent in animation. Designers and animators modify the shape of these types of curves and surfaces through manipulation of their degrees of freedom, primarily their control points (and for rational cases of their weights as well). Additional modifications are possible through changes of their knot vectors. Such curves and surfaces typically get generated via an approximation or interpolation of some primitive point data or, in the case of surfaces, through further interpolation of some set of curves. As a result of these processes, geometric design and animation is difficult because of the indirect nature of the operations involved and the need to also execute further operations on the resulting entities to make them smoother and more fair.

To address these restrictions, physically-based deformable models were developed, see for example [Barr84, Meta96b, Terz87, Celn90, Terz91, Terz94]. These models couple geometric modeling ideas and methods with physically-based laws (including inertial, damping, and elasticity effects) and result in dynamic geometric models that can respond to concentrated and distributed forces in a natural and intuitive way (see also Section 8.7 for the case of an initially straight curve (bar) with bending effects present). The resulting modeling paradigm allows the easy generation and animation of complex sculptured shapes (curves, surfaces, and volumes) with inherent smoothness and fairness, qualities that are a by-product of the formulation of such physically-based deformable models,

A short introduction to this method for the case of "elastically deformable" curves is provided below. A general treatment for curves, surfaces and solids with applications in graphics, animation, computer vision and medical imaging can be found in more specialized monographs, e.g., [Meta96a], which also includes a literature review on this subject. For the case of curves (modeled as initially straight beams under tension), an example of a partial differential equation of motion under the influence of distributed forces, suitable for shape generation and animation is given as follows (adapted from [Celn90]):

$$\mu \frac{\partial^2 \mathbf{w}}{\partial t^2} + \gamma \frac{\partial \mathbf{w}}{\partial t} + (\beta \mathbf{w}_{uu})_{uu} - (\alpha \mathbf{w}_u)_u = \mathbf{f}(u,t), \qquad (17.18)$$

where

$\mathbf{w}(u,t)$ is the position vector of the curve at parameter u and time t;

$\mu = \mu(u)$ is the mass density at parameter u;

$\gamma = \gamma(u)$ is the damping factor at parameter u;

$\alpha = \alpha(u)$ and $\beta = \beta(u)$ simulate the elastic curve-restoring force coefficients related to bending and tension effects, respectively;

$\mathbf{f}(u,t)$ is the external force at parameter u and time t;

u is a parameter describing a point on the curve and roughly approximating arc length. Subscripts u and uu denote first and second partial derivatives with respect to the parameter u.

The above partial differential equation can be solved numerically with great efficiency using the finite-element method [Zien05], and the results can be rendered for visual feedback to a designer or animator. Generalization of this method to curved elastic or plastic models of surfaces and solids is possible, and the references cited provide an introduction to the subject. Deformable surfaces can be also idealized in terms of a set of distributed linear elastic springs, which give rise to a discrete formulation. Research in this area has expanded rapidly, and animation applications have appeared that involve nonlinear motion of cloth and garments, hair, fracture of solids, propagation of cracks, simulation of fluids (liquids and gases) entraining particles or involving a free surface with gravity waves. For the case of fluid simulation, animation of jets, clouds, plumes of smoke, and breaking ocean waves have recently appeared.

17.6 Particle Systems

Previous sections presented techniques for animating concrete objects that have a specific, well-defined shape; during the animation, their shape may remain unaltered (rigid-body animation) or be subject to deterministic changes (skeletal or deformable models). Unfortunately, none of these techniques is able to realistically animate fuzzy objects such as fireworks, smoke, water, or clouds, whose shape cannot be easily described mathematically and changes seemingly randomly over time.

Particle systems were developed exactly for this purpose. Their initial application [Reev83] was the animation of a wave of fire spreading along the surface of a planet for the *Star Trek II* movie. An object or phenomenon animated as a particle system is represented by a (usually large) number of individual particles, each having its own set of attributes, such as position, velocity, color, transparency, shape, and size. Particles are animated procedurally, their attributes evolving over time according to rules that attempt to simulate the behavior of the system.

For each frame of the animation, the following steps are carried out:

1. New particles are generated and added to the system.

2. Each new particle is assigned its initial attributes.

3. Particles that have exceeded their lifetime are removed from the system.

4. Each particle currently in the system is assigned new (updated) attributes.

5. Particles currently in the system are rendered to produce the current frame.

In order to create the "fuzziness" of the object, these steps are implemented with the help of random variables, with as many degrees of freedom as the animator desires and the system can handle. For frame f, a random variable X used for any of the attributes of a particle may have the value

$$X(f) = X_{\text{mean}}(f) + \text{rand}() \cdot X_{\text{var}}(f),$$

where X_{mean} is its mean value, X_{var} is its variance, and $\text{rand}()$ is a random-number generator. The random variables X_{mean} and X_{var} may both also vary between frames if the phenomenon modeled calls for such a variation.

Particles may be rendered in many ways, depending on the application; given the sheer number of particles that make up a system in most cases, their rendering should be economical for practical reasons. In the initial application of particle systems to model the wave of fire, each particle was rendered as a point light source, emitting a small amount of light (whose color was changing over time) and affecting its neighboring pixels; light from nearby particles is accumulated and therefore no back-to-front sorting is necessary, and no shadows are cast on the particles. Alternatively, particles may be rendered as colored points or short colored lines, for example when animating fireworks. Finally, it might be necessary to render each particle as a 3D object like a sphere; in this case the complete lighting and shadow calculations will need to be applied to each particle, resulting in high computational cost. In any case, to enhance the realism of a particle system it may be necessary to apply both spatial and temporal antialiasing to the scene.

As an example of a particle system, consider the water fountain depicted in Figure 17.21. Water is emitted from a nozzle at angle α_0 from the ground. Each water particle starts off at a random angle

$$\alpha = \alpha_0 + \text{rand}() \cdot \alpha_{\text{var}}$$

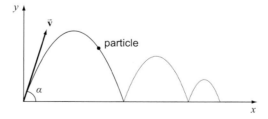

Figure 17.21. One particle from the water-fountain particle system

with a random initial velocity

$$\vec{\mathbf{v}} = \vec{\mathbf{v}}_0 + \text{rand}() \cdot \vec{\mathbf{v}}_{\text{var}}.$$

This motion can be analyzed into two components, a vertical one which is subject to the effect of gravity and a horizontal one which is constant, thus producing the parabolic trajectory of the particle until it reaches the water surface. Therefore the position of the particle over time is given by

$$x(t) = |\vec{\mathbf{v}}| \cos \alpha \, t,$$
$$y(t) = |\vec{\mathbf{v}}| \sin \alpha \, t - \tfrac{1}{2} g t^2,$$

where g is the acceleration due to gravity, which is a constant. For a frame at time t, these relations provide the position of the particle and may be used to animate the particle system. The model can be made more realistic if the color of the particles changes over time (for example, being more whitish in the first frames to simulate higher pressure and more blueish later on), if the particles are allowed to jump over when they reach the water surface, etc.

17.7 Exercises

1. If each frame of an animation takes 10 minutes to render at a resolution of $1024 \times 1024 \times 24$ bits/pixel, estimate the amount of time and space required for a 20-minute animation at 30 frames/second.

2. Create the wagon-wheel effect. Pick a circular 2D object with one or more spikes and implement its rotation at a frequency that can be increased or decreased by the user. The rotational frequency value should be simultaneously displayed.

3. Perform temporal antialiasing on the previous exercise. Use a simple 1D convolution filter, such as the one given in Section 17.2.3.

4. Implement a simple 2D rigid-body animation system. The user must be able to specify the motion of a 2D object using a Bézier or B-spline curve and the object must then follow this trajectory. In addition, the object's orientation must coincide with the tangent of the curve.

5. Implement a simple 2D keyframe animation system. Assume that objects consist of 2D line segments. The user must be able to create an initial

keyframe of line segments F_0. Then, subsequent keyframes F_i, $(i > 0)$ are created by editing (translating, rotating, scaling) the line segments of the previous keyframe F_{i-1}. The user must also be able to specify the distance in frames between adjacent keyframes. The animation system then creates the in-between frames by interpolation and produces an animation sequence.

6. (Image Morph.) Implement a simple image-morphing package using vectors as features. The user must input two images G_1 and G_2 and define corresponding vectors on them (feature-specification step). For the warp step, use a reverse mapping from $G*$ to G_1 and G_2. For the combination step, use only pixel colors as attributes and interpolate using the distance of $G*$ to G_1 and G_2. Omit the blending step.

7. Implement a simple system to handle and animate particle systems. The system may be restricted to simple shapes such as points or lines for the individual particles. The user must be able to specify the attributes of each particle, their initial values, and the way these values change over successive frames.

18

Scientific Visualization
Algorithms

Creative visualization is used by successful
people in all walks of life.
—Marisa D'Vari

18.1   Introduction

The applications of visualization are diverse; however, it is possible to form broad classes of applications according to the *type* of data (e.g., vector or scalar). Algorithms then exist for the visualization of common types of data, and one usually finds them implemented in visualization packages. This chapter examines established visualization algorithms for common types of visualization data.

Before the application of a specific visualization algorithm, it is also essential to know the data characteristics that we want to enhance. For example, when visualizing scalar data, it is possible to select between algorithms that display the entire data set or algorithms that only display isosurfaces within the data; each group has its own advantages. With every algorithm category presented here, we give a short discussion to address this point.

The choice of visualization algorithm to be applied thus depends on two main factors:

- the type of data;

- the desired visual effect.

For example, if we are given a large scalar data set which must be displayed in its entirety in order to get a global view of the data, ray-casting or splatting

643

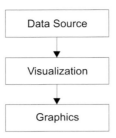

Figure 18.1. Visualization and graphics.

algorithms would be a good choice. If, on the other hand, we must examine areas of equal value more closely, the marching cubes algorithm, which extracts isosurfaces, should be selected.

It is now useful to create the link between visualization and graphics (Figure 18.1). Visualization algorithms are applied to a source of data. Visualization can be thought of as one level above graphics. The visualization algorithm creates a visualization object from the raw data and specifies its display parameters (camera parameters, color maps, transparency maps, textures, lighting parameters, etc.). Graphics algorithms are then called upon to implement these specifications and thus produce the actual images.

Let us be more specific and define the *visualization object* as a function $V(S)$ [Brod92]. The domain S of the function is the space in which the experiment or simulation took place. For example, S may consist of structured points in a 1-, 2-, 3-, or higher-dimensional space. This set of structured points is usually referred to as a *grid* and is the most common type of domain. Alternatively, S may consist of regions of a continuous space (e.g., regions of a map) or it may be an enumerated set (e.g., types of musical instruments). Often, the domain will contain a time variable. The range of $V(S)$ consists of the data items that are produced by the experiment or simulation for elements of the domain. It is the *type* of the items of the range of $V(S)$ that distinguishes between visualization methods. Common types for the range are *scalar, vector,* and *tensor*. We shall use the following notation [Spiv92] to define the type of a visualization object O:

$$O : \text{domtype1} \times \text{domtype2} \times ... \times \text{domtypeN} \rightarrow \text{rangetype}.$$

For example, the visualization object that represents two-element vector values (the range) on a three-dimensional grid plus time (the domain) would be of type $X \times Y \times Z \times T \rightarrow \text{vector2}$. If a vector plus a scalar value are the result of a simula-

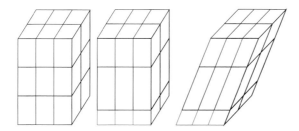

Figure 18.2. Regular, rectilinear, and structured grids.

tion on a similar grid, the type would be a multi-valued function $X \times Y \times Z \times T \rightarrow$ vector $\times$ scalar. (By default we shall assume that vectors have the dimensionality of the underlying grid). We shall use the abbreviation $O_{\text{domain\_type}}^{\text{range\_type}}$ to give the type of a visualization object more concisely. So, for example, a three-element vector field over a three-dimensional grid (Color Plate XXXIV) is a $O_{X \times Y \times Z}^{\text{vector3}}$.

At this point we should define exactly how data values are represented in a domain. Without loss of generality, let us consider the domain of 3D discrete space $X \times Y \times Z$. This domain is a grid and is called *regular*, if its elementary volume elements are cubes of the same size; *rectilinear*, if the elements are orthogonal parallelepipeds; and *structured*, if they are general parallelepipeds (Figure 18.2). In fact, the volume elements do not even have to be parallelepipeds; a common alternative representation is tetrahedral volume elements (Color Plate XXXV).

The range values can be mapped onto the grid domain in two ways (Figure 18.3):

- Range values are associated with entire volume elements (the volume elements are called *voxels*).

- Range values are associated with grid vertices (the volume elements are called *cells*).

To determine the value of an arbitrary 3D point, we thus have two options cor-

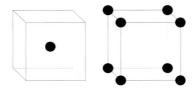

Figure 18.3. Voxel (left) and cell (right) elements.

responding to the above mappings: assign to the point the constant value of the voxel that the point belongs to or perform interpolation from the values of the vertices of the appropriate cell.

The discrete (grid) nature of visualization data becomes a problem when images with varying viewing parameters must be created, or computations be performed which require access to values on arbitrary 3D points, rather than discrete grid points. This is overcome by the use of *interpolation* techniques, which are the single most important mathematical tool in visualization. A brief presentation of interpolation techniques is given in Section 17.2.1.

18.2   Scalar Data Visualization

There are two main approaches to visualizing scalar data represented on a grid (Figure 18.4). If we are interested in observing one or more surfaces of constant value (*isosurfaces*) within the field, then we employ isosurface extraction algorithms. These are advantageous in that they create sharp renderings and by

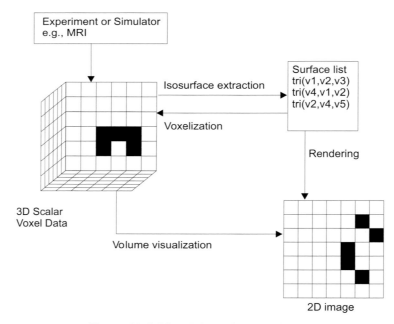

Figure 18.4. Visualizing scalar voxel data.

Figure 18.5. A solid object (middle) can be visualized using an isosurface (volume crust (left)). Not all volume information (right) can be visualized using isosurface extraction.

transforming to a standard representation (surface lists), they can take advantage of widely available graphics techniques for rendering the surfaces. However, only part of the information present in the scalar field is visible on the isosurfaces (Figure 18.5).

Alternatively, we may show the entire field by employing a direct volume-visualization technique; such techniques are however slow and generally result in blurry images. The choice depends largely on the specifics of the application. In this section we shall assume the $O_{X \times Y \times Z}^{\text{scalar}}$ object, although generalizations to other domain dimensions are possible.

Whichever method we choose for the visualization, we may want to pre-simplify a very complex scalar data set to aid the visualization process [Chia03, Cign00]. Such simplification is carried out based on the underlying grid and is described in more detail for vector fields in Section 18.3.6.

18.2.1 Isosurface Extraction Algorithms

Volume scalar data can be too complex to visualize directly. Such data often contain too much information along each ray in the viewing direction to display onto a picture element with a single color. It is often the case that such data contain clusters of values which can be separated by surfaces, much like a 3D Voronoi diagram. Isosurface algorithms determine these separating surfaces after the user inputs one or more *isosurface value(s)*. These inputs correspond to borders where the data set passes from lesser to greater values. Once these isosurfaces are established, it is quick and easy to display them with standard graphics techniques, since they consist of polygons.

The *marching cubes* algorithm [Lore87] was initially developed as a method for the efficient visualization of 3D medical data sets acquired by magnetic resonance imaging (MRI), computed tomography (CT), or other techniques that depict complex bone formations, blood vessels, or other anatomical structures. The user provides the 3D (volume) data set and an isosurface value(s) that defines the desired structure (e.g., bone density), and the algorithm computes an isosurface consisting of triangles that can be rendered efficiently. The main drawback of marching cubes is that it creates a large number of unnecessary triangles. The *splitting box* algorithm [Mull93, Star97] attempts to improve on marching cubes in this respect.

Marching cubes. The input to the marching cubes (MC) algorithm is a scalar volume data set $O_{X \times Y \times Z}^{\text{scalar}}$ and the scalar value of the desired isosurface. The output is a list of polygons which make up the isosurface. The MC algorithm visits every *cube* (volume element) of the volume data set. For example, the cubes may be created by using adjacent slices of a MRI scan. For each cube visited, the field values at its eight vertices are compared to the user-provided isosurface value. Vertices are thus labeled as 1 (*inside*, smaller than isosurface value) or 0 (*outside*, greater than isosurface value). The vertex labels are then systematically concatenated and used as an index to a list of pre-computed surface-cube intersections. More specifically, the steps are the following:

```
Void MC() {
   For (i= 0; i<maxcubeI; i++)
      For (j= 0; j<maxcubeJ; j++)
         For (k= 0; k<maxcubeK; k++) {
         // process cube (i,j,k)

            // label vertices as inside (1) or outside (0)
            l1=get_label (i,j,k);
            l2=get_label (i+1,j,k);
            ...
            l8=get_label (i+1,j+1,k+1);

            // concatenate the 8 labels (++ stands for the
            // string concatenation operator)
            index=l1++l2++l3++l4++l5++l6++l7++l8;

            // map index to one of the 15 basic cases
            // (symmetries) and get required transform
            bindex=map_2_basic_index(index);
            transform=map_2_basic_trans(index);
```

```
// use bindex to select the appropriate
// precomputed surface-cube intersection
// and reverse transform it
surface_list=
   precomputed_surfaces(bindex,transform^{-1});

// use interpolation to place the
// intersection surface precisely
for (p=0; p<num_vertices(surface_list); p++)
   compute_precise_edge_position(p,
   cube_field_values(i,j,k));
// calculate normals at intersection
// surface vertices for rendering
for (p=0; p<num_vertices(surface_list) p++)
   compute_normal(p, cube_field_values(i,j,k));
   }
}
```

An example of vertex labeling is given in Figure 18.6; the cubes are equivalent to the cell model of Figure 18.3.

Assuming a front-to-back, top-to-bottom, left-to-right vertex order, the indexes of the top and bottom cubes in Figure 18.6 are 10100010 and 11110011, respectively. There are a total of 2^8 possible ways to label the vertices of a cube

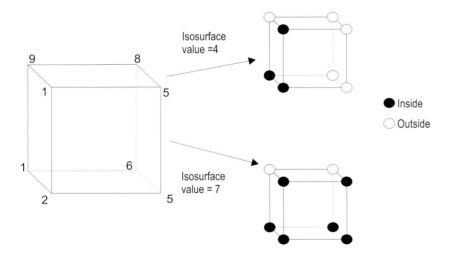

Figure 18.6. Vertex labeling.

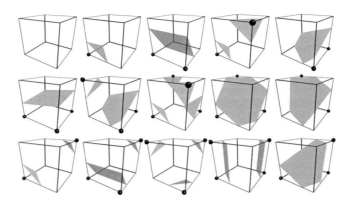

Figure 18.7. The 15 surface-cube intersections.

in this manner; therefore we require 256 pre-computed surface-cube intersection patterns. These are reduced to just 15 (Figure 18.7) by taking advantage of

- mirror symmetry;

- rotational symmetry;

- inside/outside symmetry.

Each one of the 15 intersection patterns essentially provides the topology of the polygonal intersection surface (i.e., one or more polygons) *with respect to the cube edges*. The symmetries used to go from the actual intersection pattern to one of the 15 basic cases form the transform for a cube. We next determine the exact points of intersection along each cube edge by interpolation. If the edge vertices have associated field values v and v' and the isosurface value is I ($v < I < v'$), then the intersection point p (Figure 18.8) can be expressed as a fraction of the edge length as

$$p = \frac{I - v}{v' - v}.$$

This linear interpolation assumes a linearly varying field; otherwise the computed point of intersection is only an approximation to the true point of intersection. Notice that for adjacent cubes the interpolation calculation on common edges will yield the same result, leading to locally continuous (C^0) isosurface approximations.

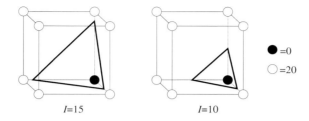

I=15 I=10

=0
=20

Figure 18.8. Interpolation along edge.

The normal vectors of the isosurface on the vertices of the resulting isosurface polygons, which are useful for the realistic rendering of the isosurface, are computed directly from the field, in two steps:

- Compute the gradient vectors of the scalar field at cube vertices;

- Interpolate the gradient vectors along cube edges and onto the vertices of the polygons (similar to the determination of the exact point of intersection p).

The gradient vectors at cube vertices are computed by taking central differences of the field values at neighboring cube vertices. Thus, if $v(i,j,k)$ and $g(i,j,k)$ are the field value and gradient vector at cube vertex (i,j,k),

$$g_x(i,j,k) = \frac{v(i+1,j,k) - v(i-1,j,k)}{\Delta x},$$

$$g_y(i,j,k) = \frac{v(i,j+1,k) - v(i,j-1,k)}{\Delta y},$$

$$g_z(i,j,k) = \frac{v(i,j,k+1) - v(i,j,k-1)}{\Delta z},$$

where Δx, Δy, Δz are the differences in the x-, y-, and z-coordinates, respectively, of the cube vertices involved. Figure 18.9 presents an example of the isosurfaces extracted from a scalar data set using the MC algorithm.

MC can be improved in a number of ways; an obvious one is to avoid recomputation for common edges of neighboring cubes. The major disadvantage of the algorithm is the large number of polygons that are created for the isosurface and the fact that this number is not proportional to the isosurface complexity but depends primarily on the density of the grid.

Still, the isosurface generated by the marching cubes algorithm is view-independent and, as such, can be computed once for a fixed density threshold and

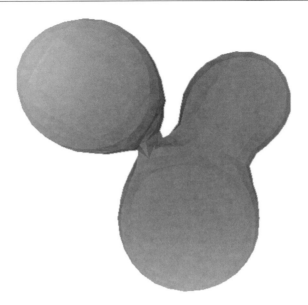

Figure 18.9. Isosurface creation with the MC algorithm.

optimized for better polygon-rendering performance using one of the many mesh-simplification algorithms [Hopp98, Hopp96, Garl99, Redd96]. Being a polygonal surface representation, the result of the MC can be fully accelerated by the GPU of modern graphics systems. The inherent disadvantage of MC is that it can only visualize volume isosurfaces (or crusts) and cannot represent any type of smooth density transitions.

Splitting box. The splitting box (SB) algorithm also creates an isosurface from volumetric scalar data sets. It creates a smaller number of polygons than MC by recursively subdividing the original volume only until the resulting elements possess a certain complexity property. Some definitions are in order here. A *box* is a rectangular parallelepiped with edges parallel to the main axes of the grid. The *length* of an edge is the number of grid vertices it contains. An edge has the *MC property* if it contains at most one isosurface transition; this is the same assumption made by the MC algorithm for neighboring vertices of a volume element (cube). The SB algorithm uses this generalised property to end the subdivision process as early as possible in the box hierarchy. A face of a box is MC if its four edges are MC. Finally a box is MC if its six faces (or twelve edges) are all MC.

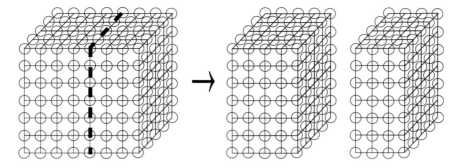

Figure 18.10. Box subdivision.

The SB algorithm recursively subdivides a box along its longest edge until boxes with the MC property are reached (Figure 18.10). It is initially called with a box which represents the entire visualization volume:

```
void SB (box); {
    if  MC_property(box)
        generate polygons using the 15 cases of MC;
    else if  size(box)=2^3
        generate polygons by analytical processing;
    else {
        subdivide box along longest edge into box1 and box2;
        SB(box1);
        SB(box2);
    }
}
```

18.2.2   Direct Volume Visualization

When we need to examine complex internal structures of data sets, volume visualization algorithms are the appropriate tool to use. In general the entire depth complexity of the data set is simultaneously displayed. The cost of displaying so much information simultaneously is, in general, unclear images that often contain cluttered information.

Three-dimensional scalar data sets consisting of sampled data or representing amorphous phenomena (such as MRI, smoke, or fire) are often hard to represent using surfaces. In such cases, we can employ visualization algorithms that display the data by directly interrogating the data set (Color Plate XXXVI). There are two main types of algorithms. *Backward projection*, or *ray casting*, fires rays for each image pixel into the data set, obtains samples and combines them into a final color. *Forward projection*, or *splatting*, does the reverse; it projects each voxel in the data set onto the image plane and establishes which pixels it affects using a filter.

Ray casting. Ray casting consists of three steps:

1. Classify each voxel according to its content;

2. Transform the rays or data so that they are aligned with the viewing direction;

3. Combine the result along each ray.

The first step classifies each voxel depending on its material content; the result is a color and transparency value. For example, in a medical scanning application we can assign color and transparency values according to the x-ray absorption values. Drebin [Dreb88] proposes a classification scheme whereby absorption values are not classified using thresholds but, rather, using a Bayesian approach. Suppose our set of possible materials is

$$\text{material} = \{\text{air, fat, soft-tissue, bone}\}$$

and that material i has an a-priori given probability distribution $P_i(I)$ to have intensity value I if it is in homogeneous form (Figure 18.11). Then the question is,

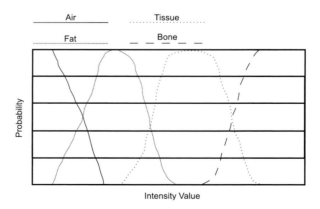

Figure 18.11. Material intensity probability distributions.

given a measured voxel intensity I, which material(s) does the voxel contain and in what proportion? If we let $P(I)$ denote the probability that a voxel has intensity value I then

$$P(I) = \sum_{i=1}^{m} \rho_i P_i(I),$$

where ρ_i is the proportion of material i in the voxel (i.e., the value we seek) and m is the number of different materials. Therefore the Bayesian estimate $\rho_i(I)$ of the amount of material i in a voxel with measured intensity value I can be computed as

$$\rho_i(I) = \frac{P_i(I)}{\sum_{j=1}^{m} P_j(I)}$$

and

$$\sum_{j=1}^{m} \rho_j(I) = 1.$$

The color/transparency C of the voxel is computed in so-called RGBA form (RGB color plus transparency):

$$C = \sum_{i=1}^{m} \rho_i C_i,$$

where $C_i = (\alpha_i R_i, \alpha_i G_i, \alpha_i B_i, \alpha_i)$ is the color and transparency value that corresponds to material i.

There are two ways of aligning the data with the viewing direction (Step 2 of the algorithm): *ray transformation* and *data transformation*. Ray transformation casts rays into the volume data and takes samples at equidistant points along each ray (Figure 18.12). The samples are computed by tri-linear interpolation from the eight nearest voxel values. (Equivalently, if the cell representation is used, they are computed from the eight values of the vertices of the cell that contains the sample point). For example, if $v_{i,j,k}|i,j,k \in \{-,+\}$ represent the values of the eight surrounding voxels for a sampling point s and d_x^-, d_y^-, d_z^- represent the distances from s to the centers of the three voxels with the smaller indices in each axis as a portion of the inter-voxel distance (Figure 18.12), then the value at s is computed as

$$v_s = (1 - d_x^-)\left[(1 - d_y^-)\left[(1 - d_z^-)v_{---} + d_z^- v_{--+}\right] + d_y^- \left[(1 - d_z^-)v_{-+-} + d_z^- v_{-++}\right]\right]$$
$$+ d_x^- \left[(1 - d_y^-)\left[(1 - d_z^-)v_{+--} + d_z^- v_{+-+}\right] + d_y^- \left[(1 - d_z^-)v_{++-} + d_z^- v_{+++}\right]\right].$$

Data transformation aligns the volume data with the viewing direction. If z is the viewing axis, then the voxel data are realigned so that voxels with the same

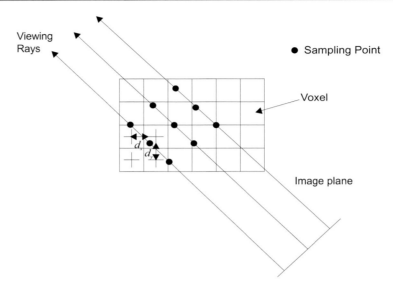

Figure 18.12. Ray transformation (parallel projection shown in 2D).

z-coordinate lie on the same viewing ray. Figure 18.13 shows this operation for
a parallel and a perspective projection. Data transformation can be achieved by
a shear-warp operation [Came92, Lacr94]. First the slices of the volume data are
sheared in the xy-plane by factors s_x and s_y (determined from the viewing transformation) and the data of each slice are re-sampled using bi-linear interpolation.
The shear matrix (see Chapter 3) for a parallel projection is

$$SH_{\mathrm{par}} = SH_{xy}(s_x, s_y) = \begin{bmatrix} 1 & 0 & s_x & 0 \\ 0 & 1 & s_y & 0 \\ 0 & 0 & 1 & 0 \\ 0 & 0 & 0 & 1 \end{bmatrix}.$$

In the case of a perspective projection, we also need to scale each slice (Figure 18.13(right)). The scale factor s is again determined from the viewing transformation and the scaling can be incorporated in the shear matrix by modifying
the homogeneous coordinate:

$$SH_{\mathrm{pers}} = \begin{bmatrix} 1 & 0 & s_x' & 0 \\ 0 & 1 & s_y' & 0 \\ 0 & 0 & 1 & 0 \\ 0 & 0 & s & 1 \end{bmatrix}.$$

Viewing Rays

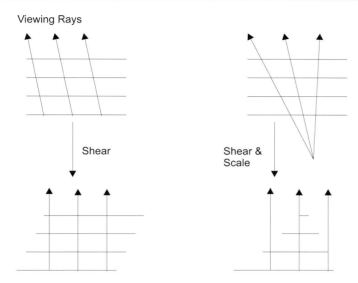

Figure 18.13. Shear operation for parallel (left) and perspective (right) projection.

A volume data slice at $z = z_0$ is thus scaled by $1/(1+sz_0)$ to return to normal homogeneous form (i.e., w-coordinate equal to 1), which achieves the desired scaling effect for the perspective projection. A problem with the perspective projection is the non-homogeneous sampling of the volume data caused by the diverging rays (Figure 18.13(right)); in other words the sampling density is a function of depth. A solution to this problem proposed by Kreeger et al. [Kree98] is to adaptively introduce extra rays as a function of depth; these rays then get sub-sampled in slices in order to end up with the initial ray resolution.

A 2D warp and re-sampling operation is needed to complete the data transformation. The warp accounts for the oblique positioning of the image plane with respect to the volume data axes, and it takes place after the volume data have been combined into a single XY image (Step 3).

The final step of the algorithm (Step 3) determines the resulting color value along each ray. This is easily achieved by combining the value at successive sample points (ray transformation) or successive voxels along the Z-direction (data transformation). For unity of presentation we shall use the term *ray samples* to refer to both cases. Remembering that the value at each ray sample is stored in RGBA form, we traverse the ray samples from back to front (Figure 18.14). At each ray sample we compute the outgoing color value RGB_{out} as a function of the

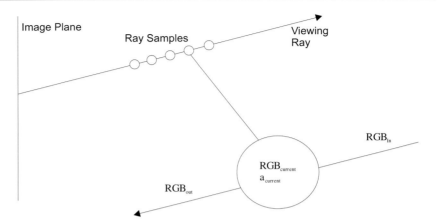

Figure 18.14. Combining the ray samples.

incoming value RGB_{in} and the color and transparency properties of the current ray sample:

$$RGB_{out} = RGB_{in}(1 - \alpha_{current}) + RGB_{current}\alpha_{current},$$

where $\alpha_{current}$ ranges from 0 (totally transparent) to 1 (totally opaque).

Splatting. The ray-casting algorithm has an outer loop for each image-space pixel and then traverses voxel space to consider which voxels affect it. In contrast, the splatting algorithm [West90] gives voxels the priority; it considers each voxel's projection onto the image plane (i.e., the pixels). This is as if the voxel was thrust onto the image plane, hence the term *splatting*.

The discrete voxel space represents a continuous volume whose values $f(x, y, z)$ can be reconstructed by the function

$$f(x, y, z) = \sum_i \sum_j \sum_k v(i, j, k) \cdot h(x - i, y - j, z - k),$$

where $v(i, j, k)$ are the discrete voxel values, h is the reconstruction kernel, and the summation is taken over a 3D volume with size equal to that of the reconstruction kernel (see Appendix E).

Instead of considering how multiple voxels contribute to the value of an arbitrary 3D point, consider the contribution $\text{contri}(x, y, z)$ of a single voxel (i, j, k) to a point (x, y, z). This is independent of the contributions of other voxels to that point and is equal to

$$\text{contri}(x, y, z) = v(i, j, k) \cdot h(x - i, y - j, z - k).$$

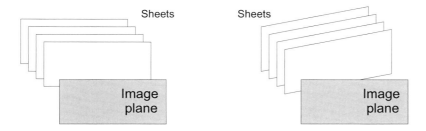

Figure 18.15. Voxel sheets and image plane.

The total contribution at a given image location (x, y) is the sum of the contributions at all points along a ray that is normal to the image plane at (x, y). Assuming z to be perpendicular to the image plane, the integral is calculated over the z-axis (for this reason $z - k$ is replaced by z):

$$\text{contri}(x, y) = \int_{-\infty}^{\infty} v(i, j, k) \cdot h(x - i, y - j, z) dz.$$

Since $v(i, j, k)$ does not depend on z it can be taken outside the integral:

$$\text{contri}(x, y) = v(i, j, k) \cdot \int_{-\infty}^{\infty} h(x - i, y - j, z) dz.$$

A kernel is centered at every voxel and its contributions to image-space pixels can be determined by projecting the kernel onto image space. All kernels have the same projection, called *footprint*:

$$\text{footprint}(\alpha, \beta) = \int_{-\infty}^{\infty} h(\alpha, \beta, z) dz,$$

where α, β represent the image-space X- and Y-displacement (in pixels) from the central pixel of the kernel projection. If the image plane is not aligned with the axes of the voxel volume, then the footprint function is slightly more complicated [West90].

The voxels are processed in *sheets*; a sheet is a plane of voxels parallel to the image plane (Figure 18.15(left)). If the image plane is not aligned with the voxel space axes, then the sheets are defined by the pair of voxel axes most parallel to the image plane (Figure 18.15(right)). Processing starts with the sheet nearest to the observer:

Figure 18.16. Volume rendering at multiple resolutions using pre-computed levels of detail and a simple step-like kernel splatting.

```
for each sheet s front-to-back
    for each voxel (x,y,s) in sheet s
        for all footprint offsets (a,b) {
            frame_buffer(x+a,y+b)=
                frame_buffer(x+a,y+b)+
                voxel(x+a,y+b,s)*footprint(a,b)*
                transparency_buffer(x+a,y+b)
            transparency_buffer(x+a,y+b)=
                transparency_buffer(x+a,y+b)+
                transp(voxel(x+a,y+b,s))
                *footprint(a,b)
        }
```

When compared to ray casting, splatting requires more computation as it processes the entire voxel space and does not take advantage of bounding volumes. On the other hand, voxels are processed independently and thus splatting is more amenable to parallel implementation.

Another useful property of the splatting algorithm and its variations is that it is very easy to integrate a multi-resolution representation of the volume data into the rendering stage. As the volume is rendered in layers, the resolution of each such planar section of the volume can be determined independently and rendered using a pre-computed lower-resolution version of the sampled scalar space, such as an octree. Figure 18.16 shows the representation of the same data set at four resolutions.

18.3   Vector Data Visualization

Vector fields are quite common results in both experiments and simulations; examples are electromagnetic fields, derivatives of scalar fields, and wind-velocity data. The visualization of vector data poses an added complexity to scalar data in

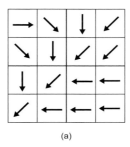

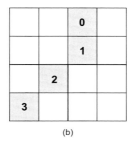

Figure 18.17. (a) A static $O_{X \times Y}^{\text{vector2}}$ vector field; (b) a streamline (see Section 18.3.2).

that each element of the field has several dimensions to represent. One can thus visualize only part of the field, show only some of the vector components, use clever color-encoding techniques, or even simplify the vector field before visualization.

The dimensionality of the definition grid and that of the vectors in the field are independent. However, although fields such as $O_{X \times Y}^{\text{vector3}}$ and $O_{X \times Y \times Z}^{\text{vector2}}$ are possible, in the usual case the dimensionality of the vectors matches that of the underlying grid; the types $O_{X \times Y}^{\text{vector2}}$ and $O_{X \times Y \times Z}^{\text{vector3}}$ are frequently encountered in experiments and simulations. An important distinction has to be made between *static* (or steady) and *dynamic* (or unsteady, time-varying) vector fields. A static field does not change over time and can represent, for example, the constant gravitational field between a set of static objects. Figure 18.17(a) shows a static 2D vector field.

In contrast, a dynamic vector field represents a dynamic vector phenomenon, for example, wind velocity and direction data over the US during the course of a day. Just like frames of an animation sequence, a dynamic vector field can be represented by taking "snapshots" of the field at discrete points in time. Each snapshot is equivalent to a static vector field. Figure 18.18 (a)–(d) represents four snapshots of a 2D dynamic vector field.

Without loss of generality, we can define the function types of three dimensional vector fields over three dimensional grids as

$$V_{\text{static}} : \quad O_{X \times Y \times Z}^{\text{vector3}},$$
$$V_{\text{dynamic}} : \quad O_{X \times Y \times Z \times T}^{\text{vector3}},$$

where the last parameter in V_{dynamic} refers to time.

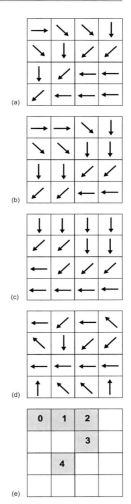

Figure 18.18. (a)–(d) Four snapshots of a dynamic $O_{X \times Y \times T}^{\text{vector2}}$ vector field at $t = t_1, t_2, t_3, t_4$; (e) a pathline (see Section 18.3.2).

18.3.1 Hedgehogs

Hedgehogs (also called *arrow plots* and *vector glyphs*) refer to the standard representation of vectors as arrows and have been extensively used to represent vector fields. The arrow length and direction represent the corresponding quantities of the vector. Figure 18.19 and Color Plate XXXVII represent a $O_{X \times Y}^{\text{vector2}}$ and a $O_{X \times Y \times Z}^{\text{vector3}}$ object, respectively.

Dynamic vector fields can be represented by animations where each frame is the arrow plot of the field at a specific time instant.

The major problems with arrow plots are:

- the *visual clutter* that arises if we construct arrow plots of dense fields;

- the *projective distortion* (foreshortening) that results when higher-dimensional vector fields are projected to 2D for display purposes.

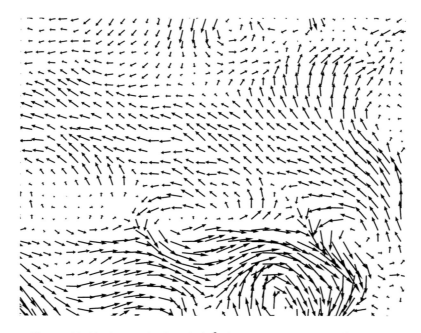

Figure 18.19. Arrow plot for $O_{X \times Y}^{\text{vector2}}$. (Image created using OpenDX.)

18.3.2 Particle Advection

Displaying dense vector fields in their entirety is often confusing, as one cannot pick out important characteristics of the field, such as flow patterns, among the large amount of information displayed. One way of fixing this is to imagine the trace of single particles through a vector field; think of a wind-tunnel experiment where we can release a small and light ping-pong ball and then observe the path that it takes. Better still, we may release a small number of colored balls at different points and observe their joint behavior. This principle finds application in the visualization of vector fields and is called *particle advection*.

Particle advection techniques rely on the existence of flow patterns in vector fields. Instead of displaying the whole vector field, we only display the effect of these flow patterns on weightless and frictionless particles that are advected through the field from their initial positions [IBM07]. Visual clutter is thus virtually eliminated, as we are in full control of the number of particles that are released into the field. If weight and friction are not negligible, they can be preincorporated in the simulation that produced the vector field.

Let us define a *visualization point* as a triplet and a *visualization line* as a set of points (this is not necessarily a straight line):

$$\text{vispoint} : [X\,Y\,Z],$$
$$\text{visline} : \{\text{vispoint}\}.$$

A *streamline* can be viewed as a function that takes a static vector field and a set of initial points and produces a set of visualization lines, one for each point:

$$\text{streamline} : V_{\text{static}} \times \{\text{vispoint}\} \rightarrow \{\text{visline}\}$$

Each streamline is the trace of a particle as it is advected through a static vector field $\overrightarrow{S}$ from its initial position. A streamline for the simple static field of Figure 18.17(a) is shown in Figure 18.17(b) while Color Plate XXXIX(left) shows a number of streamlines together. If π is the parameter of the streamline and $\mathbf{s}$ is a point on it, the following differential equation should be satisfied:

$$\frac{d\mathbf{s}}{d\pi} = \overrightarrow{S}(\mathbf{s}(\pi)).$$

The *twist* of a vector field along streamlines can be visualized by plotting *ribbons* that are the result of connecting the traces produced by pairs of neighboring particles (Color Plate XXXIX (right)). We can also plot an extra parameter along

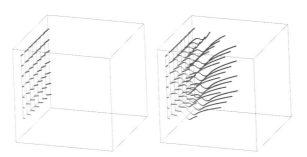

Figure 18.20. Streaklines for dynamic vector fields; after application of first field value (left) and after application of last field value (right). (Images created using OpenDX.)

a streamline (e.g., vector magnitude) by color coding the values of the parameter along its length (Color Plate XXXIX). Another variation plots a tube around a streamline; two extra parameters can thus be visualized along the path of the streamline, one coded as the color and the other as the diameter of the tube.

We can also use streamlines to visualize a single time instant t of a dynamic vector field $\overrightarrow{D}$:

$$\frac{d\mathbf{s}}{d\pi} = \overrightarrow{D}(\mathbf{s}(\pi),t).$$

Streaklines visualize a dynamic vector field by plotting the paths of particles as they are advected through the field; that is, at every discrete advection step the vector field applied to the particles is determined as a function of time. Figure 18.20 gives an example.

Let us first define the concept of a *pathline*, which is a function that, given an initial point $\mathbf{s}_0$ at an initial time t_0, produces the trace of the point through the dynamic field:

$$\text{pathline} : V_{\text{dynamic}} \times \text{initial} \rightarrow \text{visline},$$

where initial = (vispoint, time), by successively replacing the initial point by the result of advecting it through each instance of the dynamic vector field:

$$\frac{dp(\text{init},t)}{dt} = \overrightarrow{D}(p(\text{init},t),t)$$

where $p(\text{init},t)$ is the pathline starting at init = $(\mathbf{s}_0,t_0)$ at parametric time t (i.e., it is a point on the pathline). Initially $p(\text{init},t_0) = \mathbf{s}_0$. A pathline for the simple dynamic vector field of Figure 18.18(a)–(d) is shown in Figure 18.18(e).

A *streakline* can then be viewed as a function that takes a dynamic vector field and a set of initial points at given initial times and produces a set of visualization lines, one for each point:

$$\text{streakline} : V_{\text{dynamic}} \times \{\text{initial}\} \rightarrow \{\text{visline}\},$$

where initial = (vispoint, time).

The streakline S from init = $(\mathbf{s}_0, t_0)$ at time t is $S(\text{init}, t) = p(\text{init}, t)$. Streaklines do not necessarily start at the beginning of the simulation. A dynamic vector field and two associated streaklines are shown in Figure 18.21.

18.3.3   Line Integral Convolution

Particle advection techniques present only a very small portion of the information contained in a vector field; an unfortunate choice of particles can thus lead to wrong conclusions about a field. Line integral convolution (LIC) [Cabr93] was developed to allow the global visualization of dense static vector fields over 2D or 3D regular grids. An input texture with resolution equal to the cell count of the grid in the respective dimensions is "locally blurred" to produce an output texture of the same size. The vector field is thus visualized via its blurring effect on the texture. The input texture may be related to the vector field or it may be completely unrelated, such as a noise image (Figure 18.22).

Assume a $O_{X \times Y}^{\text{vector2}}$ vector field. The local behavior of a vector field can be approximated by computing a streamline that starts at the center of a certain cell (pixel), say (x, y), and extends in both the positive and the negative directions of the field, thus simulating the effect of the vector field on a particle at (x, y).

Figure 18.22. LIC on noise texture.

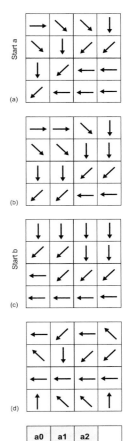

Figure 18.21.
(a)–(d) A dynamic vector field; (e) two streaklines.

Figure 18.23. 2D vector field (left) with convolution area shown shaded, 2D input image (middle), and 2D output image (right).

The value at pixel (x, y) of the output image is computed by a convolution of a 1D strip of the input image with a 1D convolution filter. The convolution is performed over L cells of the streamline of (x, y) in each direction. Figure 18.23 shows the computation of a 2D output image from a 2D vector field and a 2D input image, all of the same dimensions.

More specifically, if O and I are the output and input images, respectively, the LIC function is

$$O(x, y) = \sum_{p \in A} I(p) \cdot h(p),$$

where A is the set of cells of the streamline within a discrete cell distance L from (x, y), shown shaded in Figure 18.23(left); L is half the length of the convolution kernel

$$h(p) = \int_{\lambda_1}^{\lambda_2} k(w)dw;$$

λ_1 is the arclength of the streamline from (x, y) to the point where it enters cell p; λ_2 is the arclength of the streamline from (x, y) to the point where it exits cell p; and $k(w)$ is the convolution filter function.

The length of the convolution kernel ($2L$) is a critical parameter. A large L will cause the LIC functions of most cells to have similar values (more blurring) and a small L will result in insufficient filtering (no blurring effect) (Color Plate XL).

Note that so far only the *direction* component of vector fields was visualized. One way of visualizing the *magnitude* component is to vary the value of L (which was so far constant) according to local vector magnitude. The amount of blurring is then proportional to vector magnitude, which can be beneficial for some applications. As an example, L can be varied proportionally to wind velocity and the resulting image can be overlaid on a 2D map. Stronger winds can thus be visualized with a greater blurring effect.

It is also possible to animate the LIC technique by displaying particles that travel along the field lines [Fors95]. A simple extension maps vector magnitudes into varying animation speeds.

The generalization of the LIC technique to $O_{X \times Y \times Z}^{\text{vector3}}$ fields is relatively straightforward. However, as the number of voxels in such 3D fields can be very large (e.g., $512 \times 512 \times 512$), the computational cost can be proportionally high; in addition it is hard to visualize such a dense 3D output. Three-dimensional LIC techniques utilize the concept of a region of interest (ROI) [Helg04, Inte98]. The user defines a 3D ROI by placing constraints on some scalar value of the field, such as vector magnitude. These constraints are then used to mask out (set to 0) parts of the 3D input texture. LIC calculations are then only performed on voxels that correspond to non-zero input texture elements (Color Plate XXXVIII):

```
for each voxel v
    if (scalar_test(v) ∉ ROI) set input_texture(v) to 0
for each voxel v
    if (input_texture(v) ≠ 0) compute LIC function output O(v)
```

18.3.4 Visualization of Vector Field Topology

In order to minimize the visual clutter that is inherent in the visualization of vector fields, one solution is to concentrate only on the important features of the field and visualize its *topology*.

For a static vector field $\vec{S}$ (either $O_{X \times Y}^{\text{vector2}}$ or $O_{X \times Y \times Z}^{\text{vector3}}$), the most important elements of its topology are *critical points*, the points where the field has zero value. Critical points represent singularities of the vector field and the behavior (flow) of the field is interesting in their vicinity. Critical points can be classified according to the eigenvalues of the Jacobian matrix of the field evaluated at their position [Helm91].

For a 2D vector field $\vec{S}(x, y) = (S_x(x, y), S_y(x, y))$ the Jacobian matrix is

$$J_2 = \begin{bmatrix} \frac{\partial S_x}{\partial x} & \frac{\partial S_x}{\partial y} \\ \frac{\partial S_y}{\partial x} & \frac{\partial S_y}{\partial y} \end{bmatrix},$$

and it has two eigenvalues that are either both real or both complex; they are also conjugate to each other (i.e., their real parts are equal and their imaginary parts are opposite). Figure 18.24 presents all the possible cases. It can be seen that a positive real part of the eigenvalue corresponds to repelling behavior of the field around the critical point, while a negative value corresponds to attracting behavior; the field therefore goes both towards and away from a *saddle point* and around a *center*. Furthermore, a (non-zero) imaginary part corresponds to rotating behavior around the critical point.

For a 3D vector field, $\vec{S}(x,y,z) = (S_x(x,y,z), S_y(x,y,z), S_z(x,y,z))$, the Jacobian matrix may have either three real eigenvalues or one real and a pair of conjugate complex eigenvalues, and they correspond to behaviors of the field similarly to the 2D case.

As Figure 18.24 shows, there are different types of field flow in the vicinity of critical points, which define sectors of different kinds in the domain of the field. The boundaries of these sectors are curves (for 2D fields) and curves or surfaces (for 3D fields) called *separatrices*. A graph of the critical points and

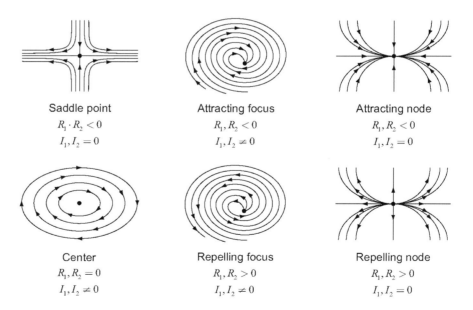

Saddle point	Attracting focus	Attracting node
$R_1 \cdot R_2 < 0$	$R_1, R_2 < 0$	$R_1, R_2 < 0$
$I_1, I_2 = 0$	$I_1, I_2 \neq 0$	$I_1, I_2 = 0$
Center	Repelling focus	Repelling node
$R_1, R_2 = 0$	$R_1, R_2 > 0$	$R_1, R_2 > 0$
$I_1, I_2 \neq 0$	$I_1, I_2 \neq 0$	$I_1, I_2 = 0$

Figure 18.24. Classification of 2D critical points. R_1, R_2 are the real parts of the eigenvalues of the Jacobian matrix, and I_1, I_2 are the respective imaginary parts.

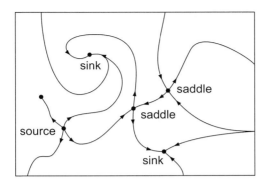

Figure 18.25. The skeleton of a vector field.

the separatrices of a vector field is called its *skeleton* and it provides a simplified representation of the field (Figure 18.25).

However, even this simplified representation of the field can be problematic, if the field contains an excessive number of densely spaced critical points. To address such situations, efforts to simplify the topology of a vector field have been presented [dL99, Tric00] that merge nearby critical points, under suitable criteria and constraints, aiming to reduce their number while preserving the characteristics of the field.

This kind of topological analysis has been developed for static vector fields, but it can be employed to visualize dynamic vector fields as well. Specifically, given consecutive time "snapshots" of a dynamic vector field, their skeletons may be joined by linking consecutive positions of the critical points and the respective separatrices. The resulting surfaces permit the observation of the evolution of the field and of its topology over time. It may then be seen that topological changes (*bifurcations*) occur; for example, the type of critical points may change, critical points may be merged, created, or destroyed over time.

18.3.5 Scalarization

A simple (but lossy) way to deal with the problems of visual clutter and projective distortion is to discard most components of the vector field, thus creating a scalar field. The scalar field can then be directly displayed by a simple color-value association, using any of the techniques presented above for scalar fields. For example, one can pick the magnitude component of the vector field for display and discard all directional information.

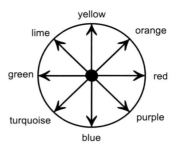

Figure 18.26. Color hues are mapped to the equator (θ) of the color sphere.

Hall [Hall93] introduced a cleverer way of using color to display vector fields. Instead of discarding vector components, he maps direction and magnitude to different color characteristics. Let vectors of an $O_{X \times Y}^{vector2}$ vector field be represented in a polar coordinate system as triplets (ρ, θ, ϕ) where ρ is the normalized vector magnitude and θ, ϕ the polar direction angles. These can then be directly mapped to a spherical color-coordinate system. For example, θ can represent hue (color hues define the equator of the color sphere (Figure 18.26)), ϕ can represent tone (shade), and ρ can represent purity. So, pure colors represent vectors of maximum magnitude, while direction is mapped to hue and tone.

Although this technique alleviates the problems of visual clutter and projective distortion, it is hard for our brain to associate color with vector characteristics. The situation can be somewhat improved if the colors are quantized before display (direction and / or magnitude), as that helps us to classify the vectors into a few major categories (Color Plate XLI).

18.3.6   Vector Field Simplification

A useful alternative technique in the case of complex vector fields, is to simplify the field before visualizing it. Simplification techniques reduce the number of vectors in the field in a controlled way while aiming to preserve important field properties, such as critical points or the boundary of the field. The risk of missing important data (as in the case of particle advection) is therefore reduced. Several such methods have been recently developed, mostly based on vector clustering techniques [Garc01, Heck99, Tele99, Tric00].

In the case of vector fields defined over *tetrahedral meshes* (i.e., where vectors are given at the vertices of a tetrahedral mesh), it is possible to use a generalization of the well established *edge-collapse* operation (see Chapter 6) to simplify

	Hedgehogs	Particle advection	LIC	Vector field topology	Scalarization	Simplification
Full field visualization	x		x		x	
Direction visualization	x	x	x	x	x[1]	x
Magnitude visualization	x	x	x		x[1]	x
No significant information loss	x		x			x
Avoids clutter		x	x	x	x	x

[1]Either vector direction or magnitude is usually visualized with this technique.

Table 18.1. Summary of vector-field visualization techniques.

the vector field [Plat04]. An edge-collapse in the tetrahedral mesh reduces the tetrahedra that share this edge to mere triangles and these are deleted; tetrahedra that share a vertex of the collapsed edge must have this vertex updated. Briefly, the algorithm is as follows:

- Create a queue of candidate edge-collapses by ordering all edges of the tetrahedral mesh according to an error metric that measures the degradation of the field as a result of each candidate edge-collapse;

- Repeat until the simplification target is reached:

  - Remove the edge from the front of the queue,

  - Apply the associated edge-collapse,

  - Re-compute the error metric for affected queue elements and reorder the queue.

Evidently the error metric used in the above algorithm is of critical importance. Platis [Plat04] recommends a compound error metric that takes into account both the tetrahedral *domain* (i.e., deviation from the original boundary) and the vector *field* (i.e., changes in the implied vector values or the positions of critical points). Color Plate XLII presents an example of a complex vector field (left) simplified to 50%, 25%, and 10% of its original number of tetrahedra using this method.

The main characteristics of the presented vector-visualization techniques are summarized in Table 18.1.

18.4   Exercises

The exercises listed below are necessarily practical. However, they have been
designed with a generic view, so that they can be implemented using any major
visualization system.

1. Write a simulation program to create a vector field $O_{X \times Y}^{\text{vector2}}$ based on the
   gravitational attraction exerted by three point masses. The vector field is
   defined over a 500×500 2D regular grid. The three point masses should
   have different mass values and be located at points of your choice within the
   bounding rectangle of the 500×500 grid. For the purpose of this exercise,
   the gravitational field of a point mass is proportional to its mass value and
   diminishes as the square of the distance from it. The value of the force field
   at any point on the grid is a vector whose magnitude and direction is the
   vector sum of the three forces that are exerted upon the point by the three
   point masses.

   Import your field in your visualization program and visualize it using the
   hedgehog technique and an appropriate color map.

2. Extend your program for the previous exercise so that it operates on a 3D
   regular grid and produces an $O_{X \times Y \times Z}^{\text{vector3}}$ field on that grid, again based on
   the forces exerted by three point masses located in positions within the 3D
   grid. Visualize this field by converting your vector field into scalar and then
   employing the following techniques:

   - cutting planes;
   - isosurfaces.

   Convert your vector field to scalar by

   - taking the vector magnitude component;
   - employing the scalarization technique described in this chapter.

3. The *Blunt Fin* data set (obtained from NASA and other sites) is a well-
   known testbed for visualization programs. It is the output of an aeronautics
   simulation and consists of three fields placed on a 3D grid. The three fields
   are:

   - density, a scalar field;

- momentum, a 3D vector field;

- stagnation, another scalar field.

Import the Blunt Fin data set and *simultaneously* display the following:

- an isosurface of the density field;

- a volume rendering of the stagnation field;

- glyphs of the vectors of the momentum field that originate from the isosurface of the density field.

In addition, add "sensible" animation capability on any of the parameters (e.g., the isosurface value).

Note: a "glyph" is an object used to represent a particular type of data; in the case of vector data a usual glyph is the arrow.

A

Vector and Affine Spaces

Points and vectors are the most basic primitives used in graphics. In this appendix we present their mathematical foundations and their most essential properties. The reader should refer to a specialized linear algebra textbook (for example, [Stra03]) for a more complete presentation and advanced topics.

A.1 Vector Spaces

A set V with elements called *vectors* and denoted $\vec{a}$, $\vec{b}$, $\vec{v}$, etc. is a *vector space* if two operations are defined:

1. *vector addition* between two vectors, denoted $\vec{a} + \vec{b}$, whose result is also a vector, and

2. *scalar multiplication* between a scalar (real number) and a vector, denoted $\lambda \cdot \vec{a}$ or simply $\lambda\,\vec{a}$, whose result is also a vector,

and the following properties are satisfied:

1. For vector addition:

    (a) *Commutativity*: $\vec{a} + \vec{b} = \vec{b} + \vec{a}$ for every $\vec{a}$, $\vec{b} \in V$.

    (b) *Associativity*: $\vec{a} + (\vec{b} + \vec{c}) = (\vec{a} + \vec{b}) + \vec{c}$ for every $\vec{a}$, $\vec{b}$, $\vec{c} \in V$.

(c) There is a *zero element* $\overrightarrow{\mathbf{0}} \in V$ such that $\overrightarrow{\mathbf{0}} + \overrightarrow{\mathbf{a}} = \overrightarrow{\mathbf{a}} + \overrightarrow{\mathbf{0}} = \overrightarrow{\mathbf{a}}$ for every $\overrightarrow{\mathbf{a}} \in V$.

(d) For every $\overrightarrow{\mathbf{a}} \in V$ its *inverse* exists in V, that is, an element $-\overrightarrow{\mathbf{a}} \in V$ such that $\overrightarrow{\mathbf{a}} + (-\overrightarrow{\mathbf{a}}) = \overrightarrow{\mathbf{0}}$.

2. For scalar multiplication:

   (a) *Associativity*: $(\lambda \mu)\overrightarrow{\mathbf{a}} = \lambda(\mu \overrightarrow{\mathbf{a}})$ for every $\lambda, \mu \in \mathbb{R}$ and $\overrightarrow{\mathbf{a}} \in V$.

   (b) 1 is the *identity element*: $1 \cdot \overrightarrow{\mathbf{a}} = \overrightarrow{\mathbf{a}}$ for every $\overrightarrow{\mathbf{a}} \in V$.

   (c) *Distributivity* of scalar multiplication over vector addition: $\lambda(\overrightarrow{\mathbf{a}} + \overrightarrow{\mathbf{b}}) = \lambda \overrightarrow{\mathbf{a}} + \lambda \overrightarrow{\mathbf{b}}$ for every $\lambda \in \mathbb{R}$ and $\overrightarrow{\mathbf{a}}, \overrightarrow{\mathbf{b}} \in V$.

   (d) *Distributivity* of vector addition over scalar multiplication: $(\lambda + \mu)\overrightarrow{\mathbf{a}} = \lambda \overrightarrow{\mathbf{a}} + \mu \overrightarrow{\mathbf{a}}$ for every $\lambda, \mu \in \mathbb{R}$ and $\overrightarrow{\mathbf{a}} \in V$.

The most familiar examples of vector spaces are the spaces $\mathbb{R}^2$ and $\mathbb{R}^3$ of 2D vectors on a plane and 3D vectors in space, respectively, with the usual operations. For 3D vectors these are

$$\overrightarrow{\mathbf{a}} + \overrightarrow{\mathbf{b}} = [a_x, a_y, a_z]^{\mathrm{T}} + [b_x, b_y, b_z]^{\mathrm{T}} = [a_x + b_x, a_y + b_y, a_z + b_z]^{\mathrm{T}},$$
$$\lambda \cdot \overrightarrow{\mathbf{a}} = \lambda[a_x, a_y, a_z] = [\lambda a_x, \lambda a_y, \lambda a_z]^{\mathrm{T}}.$$

Another example of vector space is the set of polynomials of degree k; the operations are defined as

$$\overrightarrow{\mathbf{a}} + \overrightarrow{\mathbf{b}} = (a_0 + a_1 x + a_2 x^2 + \cdots + a_k x^k) + (b_0 + b_1 x + b_2 x^2 + \cdots + b_k x^k)$$
$$= (a_0 + b_0) + (a_1 + b_1)x + (a_2 + b_2)x^2 + \cdots + (a_k + b_k)x^k.$$

$$\lambda \cdot \overrightarrow{\mathbf{a}} = \lambda(a_0 + a_1 x + a_2 x^2 + \cdots + a_k x^k)$$
$$= (\lambda a_0) + (\lambda a_1)x + (\lambda a_2)x^2 + \cdots + (\lambda a_k)x^k.$$

A.1.1   Linear Combinations and Linear Independence

Consider vectors $\overrightarrow{\mathbf{a}}_1, \overrightarrow{\mathbf{a}}_2, \ldots, \overrightarrow{\mathbf{a}}_m$ of a vector space V. An expression of the form

$$\overrightarrow{\mathbf{a}} = \lambda_1 \overrightarrow{\mathbf{a}}_1 + \lambda_2 \overrightarrow{\mathbf{a}}_2 + \cdots + \lambda_m \overrightarrow{\mathbf{a}}_m$$

for $\lambda_1, \lambda_2, \ldots, \lambda_m \in \mathbb{R}$ is called a *linear combination* of $\overrightarrow{\mathbf{a}}_1, \overrightarrow{\mathbf{a}}_2, \ldots, \overrightarrow{\mathbf{a}}_m$. Since vector addition and scalar multiplication yield vectors, the linear combination of vectors is also a vector. Special forms of linear combinations are *affine combinations* (or *barycentric combinations*), for which the coefficients sum to one,

$\sum_{i=1}^{m} \lambda_i = 1$, and *convex combinations*, which are affine combinations for which additionally the coefficients are non-negative, $\lambda_i \geq 0$.

Vectors $\vec{\mathbf{a}}_1, \vec{\mathbf{a}}_2, \ldots, \vec{\mathbf{a}}_m$ are called *linearly independent* if the equation

$$\lambda_1 \vec{\mathbf{a}}_1 + \lambda_2 \vec{\mathbf{a}}_2 + \cdots + \lambda_m \vec{\mathbf{a}}_m = \vec{\mathbf{0}}$$

has the unique solution $\lambda_1 = \lambda_2 = \cdots = \lambda_m = 0$. Otherwise these vectors are called *linearly dependent*; in this case at least one of the λ_i is non-zero and therefore at least one of $\vec{\mathbf{a}}_1, \vec{\mathbf{a}}_2, \ldots, \vec{\mathbf{a}}_m$ can be written as as linear combination of the remaining $(m-1)$ vectors.

As a consequence of this definition, we observe that if a vector $\vec{\mathbf{a}}$ can be written as a linear combination of some linearly independent vectors $\vec{\mathbf{a}}_1, \vec{\mathbf{a}}_2, \ldots, \vec{\mathbf{a}}_m$, then this expression is *unique*. Indeed, suppose that $\vec{\mathbf{a}}$ can be expressed as two different linear combinations of these vectors,

$$\vec{\mathbf{a}} = \lambda_1 \vec{\mathbf{a}}_1 + \lambda_2 \vec{\mathbf{a}}_2 + \cdots + \lambda_m \vec{\mathbf{a}}_m = \mu_1 \vec{\mathbf{a}}_1 + \mu_2 \vec{\mathbf{a}}_2 + \cdots + \mu_m \vec{\mathbf{a}}_m.$$

Then

$$\vec{\mathbf{0}} = (\lambda_1 - \mu_1) \vec{\mathbf{a}}_1 + (\lambda_2 - \mu_2) \vec{\mathbf{a}}_2 + \cdots + (\lambda_m - \mu_m) \vec{\mathbf{a}}_m,$$

but since $\vec{\mathbf{a}}_1, \vec{\mathbf{a}}_2, \ldots, \vec{\mathbf{a}}_m$ are linearly independent, all the coefficients in this expression must be zero:

$$\lambda_i - \mu_i = 0 \quad \Leftrightarrow \quad \lambda_i = \mu_i \quad \text{for all } i,$$

hence the expression of $\vec{\mathbf{a}}$ in terms of $\vec{\mathbf{a}}_1, \vec{\mathbf{a}}_2, \ldots, \vec{\mathbf{a}}_m$ is actually unique.

A.1.2   Basis and Dimension of a Vector Space

A *basis* of a vector space is a set of linearly independent vectors having the additional property that every vector of the space can be written as a linear combination of them.

According to the above discussion, the expression of every vector as a linear combination of the elements of a basis is unique. The (unique) coefficients with which a vector is written as a linear combination of the elements of a basis are called the *coordinates* of the vector in terms of this basis.

Every vector space has a basis. In fact, every vector space may have many different bases. However, it can be proven that all bases of a vector space have the same number of elements. The number of elements in a vector space basis is called the *dimension* of the vector space.

In the 3D space $\mathbb{R}^3$, the most familiar basis is

$$\overrightarrow{\mathbf{i}} = [1,0,0]^T, \quad \overrightarrow{\mathbf{j}} = [0,1,0]^T, \quad \overrightarrow{\mathbf{k}} = [0,0,1]^T.$$

Every vector is written in terms of this basis using its usual coordinates, for instance a vector $\overrightarrow{\mathbf{a}} = x\,\overrightarrow{\mathbf{i}} + y\,\overrightarrow{\mathbf{j}} + z\,\overrightarrow{\mathbf{k}}$ has coordinates $[x,y,z]^T$. Another basis of this space is

$$\overrightarrow{\mathbf{i}'} = [1,1,1]^T, \quad \overrightarrow{\mathbf{j}'} = [1,2,3]^T, \quad \overrightarrow{\mathbf{k}'} = [2,3,7]^T,$$

and, for example, the vector $\overrightarrow{\mathbf{a}} = [2,1,-6]^T$ has coordinates $\overrightarrow{\mathbf{a}'} = [5,1,-2]$ in terms of this basis.

For the vector space of k-degree polynomials, the usual basis is the one comprised of the monomials

$$1, t, t^2, \ldots, t^k,$$

and therefore this space has dimension $(k+1)$. Another basis for this vector space is comprised of the k-degree Bernstein polynomials,

$$B_i^k(t) = \binom{k}{i} t^i (1-t)^{k-i}, \quad i = 0, 1, \ldots, k.$$

See Chapter 7 for more details on this basis.

In general, if the coordinates of a vector are given in terms of an initial basis, it is possible to compute its coordinates in terms of a different basis; it suffices to know the coordinates of the vectors of the new basis in terms of the initial basis. See Section 3.15 for an example and application in $\mathbb{R}^3$.

In the following sections we shall concentrate on 2D and 3D vectors of $\mathbb{R}^2$ and $\mathbb{R}^3$, since they are useful for graphics and visualization. We will denote these vectors by their usual coordinates in a column, for example

$$\overrightarrow{\mathbf{a}} = \begin{bmatrix} x \\ y \\ z \end{bmatrix} = [x,y,z]^T.$$

Several of the properties we mention below hold equally for any vector space, but the reader should refer to a linear algebra textbook for more details.

A.1.3 Vector Norm and Unit Vectors

The *norm* of a vector $\overrightarrow{\mathbf{a}} = [x,y,z]^T$ is the non-negative real number

$$|\overrightarrow{\mathbf{a}}| = \sqrt{x^2 + y^2 + z^2}$$

and is actually the *length* of the vector. The norm of a vector has the following properties:

1. $|\vec{\mathbf{a}}| > 0$ for $\vec{\mathbf{a}} \neq \vec{\mathbf{0}}$ and $|\vec{\mathbf{a}}| = 0$ if and only if $\vec{\mathbf{a}} = \vec{\mathbf{0}}$.

2. $|\lambda \vec{\mathbf{a}}| = |\lambda||\vec{\mathbf{a}}|$ for any $\lambda \in \mathbb{R}$.

3. $|\vec{\mathbf{a}} + \vec{\mathbf{b}}| \leq |\vec{\mathbf{a}}| + |\vec{\mathbf{b}}|$.

We note that it is possible to define different kinds of vector norms in any vector space; the only requirement is that they satisfy the above three properties.

Vectors with norm equal to 1 are called *unit vectors* and in this book are denoted with a hat (ˆ) instead of an arrow on top. Given any vector $\vec{\mathbf{a}}$, a unit vector in the direction of $\vec{\mathbf{a}}$ may be computed by dividing it (coordinate-wise) by its norm:

$$\hat{\mathbf{a}} = \frac{\vec{\mathbf{a}}}{|\vec{\mathbf{a}}|} = \left[\frac{x}{|\vec{\mathbf{a}}|}, \frac{y}{|\vec{\mathbf{a}}|}, \frac{z}{|\vec{\mathbf{a}}|}\right]^{\mathrm{T}}.$$

This process is often called *normalization* of $\vec{\mathbf{a}}$.

A.1.4 Dot Product

The *dot product* (or *inner product*) of two vectors $\vec{\mathbf{a}} = [a_x, a_y, a_z]^{\mathrm{T}}$ and $\vec{\mathbf{b}} = [b_x, b_y, b_z]^{\mathrm{T}}$ is a real number and is defined as

$$\vec{\mathbf{a}} \cdot \vec{\mathbf{b}} = a_x b_x + a_y b_y + a_z b_z.$$

This formula holds for 2D vectors as well as for vectors in any vector space given in terms of their coordinates. The dot product can also be seen as a matrix multiplication: $\vec{\mathbf{a}} \cdot \vec{\mathbf{b}} = \vec{\mathbf{a}}^{\mathrm{T}} \vec{\mathbf{b}}$. It should also be noted that

$$\vec{\mathbf{a}} \cdot \vec{\mathbf{a}} = |\vec{\mathbf{a}}|^2.$$

The dot product has the following properties:

1. *Commutativity*: $\vec{\mathbf{a}} \cdot \vec{\mathbf{b}} = \vec{\mathbf{b}} \cdot \vec{\mathbf{a}}$;

2. *Bilinearity*: $\vec{\mathbf{a}} \cdot (\vec{\mathbf{b}} + \lambda \vec{\mathbf{c}}) = \vec{\mathbf{a}} \cdot \vec{\mathbf{b}} + \lambda(\vec{\mathbf{a}} \cdot \vec{\mathbf{c}})$.

The dot product of two vectors can also be written as

$$\vec{\mathbf{a}} \cdot \vec{\mathbf{b}} = |\vec{\mathbf{a}}||\vec{\mathbf{b}}|\cos\theta$$

where θ is the (oriented) angle from $\vec{\mathbf{a}}$ to $\vec{\mathbf{b}}$. This form of the dot product has important applications. First, it reveals that if two vectors are perpendicular to each other, their dot product is equal to zero, since $\theta = 90°$:

$$\vec{\mathbf{a}} \perp \vec{\mathbf{b}} \quad \Leftrightarrow \quad \vec{\mathbf{a}} \cdot \vec{\mathbf{b}} = 0.$$

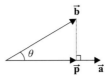

Figure A.1. Vector projection.

Second, if the coordinates of two vectors are given, the above formula can be used to compute the angle between them:

$$\theta = \arccos\left(\frac{\overrightarrow{\mathbf{a}} \cdot \overrightarrow{\mathbf{b}}}{|\overrightarrow{\mathbf{a}}||\overrightarrow{\mathbf{b}}|}\right).$$

Notice that if $\overrightarrow{\mathbf{a}}$ and $\overrightarrow{\mathbf{b}}$ are normalized, the division is avoided:

$$\theta = \arccos(\hat{\mathbf{a}} \cdot \hat{\mathbf{b}}).$$

Third, given a vector $\overrightarrow{\mathbf{a}}$, it can be observed that the projection $\overrightarrow{\mathbf{p}}$ of any vector $\overrightarrow{\mathbf{b}}$ along $\overrightarrow{\mathbf{a}}$ (Figure A.1) has length

$$|\overrightarrow{\mathbf{p}}| = |\overrightarrow{\mathbf{b}}|\cos\theta = |\overrightarrow{\mathbf{b}}|\left(\frac{\overrightarrow{\mathbf{a}} \cdot \overrightarrow{\mathbf{b}}}{|\overrightarrow{\mathbf{a}}||\overrightarrow{\mathbf{b}}|}\right),$$

where θ is the angle between $\overrightarrow{\mathbf{a}}$ and $\overrightarrow{\mathbf{b}}$; this formula can be simplified if $\overrightarrow{\mathbf{a}}$ is normalized:

$$|\overrightarrow{\mathbf{p}}| = \hat{\mathbf{a}} \cdot \hat{\mathbf{b}}.$$

A.1.5 Cross Product

The *cross product* (or *external product*) of two 3D vectors $\overrightarrow{\mathbf{a}} = [a_x, a_y, a_z]^\mathsf{T}$ and $\overrightarrow{\mathbf{b}} = [b_x, b_y, b_z]^\mathsf{T}$ is a vector perpendicular to both $\overrightarrow{\mathbf{a}}$ and $\overrightarrow{\mathbf{b}}$ (and therefore to the plane spanned by them) and is defined[1] as

$$\overrightarrow{\mathbf{a}} \times \overrightarrow{\mathbf{b}} = (a_y b_z - a_z b_y)\overrightarrow{\mathbf{i}} + (a_z b_x - a_x b_z)\overrightarrow{\mathbf{j}} + (a_x b_y - a_y b_x)\overrightarrow{\mathbf{k}}$$

or, in determinant form,

$$\overrightarrow{\mathbf{a}} \times \overrightarrow{\mathbf{b}} = \begin{vmatrix} \overrightarrow{\mathbf{i}} & \overrightarrow{\mathbf{j}} & \overrightarrow{\mathbf{k}} \\ a_x & a_y & a_z \\ b_x & b_y & b_z \end{vmatrix}.$$

---

[1] Note that the cross product is defined for 3D vectors only.

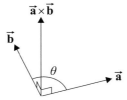

Figure A.2. The cross product of two vectors.

The direction of the cross product can be determined using the right-hand rule for $\vec{a}$, $\vec{b}$ and $\vec{a} \times \vec{b}$ as shown in Figure A.2.

The cross product has the following properties:

1. *Anti-commutativity*: $\vec{b} \times \vec{a} = -(\vec{a} \times \vec{b})$

2. *Distributivity* over vector addition: $\vec{a} \times (\vec{b} + \vec{c}) = (\vec{a} \times \vec{b}) + (\vec{a} \times \vec{c})$.

It can be verified that the cross product of two parallel vectors is zero:

$$\vec{a} \parallel \vec{b} \quad \Leftrightarrow \quad \vec{a} \times \vec{b} = 0.$$

It is noteworthy that the norm of the cross product is equal to the area of the parallelogram with sides $\vec{a}$ and $\vec{b}$, and can be computed as

$$|\vec{a} \times \vec{b}| = |\vec{a}||\vec{b}| \sin \theta$$

where θ ($0 \leq \theta \leq 180°$) is the angle between $\vec{a}$ and $\vec{b}$ (Figure A.2).

A.1.6 Orthonormal Basis

Even though every vector space has multiple bases, some bases are more useful than others! One such category are *orthonormal* bases, which are comprised of unit vectors that are pairwise perpendicular (orthogonal) to each other; therefore, $(\hat{\mathbf{b}}_1, \hat{\mathbf{b}}_2, \ldots, \hat{\mathbf{b}}_n)$ is an orthonormal basis of a vector space V when the vectors $\hat{\mathbf{b}}_i$ constitute a basis and satisfy

$$\hat{\mathbf{b}}_i \cdot \hat{\mathbf{b}}_j = \begin{cases} 1, & \text{if } i = j, \\ 0, & \text{if } i \neq j. \end{cases}$$

Because of this property, when an orthonormal basis is used the coordinates of a vector are easy to find; specifically, if $\vec{a} = \lambda_1 \hat{\mathbf{b}}_1 + \lambda_2 \hat{\mathbf{b}}_2 + \cdots + \lambda_n \hat{\mathbf{b}}_n$, then

$$\lambda_i = \vec{a} \cdot \hat{\mathbf{b}}_i.$$

The familiar bases of the Euclidean spaces $\mathbb{R}^2$ and $\mathbb{R}^3$ are orthonormal.

A.2 Affine Spaces

A set S with elements called *points* and denoted **p**, **q**, etc. is an *affine space* with an associated vector space V, if an operation called *addition* is defined between a point and a vector, denoted $\mathbf{p} + \overrightarrow{\mathbf{a}}$, whose result is a point, provided that the following properties are satisfied:

1. *Associativity* of addition: $(\mathbf{p} + \overrightarrow{\mathbf{a}}) + \overrightarrow{\mathbf{b}} = \mathbf{p} + (\overrightarrow{\mathbf{a}} + \overrightarrow{\mathbf{b}})$ for every $\mathbf{p} \in S$ and $\overrightarrow{\mathbf{a}}, \overrightarrow{\mathbf{b}} \in V$.

2. $\overrightarrow{\mathbf{0}}$ is the *zero element* for addition: $\mathbf{p} + \overrightarrow{\mathbf{0}} = \mathbf{p}$ for every $\mathbf{p} \in S$.

3. For every $\mathbf{p}, \mathbf{q} \in S$, there exists a unique vector $\overrightarrow{\mathbf{a}} \in V$ such that $\mathbf{p} = \mathbf{q} + \overrightarrow{\mathbf{a}}$; this is written equivalently as $\mathbf{p} - \mathbf{q} = \overrightarrow{\mathbf{a}}$ and is often referred to as the *difference* between **p** and **q**.

The most familiar examples of affine spaces are the 2D and 3D Euclidean spaces $\mathbb{E}^2$ and $\mathbb{E}^3$ of points on a plane or in space, respectively.

This definition is consistent with the usual perception of the interplay between points and vectors. Adding a point and a vector assumes basing the vector onto the point and yields the point at the end of the vector. Conversely, taking the difference of two points constructs the vector between them (specifically, $\mathbf{p} - \mathbf{q}$ is the vector from **q** to **p**, see Figure A.3). Points may not be added together as this operation has no sense. In general, points denote position whereas vectors denote direction and magnitude but are not based on a specific point.

Figure A.3. Operations in affine space.

A.2.1 Coordinate Systems

Consider a constant point **o** of an affine space S and a basis $(\overrightarrow{\mathbf{b}}_1, \overrightarrow{\mathbf{b}}_2, \ldots, \overrightarrow{\mathbf{b}}_n)$ of the associated vector space V. Then $(\mathbf{o}; \overrightarrow{\mathbf{b}}_1, \overrightarrow{\mathbf{b}}_2, \ldots, \overrightarrow{\mathbf{b}}_n)$ constitutes an *(affine) coordinate system* of S. The point **o** is called the *origin* of the coordinate system, and $\overrightarrow{\mathbf{b}}_1, \overrightarrow{\mathbf{b}}_2, \ldots, \overrightarrow{\mathbf{b}}_n$ define the *coordinate axes*. The dimension of the vector space V is also called the *dimension* of the affine space S. Different coordinate systems may be constructed for the same affine space by varying the origin, the basis, or both.

Using a coordinate system of an affine space, it is possible to define coordinates for the points of the space (remember that coordinates were defined only for vectors above). Specifically, given a point $\mathbf{p} \in S$ such that

$$\mathbf{p} - \mathbf{o} = \lambda_1 \overrightarrow{\mathbf{b}}_1 + \lambda_2 \overrightarrow{\mathbf{b}}_2 + \cdots + \lambda_n \overrightarrow{\mathbf{b}}_n,$$

the coefficients $\lambda_1, \lambda_2, \ldots, \lambda_n$ are called the *coordinates* of $\mathbf{p}$ with respect to the coordinate system $(\mathbf{o}; \overrightarrow{\mathbf{b}}_1, \overrightarrow{\mathbf{b}}_2, \ldots, \overrightarrow{\mathbf{b}}_n)$.

Since the coordinates of point $\mathbf{p}$ are the same as those of vector $\mathbf{p} - \mathbf{o}$ from the origin $\mathbf{o}$ to $\mathbf{p}$, it is usual to identify these two elements. Therefore some normally illegal constructs can be seen, such as multiplying a point by a scalar (which is actually a multiplication of the corresponding vector from the origin, see, for example, the scaling transformation in Chapter 3) or adding two points (which is actually an addition of the corresponding vectors from the origin); however, such practices are discouraged and the distinction between points and vectors, depending on whether a position or a direction is represented, should be respected.

In the case of Euclidean 2D and 3D spaces $\mathbb{E}^2$ and $\mathbb{E}^3$, the origin that usually accompanies the familiar bases is $\mathbf{o} = [0,0,0]^\mathrm{T}$.

The *orientation* of the coordinate system is important in graphics. Visually, for $\mathbb{E}^2$ a coordinate system may either be *counterclockwise* (the usual convention) or *clockwise*, as determined by the direction of rotation that the first coordinate axis must perform in order to be aligned with the second one. Similarly, for $\mathbb{E}^3$ a coordinate system may either be *right-handed* (the usual convention) or *left-handed* (Figure 3.1). It can thus be seen that the orientation of a coordinate system depends on the order of the basis vectors. In general, for an affine space of dimension n, two coordinate systems using different bases have the same orientation if the determinants of the $(n \times n)$ matrices formed by the coordinates of the basis vectors for the two bases have the same sign.

Differential Geometry Basics

Differential geometry, as its name suggests, studies the properties of geometric entities using differential calculus. Emphasis is placed on local characteristics such as curvature. In this appendix, we present the most fundamental concepts regarding curves and surfaces; more complete discussions of the field can be found in specialized sources such as [O'Ne66, Lips74, dC76, Opre97, Patr02].

B.1   Curves

B.1.1   Basic Definitions

A *curve* in its parametric representation is a differentiable mapping from an interval $I \subseteq \mathbb{R}$ to $\mathbb{R}^3$; therefore a curve can be written as

$$\mathbf{X}(t) = \begin{bmatrix} x(t) \\ y(t) \\ z(t) \end{bmatrix} , \quad t \in I, \tag{B.1}$$

where $x(t)$, $y(t)$, $z(t)$ are all differentiable functions of t, called the *coordinate functions* of $\mathbf{X}$. If one of the coordinate functions, for example $z(t)$, is constant everywhere, then the curve is a plane curve. The interval I may be of any type: closed, half open, open, finite or infinite.

685

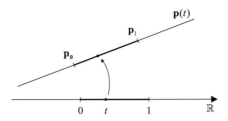

Figure B.1. Parametric equation of a line segment.

For example, the equation of a straight line through points $\mathbf{p}_0$ and $\mathbf{p}_1$ is

$$\mathbf{X}_{\text{line}}(t) = (1-t)\,\mathbf{p}_0 + t\,\mathbf{p}_1\,, \quad t \in (-\infty, +\infty). \tag{B.2}$$

If $t \in [0, +\infty)$ then $\mathbf{X}_{\text{line}}(t)$ represents the ray from $\mathbf{p}_0$ through $\mathbf{p}_1$, whereas if $t \in [0,1]$ then $\mathbf{X}_{\text{line}}(t)$ represents the line segment from $\mathbf{p}_0$ to $\mathbf{p}_1$ (Figure B.1).[1]

A physical interpretation of the above definition of a curve is to consider t to be time, and then $\mathbf{X}(t)$ is the position of a particle moving along the curve at time t. Continuing this intuition, the *tangent vector* of the curve at position t,

$$\mathbf{X}'(t) = \begin{bmatrix} x'(t) \\ y'(t) \\ z'(t) \end{bmatrix} \tag{B.3}$$

gives the velocity of this particle at time t; thus this vector is also called the *velocity vector* of $\mathbf{X}$ at point $\mathbf{X}(t)$. A curve is *regular* if its velocity vector is non-zero everywhere, i.e.,

$$\mathbf{X}'(t) \neq \vec{\mathbf{0}} \text{ for every } t \in I.$$

Such a curve does not have any cusps or corners (*singularities*) that occur at parametric points t_0 where $\mathbf{X}'(t_0) = \vec{\mathbf{0}}$; we will only consider regular curves in our discussion.

The length traveled along the curve can be computed by integrating the velocity; therefore, the *arc length* between two points $\mathbf{X}(a)$ and $\mathbf{X}(b)$ of a curve $\mathbf{X}$ can be computed as

$$L = \int_a^b |\mathbf{X}'(t)|\,dt. \tag{B.4}$$

---

[1]It should be noted that, according to the operations defined in Appendix A, the equation of the straight line should be written more correctly as $\mathbf{X}_{\text{line}}(t) = \mathbf{p}_0 + t(\mathbf{p}_1 - \mathbf{p}_0)$.

B.1.2 Parameterizations of a Curve

The path of a curve may be followed at many different speeds; these correspond to different parameterizations of the curve. Specifically, consider a differentiable function $t = t(s)$ from an interval J to I; then

$$\mathbf{Y}(s) = \mathbf{X}\big(t(s)\big), \quad s \in J \tag{B.5}$$

is a *reparameterization* of the curve $\mathbf{X}$. If the function $t(s)$ is invertible, then the two parameterizations $\mathbf{X}(t)$ and $\mathbf{Y}(s)$ of the curve are *equivalent*. Concerning the velocity vector of a reparameterized curve, the chain rule yields

$$\mathbf{Y}'(s) = t'(s)\,\mathbf{X}'\big(t(s)\big). \tag{B.6}$$

As an example, consider the linear mapping of an interval $J = [a,b]$ to $I = [0,1]$

$$t = t(s) = \frac{s-a}{b-a} \quad \Longleftrightarrow \quad s = s(t) = a + (b-a)t.$$

A reparameterization of the line segment between two points $\mathbf{p}_0$ and $\mathbf{p}_1$ such that the parameter s is in J is

$$
\begin{aligned}
\mathbf{Y}_{\text{line}}(s) = \mathbf{X}_{\text{line}}\big(t(s)\big) &= \left(1 - \frac{s-a}{b-a}\right)\mathbf{p}_0 + \frac{s-a}{b-a}\mathbf{p}_1 \\
&= \frac{b-s}{b-a}\mathbf{p}_0 + \frac{s-a}{b-a}\mathbf{p}_1, \quad s \in [a,b].
\end{aligned}
\tag{B.7}
$$

Another example of reparameterization is presented in Section 7.2.5.

Arc length parameterization. Consider now a curve $\mathbf{X}(t)$, $t \in I$ and the "arc length" function

$$s(t) = \int_a^t |\mathbf{X}'(u)|\,du, \tag{B.8}$$

for some arbitrary $a \in I$. The inverse of this function has the form $t = t(s)$ (and it can be proven that it always exists). It can also be shown that the reparameterization $\mathbf{Y}(s) = \mathbf{X}\big(t(s)\big)$ of the original curve for this $t = t(s)$ has unit velocity everywhere, $|\mathbf{Y}'(s)| = 1$; consequently, in $\mathbf{Y}(s)$ the parameter (in this case s) can be interpreted as the total length traveled along the curve. This parameterization is appropriately called *arc length parameterization*.

The arc length parameterization has great theoretical interest, since it simplifies the study of curves. It also has great practical interest, since it allows us to answer the question "at what point $\mathbf{Y}(s)$ on the curve are we after having traveled distance s from its start?" rather than "at what point $\mathbf{X}(t)$ are we at time t?" Unfortunately, it is not easy to compute the inverse of the arc length function for any but a limited class of curves, and it is even impossible for several curves, albeit common ones like, for example, the ellipse.

B.1.3   Curvature, Torsion, and the Frenet Frame

One of the aims of differential geometry is to study the local behavior of curves and surfaces. Concerning curves, their shape is characterized by two quantities, curvature and torsion. We will initially develop these notions on curves parameterized by arc length, in order to simplify our discussion, and then give the respective formulas for general curves.

Consider a curve $\mathbf{Y}(s)$ parameterized by arc length; for this curve, $|\mathbf{Y}'(s)| = 1$ everywhere. For any point $\mathbf{Y}(s)$ on the curve we define the following three unit vectors:

$$\hat{\mathbf{t}} = \hat{\mathbf{t}}(s) = \mathbf{Y}'(s),$$

$$\hat{\mathbf{n}} = \hat{\mathbf{n}}(s) = \frac{\hat{\mathbf{t}}'(s)}{|\hat{\mathbf{t}}'(s)|}, \tag{B.9}$$

$$\hat{\mathbf{b}} = \hat{\mathbf{b}}(s) = \hat{\mathbf{t}}(s) \times \hat{\mathbf{n}}(s).$$

Regarding these vectors,

- $\hat{\mathbf{t}}$ is the *tangent vector* mentioned above.

- $\hat{\mathbf{n}}$ is called the *principal normal vector* and it can be proven to be perpendicular to $\hat{\mathbf{t}}$: remember that $|\mathbf{Y}'(s)| = 1$, therefore $1 = |\hat{\mathbf{t}}| = \sqrt{\hat{\mathbf{t}} \cdot \hat{\mathbf{t}}}$ and thus $\hat{\mathbf{t}} \cdot \hat{\mathbf{t}} = 1$. Then $(\hat{\mathbf{t}} \cdot \hat{\mathbf{t}})' = 0$ which yields $2(\hat{\mathbf{t}} \cdot \hat{\mathbf{t}}') = 0$, hence $\hat{\mathbf{t}} \cdot \hat{\mathbf{t}}' = 0$ which means that $\hat{\mathbf{t}}'$ (and also $\hat{\mathbf{n}} = \hat{\mathbf{t}}'/|\hat{\mathbf{t}}'|$) is perpendicular to $\hat{\mathbf{t}}$.

- $\hat{\mathbf{b}}$ is called the *binormal vector* and is by definition perpendicular to both $\hat{\mathbf{t}}$ and $\hat{\mathbf{n}}$.

These three vectors define, for every point $\mathbf{Y}(s)$ of the curve, a local orthonormal coordinate system, called the *Frenet frame* (Figure B.2). The Frenet frame changes orientation as its origin $\mathbf{Y}(s)$ moves along the curve, and this change of orientation can help the study of the shape of the curve.

Curvature and torsion are defined in terms of the Frenet frame unit vectors, as follows:

$$\kappa = \kappa(s) = |\hat{\mathbf{t}}'(s)|,$$

$$\tau = \tau(s) = -\hat{\mathbf{n}} \cdot \hat{\mathbf{b}}. \tag{B.10}$$

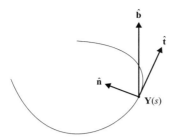

Figure B.2. The Frenet frame of a parametric curve

- κ is the *curvature*, which measures how much the curve deviates from the straight line at parametric position s. For an explanation of this fact, consider that the derivative $\hat{\mathbf{t}}'(s)$ measures the rate of change of the tangent vector $\hat{\mathbf{t}}$ along the curve, but since $\hat{\mathbf{t}} = \mathbf{Y}'$ has unit length everywhere on the curve, $\hat{\mathbf{t}}'$ measures only the rate of change of its direction; therefore, $\kappa = |\hat{\mathbf{t}}'(s)|$ provides a numerical estimate of the turning of the curve.

  It is evident that $\kappa(s) \geq 0$. We note that if $\kappa(s) = 0$ for all s then the curve is a straight line and vice versa. Moreover, the larger $\kappa(s)$ is, the sharper the curve at $\mathbf{Y}(s)$.

  Using the curvature, we may define the *osculating circle* of the curve at point $\mathbf{Y}(s)$. It is a circle that has radius $\rho(s) = 1/k(s)$ (the *radius of curvature*) and center $\mathbf{c}(s) = \mathbf{Y}(s) + \rho(s)\hat{\mathbf{n}}(s)$ (the *center of curvature*). The osculating circle is tangent to the curve at $\mathbf{Y}(s)$ and their first and second derivatives are equal.

- τ is the *torsion*, which measures how much the curve deviates from being a plane curve at parametric position s; the reference plane is the one spanned by the point $\mathbf{Y}(s)$ and the vectors $\hat{\mathbf{t}}(s)$ and $\hat{\mathbf{n}}(s)$, called the *osculating plane*. Unfortunately, it is not possible to present an intuitive derivation for torsion within the space limits of this appendix; we note that just as curvature provides a measure of the change of orientation of the tangent vector $\hat{\mathbf{t}}$, torsion provides a measure of the change of orientation of the binormal vector $\hat{\mathbf{b}}$ as the Frenet frame moves along the curve.

  Torsion can be either positive (for right-handed curves) or negative (for left-handed curves). If $\tau(s) = 0$ then the curve lies on a plane and vice versa.

It is important to note that the curvature and torsion of a curve do not depend on its parameterization, and therefore they characterize the curve itself; they are *intrinsic properties* of the curve; in fact, if a curve $\mathbf{Y}(s)$ has curvature $\kappa(s)$ and torsion $\tau(s)$, then any other curve with the same curvature and torsion differs from $\mathbf{Y}(s)$ only by a rigid motion (in other words, their shapes are identical and only their absolute positions in space and orientations may be different).

Our final tool for studying the shape of a curve is provided by the derivatives of $\hat{\mathbf{t}}, \hat{\mathbf{n}}, \hat{\mathbf{b}}$, which express the change of orientation of the Frenet frame as it moves along the curve. They are given by the *Frenet-Serret formulas* (we omit the parameter s):

$$
\begin{aligned}
\hat{\mathbf{t}}' &= &+\kappa\hat{\mathbf{n}}, \\
\hat{\mathbf{n}}' &= -\kappa\hat{\mathbf{t}} &+\tau\hat{\mathbf{b}}, \\
\hat{\mathbf{b}}' &= &-\tau\hat{\mathbf{n}}.
\end{aligned}
\tag{B.11}
$$

All the formulas given above for a curve parameterized by arc length $\mathbf{Y}(s)$ can be generalized for a regular curve $\mathbf{X}(t)$ with arbitrary parameterization. The Frenet frame is defined as

$$
\hat{\mathbf{t}} = \hat{\mathbf{t}}(t) = \frac{\mathbf{X}'(t)}{|\mathbf{X}'(t)|},
$$

$$
\hat{\mathbf{n}} = \hat{\mathbf{n}}(t) = \hat{\mathbf{b}}(t) \times \hat{\mathbf{t}}(t),
\tag{B.12}
$$

$$
\hat{\mathbf{b}} = \hat{\mathbf{b}}(t) = \frac{\mathbf{X}'(t) \times \mathbf{X}''(t)}{|\mathbf{X}'(t) \times \mathbf{X}''(t)|}.
$$

Curvature and torsion are defined as

$$
\kappa = \kappa(t) = \frac{|\mathbf{X}'(t) \times \mathbf{X}''(t)|}{|\mathbf{X}'(t)|^3},
$$

$$
\tau = \tau(t) = \frac{\det[\mathbf{X}'(t), \mathbf{X}''(t), \mathbf{X}'''(t)]}{|\mathbf{X}'(t) \times \mathbf{X}''(t)|^2},
\tag{B.13}
$$

where $\det[\mathbf{a}, \mathbf{b}, \mathbf{c}]$ is the determinant of the matrix with columns $\mathbf{a}, \mathbf{b}, \mathbf{c}$. Finally, the derivatives of the Frenet frame are (we omit the parameter t)

$$
\begin{aligned}
\hat{\mathbf{t}}' &= &+\kappa v\hat{\mathbf{n}}, \\
\hat{\mathbf{n}}' &= -\kappa v\hat{\mathbf{t}} &+\tau v\hat{\mathbf{b}}, \\
\hat{\mathbf{b}}' &= &-\tau v\hat{\mathbf{n}},
\end{aligned}
\tag{B.14}
$$

where $v(t) = s'(t) = |\mathbf{X}'(t)|$ is the velocity function of the curve (see Equation (B.8)).

B.2 Surfaces

B.2.1 Basic Definitions

A *surface* in its parametric representation is a differentiable mapping from a region $\mathbf{I} \subseteq \mathbb{R}^2$ to $\mathbb{R}^3$; therefore a surface can be written as

$$\mathbf{X}(u,v) = \begin{bmatrix} x(u,v) \\ y(u,v) \\ z(u,v) \end{bmatrix}, \quad (u,v) \in \mathbf{I}, \tag{B.15}$$

where $x(u,v)$, $y(u,v)$, and $z(u,v)$ are all differentiable functions of u and v, called the *coordinate functions* of $\mathbf{X}$. The region $\mathbf{I}$ may be of any type: closed, half open, open, finite, or infinite.

By fixing one of the parameters and letting the other one vary, we get *isoparametric curves* on the surface. More concretely, if we fix $v = v_0$ we get the *u-parameter curve* $\mathbf{X}(u,v_0)$ and similarly, if we fix $u = u_0$ we get the *v-parameter curve* $\mathbf{X}(u_0,v)$ (see Figure 7.16).

Isoparametric curves allow us to derive a physical meaning for the parametric equation of a surface: starting, for instance, with a *u*-parameter curve and letting each of its points trace a *v*-parameter curve, the outcome is the surface $\mathbf{X}(u,v)$; the result is the same if the roles of u and v are interchanged.

Curves may be constructed on a surface in a more general way as follows. Consider a surface $\mathbf{X}(u,v)$, $(u,v) \in \mathbf{I} \subseteq \mathbb{R}^2$, and a (regular) parametric curve $\mathbf{B}(t)$ whose image lies in the parametric space $\mathbf{I}$ of the surface, $\mathbf{B}(t) = \begin{bmatrix} u(t) & v(t) \end{bmatrix}^{\mathrm{T}}$; then the composition $\mathbf{C}(t) = \mathbf{X}(\mathbf{B}(t)) = \mathbf{X}(u(t),v(t))$ is a curve that lies on the surface $\mathbf{X}$, a *surface curve* of $\mathbf{X}$.

Tangent vectors (also called *velocity vectors*) on a surface are defined by differentiating surface curves. The tangent vectors of the isoparametric curves are the most straightforward ones, since they are computed by partially differentiating the surface with respect to each of the parameters u and v. We will use the following notation for the partial derivatives of the surface $\mathbf{X}(u,v)$:

$$\mathbf{X}_u = \frac{\partial \mathbf{X}}{\partial u}, \quad \mathbf{X}_v = \frac{\partial \mathbf{X}}{\partial v}, \quad \mathbf{X}_{uu} = \frac{\partial^2 \mathbf{X}}{\partial u^2}, \quad \mathbf{X}_{uv} = \frac{\partial^2 \mathbf{X}}{\partial u\,\partial v}, \quad \text{etc.} \tag{B.16}$$

For an arbitrary surface curve $\mathbf{C}(t) = \mathbf{X}(u(t),v(t))$, the tangent vector is, by the chain rule,

$$\mathbf{C}'(t) = \frac{\partial \mathbf{X}}{\partial u}\frac{du}{dt} + \frac{\partial \mathbf{X}}{\partial v}\frac{dv}{dt} = \mathbf{X}_u u'(t) + \mathbf{X}_v v'(t) \tag{B.17}$$

where the partial derivatives $\mathbf{X}_u$ and $\mathbf{X}_v$ are evaluated at $(u(t),v(t))$.

A surface is *regular* if

$$\mathbf{X}_u \times \mathbf{X}_v \neq \vec{\mathbf{0}} \text{ for every } (u,v) \in \mathbf{I}. \tag{B.18}$$

This relation implies that all its isoparametric curves are regular curves and they are nowhere tangent to each other. Such a surface does not have ridges or cusps (*singularities*). We will only consider regular surfaces in our discussion.

Any point $\mathbf{X}(u,v)$ on the surface together with the two tangent vectors $\mathbf{X}_u(u,v)$ and $\mathbf{X}_v(u,v)$ defines the *tangent plane* to the surface at that point; in fact, the tangent vector of *any* surface curve passing from $\mathbf{X}(u,v)$ lies on this tangent plane. The (unit) normal vector of this plane,

$$\hat{\mathbf{n}} = \hat{\mathbf{n}}(u,v) = \frac{\mathbf{X}_u \times \mathbf{X}_v}{|\mathbf{X}_u \times \mathbf{X}_v|}, \tag{B.19}$$

is the *normal vector* of the surface at $\mathbf{X}(u,v)$; it follows from relation (B.18) that the normal vector exists everywhere on a regular surface.

The three vectors $\mathbf{X}_u(u,v)$, $\mathbf{X}_v(u,v)$, and $\hat{\mathbf{n}}(u,v)$ define a local coordinate system at $\mathbf{X}(u,v)$. This coordinate system is analogous to the Frenet frame defined on the points of a curve; it should be noted, however, that unlike the Frenet frame, this coordinate system is not orthonormal and is dependent on the parameterization of the surface.

B.2.2 Fundamental Coefficients

In the next section we will study the local properties of surfaces by analyzing several measures of their curvature. We will make use of the following quantities:

- the *first-order fundamental coefficients*,

$$\begin{aligned}
E &= E(u,v) = \mathbf{X}_u \cdot \mathbf{X}_u, \\
F &= F(u,v) = \mathbf{X}_u \cdot \mathbf{X}_v, \\
G &= G(u,v) = \mathbf{X}_v \cdot \mathbf{X}_v,
\end{aligned} \tag{B.20}$$

and

- the *second-order fundamental coefficients*,

$$\begin{aligned}
L &= L(u,v) &&= -\mathbf{X}_u \cdot \hat{\mathbf{n}}_u &&= \mathbf{X}_{uu} \cdot \hat{\mathbf{n}}, \\
M &= M(u,v) &&= -\tfrac{1}{2}(\mathbf{X}_u \cdot \hat{\mathbf{n}}_u + \mathbf{X}_v \cdot \hat{\mathbf{n}}_v) &&= \mathbf{X}_{uv} \cdot \hat{\mathbf{n}}, \\
N &= N(u,v) &&= -\mathbf{X}_v \cdot \hat{\mathbf{n}}_v &&= \mathbf{X}_{vv} \cdot \hat{\mathbf{n}},
\end{aligned} \tag{B.21}$$

where $\hat{\mathbf{n}}$ is the surface normal at point $\mathbf{X}(u,v)$ defined in Equation (B.19). We note that the rightmost equalities in (B.21) can be confirmed by recalling that $\hat{\mathbf{n}}$ is perpendicular to $\mathbf{X}_u$ and $\mathbf{X}_v$ and differentiating $\hat{\mathbf{n}} \cdot \mathbf{X}_u = 0$ and $\hat{\mathbf{n}} \cdot \mathbf{X}_v = 0$.

These quantities are thus called because they appear in the definitions of the *first* and *second fundamental form*, respectively, which are two important tensors used for the study of the local properties of a surface; we will not elaborate on the fundamental forms in this appendix.

Apart from the formulas for surface curvatures that we will present below, further important computations on a surface can be expressed with the help of the fundamental coefficients. Given a surface curve $\mathbf{C}(t) = \mathbf{X}\big(u(t), v(t)\big)$, its *arc length* between parametric points a and b is given by (see (B.4) and (B.17))

$$s = \int_a^b \sqrt{E(u')^2 + 2Fu'v' + G(v')^2}\, dt. \tag{B.22}$$

Also, the *area* of the surface corresponding to a parametric region $\mathbf{U}$ can be expressed as

$$A = \iint_{\mathbf{U}} \sqrt{EG - F^2}\, du\, dv. \tag{B.23}$$

B.2.3   Surface Curvatures

Consider a point $\mathbf{P} = \mathbf{X}(u,v)$ on a surface, the normal vector $\hat{\mathbf{n}} = \hat{\mathbf{n}}(u,v)$ at that point, and a plane Π that contains both $\mathbf{P}$ and $\hat{\mathbf{n}}$ (Figure B.3). The intersection of the plane Π and the surface is a surface curve $\mathbf{C}(t) = \mathbf{X}\big(u(t), v(t)\big)$. The curvature of $\mathbf{C}(t)$ at the point $\mathbf{X}(u,v)$ is the *normal curvature* κ_n of the surface at $\mathbf{X}(u,v)$ along the direction $\mathbf{C}'(t)$. The normal curvature can be expressed using the fundamental coefficients as

$$\kappa_n = \frac{L(u')^2 + 2Mu'v' + N(v')^2}{E(u')^2 + 2Fu'v' + G(v')^2}. \tag{B.24}$$

The normal curvature κ_n at a surface point clearly depends on the direction chosen, and it varies periodically as the cutting plane Π is rotated around $\hat{\mathbf{n}}$. It can be proven that κ_n has at most two extreme values, called the *principal curvatures* κ_1 (the maximum) and κ_2 (the minimum) of the surface at the point considered. The directions along which κ_1 and κ_2 are obtained are called the (first and second, respectively) *principal curvature directions*, and they are perpendicular to each other.

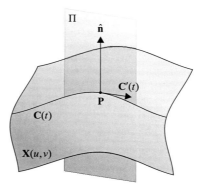

Figure B.3. Normal section of a surface.

The product of the principal curvatures

$$K = \kappa_1 \kappa_2 \tag{B.25}$$

is called the *Gaussian curvature* of the surface at the point $\mathbf{X}(u,v)$. Using the fundamental coefficients, the Gaussian curvature can be expressed as

$$K = \frac{LN - M^2}{EG - F^2}. \tag{B.26}$$

The mean of the principal curvatures

$$H = \tfrac{1}{2}(\kappa_1 + \kappa_2) \tag{B.27}$$

is called the *mean curvature* of the surface at the point $\mathbf{X}(u,v)$. It can be expressed as

$$H = \frac{1}{2}\frac{EN - 2FM + GL}{EG - F^2}. \tag{B.28}$$

Using (B.25) and (B.27), the two principal curvatures can be computed as

$$\kappa_1 = H + \sqrt{H^2 - K} \quad \text{and} \quad \kappa_2 = H - \sqrt{H^2 - K}. \tag{B.29}$$

The normal and principal curvatures are related by *Euler's formula*,

$$\kappa_n = \kappa_1 \cos^2 \phi + \kappa_2 \sin^2 \phi, \tag{B.30}$$

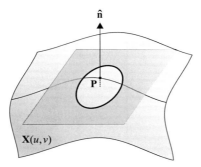

Figure B.4. Approximation of the Dupin indicatrix.

where ϕ is the angle between the tangent direction of the cutting plane considered for κ_n and the first principal direction. In Euler's formula, if we substitute $\xi = \cos\phi/\sqrt{\kappa_n}$ and $\eta = \sin\phi/\sqrt{\kappa_n}$, we get

$$1 = \kappa_1\xi^2 + \kappa_2\eta^2,\qquad(\text{B.31})$$

which is the equation of a conic section, called the *Dupin indicatrix*. An approximation of the Dupin indicatrix can be visualized as the intersection of the surface with a plane parallel to its tangent plane at a small distance ε along the direction of the surface normal (Figure B.4). The shape of the Dupin indicatrix depends on the values of κ_1 and κ_2, and the point on the surface is characterized accordingly:

- if κ_1 and κ_2 have the same sign ($K > 0$), the Dupin indicatrix is an ellipse whose axes correspond to the principal directions, and the point on the surface is called *elliptic*;

- if they have opposite signs ($K < 0$), it is a hyperbola whose axes correspond to the principal directions, and the point is called *hyperbolic*;

- if one of the principal curvatures is zero ($K = 0$), the indicatrix is a pair of parallel lines, in which case the principal direction that corresponds to the non-zero principal curvature is perpendicular to these lines and the other one is parallel, and the point is called *parabolic*;

- if the principal curvatures are equal, signifying that any direction is principal, then the indicatrix is a circle and the point is called *umbilical*;

- finally, if both principal curvatures are zero ($K = 0$ as well), the Dupin indicatrix does not exist and the point on the surface is *flat*.

Another curvature measure is the *absolute curvature*, defined as follows:

$$\kappa_a = |\kappa_1| + |\kappa_2|. \tag{B.32}$$

The last form of curvature that we will introduce is the *geodesic curvature* of a surface curve. This is the equivalent for surface curves of the usual curvature defined on simple parametric curves: given a parametric curve, its curvature on a specific point measures how much the curve deviates from being a straight line—which is the shortest path between two points in 2D or 3D space—in the neighborhood of this point; similarly, the geodesic curvature at a point of a surface curve measures how much the curve deviates from the shortest path *on the surface* between two (arbitrarily close) points in the neighborhood of this point.

Given an *arc length parametrized* surface curve $\mathbf{C}(s) = \mathbf{X}(u(s), v(s))$, the geodesic curvature κ_g at a given point is given by

$$\kappa_g = \mathbf{C}' \times \mathbf{C}'' \cdot \hat{\mathbf{n}}, \tag{B.33}$$

where $\hat{\mathbf{n}}$ is the normal vector of the surface at that point. Using (B.17) (but differentiating with respect to s in this case), it is possible to formulate an expression for κ_g that involves the derivatives of the surface $\mathbf{X}$:

$$
\begin{aligned}
\kappa_g = \big[\quad & (\mathbf{X}_u \times \mathbf{X}_{uu})(u')^3 \\
& + (2\mathbf{X}_u \times \mathbf{X}_{uv} + \mathbf{X}_v \times \mathbf{X}_{uu})(u')^2 v' \\
& + (\mathbf{X}_u \times \mathbf{X}_{vv} + 2\mathbf{X}_v \times \mathbf{X}_{uv})u'(v')^2 \\
& + (\mathbf{X}_v \times \mathbf{X}_{vv})(v')^3 \\
& + (\mathbf{X}_u \times \mathbf{X}_v)(u'v'' - u''v') \big] \cdot \hat{\mathbf{n}}
\end{aligned}
\tag{B.34}
$$

A surface curve whose geodesic curvature is zero everywhere is called a *geodesic curve* (or simply a *geodesic*) and it typically represents the shortest path on the surface between any two nearby points. For example, the great circles of a sphere are geodesics.

C

Intersection Tests

This appendix presents algorithms for the intersection tests encountered through-out the book. Valuable resources on this topic are the *journal of graphics tools*, the online newsletter *Ray Tracing News* (http://www.raytracingnews.org/) and several specialist books (e.g. [Schn03, Eric05]).

The intersection tests that we shall consider involve a line and another object. Given a line specified by two points $\mathbf{p}_1$, $\mathbf{p}_2$, the algorithms presented in the following use its parametric equation,

$$\mathbf{p}(t) = \mathbf{p}_1 + t\,(\mathbf{p}_2 - \mathbf{p}_1)$$

and compute the parametric value t for the point of intersection. We note that this equation represents the whole *directed line* through these two points if $t \in \mathbb{R}$, the *ray* from $\mathbf{p}_1$ through $\mathbf{p}_2$ if $t \in [0, +\infty)$, and the *line segment* from $\mathbf{p}_1$ to $\mathbf{p}_2$ if $t \in [0, 1]$. Therefore, depending on whether a ray or a line segment is considered, the parametric value computed should be post-checked for inclusion in the appropriate interval; otherwise the intersection point falls outside the bounds of the ray or line segment.

It should also be noted that it is sometimes important to determine at an initial stage if an intersection *does not* exist between the primitives examined, so that any computations relevant only to the calculation of the intersection point(s) can be skipped. This should be taken into account when implementing the algorithms below.

C.1   Planar Line-Line Intersection

Suppose that each of the two lines is specified by two points, $\mathbf{p}_1 = [x_1, y_1]^T$, $\mathbf{p}_2 = [x_2, y_2]^T$ and $\mathbf{p}'_1 = [x'_1, y'_1]^T$, $\mathbf{p}'_2 = [x'_2, y'_2]^T$, respectively. Then the parametric equations of the two lines can be written as

$$x(t) = x_1 + t\,\Delta x,$$
$$y(t) = y_1 + t\,\Delta y$$

and

$$x'(s) = x'_1 + s\,\Delta x',$$
$$y'(s) = y'_1 + s\,\Delta y',$$

respectively, where

$$\Delta x = x_2 - x_1, \qquad\qquad \Delta x' = x'_2 - x'_1,$$
$$\Delta y = y_2 - y_1, \qquad\qquad \Delta y' = y'_2 - y'_1.$$

At their point of intersection the following must simultaneously hold:

$$x(t) = x'(s),$$
$$y(t) = y'(s),$$

giving two equations with two unknowns (s and t). Solving these equations for s gives

$$s = \frac{(y'_1 - y_1)\Delta x - (x'_1 - x_1)\Delta y}{\Delta x'\,\Delta y - \Delta x\,\Delta y'},$$

and substituting this value of s into the parametric equation of the second line gives the point of intersection. Note that if the denominator in the expression for s is 0 then the two lines are parallel.

Often one of the two lines is axis aligned, as in the case of a clipping window. Then a simpler calculation can be used. For example suppose that one of the lines is $x = x_{min}$ and the other is again given by its parametric equation as before

$$x(t) = x_1 + t\,\Delta x,$$
$$y(t) = y_1 + t\,\Delta y.$$

At the point of intersection we must have $x(t) = x_{min}$, so solving for t gives

$$t = \frac{x_{min} - x_1}{\Delta x},$$

and plugging this value of t into the parametric line equation gives the point of intersection.

C.2   Line-Plane Intersection

Suppose that the equation of the plane is

$$\vec{\mathbf{n}} \cdot \mathbf{p} + d = 0,$$

where $\vec{\mathbf{n}}$ is the normal to the plane. Then the intersection of the line and the plane is found by substituting the equation of the line for the point $\mathbf{p}$ of the plane:

$$\vec{\mathbf{n}} \cdot \left(\mathbf{p}_1 + t\left(\mathbf{p}_2 - \mathbf{p}_1\right)\right) + d = 0.$$

This gives the value of t corresponding to the point of intersection,

$$t = -\frac{\vec{\mathbf{n}} \cdot \mathbf{p}_1 + d}{\vec{\mathbf{n}} \cdot \left(\mathbf{p}_2 - \mathbf{p}_1\right)},$$

and substituting this value of t into the equation of the line gives the point of intersection. Note that if the denominator is 0 then the line is parallel to the plane; also if the denominator is positive then the value of t is negative, corresponding to an intersection point outside the ray or line segment.

C.3   Line-Triangle Intersection

The intersection test between a line and a triangle is probably the one most often used in graphics applications, since the majority of objects are represented as triangle models. Consequently, this test has been studied extensively in an effort to determine the most efficient algorithm in varying circumstances. The implementation that is best suited to each application should be chosen among the many available ones based on the specific set-up (for example, if the triangle normals are pre-computed or not) and constraints (for example, how much auxiliary information can be pre-computed and stored per triangle).

   The algorithm that we present here [Mö97] is considered very efficient in most common cases and can be further optimized if more data can be pre-computed and stored per triangle.

   Given a triangle $\mathbf{T} = \triangle(\mathbf{t}_1, \mathbf{t}_2, \mathbf{t}_3)$, its parametric equation in terms of its barycentric coordinates is

$$\mathbf{T}(u_2, u_3) = (1 - u_2 - u_3)\mathbf{t}_1 + u_2\mathbf{t}_2 + u_3\mathbf{t}_3.$$

To find its intersection with the line, we equate this equation with the parametric equation of the line:

$$(1 - u_2 - u_3)\mathbf{t}_1 + u_2\mathbf{t}_2 + u_3\mathbf{t}_3 = \mathbf{p}_1 + t(\mathbf{p}_2 - \mathbf{p}_1)$$
$$\Leftrightarrow (\mathbf{p}_1 - \mathbf{p}_2)t + (\mathbf{t}_2 - \mathbf{t}_1)u_2 + (\mathbf{t}_3 - \mathbf{t}_1)u_3 = \mathbf{p}_1 - \mathbf{t}_1.$$

This constitutes a 3×3 linear system for t, u_2, and u_3. By solving it, we get the parametric value t of the intersection point along the line (which, as usual, should be checked for inclusion in the appropriate interval if a ray or line segment is considered) as well as the barycentric coordinates of the intersection point with respect to the triangle. The point lies inside the triangle if $0 \le u_2, u_3 \le 1$ (which implies $0 \le 1 - u_2 - u_3 \le 1$ as well).

The system can be solved efficiently, reusing many calculations. We set the coefficients of the system,

$$\vec{\mathbf{c}}_1 = \mathbf{p}_1 - \mathbf{p}_2,$$
$$\vec{\mathbf{c}}_2 = \mathbf{t}_2 - \mathbf{t}_1,$$
$$\vec{\mathbf{c}}_3 = \mathbf{t}_3 - \mathbf{t}_1,$$
$$\vec{\mathbf{c}} = \mathbf{p}_1 - \mathbf{t}_1,$$

and by Cramer's rule, the solution is

$$\begin{bmatrix} t \\ u_2 \\ u_3 \end{bmatrix} = \frac{1}{\det[\vec{\mathbf{c}}_1 \quad \vec{\mathbf{c}}_2 \quad \vec{\mathbf{c}}_3]} \begin{bmatrix} \det[\vec{\mathbf{c}} \quad \vec{\mathbf{c}}_2 \quad \vec{\mathbf{c}}_3] \\ \det[\vec{\mathbf{c}}_1 \quad \vec{\mathbf{c}} \quad \vec{\mathbf{c}}_3] \\ \det[\vec{\mathbf{c}}_1 \quad \vec{\mathbf{c}}_2 \quad \vec{\mathbf{c}}] \end{bmatrix}.$$

Furthermore, since $\det[\vec{\mathbf{x}} \quad \vec{\mathbf{y}} \quad \vec{\mathbf{z}}] = \vec{\mathbf{x}} \cdot (\vec{\mathbf{y}} \times \vec{\mathbf{z}}) = -\vec{\mathbf{x}} \cdot (\vec{\mathbf{z}} \times \vec{\mathbf{y}})$ etc., the solution can be rewritten as

$$\begin{bmatrix} t \\ u_2 \\ u_3 \end{bmatrix} = \frac{1}{d} \begin{bmatrix} \vec{\mathbf{c}} \cdot \vec{\mathbf{n}} \\ \vec{\mathbf{c}}_3 \cdot \vec{\mathbf{e}} \\ -\vec{\mathbf{c}}_2 \cdot \vec{\mathbf{e}} \end{bmatrix},$$

where

$$\vec{\mathbf{n}} = \vec{\mathbf{c}}_2 \times \vec{\mathbf{c}}_3,$$
$$\vec{\mathbf{e}} = \vec{\mathbf{c}}_1 \times \vec{\mathbf{c}},$$
$$d = \vec{\mathbf{c}}_1 \cdot \vec{\mathbf{n}}.$$

C.4   Line-Sphere Intersection

The number of intersection points between a line and a sphere may be zero (when the ray avoids the shere), one (when the line is tangent to the sphere), or two (when the line crosses the sphere). Note that in many applications when two intersection points exist, only the *first* one along the ray is important, for instance when a light ray hits the sphere.

For this test we rewrite the equation of the line in terms of its direction $\overrightarrow{\mathbf{d}} = \mathbf{p}_2 - \mathbf{p}_1$:

$$\mathbf{p}(t) = \mathbf{p}_1 + t\,\overrightarrow{\mathbf{d}}.$$

The algorithm uses the equation of the sphere of center $\mathbf{c}$ and radius r: a point $\mathbf{p}$ lies on the sphere if

$$(\mathbf{p} - \mathbf{c}) \cdot (\mathbf{p} - \mathbf{c}) = r^2.$$

We will also denote the vector between the first point on the line (the start of the ray or line segment) and the center of the sphere by

$$\overrightarrow{\mathbf{m}} = \mathbf{p}_1 - \mathbf{c}.$$

The intersection of the line and the sphere is found by substituting the parametric equation of the line for the point $\mathbf{p}$ in the equation of the sphere, which yields a quadratic equation for t:

$$(\mathbf{p}_1 + t\,\overrightarrow{\mathbf{d}} - \mathbf{c}) \cdot (\mathbf{p}_1 + t\,\overrightarrow{\mathbf{d}} - \mathbf{c}) = r^2$$
$$\Leftrightarrow (\overrightarrow{\mathbf{m}} + t\,\overrightarrow{\mathbf{d}}) \cdot (\overrightarrow{\mathbf{m}} + t\,\overrightarrow{\mathbf{d}}) = r^2$$
$$\Leftrightarrow (\overrightarrow{\mathbf{d}} \cdot \overrightarrow{\mathbf{d}})t^2 + 2(\overrightarrow{\mathbf{m}} \cdot \overrightarrow{\mathbf{d}})t + (\overrightarrow{\mathbf{m}} \cdot \overrightarrow{\mathbf{m}}) - r^2 = 0$$

The result depends on the discriminant of this equation. If we rewrite it as $at^2 + 2bt + c = 0$, then the discriminant is $D = b^2 - ac$, and

- if $D < 0$, then no real roots exists and the line does not intersect the sphere.

- if $D = 0$, then one (double) root exists and the line is tangent to the sphere. The value of t for the root should be checked for inclusion in the appropriate interval if a ray or line segment is considered.

- if $D > 0$, then two roots exist corresponding to two intersection points. The smallest root is $t = (-b - \sqrt{D})/a$ and it corresponds to the first point of intersection along the directed line.

If a ray is considered and the smallest value of t it is negative, then the second root, $t = (-b + \sqrt{D})/a$ is the correct one, unless it is negative as well (in which case the ray actually points away from the sphere). If a line segment is considered, similar checks are required.

Note that the above calculations are simplified if the direction vector of the line, $\overrightarrow{\mathbf{d}}$, is pre-normalized, since in this case $a = (\overrightarrow{\mathbf{d}} \cdot \overrightarrow{\mathbf{d}}) = |\overrightarrow{\mathbf{d}}|^2 = 1$.

C.5   Line-Convex Polyhedron Intersection

The basic principle for testing the intersection between a line and a convex polyhedron is the same as for the Liang-Barsky line clipping-algorithm (see Section 2.9.2 for the 2D algorithm and Section 5.3.1 for the 3D algorithm).

Considering a (directed) line and a general convex polyhedron [Hain91], the faces of the polyhedron can be partitioned into three sets: those for which the line is "incoming," those for which the line is "outgoing," and those to which the line is parallel (see Figure C.1 for the 2D analog). The algorithm computes the maximum parametric value of the incoming intersections, t_{in}, and the minimum parametric value of the outgoing intersections, t_{out}. If $t_{in} < t_{out}$ then the line segment corresponding to $[t_{in}, t_{out}]$ is inside the polyhedron; otherwise there is no intersection. For faces parallel to the ray, one of the points defining the line may be checked for being on the "inside" or the "outside" of the face, and in the latter case the algorithm may terminate since no intersection exists.

The faces of the polyhedron should be specified as planes in the form $\overrightarrow{\mathbf{n}} \cdot \mathbf{p} + d = 0$ with $\overrightarrow{\mathbf{n}}$ being the outward-pointing normal vector. The intersection points between each face and the line can be computed as shown in Section C.2. Then

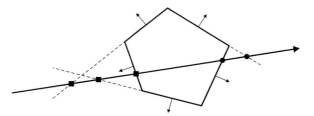

Figure C.1. A ray intersecting a convex polygon: the ray "enters" the polygon through the points marked with a square, and "leaves" the polygon through the points marked with a disk.

the choice whether the line enters, leaves, or is parallel to the face is determined by the sign of the inner product $\overrightarrow{\mathbf{n}} \cdot (\mathbf{p}_2 - \mathbf{p}_1)$:

- If $\overrightarrow{\mathbf{n}} \cdot (\mathbf{p}_2 - \mathbf{p}_1) = 0$, the ray is parallel to the plane; then if $\overrightarrow{\mathbf{n}} \cdot \mathbf{p}_1 + d < 0$, $\mathbf{p}_1$ is on the "outside" of the polyhedron and so no intersection exists.

- If $\overrightarrow{\mathbf{n}} \cdot (\mathbf{p}_2 - \mathbf{p}_1) < 0$, the ray enters the polyhedron.

- If $\overrightarrow{\mathbf{n}} \cdot (\mathbf{p}_2 - \mathbf{p}_1) > 0$, the ray leaves the polyhedron.

It can be seen that the computations required are exactly the same as those needed to determine the intersection point.

In the special case that the polyhedron is an AABB (axis-aligned bounding box), the 3D Liang-Barsky Algorithm can be applied with only minor modifications: similarly to the line-sphere intersection problem, most applications are concerned only with the first point of intersection (the one through which the line enters the AABB). Again, if a ray or line segment is considered, its parametric value should be checked for inclusion in the appropriate interval.

D

Solid Angle Calculations

The solid angle ω subtended by a surface patch A is defined as the area of the projection A' of A on the surface of a sphere of radius r, divided by r^2 (Figure D.1):

$$\omega = \frac{A'}{r^2}.$$

(D.1)

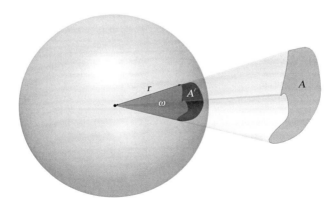

Figure D.1. Definition of the solid angle.

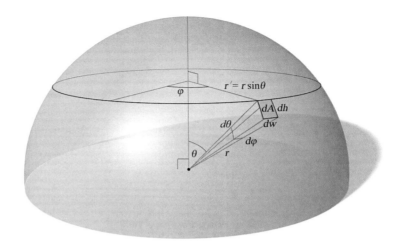

Figure D.2. Calculation of a differential solid angle.

In practical terms, a solid angle measures the aperture of the semi-infinite conical slice of space, with its peak at the center of the sphere and its sides touching the boundary of the surface patch (or its projection on the unit sphere). Essentially, a solid angle is not associated with any physically meaningful unit. Instead, a mathematical unit, the *steradian* (sr) is assigned to this quantity.

A unit of 1 sr corresponds to a solid angle that extends from the center of a sphere with radius r such that it subtends a spherical patch with area equal to r^2.

The estimation of the solid angle of an arbitrary spherical patch is usually performed by integrating a *differential solid angle* over the patch. A differential solid angle is the solid angle $d\vec{\omega}$ that corresponds to an infinitesimally small spherical patch dA that contains a point on the sphere with polar coordinates (θ, φ) (Figure D.2). Sometimes, when the direction of a particular differential solid angle is not of importance to the calculations, the arrow above the variable can be dropped.

Let us now derive a formula that associates $d\vec{\omega}$ with the polar coordinates, in order to be able to integrate over two intuitive and manageable variables. The area of dA is given as the product of the arc-length of its sides, dw and dh. Both differential arcs are part of the circumferences of the corresponding circles spanning the sphere horizontally and vertically (Figure D.2). The arc-lengths dw and dh are fractions of these circumferences:

$$dh = 2\pi r \frac{d\theta}{2\pi} = r d\theta,$$
$$dw = 2\pi r' \frac{d\varphi}{2\pi} = r' d\varphi.$$

(D.2)

But r' depends on the latitude of the patch and is equal to $r \sin\theta$. Using Equation (D.2), the area of the patch becomes

$$dA = r^2 \sin\theta d\theta d\varphi,$$

(D.3)

and according to the definition of the solid angle, the corresponding differential solid angle is

$$d\vec{\omega} = \frac{dA}{r^2} = \sin\theta d\theta d\varphi.$$

(D.4)

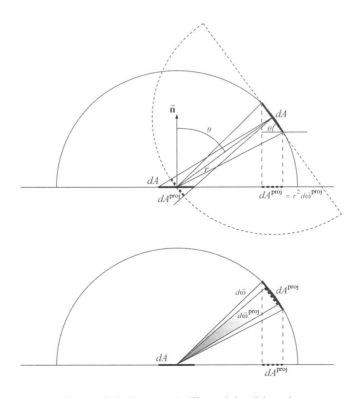

Figure D.3. Projected differential solid angle.

The solid angle that corresponds to a sphere can be found by integrating $d\vec{\omega}$ over the full range of φ and θ. Remember that θ is measured relative to the North pole according to the set-up of Figure D.2:

$$\omega_{\text{sphere}} = \int\limits_{\theta=0}^{\pi} \int\limits_{\varphi=0}^{2\pi} \sin\theta\, d\varphi\, d\theta = 2\pi \int\limits_{\theta=0}^{\pi} \sin\theta\, d\theta = 4\pi. \qquad (D.5)$$

This result is of course consistent with the area of a sphere of radius $r(4\pi r^2)$, according to the definition of the solid angle.

In photometric calculations, it is often useful to introduce the term *projected differential solid angle* $d\vec{\omega}^{\text{proj}}$. It is a quantity devised for measuring solid angles defined by oblique orientations of a differential patch dA. Observe the hemisphere of radius r that surrounds patch dA in Figure D.3. The solid angle $d\vec{\xi}$ that is formed using as "observation" center any point on the hemisphere and dA, involves, according to definition, the projection of dA on the line of sight (radial direction) between the patch and that point:

$$d\xi = \hat{\mathbf{n}} \cdot \hat{\mathbf{r}}\, dA/r^2 = \cos\theta\, dA/r^2. \qquad (D.6)$$

But in Equation (D.6), dA/r^2 is also the solid angle corresponding to a differential patch equal to dA on the hemisphere as seen from its center. The solid angle $d\vec{\xi}$ then equals the projection $d\vec{\omega}^{\text{proj}}$ of $d\vec{\omega} = dA/r^2$ on the hemisphere's base:

$$d\vec{\omega}^{\text{proj}} = \cos\theta\, d\vec{\omega}. \qquad (D.7)$$

In broad terms, the projected differential solid angle gives us a measure of how much of the patch is perceived from various directions.

Elements of Signal Theory

E.1 Sampling

An *N*-dimensional continuous signal can be sampled to produce an *N*-dimensional *discrete signal*. The *sampling* procedure involves the selection of the appropriate points in the signal domain and the recording of sample values at these locations. When the samples acquired are digitized, they are *quantized* to match the resolution of the discrete storage type used (e.g., 8, 16, 24 bits per sample). Quantization is the conversion of a continuous range of values to discrete levels (Figure E.1(b)). The continuous signal is sampled using a sampling pattern. The most common pattern of signal discretization is *uniform sampling*, where each sample is taken at regular intervals in the continuous domain (Figure E.1(a)).

Various signals are sampled in graphics and visualization algorithms, and we often attempt to reconstruct the original signal from the samples taken. A good example of this procedure is texture mapping, where a bitmap represents a discretization of a real surface appearance. This signal is then re-sampled in an attempt to reconstruct the appearance of the original surface in the rendered image. In polygon rasterization or ray tracing, we sample the light-field that reaches the camera location in order to record a two-dimensional image of what is seen from that particular viewpoint. In order to be able to reconstruct the original visible signal and, therefore, to produce a faithful rendering of the objects in space, we need to adequately sample the continuous domain signal so that we capture every

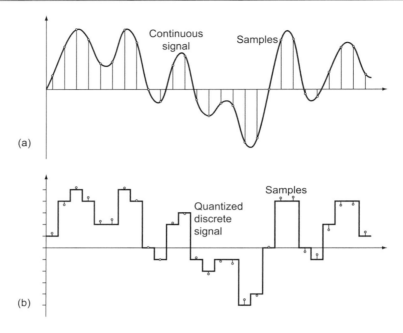

Figure E.1. Regular sampling. (a) Discrete samples of a continuous signal. (b) Quantized samples (11 levels).

detail. The detail information of a periodic signal is actually the rate at which the values change with respect to the N-dimensional input domain. Higher detail reflects the presence of more rapid changes in the signal values or higher *frequencies*. A periodic signal can be expressed as a weighted sum of N-dimensional sinusoidal terms. The finer the details present in the signal, the smaller the period of the sinusoidal terms that correspond to them and the higher the upper frequency bound of these periodic components.

E.2   Frequency Domain

A signal defined in an N-dimensional domain can be expressed in terms of the frequency of its components, i.e., as a set of coefficients that specify the contribution of each frequency of sinusoidal terms to the signal. This is called the *frequency domain* of a signal and describes what and how harmonic waveforms contribute to the construction of the signal. For periodic signals, the linear combination of sinusoidal terms with coefficients a_k that comprise the signal is called the *Fourier series*. For a one-dimensional periodic signal, the Fourier series is given by

$$f(x) = \sum_{k=-\infty}^{\infty} a_k e^{jk2\pi x/T},$$ (E.1)

where $e^{jk2\pi}$ is the kth harmonic and T is the period of the signal. Note that the Fourier coefficients are complex numbers, the real part representing the amplitude of the specific harmonic and the imaginary part providing the phase (offset) of the sinusoidal term.

For arbitrary aperiodic signals defined on an N-dimensional input domain, the corresponding *Fourier synthesis* composes the signal from the contribution of each frequency $F(\mathbf{u})$ (continuous frequency domain), $\mathbf{u}$ being the vector of frequency in each direction (N total):

$$f(\mathbf{x}) = \int_{-\infty}^{+\infty} F(\mathbf{u}) e^{j2\pi \mathbf{x} \cdot \mathbf{u}} du_1 du_2 ... du_N.$$ (E.2)

The integral is N-dimensional. The function $F(\mathbf{u})$ is the *Fourier transform* (*Fourier analysis*) of the signal $f(\mathbf{x})$ and is given by:

$$F(\mathbf{u}) = \int_{-\infty}^{+\infty} f(\mathbf{x}) e^{-j2\pi \mathbf{x} \cdot \mathbf{u}} dx_1 dx_2 ... dx_N.$$ (E.3)

For example, the images (a), (b), and (c) of Figure E.2 are two-dimensional signals that depict the same pattern but with different detail. The intensity in Figure E.2(a) varies slowly, and the image is devoid of any abrupt intensity change that would signify a fine detail. As can be observed by the amplitude of the Fourier transform above each version of the pattern (logarithmic scale), the finer the details present in the two-dimensional signal of the image, the more the higher frequencies (smaller sinusoidal waveform periods) contribute to the signal.

E.3   Convolution and Filtering

A system is classified as *linear* if for an arbitrary number of input signals $s_1(\mathbf{x})$, $s_2(\mathbf{x})$,..., $s_M(\mathbf{x})$, the combined output of the system for each one of them $y(s_1(\mathbf{x}))$, $y(s_2(\mathbf{x}))$,..., $y(s_M(\mathbf{x}))$ is identical to the output of the system on the superimposed input signals, for any $\mathbf{x}$ in $\mathbb{R}^N$:

$$y(a_1s_1(\mathbf{x}) + a_2s_2(\mathbf{x}) + ... + a_Ms_M(\mathbf{x})) =$$
$$a_1y(s_1(\mathbf{x})) + a_2y(s_2(\mathbf{x})) + ... + a_My(s_M(\mathbf{x})). \quad \text{(E.4)}$$

where a_i are arbitrary weights.

A signal value $s(x)$ can be represented as an infinite sum of values over the input domain, when multiplied with a coefficient that is non-zero only for x:

$$s(x) = \int_{-\infty}^{+\infty} \delta(x-t)s(t)dt. \quad \text{(E.5)}$$

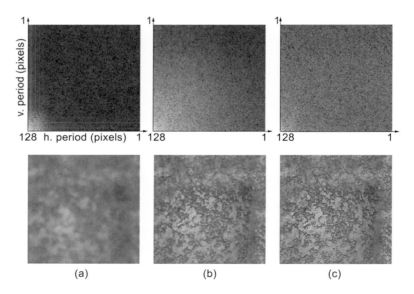

(a)   (b)   (c)

Figure E.2. Frequency domain (logarithmic amplitude - top row) for 2D image data. (a) Blurred, low-detail version of the sample image. Note the concentration of high energy in the low frequencies (longer period). (b) Less blurred image; the spectrum contains higher frequencies. (c) The original, crisp image exhibits a lot of detail, which is reflected in the Fourier transform of the signal as a more even distribution of energy in the entire frequency domain.

The function $\delta(x)$ (*Delta* or *Dirac* function) is defined as a spike of unit amplitude at zero:

$$\delta(x) = \begin{cases} 1, & x = 0, \\ 0, & x \neq 0. \end{cases} \qquad (E.6)$$

Now consider a superposition of every shifted version of the input signal $s(x)$ by t multiplied by a corresponding weighting coefficient $h(x,t)$. The output of the linear system that is characterized by $h(x,t)$ is similar to Equation (E.5) and is given by

$$y(x) = \int_{-\infty}^{+\infty} h(x,t)s(t)dt, \qquad (E.7)$$

or for time-invariant linear systems

$$y(x) = \int_{-\infty}^{+\infty} h(x-t)s(t)dt. \qquad (E.8)$$

Equation (E.8) is the *convolution* of the input signal $s(t)$ and another signal $h(x)$ and is denoted by an asterisk $(*)$; $y(x) = h(x) * s(x) = s(x) * h(x)$. When referring to a linear system, $h(x)$ is the *impulse response* of the system. The impulse response characterizes the system's behavior and is so named because it is equal to the application of the system on a Dirac input signal (see Figure E.3):

$$h(x) = \int_{-\infty}^{+\infty} h(x-t)\delta(t)dt. \qquad (E.9)$$

In theory, the impulse response for continuous domain signals can be obtained for any arbitrary unknown linear system by applying it on a Dirac signal. For discrete signals, this is practical, indeed, and the corresponding convolution is given by

$$y(n) = \sum_{k=-\infty}^{+\infty} h(n-k)s(k), \ n \in \mathbb{Z}, \qquad (E.10)$$

$$y(n_1,...,n_N) = \sum_{k_1=-\infty}^{\infty} ... \sum_{k_N=-\infty}^{+\infty} h(n_1 - k_1,...,n_N - k_N)s(k_1,...,k_N). \qquad (E.11)$$

The impulse response h implements a linear *filter kernel*. The input signal is *filtered* by convolution in the signal domain. When the impulse response is non-zero only for a bounded region of the input domain, i.e., it has a finite support,

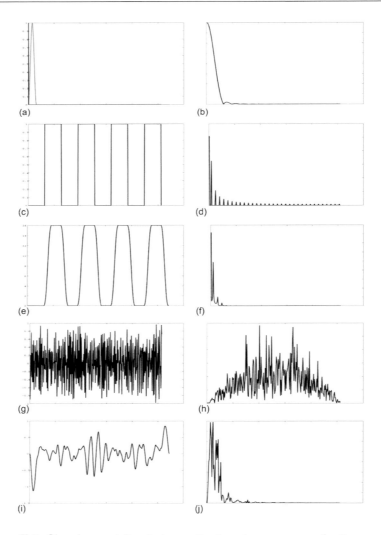

Figure E.3. Signal convolution between the impulse response of a linear system and various signals. Convolution in the signal domain results in multiplication of the corresponding spectra. (a) The impulse response h (light grey) and the Dirac function. (b) Power spectral density (PSD) of $y(x) = h(x) * \delta(x) = h(x)$. (c) A square input pulse. (d) PSD of the square input pulse of (c). (e) Convolution of the square pulse with the impulse response h of figure (a). (f) Resulting PSD of the filtered signal of (e). (g) Noise. (h) The PSD of the noise signal of (g). (i) The filtered noise. (j) The resulting PSD (magnified in the vertical axis).

then the filter is characterized as *finite impulse response* (FIR), otherwise it is an *infinite impulse response* (IIR) filter. Most practical linear filters are FIR.

An important property of convolution is that when the signals can be expressed in the frequency domain, convolution in the input domain corresponds to multiplication of the Fourier transforms Y, H and S of the signals:

$$y(\mathbf{x}) = h(\mathbf{x}) * s(\mathbf{x}) \Leftrightarrow Y(\mathbf{u}) = H(\mathbf{u})S(\mathbf{u}). \qquad (\text{E}.12)$$

The Fourier transform of the impulse response $h(\mathbf{x})$ is called the *transfer function*. Often it is preferable to perform filtering in the frequency domain, especially when multiple filters must be consecutively applied to the input signal or when the shape (waveform) of the transfer function is more conveniently described than that of the impulse response. For example, cutting off the middle frequencies of an input signal may require the design of a complex impulse response. On the other hand, it is more intuitive to construct a transfer function that selectively zeroes the required frequencies.[1]

E.4   Sampling Theorem

In order to ensure that the reconstructed signal is identical to the original, the *Nyquist-Shannon sampling theorem* states that the original signal has to be band-limited and the sampling rate f_{sampling} must be at least twice the highest frequency of the original signal:

$$2|f_{\text{max}}| \leqslant f_{\text{sampling}}. \qquad (\text{E}.13)$$

The minimum adequate rate f_{sampling} at which to sample the signal in order to correctly reconstruct it is called the *Nyquist* rate. Failure to satisfy the above criteria leads to poor sampling of the initial signal and the phenomenon of *aliasing*. Aliasing is the misinterpretation of the samples as a different signal than the original during the reconstruction. This happens because more than one signal could actually pass through the recorded samples.

In practice, as we do not actually know or cannot guarantee the spectrum extents of the signal, the original signal is first low-pass filtered to explicitly cut off frequencies higher than half the sampling rate. A low-pass filter allows, as the name implies, only the low frequencies to pass to the output of the filter.

---

[1]In practice, the creation of a good transfer function is tricky, as discontinuities in the frequency domain expand the signal input domain support, and the resulting impulse response must be truncated to be applicable, leading to distortions.

Bibliography

[Adob07] Adobe. Available online at http://www.adobe.com, 2007.

[Agar03] Sameer Agarwal, Ravi Ramamoorthi, Serge Belongie, and Henrik Wann Jensen. "Structured Importance Sampling of Environment Maps." *ACM Transactions on Graphics* 22:3 (2003), 605–612.

[Ahne87] P. K. Ahnelt, H. Kolb, and R. Pflug. "Identification of a Subtype of Cone Photoreceptor, Likely to be Blue Sensitive, in the Human Retina." *J. Comp. Neurol.* 255 (1987), 18–34.

[Aire91] J. Airey. "Increasing Update Rates in the Building Walkthrough System with Automatic Model-Space Subdivision and Potentially Visible Set Calculations." Ph.D. thesis, University of North Carolina at Chapel Hill, 1991.

[Aman87] J. Amanatides and A. Woo. "A Fast Voxel Traversal Algorithm for Ray Tracing." In *Eurographics '87*, pp. 3 – 10. Amsterdam, North-Holland: Elsevier Science Publishers, 1987.

[Appe68] A. Appel. "Some Techniques for Shading Machine Rendering of Solids." In *AFIPS 1968 Spring Joint Computer Conf., Vol. 32*, pp. 37–45, 1968.

[Augs06] U. H. Augsdörfer, N. A. Dodgson, and M. A. Sabin. "Tuning Subdivision by Minimising Gaussian Curvature Variation Near Extraordinary Vertices." *Computer Graphics Forum (Proc. Eurographics '06)* 25:3 (2006), 263–272.

[Barr84] A. H. Barr. "Global and Local Deformations of Solid Primitives." *Computer Graphics (SIGGRAPH '84 Proceedings)* 18:3 (1984), 21–30.

[Barr97] B. Barraquand, L.E. Kavraki, J.-C. Latombe, T.-Y. Li, R. Motwani, and P. Raghavan. "A Random Sampling Scheme for Robot Path Planning." *International Journal of Robotics Research* 16:6 (1997), 759–774.

[Bart87] Richard H. Bartels, John C. Beatty, and Brian A. Barsky. *An Introduction to Splines for Use in Computer Graphics and Geometric Modeling.* San Francisco, CA: Morgan Kaufmann, 1987.

[Bart92] P. Barten. "Physical Model for the Contrast Sensitivity of the Human Eye." In *Human Vision, Visual Processing, and Digital Display III, Proc. SPIE*, 1666, 1666, pp. 57–72, 1992.

[Bart93] P. Barten. "Spatio-Temporal Model for the Contrast Sensitivity of the Human Eye and Its Temporal Aspects." In *Human Vision, Visual Processing and Digital Display IV. Vol. 1913*, edited by J. Allenbach B. Rogowitz, pp. 2–14. Bellingham, WA: SPIE Press, 1993.

[Bart04] L. Barthe and L. Kobbelt. "Subdivision Scheme Tuning Around Extraordinary Vertices." *Computer Aided Geometric Design* 21 (2004), 561–583.

[Bart05] L. Barthe, C. Gerot, M.A. Sabin, and L. Kobbelt. "Simple Computation of the Eigencomponents of a Subdivision Matrix in the Fourier Domain." In *Advances in Multiresolution for Geometric Modelling*, edited by N.A. Dodgson, M.S. Floater, and M.A. Sabin, pp. 245–257. Berlin / Heidelberg: Springer-Verlag, 2005.

[Bata99] H. C. Batagelo and I. C. Junior. "Real Time Shadow Generation Using BSP Trees and Stencil Buffers." In *Proceedings of SIGGRAPH 99, Computer Graphics Proceedings, Annual Conference Series*, pp. 93–102. Reading, MA: Addison Wesley Longman, 1999.

[Baum72] Bruce G. Baumgart. "Winged Edge Polyhedron Representation." Technical Report CS-TR-72-320, Stanford University, 1972.

[Beck63] P. Beckmann and A. Spizzichino. *The Scattering of Electromagnetic Waves from Rough Surfaces*. New York: Mac Millan, 1963.

[Bilo99] B. Bilodeau and M. Songy. "Real Time Shadows." In *Creativity '99*, 1999. Creative Labs Inc. sponsored game developer conferences Los Angeles, CA and Surrey, England.

[Blin76] J. F. Blinn and M. E. Newell. "Texture and Reflection in Computer Generated Images." *Communications of the ACM* 19 (1976), 542–546.

[Blin77] J. F. Blinn. "Models of Light Reflection for Computer Synthesized Pictures." 11:2 (1977), 192–198.

[Boeh80] W. Boehm. "Inserting New Knots into B-Spline Curves." *Computer Aided Design* 12:4 (1980), 199–201.

[Bres65] J.E. Bresenham. "Algorithm for Computer Control of a Digital Plotter." *IBM System Journal* 4:1 (1965), 25–30.

[Bres77] J.E. Bresenham. "A Linear Algorithm for Incremental Digital Display of Circular Arcs." *Communications of the ACM* 20:2 (1977), 100–106.

[Brod92] K. W. Brodlie, L. A. Carpenter, R. A. Earnshaw, J. R. Gallop, R. J. Hubbold, A. M. Mumford, C. D. Osland, and P. Quarendon, editors. *Scientific Visualization: Techniques and Applications*. Berlin / Heidelberg: Springer-Verlag, 1992.

[Bunn04] M. Bunnel and F. Pellacini. "Shadow Map Antialiasing." In *GPU Gems*, edited by R. Fernando. Reading, MA: Addison-Wesley, 2004.

[Burk05] David Burke, Abhijeet Ghosh, and Wolfgang Heidrich. "Bidirectional Importance Sampling for Direct Illumination." In *Rendering Techniques 2005: 16th Eurographics Workshop on Rendering*, pp. 147–156. Aire-la-Ville, Switzerland: Eurographcs Assoc., 2005.

[Cabr93] B. Cabral and L. (C.) Leedom. "Imaging Vector Fields Using Line Integral Convolution." In *Proceedings of SIGGRAPH 93, Computer Graphics Proceedings, Annual Conference Series*, pp. 263–270. New York: ACM Press, 1993.

[Cabr99] B. Cabral, M. Olano, and P. Nemec. "Reflection Space Image Based Rendering." In *Proceedings of SIGGRAPH 99, Computer Graphics Proceedings, Annual Conference Series*, pp. 165–171. Reading, MA: Addison Wesley Longman, 1999.

[Came90] S.A. Cameron. "Collision Detection by Four-Dimensional Intersection Testing." *IEEE Trans. on Robotics and Automation* 6:3 (1990), 291–302.

[Came92] G. G. Cameron and P. E. Undrill. "Rendering Volumetric Medical Image Data on a SIMD-Architecture Computer." In *Third Eurographics Workshop on Rendering*, pp. 135–145. Aire-la-Ville: Eurographics Association, 1992.

[Carm00] J. Carmack. "Carmack on Shadow Volumes.", 2000. Email to private list May 23, 2000; Also published on the NVIDIA website: http://developer.nvidia.com/object/robust_shadow_volumes.html.

[Carp84] L. C. Carpenter. "The A-Buffer, An Antialiased Hidden Surface Method." *Computer Graphics (Proc. SIGGRAPH '84)* 18:3 (1984), 103–108.

[Catm74] E. Catmull. "A Subdivision Algorithm for Computer Display of Curved Surfaces." Ph.D. thesis, Department of Computer Science, University of Utah, Salt Lake City, Utah, 1974.

[Catm78] E. Catmull. "A Hidden Surface Algorithm with Antialiasing." *Computer Graphics (Proc. SIGGRAPH '78,)* 12:3 (1978), 6–11.

[Cava91] A. S. Cavaretta, W. Dahmen, and C. A. Micchelli. *Stationary Subdivision*. Memoirs of the American Mathematical Society, Providence, RI: American Mathematical Society, 1991.

[Celn90] G. Celniker and D. Gossard. "Continuous Deformable Curves and their Application to Fairing 3-D Geometry." In *Proceedings of the IFIP Conference on Geometric Modeling in Computer-Aided Design*. Rensselaerville, NY, 1990.

[Chai74] G. M. Chaikin. "An Algorithm for High-Speed Curve Generation." *Computer Graphics and Image Processing* 3 (1974), 346–349.

[Chal98] A. Chalmers and E. Reinhard. "Parallel and Distributed Photo-Realistic Rendering." In *ACM SIGGRAPH '98 Course Notes*, 1998.

[Chen95] S. E. Chen. "QuickTime VR - An Image-Based Approach to Virtual Environment Navigation." In *Proceedings of SIGGRAPH 95, Computer Graphics Proceedings, Annual Conference Series*, pp. 29–38. Reading, MA: Addison Wesley, 1995.

[Cher73] H. Chernoff. "Using Faces to Represent Points in K-Dimensional Space Graphically." *Journal of the American Statistical Association* 68 (1973), 361–368.

[Chia03] Y.-J. Chiang and X. Lu. "Progressive Simplification of Tetrahedral Meshes Preserving All Isosurface Topologies." *Computer Graphics Forum* 22:3 (2003), 493–504.

[Cho03] W. Cho, E. M. Sachs, N. M. Patrikalakis, and D. E. Troxel. "A Dithering Algorithm for Local Composition Control with Three-Dimensional Printing." *Computer Aided Design* 35:9 (2003), 851–867.

[Cign98] Paolo Cignoni, Claudio Roccini, and Roberto Scopigno. "Metro: Measuring Error on Simplified Surfaces." *Computer Graphics Forum* 17:2 (1998), 167–174.

[Cign00] P. Cignoni, D. Constanza, C. Montani, C. Rocchini, and R. Scopigno. "Simplification of Tetrahedral Meshes with Accurate Error Evaluation." In *Proceedings of IEEE Visualization*, pp. 85–92. Loas Alamitos, CA: IEEE Computer Society, 2000.

[Cira00] F. Cirak, M. Ortiz, and P. Schröder. "Subdivision Surfaces: A New Paradigm for Thin-Shell Finite-Element Analysis." *International Journal for Numerical Methods in Engineering* 47:12 (2000), 2039–72.

[Clar76] James H. Clark. "Hierarchical Geometric Models for Visible Surface Algorithms." *Communications of the ACM* 19:10 (1976), 547–554.

[Clar82] J. Clark. "The Geometry Engine: A VLSI Geometry System for Graphics." *Computer Graphics (Proc. SIGGRAPH '82)* 16:3 (1982), 127–133.

[Clar05] Petrik Clarberg, Wojciech Jarosz, Tomas Akenine-Möller, and Henrik Wann Jensen. "Wavelet Importance Sampling: Efficiently Evaluating Products of Complex Functions." *ACM Transactions on Graphics* 24:3 (2005), 1166–1175.

[CO03] D. Cohen-Or, Y. Chrysanthou, C.T. Silva, and F. Durand. "A Survey of Visibility for Walkthrough Applications." *IEEE Transactions on Visualization and Computer Graphics* 9:3 (2003), 412–431.

[Cohe80] E. Cohen, T. Lyche, and R. Riesenfeld. "Discrete B-Splines and Subdivision Techniques in Computer Aided Geometric Design and Computer Graphics." *Computer Graphics and Image Processing* 14:2 (1980), 87–111.

[Cohe86] M. F. Cohen, D. P. Greenberg, D. S. Immel, and P. J. Brock. "An Efficient Radiosity Approach for Realistic Image Synthesis." *IEEE Computer Graphics and Applications* 6:3 (1986), 26–35.

[Cohe88] M. F. Cohen, S. E. Chen, J. R. Wallace, and D. P. Greenberg. "A Progressive Refinement Approach to Fast Radiosity Image Generation." *Computer Graphics (Proc. SIGGRAPH '88)* 22:4 (1988), 75–84.

[Cohe92] A. Cohen and J.-P. Conze. "Regularité des bases d'ondelettes et mésures ergodiques." *Revista Matematica Iberoamer* 8 (1992), 351–366.

[Cohe93] M. F. Cohen and J. R. Wallace. *Radiosity and Realistic Image Synthesis.* Boston, MA: Academic Press Professional, 1993.

[Cohe98] J. Cohen, M. Olano, and D. Manocha. "Appearance Preserving Simplification." In *Proceedings of SIGGRAPH 98, Computer Graphics Proceedings, Annual Conference Series*, pp. 115–122. Reading, MA: Addison Wesley, 1998.

[Cook82] R. L. Cook and K. E. Torrance. "A Reflectance Model for Computer Graphics." *ACM Transactions on Graphics* 1:1 (1982), 7–25.

[Cook84] Robert L. Cook. "Shade Trees." *Computer Graphics (Proc. SIGGRAPH '84)* 18:3 (1984), 223–231.

[Cook86] R. L. Cook. "Stochastic Sampling in Computer Graphics." *ACM Transactions on Graphics* 5:1 (1986), 51 – 72.

[Cook89] R. L. Cook. "Stochastic Sampling and Distributed Ray Tracing." In *An Introduction to Ray Tracing*, edited by A. Glassner. London: Academic Press Limited, 1989.

[Coon67] S.A. Coons. "Surfaces for Computer-Aided Design of Space Forms." Technical Report MIT/LCS/TR-41, Massachusetts Institute of Technology, 1967.

[Coor97] S. Coorg and S. Teller. "Real-Time Occlusion Culling for Models with Large Occluders." In *ACM Symposium on Interactive 3D Graphics*, pp. 83–90. New York: ACM Press, 1997.

[Cox72] M. Cox. "The Numerical Evaluation of B-Splines." *IMA Journal of Applied Mathematics* 10:2 (1972), 134–149.

[Crow77] F. C. Crow. "Shadow Algorithms for Computer Graphics." *Computer Graphics (Proc. SIGGRAPH '77)* 11:2 (1977), 242–248.

[Crow81] F.C. Crow. "A Comparison of Antialiasing Techniques." *IEEE Computer Graphics and Applications* 1:1 (1981), 40–48.

[Cull86] R.K. Culley and K.G. Kempf. "A Collision Detection Algorithm Based on Velocity and Distance Bounds." In *IEEE Int. Conf. on Robotics and Automation, Volume 2*, pp. 1064–1069. Washington, D.C.: IEEE, 1986.

[Cunn90] S. Cunningham. *3D Viewing and Rotation Using Orthonormal Bases*, pp. 516–521. Boston, MA: Academic Press, 1990.

[Daub99] I. Daubechies, I. Guskov, and W. Sweldens. "Regularity of Irregular Subdivision." *Constructive Approximation* 15:3 (1999), 381–426.

[dB72] Carl de Boor. "On Calculating with B-splines." *J. Approx. Theory* 6:1 (1972), 50–62.

[dC76] Manfredo P. do Carmo. *Differential Geometry of Curves and Surfaces*. Englewood Cliffs, NJ: Prentice-Hall, 1976.

[Debe96] P. E. Debevec, C. J. Taylor, and J. Malik. "Modeling and Rendering Architecture from Photographs: A Hybrid Geometry and Image-Based Approach." In *Proceedings of SIGGRAPH 96, Computer Graphics Proceedings, Annual Conference Series*, pp. 11–20. Reading, MA: Addison Wesley, 1996.

[Deer88] M. F. Deering, S. Winner, B. Schediwy, C. Duffy, and N. Hunt. "The Triangle Processor and Normal Vector Shader: a VLSI System for High-Performance Graphics." *Computer Graphics)Proc. SIGGRAPH '88* 22:4 (1988), 21–30.

[Delv85] L. M. Delves and J. L. Mohamed. *Computational Methods for Integral Equations*. Cambridge, UK: Cambridge University Press, 1985.

[DeRo98] T. DeRose, M. Kass, and T. Truong. "Subdivision Surfaces in Character Animation." In *Proceedings of SIGGRAPH '98, Computer Gaphics Proceedings, Annual
Conference Series*, pp. 85–94. New York: ACM, 1998.

[Dey99] Tamal K. Dey, Herbert Edelsbrunner, Sumanta Guha, and Dmitry V. Nekhayev.
"Topology Preserving Edge Contraction." *Publications de l'Institut Mathématique
(Beograd)* 66:80 (1999), 23–45.

[DF97a] Leila De Floriani, Paola Magillo, and Enrico Puppo. "Building and Traversing a
Surface at Variable Resolution." In *Proceedings of IEEE Visualization '97*, pp. 103–
110. Los Alamitos, CA: IEEE, 1997.

[DF97b] Leila De Floriani, Enrico Puppo, and Paola Magillo. "A Formal Approach to
Multiresolution Modeling." In *Geometric Modeling: Theory and Practice*, edited
by Wolfgang Straßer, Reinhard Klein, and René Rau. Berlin / Heidelberg: Springer-
Verlag, 1997.

[DF98] Leila De Floriani, Paola Magillo, and Enrico Puppo. "Efficient Implementation
of Multi-Triangulations." In *Proceedings of IEEE Visualization '98*, pp. 43–50. Los
Alamitos, CA: IEEE, 1998.

[Dief96] P. J. Diefenbach. "Multi-Pass Pipeline Rendering: Interaction and Realism
through Hardware Provisions." Ph.D. thesis, University of Pennsylvania, 1996.

[dL99] W. de Leeuw and R. van Liere. "Collapsing Flow Topology Using Area Metrics."
In *Proceedings IEEE Visualization*, pp. 349–354. Los Alamitos, CA: IEEE, 1999.

[Doo78] D. Doo and M. A. Sabin. "Behaviour of Recursive Subdivision Surfaces Near
Extraordinary Points." *Computer Aided Design* 10:6 (1978), 356–360.

[Dreb88] R. A. Drebin, L. Carpenter, and P. Hanrahan. "Volume Rendering." *Computer
Graphics (Proc. SIGGRAPH '88)* 22:4 (1988), 65–74.

[Duff85] T. Duff. "Compositing 3D Rendered Images." *Computer Graphics (Proc. SIG-
GRAPH '85)* 19:3 (1985), 41–44.

[Dura02] F. Durand and J. Dorsey. "Fast Bilateral Filtering for the Display of High-
Dynamic-Range Images." *ACM Transactions on Graphics (SIGGRAPH 2002)* 21:3
(2002), 257–266.

[Dyn90] Nira Dyn, David Levin, and John A. Gregory. "A Butterfly Subdivision Scheme
for Surface Interpolation with Tension Control." *ACM Transactions on Graphics* 9:2
(1990), 160–169.

[Dyn92] N. Dyn. "Subdivision Schemes in Computer Aided Geometric Design." In *Advances in Numerical Analysis II, Wavelets, Subdivision Algorithms, and Radial Basis
Functions*, edited by W. A. Light, pp. 36–104. Oxford, UK: Oxford University Press,
1992.

[Dyn02] N. Dyn and D. Levin. "Subdivision Schemes in Geometric Modelling." *Acta
Numerica* 12 (2002), 73–144.

[Edi05] University of Edinburgh. *Visualization*, 2005. Available online at http://www.dcs.
ed.ac.uk/teaching/cs4/handbook/html/node45.html.

[Eric05] Christer Ericson. *Real-Time Collision Detection*. San Francisco, CA: Morgan Kaufmann, 2005.

[Ever02] C. Everitt and M. J. Kilgard. "Practical and Robust Stenciled Shadow Volumes for Hardware-Accelerated Rendering." Online technical report, nVidia Corp., 2002. Available online at http://developer.nvidia.com/object/robust_shadow\ _volumes.html.

[Fari01] G. Farin. *Curves and Surfaces for CAGD: A Practical Guide*. Morgan Kaufmann, 2001.

[Floy75] R. Floyd and L. Steinberg. "An Adaptive Algorithm for Spatial Gray Scale." In *Society for Information Display 1975 Symposium Digest of Technical Papers*, pp. 36–37. San Jose, CA: Society for Information Display, 1975.

[Fors89] D. Forsyth and A. Zisserman. "Mutual Illumination." In *IEEE Computer Vision and Pattern Recognition*, pp. 466–473. Los Alamitos, CA: IEEE, 1989.

[Fors95] L. K. Forssell and S. D. Cohen. "Using Line Integral Convolution for Flow Visualization: Curvilinear Grids, Variable-Speed Animation, and Unsteady Flows." *IEEE Transactions on Visualization and Computer Graphics* 1:2 (1995), 133–141.

[Frie91] R. M. Friedhoff. *Visualization: The Second Computer Revolution*. New York: W.H. Freeman & Company, 1991.

[Fuch77] H. Fuchs. "Distributing a Visible Surface Algorithm over Multiple Processors." In *ACM '77: Proceedings of the 1977 Annual Conference*, pp. 449–451. New York, NY, USA: ACM, 1977.

[Fuch80] H. Fuchs, Z. Kedem, and B. Naylor. "On Visible Surface Generation by a priori Tree Structures." *Computer Graphics (Proc. SIGGRAPH '80)* 14:3 (1980), 124–133.

[Fuch83] H. Fuchs, G. D. Abram, and E. D. Grant. "Near Real-Time Shaded Display of Rigid Objects." *Computer Graphics (Proc. SIGGRAPH '83)* 17:3 (1983), 65–72.

[Fuch85] H. Fuchs, J. Goldfeather, J. P. Hultquist, S. Spach, J. D. Austin, F. P. Brooks Jr, J. G. Eyles, and J. Poulton. "Fast Spheres, Shadows, Textures, Transparencies and Image Enhancements in Pixel-Planes." *Computer Graphics (Proc. SIGGRAPH '85)* 19:3 (1985), 111–120.

[Fuji86] A. Fujimoto, T. Tanaka, and K. Iwata. "ARTS: Accelerated Ray-Tracing System." *IEEE Computer Graphics and Applications* 6:4 (1986), 16 – 26.

[Garc01] H. Garcke, T. Preusser, M. Rumpf, A. Telea, U. Weikard, and J. J. van Wijk. "A Phase Field Model for Continuous Clustering on Vector Fields." *IEEE Transactions on Visualization and Computer Graphics* 7:3 (2001), 230–241.

[Garl97] Michael Garland and Paul S. Heckbert. "Surface Simplification Using Quadric Error Metrics." In *SIGGRAPH '97: Proceedings of the 24th Annual Conference on Computer Graphics and Interactive Techniques*, pp. 209–216. New York: ACM Press/Addison-Wesley Publishing Co., 1997.

[Garl98] Michael Garland and Paul S. Heckbert. "Simplifying Surfaces with Color and Texture using Quadric Error Metrics." In *Proceedings of IEEE Visualization '98*, pp. 263–270. Los Alamitos, CA: IEEE, 1998.

[Garl99] M. Garland. "Quadric-Based Polygonal Surface Simplification." Ph.D. thesis, School of Computer Science, Carnegie-Mellon University, 1999.

[Gero05] C. Gerot, L. Barthe, N. A. Dodgson, and M.A. Sabin. "Subdivision as a Sequence of Sampled C^p Surfaces." In *Advances in Multiresolution for Geometric Modelling*, edited by N.A. Dodgson, M.S. Floater, and M.A. Sabin, pp. 259–270. berlin / Heidelberg: Springer-Verlag, 2005.

[Gink06] I. Ginkel and G. Umlauf. "Loop Subdivision with Curvature Control." In *Proc. Eurographics Symposium on Geometry Processing '06*, pp. 163–171. Aire-la-Ville, Switzerland, Switzerland: Eurographics Association, 2006.

[Glas84] A. S. Glassner. "Space Subdivision for Fast Ray Tracing." *IEEE Computer Graphics and Applications* 4:10 (1984), 15 – 22.

[Glas95] A. S. Glassner. *Principles of Digital Image Synthesis (two-volume set)*. San Francisco, CA: Morgan-Kaufmann, 1995.

[Gold71] R. A. Goldstein and R. Nagel. "3-D Visual Simulation." *Simulation* 16:1 (1971), 25–31.

[Gold87] J. Goldsmith and J. Salmon. "Automatic Creation of Object Hierarchies for Ray Tracing." *IEEE Computer Graphics and Applications* 7:5 (1987), 14 – 20.

[Gome99] J. Gomes, L. Darsa, B. Costa, and L. Velho. *Warping and Morphing of Graphical Objects*. San Francisco, CA: Morgan-Kaufmann, 1999.

[Gord94] D. Gordon, M.A. Peterson, and R.A. Reynolds. "Fast Polygon Scan Conversion with Medical Applications." *IEEE Computer Graphics and Applications* 14:6 (1994), 20–27.

[Gort96] S. J. Gortler, R. Grzeszczuk, R. Szeliski, and M. F. Cohen. "The Lumigraph." In *Proceedings of SIGGRAPH 96, Computer Graphics Proceedings, Annual Conference Series*, pp. 43–52. Reading, MA: Addison Wesley, 1996.

[Gott96] S. Gottschalk, M. C. Lin, and D. Manocha. "OBBTree: A Hierarchical Structure for Rapid Interference Detection." In *Proceedings of SIGGRAPH 96, Computer Graphics Proceedings, Annual Conference Series*, pp. 171–180. Reading, MA: Addison Wesley, 1996.

[Gour71] H. Gouraud. "Continuous Shading of Curved Surfaces." *IEEE Transactions on Computers* C-20 (1971), 623–628.

[Gray97] Alfred Gray. *Modern Differential Geometry of Curves and Surfaces*. Boca Raton, FL: CRC Press, 1997.

[Gree86] N. Greene and P. S. Heckbert. "Creating Raster Omnimax Images from Multiple Perspective Views Using the Elliptical Weighted Average Filter." *IEEE Computer Graphics and Applications* 6:6 (1986), 21–27.

[Gree04] S. Green and G. Turkiyyah. "Second Order Accurate Constraint Formulation for Subdivision Finite Element Simulation of Thin Shells." *International Journal for Numerical Methods in Engineering* 61 (2004), 380–405.

[Gree05] S. Green and G. Turkiyyah. "A Rotation-Free Quadrilateral Thin Shell Subdivision Finite Element." *Communications in Numerical Methods in Engineering* 21 (2005), 757–767.

[Greg97] R. L. Gregory. *Eye and Brain: The Physiology of Seeing*, Fifth edition. Princeton, NJ: Princeton University Press, 1997.

[Grei98] G. Greiner and K. Hormann. "Efficient Clipping of Arbitrary Polygons." *ACM Transactions on Graphics* 17:2 (1998), 71–83.

[Grin02] E. Grinspun, P. Krysl, and P. Schröeder. "CHARMS: A Simple Framework for Adaptive Simulation." *ACM Transanctions on Graphics* 21:3 (2002), 281–290.

[Gu02] X. Gu, S. J. Gortler, and H. Hoppe. "Geometry Images." *Transactions on Graphics (Proc. SIGGRAPH '02)* 21:3 (2002), 355–361.

[Guen05] E. Guendelman, A. Selle, F. Losasso, and R. Fedkiw. "Coupling Water and Smoke to Thin Deformable and Rigid Shells." pp. 973–981. New York: ACM, 2005.

[Guib85] Leonidas Guibas and Jorge Stolfi. "Primitives for the Manipulation of General Subdivisions and the Computation of Voronoi Diagrams." *ACM Transactions on Graphics* 4:2 (1985), 74–123.

[Hain91] Eric Haines. "Fast Ray-Convex Polyhedron Intersection." In *Graphics Gems II*, edited by James Arvo, pp. 247–250 and code. San Diego: Academic Press, 1991.

[Hall93] P. Hall. "Volume Rendering for Vector Fields." *The Visual Computer* 10:2 (1993), 69–78.

[Hals93] M. Halstead, M. Kass, and T. DeRose. "Efficient, Fair Interpolation Using Catmull-Clark Surfaces." In *SIGGRAPH '93: Proceedings of the 20th Annual Conference on Computer Graphics and Interactive Techniques*, pp. 35–44. New York: ACM, 1993.

[Hamm64] J. M. Hammersley and D. C. Handscomb. *Monte Carlo Methods*. London, UK: Methuen London/Chapman and Hall, 1964.

[Han03] B. Han. "Computing the Smoothness Exponent of a Symmetric Multivariate Refinable Function." *SIAM Journal on Matrix Analysis and Applications* 24:3 (2003), 693–714.

[Hanr91] P. Hanrahan, D. Salzman, and L. Aupperle. "A Rapid Hierarchical Radiosity Algorithm." In *Computer Graphics (Proc. SIGGRAPH '91)*, 25, 25, pp. 197–206, 1991.

[Hanr98] P. Hanrahan. "Scan Conversion: Lines and Curves." Stanford Course Notes, 1998. Available online at http://graphics.stanford.edu/courses/cs248-97-winter/Lectures/lecture7/.

[Hanr05] P. Hanrahan. "Teaching Visualization." *Computer Graphics* 39:1 (2005), 4–5.

[Harr04] M.A. Harris and E.M. Reingold. "Line Drawing, Leap Years, and Euclid." *ACM Computing Surveys* 36:1 (2004), 68–80.

[Heck89] P. S. Heckbert. "Fundamentals of Texture Mapping and Image Warping." Master's thesis, University of California, Berkeley, 1989.

[Heck91] P. S. Heckbert and H. P. Moreton. "Interpolation for Polygon Texture Mapping and Shading." In *State of the Art in Computer Graphics, Visualization and Modeling*, edited by D. F. Rogers and R. A. Earnshaw, pp. 101–111. New York: Springer-Verlag, 1991.

[Heck99] B. Heckel, G. Weber, B. Hamann, and K. I. Joy. "Construction of Vector Field Hierarchies." In *IEEE Visualization '99*, pp. 19–25. los Alamitos, CA: IEEE, 1999.

[Heid91] T. Heidmann. "Real Shadows Real Time." *IRIS Universe* 18 (1991), 28–31.

[Heid99] Wolfgang Heidrich and Hans-Peter Seidel. "Realistic, Hardware-Accelerated Shading and Lighting." In *SIGGRAPH '99: Proceedings of the 26th Annual Conference on Computer Graphics and Interactive Techniques*, pp. 171–178. New York: ACM Press/Addison-Wesley Publishing Co., 1999.

[Helg04] A. Helgeland and O. Andreassen. "Visualization of Vector Fields Using Seed LIC and Volume Rendering." *IEEE Transactions on Visualization and Computer Graphics* 10:6 (2004), 673–682.

[Helm91] J. L. Helman and L. Hesselink. "Visualizing Vector Field Topology in Fluid Flows." *IEEE Computer Graphics and Applications* 11:3 (1991), 36–46.

[Hink93] Paul Hinker and Charles Hansen. "Geometric Optimization." In *Proceedings of IEEE Visualization '93*, pp. 189–195. Los Alamitos, CA: IEEE, 1993.

[Hoff99] K.E. Hoff.III, T. Culver, J. Keyser, M. Lin, and D. Manocha. "Fast Computation of Generalized Voronoi Diagrams Using Graphics Hardware." In *Proceedings of SIGGRAPH 99, Computer Graphics Proceedings, Annual Conference Series*, pp. 277–286. Reading, MA: Addison Wesley Longman, 1999.

[Hopp93] Hugues Hoppe, Tony DeRose, Tom Duchamp, John McDonald, and Werner Stuetzle. "Mesh Optimization." In *SIGGRAPH '93: Proceedings of the 20th Annual Conference on Computer Graphics and Interactive Techniques*, pp. 19–26. New York, NY, USA: ACM, 1993. Also available as the more detailed Technical Report TR UW CSE 1993-01-01.

[Hopp94] H. Hoppe, T. deRose, T. Duchamp, M. Halstead, H. Jin, J. McDonald, J. Schweitzer, and W. Stuetzle. "Piecewise Smooth Surface Reconstruction." In *Proceedings of SIGGRAPH 94, Computer Graphics Proceedings, Annual Conference Series*, edited by A. Glassner, pp. 295–302. New York: ACM Press, 1994.

[Hopp96] H. Hoppe. "Progressive Meshes." In *Proceedings of SIGGRAPH 96, Computer Graphics Proceedings, Annual Conference Series*, pp. 99–108. Reading, MA: Addison Wesley, 1996.

[Hopp97] Hugues Hoppe. "View-Dependent Refinement of Progressive Meshes." In *SIGGRAPH '97: Proceedings of the 24th Annual Conference on Computer Graphics and Interactive Techniques*, pp. 189–198. New York: ACM Press/Addison-Wesley Publishing Co., 1997.

[Hopp98] H. Hoppe. "Efficient Implementation of Progressive Meshes." *Computers & Graphics* 22:1 (1998), 27–36.

[Horn05] S. Hornus, J. Hoberock, S. Lefebvre, and J. C. Hart. "ZP+: Correct Z-pass Stencil Shadows." In *ACM Symposium on Interactive 3D Graphics and Games (I3D'05)*, pp. 195–202. New York: ACM, 2005.

[Hosc96] Josef Hoschek and Dieter Lasser. *Fundamentals of Computer Aided Geometric Design*. Wellesley, MA: A K Peters, 1996.

[Huds97] T. Hudson, D. Manocha, J. Cohen, M. Lin, K. Hoff, and H. Zhang. "Accelerated Occlusion Culling Using Shadow Frustra." In *13th Annual ACM Symposium on Computational Geometry*, pp. 1–10. New York: ACM, 1997.

[IBM07] IBM. *OpenDX User Guide, Version 4.4*, 2007. Available online at http://www.opendx.org.

[Illi00] V. Illingworth. *The Penguin Dictionary of Physics*. London, UK: Penguin, 2000.

[Inte98] V. Interrante and C. Grosch. "Visualizing 3D Flow." *IEEE Computer Graphics and Applications* 18:4 (1998), 49–53.

[Ione03] A. Iones, A. Krupkin, M. Sbert, and S. Zhukov. "Fast Realistic Lighting for Video Games." *IEEE Computer Graphics and Applications* 23:3 (2003), 54–64.

[Ivri03] Ioannis Ivrissimtzis, Kanishka Shrivastava, and Hans-Peter Seidel. "Subdivision Rules for General Meshes." In *Curve and Surface Fitting: Saint-Malo 2002, Volume 2, Proceedings of the 5th Conference on Curves and Surfaces*, edited by Albert Cohen, Jean-Louis Merrien, and Larry Schumaker, pp. 229–238. L' Association Française d'Approximation (AFA), Brentwood, NJ: Nashboro Press, 2003.

[Jarv76] J.F. Jarvis, C.N. Jundice, and W.H. Ninke. "A Survey of Techniques for the Display of Continuous Tone Pictures on Bilevel Displays." *Computer Graphics and Image Processing* 5 (1976), 13–40.

[Jens95] H. W. Jensen and N. J. Christensen. "Photon Maps in Bidirectional Monte Carlo Ray Tracing of Complex Objects." *Computers & Graphics* 19:2 (1995), 215–224.

[Jens96a] H. W. Jensen. "Global Illumination using Photon Maps." In *Eurographics Rendering Workshop*, pp. 21–30. aire-la-Ville, Switzerland: Eurographics, 1996.

[Jens96b] H. W. Jensen. "Rendering Caustics on Non-Lambertian Surfaces." In *Proceedings of Graphics Interface*, pp. 116–121. Toronto, Ontario: Canadian Information Processing Society, 1996.

[Jens01] H. W. Jensen. *Realistic Image Synthesis Using Photon Mapping*. Natick, MA: A K Peters, 2001.

[Jia95] R. Q. Jia. "Subdivision Schemes in l_p Spaces." *Advances in Computational Mathematics* 3 (1995), 309–341.

[Jime01] P. Jimenez, F. Thomas, and C. Torras. "3D Collision Detection: A Survey." *Computers and Graphics* 25:2 (2001), 269–285.

[Jirk02] T. Jirka and V. Skala. "Gradient Vector Estimation and Vertex Normal Computation." Technical report, University of West Bohemia in Pilsen, Czech Republic, TR DCSE/TR-2002-08, 2002.

[Jord87] Camille Jordan. *Cours d'Analyze de l'Ecole Polytechnique*, 1887.

[Jr.04] R.S. Wright. Jr. and B. Lipchak. *OpenGL Superbible, Third Edition*. Indianapolis, IN: SAMS Publishing, 2004.

[Kaji85] J. T. Kajiya. "Anisotropic Reflection Models." *Computer Graphics (Proc. SIGGRAPH '85)* 19:3 (1985), 15–21.

[Kaji86] J. T. Kajiya. "The Rendering Equation." *Computer Graphics (Proc. SIGGRAPH '86)* 20:4 (1986), 143–150.

[Kalo86] M. H. Kalos and P. Whitlock. *The Monte Carlo Method. Volume 1: Basics*. New York: J. Wiley and Sons, 1986.

[Kalv96] Alan D. Kalvin and Russell H. Taylor. "Superfaces: Polygonal Mesh Simplification with Bounded Error." *IEEE Computer Graphics and Applications* 16:3 (1996), 64–77.

[Kara99] E.A. Karabassi, G. Papaioannou, and T. Theoharis. "A Fast Depth-Buffer-Based Voxelization Algorithm." *ACM Journal of Graphics Tools* 4:4 (1999), 5–10.

[Karc04] K. Karciauskas, J. Peters, and U. Reif. "Shape Characterization of Subdivision Surfaces: Case Studies." *Computer Aided Geometric Design* 21:6 (2004), 601–614.

[Kats05] P. Katsaloulis, P. Simos, D. Francis, A. Papanicolaou, I. Kakadiaris, and T. Theoharis. "3D Visualization of MEG Activation Records within a Semi-Transparent Talairach Model Brain." In *1st International Conference on Geometric Modeling, Visualization & Graphics (GMV)*. Joint Conference on Information Sciences UT, 2005. Available online at http://fs.mis.kuas.edu.tw/~cobol/JCIS2005/jcis05/prof390.html.

[Kauf86] A. Kaufman and E. Shimony. "3D Scan-Conversion Algorithms for Voxel-Based Graphics." In *Proc. ACM Workshop on Interactive 3D Graphics*, pp. 45–76. New York: ACM, 1986.

[Kava03] L. Kavan and J. Zara. "Real Time Skin Deformation with Bones Blending." In *The 11th International Conference in Central Europe on Computer Graphics, Visualization and Computer Vision*, 2003. Available online at http://wscg.zcu.cz/wscg2003/Papers_2003/G61.pdf.

[Kay86] T. Kay and J. Kajiya. "Ray Tracing Complex Scenes." 20:4 (1986), 269–278.

[Kilg00] M. J. Kilgard. "Improving Shadows and Reflections via the Stencil Buffer." nvidia white paper, nVidia Corp., 2000.

[Klos98] J. T. Klosowski, M. Held, J. S. Mitchell, H. Sowizral, and K. Zikan. "Efficient Collision Detection Using Bounding Volume Hierarchies of k-DOPs." *IEEE Visualization and Computer Graphics* 4:1 (1998), 21–36.

[Kobb00] Leif Kobbelt. "$\sqrt{}(3)$ Subdivision." In *Proceedings SIGGRAPH '00, Computer Graphics Proceedings, Annual Conference Series*, pp. 103–112. New York: ACM Press/Addison-Wesley Publishing Co., 2000.

[Kolb95] C. Kolb, D. Mitchell, and P. Hanrahan. "A Realistic Camera Model for Computer Graphics." In *Proceedings SIGGRAPH '95, Annual Conference Series*, pp. 317–324. New York: ACM, 1995.

[Koll03] Thomas Kollig and Alexander Keller. "Efficient Illumination by High Dynamic Range Images." In *14th Eurographics Workshop on Rendering*, pp. 45–51. Aire-la-Ville, Switzerland: Eurographics Association, 2003.

[Kozl04] S. Kozlov. "Perspective Shadow Maps: Care and Feeding." In *GPU Gems*, edited by R. Fernando, pp. 217–244. Reading, MA: Addison-Wesley, 2004.

[Kree98] K. Kreeger, I. Bitier, T. Dachille, B. Chen, and A. Kaufman. "Adaptive Perspective Ray Casting." In *IEEE Symposium on Volume Visualization*, pp. 55–62. New York, NY, USA: ACM, 1998.

[Kres89] R. Kress. *Linear Integral Equations*. Berlin /Heidelberg: Springer Verlag, 1989.

[Krey06] E. Kreyszig. *Advanced Engineering Mathematics*. New York: J. Wiley & Sons, 2006.

[Lacr94] P. Lacroute and M. Levoy. "Fast Volume Rendering using a Shear-Warp Factorization of the Viewing Transformation." In *Proceedings of SIGGRAPH 94, Computer Graphics Proceedings, Annual Conference Series*, pp. 451–457. New York: ACM Press, 1994.

[Lafo94] E. P. Lafortune and Y. D. Willems. "A Theoretical Framework for Physically Based Rendering." *Computer Graphics Forum* 13:2 (1994), 97–107.

[Lamb60] J. H. Lambert. *Photometria sive de mensura et gradibus luminis, colorum et umbrae (in Latin)*, 1760.

[Lars97] G. W. Larson, H. Rushmeier, and C. Piatko. "A Visibility Matching Tone Reproduction Operator for High Dynamic Range Scenes." *IEEE Trans. on Visualization and Computer Graphics* 3:4 (1997), 291–306.

[Lars98a] G.W. Larson. "LogLuv Encoding for Full-Gamut, High-Dynamic Range Images." *journal of graphics tools* 3:1 (1998), 15–31.

[Lars98b] G.W. Larson. "Overcoming Gamut and Dynamic Range Limitations in Digital Images." In *Proc. of 1S&T 6th Color Imaging Conf.* Springfield, VA: Society for Imaging Science and Technology, 1998.

[Ledo02] J. Ledoux. *Synaptic Self: How Our Brains Become Who We Are*. London: Penguin Books, 2002.

[Leng04] E. Lengyel. *Mathematics for 3D Game Programming & Computer Graphics, 2nd Edition*. Hingham, MA: Charles River Media Inc., 2004.

[Levi99] A. Levin. "Interpolating Nets of Curves by Smooth Subdivision Surfaces." In *Proceedings of SIGGRAPH 99, Computer Graphics Proceedings, Annual Conference Series*, pp. 57–63. New York: ACM Press/Addison-Wesley Publishing Co., 1999.

[Levi06] A. Levin. "Modified Subdivision Surfaces with Continuous Curvature." *ACM Transactions on Graphics* 25:3 (2006), 1035–1040.

[Levo96] M. Levoy and P. Hanrahan. "Light Field Rendering." In *Proceedings of SIGGRAPH 96, Computer Graphics Proceedings, Annual Conference Series*, pp. 31–41. Reading, MA: Addison Wesley, 1996.

[Levo00] Marc Levoy, Kari Pulli, Brian Curless, Szymon Rusinkiewicz, David Koller, Lucas Pereira, Matt Ginzton, Sean Anderson, James Davis, Jeremy Ginsberg, Jonathan Shade, and Duane Fulk. "The Digital Michelangelo Project: 3D Scanning of Large Statues." In *Proceedings SIGGRAPH '00, Computer Graphics Proceedings, Annual Conference Series*, pp. 131–144. New York: ACM Press/Addison-Wesley Publishing Co., 2000.

[Levy02] B. Levy, S. Petitjean, N. Ray, and J. Maillot. "Least Squares Conformal Maps for Automatic Texture Atlas Generation." *ACM Transactions on Graphics* 21:3 (2002), 362–371.

[Lian84] Y.D. Liang and B. Barsky. "A New Concept and Method for Line Clipping." *ACM Transactions on Graphics* 3:1 (1984), 1–22.

[Limb69] J. O. Limb. "Design of Dither Waveforms for Quantized Visual Signals." *Bell Systems Technical Journal* 48 (1969), 2555–2582.

[Lin91] M. C. Lin and J. F. Canny. "A Fast Algorithm for Incremental Distance Calculation." In *IEEE International Conference on Robotics and Automation*, pp. 1008–1014. Washington, DC: IEEE, 1991.

[Lin98] M.C. Lin and S. Gottschalk. "Collision Detection Between Geometric Models: A Survey." In *Proceedings of IMA Conference on Mathematics of Surfaces*. Essex, UK: Institute of Mathematics and Its Applications, 1998.

[Lips74] Martin Lipschutz. *Differential Geometry*. Schaum's Outlines Series, New York: McGraw-Hill, 1974.

[Lisc94] Dani Lischinski. "Incremental Delaunay Triangulation." In *Graphics Gems IV*, edited by Paul Heckbert, pp. 47–59. San Diego, CA: Academic Press, 1994.

[Loop87] C. T. Loop. "Smooth Subdivision Surfaces Based on Triangles." Master's thesis, University of Utah, Department of Mathematics, 1987.

[Loop98] C. T. Loop. "Bounded Curvature Triangle Mesh Subdivision With the Convex Hull Property." *The Visual Computer* 18:5–6 (1998), 316–325.

[Lore87] W. E. Lorensen and H. E. Cline. "Marching Cubes: A High Resolution 3D Surface Construction Algorithm." *Computer Graphics (Proc. SIGGRAPH '87)* 21:4 (1987), 163–169.

[Lueb95] D. Luebke and C. Georges. "Portals and Mirrors: Simple, Fast Evaluation of Potentially Visible Sets." In *ACM Interactive 3D Graphics Conference*. New York: ACM, 1995.

[Malv69] L. E. Malvern. *Introduction to the Mechanics of a Continuous Medium*. englewood Cliffs, NJ: Prentice-Hall, 1969.

[Mand75] B. Mandelbrot. *Les objets fractals*. Paris: Flammarion, 1975.

[Marc77] R. E. Marc and H. G. Sperling. "Chromatic Organization of Primate Cones." *Science* 196 (1977), 454–456.

[Mass04] Vincent Masselus. "A Practical Framework for Fixed Viewpoint Image-based Relighting." Ph.D. thesis, Dept. of Computer Science, Katholieke Universiteit Leuven, 2004.

[McGu03] M. McGuire, J. F. Hughes, K. T. Egan, M. J. Kilgard, and C. Everitt. "Fast, Practical, and Robust Shadows." Technical report, nVidia Corp., 2003. Avalable online at http://developer.nvidia.com/object/fast_shadow_volumes.html.

[Meta96a] D. N. Metaxas. *Physics-Based Deformable Models: Applications to Computer Vision, Graphics and Medical Imaging.* Berlin / Heidelberg: Springer, 1996.

[Meta96b] D. N. Metaxas and I. A. Kakadiaris. "Elastically Adaptive Deformable Models." In *Computer Vision - ECCV '96: Fourth European Conference on Computer Vision, Cambridge, UK April 14-18, 1996. Proceedings, Volume II (Lecture Notes in Computer Science)*, pp. 550–559. Berlin / Heidelberg: Springer, 1996.

[Meye03] M. Meyer, M. Desbrun, P. Schroeder, and A.H. Barr. "Discrete Differential-Geometry Operators for Triangulated 2-Manifolds." In *Visualization and Mathematics III*, edited by Hans-Christian Hege and Konrad Polthier, pp. 35–57. Heidelberg: Springer-Verlag, 2003.

[Miha91] T. Mihalisin, J. Timlin, and J. Schwegler. "Visualizing Multivariate Functions, Data and Distributions." *IEEE Computer Graphics and Applications* 11:3 (1991), 28–35.

[Mö97] T. Möller and B. Trumbore. "Fast, Minimum Storage Ray-Triangle Intersection." *journal of graphics tools* 2:1 (1997), 21–28.

[Moln94] S. Molnar, M. Cox, D. Ellsworth, and H. Fuchs. "A Sorting Classification of Parallel Rendering." *IEEE Computer Graphics and Applications* 14:4 (1994), 23–32.

[Muel95] C. Mueller. "The Sort-First Rendering Architecture for High-Performance Graphics." In *SI3D '95: Proceedings of the 1995 symposium on Interactive 3D graphic*, pp. 75–84. New York: ACM, 1995.

[Mull93] H. Muller and M. Stark. "Adaptive Generation of Surfaces in Volume Data." *The Visual Computer* 9:4 (1993), 182–199.

[Muns41] A. H. Munsell and R. B. Farnum. *A Color Notation: An Illustrated System Defining All Colors And Their Relations by Measured Scales of Hue, Value, and Chroma.* Munsell Color Company, 1941.

[Murc84] G. Murch. "Physiological Principles for the Effective Use of Color." *IEEE Computer Graphics & Applications* 4:11 (1984), 49–54.

[Murr96] James D. Murray and William Van Ryper. "Wavefront OBJ File Format Summary." In *Encyclopedia of Graphics File Formats*, Second edition, 1996. Available online (http://www.fileformat.info/format/wavefrontobj/).

[Nasr87] A. Nasri. "Polyhedral Subdivision Methods for Free-Form Surfaces." *ACM Transactions on Graphics* 6:1 (1987), 29–73.

[Nasr91] A. Nasri. "Boundary Corner Control in Recursive Subdivision Surfaces." *Computer Aided Design* 23:6 (1991), 405–410.

[Nasr95] A. Nasri. "Interpolation of Meshes of Curves by Recursive Subdivision Surfaces." In *Fourth SIAM Conference on Geometric Design.* Philadelphia, PA: SIAM, 1995.

[Nasr97] A. Nasri. "Curve Interpolation in Recursively Generated B-spline Surfaces Over Arbitrary Topology." *Computer Aided Geometric Design* 14:1 (1997), 13–30.

[Nasr00] A. Nasri. "Recursive Subdivision of Polygonal Complexes and its Applications in CAGD." *Computer Aided Geometric Design* 17:7 (2000), 595–619.

[Nasr02a] A. Nasri and A. Abbas. "Designing Catmull-Clark Subdivision Surfaces with Curve Interpolation Constraints." *Computer & Graphics* 26:3 (2002), 393–400.

[Nasr02b] A. Nasri and M. Sabin. "Taxonomy of Interpolation Conditions in Recursive Subdivision Curves." *The Visual Computer* 18:4 (2002), 259–272.

[Nasr02c] A. Nasri and M. Sabin. "Taxonomy of Interpolation Conditions in Recursive Subdivision Surfaces." *The Visual Computer* 18:6 (2002), 382–403.

[Nasr03a] A. Nasri. "Interpolating an Unlimited Number of Curves Meeting at Extraordinary Points on Subdivision Surfaces." *Computer Graphics Forum* 22:1 (2003), 87–97.

[Nasr03b] A. Nasri, A. Abbas, and I. Hasbini. "Skinning Catmull-Clark Subdivision Surfaces with Incompatible Cross-sectional Curves." In *Pacific Graphics 2003*, pp. 102–111. Washington, DC: IEEE Press, 2003.

[Newe72] M.E. Newell, R.G. Newell, and T.L. Sancha. "A Solution to the Hidden Surface Problem." In *ACM'72: Proceedings of the ACM Annual Conference*, pp. 443–450. New York: ACM, 1972.

[Newm81] W.M. Newman and R.F. Sproull. *Principles of Interactive Computer Graphics.* McGraw Hill, 1981.

[Ngo93] J. T. Ngo and J. Marks. "Spacetime Constraints Revisited." In *Proceedings of SIGGRAPH 93, Computer Graphics Proceedings, Annual Conference Series*, pp. 343–350. New York: ACM Press, 1993.

[Nico77] F. E. Nicodemus, J. C. Richmond, J. J. Hsia, I. W. Ginsberg, and T. Limperis. "Considerations and Nomenclature for Reflectance." Technical report, U.S. Department of Commerce, 1977.

[Nire02] S. Nirenstein, E. Blake, and J. Gain. "Exact From Region Visibility Culling." In *Rendering Techniques 2002: Proceedings of the 13th Eurographics Workshop on Rendering*, pp. 191–202. Berlin / Heidelberg: Springer-Verlag, 2002.

[NSF87] NSF. "Visualization in Scientific Computing." Technical report, NSF Panel on Graphics, Image Processing, and Workstations, 1987.

[O'Ne66] Barrett O'Neill. *Elementary Differential Geometry.* New York: Academic Press, 1966.

[Open07a] OpenDX. "The Open Source Software Project Based on IBM'S Visualization Data Project." Available online at http://www.opendx.org, 2007.

[Open07b] OpenGL. "OPenGL Homepage.", 2007. Available 0nline at www.opengl.org.

[Opre97] John Oprea. *Differential Geometry and its Applications.* englewood Cliffs, NJ: Prentice-Hall, 1997.

[Oren92] M. Oren and S. K. Nayar. "Generalization of the Lambertian Model and Implications for Machine Vision." Technical Report CUCS-057-92, Department of Computer Science, Columbia University, New York, USA, 1992.

[Oren94] M. Oren and S. K. Nayar. "Generalization of Lambert's Reflectance Model." In *Proceedings of SIGGRAPH 94, Computer Graphics Proceedings, Annual Conference Series*, pp. 239–246. New York: ACM Press, 1994.

[O'Ro98] Joseph O'Rourke. *Computational Geometry in C*, Second edition. Cambridge, UK: Cambridge University Press, 1998.

[Over97] C.W.A.M. Overveld and B. Wyvill. "Phong Normal Interpolation Revisited." *ACM Transactions on Graphics* 16:4 (1997), 397–410.

[Owen99] G. Scott Owen. "Emotional Response to Color.", 1999. Available online (http://www.siggraph.org/education/materials/HyperGraph/color/coloremo.htm).

[Oxf04] *Concise Oxford English Dictionary*, 11th edition. Oxford, UK: Oxford University Press, 2004.

[Pakd05] H.-R. Pakdel and F.F. Samavati. "Incremental Catmull-Clark Subdivision." In *5th International Conference on 3-D Digital Imaging and Modeling*, pp. 95–102. Los Alamitos, CA: IEEE Computer Society Press, 2005.

[Palm95] J.M. Palmer. "Getting Intense on Intensity." *Optics and Photonics News*, pp. 6–6.

[Palm05] J.M. Palmer. *Radiometry and Photometry FAQ*. University of Arizona, Optical Sciences Center, http://www.optics.arizona.edu/Palmer/rpfaq/rpfaq.htm, 2005.

[Papa00] G. Papaioannou, E. A. Karabassi, and T. Theoharis. "Segmentation and Surface Characterization of Arbitrary 3D Meshes for Object Reconstruction and Recognition." In *IEEE International Conference on Pattern Recognition*, pp. 734–737. Washington, DC: IEEE, 2000.

[Papa02] G. Papaioannou, E.A. Karabassi, and T. Theoharis. "Reconstruction of Three-Dimensional Objects through Matching of their Parts." *IEEE Transactions on Pattern Analysis and Machine Intelligence* 24:1 (2002), 114–124.

[Papa06] G. Papaioannou, A. Gaitatzes, and D. Christopoulos. "Efficient Occlusion Culling using Solid Occluders." In *14th International Conference in Central Europe on Computer Graphics, Visualization and Computer Vision (WSCG '2006)*, pp. 87–94. Plzen, Czech Republic: University of West Bohemia, 2006.

[Pare01] R. Parent. *Computer Animation: Algorithms and Techniques*. San Francisco: Morgan Kaufmann, 2001.

[Pass04] G. Passalis, I. Kakadiaris, and T. Theoharis. "Efficient Hardware Voxelization." In *Computer Graphics International 2004*, pp. 374–377. Washington, DC: IEEE, 2004.

[Pass06] G. Passalis, T. Theoharis, and I.A. Kakadiaris. "PTK: A Novel Depth Buffer-Based Shape Descriptor for Three-Dimensional Object Retrieval." *The Visual Computer* 23:1 (2006), 5–14.

[Past02] M. J. Pastizzo, R. F. Erbacher, and L. B. Feldman. "Multi-Dimensional Data Visualization." *Behavior Research Methods, Instruments, and Computers* 34:2 (2002), 158–162.

[Patr02] N. M. Patrikalakis and T. Maekawa. *Shape Interrogation for Computer Aided Design and Manufacturing (Mathematics and Visualization).* Berlin /Heidelberg: Springer, 2002.

[Perl85] K. Perlin. "An Image Synthesizer." *Computer Graphics (Proc. SIGGRAPH '85)* 19:3 (1985), 287–296.

[Perl89] K. Perlin and E. M. Hoffert. "Hypertexture." *Computer Graphics (Proc. SIGGRAPH '89)* 23:3 (1989), 254–262.

[Pete97] Jörg Peters and Ulrich Reif. "The Simplest Subdivision Scheme for Smoothing Polyhedra." *ACM Transactions on Graphics* 16:4 (1997), 420–431.

[Pete98] J. Peters and U. Reif. "Analysis of Algorithms Generalizing B-Spline Subdivision." *SIAM Journal on Numerical Analysis* 35:2 (1998), 728–748.

[Pete00] J. Peters and G. Umlauf. "Gaussian and Mean Curvature of Subdivision Surfaces." In *Proc. Ninth IMA Conference on The Mathematics of Surfaces*, pp. 59–69. London, UK: Springer-Verlag, 2000.

[Pete03] J. Peters and J. L. Shiue. "4-3 Directionally Ripple-free Subdivision." *ACM Transactions on Graphics* 23:4 (2003), 980–1003.

[Pete04] J. Peters and U. Reif. "Shape Characterization of Subdivision Surfaces: Basic Principles." *Computer Aided Geometric Design* 21:6 (2004), 585–599.

[Phon75] B.T. Phong. "Illumination for Computer Generated Pictures." *Communications of the ACM* 18:6 (1975), 311–317.

[Pitt80] M.L.V. Pitteway and D.J. Watkinson. "Bresenham's Algorithm with Gray Scale." *Communications of the ACM* 23:11 (1980), 625–626.

[Plak05] E. Plaku, K.E. Bekris, B.Y. Chen, A.M. Ladd, and L.E. Kavraki. "Sampling-Based Roadmap of Trees for Parallel Motion Planning." *IEEE Transactions on Robotics* 21:4 (2005), 597–608.

[Plat03] N. Platis and T. Theoharis. "Progressive Hulls for Intersection Applications." *Computer Graphics Forum* 22:2 (2003), 107–116.

[Plat04] N. Platis and T. Theoharis. "Simplification of Vector Fields over Tetrahedral Meshes." In *CGI '04: Proceedings of the Computer Graphics International (CGI'04)*, pp. 174–181. Washington, DC, USA: IEEE Computer Society, 2004.

[PLY07] "The PLY File Format.", 2007. Available online (http://www.cc.gatech.edu/projects/large_models/ply.html).

[Popo00] J. Popovic, S.M. Seitz, M. Erdmann, Z. Popovic, and A. Witkin. "Interactive Manipulation of Rigid Body Simulations." In *Proceedings of SIGGRAPH 2000, Computer Graphics Proceedings, Annual Conference Series*, pp. 209–217. Reading, MA: Addison-Wesley, 2000.

[Port84] T. Porter and T. Duff. "Compositing Digital Images." *Computer Graphics (Proc. SIGGRAPH '84)* 18:3 (1984), 253–259.

[Poul90] P. Poulin and A. Fournier. "A Model for Anisotropic Reflection." *Computer Graphics (Proc. SIGGRAPH '90)* 24:4 (1990), 273–282.

[Prau98] H. Prautzsch and G. Umlauf. "A G^2 Subdivision Algorithm." In *Geometric Modeling, Computing Supplements*, edited by G. Farin, H. Bieri, G. Brunnet, and T. DeRose, pp. 217–224. Berlin / Heidelberg: Springer-Verlag, 1998.

[Prau99] H. Prautzsch and U. Reif. "Degree Estimates for C^k-Piecewise Polynomial Subdivision Surfaces." *Advances in Computational Mathematics* 10:2 (1999), 209–217.

[Prep85] Franco P. Preparata and Michael I. Shamos. *Computational Geometry: An Introduction.* New York: Springer-Verlag, 1985.

[Pupp97] Enrico Puppo and Roberto Scopigno. *Simplification, LOD and Multiresolution—Principles and Applications.* Eurographics '97 Tutorial Notes, Aire-la-Ville, Switzerland: The Eurographics Association, 1997.

[Pupp98] Enrico Puppo. "Variable Resolution Triangulations." *Computational Geometry* 11:3–4 (1998), 219–238.

[Purn04] B. Purnomo, J. D. Cohen, and S. Kumar. "Seamless Texture Atlases." In *Eurographics Symposium on Geometry Processing*, pp. 67–76. Aire-la-Ville, Switzerland: Eurographics, 2004.

[Raub93] T. Rauber. *Algorithmen in der Computergraphik.* Berlin: B.G. Teubner, 1993.

[Redd96] M. Reddy. "SCROOGE: Perceptually Driven Polygon Reduction." *Computer Graphics Forum* 15:4 (1996), 191–203.

[Reev83] W. T. Reeves. "Particle Systems—A Technique for Modeling a Class of Fuzzy Objects." *Computer Graphics (Proc. SIGGRAPH '83)* 17:3 (1983), 359–375.

[Reev87] W. T. Reeves, D. H. Salesin, and R. L. Cook. "Rendering Antialiased Shadows with Depth Maps." *Computer Graphics (Proc. SIGGRAPH '87)* 21:4 (1987), 283–291.

[Reif79] J.H. Reif. "Complexity of the Mover's Problem and Generalizations." In *20th IEEE Symposium on Foundations of Computer Science*, pp. 421–427. Washington, DC: IEEE, 1979.

[Reif96] U. Reif. "A Degree Estimate for Subdivision Surfaces of Higher Regularity." *Proceedings of the American Mathematical Society* 124:7 (1996), 2167–2174.

[Reif06] U. Reif and J. Peters. "Structural Analysis of Subdivision Surfaces—A Summary." In *Topics in Multivariate Approximation and Interpolation*, edited by K. Jetter, M. Buhmann, W. Haussmann, R. Schaback, and J. Stoeckler, pp. 149–190. Amsterdam: Elsevier Science Ltd, 2006.

[Rein05] E. Reinhard, G. Ward, S. Pattanaik, and P. Debevec. *High Dynamic Range Imaging: Acquisition, Display, and Image-Based Lighting.* San Francisco: Morgan Kaufmann Publishers, 2005.

[Reyn87] C.W. Reynolds. "Flocks, Herds and Schools: A Distributed Behavioral Model."
          Computer Graphics 21:4 (1987), 25–34.

[Ries75] R. F. Riesenfeld. "On Chaikin's Algorithm." *Computer Graphics and Image
          Processing* 4 (1975), 304–310.

[Riou92] O. Rioul. "Simple Regularity Criteria for Subdivision Schemes." *SIAM Journal
          on Mathematical Analysis* 23:6 (1992), 1544–1576.

[Rost04] R. J. Rost. *OpenGL Shading Language.* Boston: Addison Wesley, 2004.

[Rouj04] J.-L. Roujean, C. B. Schaaf, and W. Lucht. "Fundamentals of Di-Directional
          Reflectance and BRDF Modeling." In *Reflective Properties of Vegetation and Soil*,
          edited by M. von Schoenmark, B. Geiger, and H.P. Roeser, pp. 105–120. Berlin:
          Wissenshaft und Technik Verlag, 2004.

[Rubi80] S. M. Rubin and T. Whitted. "A 3-Dimensional Representation for Fast Render-
          ing of Complex Scenes." *Computer Graphics (Proc. SIGGRAPH '80)* 14:3 (1980),
          110–116.

[Sabi91] M. Sabin. "Cubic Recursive Division with Bounded Curvature." In *Curves And
          Surfaces*, edited by P.J.Laurent, A. Le Méhauté, and L. L. Schumaker, pp. 411–414.
          New York: Academic Press, 1991.

[Sabi02] M. A. Sabin. "Eigenanalysis and Artifacts of Subdivision Curves and Surfaces."
          In *Tutorials on Multiresolution in Geometric Modelling*, edited by A. Iske, E. Quak,
          and M. S. Floater, pp. 69–97. Berlin / Heidelberg: Springer-Verlag, 2002.

[Sabi03] M. A. Sabin and L. Barthe. "Artifacts in Recursive Subdivision Surfaces." In
          Proc. Curve and Surface Fitting '02, pp. 353–362. Brentwood, TN: Nashboro Press,
          2003.

[Sabi04] Malcolm Sabin. "Recent Progress in Subdivision: A Survey." In *Advances in
          Multiresolution for Geometric Modelling*, edited by Neil Dodgson, Michael Floater,
          and Malcom Sabin, pp. 203–230. Berlin / Heidelberg: Springer, 2004.

[Sand00] P. V. Sander, X. Gu, S. J. Gortler, H. Hoppe, and J. Snyder. "Silhouette Clip-
          ping." In *Proceedings of SIGGRAPH 2000, Computer Graphics Proceedings, Annual
          Conference Series*, pp. 327–334. Reading, MA: Addison-Wesley, 2000.

[Sand01] P. V. Sander, J. Snyder, S. J. Gortler, and H. Hoppe. "Texture Mapping Progres-
          sive Meshes." In *Proceedings of SIGGRAPH 2001, Computer Graphics Proceedings,
          Annual Conference Series*, pp. 409–416. Reading, MA: Addison-Wesley, 2001.

[Sand03] P. Sander, Z. Wood, S. Gortler, J. Snyder, and H. Hoppe. "Multi-Chart Geom-
          etry Images." In *Eurographics Symposium on Geometry Processing*, pp. 146–155.
          Aire=la=Ville, Switzerland: Eurographics, 2003.

[Scha04] S. Schaefer, D. Zorin, and J. Warren. "Lofting Curve Networks with Subdivi-
          sion Surfaces." In *Proceedings of Eurographics Symposium on Graphics Processing*,
          pp. 105–116. Aire-la-Ville, Switzerland: Eurographics, 2004.

[Schm02] J. Schmittler, I. Wald, and P. Slusallek. "SaarCOR—A Hardware Architecture
          for Ray Tracing." In *Proc. EUROGRAPHICS Graphics Hardware 2002*, pp. 1–11.
          Aire-la-Ville: Eurographics, 2002.

[Schn03] P. J. Schneider and D. H. Eberly. *Geometric Tools for Computer Graphics*. San Francisco: Morgan Kaufmann, 2003.

[Sede98] T. W. Sederberg, J. Zheng, D. Sewell, and M. Sabin. "Non-Uniform Subdivision Surfaces." In *Proceedings of SIGGRAPH 98, Computer Graphics Proceedings, Annual Conference Series*, edited by M. Cohen, pp. 387–394. Reading, MA: Addison Wesley, 1998.

[Seet04] Helge Seetzen, Wolfgang Heidrich, Wolfgang Stuerzlinger, Greg Ward, Lorne Whitehead, Matthew Trentacoste, Abhijeet Ghosh, and Andrejs Vorozcovs. "High Dynamic Range Display System." *ACM Trans. Graph.* 23:3 (2004), 760–768.

[Seg04] "The OpenGL Graphics System: A Specification, Version 2.0.", 2004. Available online at www.opengl.org/documentation/specs/version2.0/glspec20.pdf.

[Sega92] M. Segal, C. Korobkin, R. van Widenfelt, J. Foran, and P. Haeberli. "Fast Shadows and Lighting Effects Using Texture Mapping." *Computer Graphics (Proc. SIGGRAPH '92)* 26:2 (1992), 249–252.

[Shad98] J. Shade, S. Gortler, L. W. He, and R Szeliski. "Layered Depth Images." In *Proceedings of SIGGRAPH 98, Computer Graphics Proceedings, Annual Conference Series*, pp. 231–242. Reading, MA: Addison Wesley, 1998.

[Shao06] W. Shao and D. Terzopoulos. "Populating Reconstructed Archaeological Sites with Autonomous Virtual Humans." In *Intelligent Virtual Agents (IVA 06), Lecture Notes in Computer Science, 4133*, pp. 420–433. Berlin / Heidelberg: Springer, 2006.

[Shao07] W. Shao and D. Terzopoulos. "Autonomous Pedestrians." *Graphical Models* 69:5-6 (2007), 246–274.

[Shef05] A. Sheffer, B. Levy, M. Mogilnitsky, and A. Bogomyakov. "ABF++: Fast and Robust Angle Based Flattening." *ACM Transactions on Graphics* 24:2 (2005), 311–330.

[Shir97] Peter Shirley and Kenneth Chiu. "A Low Distortion Map Between Disk and Square." *journal of graphics tools* 2:3 (1997), 45–52.

[Shir00] P. Shirley. *Realistic Ray Tracing*. Wellesley, MA: A K Peters, 2000.

[Shoe85] Ken Shoemake. "Animating Rotation with Quaternion Curves." *Computer Graphics (Proc. SIGGRAPH '85)* 19:3 (1985), 245–254.

[Shoe87] Ken Shoemake. *Quaternion Calculus and Fast Animation*. New York: ACM, 1987.

[Shor05] Nicholas Short. *The Remote Sensing Tutorial*. NASA, 2005. Available online at http://rst.gsfc.nasa.gov/.

[SIGG01] ACM SIGGRAPH. "SIGGRAPH Education Materials on Anti-Aliasing." Available online at http://www.siggraph.org/education/materials/HyperGraph/aliasing/alias0.htm, 2001.

[Sigg05] C. Sigg and M. Hadwiger. "Fast Third-Order Texture Filtering." In *GPU Gems 2*, edited by M. Pharr, pp. 313–329. Reading, MA: Addison-Wesley, 2005.

[Sill94] F. Sillion and C. Puech. *Radiosity and Global Illumination*. San Francisco: Morgan Kaufmann, 1994.

[Skal05] V. Skala. "A New Approach to Line and Line Segment Clipping in Homogeneous Coordinates." *The Visual Computer* 21:11 (2005), 905–914.

[Spiv92] J. M. Spivey. *The Z Notation: A Refernce Manual*, Second edition. Englewood Cliffs, NJ: Prentice Hall, 1992.

[Spro82] R.F. Sproull. "Using Program Transformations to Derive Line-Drawing Algorithms." *ACM Transactions on Graphics* 1:4 (1982), 259–273.

[Stam98] J. Stam. "Exact Evaluation of Catmull-Clark Subdivision Surfaces at Arbitrary Parameter Values." In *SIGGRAPH '98: Proceedings of the 25th Annual Conference on Computer Graphics and Interactive Techniques*, pp. 395–404. New York, NY, USA: ACM, 1998.

[Stam02] M. Stamminger and G. Drettakis. "Perspective Shadow Maps." *Transactions on Graphics (Proc. SIGGRAPH '02)* 21:3 (2002), 557–562.

[Stam03] Jos Stam and Charles Loop. "Quad/Triangle Subdivision." *Computer Graphics Forum* 22(1) (2003), 79–85.

[Star97] M. Stark, H. Muller, and U. Welsch. "Variations of the Splitting Box Scheme for Adaptive Generation of Contour Surfaces in Volume Data." In *Scientific Visualization*, edited by G. M. Nielson, H. Hagen, and H. Muller. washington, DC: IEEE Press, 1997.

[Stra90] P. S. Strauss. "A Realistic Lighting Model for Computer Animators." *IEEE Computer Graphics & Applications* 10:6 (1990), 56–64.

[Stra03] G. Strang. *Introduction to Linear Algebra*. Wellesley, MA: Wellesley-Cambridge Press, 2003.

[Suth63] I.E. Sutherland. "Sketchpad: A Man-Machine Graphical Communication System." In *AFIPS Conference proceedings Vol. 23 of the Spring Joint Computer Conference*, 1963.

[Suth74a] I.E. Sutherland and G.W. Hodgman. "Reentrant Polygon Clipping." *Communications of the ACM* 17:1 (1974), 32–42.

[Suth74b] I.E. Sutherland, R.F. Sproull, and R.A. Schumacker. "A Characterization of Ten Hidden Surface Algorithms." *ACM Computing Surveys* 6:1 (1974), 1–55.

[Talb05] Justin Talbot, David Cline, and Parris Egbert. "Importance Resampling for Global Illumination." In *Rendering Techniques 2005: 16th Eurographics Workshop on Rendering*, pp. 139–146. Aire-la-Ville, Switzerland: Eurographics, 2005.

[Tecc02] F. Tecchia, C. Loscos, and Y. Chrysanthou. "Image-Based Crowd Rendering." *IEEE Computer Graphics and Applications* 22:2 (2002), 36–43.

[Tele99] A. Telea and J. J. Van Wijk. "Simplified Representation of Vector Fields." In *VIS '99: Proceedings of the conference on Visualization '99*, pp. 35–42. Los Alamitos, CA, USA: IEEE Computer Society Press, 1999.

[Tell91] S. Teller and C.H. Sequin. "Visibility Preprocessing for Interactive Walk-throughs." *Computer Graphics (SIGGRAPH '91)* 25:4 (1991), 61–69.

[Tera05] J. Teran, J., E. Sifakis, G. Irving, and R. Fedkiw. "Robust Quasistatic Finite Elements and Flesh Simulation." In *Proceedings of ACM SIGGRAPH/Eurographics Symposium on Computer Animation*, edited by K. Anjyo and P. Faloutsos, pp. 181–190. New York: ACM, 2005.

[Terz87] D. Terzopoulos, J. Platt, A. Barr, and K. Fleisher. "Elastically Deformable Models." *Computer Graphics (Proc. SIGGRAPH '87)* 21:4 (1987), 205–214.

[Terz91] D. Terzopoulos and D. N. Metaxas. "Dynamic 3D Models with Local and Global Deformations: Deformable Superquadrics." *IEEE Transactions on Pattern Analysis and Machine Intelligence* 13:7 (1991), 703–714.

[Terz94] D. Terzopoulos and H. Qin. "Dynamic NURBS with Geometric Constraints for Interactive Sculpting." *ACM Transactions on Graphics* 13:2 (1994), 103–136.

[Theo89a] T. Theoharis. *Algorithms for Parallel Polygon Rendering.* Lecture Notes in Computer Science 373, Berlin: Springer-Verlag, 1989.

[Theo89b] T. Theoharis and I. Page. "Two Parallel Methods for Polygon Clipping." *Computer Graphics Forum* 8 (1989), 107–114.

[Theo90] T. Theoharis, A. Travis, and N. Wiseman. "3D Display: Simulation and Synthetic Image Production." *Computer Graphics Forum* 9 (1990), 337–348.

[Theo01] T. Theoharis, G. Papaioannou, and E.A. Karabassi. "The Magic of The Z-Buffer: A Survey." In *WSCG '98 (Ninth European Conference in Central Europe on Computer Graphics and Visualization)*, pp. 379–386. Plzen, Czech Republic: University of West Bohemia, 2001.

[Thom06] B. Thomaszewski, M. Wacker, and W. B. Straber. "A Consistent Bending Model for Cloth Simulation with Corotational Subdivision Finite Elements." In *Proceedings of ACM SIGGRAPH/Eurographics Symposium on Computer Animation*, edited by M.-P. Cani, J.O'Brien. New York: ACM, 2006.

[Thue98] G. Thuermer and A. Wuthrich. "Computing Vertex Normals from Polygonal Facets." *journal of graphics tools* 3:1 (1998), 43–46.

[Torr67] K. E. Torrance and E. M. Sparrow. "Theory for Off-Specular Reflection from Roughened Surfaces." *Journal of the Optical Society of America* 57:9 (1967), 1105–1114.

[Tric00] Xavier Tricoche, Gerik Scheuermann, and Hans Hagen. "A Topology Simplification Method For 2D Vector Fields." In *Proc. IEEE Visualization 2000*, pp. 359–366. Washington, DC: IEEE, 2000.

[Tu94] X. Tu and D. Terzopoulos. "Artificial Fishes: Physics, Locomotion, Perception, Behavior." In *Proceedings of SIGGRAPH 94, Computer Graphics Proceedings, Annual Conference Series*, pp. 43–50. New York: ACM Press, 1994.

[Tumb99] J. Tumblin and G. Turk. "LCIS: A Boundary Hierarchy for Detail-Preserving Contrast Reduction." In *Proceedings of SIGGRAPH 99, Computer Graphics Proceedings, Annual Conference Series*, pp. 83–90. Reading, MA: Addison Wesley Longman, 1999.

[Umla00] G. Umlauf. "Analyzing the Characteristic Map of Triangular Subdivision Schemes." *Constructive Approximation* 16:1 (2000), 145–155.

[Umla05] G. Umlauf. "Analysis and Tuning of Subdivision Algorithms." In *Proc. 21st Spring Conference on Computer Graphics*, pp. 33–40. New York, NY, USA: ACM, 2005.

[Upso89] C. Upson, Jr. T. Faulhaber, D. Kamins, D.H. Laidlaw, D. Schlegel, J. Vroom, R. Gurwitz, and A. van Dam. "The Application Visualization System: A Computational Environment for Scientific Visualization." *IEEE Computer Graphics and Applications* 9:4 (1989), 30–42.

[Vatt92] B.R. Vatti. "A Generic Solution to Polygon Clipping." *Communications of ACM* 35:7 (1992), 57–63.

[Veac94] E. Veach and L. J. Guibas. "Bidirectional Estimators for Light Transport." In *Fifth Eurographics Workshop on Rendering*, pp. 147–162. Aire-la-Ville, Switzerland: Eurographics, 1994.

[Veac97] E. Veach. "Robust Monte Carlo Methods for Light Transport Simulation." Ph.D. thesis, Stanford University, Department of Computer Science, 1997.

[Velh01a] L. Velho. "Quasi 4 − 8 Subdivision." *Computer Aided Geometric Design* 18:4 (2001), 345–357.

[Velh01b] L. Velho and D. Zorin. "4 − 8 Subdivision." *Computer Aided Geometric Design* 18:5 (2001), 397–427.

[Wald01] I. Wald and P. Slusallek. "State of the Art in Interactive Ray Tracing." In *State of the Art Reports, EUROGRAPHICS 2001*, pp. 21–42. Aire-la-Ville, Switzerland: Eurographics, 2001.

[Wald02] I. Wald, C. Benthin, and P. Slusallek. "A Flexible and Scalable Rendering Engine for Interactive 3D Graphics." Technical Report TR-2002-01, Computer Graphics Group, Saarland University, 2002.

[Ward91] G. Ward. "Real Pixels." In *Graphics Gems II*, edited by J. Arvo, pp. 80–82. San Diego: Academic Press, 1991.

[Ward92] G. J. Ward. "Measuring and Modeling Anisotropic Reflection." *Computer Graphics (Proc. SIGGRAPH '92)* 26:2 (1992), 265–272.

[Ward94] G. Ward. "The RADIANCE Lighting Simulation and Rendering System." In *Proceedings of SIGGRAPH 94, Computer Graphics Proceedings, Annual Conference Series*, pp. 459–472. New York: ACM Press, 1994.

[Ward01] G. Ward. "High Dynamic Range Imaging." In *IS&T/SID's Ninth Color Imaging Conference*. Springfield, VA: Society for Imaging Science and Technology, 2001.

[Warn69] J. Warnock. *A Hidden Surface Algorithm for Computer Generated Half-Tone Pictures*. University of Utah, Department of Computer Science, Salt Lake City, Utah, TR 4-15, 1969.

[Warr01] J. Warren and H. Weimer. *Subdivision Methods for Geometric Design*. San Francisco: Morgan Kaufmann, 2001.

[Watt01] A. Watt and F. Policarpo. *3D Games: Real-Time Rendering and Software Technology*, 1. Harlow, UK: Addison-Wesley, 2001.

[Weil85] K. Weiler. "Edge-Based Data sSructures for Solid Modeling in Curved-Surface Environments." *IEEE Computer Graphics and Applications* 5:1 (1985), 21–40.

[Weis04] Eric W. Weisstein. "Conic Section." MathWorld – A Wolfram Web Resource, 2004. Available online (http://mathworld.wolfram.com/ConicSection.html).

[West90] L. Westover. "Footprint Evaluation for Volume Rendering." *Computer Graphics (Proc. SIGGRAPH '90)* 24:4 (1990), 367–376.

[Whit80] T. Whitted. "An Improved Illumination Model for Shaded Display." *ACM Communications* 26:6 (1980), 342–349.

[Whit92] S. Whitman. *Multiprocessor Methods for Computer Graphics Rendering*. Boston, MA: Jones and Bartlett, 1992.

[Will78] L. Williams. "Casting Curved Shadows on Curved Surfaces." *Computer Graphics (Proc. SIGGRAPH '78)* 12:3 (1978), 270–274.

[Will83] L. Williams. "Pyramidal Parametrics." *Computer Graphics (Proc. SIGGRAPH '83)* 17:3 (1983), 1–11.

[Will98] L. Williams. "Casting Curved Shadows on Curved Surfaces." In *Seminal Graphics: Pioneering Efforts that Shaped the Field*, pp. 51–55. New York: ACM, 1998.

[Will06] P. Willis. "Projective Alpha Color." In *Proceedings Eurographics 2006*, pp. 557–566. Aire-la-Ville, Switzerland: Eurographics, 2006.

[Witk88] A. Witkin and M. Kass. "Spacetime Constraints." *Computer Graphics (Proc. SIGGRAPH '88)* 22:4 (1988), 159–168.

[Wysz00] G. Wyszecki and W.S. Stiles. *Color Science: Concepts and Methods, Quantitative Data and Formulae*. New York: Wiley, 2000.

[Wyvi95] G. Wyvill. "Practical Ray Tracing." Computer Graphics International 1995 Course Notes, 1995.

[Xia96] Julie C. Xia and Amitabh Varshney. "Dynamic View-Dependent Simplification for Polygonal Models." In *Proceedings of IEEE Visualization '96*, pp. 327–334. Washington, DC: IEEE, 1996.

[Zhan02] Hong-xin Zhang and Guo-jin Wang. "Honeycomb Subdivision." *J. of Software* 13:5 (2002), 1199–1208.

[Zhuk98a] S. Zhukov, A. Iones, and G. Kronin. "An Ambient Light Illumination Model." In *Rendering Techniques (Proc. Eurographics Rendering Workshop)*, pp. 45–55. Eurographics, Vienna: Springer-Wien, 1998.

[Zhuk98b] S. Zhukov, A. Iones, and G. Kronin. "Using Light Maps to Create Realistic Lighting in Real-time Applications." In *Central European Conference on Computer Graphics and Visualization (WSCG98)*, pp. 464–471. Plzen, Czech Republic: University of West Bohemia, 1998.

[Zien05] O. C. Zienkiewicz and R. L. Taylor. *The Finite Element Method for Solid and Structural Mechanics*, 6th edition. Amsterdam: Butterworth-Heinemann / Elsevier, 2005.

[Zori96] Denis Zorin, Peter Schröder, and Wim Sweldens. "Interpolating Subdivision for Meshes with Arbitrary Topology." In *Proceedings of ACM SIGGRAPH '96*, pp. 189–192. New York: ACM Press, 1996.

[Zori00] D. Zorin, P. Schröder, A. DeRose, L. Kobbelt, A. Levin, and W. Sweldens. "Subdivision for Modeling and Animation." ACM SIGGRAPH '00 Course Notes, 2000.

[Zuff02] M. K. Zuffo and H. Kaczmarski. "Commodity Clusters for Immersive Projection Environments." *SIGGRAPH Course Notes*.

[Zult06] A. Zulti, A. Levin, D. Levin, and M. Teicher. "C^2 Subdivision Over Triangulations With One Extraordinary Point." *Computer Aided Geometric Design* 23:2 (2006), 157–178.

Index

For Product Safety Concerns and Information please contact our EU
representative GPSR@taylorandfrancis.com Taylor & Francis Verlag GmbH,
Kaufingerstraße 24, 80331 München, Germany

Printed and bound by CPI Group (UK) Ltd, Croydon, CR0 4YY
08/06/2025
01897014-0001